The Third Option

ALSO BY LOCH K. JOHNSON

Advanced Introduction to American Foreign Policy (2021)

Intelligence: The Secret World of Spies, 5th ed., ed. with James J. Wirtz (2019)

Spy Watching: Intelligence Accountability in the United States (2018)

National Security Intelligence: Secret Operations in Defense of the Democracies, 2d ed. (2017)

A Season of Inquiry Revisited: The Church Committee Confronts America's Spy Agencies (2015)

Essentials of Strategic Intelligence, ed. (2015)

American Foreign Policy and the Challenges of World Leadership: Power, Principle, and the Constitution (2015)

The Threat on the Horizon: An Inside Account of America's Search for Security After the Cold War (2011)

Intelligence: Critical Concepts in Military, Strategic, and Security Studies, Vols. I–IV, ed. (2011)

The Oxford Handbook of National Security Intelligence, ed. (2010)

The Study of Strategic Intelligence, Vols. I–V, ed. (2007)

Handbook of Intelligence Studies, ed. (2007)

Seven Sins of American Foreign Policy (2007)

Who's Watching the Spies? Establishing Intelligence Service Accountability, ed. with Hans Born and Ian Leigh (2005)

American Foreign Policy: History, Politics, and Policy with John Endicott and Daniel S. Papp (2005)

Fateful Decisions: Inside the National Security Council, ed. with Karl F. Inderfurth (2004)

Bombs, Bugs, Drugs, and Thugs: Intelligence and America's Quest for Security (2000)

Secret Agencies U.S. Intelligence in a Hostile World (1996)

America as a World Power (1995)

Runoff Elections in the United States with Charles S. Bullock III (1993)

America's Secret Power: The CIA in a Democratic Society (1989)

Decisions of the Highest Order: Perspectives on the National Security Council, ed. with Karl F. Inderfurth (1988)

Through the Straits of Armageddon: Arms Control Issues and Prospects, ed. with Paul F. Diehl (1987)

A Season of Inquiry: The Senate Intelligence Investigation (1985)

The Making of International Agreements: Congress Confronts the Executive (1984)

The Third Option

Covert Action and American Foreign Policy

LOCH K. JOHNSON

OXFORD
UNIVERSITY PRESS

OXFORD
UNIVERSITY PRESS

Oxford University Press is a department of the University of Oxford. It furthers
the University's objective of excellence in research, scholarship, and education
by publishing worldwide. Oxford is a registered trade mark of Oxford University
Press in the UK and certain other countries.

Published in the United States of America by Oxford University Press
198 Madison Avenue, New York, NY 10016, United States of America.

© Oxford University Press 2022

All rights reserved. No part of this publication may be reproduced, stored in
a retrieval system, or transmitted, in any form or by any means, without the
prior permission in writing of Oxford University Press, or as expressly permitted
by law, by license, or under terms agreed with the appropriate reproduction
rights organization. Inquiries concerning reproduction outside the scope of the
above should be sent to the Rights Department, Oxford University Press, at the
address above.

You must not circulate this work in any other form
and you must impose this same condition on any acquirer.

CIP data is on file at the Library of Congress
ISBN 978-0-19-760441-0

DOI: 10.1093/oso/9780197604410.001.0001

1 3 5 7 9 8 6 4 2

Printed by Sheridan Books, Inc., United States of America

*To my former students at the University of Georgia,
with heartfelt thanks for their inspiration, friendship, and dedication
to public service*

And, as always, to Leena

But I remember now
I am in this earthly world, where to do harm
Is often laudable, to do good sometime
Accounted dangerous folly.

—William Shakespeare
Macbeth
Lady Macbeth
III, v

Contents

Figures ix
Preface xi

Introduction: The Mysterious World of Clandestine Interventions 1

I. TRADECRAFT

1. The Forms of Covert Action 19
2. A Ladder of Clandestine Escalation 40

II. PRACTICE, 1947–1975

3. A Shadowy Foreign Policy, 1947–1960 69
4. Murder Most Foul, 1960–1975 93

III. PRACTICE, 1975–2020

5. A New Approach to Covert Action, 1975–2000 117
6. The Third Option in an Age of Terror, 2000–2020 143

IV. LAW AND ACCOUNTABILITY

7. Legal Foundations 167
8. Decision Paths and Accountability 194

V. ETHICS AND ASSESSMENTS

9. Drawing Bright Lines: Ethics and Covert Action 223
10. The Third Option Reconsidered 252

Acknowledgments	279
Appendix A: Intelligence Leadership in the United States, 1946–2021	281
Appendix B: Intelligence Oversight Act of 1980	283
Notes	285
Abbreviations and Codenames	335
Selected Bibliography	343
About the Author	367
Index	369

Figures

1.1. The Directorates of the Central Intelligence Agency	20
1.2. The CIA Operations Directorate During the Cold War	21
1.3. The Organization of the US Intelligence Community	22
2.1. A Ladder of Clandestine Escalation	41
2.2. "The C.I.A. Did It." *New Yorker*, cartoon	58
3.1. Key Targeting in the Evolution of Covert Action, 1947–1975	70
5.1. Key Targeting in the Evolution of Covert Action, 1975–2020	118
6.1. Fluctuating Flows and Main Currents in the "River" of Covert Actions, Since 1947	159
7.1. Examples of Presidential Findings on Covert Actions, 1981	185
8.1. Decision and Reporting Paths for Covert Action, Established in 1975	196
9.1. An Ethical Profile of America's Covert Actions Since 1947	250
10.1. Covert Action Targeting, by Level of Development and Region, 1947–2020	274

Preface

Hello, and welcome.

Here is a trail map for this book. The Introduction that follows this Preface discusses, in brief, the three major instruments that guide this nation's activities abroad: the Treaty Power, the War Power, and the Spy War. Within the category of Spy Power one finds the Third Option: the use of "covert action" as a means for secretly influencing world events. The Introduction also sets the stage for an understanding of how the philosophies of anti-communism and counterterrorism have driven the adoption of clandestine interventions overseas as a central strand of American foreign policy.

An attraction of the nation's leaders to the Third Option as an important foreign policy tool is as old as the Republic. Indeed, this approach preceded the nation's founding. Prior to the Revolutionary War, Benjamin Franklin planted disinformation in French newspapers while serving the colonies as a diplomatic representative in Paris; and he secretly shipped weapons back from France to the army of General George Washington. After the establishment of the new nation, America's third president, Thomas Jefferson, ordered paramilitary operations directed against the Barbary Pirates of North Africa, terrorists of that era who regularly marauded commercial shipping in the Mediterranean.

A number of additional presidents have relied on covert action, in one form or another, during the early decades of the Republic. In 1843, for example, President John Tyler sent an agent to Great Britain for the purpose of quietly shaping public opinion in America's favor; in 1845, President James K. Polk resorted to furtive operations meant to prevent Mexico from ceding California to the British; and, in 1870, President Ulysses S. Grant turned to covert propaganda in hopes of convincing Canadians to join the United States rather than go their own way.[1] This book, though, concentrates on America's uses of covert action since 1947, as planned and carried out by one of the nation's premier secret services: the Central Intelligence Agency or CIA, known by insiders as "the Agency."[2]

Chapter 1 explores the forms that Third Option has assumed, such as clandestine radio broadcasts and sabotage. A hush-hush organization like the CIA runs counter to the ethos of an open, democratic society. Given the forbearance in this country for this incongruity, a fundamental question ties the chapters of this book together: Of what value has the Agency actually been in trying to contour global events, as a complement to the federal government's more open national security organizations, such as the Department of State (DoS) and the Department of Defense (DoD)?

Chapter 2 presents a Ladder of Clandestine Escalation. The ladder metaphor provides a device for arraying examples of the Third Option. Its rungs move from minimal risk and moral doubt at the bottom of the ladder, to rising levels that pose acute dangers and profound ethical implications for the United States.

Chapter 3 gazes into the rearview mirror at America's covert actions during the opening years of the Cold War, from 1947 to 1960. Several questions are addressed in this chapter: What was the evolutionary arc for covert action throughout the inaugural years of the Cold War? Specifically, what nations and groups were targeted for secret interventions, and toward what purposes? How have the methods of covert action—"tradecraft" is the amusing term adopted by the CIA—changed over the years?

Chapters 4 through 6 further unspool this historical thread, exploring these same questions for later decades. The exploration begins with the closing years of the Eisenhower administration, when it turned to murder as a means of advancing US interests in Africa. On the heels of this chilling initiative in the Congo came the first major setback for covert action in the modern era, a paramilitary operation at the Bay of Pigs in Cuba during the Kennedy administration. This capsule history of the Third Option continues through Chapters 5 and 6, moving toward America's contemporary struggle against international terrorism and the reemergence of a superpower rivalry with the Russian Federation and the Chinese. To what degree did the standoff with the Soviet Union during the Cold War, followed by an Age of Terror and renewed aggression by the communist powers, lead to a metamorphosis in the forms and objectives of clandestine interventions carried out by the CIA on behalf of the United States?

Several outstanding case studies have been written on the episodes discussed in the historical chapters. The objective in these pages is to draw on the existing research literature as a means for highlighting key illustrations of America's secret operations abroad. A meta-analysis of this kind has its place, but it also has its limitations: complex events are summarized in just a few pages, or sometimes in only a paragraph or so. In choosing to look at a wide sampling of covert action examples, history is condensed in a search for overarching motifs. The result is something of a "motorcycle ride through the art gallery," to borrow a phrase from a former CIA deputy director, Admiral William O. Studeman. The reader is encouraged to explore entries in this book's bibliography for a more in-depth account of any given case.

In Chapter 7, the legal foundations for the Third Option are perused: the set of executive orders and statutes that have shaped America's hidden interventions abroad. At first, these official guidelines were flimsy and based solely on executive orders, until covert action was finally addressed in a series of landmark laws enacted from the mid-1970s through the early 1980s—some three decades after the CIA launched its first clandestine operations in 1947. Even in the aftermath of enacting these unprecedented intelligence oversight laws, ambiguities have persisted over the proper legal boundaries for the Third Option. Moreover, from time to time, presidential administrations have chosen simply to ignore the established statutory limits—a deeply troubling failure of democracy within the most concealed recesses of America's government.

The decision paths followed by Washington officials in authorizing the Third Option are placed under the microscope in Chapter 8. In places like Russia and China, dictators call the shots; in the democracies, the people have a say in their destiny. With respect to the United States, diplomacy and war-making are relatively transparent endeavors; in these domains, the Constitution explicitly requires members of Congress and the courts to provide checks on the actions of the White House and its executive bureaucracy. Debate has the potential to be thorough on Capitol Hill when it comes to the use of military force, as well as in the forging of major international accords from trade pacts to arms-control agreements. What about covert action, though? Are these operations, which go unmentioned in the Constitution, so sensitive that normal democratic procedures must be set aside, in deference to secrecy, efficiency, and deniability? As well, Chapter 8 examines the ups-and-downs of accountability for covert action. How well are these "black" operations supervised by the White House and the Congress?

Some would argue that to utter in the same breath "ethics and covert action" is to speak an oxymoron. Yet the United States often espouses lofty human values at home and abroad; therefore, it is reasonable to ask whether these values are as valid for the nation's covert operations as for its more open activities. This contrast lies at the heart of Chapter 9, which draws back the curtain on America's hidden interventionist activities around the globe to appraise their moral legitimacy. What clandestine methods, if any, should be considered beyond the pale of acceptability for the United States, a democratic nation that advocates high ethical principles in its founding documents and ongoing political rhetoric? Chapter 9 also offers a balance sheet of pluses and minuses on the outcomes of this nation's major covert intrusions during the modern era, as gauged by an ethical accounting. What have been the successes and failures of this approach to world affairs, and at what cost to America's moral standing in the world?

Last, Chapter 10 presents an overall assessment of the Third Option. The focus for this chapter, and for the book as a whole, reduces to these core questions: Does the Third Option merit retention as an instrument of American foreign policy? And, if so, what safeguards should be in place to ensure its proper conduct?

The Challenges of Studying Covert Action

This book delves into what is, at times, the seamy side of America's relations with other countries, including activities that range from secret political bribes and major economic disruptions to extreme paramilitary attacks and even assassination plots against individuals overseas considered enemies of the United States. Dean Rusk, secretary of state during the Kennedy and Johnson administrations, referred to these controversial activities as "a tough struggle going on in the back alleys all over the world"—in essence, subterranean wars between the superpowers in which the CIA and its associated intelligence agencies had become the first line of defense for the American homeland. Leon E. Panetta, director of the CIA during the Obama administration, has emphasized that covert action is "a hard business of agonizing choices." Critics have been more blunt, castigating this method as the "dirty tricks" side of US foreign policy.[3]

Government investigative panels have been consistently wary of staring into the covert action abyss. Indeed, no major investigation into the Third Option was carried out until 1975, when the Senate entered into the most thorough inquiry ever undertaken into America's Spy Power.[4] At the time, concerns abounded among lawmakers and citizens alike that the CIA may have become a force unto its own, skulking around the planet and perhaps even at home with little—if any—monitoring by lawmakers, the courts, or the White House. Senator Frank Church (D, Idaho), who led the Senate investigation, suggested on a nationally televised news show that the CIA had become a "rogue elephant rampaging out of control."[5] He soon withdrew this characterization, conceding that it had been proffered prematurely while his committee was still in the beginning stages of its probe. Nevertheless, as the work of the panel progressed, Church continued to harbor reservations about how accountable the Agency really was, especially when it came to the launching of coups, assassinations, and other radical forms of the Third Option.

Additional members of Congress, then and in years to follow, also raised the specter of elephant roguery at the CIA, among them Edward P. Boland (D, Massachusetts), a mild-mannered and well-regarded member of the House of Representative, a Bostonian who never lost an election and served in Congress for more than three decades. From 1977 to 1983, he stood at the helm of the House Permanent Select Committee on Intelligence, known simply as HPSCI (pronounced "hip-see") and established in 1977. He observed with reference to America's secret operations in Nicaragua that "the CIA was almost like a rogue elephant doing what it wanted to do."[6]

The Church Committee inquiry brought to light Agency spying within the United States against anti-war protestors and, abroad, CIA schemes to murder foreign leaders. The Committee revealed, as well, disquieting attempts by the United States to manipulate a presidential election in Chile in the 1970s, followed by operations meant to instigate a coup in that democratic nation. Even the prestigious Church Committee ran into significant roadblocks imposed by the Ford administration, however, and had to limit its examination of the nation's covert interventions. The second most exhaustive investigation of the CIA, the Aspin-Brown Commission in 1995–96, avoided the subject of the Third Option almost completely, bracketing this part of its inquiry at an early meeting in lieu of a later review—one that never occurred.[7] Experience has shown that few subjects in the realm of intelligence activities are as sacrosanct, as highly classified, and as deeply under lock and key within the vaults of the CIA as covert action.

A democracy, though, demands candor with its citizens on all of their government's activities—not on details about CIA agents and officers serving abroad, of course, which would endanger their lives; or sensitive operational specifics, known by insiders as "sources and methods," regarding how the United States carries out its intelligence activities. Nonetheless, the broader purpose, scope, and effectiveness of this nation's heavily veiled intrusions against other nations and terrorist organizations are topics that do warrant scrutiny. After all, citizen awareness of decisions made by their elected officials is a central tenet of democracy. The American people have the right to judge the covert action record, then to determine whether to continue on with these endeavors as practiced in the past or to make course corrections.

A research note: studying the Third Option is a daunting challenge, given its status as the ultimate confidential topic in government, surrounded by layers of darkness and mythology. No one is currently able to write a definitive analysis of America's covert actions because so many of the detailed operational records remain classified. To the best of my ability, though, I have scoured both the scholarly and the more anecdotal commentary in the public domain for core findings. In addition, I had the opportunity to serve as senior aide to Senator Church during his panel's inquiry; and twenty years later, in 1995, in that same capacity with Chairman Les Aspin on the Aspin-Brown Presidential Commission that looked into America's post–Cold War intelligence activities. In between, I had the privilege of being the first staff director of HPSCI's Subcommittee on Intelligence Oversight. These experiences allowed rare access for a professor of political science into the charmed circle of America's secret agencies. I had the opportunity and privilege of regularly attending meetings and briefings at the CIA's Headquarters Building in northern Virginia, in addition to several of its "stations" overseas.

I have supplemented these stints as a "participate observer" (social science jargon meant to convey the notion of researching how Washington, DC, works by serving among its officials for a time) with an additional forty-five years of monitoring the US intelligence services as a university researcher. Since 1975, I have kept up with the public record on this subject, as recorded in congressional hearings and reports, newspaper and other media accounts, commission findings, library archives, and memoirs. From 2002 to 2019, I also had the honor of serving as the senior editor of the premier international journal on intelligence studies, entitled *Intelligence and National Security* and published in the United Kingdom. In this capacity, I was able to track many of the best scholarly articles on the Spy Power published by fellow academicians in the United States and around the world.

Further, I have spoken with, and often formally interviewed, hundreds of intelligence professionals during these decades, including most of the directors of Central Intelligence (DCIs), whether retired or still serving as the nation's spymasters, a list that extends from Richard Helms (1966–73) forward. I have also had the privilege of having multiple interview sessions with the nation's longest serving director of National Intelligence (DNI), Lieutenant General James R. Clapper, a high school friend with whom I have kept in touch. These circumstances provided me with a further understanding of the US intelligence mission, even though I have never served as an officer in any of the secret services.

In all of my writings on America's spy agencies, I have been interested in reviewing the public record on their activities, evaluating the merits of intelligence operations that have come into open light. These activities have included most all of the large and significant uses of the Third Option. An insider argument that "if you only knew . . ." simply doesn't hold water when it comes to an objective appraisal of America's major covert actions, though one frequently hears this refrain from intelligence professionals. A seasoned CIA veteran has written, for example, "the main body of the clandestine warfare is unknown to all but a few people in the inner sancta of the various governments."[8] Yet, after decades of service at high perches in the US national security apparatus, former Secretary of State Rusk concluded: "The argument that 'If you only knew what I knew, you would agree with me' is a phony."[9]

~~~

So down the rabbit hole we go, into a dimly lit world of secret agents; poison-dart guns; vials of curare, cobra venom, and shellfish toxins; barrels of ink for writing propaganda tracts; weaponry of all makes and calibers; heavily armed drones and high-powered missiles; speed boats, bombers, and explosives; masks and fake prosthetics; CIA crafted political campaign buttons, bumper stickers, and TV ads written in foreign tongues for use in elections overseas; counterfeit foreign currencies—a largely invisible realm of clandestine activities governed by the best of intentions, yet sometimes yielding the worst of results; a world that merits the thoughtful attention and judgment of every citizen. The purpose here is to offer a frank assessment of this obscure but vital component of America's foreign policy.[10]

—Loch K. Johnson
Northwest Hills, Connecticut

Introduction

The Mysterious World of Clandestine Interventions

The Treaty, War, and Spy Powers

Since the creation of the Central Intelligence Agency (CIA) in 1947, the United States has often turned to this secretive organization for implementation of a "Third Option" in pursuit of its foreign policy objectives—a pathway between the alternatives of diplomacy, on the one hand, and war-fighting, on the other hand. This middle option is more commonly known by government insiders as "covert action": clandestine intervention in the affairs of other nations for the purpose of advancing the global interests of the United States.[1] No approach to international affairs has been consistently more controversial.

These opening pages place this shadowy approach to foreign policy into the broader context of America's international activities. Among the orienting questions explored in this Introduction are these:

What are the objectives of US foreign policy?
What options are available to Washington officials as they confront an uncertain global environment?
What institutional approach to foreign policy best serves the nation: reliance on a strong president, or one that includes participation by lawmakers as well?

The Objectives of American Foreign Policy

In 1975, the Murphy Commission on Foreign Policy lamented the fact that "we must live in the world we find, not the world we might wish."[2] That world has seen two global wars and scores of other military conflicts, with the United States involved one way or another in much of this strife. In the twentieth century, the Second World War (1939–1945) led to the deaths of over 400,000 Americans; and the war in Vietnam (1964–1975) yielded an additional 58,000 who gave their full measure of devotion. America's most recent and longest wars—in Iraq (2003–2011) and Afghanistan (2001–2021), this nation's "forever wars"—have emptied the national treasury of some $6 trillion and sent to an early grave more than 15,000 US troops and war-zone contractors, as well as at least nineteen CIA officers.

This world we must live in has brought violent calamity directly to America's shores as well, most shockingly on September 11, 2001 ("9/11") with the destruction by aerial terrorism of the World Trade Center in New York City and a hit against the Pentagon in Virginia. Almost 3,000 Americans perished in these attacks. In this age of intercontinental ballistic missiles and the ongoing development of long-range military drones, the Atlantic and Pacific Oceans no longer provide the reassuring moats once enjoyed by Americans during the first 150 years of the nation's existence. Moreover, the dangers to the United States go beyond surprise terrorist attacks from overseas. In 2020, the deadly COVID-19 virus tragically demonstrated anew how pandemics can also kill large numbers of people. Over 400,000 Americans had died of the disease by early 2021, following the arrival of this virus into the United States from China in January of the previous year—a number that is greater than all of the US soldiers killed in warfare during the Second World War.[3] Yet another danger springs from domestic terrorism, stunningly demonstrated on January 6, 2021, when homegrown insurgents stormed the US Capitol in a violent attack inflamed by the false rhetoric of President Donald J. Trump that Democrats had resorted to election fraud as a means for thwarting his re-election bid. Far fewer people were killed in this event than on 9/11, but the assault on democracy that day was profoundly disturbing and continues to haunt a nation fearful that it could happen again---perhaps this time led by a fully armed rebel militia.

As with other governments around the world, leaders in Washington, DC, maintain a top-secret "threat assessment" of foreign and domestic perils. At the top of the list are military conflicts in locations abroad where US forces face imminent danger, whether on acknowledged battlefields like Afghanistan or in more ambiguous settings like the Maghreb or Somalia in Africa. As a result of the blow against the Capitol in January of 2021, domestic terrorism now shares a spot with foreign wars at the top of the government's list of perils to the nation's security. Almost as worrisome in this tabulation of threats are ongoing, or potential, cyberattacks. In this computer-dependent age, the risk is ever present of an electronic Pearl Harbor—a sudden meltdown of power grids across the country, with the possible collapse of the stock exchange on Wall Street, a disruption of the nation's energy grid, and a blackout of personal computers on every desk in every home, hospital, and office building across the land.

Further electronic challenges are presented by computer hackers in Russia, China, Iran, North Korea, and other locations where trollers seek to steal not only America's industrial secrets but also classified government data from computers in the Departments of Defense and State, as well in the nation's intelligence agencies. A massive Russian cyberattack against the United States, discovered in December 2020 and known as the "SolarWinds" case (after the name of a key software provider targeted in the attack), underscored these vulnerabilities and sent Washington officials scrambling to strengthen US cyberdefenses. Moreover, foreign computer hackers working for hostile spy agencies have attempted to undermine the American electoral system by tampering with voter registration systems and electronic voting machines in all fifty states, and by infusing social media with propaganda related to candidates either liked or disliked in Moscow, Beijing, Tehran, Pyongyang, or wherever else dictators ply their regime's insidious cyber skills—all in an effort to weaken and, they hope, ultimately destroy the Western democracies. Additional hackers based in remote cities around the world have engaged in the theft of computer data from both the public and private sectors within the United States, demanding ransom payoffs in exchange for return of the data.

High, too, on the list of blinking red lights for US government officials are foreign nuclear, biological, and chemical (NBC) weapons that are, or could be, aimed at America's population centers at home or its troops on distant battlefields. The proliferation of weapons of mass destruction (WMD) is a source of great, ongoing concern. The possibility of a further burgeoning of the North Korean nuclear arsenal, followed perhaps by similar outcomes in Iran, Saudi Arabia, Syria, and on down the list, conjures a dismaying portrait of a future whose hallmark would be the global spread of enough potential firepower to destroy whole nations if these weapons were used in anger. Even the planet itself could be turned into a frozen wasteland, after the initial scorching subsided. According to computer modeling, the widespread use of nuclear bombs in a Third World War could throw so much soot and debris into the Earth's atmosphere that the sun's warming rays would be blocked out for months on end, trapping the human race and every other species in a deadly and inescapable global icebox—a nuclear winter.[4]

Both Russia and China have a sufficient number of nuclear weapons to annihilate the United States from Maine to California in a thirty-minute hailstorm of ballistic missiles, carrying warheads with multiple-megaton yields of explosive force. Russian submarines off America's coastlines have the capacity to level Washington, DC, New York City, Boston, Los Angeles, San Francisco, and San Diego (among other cities) within five minutes of missile-launch—virtually no time for Americans to seek shelter. And even if one could find a place to hide, what would be left when one emerged, other than a landscape covered in charred rubble and pulsating with deadly radiation?

This review of military, cyber, and terrorist threats underscores the importance of having effective intelligence agencies to help provide an early warning of dangers to the nation.

Beyond the constant quest for a strong shield against the use of hostile force against the American homeland, this nation's foreign policy also includes a search for economic opportunities around the world. Further, citizens of the United States—and in every other country—seek a better quality of daily life by reversing environmental degradation, establishing immunities against pandemics, and advancing universal human rights. With the exception of the Trump administration, those who have governed the United States since the Second World War have found it unwise—if not impossible—to retreat from this tumultuous world, as Americans had fecklessly attempted to do after the First World War. Like it or not, citizens of the United States are part of a vast, interwoven tapestry of global interdependence, with strands that reach from across North America to Latin America, Europe, the Middle East, Asia, and Africa. The prevention of future 9/11s, or perhaps even the Armageddon of a nuclear war, may depend on the skill of Washington leaders in their conduct of international relations.

Efforts to cope with this complex world have proven doubly difficult as a result of periodic disagreements in the nation's capital over what instruments of foreign policy should be adopted in the pursuit of national security and other international objectives.

Key Instruments of American Foreign Policy

Three prominent foreign policy options are most often adopted by Washington officials as they try to advance America's interests abroad: the Treaty Power, the War Power, and the Spy Power.[5] Like the proverbial onion, America's relationships with other countries have many layers, in response to a planet that is vast in size; multilingual and multicultural; fractious; spiked with dangerous weapons, failing nations, terrorist factions, and lethal diseases; led in many places by ruthless autocrats; and plagued by uncertainties as adversaries attempt to keep closely veiled their intentions and military capabilities (as when North Korea constructs its nuclear weapons underground, away from the watchful eyes of US high-altitude surveillance satellites). Will diplomacy meet America's needs in certain circumstances, whether through political alliances, military pacts, trade agreements, arms control accords, or environmental commitments? Is the use of force necessary, as during the Second World War in response to Hitler's drive for *lebensraum* and world domination, and against the Japanese intention to vanquish all of East Asia, Australia, and the Pacific islands? Or to counter Al Qaeda, ISIS, violent hate groups, and other terrorist organizations based within the United States and abroad? If diplomacy fails and the use of military force proves too fraught, will America's resort to a stealthier Third Option succeed in their place?

The Treaty Power. Derived from the Greek word *diplomata*, meaning "folded documents," diplomacy is the tool of foreign policy most widely and consistently embraced by officials in Washington—the First Option. It may be more formally defined as the art of adjudicating international disputes through negotiations, including the search for trade deals abroad (often referred to as "economic statecraft"). As a thoughtful Israeli foreign minister has written, diplomacy attempts to achieve national goals "by persuasion, eloquence, inducement, threat or deterrence, and not only by physical domination and war."[6]

The War Power. Taking up arms—the Second Option—can be a beguiling alternative to diplomacy at times, as administrations in Washington make their way in a prickly world through means less painfully slow and indeterminate than is often the case with diplomatic negotiations.[7] "War, war" replaces "jaw, jaw" (in a contrast made famous by Winston Churchill). Moreover, sometimes a military response is pressed upon the United States, as when Nazi U-boats began to sink American passenger liners in the Atlantic, or when Tokyo bombed Pearl Harbor. As well, presidents may strike out with military muscle in a fit of rage, as was reportedly the case when President Trump ordered an attack against Syria in 2018. Fifty-nine US Tomahawk missiles rained down on that nation, without congressional authority or even a debate within the House or Senate—and to no appreciable effect on resolving America's continuing disputes with Syria. As presidents soon discover, war-making is noisy, expensive, difficult to manage (the "fog of war"), and often indecisive.

The Spy Power. In light of diplomacy's limitations (chiefly its glacial pace), as well as the risks—and the staggering erosion of the federal treasury—that accompany warfare, one can readily understand why America's leaders have found covert action an attractive alternative in this triad of foreign policy options. In testimony before a Senate investigative committee in 1975, Director of Central Intelligence (DCI) William E. Colby cited a passage from the Murphy Commission's report in his advocacy of the Third Option:

> There are many risks and dangers associated with covert action ... but ... our adversaries deny themselves no forms of action which might advance their interests or undercut ours.... In many parts of the world a prohibition on our use of covert action would put the U.S. and those who rely on it at a dangerous disadvantage ... therefore ... covert action cannot be abandoned."[8]

This clandestine method of confronting America's international vexations is also known by practitioners as "special activities"—*Actiones Praecipuae*, in the Latin phrase etched on a windowpane at the entrance to the suite of offices that house the Directorate of Operations (DO), the inner sanctum where contemporary practitioners of covert action reside at CIA Headquarters in Langley, Virginia. (A waggish friend of the author has suggested that beneath this Latin phase might be etched another one: *Picaro Pachydermata* or "rogue elephant," a term sometimes used by critics who question the quality of supervision by Congress and even the White House over the CIA's use of covert actions.) In theory at least, covert action promises a quicker remedy than diplomacy to problems overseas. Furthermore, this *modus operandi* is usually far less cacophonous than overt warfare. In light of this feature, covert action is sometimes referred to as "the Quiet Option." It could also be called "the Frugal Option," since these secret operations tend to tap into the federal treasury far less deeply than does mobilizing the US military for major warfare. More important still, fewer lives are lost in covert endeavors than in outright battlefield confrontations.

In an additional description of the Third Option, an experienced officer in the Agency's Directorate of Operations has referred to this approach as a bag of "knavish tricks."[9] Yet a further tag: "irregular methods." Whatever label one prefers, this hidden dimension of foreign policy has been defined in more detail by a former DO leader as "influencing people, organizations, and events in other counties secretly, using a variety of inducements and pressures while attempting to conceal sponsorship."[10] Influencing others, shaping their sense of reality—these are core objectives of covert action.

In a further illustration of its alluring attributes, covert action is normally more subtle than a resort to military force. As former DCI and later secretary of defense James R. Schlesinger once observed, "The military can't do anything small and quiet."[11] In contrast, the CIA can be quick, nimble, and stealthy, moving with cat's eyes in the dark. Journalist Steve Coll observes that the Defense Department usually needs weeks or months to put in place just its logistical support for ground operations overseas. In comparison, "the CIA's value to the White House over decades—part myth, part valid history—had always been that a hundred operations officers with M4 rifles could go anywhere in a week and create mayhem without a lot of care and feeding."[12]

Another consideration: if adversaries such as the Soviet Union during the Cold War were faced with a direct and open slap in the face from the United States by way of a military attack against the USSR or its satellite nations, the Kremlin would almost certainly have slapped back. By avoiding such overt showdowns, covert action significantly reduced the chances of an escalating conflict between the superpowers. When dealing with America's Third Option, adversaries feel less backed into a corner than they would if faced with direct armed aggression.

Put even more simply, the idea behind covert action—an ambitious one—is to channel world affairs in a direction favorable to the United States. Such a goal is, of course, difficult to achieve. History is a vast river with strong currents; it has a mind of its own, and the dragon of Chance is ever near. Still, in hopes of gaining some headway toward the dream of controlling destiny, the United States might (for instance) provide friendly foreigners with "arms or money or encouragement and training," delivered through intermediaries—or "cut-outs" in spy talk.[13] Former secretary of state and national security adviser Henry Kissinger of the Nixon and Ford administrations stated this case for the Third Option: "We need an intelligence community that, in certain complicated situations, can defend the American national interest in the gray areas where military operations are not suitable and diplomacy cannot operate."[14] The fundamental purpose of covert action, then, as a DO officer has put it sparsely, is to "give history a push."[15]

Constitutional Disputes over the Making of American Foreign Policy

Two broad perspectives on governing and foreign policy have evolved in the United States since the nation's Founding Convention in Philadelphia in 1787. The first is a belief that both Congress and the president, working together, have important and interwoven roles to play in determining America's relationship with the rest of the world. While the Constitution has some ambiguities, its key features are as clear as a blue summer sky. First, Congress has the right to declare war—today, we would say "authorize war," since formal declarations have fallen into disuse. This requires a majority vote in each chamber, the House and the Senate. In addition, lawmakers control the nation's purse strings; have authority to maintain accountability over executive agencies; and, ultimately, can impeach and convict a sitting president. All of these rights are listed in Article I of the Constitution.

A second perspective points to Article II, which designates the president as the nation's chief administrator and commander-in-chief; therefore, by implication, this office is basically in charge of foreign policy, whether one is talking about treaty-making, war-making, or the use of covert action. At least so runs the argument from Article II devotees.[16] President Trump seemed intoxicated by this interpretation. "I have an Article II," he told an audience in 2019, "where I have the right to do whatever I want as president."[17]

This simplistic dichotomy between Article I and Article II advocates shunts aside the basic reality of the Constitution: government powers were meant to be *shared* between the two branches of government, Congress and the presidency.[18] Preventing the disintegration of democracy by an executive grown too strong was the core value that animated the nation's founders, and their wisdom continues to reside at the center of America's traditional values. "Checks-and-balances" we call it in the civic books, a doctrine vital to restraining the misuse of governmental powers. The fatal flaw in the argument of those who champion

Article II is the absence of day-to-day accountability exercised over the executive branch by other elected representatives of the American people—that is, by members of Congress.

As a Supreme Court justice has emphasized, the most important idea put forth by the nation's founders was "not to promote efficiency but to *preclude the exercise of arbitrary power*. The purpose was, not to avoid friction, but by means of the inevitable friction incident to the distribution of governmental powers among three departments, *to save the people from autocracy*."[19] By involving other elected officials in the making of foreign and domestic policy, a president—one person—could not dominate the nation, most importantly in the great decisions of war and peace. This is not an antiquated philosophy relevant only to the eighteenth century, but rather the most significant and enduring principle of governance undergirding the existence of the United States as a free and democratic nation over the past 234 years.

Because they regularly visit their constituencies, members of Congress are more exposed to the currents of public opinion from across the United States than are intelligence officers at the CIA or members of the National Security Council (NSC, a presidential forum for White House deliberation over key foreign policy issues). Moreover, lawmakers have considerable knowledge and experience with respect to the crafting of the nation's international affairs, whether the approach involves overt or covert action. Some members of Congress have served for decades on committees that deal with foreign relations, intelligence, armed services, and appropriations. They offer a valuable corporate memory on how the United States has conducted itself on the world stage over the decades—on what has worked and what hasn't.

Of course, the legislative branch can appear unwieldy at times in its debates and deliberations; it is, after all, a large committee of 535 individuals who represent places as different from one another as Vermont is to Arizona. Further, sometimes its leaders seem more dedicated to obstructionism—ensuring that the government does little or nothing—than they are to working across the aisle in search of solutions to the nation's problems. When necessary, though, the more constructive members of Congress can bypass the obstructionists, moving forward with alacrity and a sense of national purpose. Neither branch is perfect; both comprise mortals. Presidents have erred ("To err is Truman," was a favorite GOP saying during the Korean War); and lawmakers have made mistakes, too, as epitomized by the McCarthy era. Working together, though, they may have a better chance of doing the right thing, helping the American people while at the same time reducing the odds of power abuse. At least, that is the essence and hope of democracy, which continues to be (as Churchill observed) better than any other form of governance yet devised, however flawed.

Diplomatic Disputes. In the diplomatic realm, controversy in Washington over power sharing always simmers—and periodically boils over. Tired of being relegated to the sidelines by the executive branch during international negotiations, Congress enacted the landmark Case-Zablocki Act in 1972, which required the executive to report to lawmakers on all agreements consummated by the executive branch with other nations.[20] Before this law, members of Congress often had no idea what foreign pacts the president and his aides had approved with heads of state overseas; with Case-Zablocki, there would be a record of these negotiations. Lawmakers were, at last, in a position to evaluate whether America's agreements were routine and appropriately relegated to executive action or should have been introduced first to the Senate as a solemn treaty proposal—or acted on at least as a "statutory international agreement" requiring a majority vote of approval in both chambers.[21]

The Case-Zablocki law was a meaningful step taken by the legislative branch toward the challenging task of restoring its authority over foreign policy decisions, which had severely eroded with the rise of the "imperial presidency" during the era of the Vietnam War. If Congress was expected to pay for a US commitment made overseas, its members wanted to be part of the decision—in on the takeoffs, not just for the crash landings, in a popular mantra on Capitol Hill.

War Disputes. Similarly, though with even more untoward effects, the White House displayed throughout the Cold War a proclivity to decide on its own when and where US military force would be used. In 1964, for example, President Lyndon B. Johnson misled lawmakers into believing that the North Vietnamese had fired torpedoes at US Navy vessels in the Gulf of Tonkin. The president then requested authority from Congress to build up additional forces in Vietnam to protect the limited American presence he and President John F. Kennedy had already sent there. Gullible at the time, lawmakers readily passed the broadly worded Gulf of Tonkin Resolution, without realizing that Johnson would use this short-term authority to escalate the presence of US troops in South Vietnam and turn Indochina into a major war zone.[22]

Just as Congress decided it had had enough with executive branch dominance over diplomacy, now—just a year after Case-Zablocki—its dismay over unilateral, secretive war-making by the White House reached a head and lawmakers enacted the War Powers Resolution (WPR). This law mandated reporting to Capitol Hill on the use of military force by the executive branch.[23] Moreover, Congress added the bold proviso that henceforth US troops would have to be withdrawn automatically from foreign conflicts within sixty days, unless lawmakers decided to keep them engaged in the fighting for a longer period. In addition, the president would have to withdraw troops at any time *before* the sixty-day period ended, if Congress so decreed by majority vote in both chambers (a "legislative veto" provision struck down by the Supreme Court in 1983 as unconstitutional).

Lawmakers cede their role as a check-and-balance from time to time, but at some point members of Congress remember the wisdom of the Constitution, rue their quiescence, and swing back the pendulum of power in Washington toward a more constitutional executive-legislative balance, as with Case-Zablocki and the WPR.[24] Reflecting with pride on the war powers initiative, a Senate majority leader reminded Americans: "If you've got children or grandchildren who might have to go to war, you'd feel much better with Congress being brought in, than leaving it to one man."[25] Logically, this principle—a distrust of concentrated governmental powers, the greatest insight of the nation's founders—would apply as well to covert actions.

Third Option Disputes. Parallel to the quarrels in Washington that rocked the powers of diplomacy and war-making in the mid-1970s, institutional conflicts between Article I and Article II proponents also roiled the waters surrounding America's use of the Spy Power. Lawmakers were a little slower in confronting institutional imbalances in this dark domain; however, soon after enactment of the WPR and in the wake of a domestic CIA spy scandal,[26] Congress attempted in the years from 1974 to 1977 to tighten controls as well over America's secret agencies, carrying its reassertion of constitutional authority over foreign policy even further into this highly secretive sphere of government than it had with matters of diplomacy and war-making.

The central controversy over the Spy Power during this period of intelligence reform in the 1970s became initially riveted, as had been true for diplomacy and war-making, on whether lawmakers should be privy to information about US foreign policy initiatives: in this case, the CIA's use of clandestine operations abroad—and especially, at that time, against the democratic government of Chile. The nature of the Spy Power as manifested in the Third Option, and efforts by lawmakers to control its use, is explored in the chapters that follow, beginning with a look at the different forms that covert action can assume. First, though, this Introduction briefly reconstructs the kind of world the United States faced in 1947 when it established the CIA and a covert action capability.

The Emergence of a Chilling Global Rival

The end of the Second World War brought the joy of victory to the United States. At last the troops were coming home and Americans could return to a normal life. Yet the war had brought great loss to the nation and had left the world in a state of exhaustion and disarray. Europe and much of Asia lay prostrate, wrecked by the carnage of modern warfare. Nations and families were torn asunder;

refugees uprooted and crowded into makeshift camps; hunger and unemployment, rampant; Dresden and other European cities, burned-out skeletons; Hiroshima and Nagasaki, moonscapes covered in a blanket of nuclear radiation.

After the war, the Truman administration rapidly demobilized US troops and concentrated on the challenge of helping veterans begin new lives in civilian society. The Soviet Union, though, had a rather different approach to the new peace. America's erstwhile ally had lost a staggering 27 million troops and civilians while fighting the Nazis, more than a tenth of its population and ninety times the number of Americans who perished in the war.[27] Russia had been popular among Americans, who appreciated the sacrifices its people had endured during the war once the Kremlin awoke to the fact that the Third Reich had become an enemy. In 1945, though, the world seemed to change overnight as the Soviets immediately displayed aggressive intentions toward the West. "Within six months after war's end all pretense at friendship was being dropped," writes political scientist David S. McLellan. "Henceforth each side would interpret all moves as basically hostile and therefore would act accordingly. The Cold War had begun."[28]

Soviet leader Joseph Stalin, a crafty and ruthless autocrat, had ordered the murder of millions of Russians during his rule (1923–1953), including not only personal rivals but an entire class of citizens—some 1 million people—known as *kulaks*, the backbone of the entrepreneurial class of small landholders in Russia who resisted his plans for forced agricultural collectivization. Stalin kept his armies in uniform and, augmented by guerilla cadres, used these soldiers at the end of the war to rob banks in Germany and elsewhere in Europe, accumulating an illicit treasure chest to fund the development of communist parties in every nation on the European Continent, in Asia, and most everywhere else he could.

Stalin also directed his standing army to subjugate and exploit smaller nations on Russia's borders. Overnight, the Red Army crushed the budding tendrils of freedom in Eastern Europe, from Estonia to Yugoslavia. Taking up covert action with a vengeance ("active measures" in Soviet terminology, or what some Russian intelligence officers refer to as "wrecking"), the Stalin regime and its key foreign intelligence apparatus, the KGB, set out to influence elections in France and Italy in 1946 (just as another Russian leader, Vladimir V. Putin, would do with his troll farms against the United States in 2016 and 2020, and on matters other than elections as well).[29] British historian Christopher Andrew writes that throughout the Cold War, the KGB would use covert action "on a larger scale than the CIA."[30]

America now faced an unexpected and muscular nemesis, one hell-bent—as Stalin's truculent speeches made abundantly clear—on spreading communism around the globe at the expense of Western democratic alliances and the freedom of neutral regimes in Asia, Africa, and Latin America. Any appraisal of the Third

Option during this time and throughout the Cold War must take into account the tenor of these times and the understandable fear that Stalin induced in the West, further inflamed inside the United States during the 1950s by Senator Joe McCarthy (R, Wisconsin) and others who profited politically from an epidemic of anti-communist fearmongering.[31]

Hitler had intended to rule the Third Reich from Nürnberg, a city in Bavaria known for its beautiful parks, lakes, and spacious athletic fields; for Stalin, Moscow would be the center of the universe, with the capitalist nations subservient to the will of the Soviet Communist Party and its expanding military arm. From Stalin's point of view, the Second World War had demonstrated how "the development of world capitalism proceeds . . . through crises and military conflicts."[32] According to his worldview, capitalism was an evil force that had to be vanquished and replaced with a superior form of society: the Soviet brand of communism.

Stalin was used to having his way, but President Truman and his secretary of state Dean Acheson were not in the habit of being pushed around. The president was known for his feisty personality, honed as a combat leader in the trench warfare of the First World War. "I do not think we should play compromise any longer," he told Acheson. "I'm tired of babying the Soviets."[33] The crude thump of reality in the form of the rising Red Army and a global web of intelligence agents run by the KGB (the Soviet equivalent of the CIA during the Cold War), along with the realization that the Russians were developing their own nuclear weapons—with much of the necessary technology stolen from America's Manhattan Project by the Kremlin's "atomic spies" during the waning months of the Second World War—forced the United States to abandon its tradition of isolationism and assume the stance of a world leader, one that began to see world events largely through an anti-communism prism.

In light of this unsettling new threat, one of President Truman's first moves after the war ended was to improve America's intelligence capabilities. The potential use of covert action was far from his mind, but better intelligence collection and analysis became a White House priority: making sense of world developments, guarding against another Pearl Harbor surprise from the Soviets or anyone else, and—above all—tracking what Stalin, the Red Army, and the KGB were plotting across the latitudes and longitudes. Truman had been dismayed by the disorganized nature of America's intelligence efforts during the war. Afterward, he grew increasingly weary of the multiple stacks of intelligence reporting that arrived each day on his desk in the Oval Office (the "Oval"). In frustration, Truman told his top aides that he didn't have time to wade through "a bunch of papers two feet high." Intelligence had to be "centralized," with a director "coordinating all intelligence activities."[34] Even more worrisome than this intelligence fragmentation and inefficiency was the memory of the Japanese surprise attack, and—above all else—the mushrooming military might of the Soviet Union. The United States had to know what weaponry, troop battalions, and naval capabilities the Soviets had, where they were located, and how they might be deployed; and that information needed to be communicated succinctly and accurately to the White House.

The Truman administration recommended to Congress the establishment of a Central Intelligence Agency to establish improved interagency integration of intelligence activities. The goal would be, in spy vernacular, "all-source fusion"—a more manageable collation of the intelligence gathered from around the world by America's espionage services. In 1947, the CIA became the first foreign intelligence organization in any major nation set up as a result of a law passed by the legislative branch of government.[35] America's new Intelligence Community or IC, under the leadership of a director of Central Intelligence based at the CIA, ended up being far less centralized, though, than Truman had originally envisioned. The Pentagon balked at giving too much power to the new spy agency, particularly over intelligence related to military matters (as most intelligence is). Thus, America's first spymaster, the DCI, remained something of a figurehead. The director had control over the CIA but was granted only limited authority to coordinate intelligence organizations throughout the government. This weakness, with individual intelligence agencies operating within their own separate "silos" or "stovepipes," would consistently plague the government in the years to come.

The law that created the CIA, entitled the National Security Act of 1947, was devoted primarily to the creation of a modern Department of Defense that would replace the old Departments of Navy and War. At its core, this meant strengthening cooperation ("jointness") among the US armed services, which had often failed to dovetail their activities effectively during the war. Only six paragraphs of the lengthy document dealt with intelligence; they addressed the DCI's powers, limited as they were, and emphasized that the CIA would be essentially a collection-and-analysis organization. The words "covert action" or "counterintelligence" never appeared in the statute, although both of these missions would soon become important as America's intelligence officers focused on what was rapidly becoming their most important responsibility: checking the global appetite of the Soviet Union.

An oblique nod in the direction of the Third Option could be imagined, though, in language embedded at the very end of the intelligence portion of the 1947 law. White House counsel Clark Clifford, the main drafter of the National Security Act, capped off the section on intelligence with a boilerplate phrase designed to cover unforeseen secret directions the government might need to take in pursuit of its foreign policy objectives. This last-minute language noted that the government—the CIA—might have to engage in "such other functions and duties related to intelligence affecting the national security as the National Security Council may from time to time direct."

After leaving office, Truman expressed concern about this vague invitation to a more aggressive use of America's premier spy agency, as opposed to its collection-and-analysis mission. "For some time I have been disturbed by the way CIA has been diverted from its original assignment," he recalled in retirement. "It has become an operational and at times a policy-making arm of the government." The former president worried that the Agency was now "so removed from its intended role that it is being interpreted as a symbol of sinister and mysterious foreign intrigue—and a subject for Cold War enemy propaganda."[36]

In 1947, however, Truman's aides enthusiastically embraced the spongy "other functions and duties" phrase of the Security Act to justify the rapid establishment of a Third Option capability within the Agency. Here was a secretive foreign policy tool that could be used in such a manner as to avoid more open and risky military confrontations with the Soviet empire; and it would be far less costly to carry out than overt warfare, with its great disruptions, loss of lives, and expensive weaponry. Legally scholars Reisman and Baker have underscored this attractive attribute of covert action: "The costs, in terms of lives, materiel and social and economic disruption, to the United States, to particular target states and to non-targeted third states might be substantially less if the modality of implementation selected were in whole or in part covert."[37]

Within days of the law's enactment, planners at the CIA were busy devising propaganda themes the Agency could use secretly in foreign countries to counter the negative information onslaught that the Soviet Union had already unleashed against the United States around the globe. The climate of the times—the disquieting emergence of a Cold War between the two superpowers (the Soviets had "the Bomb" by 1949, much to the surprise of the CIA)—demanded no less than an energetic response by all of America's national security agencies, from the Pentagon to the various espionage organizations.

At any rate, this was the thinking at the time. A presidential commission would state the case in stark terms during the early years of the Eisenhower administration:

> It is clear that we are facing an implacable enemy whose avowed objective is world domination by whatever means at whatever cost. There are no rules in such a game. Hitherto acceptable norms of human conduct do not apply. If the U.S. is to survive . . . we must learn to subvert, sabotage and destroy our enemies by more clever, more sophisticated and more effective methods than those used against us. It may become necessary that the American people will be made acquainted with, understand and support this fundamentally repugnant philosophy.[38]

This climate of fear, stirred by the prospects of communist global expansion, had become palpable across the American landscape by the 1950s.[39] As early as 1946, the Soviets had gobbled up the Iranian province of Azerbaijan; and, that same year, Soviet-sponsored communist rebels initiated a civil war in Greece. Germany stood divided between East and West; the Baltic nations had fallen into the Kremlin's grasping hands as early as 1944; and, by 1947 when the CIA was created, communists had taken over as well as in Poland, Hungary, and Romania. Further, Moscow was secretly sponsoring communist-led insurrections in the Philippines. The next year, Czechoslovakia succumbed to communist guerrillas funded by the KGB, as the Kremlin tightened its grip over Eastern Europe. As these events were under way, France and Italy suffered from debilitating communist-instigated labor strikes.

Moscow seemed to be pulling the strings on a massive global movement that aspired to universal Soviet control. All the while, Stalin was spouting vitriolic anti-Western rhetoric. Little wonder a sense of "war scare" possessed Washington officials, a nervousness that would only be intensified by further communist successes in mainland China and during the Korean War—not to mention the sense of panic stirred within the United States by Senator McCarthy. Little wonder that Dwight D. Eisenhower rode to an easy victory on a strident anti-communist platform during the 1952 presidential election, blaming the Truman administration for (among other things) "losing China." And that a stealthy, and increasingly aggressive, CIA held appeal as a means for coping with this rising Red Menace.

The United States could ill afford to stumble in the struggle to win the hearts and minds of people around the world (in a popular trope of the times). Would the planet be painted in crimson hues by a Soviet brush or would the democracies and capitalism prevail? Much hung in the balance. According to a chief of covert action at the CIA in these early years, the foremost duty of his unit was to take on "the global challenge of communism . . . to be confronted whenever and wherever it seemed to threaten our interests."[40] A chairman of the Armed Services Committee in the House of Representatives graphically described the road ahead as "a fight between Jesus Christ and the Hammer-and-Sickle."[41] Readers of Jack London's still popular novel, *The Call of the Wild*, published in 1903, could recognize in this overheated rhetoric the code of club and fang, where "kill or be killed, eat or be eaten was the law."[42] Not only for huskies in the Yukon but for Americans in a dangerous world, only the strong would prevail. The United States found itself in a world of battle and blood: Americanism versus communism.

"The Soviets would try to achieve their purposes by the penetration and subversion of governments all over the world," writes historian Anne Karalekas. "The accepted role of the United States was to prevent that expansion."[43] This state of affairs gave birth to the containment doctrine, and provided the CIA with its marching orders. Even decades later in the 1970s, President Gerald R. Ford would declare that the primary objective of covert action was to buttress the world's democracies against communist influence.[44]

The Treaty Power, the Spy Power, and—if necessary—maybe even the War Power would have to be adroitly administered if, at the end of the day, the American way of life would continue to exist. At the CIA, intelligence officials took up the tasks of improving collection and analysis; crafted methods of counterintelligence to block Soviet espionage and active measures against the United States; and, last but not least, developed an array of Third Option techniques designed to stymie Soviet global adventurism.

More specifically, covert actions would help to seek victory for the United States in the incipient Cold War by such measures as these:

- fostering democratic solutions to dauntingly complex challenges facing countries in the developing world, most notably hunger and poverty;
- resisting communist subversion;
- assisting, behind the scenes, governments favorably disposed toward the United States and democracy;
- encouraging developing nations to join pro-Western regional pacts, such as the Alliance for Progress, created by the Kennedy administration to improve US economic cooperation with Latin America and, thereby, curb the appeal of communism;
- helping trade unions, student groups, and other organizations around the world in the fight against communist takeovers; and,
- driving communists and their bedfellows from public office on every continent.

Both the Truman and Eisenhower administrations decided it would be useful to have a handy covert instrument available for foreign intervention in the absence of a national consensus for the overt use of military force against a threatening nation or faction.[45] So on the covert action front there was much work to be done by the fledgling CIA, even if its main job was supposedly the collection and interpretation of information from all points of the compass. As Chapter 1 relates, the Agency set out to develop a lively packet of tricks to advance this added mission of clandestine interventions abroad.

PART I
TRADECRAFT

1
The Forms of Covert Action

From Propaganda to Paramilitary Operations

Since 1947, the scope of US covert actions carried out by the Central Intelligence Agency (CIA) has been wide.[1] Usually these operations were driven by an anticommunist blueprint, directed against nations that had been drawn into an orbit around the Soviet Union and Mainland China, or against neutral countries that had leaned toward Moscow or Beijing more than Washington officials found tolerable—an emerging ABC foreign policy ("Anybody But Communists"). Toward this end, the Agency targeted the Third Option not only against the governments and leaders of foreign nations but at their citizens as well: political parties, labor unions, student and faculty groups, women's clubs, civic associations, religious organizations, newspapers and journals, publishing houses. Targeted, too, especially in more recent years, have been hostile non-state organizations. Highest on this list: terrorist factions, narcotics cartels, illicit arms dealers, and human traffickers. Moreover, threatening individuals—hostile leaders, terrorists—have been in the Agency's crosshairs from time to time, sometimes literally.

The covert actions directed against these nations, groups, and individuals may be divided into four general categories or forms: propaganda, political, economic, and paramilitary operations. As a former CIA officer has written, these approaches "cover a broad front" that includes "dropping arms and money to guerrilla groups, supplying funds to a political party or leader, subsidizing a labor union, funding an editor or giving him an outline for an editorial, supporting an ostensibly private radio or magazine, supplying an airline ticket, taking a man to dinner."[2]

Far and away the most extensively pursued method has been the use of propaganda, in part because it is the easiest to pull off. In an earlier era, this response to world events was known in US military circles as psychological warfare, psychological operations, politico-psychological operations, or just plain "psy ops." Today it is often referred to as "information operations" ("info ops") or, in a notably creative Agency euphemism, "perception enhancement."

Covert Action as Propaganda

Since 1947, in a worldwide anti-communist ideological campaign, the CIA has disseminated (through an undercover network that reaches to far-flung areas of the earth's surface) thousands of themes on international affairs ("perspectives," in Agency terminology). This approach, studded with many possibilities for extolling the virtues of the United States and denigrating its adversaries, has portrayed this country in a uniformly favorable light and international opponents—mainly the USSR and, today, Russia—as villainous.

Hoping to dominate the global information space with anti-communist and pro-democracy stories, the Agency inserted its messages into foreign media channels wherever possible across the globe: newspapers, magazines, television, and, more recently, social media. This outpouring, a veritable floodtide of attempted influence-peddling operations—critics might say "brainwashing"—is dispersed by way of local journalists hired by the CIA and known as "media assets," in the parlance of the Directorate of Operations or DO, the Agency's nerve center for covert action starting in 1973 (and known earlier as the Directorate of Plans or DP). For a blueprint of how the CIA is organized into "directorates," which a former DCI has described as "separate baronies rather than a strategic planning system," see Figure 1.1. These directorates have changed little over the

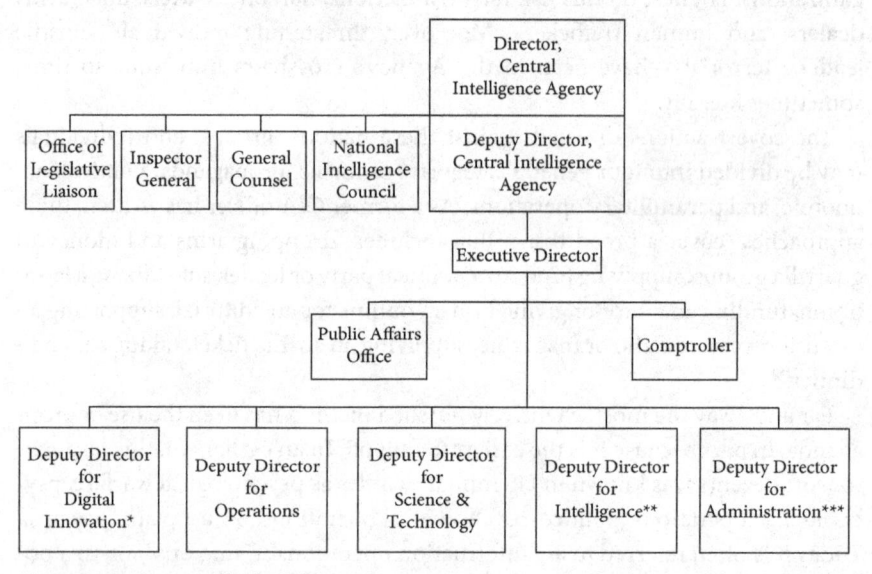

*A new Directorate created by the CIA in 2015
**Now the Deputy Director of Analysis for the Directorate of Analysis
***Now the Deputy Director for Support for the Directorate of Support

Figure 1.1 The Directorates of the Central Intelligence Agency

THE FORMS OF COVERT ACTION   21

years, although now include a Directorate for Digital Innovation and, within the DO, a Special Activities Center.[3]

Assets, or "agents" as they are portrayed in the media and Hollywood movies, are locals in foreign countries who are secretly recruited by DO "case officers" ("human operations officers," or simply "operations officers" in more recent CIA diction). The job description for an asset: influence the media—or possibly pursue more nefarious roles, such as paramilitary activities if the asset has the requisite talents and access to targets. The Agency's worldwide network of media assets is known in the DO as the "infrastructure" or, in more colloquial terms, the "plumbing," which the Agency relies on overseas for both intelligence collection and carrying out the Third Option. The top Agency official in the field within each country where the organization has a presence is the chief of station

```
                    Directorate of Operations
                              │
                    Deputy Director for
                     Operations (DDO)
                              │
  ┌─────────┬─────────┬─────────┬─────────┬─────────┬─────────┐
 Covert    Special  Counter-   Counter-  Counter-   Other
 Action    Operations Intelligence Terrorism Narcotics Specialized
 Staff (CAS) (SO)    Staff (CIS)                      Statts
  └─────────┴─────────┴─────────┴─────────┴─────────┴─────────┘
                              │
                     Regional Divisions
                              │
  ┌─────────┬─────────┬─────────┬─────────┬─────────┬─────────┐
 Soviet/    Near     Europe    East      Africa    Western
 East Europe East                Asia                Hemisphere
  └─────────┴─────────┴─────────┴─────────┴─────────┴─────────┘
                              │
                         Specific
                         Countries
                              │
                          Chief
                        of Station
                          (COS)
                              │
                           CIA
                         Officers
                              │
                          Assets
```

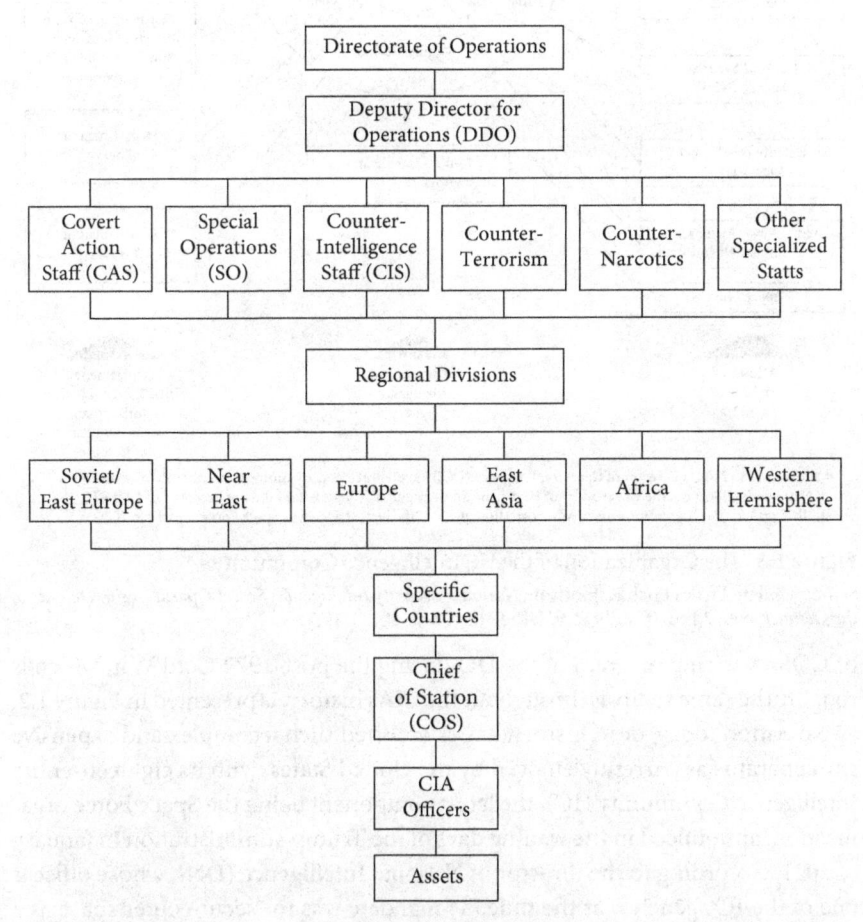

Figure 1.2 The CIA Operations Directorate During the Cold War

22 THE THIRD OPTION

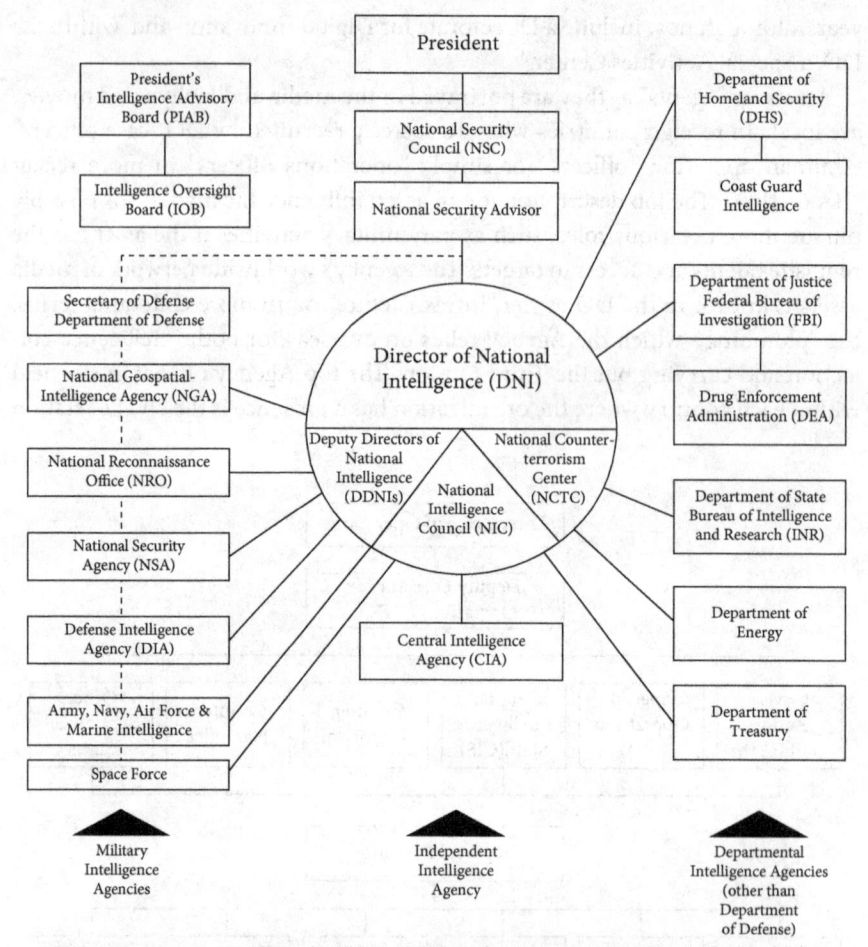

Figure 1.3 The Organization of the US Intelligence Community

Source: Updated from Loch K. Johnson, *National Security Intelligence: Secret Operations in Defense of the Democracies*, 2d ed. (Cambridge, UK: Polity Press, 2017): 17.

or COS. A wiring diagram of the DO during the post-1972 Cold War, which is roughly the same setup as throughout the CIA's history, is presented in Figure 1.2.

No nation today, or in history, has established such a complex and expensive spy apparatus as currently enjoyed by the United States, with its eighteen-entity Intelligence Community (IC), the latest component being the Space Force organization, announced in the waning days of the Trump administration in January of 2021. According to the director of National Intelligence (DNI, whose office is one of the IC agencies) at the time, its mandate was to "secure outer space as a safe and free domain for America's interests."

This array of cloistered organizations (see Figure 1.3) costs some $80 billion per annum and stretches from espionage assets in the world's back alleys—a CIA specialty—to elaborate space-based surveillance satellites carrying every possible bell and whistle for peering down at Planet Earth. The satellite side of US intelligence is the preserve of other giant, three-letter agencies in the Community: the National Security Agency (NSA), the National Geospatial-Intelligence Agency (NGA), and the National Reconnaissance Office (NRO). Among the full cluster of entities in the IC, five have principally an intelligence mission: CIA, NSA, NGA, NRO, and Defense Intelligence Agency (DIA)—these last four all within the framework of the Defense Department, with the CIA the only organization outside of a cabinet department. Some IC leaders think of these five organizations as the true intelligence "agencies," with the remaining thirteen as IC "components" that support a larger policy department in a range of assignments. In another variation, the Federal Bureau of Investigation (FBI) is sometimes viewed as the sixth agency, since intelligence (along with law enforcement) is such a prominent responsibility at "the Bureau" (see Figure 1.3).

The CIA has relied on a broad portfolio of other methods to undermine foreign leaders and regimes opposed by the United States, including the use of counterfeit documents, the testimony of fake experts, the spreading of rumors, and letter-writing campaigns. An example of a letter-writing campaign: in an effort to shift the Italian electorate away from the Communist Party and toward the pro-Western Christian Democratic Party in Italy during the early decades of the Cold War, the Agency stimulated a large-scale mailing blizzard. At the request of the CIA, Italian-Americans in the United States sent some 10,000 messages to relatives back home in Italy, urging an anti-communist vote.[4] As well, the Agency regularly leaks favorable news stories to the foreign media about the United States (true or exaggerated), as well as negative stories (often true) and—though rarely—fabricated documents about the governments in communist countries.

The theory behind covert propaganda is uncomplicated. To use a hypothetical illustration from Germany, a reader in Munich is likely to put more stock in an op-ed written in a local newspaper by, let us say, the journalist Hans Bauermann (a made-up name) than in an official White House or US embassy press release. Unbeknownst to his readers, Herr Bauermann is the recipient of a monthly stipend from the CIA. In return for the non-taxed Euros and the vacation they will purchase on a Greek isle, he adopts the American point-of-view in his columns. If Herr Bauermann is energetic, he may pen the pieces himself based on a few CIA guidelines; or, depending on how lazy (or malleable) he is, the DO will write the copy for him, in perfect German and ready for print.

Covert propaganda can take three general forms. One is "white," in which the message is truthful: telling it like it is, for which the British Broadcasting Company (BBC, founded in 1926) had an enviable reputation during the Cold

War, and still does. Credibility is the hallmark of this approach. Propaganda can also be "black," that is, consisting of attempts to assault the ears of listeners and the eyes of readers with counterfeit truth, whether outright falsehoods or exaggerations; in a word, disinformation, often designed to make it appear as though it emanated from Moscow or some other adversarial source. This particularly controversial form of propaganda amounted to only about 2 percent of the total CIA dissemination during the Cold War. Propaganda may be gray, as well: an alloy of white and black—clandestine spin-doctoring, with a premium on making the United States look good.

Examples of the Agency's use of propaganda during the Cold War might include commentaries about the human tragedies caused by East Germany's erection of the Berlin Wall; op-eds to drum up support for America's involvement in the Vietnam War (a sore point among many Europeans in the 1960s who otherwise liked the United States); or an excoriation of the Soviet invasion into Czechoslovakia in 1968. Today, perhaps an article might claim that Russia has been arming certain terrorist groups; inveigh against the Russian development of destabilizing "supersonic" missiles; or accuse the Chinese of causing a worldwide pandemic with the COVID-19 virus. Of course, similar kinds of invective are routinely spread by Russian, Chinese, Iranian, North Korean, and other foreign intelligence services against the United States and its allies—an ongoing war of words that adds daily to the pollution of the world's air waves.

A further illustration is America's advocacy in the 1980s of a US intermediate-range nuclear force (INF), a category of nuclear-tipped missiles placed on West German soil to serve as an added deterrent against the Soviet Union. The Kremlin precipitated this new Cold War arms race when it installed a comparable category of weaponry in East Europe, along the West German border. The Green Party and others on the left in West German politics strenuously opposed the INF counterresponse by the United States, despite the initial provocative move by Moscow. Many West Germans feared that the US missiles (Pershing IIs) would attract immediate retaliation by the Kremlin, should a Third World War break out between the superpowers. They balked at the possibility of turning *Deutschland* into a smoldering radioactive heap. The US government sought to neutralize this opposition to the INF through a hidden media campaign, fashioned by the DO and crafted to reinforce the official government position in Washington that the American missiles were a positive, vital part of the West's defensive shield against potential Soviet aggression.

The argument secretly disseminated by the CIA was essentially truthful, but the Agency had sidestepped the question of whether these missile placements would, in fact, make West Germany a more likely prime target for a preemptive military strike by the Soviet Union in wartime. The "perception enhancement" in this example was mostly white, but with some significant omissions regarding the implications of the INF weapon sites. German public opinion moved toward accepting the INF initiative, although it is impossible to measure the effects (if any) of the Agency's covert propaganda program in nurturing this support. The view at the CIA was that it didn't hurt and maybe it helped. This rationale is comparable to what intelligence scholar Rory Cormac refers to as the British intelligence point-of-view on its global propaganda activities during the 1960s. The policy was one of "hoping for the best and seeing what happened."[5]

Measuring the effects of media in any capacity is notoriously difficult, but proponents of the Agency's covert propaganda cite interviews with Soviet dissidents to make their case. These émigrés periodically fled the Soviet Bloc during the Cold War and, once settled in the West, testified to US intelligence debriefers that the copies of *Time*, *Newsweek*, and other magazines smuggled into the USSR by Agency assets, along with anti-Soviet audiotapes, recordings, and books, gave them hope and courage to continue their resistance. The Agency's "book program," started in 1956, was particularly popular among dissidents. A miniaturized edition of the *Gulag Archipelago* was a hot underground item, for instance, infiltrated into Eastern Europe and the Soviet Union by CIA assets. The book, banned throughout the Soviet empire, was a searing account of Russia's political prisons, published in 1973 by the exiled Russian winner of the Nobel Prize for Literature (awarded in 1970), Aleksandr Solzhenitsyn. Much sought after, too, in Poland, was a book on the Soviet massacre of some 22,000 Polish military officers and intelligentsia in the spring of 1940.

The CIA did its best to flood Soviet and Red Chinese territories with pro-West, anti-communist literature through a range of secret routes ("ratlines") into Eastern Europe and other nations bordering the communist superpowers. This infiltration relied on a variety of ingenious techniques that would have impressed the *Capos* of an experienced drug cartel, including the hiding of contraband literature in costume wardrobes worn by visiting ballet troupes from behind the Iron Curtain, as well as within the athletic gear of touring athletes and the Lederhosen of backpackers. Handy hiding places also included the confines of thick conference papers lugged by academics to international conferences, and the suitcases of individuals wearing the clerical collar. Other places included concealment inside exported goods, from automobiles to fire extinguishers; trucks, boats, tour buses, small boats traveling at midnight along the coastline; even homing pigeons and helium-filled balloons dependent on favorable wind currents—whatever might work became a method for permeating suppressed nations with propaganda.

Through hundreds of media channels around the world, the CIA pumped roughly seventy to eighty insertions per day during the Cold War from 1947 to 1974, according to Church Committee investigators—a substantial outpouring of propaganda known proudly at the Agency in these years as a "Mighty Wurlitzer."[6] These Third Option methods assisted in the ousting of an Iranian leader in 1953 and played an important role in another coup in Guatemala the following year (both examined in Chapter 3). According to CIA officials, propaganda programs significantly helped as well to shield fledgling democracies against lies about the United States and the supposed bankruptcy of the democratic model of governance, all concocted and propagated by the KGB (the Soviet foreign intelligence service).

In its efforts first to defeat, and then—when he was elected anyway, in a free and open balloting in 1970—to topple the president of Chile, Salvador Allende, the CIA spent millions of dollars on propaganda operations designed to crater his fledgling regime. Allende had had the nerve to invite Fidel Castro for a visit to Chile for a month, putting an exclamation mark behind the belief of the Nixon administration that the Chilean leader was a serious threat to stability in the Western Hemisphere. The Agency's propaganda operations in this case relied heavily on newspaper articles, including one-a-day in the top Santiago paper, *El Mercurio*, during the 1970 presidential election. The CIA would soon secretly fund this entire newspaper, going beyond its norm of recruiting only individual reporters employed by a foreign paper, magazine, or broadcast station. According to the Church Committee, other propaganda venues against Allende included radio transmissions; cartoons; films; pamphlets, posters, and banners; paper streamers; leaflets and direct mailings; wall paintings; and, drawing the Catholic Church into the fray, copies of an anti-communist pastoral letter written by Pope Pius XI. Winning regardless, Allende remained in power until 1973, when he was overthrown by a military coup supported by the CIA (examined later in this book).

Further, the Agency ran its own radio stations in different parts of the world, such as Radio Free Europe (RFE, set up in 1950 to beam into Poland and elsewhere in Eastern Europe) and Radio Liberty (RL, established the next year as a complement to RFE). Both stations delivered anti-communist messages around the world, with a special focus on whatever audiences might be listening behind the Soviet Iron Curtain. The goal was to inspire hope among dissidents as well as to encourage their resistance to communism—maybe even inspiring a few high-level government officials and societal notables to defect to the Western camp. To assist in its propaganda transmissions, the Agency has periodically distributed transistor radios—tunable only to the CIA's stations—lofted by balloons into the arms of villagers located in remote parts of the world, if the prevailing winds cooperated. Example targets were communist-held regions of Laos during the 1960s, and Polish townships in the 1980s.[7] In 1972, RFE and RL stations were outed as CIA tools of propaganda, but they soon began to serve the same purposes as overt arms of the State Department. Today, a considerable portion of additional radio propaganda for foreign audiences is openly funded by the United States, as with Radio Sawa and its companion station Al Hurra TV, both becoming operational in 2002 and dedicated to enhancing America's image among Arabs in the Middle East.

During the Cold War, the CIA sowed comparable anti-communist materials, including again *Time* and *Newsweek* magazines, into China and other communist countries. The Agency also expanded its secret sponsorship of influential newspapers and journals abroad, such as *Der Monat* in West Germany. Moreover, it recruited Eastern European dissidents and expatriates who, given the right financial encouragement, would establish magazines and newspapers critical of communism. An example during the 1980s was the publication *Kultura*, based in Paris, run by expats, and aimed at their Polish homeland; and *Tygodnik Mazowsze*, a weekly newspaper inside Poland, operated by members of the Solidarity trade union movement. As well, the Agency financed (with "research funding") anti-communist tracts written by Western authors, including American university professors—some knowledgeable and others not about the true source of their "government" awards.

One former CIA officer has concluded that the Agency's propaganda programs delivered "dubious benefits."[8] The DCI in the Carter administration, Admiral Stansfield Turner, also had little use—at first—for the notion of secretly distributing books and periodicals as instruments of propaganda. The admiral considered it a waste of time and money. The program eventually grew on him, though. "Certainly one thinks that the book program, the broadcast programs (most notably, Radio Free Europe), the information programs do good," Turner recalled to an interviewer after his retirement as CIA chief. "When you get facts into a country where the truth is not a common commodity, you're doing some good."[9]

Today the available social media "advertising channels" for possible use by the Agency, and every other spy service in the world, have proliferated like spring poppyseeds: Facebook, Google, Twitter, YouTube, and the rest. Nevertheless, some of the old tried-and-true methods have continued to play a role, as when "night letters" were used in covert actions against the Taliban regime in Afghanistan after the September 11, 2001, terrorist attacks on the United States. As former DO officer Robert L. Grenier remembers, these letters were "propaganda sheets slid under doors or tossed over compound walls in the dark of night—in and around Kandahar, decrying bin Laden and the pernicious presence of Arab foreigners."[10]

While usually in the form of a tame distribution of truthful information in support of US foreign policy objectives, sometimes the CIA's propaganda activities have slipped into an irresponsible encouragement of local rebellions despite the exceedingly poor odds of success—an unethical approach to anti-communism or any other adversarial ideology. A classic illustration is Hungary in 1956, when Agency propaganda—most notably, RFE—may have encouraged young people in Budapest to rise up against communist rule, with the hinted inducement that the United States would have their back once the rebellion began. The inspirational message: students, heroically, could roll back the Iron Curtain and the United States would help. If this Agency incitement actually occurred (reports differ), the promises were a tragic lie, indeed an invitation to mass suicide. In response to the rebellion, the Soviet Army engaged in wholesale slaughter against mainly young Hungarian idealists—with many thousands of deaths in Budapest and across that nation's bloodied landscape.[11]

Similarly, in 1991 during the First Persian Gulf War, the Agency encouraged Kurds and Shiites in Iraq to rebel against Saddam Hussein and his Sunni regime, by broadcasting through a CIA clandestine radio station ("Voice of Free Iraq") that the dictator was on the verge of fleeing the country and the moment was propitious for insurrection. The rebellion never materialized; fear among Iraqi citizens over the viciousness of Saddam's internal security forces was too strong, and rightly so. By 1995, however, the Agency's cumulative propaganda promises had their desired effect and some Iraqis—mostly the hapless Kurds in the north of Iraq, held together by cobwebs of hope—did rebel, in a dreamy belief that the US military would return immediately to Iraq and take up their cause. Yet another misperception, another Third Option come unstuck, a swirl of shattered hopes, more massacres: this time in the streets of cities and villages across northern Iraq. The failure of these operations left a bad taste in President Clinton's mouth regarding the value of covert action and raised doubts in his administration about the leadership acumen of the DCI at the time, John Deutch (discussed further in Chapter 5).

One of the CIA's most spectacular propaganda operations involved circulating, throughout Eastern Europe and beyond, copies of Soviet President Nikita Khrushchev's notorious "secret speech" to the 20th Communist Party Congress in 1956. This document was strongly critical of the Stalin years. (The Soviet dictator died in March 1953.) Israeli intelligence had obtained a copy and passed it along to James J. Angleton, their favorite contact inside the Directorate of Plans (DP, the precursor to the DO). Astonishingly, in the speech Khrushchev revealed to his comrades a blood-curdling glimpse into the purgatory of the Stalin regime—great material for the CIA's psy-war specialists. Some say the speech was doctored by the DP before its circulation into Eastern Europe by its local *agents provocateurs*. The idea was to portray Stalin as even more of a monster than he was, a twist of the screw that may have been an Angleton brainstorm.[12]

Over the years, the Agency has gone so far as to encourage its copious media contacts inside the United States to write negative reviews and commentary about books critical of the CIA, or thumbs-up evaluations of volumes that portray the Agency in a more positive light. The reward to compliant writers: newsworthy leaks, maybe even Pulitzer prize–winning scoops. Through at-home media channels, the Agency has also attacked investigating congressional committees.[13] These are disturbing illustrations of how the CIA's psy-ops machine has been directed against an American audience in an effort to marginalize the organization's critics.[14]

Recently, the CIA promulgated a steady, positive drumbeat of media coverage inside the United States on the subject of its torture practices against suspected terrorists in the aftermath of the 9/11 terrorist strikes, a counterattack aimed at a report from the Senate Select Committee on Intelligence that had been critical of these harsh methods of counterterrorism. Current and former intelligence officers regularly appeared on television and radio talk shows and sent out emails and tweets, each similarly worded, to defend the Agency's "enhanced interrogation" methods (in another of Langley's gentle-sounding euphemisms).[15] Defaming foreign leaders disliked by Washington administrations is a finely honed CIA specialty: deepfakes; pornographic movies starring fake stand-ins resembling foreign leaders; poison-pen and fabricated letters; entirely forged or altered documents—all number among its methods of discrediting communists and other foreign adversaries.[16] Turning these skills against critics inside the United States, or against America's ambassadors overseas who may be giving the Agency trouble in the field, is an easy transition.[17]

Another controversial aspect of CIA propaganda has been the problem of "blowback" or "replay," whereby the Agency's attempts at foreign influence have wafted back to the United States on the airwaves of a media-compressed globe, thereby manipulating America's citizens rather than just foreign adversaries. The irony is obvious: in its designs to fool US foes abroad, the CIA ends up inadvertently fooling Americans at home. Former DCI William Colby maintained that blowback occurs "very rarely"; but, in one of several examples, the Church Committee came across a DP memo that boasted how "a replay of Chile theme materials" (part of the Agency's effort to depose Allende) had surfaced in the *New York Times* and the *Washington Post*. Further, a high-level analyst at the CIA, Ray S. Cline, recalled how it worried him "a lot that false CIA propaganda about mainland China might fool China experts in the Department of State, skewing their analysis."[18]

Blowback remains a dilemma for the Agency. One remedy, exercised in an uneven manner, is for DCIs (and now directors of Central Intelligence or D/CIAs, an office that replaced the DCI position in 2004) to contact prominent media managers at leading American newspapers to warn them in advance—under strict rules of confidentiality—about selected propaganda stories the CIA had planted abroad or was about to plant. Another Agency approach to blowback was use of this device intentionally to generate support from US citizens for covert actions in one part of the world or another, with the source of this advocacy unknown to them. To illustrate, propaganda plants during the Agency's early efforts in Indochina to discredit and thwart the rise of Ho Chi Minh, the communist leader of North Vietnam, reportedly floated back to influence an American audience.[19] The celebrated *New York Times* journalist James Reston reported, too, that now and then the CIA "had tried to pass on to our reporters false information."[20]

Political Covert Action

Covert action is usually most successful when all four of its components function together in a synergistic manner, using every stitch of canvas—or at least some combination. The snake oil of propaganda combined with the allure of greenback dollars is a common duo. For instance, the CIA's early efforts to thwart communist takeovers in countries around the world included not only propaganda materials but also financial support to political groups, democratic trade unions, and individuals likely to be friendly toward the United States in the future. Most covert actions follow a sequence: they start off with propaganda, often by setting up a radio station and a newspaper at first; they move next to political activities; and then, if necessary, they stir into the pot more severe economic and even paramilitary (PM) operations. As this sequence progresses, the effort can expand dramatically as all forms of the Third Option flow together into a deluge of secret pro-American operations that sweep across the seas and continents.

On some occasions, the CIA's enthusiasm for taking on global communism in every possible way has led to a violation of its 1947 mandate on limiting its activities strictly to foreign targets. For example, the DP infiltrated and funded the US National Student Association, relying on this "NSA" (not to be confused with the spy agency with that same acronym) to spread pro-American propaganda abroad, as well as to organize support for the United States during the group's participation at international youth convocations. Former DP operative Rositzke recalls that, in this manner, "the earliest links with dissident groups in Moscow were forged at the Moscow Youth Festival in 1957."[21] A decade later, the left-leaning magazine *Ramparts* revealed these questionable Agency ties to American youth groups, leading to an executive order from the Johnson administration that reinforced the already existing prohibition against CIA involvement with organizations inside the United States.

Another illustration of the Agency's financial support to friendly groups, this time abroad, was its connection to anti-communist trade unions (often run by Mafia and Corsican gangsters) in the Mediterranean ports of Marseilles and Naples after the Second World War. These longshoremen assisted US efforts to unload military weapons and ammunition for later distribution to anti-Soviet resistance factions in Eastern Europe, notably inside Ukraine and Poland. They also protected, sometimes with brass knuckles or bare fists, US aid being brought to Europe under the auspices of the Marshall Plan. These ties to the mob in Europe foreshadowed the Agency's ongoing contacts with Mafia figures in Chicago, New York, and Miami, which the DP would turn to during the Kennedy administration for aid in carrying out a series of assassination attempts in Havana against Cuban leader Fidel Castro.

The British foreign intelligence service, MI6, has a saying (though its origins remain obscure) that captures the attempt of spy agencies to influence political events abroad through the judicious dispersal of money to friendly personalities and political parties. The expression is "King George's cavalry," which translates into "cold cash to the rescue"—a sure-fire motivational magic to influence some individuals and organizations in foreign lands.[22] The CIA ladled out secret funding to promote the 1953 and 1954 coups in Iran and Guatemala, in two well-known examples.

In addition, from practically the first day it went into business, the Agency financially supported anti-communist intelligence services, parties, and interest groups in France and West Germany. These operations ran parallel to the CIA's funding for the Christian Democratic Party in Italy from 1947 to 1967, and later during the Ford administration in the 1970s.[23] Throughout the Cold War, the Agency frequently engaged in hidden efforts to bend foreign electoral outcomes in a manner that favored America's favorite candidate: in Chile, El Salvador, Guyana, and Japan, just to scratch the surface of places where the CIA and the KGB squared off behind the scenes in their attempts to manipulate public opinion and voting behavior.[24]

Italy in particular was an electoral battleground where the Agency made its bones in developing the art of clandestine political intervention, augmented by propaganda operations. The Italian Communist Party was bolstered just as vigorously by covert financing from the KGB. Neither superpower thought it wise to make these cash gifts a matter of public record, out of concern that Italian voters might recoil at the notion of casting a ballot for a candidate who seemed to be dancing on the strings of an outside superpower. As underscored by John Bross, a CIA division chief for Central and Eastern Europe, "Identification with foreign support turns what looks like patriotic opposition into what looks like treason."[25]

To put a harsh light on this methodology, political covert action can be interpreted as bribery: we will secretly help you win an election but, once in office, we expect you to follow the US lead in international affairs. A kinder interpretation would be the argument that secret funding is merely a benign way of assisting fellow democratic parties and candidates overseas, or anyone else who embraces democracy and opposes America's foes—or at least opposes communism. An illustration of a CIA funding initiative: the Northern Alliance, a coalition of anti-Taliban warlords in Afghanistan, after the US invasion of that nation in 2001. "I acknowledge receipt of USD 1,000,000.00 from the CIA for passage to Foxtrot Team" read an Agency document, signed by a Northern Alliance team leader after a paramilitary operative handed him a leather satchel bulging with US currency on December 15, 2001.[26]

"When threats arise to America's interests in the world," argued Colby in 1978, "it is better that we have the ability to help people in those countries where that will happen, quietly and secretly, and not wait until we are faced with a military threat that has to be met by armed force."[27] Earlier, while serving as DCI, he observed in the midst of the Church Committee investigation into covert action that "if the United States is unable to assist its friends, this is a sorry state."[28] According to another DCI, R. James Woolsey of the Clinton administration (1993–95), the whole purpose behind the use of the Third Option was "to avoid communists taking over."[29] Worth emphasizing is the cost-effective dimension of this method, too, especially when it comes to paramilitary activities. As stated by a former CIA inspector general, the United States "could use the Marines and 5,000 guns or we [the Agency] use six agents and $50,000."[30]

For many elections around the world, the CIA's assets have been on the scene armed with attaché cases brimming with local currency to purchase media time for local pro-Western politicians, as well as to provide electioneering paraphernalia designed to enhance their chances for victory (in those nations with democratic balloting). These materials have included a plethora of the usual campaign materials: leaflets; banners; stickers; placards; handbills; photos; motion pictures; videos; TV ads; bumper stickers, even in countries with few automobiles; thousands of lapel pins or buttons (including 50,000 that said "I am a member of the FNLA Party, in an example from Angola promoting the National Front for the Liberation of Angola, designed for attachment to the fatigues of soldiers in a jungle setting with few voters around to ponder the party acronym); and yard signs, sometimes for distribution in countries with few suburban lawns. Practically everything necessary for advertising, short of sandwich boards. For non-democratic regimes, the goal would be to fund groups and individuals toiling, usually underground, to bring about the establishment of a more open, pro-US society, or one that was neutral at any rate.

Although at times these methods were a reach (as with lapel buttons in jungle settings), overall the Agency proved quite effective in the use of secret propaganda and funding for favored groups and individuals overseas. It benefited from its relatively small size (in its early days, at least), which allowed for a certain agility far beyond what the hulking Pentagon could even imagine. Covert actions are meant to be small and quiet; the US military, prior to the development of its furtive Special Forces, was large and noisy—and still is when it mobilizes for open warfare.

Economic Covert Action

In the realm of economic activities, the Third Option presents a much nastier portrait of America's secret foreign policy. Examples include proposals to incite labor strikes; the mining of harbors to discourage shipping with US adversaries (a radical assault on international laws that protect sea trade among nations); instigating power blackouts; turning oil refineries into smoke; severing telephone lines; bombing or twisting rail lines to halt train shipments (what General William Tecumseh Sherman called "unbuilding railroads" as he marched across Georgia during the American Civil War); blowing up electrical power lines, power plants, bus depots, and bridges; disabling ships in foreign ports through the use of Underwater Demolition Teams (UDTs); contaminating lubricants, in an effort to bring about a breakdown of machinery in adversarial nations; and engaging in high-tech computer hacking. An NSC memo from the Johnson administration comments on two uses of the Third Option against the Castro regime designed to harm the Cuban economy: a commando sabotage operation against a warehouse and pier, and against a moored fuel barge; and a sabotage operation against a fuel barge proceeding in coastal waters.[31]

These are classic sabotage operations. In addition, according to the public record (chiefly declassified NSC documents), the CIA has counterfeited foreign currency to trigger inflationary pressures in target countries; forged food stamps and bank drafts; and depressed the world price of agricultural products vital to the economies of adversaries, an approach that can be especially devastating in small, one-crop countries.[32] No doubt Russian intelligence agencies—the KGB during the Cold War and its modern replacements today—have been involved in such activities, as well, and likely worse.[33]

One can also imagine, hypothetically, a nation using covert interventions to taint foreign agricultural products; disrupt food-supply chains; and destroy livestock. While proposals for food and livestock meddling have been consistently rejected at high government levels in the United States (with a shocking exception discussed further in Chapter 9), the other sabotage activities listed here have gone forward from time to time in far-flung places, usually in the broader context of CIA paramilitary operations. Another hypothetical case to illustrate the possibilities would be the sudden and mysterious disappearance of money that President Putin has stashed away in international banks, as payback for Russian tampering with US elections and computer hacking against US security agencies.[34]

Paramilitary Operations

With paramilitary operations (PM ops, sometimes referred to in CIA documents as "preventive direct action" or, in the wry patois of British intelligence, "ungentlemanly warfare"), one enters an even more extreme, expensive, and treacherous domain of covert action. This category includes everything from from "extraordinary rendition" (the abduction) of suspected terrorists by CIA "snatch teams," to the killing of foreign public officials deemed unfriendly toward the United States.

The Agency's "snatch" operations are not a main focus in this book, but it is worth noting that almost always such activities are beneath the dignity of the United States. The exception are those rare cases when outstanding foreign arrest warrants are being lawfully pursued by the FBI, say, related to international banking fraud. During the second Bush administration, the CIA had "Special Removal Units" that grabbed terrorist suspects off the streets in foreign nations (Stockholm, for example) and flew them to "black sites" abroad where torture is a common practice. Egypt was a favorite destination, but Afghanistan, Jordan, Morocco, Syria, Thailand, Qatar, and Uzebkistan were in the mix as well. As Vice President Dick Cheney put it on "Meet the Press" a few days after the 9/11 attacks, "So it's going to be vital for us to use any means at our disposal, basically, to achieve our objective." In 2005, a CIA lawyer, John Radsan, would tell journalist Jane Mayer of the *New Yorker* that, when it came to dealing with global terrorism, "It's the law of the jungle."

A CIA internal budget document, dated December 15, 1963, noted some forms of PM activity directed against the Castro regime in Cuba, among them "maritime operations, air operations, training, military hardware and the formation, development, and dispatch of groups in paramilitary operations."[35] Stephen Kinzer has pointed to another off-the-charts form of PM activity: mind-control, which he considers "the ultimate covert action weapon." Although the Agency has spent much time and money attempting to develop a capacity for brainwashing or "psycho-war," based on mind-control drugs and other means for incapacitating adversaries overseas, the results have never panned out—fortunately for the honor and reputation of the United States.[36]

An HPSCI chairman has underscored the controversial nature of PM activities. "During my six years on the Intelligence Committee, over 90 percent of the covert actions that were recommended to us by the president were supported and approved," remembers Representative Lee H. Hamilton (D, Indiana). "And only the large-scale paramilitary operations, which really could not be kept secret, were challenged."[37] Often working hand in glove with the Pentagon's Special Forces, these activities are carried out by the Special Operations Group (SOG), located along with the Covert Action Staff (CAS) in the Agency's Special

Activities (SA) Division—all units that are part of the DP and (later) the DO, in the dizzying "alphabet soup" common to Washington's jargon-addled national security bureaucracies. The officers in SOG, the toughest of whom seem half horse and half alligator, are often recruited from the US military for short-term assignments ("sheep-dipped," in a peculiar phrase).

The CIA's initial engagement in these warlike operations occurred soon after it came into being. In those days, the Agency's paramilitary operatives ("snake-eaters" in DP jargon, or what Orwell would have referred to as "rough men") fought *directly* against their Soviet counterparts on occasion, as when in support of Ukrainian partisans—a rare and perilous Cold War face-to-face match-up of CIA and KGB secret warriors.[38] The Agency and its Soviet counterpart soon backed away from such direct confrontations with one another, their governments wary of how this close-quarter combat between the superpowers might escalate out of control. Beyond periodic involvement in nitty-gritty battlefield activities in Third World nations, SOG officers are in the business as well of supplying weapons to US friends overseas, such as security forces in pro-Western developing countries. A controversial aspect of this program has been the Agency's assistance to these governments in dealing with—some would say "repressing"—home-grown dissidents. Among the most popular items of CIA support of this kind have been secure communications equipment, billy clubs, tear-gas grenades, and gas masks.

Training, supplying equipment for war-fighting and internal security, and even occasionally forming a foxhole partnership against a common adversary: this is the secret catnip the CIA can offer foreign military and intelligence officers allied with the United States. At a building in a remote Agency base inside the United States, an impressive collection of foreign arms is stockpiled, from pistols and grenades to high-caliber automatic rifles, available for issuing to surrogate paramilitary armies fighting on behalf of the United States in their own countries. These weapons are "sterilized" to prevent them from being traced back to their origin. Among the items from this armory favored by America's friends in the developing world during the Cold War were .38-caliber pistols, submachine guns, and grease guns, along with crates packed full of ammunition. During the early decades of the superpower struggle, the Agency's "stay-behind" guerrilla forces in Eastern Europe and elsewhere required armaments as well for the purpose of carrying out sabotage operations against the Soviet Army in case a Third World War erupted.

An illustration of a proud SOG operation involved Stinger missiles, with their lethal five-mile firing radius, which the Agency requisitioned to the *mujahideen* in their struggle against a Soviet army occupying their country, Afghanistan, during the 1980s (Chapter 5). A director of National Intelligence (DNI, a position created in 2004 to provide overall supervision for the Intelligence Community) has called this intervention "the most successful covert action in history."[39] In another example, Stingers were provided to a pro-American faction in Chad during this same time frame.

During the Cold War, Agency guns and grenades were passed along to various coup-schemers, as in Chile and Afghanistan, or used for planting "evidence" in some nation as a way of incriminating and embarrassing the Soviets or other foes. This approach might be adopted, as well, to sell a covert action proposal to congressional overseers during the Cold War. As an illustration of the latter, consider, say, the possibility of planting Russian Kalashnikov assault rifles in Country X to make it appear as though Moscow had provided the armaments; through this legerdemain, lawmakers might be spooked into funding the Agency to combat this new "danger." Such "revelations" regarding KGB adventurism would be leaked by the CIA to the media, providing a pretext for covert intervention. As an actual example, in 1954 the DP sneaked Soviet weaponry into Nicaragua, allowing the Agency to claim that the Russians were secretly establishing a beachhead near the very borders of the United States to aid Guatemalans in their resistance to a US-sponsored coup.[40]

Of course, periodically the Soviets *did* in fact sell or give weaponry to one neutral country or another in hopes of gaining additional adherents in its ideological struggle with the United States. This is a lucrative game engaged in by US, Russian, and Chinese arms merchants as well, in another hidden economic dimension of the superpower rivalry. The Agency's storehouse of weapons has been deployed, further, for its own "covert" wars, as in Laos during the 1960s—as if anything so large in scale could remain covert for long. (With tongue in cheek, journalists have labeled this phenomenon an "overt-covert action.") Moreover, SOG has supported US troops fighting in major, open combat, as in Korea, Vietnam, Iraq, and Afghanistan. This is the deadliest form of PM intervention for Agency officers, in which several have been killed or badly wounded.

A new wrinkle in PM operations is its privatization: the hiring of outside contractors to carry out potentially dicey activities. Most of these hires have been valuable, especially as security personnel to help protect US embassies in perilous locations. Government "outsiders" can cause problems, however, since now and then a few can be as unprincipled as they are energetic. They may know little to nothing about such niceties as the legal restrictions laid out in various intelligence oversight statutes, or even the existence of the congressional Intelligence Committees.

A group based in North Carolina known as Blackwater, with the subsequent names of Xe Services, then Academi, provides an illustration. The CIA included Blackwater in its planning to kill terrorist leaders in the Middle East and Southwest Asia. The DO fired the group, though, when it developed a "cowboy" reputation for overzealous behavior. In one instance from 2007, four Blackwater personnel (which included former CIA, NSA, and FBI officers) turned their machine guns and grenade launchers against seventeen Iraqi civilians, including children, at Nisour Square in Baghdad. According to the FBI case agent who led the inquiry into this mass killing of civilians, it was a "massacre along the lines of My Lai in Vietnam."[41] Those among the Blackwater team involved in these murders were tried in a US court of law, found guilty, and sentenced to prison. As he was about to leave office, President Trump issued each of the Nisour killers a pardon. Erik Prince, the brother of Secretary of Education Betsy DeVos in the Trump administration, led the Academi consulting group. He remained influential despite the Nisour scandal and, in 2015, had one of his men selected as staff director for HPSCI, under the chairmanship of Devin Nunes (R, California), who was awarded the Medal of Freedom by President Trump. Reportedly, Prince also offered his clandestine skills to the Trump administration for use against Democrats in the 2020 elections.[42]

Monitoring CIA covert action is challenging enough, let alone adding into the mix outside organizations only loosely aware of America's intelligence laws, executive orders, and traditions—and operating outside the government's normal chain-of-command. One contractor prepared an inappropriate CIA *Assassination Manual* for use in Nicaragua during the Reagan years, despite the existence of an executive order against assassinations signed by President Ford in 1975 and endorsed by subsequent presidents. An HPSCI report sharply lambasted this operation, seeing it as yet another sign that "the CIA did not have adequate command and control of the entire Nicaraguan covert action."[43] Coll notes, in addition, that "about 85 percent of the C.I.A. personnel who conducted interrogations [of suspected terrorists] after 2001 were contractors."[44] Torture has never been a subject on the curriculum at "the Farm" (or "Camp Swampy"), a bucolic facility in rural Virginia where career CIA officers receive their initial training. One of the most bizarre examples of the outsourcing problem was reported by legendary CIA operative Ted Shackley. He recalled how a young group of anti-Castro activists in Miami whom he had hired suddenly decided, on their own volition, to take a boat to the Havana harbor and spray its waterfront boulevard with machine-gun fire.[45] Shackley quickly separated himself from this rogue element.

Cuban exiles, another group of contractors involved in the Bay of Pigs covert action in 1961 against their former homeland, presented a special challenge for the CIA, which is sometimes referred to as the "disposal problem." Approaching D-day for the paramilitary invasion of Cuba, Agency planners were reluctant to shut down the operation despite their growing misgivings based on a whole suite of reasons—foremost among them, considerable uncertainty about the strength and determination of Castro's military. The more the planners weighed the chances, the more their concern rose. Yet a cancellation, they worried, would have led to angry public criticism by the exiles and made President Kennedy appear weak on communism. The planners pushed aside disturbing facts about the likelihood of failure (examined in Chapter 4) that, in retrospect, they wish had been taken more seriously before the operation split apart at the seams on the Cuban beaches. The exiles continued on as a problem for the CIA. In May of 1964, for instance, NSC aides noted that "exile raids [into Cuba] were becoming completely beyond U.S. control despite CIA financial support to the groups."[46]

Beyond the serious challenge of controlling contractors is the added inside difficulty of managing the Agency's own paramilitary officers. As a deputy director for Operations (DDO), the head of covert actions at Langley, once fretted out loud: "What do you do with the fire horses when there's no fire?"[47] Tough, combat-ready intelligence officers are good to have around in times of emergency; however, they are often restless, happy only when they are parachuting out of aircraft, scaling enemy walls, crawling through jungles on their bellies, and shooting long guns at commies or terrorists. What does one do with these warriors during normal times? "Lock them in a box," a CIA manager has suggested in exasperation.[48] These PM officers can make important contributions to America's safety and foreign policy objectives; consider their intrepid performance in spearheading the invasion into Afghanistan, as they hunted down Qaeda members and their Taliban hosts after the 9/11 attacks. Like firefighters in local communities, they are crucial at key moments of disaster; however, as with firefighters, they also must be carefully selected and trained to extinguish fires while being good citizens in between alarms. Most observers would agree with the judgment reached long ago by the top intelligence staff aide on the National Security Council during the Johnson years. A paramilitary force "is a good capability to keep on hand if we possibly can," Gordon Chase argued in 1965. "I would agree to an abandonment of this capability only if it were demonstrated that we could crank it up again in a very short space of time."[49] This kind of "cranking up" is unrealistic, any more than one could crank up an effective local fire department. One must have seasoned, well-prepared professionals in place.

At still lower ranks where one is dealing directly with the Agency's foreign assets, the train can really come off the tracks. A senior operations officer has said that these recruits can be "goof balls—unreliable and uncontrollable."[50] As a DDO emphasized in testimony before the Aspin-Brown Commission, "We deal with thugs, not church elders."[51] In 1975, the Church Committee came across an unsettling paramilitary asset involved in the Agency's plotting against the life of President Patrice Lumumba in the Congo. The asset's codename was, appropriately enough, WI/ROGUE. A former Africa Division officer at Langley recalls that this man was an "essentially stateless" soldier of fortune, with a past history of forgery and bank robbing. After giving WI/ROGUE plastic surgery and a toupee, the DO sent him to the CIA's station in the Congo, where—acting without higher authority—he attempted to recruit another individual to join him as an "execution squad." The frantic Chief of Station cabled back to Langley Headquarters: "WI/ROGUE FREE WHEELING AND LACK OF SECURITY . . . NOT WILLING TO FOLLOW INSTRUCTIONS."[52] The DP leadership fired the soldier-of-fortune.[53]

~~~

Here, then, are the primary forms assumed by the Third Option over the years since 1947. Against what nations and factions have these methods been directed since the end of the Second World War, and for what purposes? Chapters 3 through 6 explore the practice of CIA covert actions around the world. Beforehand, though, this book presents an additional perspective on the forms of covert action. The Ladder of Clandestine Escalation in Chapter 2 evokes a sense of their degree of severity, risk, and probity as one travels upward on the rungs from relatively benign uses to activities that can spill blood and stun the conscience.

2
A Ladder of Clandestine Escalation

The Rising Risks of Covert Action

In the 1960s, strategist Herman Kahn of the Hudson Institute in New York devised an "escalation-ladder metaphor" in which he listed an array of overt options available to US government officials in dealing with the Soviet Union, all the way from modest diplomatic gestures to full-scale nuclear war.[1] His metaphor is suggestive, too, for envisioning a range of clandestine interventions, as the United States ponders the need to intrude overseas secretly when warranted. Kings and queens, prime ministers and presidents, czars and shahs, emirs, pashas, sultans, drug thugs, human traffickers, illicit arms dealers, *jihadists* around the globe—the CIA has tried to assess their degree of enmity toward the United States and defend against dangers they might pose.

As presented in Figure 2.1, the "Ladder of Clandestine Escalation" is a refinement of earlier attempts to display Third Option methods along a continuum, rising from relatively benign activities to those only a nation devoid of a moral compass would adopt.[2] The ladder provides a framework for understanding a series of practical and moral considerations presented to the United States as its leaders move from low-level operations (say, Herr Bauermann's CIA-sponsored propaganda op-eds in Munich) to the highest rung on the ladder where—fortunately, only in theory so far—nuclear, biological, and chemical (NBC) weapons of mass destruction are covertly used against a foe. The upward movement ascends from modest attempts at media manipulations at the bottom of the ladder to the widespread killing of civilians at the top.

"At the CIA you get into moral ambiguities more than you do in other agencies," observes long-time senior Agency officer, Charlie Allen. "Hard decisions are made. And there are high-risk stakes, particularly as you move into covert action."[3] As one rises toward the top rungs—the risker segment of the ladder depicted in Figure 2.1—the weight of ethics becomes especially pressing. For purposes of highlighting this risk gradation, the steps on the ladder are divided into four "thresholds," each indicating a cluster of covert actions that have a similar moral coloration, whether light (relatively benign) at the bottom of the ladder or dark (with horrific implications) at the top, along with a variety of hues in between.

Threshold Three: High-Risk Operations

36. CIA officers directly involved in paramilitary operations within a "neutral" country [PM]
35. Propaganda aimed at inciting rebellion or other forms of violence within a target nation or faction [P]
34. Supply of advanced weaponry provided to "neutral" nations [PM]
33. Sophisticated arms supplies and counsel provided to pro-Western nations [PM]
32. Massive increases in funding for a party or faction within a pro-Western nation [POL]
31. Massive increases in funding for a party or faction within a non-democratic adversarial nation [POL]
30. Massive increases in funding for a party or faction within a "neutral" nation [POL]
29. False (black) propaganda aimed at fellow democratic nations with a free press [P]
28. Limited arms supplies to "neutral" nations (or factions therein) for offensive purposes [PM]
27. Limited arms supplies to pro-Western nations for offensive purposes [PM]
26. Limited arms supplies to "neutral" nations for defensive balancing purposes, or for a *quid pro quo* deal [PM]
25. Limited arms supplies to pro-Western nations for defensive balancing purposes [PM]
24. Economic disruptions without loss of life [E]
23. Operations carried out against a target nation or organization without a local allied faction [PM, POL]
22. Operations that target a particularly dangerous nation or organization [PM, POL, E]
21. Operations targeted against a nation or organization that have resulted in significant prior CA failures [PM, POL, E]
20. Joint CA operations [PM, POL, E]
19. Operations that have a price tag above $5 million [PM, POL, E, P]
18. Military guidance to pro-Western nations [PM]
17. Military guidance to the "neutral" nations [PM]
16. Moderate increases in funding for a party or faction within a pro-Western nation [POL]
15. Large increases in funding for a party or faction within a "neutral" nation [POL]
14. Moderate increases in funding for a party or faction within a "neutral" nation [POL]
13. Truthful, yet contentious, propaganda aimed at fellow democratic nations [P]

Threshold Two: Modest Intrusions

12. Low-level funding of nations and groups friendly toward the democratic regimes, when overt funding is rejected for one reason or another [POL]
11. Truthful, benign propaganda aimed at fellow democratic nations [P]
10. False propaganda aimed at "neutral" nations [P]
9. Intensified false propaganda aimed at US non-democratic adversaries [P]

Threshold One: Routine Operations

8. Political and economic counsel to pro-Western nations in resisting encroachment by the autocracies [POL, E]
7. CIA security advisement to neutral nations seeking counterintelligence and counterterrorism guidance from the United States in resisting encroachment by autocrats or terrorists [PM]
6. CIA security advisement to pro-Western nations seeking counterintelligence and counterterrorism guidance from the United States in resisting encroachment by autocrats or terrorists [PM]
5. Truthful, but contentious, propaganda aimed at "neutral" nations [P]
4. Truthful, benign propaganda aimed at nations "neutral"—neither pro-US or pro-US adversaries—but with no free press involved [P]
3. False propaganda aimed at US non-democratic adversaries [P]
2. Truthful, but contentious, propaganda aimed at US non-democratic adversaries [P]
1. Truthful benign propaganda aimed at US non-democratic adversaries, with no free press involved [P]

Threshold Four: Extreme Operations

55. Use of NBC (nuclear, biological, chemical) and radiological weapons [PM]
54. Violence targeted against groups of innocent civilians, torture against anyone, and other gross violations of human rights [PM]
53. An assault on the US Constitution [P, POL, E, PM]
52. A defiance of US law governing covert actions [P, POL, E, PM]
51. Major cyberattack against a powerful foreign government [PM, E, POL, P]
50. Major "secret" coup against a fellow democratic regime, with a paramilitary component [PM, POL, E, P]
49. Major "secret" *coup d'état* against a powerful autocrat regime [PM, POL, E, P]
48. Major "secret" *coup d'état* against a populous "neutral" regime [PM, POL, E, P]
47. Use of CIA drones or other violent means to target for death high-ranking public officials overseas, in contrast to uniformed soldiers and terrorists on an acknowledged battlefield, or (below on Rung 46) suspected terrorists outside a battlefield [PM]
46. Assassination of suspected terrorists [PM]
45. Small-scale *coup d'état* that includes a paramilitary component [PM]
44. Small-scale *coup d'état* without a paramilitary component [POL, E, P]
43. Major economic dislocations, including the creation of food shortages, crop or livestock destruction, the mass destruction of property, and even the loss of life [E]
42. Major environmental alterations, such as the covert use of poisonous defoliates or the creation of floods [PM, E]
41. Limited environmental alterations, such as cloud-seeding [PM, E]
40. Limited cyberattacks [PM, E, POL, or P]
39. Supply of advanced weaponry to factions within a non-democratic adversarial nation [PM]
38. Hostage-taking and "snatch" operations ("extraordinary renditions") [PM]
37. Major hostage-rescue attempts [PM]

Figure 2.1 Ladder of Clandestine Escalation*

* Revised from Loch K. Johnson, *US Intelligence in a Hostile World: Secret Agencies* (New Haven, CT: Yale University Press, 1996: 62–63), which was based on an earlier iteration in Loch K. Johnson, "On Drawing a Bright Line for Covert Operations," *American Journal of International Law* 86 (April 1992): 284–309. The rungs are meant to be heuristic rather than definitive, since there are many more covert-action scenarios than those represented in the steps shown here. The purpose of the ladder is to suggest a range of possibilities.

P = covert propaganda
POL = covert political activities
E = covert economic activities
PM = covert paramilitary (warlike) activities

In climbing the ladder, a nation opts for increasingly serious intrusions into the sovereignty of other nations accompanied by breaches of international law and other widely recognized moral "bright lines." In the 1960s, a team of *New York Times* journalists stated the central question embedded in this idea of a Third Option ladder (although without using this metaphor). "How far should the political leaders of the United States go in approving the clandestine violation of treaties and borders, financing of coups, influencing of parties and governments," they asked, "without tarnishing and retarding these ideas of freedom and self-government they proclaim to the world?"[4]

Threshold One: Routine Covert Actions

Lower-Level Propaganda

If covert intervention can ever be thought of as routine—and, in the modern era, such has become the case for a host of countries—some operations are relatively harmless and may be placed on the lowest rungs of the clandestine escalation ladder. Using the CIA as a conduit for secret, entirely truthful propaganda directed toward people living under the heavy-handed rule of autocratic adversaries of the United States—that is, the use of propaganda to extol freedom, democracy, and related values associated with open societies—can well be considered a benign activity. The purpose is to open the windows of consciousness to a world that is shut off by the oppressive, high barriers erected by totalitarian and authoritarian regimes (*Rung 1*). The leaders of a targeted nation, though— say, North Korea—would obviously not see this type of intervention as benign. Nonetheless, viewed through the prism of democratic values, providing accurate depictions of the real world would be a gift to these sequestered people, giving them at least a glimpse of contemporary global realities, along with perhaps a sense of purpose and a spark of hope that one day they might be able to breathe in the air of freedom, uncontaminated by state lies.

As former DCI Robert M. Gates has written, CIA propaganda programs aimed at the Soviet Union and Eastern Europe during both the Ford and Carter presidencies "gave new heart, resolve, and courage" to those trapped inside their totalitarian cages, especially nascent human rights groups. The adoption of these programs during the Carter years, pushed strongly by National Security Adviser and Polish émigré Zbigniew Brzezinski, produced in Gates's view "tiny fissures in the Soviet structure that ultimately helped bring about its collapse."[5] Yes, Agency propaganda would represent an intrusion into a foreign regime; but if the regime's government is morally bankrupt to begin with, based on Kafkaesque layers of repression, efforts to engage its population with communications about accurate news and some encouragement for the future may be considered a modestly valuable contribution to the goal of expanding freedom and the democratic way of life around the globe (even if the precise effects of the propaganda will remain difficult to measure).

The use of propaganda operations becomes immediately more tangled even just one step upward, on *Rung 2*, when they take on a combative tone, raising contentious issues that could rile a population into adopting some form of action against its oppressive leaders—say, CIA clandestine radio themes transmitted into a closed society that focus on the lack of adequate food for its people. Then, rising a further step, on *Rung 3* the propaganda shades into "black" (false propaganda of one degree or another—attempts to shape the disinformation landscape), perhaps claiming in exaggeration that the nation's leadership enjoys swollen bank accounts in London and yachts in Monaco while most of the nation's citizens must tighten their belts each day.

The ladder starts off with propaganda operations because information flows are generally less provocative than on-the-ground political maneuvering, economic disruption, or—truly raising the stakes—paramilitary actions undertaken in-country against a foreign government. This is not to say, though, that propaganda operations are merely a faint echo from CIA headquarters of well-known American government themes; taken at full tide, they can incite rebellion, as was possibly the case with Agency perspectives directed by Radio Free Europe toward the anti-communist youth of Hungary in 1956. At its extreme, covert propaganda can trigger a cascading chain of events, stirring populations into violent responses against a regime (a leap upward on the ladder to *Rung 35*). Still, when compared to political, economic, and paramilitary activities, propaganda normally stands at the lower levels of provocation found within Threshold One.

Russian efforts to influence the American presidential elections in 2016 and 2020 through propaganda methods—as well as, even more provocatively, through attempted cyber-manipulation of ballot boxes and other interventions into election processes at the local level, not to mention efforts to place malware on US national security computers (2020)—ignited a strong sense of resentment in the United States. The allegations led to a major investigation in 2019, chaired by Special Prosecutor Robert S. Mueller III, which confirmed the validity of reported Russian influence operations that were undertaken during the election; and to the launching of further US inquiries in 2021 into massive Russian cyberattacks against America's security agencies in 2020.

Imagine, further, a scenario in which the Kremlin had dispatched its operatives in 2016 and 2020 to participate undercover in the Iowa, New Hampshire, South Carolina, and the Super Tuesday primaries, spreading money around secretly (through cut-outs) to Donald J. Trump and other candidates favored in the Kremlin. Or ratcheting things up even more, what if the Russian government—in further attempts to shape electoral outcomes—resorted to economic intrigues inside the United States (inciting anti-police unrest, for example) and even paramilitary activities (maybe sidelining a candidate by infecting her or him with the COVID-19 virus). Such highly aggressive "active measures" by the Russians would have brought the American people and their leaders to a boiling point, with potentially far-reaching retaliatory consequences. Edging in this direction, Russian cyber-terrorists reportedly attacked US hospital computers in 2020, hoping to induce further chaos during the COVID crisis.[6]

During the Cold War, the KGB frequently spread vitriolic secret propaganda (*agitprop*) against the United States. In 1968, for instance, Soviet disinformation (*dezinformatsia*) claimed that US forces in Vietnam had resorted to the use of bacteriological weapons against the North Vietnamese, a story published in the Bombay *Free Press Journal* and picked up by the *New York Times* and other media around the world, despite the pungent odor of mendacity that surrounded the allegation. In the 1980s, a favorite theme concocted by the KGB (working in tandem with the East German intelligence service, Stasi) claimed that the United States started the AIDS epidemic in Africa. As ludicrous as that story was, many gullible people around the world believed it. Former DCI Robert M. Gates recalls additional Soviet black propaganda intended to discredit the United States on the world stage. "In South Asia, the KGB spent much time and money trying to blame the United States for the assassination of Prime Minister Indira Gandhi," he writes. "Throughout the Third World, they spread the story that the United States was kidnapping babies there to use their body parts in transplant operations." Gates adds: "Some of these tales would take on a life of their own and continue long after the Soviet Union had collapsed."[7]

In 2020, both Russia and China spread alarm and political unrest in Europe by disseminating conspiracy stories claiming the United States was responsible for the coronavirus pandemic.[8] Russia propagated the theme that American scientists invented COVID-19 as a germ bioweapon designed to destroy its foreign enemies. One variation charged that the US Army was responsible for the germ as a way of harming the reputation of China—never mind that the virus clearly emanated from China and led to the deaths of multiple thousands of citizens in both the democracies and the communist nations. Well over 1 million people worldwide had succumbed to the disease as 2020 came to a close, and the numbers were continuing to climb.

The *New York Times* concluded that "Mr. Putin [Vladimir Putin, the Russian president, a former KGB officer] has spread misinformation on issues of personal health for more than a decade." This propaganda list included allegations related to flu outbreaks, Ebola, and the coronavirus—which were all sown by American scientists, according to wordsmiths inside the Russian intelligence services who managed to infect every social media account they could find in the United States and the other democracies with this form of blather.[9] Among other favorite Russian themes: the US manipulates the world's radio waves, and it bioengineers genes and hazardous industrial chemicals. Not to be outdone, Beijing—whose "wet markets" have been notorious wellsprings of zoonotic pandemics over the years—attempted, farcically, to blame the COVID-19 virus outbreak on visits by American soldiers to the Chinese city of Wuhan, the recognized global epicenter of the disease.

Continuing on with the CIA's clandestine propaganda operations, *Rungs 4* and *5* rest on the notion that truthful themes are less intrusive than contentious ones—particularly false themes. Further, these rungs underscore that the nature of the target nation is important to consider, with autocracies fair game; but Third Option operations aimed at "neutral" regimes, which are neither autocratic adversaries of the United States nor pro-Western democracies, increase the chances of moral hazard. These neutral countries may not oppose the Western democracies but rather just choose to be politically independent, as with India and other non-aligned nations during the Cold War—playing both sides for their own benefit, by the lights of a more cynical interpretation of this neutral posture.

Covert Security Consultations

In addition to the limited propaganda measures depicted at Threshold One, this lower set of rungs also includes private CIA consultations with pro-Western democracies on intelligence and national security matters of common interest, such as counterintelligence and counterterrorism at *Rung 6*; or similar guidance to neutral nations at *Rung 7*. At its highest step (*Rung 8*), Threshold One envisions stepped up, on-the-ground covert political and economic advisement by CIA officers to security officials in pro-Western democracies, in a mutual effort to thwart encroachments by the world's totalitarian and authoritarian nations, as well as terrorist cells. This step indicates a shift from hidden information flows (propaganda) to on-the-ground, hands-on, in-country advice regarding best practices in the uses of political and economic resistance against the predatory practices engaged in by the Kremlin and other anti-democratic governments.

Threshold Two: Modest Intrusions

Black Propaganda

The "Modest Intrusion" segment of the ladder returns to the use of untruthful propaganda directed against non-democratic regimes (*Rung 3*), but this time the dissemination is wider and more intensive (*Rung 9*), or directed against neutral regimes (*Rung 10*). These programs up the propaganda ante. Going further, any propaganda operations aimed at a fellow democratic nation enters into a notably questionable moral realm, even when the information communicated is factual (*Rung 11*), let alone contentious (*Rung 13*, examined below) or outright false (a leap upward in propaganda activities all the way to a Threshold Three level at *Rung 29*).

Political Manipulation

This Second Threshold introduces, as well, an opening charge of "King George's cavalry": the use of covert funding for worthy democratic causes when, for whatever reason, the party or political leaders in the targeted nation determine that open financial support from the United States would produce a negative reaction among their citizenry. In a CIA expression, it is necessary from time to time to apply some "financial lubrication" (*Rung 12*) to frictional circumstances abroad.

Threshold Three: High-Risk Operations

Ascending to Threshold Three, covert action arrives at a high-risk segment of the ladder, where each envisioned operation poses (or should pose) serious ethical qualms about the wisdom of proceeding farther upward.

Aiming at Democracies on the Target Range

As mentioned above, at *Rung 13* the United States would prod fellow democracies into a preferred direction through the use of controversial propaganda themes, set loose in a society that cherishes a free press. If the intervention were made public, the local citizens would surely recoil in anger and disgust toward the United States, just as the reverse would be true if Americans were so targeted by an allied nation. The initial rung at this level poses the fundamental question of whether the CIA should have *any* media assets at all operating inside fellow democratic societies, even of the *Rung 11* truthful variety. Clearly, Americans would not be amused to learn (in a hypothetical illustration) that the German intelligence service, the Bundesnachrichtendienst or BND, was recruiting and manipulating reporters on the payroll of the *New York Times*, the *Washington Post*, or any other US publication. Understandably the citizens of Germany are, in turn, unlikely to appreciate attempts by the CIA to suborn their free press.

That is why this approach to propaganda dissemination is listed within the ladder heading of "High-Risk": it escalates this use of covert action by manipulating information flows in companion open societies—a large step to take, even if still only on the initial rung of Threshold Three. At this level, comity within the Western alliance faces a degree of jeopardy stemming from freedom-of-the-press violations by the United States. Whether carried out through the venues of traditional or new media (Facebook, YouTube, Twitter, Telegram, and others), these clandestine activities are directed against fellow members in the precious and fragile global association of democratic societies. Former CIA officer Michael A. Turner has commented on the drawback of this approach: "Secret propaganda undermines the free press, in that journalists in free countries should not be bought and their media compromised for questionable gains by the US government."[10]

Secret Political Funding and Military Consultations

With the next three ladder increments (*Rungs 14, 15,* and *16*), America's covert actions open the funding spigots more freely for foreign political operations, moving from a trickle at *Rung 14* to a stream of cash pouring into the hidden coffers of favored parties and politicians at *Rung 16*. Returning to the King George's calvary metaphor, one moves from a canter to a gallop. Then, at *Rungs 17 and 18*, covert action takes a still more aggressive turn, undergoing a notable expansion by virtue of the Agency's focus on military matters—always a potentially dangerous realm. At these rungs, though, the covert interventions remain at the talking level of offering guidance and training with respect to the uses of armed force, as opposed to an actual dissemination of weaponry (a possibility reserved for higher rungs).

The next several steps point to various idiosyncratic features of Third Option activities that thicken the chances of moral hazard, as well as complicate the opportunities for success. For example, *Rung 19* underscores the importance of high spending levels as a benchmark for stimulating concern among CIA planners and overseers about how far a specific covert action might unspool beyond their original intentions. A $5 million figure is suggested here as a cautionary yellow light that signals overly ambitious aspirations for what is supposed to be a limited, clandestine venture. Large and expensive Third Options run counter to the basic instinct and hopes that rest behind secret interventions: the desire for non-attribution, accompanied by a quiet, relatively unobtrusive resolution to a foreign policy problem.

Covert Action as a Delicate Tango

Joint covert actions (*Rung 20*)—say, with CIA and MI6, CIA and Mossad, or CIA and the BND—raise significant potential problems of operational security. As intelligence scholars Gill and Phythian point out, "The more complex the operation or the greater the number of people involved, then the harder it becomes to maintain secrecy."[11] Especially, one might add, when the intelligence officers involved are from different countries, with divergent languages, cultures, and traditions. These activities can work, but they must be handled with extra attention to detail. An illustration of a joint operation that met its goal is when the CIA in 2008 provided a specially crafted bomb to Mossad, which then used the explosive to kill a Hezbollah leader in Lebanon by the name of Imad Mughniyah (nicknamed "Maurice" by Agency officers). He was a notorious terrorist and munitions expert with the blood of hundreds of US Marines, CIA personnel, and foreign service officers on his hands from an explosion at the American Embassy in Beirut in 1983 as well as many other attacks against American and Israeli facilities and personnel.[12]

Further, the CIA and Israeli intelligence have combined forces in cyberwar efforts aimed at crippling Iran's nuclear-weapons program. They have successfully caused a series of breakdowns in that nation's nuclear facilities, including the malfunctioning of computers, centrifuges, and transformers. In one operation, carried out from 2005 to 2010 and labeled "Olympic Games," the National Security Agency (NSA) and Israel's Unit 8200 intelligence agencies injected computer viruses—the most notorious known as "Stuxnet"—into Iranian computers located in Natanz. The covert action severely damaged Iran's uranium enrichment facilities, including the destruction of about 1,000 centrifuges. In this instance, the NSA entered into the covert action field because of its technical acumen. Its authority to engage in the operation stemmed, though, from an initial CIA request for permission to mobilize the Third Option against the Iranian nuclear program. Journalist David E. Sanger, who helped break the Stuxnet story, wondered if "Olympic Games was a sign of where American covert action was headed" and whether we were "ready as a nation to open this Pandora's box"— which, once opened, might be impossible to close.[13]

The CIA-Mossad alliance had joined forces for an earlier anti-Iranian scheme designed, as well, to cripple the Iranian nuclear program. This operation was known as "Merlin," conceived during the Clinton administration and carried out in the next administration led by George W. Bush. The plan was to prepare bogus technical blueprints for building a nuclear bomb. These misleading instructions were meant to reach the hands of Tehran's scientists via an unwitting Russian intermediary, thereby sending the Iranians on a wild goose chase. The flaws in the blueprints were so obviously contrived, though, that the Iranian experts never fell for the trick.[14] In another illustration of a joint covert action (CA), the Agency banded with the Government Communications Headquarters in the United Kingdom (GCHQ, the British signals intelligence agency) to contaminate Iraqi computer hardware in 1991.[15]

The Third Option requires competent tradecraft, which is made doubly hard when two (or more) nations must coordinate their activities while retaining the requisite invisibility. Sometimes, moreover, one of the nations involved may go too far, legally or morally. Against Iran's nuclear weapons program, for instance, Mossad began a program of slaying nuclear scientists in Tehran and at various scientific labs around that nation—a step covert action planners in Washington were unwilling to take.[16] In addition, when engaged in joint operations, the CIA must always be concerned that its partner may have been penetrated by a mole recruited by the Russian, Chinese, Iranian, or some other nation's foreign intelligence service.

The Third Option as a Form of Gambling

Sometimes CAs against a target repeatedly fail, such as the Agency's multiple attempts against the life of the Cuban president, Fidel Castro, during the early 1960s. A history of failure should instill a sense of humbleness and skepticism among CIA planners, causing them to ponder the questionable chances of success in yet another attempt (a *Rung 21* consideration). For example, despite limited success in the past, the CIA proposed an anti-Cuban maritime PM venture to the Johnson administration in January of 1965. The operation would

> use the underwater demolition team to sink Cuban navy patrol vessels or other Cuban targets of opportunity . . . in the Port of La Isabela. . . . The team would approach the harbor during darkness in a 50-foot Swift or similar vessel until it reaches a point three miles north of La Isabel. At this point it would embark on a smaller boat in which it will slowly proceed to Caye Arbolite, a small island near the mouth of the harbor. The boat and crew would remain hidden on the island; after a brief reconnaissance and final briefing by the leader, the team itself would swim into the harbor. It would then split into three sub-teams and attach charges to hulls of Cuban vessels lying at anchor. Pre-set timing devices would explore the charges five hours after placement.[17]

Engaging in Third Option activities that have a high likelihood of ending badly is a form of immorality, since DO officers and their foreign assets are placed at risk even though their leaders know that the odds of a favorable outcome are slim. Into this cluster of rungs fall, too, operations that seek to target a particularly dangerous adversary—one with a known record of capable counterintelligence defenses, along with both a capacity and an ideological inclination to strike back at the CIA and the United States in a disproportionate and perhaps lethal manner (*Rung 22*).

Cannibals and Other Hazards

At *Rung 23*, America's past experience with the Third Option has taught US national security officials that favorable outcomes are a long shot unless the Agency has a reliable and effective local partner inside the targeted country, as was the case in 2001–2 with the Northern Alliance in Afghanistan following the 9/11 attacks. Who the local ally is matters, from both a practical and an ethical point of view. Is the ally strong enough to truly help; and would the American people be comfortable with the company their nation has chosen to keep ("birds of a feather")? When it has engaged in covert actions in partnership with mobsters and hitmen, the CIA has shredded any adherence to traditional American values and indelibly stained its own reputation and that of the United States.

A prominent former Agency official quotes a colleague as believing "the CIA would associate itself with cannibals if it were to find itself in a country where cannibalism was a way of life, and if it were in the interests of the American people to associate itself with the government or with one or another of the local political groups."[18] On the contrary, the interests of the United States lie not in partnerships with cannibals, or any other deviant or criminal group. Former Director of the CIA (D/CIA) John O. Brennan pointed to a fundamental challenge in any national security organization. He told an interviewer that the Agency's Operations Directorate is comprised of "some of the country's greatest heroes . . . but there were also people who thought the end justifies the mean."[19]

The writings of Machiavelli are useful to remind us of the rough-and-tumble world we live in, but his ruthless recommendations on political and policy tactics in the Middle Ages are a poor guide to honorable behavior and a strengthening of America's worldwide reputation for decency today. Yes, keep a big stick in reserve, as Teddy Roosevelt properly advocated, in case an Adolf Hitler comes along; but behave on the world stage—speak softly, as Roosevelt added—as if one were a civilized human being. The world needs fewer Florentine Renaissance princes with their treachery and ruinous disorders and more democratic nations with a sensitivity to the Golden Rule.

Non-Violent Economic Sabotage

The Chile case in the early 1970s provides a memorable example of a *Rung 24* operation: economic disruption without loss of life. The CIA-supported a truckers strike during the Allende years that ground Chile's economy to a halt. No one perished as a result of the labor unrest, but the strike had a profound effect on bread-and-butter issues in Chile and a rise in poverty levels. The outcome was, as the Agency intended, a sharp decline in the popularity of the Allende government (Chapter 3). Similarly, an adversary's harbors may be mined, as in Vietnam during the 1960s and Nicaragua during the 1980s, perhaps again without the loss of life—although, in fact, locals were killed in both of these well-known instances—but in a callous disregard for Law of the Seas considerations related to vital networks of international trade.

Weaponry

The next four rungs deal with modest increments of weaponry supplied by the CIA to either allied democracies or neutral regimes, with the latter posing greater moral and practical risks than the former, because fellow democracies are more apt to honor any restrictions that might be placed on the use of the weapons by the United States. At *Rung 25*, arms are supplied to pro-Western democracies so they might adequately defend themselves against predatory autocrats—a regional security "balancing" objective. This clandestine activity is risky only in the sense that spreading weaponry around the planet can be an intrinsically perilous policy, if only because it may lead to a local arms race or possibly even increase the likelihood that war might break out in a region.

At *Rung 26*, weapons flow to neutrals, also for defensive balancing but with less predictable outcomes, since the country in question is not a tried-and-true democratic partner. Or at this step the weapons may be used in a deal struck to assist a US foreign policy objective, such as providing missiles to Iran in exchange for its help (which proved feckless) in freeing the Agency's Chief of Station in Lebanon, William Buckley, from the grip of terrorists during the Iran-*contra* affair of the 1980s. In another example, the decision by the Reagan administration against providing weapons to the anti-communist Solidarity movement in Poland was based on a concern that supplying guns to an Eastern European nation might cross a bright line that could prove intolerable to the Kremlin. As National Security Adviser Admiral John M. Poindexter recollects: "We tempered what we would do for Solidarity by not doing those things that would provide the trigger that would provoke the Soviets into military intervention."[20]

Weaponry is involved at *Rung 27*, too, but this time the emphasis is on an expectation that the recipient will use the arms in an *offensive* manner against an autocratic predator, if necessary. This arrangement holds the potential to incite a war, should the balancing fail. At least, though (as opposed to the next rung), the weapons are in the hands of a vulnerable, but venerable, ally of democratic persuasion. With *Rung 28*, the weapons are provided to neutrals, with the understanding again that they could be used for offensive purposes, but this time with fewer controls exercised by the United States over the arms.

More Provocative Propaganda, Politics, and Weaponry

The ladder returns again to propaganda, as well as political covert actions, on the next few rungs, but at this stage in an increasingly aggressive manner. At *Rung 29*, the CIA directs the dissemination of false information against a genuine democracy—an action that, if aimed at Americans by an ally, could well result in a rupture of bilateral relations. Secretary of State Henry Kissinger takes this prohibition against CIA disinformation even further, saying: "I don't believe that putting misleading information out as news is *ever* justifiable." He continued: "I would think that any information that is placed through *any* American governmental organization should be such that it could be published here without misleading the American people."[21]

Kissinger's stance (at least in this public record) would evidently apply to whatever type of regime is being targeted: no more disinformation from the CIA, period. Such a position would help greatly to diffuse the problem of blowback, although not entirely eliminate it; the widespread dissemination of truthful propaganda can also distort reality in the direction of an unwarranted belief that a certain point of view is widely held and overwhelmingly correct.

Rung 30, which is focused on neutrals, is infused with the possibility of loss or injury. At this level on the ladder, "massive" secret political spending takes place in hopes of shaping events on the ground toward a pro-US outcome—far more than the earlier tipping point of $5 million spent against the targeted nation. The expenditure of enormous sums of money is always an important flashing dashboard light in covert action calculations. More provocative still is the similar targeting of a group or faction within an adversarial autocracy (*Rung 31*), since such an endeavor would likely stimulate a tit-for-tat retaliation against the United States by a determined and well-funded foe who is unrestricted by moral constraints. Most controversial of all among this trio of "high-risk" funding rungs is the attempted manipulation of politics—siding with one party over another—within a fellow democracy (*Rung 32*). Covert attacks within open societies are discouraged from top to bottom on the escalation ladder; and they become all the more objectionable when sizable sums of cash are involved in hopes of influencing political outcomes.

When one is dealing with the covert transfer of large caches of weaponry to another country (*Rungs 33* and *34*), the ladder's risk index climbs sharply upward—even when the recipients are democratic regimes. By engaging in these practices, the United States sets itself up as a legitimate target for the threatened third party, as when Germany began attacking American ships because they were secretly carrying weapons to the United Kingdom during the early stages of the Second World War. Moreover, it is worth remembering that international relations over the years has taught that today's ally can become tomorrow's adversary.

A substantial transfer of weaponry is inherently provocative at any level on the Third Option ladder, but especially problematic when the recipient is a neutral nation. What assurances does the CIA have that these armaments will be used in the manner initially agreed upon; or where the guns, bullets, tanks, and missiles will eventually end up, as when some Stinger missiles were never returned to the Agency by the *mujahideen* after the covert war in Afghanistan during the 1980s?

On *Rung 35*, propaganda appears in its most sobering form: the encouragement of violent rebellion in another country. Here deaths are practically guaranteed. *Rung 36* presents another significant step, with the insertion of a small contingent of CIA officers directly into a paramilitary operation within a neutral country. The assignment of Agency PM personnel as "advisers" in Vietnam during the 1950s and early 1960s reminds us of where such activities can lead.

Threshold Four: Extreme Operations

When arriving at this uppermost threshold on the escalation ladder, one enters a potential purgatory where grievous harm can be inflicted.

Hostage Situations

Rungs 37 and *38* are related to hostage situations, which—whether trying to rescue hostages or snatching them for bargaining purposes (or for obtaining intelligence)—can be laden with risk and moral opprobrium. With respect to hostage rescue attempts, an illustration of the danger is the multiple snafus that occurred when the United States tried to rescue US embassy captives in Iran during the Carter years (examined in Chapter 4). Former Secretary of State Dean Rusk offered wise words about the reaction of the US government to the Iranian standoff. The Carter administration chose not to retaliate by seizing Iranian diplomats in Washington, and Rusk applauded the decision. "We are not that kind of country," he said, underlining the fact that America can take the high ground in foreign affairs and is widely respected for doing so.[22] Given America's experience with selecting and propping up the unpopular Shah of Iran in 1953, one could have some empathy for the view of people in Tehran at the time. Who knows how Americans might have reacted had the tables been reversed? As a colleague has pointed out, "Iran did not use a covert operation to remove a US president and replace him with someone loyal to Iran."[23]

As for snatch operations, in the post-9/11 years the CIA has sometimes grabbed the wrong person off the streets overseas as a suspected terrorist wanted for intelligence gathering purposes—tragic cases of mistaken identity. Moreover, as mentioned in the previous chapter, highly questionable has been the Agency's practice of "extraordinary rendition" (a fancier word for snatching) of suspected terrorists from the streets in Stockholm, Berlin, or other locations, then transporting them to "third countries" for the harshest modes of questioning—"interrogation in depth" or torture—by less law-abiding intelligence services. Cairo has been a top-tier destination for these purposes.

At the CIA, this program is known as "rendition, detention, and interrogation" or RDI. The practice made the United States just as complicitous as if DO officers had carried out the torture techniques themselves. Again, from a Machiavellian point-of-view, covert action—with its attractive feature of plausible denial—can come in handy, allowing the White House to hide its involvement in a controversial secret operation that comes to light. The leaders of Egypt and Thailand, as well as other countries that have secretly assisted the United States and the CIA by providing "black sites" for RDI purposes, may have been far less willing to help if they had thought these activities would become a matter of public record, thereby making them vulnerable to citizen opprobrium within in their own countries.

Beyond the question of torture lies the matter of incarcerating suspected enemies of the United States in American prisons, as has been the case since the capture and internment of alleged terrorists at US brigs in Guantánamo (some of whom are no doubt guilty, while others may be innocent). In reference to an earlier counterintelligence episode involving the Soviet defector Yuriy Nosenko, who was held at a CIA facility for over three years without the benefit of counsel or a chance to prove his bone fides in a court of law, former DCI William Colby has offered this judgment: "The assassination of a foreign leader may be dumb; but to take someone and put him in jail in the United States—what the hell happened to habeas corpus? This is pretty fundamental. For an intelligence agency to do that in this country—Jesus!"[24]

Stepped-Up Arms Supplies and the Thwarting of Cyber Assaults

The next step (*Rung 39*) marks a return to the supply of arms abroad, this time involving the bold move of providing weapons to factions operating within the borders of a major adversary—poking an enemy, who is often well armed, directly in the eye. In another step upward, *Rung 40* represents one of the most unsettling developments in the contemporary world: dealing with cyberattackers, whether misguided teens or—the infinitely larger problem—officers in foreign intelligence and military services. By responding at this level, the United States goes beyond a defensive counterintelligence shield; now this nation takes to the offense with the targeting of electronic disruptions of its own making, although still within a narrow focus at this rung rather than attempts to wreck the full Web-based capacities of a foreign adversary.

Attacking Mother Nature

The Third Option can be directed against the environment, also, as if that green domain were insufficiently punished already by the fossil-fuel industry and global-warming deniers. At a preliminary level of environmental intervention (*Rung 41*), cloud-seeding was tried during the Vietnam War, for instance, in an attempt to complicate North Vietnamese troop movements southward along the Ho Chi Minh Trail (although these attempts met with only limited success). More damaging environmental tampering is attempted at *Rung 42*. This step undertakes major dislocations caused by, say, sabotaging dams to create flooding, or by the secret dissemination of harsh chemicals, such as Agent Orange during the Vietnam War, to defoliate tree cover used by the enemy and thereby make them more visible for a kill.

In the process, the chemicals themselves end up killing or horribly injuring enemies as well as innocent civilians: producing malformed limbs; babies and fetuses born with severe birth defects, including club feet, cleft palates, and missing eyes; farm animals with extra limbs—the cruel side effects of spreading carcinogenic herbicides against an adversary. As the United States discovered the hard way in Indochina, these kinds of operations may coincidentally send one's own personnel to an early grave or a life of disability, as the poisons washed back against American soldiers. While Agent Orange was an overt Pentagon operation during the war in Vietnam, it is presented in the context of this clandestine escalation ladder because such substances could just as easily have been spread by Agency operatives—and reportedly were dropped by CIA C-123 aircraft onto Laos during the 1960s.[25]

Targeting Crops and Livestock

Disquieting, too, and leading to even more widespread suffering, is the possible use of the Third Option to destroy agricultural fields and even livestock, with the intent of bringing a nation to its knees by collapsing its food-chain (*Rung 43*). One such proposed operation that arose during the Kennedy years—among the most bone-chilling proposals in the annals of US covert actions—bore the codename Operation "Square Dance." This recommendation came from the overheated mind of a Pentagon strategist, as he attempted in the early 1960s to edge the military into the business of clandestine interventions. Stunningly, the Joint Chiefs of Staff then recommended the operation to Secretary of Defense Robert S. McNamara. Square Dance envisioned nothing less than the destruction of the Cuban economy and Castro's resulting demise by dropping from aircraft onto the island late at night batches of a parasite known as Bunga. This pest has a craving for sugar cane and would presumably destroy Cuba's main export crop.[26]

The proposal was reminiscent more of what the KGB might come up with than the Defense Department of the United States. An exasperated National Security Adviser, McGeorge Bundy, caught wind of the proposal through DC's national security grapevine and in private conversations with McNamara put a quash to this madness (a view shared by the Secretary of Defense) before Bunga had a chance to dine *al fresco* in Cuba.[27] Related proposals, though, involving the dilution of Cuban pesticides as well as the poisoning of rice paddies in South Vietnam (a scheme that did move forward) are further examined in Chapter 9 in the context of an ethical examination of extreme uses of the Third Option.

Limited Coup Attempts

At *Rung 44*, the Third Option resorts initially to a modest package of propaganda, political, and economic activities meant to topple a government in a small- to medium-sized nation; and then, at *Rung 45*, this strategy is augmented by potentially lethal PM activities (though still at a limited level). Here is the CIA in its most stereotypical portrayal: the standard operating procedure (SOP) of busily overthrowing regimes around the world. Its involvement in coups d'état in every corner of the globe has been vastly exaggerated, with the DO often considered the culprit behind practically every untoward event that occurs in the world, as depicted in a *New Yorker* drawing from the 1960s (Figure 2.2). Hyperbole notwithstanding, attempted and sometimes successful CIA-sponsored coups have in fact occurred periodically around the globe—usually against small, defenseless nations with populations of color (a target selection discussed in Chapter 10).[28]

The Assassination Rungs

The most deadly contemporary instrument of paramilitary activity—the missile-laden drone, deployed by both the CIA and the Pentagon—debuts at *Rung 46*. Used for specific, premeditated purpose of hunting down and incinerating suspected terrorists worldwide, both inside and outside the scope of acknowledged US battlefields like Afghanistan from 2001 to 2021, these quietly flying aerial robots have "disappeared" many members of Al Qaeda, ISIS, and other

58 THE THIRD OPTION

"The C.I.A. did it. Pass it along."

Figure 2.2 "The C.I.A. Did It." *New Yorker*, cartoon
Source: Alan Dunn, *The New Yorker* (1965).

dangerous terrorist factions. Targeted, too, have been some US citizens overseas considered terrorists, Anwar al-Awlaki (living in Yemen at the time) the most prominent among them.[29] Here the clandestine escalation ladder arrives at the direct, immediate death of individuals as a result of a covert action, in contrast to human beings maybe or maybe not dying by exposure to defoliate sprays, induced flooding, agricultural contamination (all operations listed at slightly lower tiers), or limited coup attempts. This question of clandestine assassinations warrants closer inspection, beginning with a look at counterterrorist operations, then turning to the hot-button topic of killing foreign public figures.

Counterterrorism, ALEC Station, and Osama Bin Laden. Basic questions of morality always hover over Third Option initiatives, and especially so when loss of life is involved in a "civilian" setting. The hunt for Osama bin Laden (OBL), the Al Qaeda leader and a *Rung 46* target, illustrates some of the dilemmas. Al Qaeda had become a terrorist organization of special interest to the CIA after the DO suspected the presence of the cell's hidden hand behind US embassy bombings in Africa in 1998, and against the USS *Cole* naval ship in waters off Yemen in 2000. Several sightings of bin Laden during the Clinton years might have led to his capture or death long before Al Qaeda struck directly against the United States on 9/11. In most instances, though, ethical reservations arose among some of the administration's senior officials who were concerned about the possible inadvertent killing of nearby women and children. Or, on some occasions, a calculation was made that the chances of hitting Bin Laden seemed too low to warrant the launching of Cruise missiles against him from US ships in the Arabian Sea.[30] In one instance, the Intelligence Community had located the Qaeda leader at Tarnak Farms in an isolated desert region near Kandahar in Afghanistan. The National Security Council never met to approve the attack, though, because its staff working group on this subject found the plan inappropriate; the many civilians living at the Farms, including several of Bin Laden's wives and children, risked the likely deaths of innocent bystanders.

The inhouse CIA group responsible for locating and capturing, or at least disrupting bin Laden and Al Qaeda, known as ALEC Station at the CIA (part of the Counterterrorism Center within the DO at Agency Headquarters), was furious at this lost opportunity.[31] In contrast, those who place a value on ethics above a more narrow definition of success (in this case, OBL's removal) will give the Clinton team high marks for its judgment in rejecting a PM operation that would have snuffed out the lives of innocent women and children. Beyond the intrinsic importance of their lives, the wanton killing also would have had sharply negative repercussions among Muslim communities around the world—the very people the United States hoped to win over. Whether a sense of ethics drove the Clinton White House decisions to back away from some bin Laden assassination attempts, or the decision was simply a determination by its top officials that the chances for success were too low, remains a matter of dispute among those who have studied these plots. Coll writes: "Neither they [the Clinton national security team] nor the president ever hesitated to shoot only because of the fear of innocent deaths. The real problem, they said was the '40 percent chance,' as Clinton put it, of actually killing bin Laden." Yet, as Coll also reports, the president clearly fretted as well over the possible deaths of innocents during a US raid.[32]

On another occasion, less a gnawing sense of morality in the White House than bin Laden's own good luck saved him. Missiles fired under President Clinton's orders destroyed his camp at Khost, Afghanistan, but he had already departed. In a further example, the Qaeda leader was bird hunting in the desert with bigwigs from the United Arab Emirates. Clinton decided it would be unwise to send missiles against the target when, accidentally, the UAE officials—supposedly allies of the United States (though, really? hunting with OBL?)—might be caught in the firestorm. The hit was also opposed by DCI George Tenet. A couple of other times President Clinton's vacillation on the ethics of assassination saved the terrorist chief. These moments of indecision left Agency officials unsure about the wishes of the White House, and so they called down further attempts to eliminate Bin Laden—an ambiguity about clear presidential authority that never seemed to bother DCI Helms during assassination plotting against Fidel Castro thirty years earlier (see Chapter 4).

The ALEC Station staff was miffed with these moments of indecision in the Clinton White House, to put it mildly, and its chief finally resigned in a huff. In the COS's view, his team had worked hard to find OBL, no easy task, only to lose golden opportunities to bring the terrorist's deadly scheming to an end—and all because of Bill Clinton's indecision and moral qualms.[33] They had every right to be unhappy with the president's periodic vacillations; but, in several of the attack scenarios, Clinton and his national security aides displayed commendable moral instincts against the murder of non-combatants. Another feature of these attacks is worthy of note: they were hugely expensive—always a consideration as one climbs up the ladder. In one of the attempts to eliminate bin Laden, the Clinton White House ordered the firing of seventy-five Tomahawk cruise missiles into the Zahar Kili encampment in Afghanistan, where the terrorist leader was thought to be holding a secret meeting. While OBL had departed several hours before the strike, others gather for the powwow were obliterated. The cost to the American taxpayer: $750,000 per cruise missile.

The Targeting of Foreign Public Officials. Assassination plots against foreign heads of state and other leading government officials enter the picture at *Rung 47*, in an especially controversial step up the ladder. At this rung lies the potential disaster of a Wild West free-for-all, with shootouts around the globe at the highest levels of government, a dystopian affliction that plagued *fin de siècle* European capitals. American political officials would find themselves in the crosshairs just as readily as their foreign counterparts; indeed, given the openness of US society, they would be far more vulnerable targets.

This was the great danger, and a legitimate cause for public controversy, surrounding the order from President Trump to assassinate by drone a high-ranking Iranian public official—Major General Qasem Soleimani—during his visit to Baghdad in 2020.[34] A military Reaper drone carried out the attack, although it could just as well have been a CIA aircraft. Whichever agency called on (the differences between DoD and CIA drone attacks are explored further in Chapters 6 and 7), the result was the same: an invitation to retaliate against US officials by Tehran's secret agents. Soon after this attack against Soleimani, Iran struck back at US troops at an Iraqi-based compound with ground combat weaponry, causing severe brain damage among several victims. Experts predicted that further revenge will come from Tehran sometime in the future against an American officeholder. Trump had sown the wind; the whirlwind would await harvesting by later officials.

Former DCI Stansfield Turner has commented on assassinations, distinguishing between a battlefield and a political setting:

> [Assassination] is tempting to me only in wartime. I would have approved assassinating Saddam Hussein after the 16th of January [1991, the date when Congress gave its authority to use military force against Iraq in the First Persian Gulf War]. And that's exactly the reason: there's a big difference between a President—and, heaven help us, somebody below him—taking on him- or herself to say, "Noriega [the leader of Panama] ought to die," and the Congress of the United States and the public of the United States saying, "We're going to war with Panama, and Noriega is just as much a target as Joe Jones, Private First-Class." And if you happen to target Noriega specifically—and surely we targeted Saddam Hussein (it didn't work)—I think that is all right.[35]

Reisman and Baker have written more broadly that "assassination should be viewed as an unlawful covert action and should not be given any color of law."[36] Among many others, they are joined by W. Hays Parks, chief of the Army's International Law Branch. "Assassination is unlawful killing," he concludes, "and would be prohibited by international law even if there were no executive order proscribing it."[37]

Another DCI, William Colby, has commented on the use of assassination as a Third Option. Looking back on the debates within the Bush I administration over whether the leader of Panama, Manuel Noriega, should be assassinated, or whether if he died collaterally during a coup against his regime his demise would amount to an assassination of a foreign leader, the administration decided not to make a coup attempt against the regime. This decision was reached in part over concern with the ethical implications if Noriega died. Instead, on December 20, 1989, President Bush sent 24,000 US troops into Panama, in an overt invasion that killed several hundred Panamanians. Noriega survived the invasion and was arrested as a prisoner of war. "I suspect that was the right decision," Colby concluded, "because you'd still be hearing about the assassination of Noriega for the next hundred years, but you will not be hearing about the attack on Panama for the next hundred years, as with many previous examples in Latin America." The former CIA viewed this decision as "a tough moral issue. A very close call. But I think from this country's point-of-view, it's better to have a flat prohibition against the killing of a foreign leader." The exception to this rule, Colby added, was when America was at war. "Then," he said, "you can go after the top man."[38]

One thing is certain: the use of assassination as a political tool takes the world onto an off-ramp that departs from civilized society and heads toward international anarchy. The late 1800s witnessed a period of rampant assassinations, with almost every European head of state the target of a murder plot, including Tsars

Alexander II, Alexander III, and Nicholas II of Russia; Emperor Franz Joseph of Austria; Kaisers Wilhelm I, Friedrich III, and Wilhelm II of Germany; Kings Victor Emmanuel II, Umberto I and Victor Emmanuel III of Italy; several French presidents; and many prominent politicians.[39] This is not the kind of chaotic world culture one would like to see again.

Major Clandestine Warfare

The next three rungs envision major secret combat led by the CIA's paramilitary officers, with multiple casualties on the ground a high likelihood. They represent full-scale coups—that is, using all the P, POL, E, and PM forms of the Third Option—against major neutral nations (*Rung 48*); major autocratic regimes (*Rung 49*), and democracies (*Rung 50*). These coup targets, though dramatically different in regime type, would include paramilitary activity bound to produce a significant retaliation against the United States by nations well equipped to respond in kind—perhaps moving rapidly to an overt warfare or a terrorist response. Taking on a major autocratic regime is particularly risky, because it could likely trigger a significant overt military retaliation; and the launching of a coup against a fellow democracy is unacceptable on its face, given the supposition that democracies should eschew use of covert action against one another altogether—and especially when a PM component is involved.

At *Rung 51*, cyberattacks are aimed at everything from an adversary's command-and-control facilities and nuclear reactors to energy grids and airport terminals—an all-encompassing cyberwar. The end result: a potential nationwide electronic collapse in the targeted regime, accompanied by the high probability of retaliation in kind that such action would invite.

Destruction of the Rule of Law: Climbing the Rungs of Democratic Catastrophe

Finally, near the top perch on the ladder are two uses of covert action that are utterly dismaying in their recklessness and potentially far-reaching consequences for the future of democratic rule in the United States, whose fragility was demonstrated for all to see in the appalling attack against the US Capitol that occurred on January 6, 2021. At *Rung 52* stands a willingness by the CIA, and presumably its White House handlers, to violate the laws of the land in the conduct of a covert action; and *Rung 53* goes even a step farther into darkness with an assault on America's Constitution, as occurred during the Iran-*contra* affair of the 1980s. These transgressions, which receive further attention in subsequent chapters, present profound ethical concerns regarding the possibility of a renegade CIA (or other US intelligence agency) unmoored from the law and the Constitution, and operating inside the United States. Here is the scenario of the CIA, or some off-the-grid auxiliary entity created by the government for purposes of super-secrecy, with well-practiced propaganda, political, economic, and paramilitary skills, turned against the citizens of the United States.

Crossing the River Styx

Positioned higher still on the ladder, because a large number of lives could be immediately at stake, *Rung 54* suggests the possibility of an intelligence "My Lai": the monstrous killing of innocent civilians en masse through clandestine means. Such actions have never been taken by a US intelligence agency, but history records wanton cruelty by some foreign spy services. Examples include Hitler's Gestapo and Stalin's secret police, the NKVD. The treacherous deeds of the former are well known, the latter less so—even though the NKVD murdered 15,000 Polish prisoners during the Second World War in what is known as the Katyn Massacre (after the forest in Russia where the bodies were found). This rung on the ladder includes, as well, the use of torture against anyone, or aiding and abetting this practice through rendition—both activities falling beyond the pale of America's traditions and values. Further, this rung encompasses all other gross violations of human rights.

Finally, *Rung 55* at the very top of the ladder holds the horrifying potential of a clandestine NBC operation, or one using radiological weapons, against a target. A cataclysmic event of this kind would likely lead to the bleakest of international repercussions, quite possibly an overt NBC response that could result in the mutual annihilation of whole societies—even the planet itself.

~~~

Above all, the Ladder of Clandestine Escalation for the Third Option is a reminder that, on moral grounds alone (setting aside, for the moment, practical consequences), the United States should reject the use of high-risk covert interventions that have a strong chance of leading down a pathway toward violent outcomes that involve the death of innocents. An operation carried out in 1983 by French foreign intelligence service (Direction Générale de la Sécurité Extérieure, DGSE) against the *Rainbow Warrior*, a ship operated by the Greenpeace environmental organization that led protests against France's nuclear tests in the South Pacific, provides an illustration of how important honoring non-violence principles can be in the world of covert action, even at a level of clandestine intervention that doesn't target large numbers of people.

The Greenpeace demonstrators sailed their rickety old vessel into the ocean test site, 780 miles southeast of Tahiti, hoping to prevent nuclear weapons from being detonated and poisoning the earth's atmosphere with the release of radioactive particles into the air. In response, Paris dispatched intelligence commandos to end the protest. In the darkness of night, a French paramilitary team placed a bomb on the *Rainbow*'s hull as it moored in Auckland harbor, New Zealand, before sailing into the test zone. The French team swam away from the ship, then detonated the weapon, sending this international avatar of peace to a watery grave and killing a photographer asleep on board. If the French felt compelled to use covert action against this non-violent protest group, its operatives could have at least limited the intervention to a disabling of the ship's propeller shaft or rudder. Instead, the DGSE had no reservations about moving directly to a violent solution, starting off at *Rung 36* on the escalation ladder (or *Rung 46*, if the French were aware that a person was on board the ship that night whom they might have labeled a "terrorist" trying to disrupt French national security activities). In the process, these French intelligence officers sullied their nation's reputation for fair play and and left New Zealand's sovereignty in tatters.[40] The French government, though, proved unaffected by the immorality of its activities and, on their return to Paris, the commandos were decorated for this brazen action.

There may be a situation in the future in which the United States might be compelled to ignore Third Option laws and ethics altogether, engaging in an unrestrained approach to foreign affairs that relies on every available overt and covert policy instrument. This book places the Constitution and American law in a prominent position when it comes to a moral evaluation of covert actions. Without proper process, without debate, without White House *and* congressional review, the Third Option lacks legitimacy (the focus of Chapter 9). Yet President Abraham Lincoln, America's greatest chief executive, pushed aside key provisions of the Constitution for a time, and quite properly so as he gathered the presidential powers necessary to preserve the Union from disintegration while Congress was out of session. He explained his actions clearly and publicly at the time and vowed to return the government to normalcy as soon as possible—or suffer impeachment from office and eternal ignominy. When lawmakers returned to Washington, they reviewed and approved his emergency initiatives.

A time may come—one hopes not, of course—when, similarly, the ladder of escalation may be rendered moot and an American president will have to use whatever rungs might be necessary to thwart the destruction of the United States or some other major calamity. Imagine that Hitler's extermination of Jews during the Third Reich could have been prevented by radical use of America's clandestine capabilities. If so, such operations should have been adopted. Or, in Copeland's good example, imagine "a new Hitler intent upon using atomic warfare."[41] More generally, what if covert intervention today could help rescue a population from enslavement, brutality, or genocide? Surely, in such scenarios, a harsh hidden hand would have to be taken seriously as a temporarily acceptable foreign policy option. Most likely, though, such levels of barbarity within a foreign regime would require not so much covert action as a full-scale overt intervention, just as major warfare proved a necessity against Hitler.

Ideally, these extreme secret interventions would include prior closed-session reviews by the congressional intelligence committees as well, not just the White House and the CIA. Moreover, subsequent actions would entail collective action by a coalition of nations rather than the solitary American use of overt or covert force. Barring ultra-extreme situations, however, ethical restraints on the conduct of the Third Option will remain fitting and possible for a democratic society, a subject returned to in Chapter 9 on the ethics of secret interventions.

Which of the rungs on the ladder has the CIA grasped over the years? That question is addressed in the following four historically oriented chapters, which look at America's most significant uses of the Third Option since 1947. As social critic Louis Menard has put it, "The palette of covert activities was broad."[42]

PART II
PRACTICE, 1947–1975

3
A Shadowy Foreign Policy, 1947–1960

The Third Option Evolves

The list is extensive, in even an incomplete accounting, of publicly disclosed locations where the United States has labored secretly to advance its interests in the world through covert action.[1] This chapter examines some of the more prominent examples from 1947 to 1960, followed by a review of the years between 1960 and 1975 in Chapter 4. (See the timeline in Figure 3.1.)

Early Covert Action Targets

Neither President Harry S. Truman nor his mysterious new spy organization, the Central Intelligence Agency, were enthusiastic about the Third Option at first. The president was skeptical that clandestine interventions abroad would have any appreciable effect. So were the Agency's leaders for that matter. In the CIA's early days, intelligence officers would have preferred to concentrate on what the National Security Act of 1947 spelled out as their expected duty: the collection and assessment of information from around the world. Moreover, the president was concerned about the ethical aspects of the United States engaging in "dirty tricks" overseas.[2]

Nevertheless, during these opening years of the Cold War, the CIA experienced some success in countering KGB influence in such nations as Greece and Turkey through a range of covert actions.[3] Even critics of the Third Option understood this approach was preferable to military interventions against the Soviets, which might have triggered yet another major war. Funding was a factor as well. Former director of Central Intelligence (DCI), Robert M. Gates, writes that, as the size of the US military budget was sharply reduced after the Second World War, "... Truman turned to nonmilitary forms of power to thwart further communist expansionism," with the Third Option high on the list.[4]

The Truman Doctrine of March 1947 and the Marshall Plan a year later provided overt financial and military aid to nations being subjected to the Soviet Union's covert actions, its "active measures." America's widely publicized and well-funded overt foreign policy programs were the most influential means to help keep the countries being targeted by the Soviets safely within the Western

Containment & stay-behind operations against the **SOVIET BLOC****
GREECE, Turkey
ITALY, FRANCE, West Germany, Iran
Czechoslovakia, East Germany, Estonia, Latvia, Lithuania
ALBANIA, Belarus, Bulgaria, Poland, Romania, Ukraine
NORTH KOREA, CHINA, Japan
Burma, India
IRAN, Philippines
GUATEMALA, Brazil
HUNGARY, N. Vietnam, Cuba, Dominican Republic
Costa Rica, Ecuador, **USSR, WARSAW PACT*****
1947 1948 1949 1950-52 1953 1954-56 1958 1960 1961 1962 1963 1964 1967 1970-75
Tibet, **SYRIA, LEBANON, *INDONESIA***, Ghana
CONGO, Dominican Republic, N. Vietnam
CUBA, LAOS, S. VIETNAM, Angola
Ecuador, Chile, Mozambique
Somalia, British Guiana
Angola, Thailand
Cambodia
Brazil, Greece
CHILE, Iraq, Italy

*The cases commented on in this chapter are in bold capital letters.
**During the Cold War, the Soviet Bloc included, in addition to the Soviet Union: Bulgaria, Cuba, Czechoslovakia, East Germany, Hungary, Poland, and Romania.
***The Warsaw Pact was founded in 1955 and included the same nations as the Soviet Bloc (above), plus Albania (until 1968) but without Cuba.

Figure 3.1 Key Targeting in the Evolution of Covert Action, 1947–1975*

camp of democratic societies.[5] The secret interventions of the United States, though, also served a role as part of the Western bulwark against Soviet expansion. Western Europe was the initial critical battleground for the Third Option because it was the region of the world most energetically encroached upon by the Soviets. Moreover, the imperious General Douglas MacArthur, who controlled US foreign policy activities in the Far East, made it clear that he wanted nothing to do with the CIA interfering in "his" part of the world, just as he had successfully reined in Office of Strategic Services (OSS) espionage activities in Asia during the war. Not until April of 1949 did MacArthur begrudgingly allow Agency operations in that part of the world. The United States had good reason to be concerned, above all, about Chinese activities throughout Asia during the 1950s. The revolutionary leader of China, Mao Zedong, even viewed nuclear war against the democratic "imperialists" as a plausible route to a communist global victory over capitalism, as then the West would be destroyed "and the whole world could become socialist."[6] He secretly financed a wide range of operations against the democracies around the world, including those in Latin America.

The CIA's first covert action of major scope in these early years took place not against China, though, but in Italy. The Agency's behind-the-scenes involvement in Italian politics began in 1948 and continued for twenty years (then periodically thereafter), as the United States sought to shore up that nation's Christian Democratic Party as a counter to the Italian Communist Party.[7] Protecting Italian democracy was not the only motivation. The North Atlantic Treaty Organization (NATO) was established in 1949, and keeping Italy free of communist control was important to ensure that classified documents related to NATO's activities were kept out of the hands of a communist government in Rome. The Italian communists would have instantly shared the security organization's secrets with the Kremlin.

Moreover, as intelligence historian Jeffreys-Jones notes, Italy was strategically located, both militarily if war broke out with the USSR and commercially as a transit point for Middle East oil.[8] Soviet covert activities in France, Germany, and other nations in Western Europe were of concern, too. Indeed, Germany was considered by some operatives as "the cradle of the intelligence struggle of the Cold War."[9] The fear was that Moscow was using concealed financial resources to gain control over Western democratic institutions: publishing houses, the media, labor unions, and civic organizations of all stripes—the "key elements of life," as US diplomat George F. Kennan recalled.[10]

Other Third Option targets of the United States included countries in Africa, Latin America, Asia, and the Middle East—practically everywhere over sea and land where Moscow was trying to exercise its influence. One early instance was a successful CIA effort to aid a coup in Syria in 1949. This operation was among the Agency's "first out-and-out clandestine operation," recalls a participant who was one of a handful of young Ivy League officers enthralled by the chance to serve as the tip of the spear in America's global anti-communist crusade.[11] The Agency also reached its hidden hand into every country it could within the Soviet Empire, with a special focus on Poland and Ukraine (the latter being the site of the CIA's most lucratively funded field operation in these early days). By the 1950s, forty or so covert actions were under way in "one central European country alone."[12]

The fledgling Agency's intentions to establish guerrilla movements in Eastern Europe made up of émigrés failed, however, running into a formidable counterintelligence shield forged by the Soviet foreign intelligence service, the KGB, and its companion military spy agency, the GRU. Time and again, the CIA's infiltrating assets thought they were being greeted by allied underground resistance fighters only to find that these welcoming parties were "catchment basins" for the KGB.[13] These courageous operatives were imprisoned, tortured, or killed, with many suffering the entirety of this gruesome Soviet triad of counterintelligence methods, one following the other. The most challenging target for the CIA was Russia itself, the object of extensive propaganda and sabotage activities. These operations had little appreciable effect on the communist behemoth. Against China, the CIA was engaged in similar efforts from 1949 to 1954—a so-called Third Force resistance, ready to support any anti-communists it could locate on the mainland to carry out guerrilla PMs against Mao Zedong and his forces.[14] A recent review of these activities concludes: "The Third Force enterprise, as a paramilitary or political project, was a grand failure."[15]

In 1950, in the Far East, Lieutenant Colonel Edward G. Lansdale, on loan to the Agency from the US Air Force, led a CIA operation to help subdue communist-supported Hukbalahap ("Huk") guerrillas in the Philippine jungles. He managed to steer a local politician by the name of Ramon Magsaysay into that nation's presidency. Lansdale became something of an overnight celebrity within Washington's national security apparatus for his successful covert actions, although he would meet his demise a decade later with Operation "Mongoose," the failed attempts to oust Castro from the Cuban presidency (Chapter 4). In between these bookmarks, he had some remarkable—and clever—victories. For example, Lansdale aided the effort to engineer Ngo Dinh Diem into power in South Vietnam in 1955, by influencing the design of the ballot for presidential elections in that nation. According to one account, "He used red, the Asian good luck color, for Diem and green—signifying a cuckold—for Diem's opponent."[16]

Further, in 1950, the Agency attempted a coup against the pro-Moscow government in Albania, in a paramilitary plot codenamed Operation "Valuable" during the Truman administration and then Operation "BG/FIEND" when it was inherited from the United Kingdom (UK) by the Eisenhower administration in 1953. Initially, this venture was carried out in tandem with MI6, the British foreign intelligence service that is also known as the Secret Intelligence Service or SIS. The plan called for the United States to provide secret funding to MI6, which over the years had accrued much greater experience in that part of the world than had the CIA. The Americans and the British would infiltrate exiled guerrilla commando teams into Albania—ten times the number of fighters that the CIA would send into battle at the Bay of Pigs in Cuba a little over a decade later. The most common means of positioning these teams was by airdrop onto remote runways northwest of Athens, Greece, with the Agency using unmarked Douglas C047 aircraft on loan from the US Air Force.

It became clear, however, after much loss of life, that these fearless commandos had little chance of success. Soon after they arrived, most of the squads were wrapped up by Soviet-trained local security forces. The subsequent Eisenhower administration eventually backed out of the paramiitary side of the BG/FIEND operation, focusing instead on a more limited program of anti-Soviet propaganda aimed at Albania. The British went ahead on their own. Still more failure came—quickly and tragically—for the individuals who had volunteered for the UK operation, only to fall into the ready jaws of the communist counterintelligence services that operated throughout the Soviet satellite nations.

The infiltration teams run by MI6 kept drawing deuces, with bad luck that had nothing to do with their bravery or brio of the team members. Rather, the deck was stacked against them from the beginning. The KGB enjoyed a well-placed mole inside Her Majesty's Secret Service: a debonair counterintelligence officer by the name of Kim Philby. As a result, the Soviets knew every detail of these operations long before the guerrilla forces landed on Albanian soil, just as Moscow had been alerted by Philby (it was later discovered) to many of the earlier Eastern European infiltration attempts.

Vast sums of money were spent and, during these ill-fated attempts to establish resistance movements throughout Eastern Europe, many an Agency asset vanished into the awaiting belly of the communists—"hundreds," in one authoritative estimate.[17] The groups of infiltrators were determined anti-communist émigrés recruited from, and trained in, refugee camps across Germany and Italy. They longed to drive the Red Army from their homelands. The notion that they could serve as an invisible internal resistance against Russia if another war broke out, or that they could take part with CIA paramilitary officers in a "roll-back" of the Iron Curtain during the 1950s, was, however, a fatal delusion for them and their Agency handlers, as well as a costly and poor investment for the United States. As an Agency inhouse historian has written, most of these covert actions during the first years of the Cold War "met with failure."[18] The "roll-back" slogan did win votes for the Eisenhower presidential campaigns in 1952 and 1956, however, along with a long-term political commitment to the GOP in southern California and other enclaves in the United States where Estonian and fellow Eastern Europe émigrés had fled after the war. A key plank in the GOP platform at the 1952 presidential nominating convention called for the "liberation" of Eastern European nations.

In 1952, the same group of Agency officers behind the earlier Syrian coup turned their attention to Egypt and supported a putsch against King Farouk, a grossly obese and corrupt monarch. Out of this coup emerged a young colonel by the name of Gamal Abdel Nasser. He would soon butt heads with the United States as he became leader of the non-aligned nations during the Cold War. The spirited, if small-scale, clandestine interventions like the one against King Farouk were early trials in Washington's efforts, via the CIA, to rebuff KGB and GRU activities aimed at herding foreign countries into Moscow's corral. The Agency was trying out its covert action skills around the world and they worked in some instances, at least in providing some hidden assistance to indigenous anti-communist organizations besieged by Soviet counterintelligence operations.

The Agency also played a major role in the creation of a West German foreign intelligence agency with a typically German jaw-breaking name, Bundesnachtrichtendienst, mercifully known as the BND for short. It was housed in dilapidated, yellow paint-peeling, formerly Nazi intelligence buildings in Pullach, a suburb of Munich. The BND soon joined forces with the CIA in tandem anti-Soviet activities throughout Eastern Europe. The German intelligence service included several former Nazi officials recently engaged in fighting against Russians on Germany's Eastern Front during the Second World War and, as a result, they knew the Soviet enemy well. Too well, in some cases; several of these former Nazi officers had already been secretly recruited by the KGB during the days of the Third Reich and, as a consequence, the BND was riddled with Moscow moles from the beginning of the Cold War.

An Agency focus during this period consisted of guerrilla raids directed against the giant communist powers, Russia and Red China. In the grand scheme of things, though, raids into such vast territories were akin to poking a fist into an elephant-sized pillow—just as had been true with the CIA's secret forays into Eastern Europe. In Western Europe, the chances of success were better and the Agency experimented in the use of the Third Option within fellow democracies, including bribes to selected Western European politicians as an encouragement for them to take pro-American stances on the world stage. The idea of derailing the creation of a European Defense Community was another early example of a failed covert action, as the EDC moved forward despite the CIA's best efforts to fan the flames of opposition on grounds that this organization might make Western Europe too independent from the United States. Although such setbacks occurred from time to time, the Agency's covert action programs blossomed as the Cold War began to warm up. By 1951, the budget for the Third Option had increased dramatically over 1948 levels of spending, in a sum that raced past funding for the CIA's collection-and-analysis Directorate by a ratio of three to one. As an experienced former Agency officer has observed, collection and analysis may have been formally the Agency's premier mission, but "what rings the cash registers is .... covert action."[19]

Korea

The Agency's operations in Korea were another important challenge for the fledgling organization. As would be the case whenever the United States was involved in an overt war, the CIA was expected to do its share of the heavy lifting during the conflict by way of paramilitary (PM) operations and associated clandestine activities. It joined America's troops battling arm in arm with South Koreans against North Korea communists and their Chinese ally during the overt war on the Korean Peninsula, which lasted from 1950 to 1953 and led to the deaths of 54,246 Americans. Here was a significant test by fire of the Agency's start-up PM capabilities, mobilized at the request of the State Department and the Joint Chiefs of Staff in the Defense Department.

With the outbreak of the Korean War in June of 1950, the superpowers escalated the East-West confrontation. Communist fighters from the North would not have been able to attack the government of South Korea without a green light from the Kremlin. This was out-and-out war between the communists and the democracies. The Third Option rose dramatically in importance for US government officials, becoming "the largest component in the agency" as its expenditures "skyrocketed" (according to the Church Committee). Funding for these secret activities rose from approximately $5 million in 1949 to $82 million in 1952 and was moving steadily upward by the time that conflict ended in a draw in 1953.[20]

Covert action would continue to attract the Agency's largest portion of spending until the 1970s, as propaganda, political, and economic activities melded with paramilitary ventures into a full Black & Decker toolbox for secret interventions overseas.[21] "Europe had put the CIA into the business of covert political action," writes intelligence expert Gregory F. Treverton. "It was Asia, however, that got the Agency into secret paramilitary operations in the Korean War, a pattern repeated a decade later in another Asian war, Vietnam."[22]

As a result of its failure to anticipate the outbreak of war on the Korean Peninsula, the reputation of the young CIA took a big hit in Washington on the analytic side during this stage of its infancy—a disquieting stumble in its primary mission laid out by the National Security Act of 1947. No doubt the CIA's performance would have been better if at least someone among its 200 CIA officers assigned to the war effort had been able to speak the Korean language.[23] As time passed, the Agency would become more proficient in foreign tongues (although it has never had as many fluent non-English speakers among its officers as it would like). Soon after the Korean War, its analysts would begin to draw praise for the impressive strides they had made in their understanding of other countries, as well as—an especially difficult assignment for the human mind—in their forecasting of world events.

President Truman had set up the CIA to help protect the United States and the Free World against communist aggression by providing accurate information about Russian and Chinese activities, especially anything of a military nature. While at first the president was a leading skeptic when it came to the value of the Agency's operations side, the Korean War had demonstrated how the spy organization and its paramilitary capabilities could assist in major overt brawls against communists, this time in Asia. The US military carried the heaviest burden of the war-fighting, of course; but the CIA had helped by bringing all four forms of covert action into the effort against the North Koreas and their superpower sponsors in Moscow and Beijing. General Walter Bedell ("Beetle") Smith, DCI at this time, understood that the Agency's Directorate of Plans was still finding its legs. As he observed in the midst of the war, the CIA "would have to hold its activities to the limited number of operations that it could do well rather than to attempt to cover a broad field with poor performance."[24]

In an appraisal offered by *New York Times* reporter Tim Weiner, the CIA "failed on all fronts in Korea"—even within Smith's limited parameters. Another journalist concurs, observing that "the CIA failed in Korea because it entered the game too late and had no reliable network of agents on the ground."[25] An assassination plot to kill the president of North Korea, Kim Il Sung, is said to have collapsed; PM teams of guerrilla forces trained by the Agency parachuted into North Korea and were never heard from again—"suicide missions," in Weiner's characterization. As in Eastern Europe, operation after operation resulted in disaster. Even according to an internal Agency assessment, the PM ops during the Korean War were "not only ineffective but probably morally reprehensible in the number of lives lost."[26]

Other observers, though, have been gentler in their judgments. An account written by a Church Committee historian simply noted that the war in Korea led to "an enormous impetus for growth," with the CIA becoming "six times the size it had been at its birth." Moreover, "by 1953, the Agency was an established element of government. Its contributions in the areas of political action and paramilitary warfare were recognized and respected. It alone could perform many of the kinds of activities seemingly required to meet the Soviet threat."[27] Critics to the contrary notwithstanding, given its burgeoning staff and budget, the Agency must have impressed the Eisenhower administration to some extent. No doubt during the war, the CIA's propaganda activities fared better than its PM ventures, in part because the former had been practiced since 1947 and, as well, they were less daunting to carry out. Another history, written by a CIA officer for the Aspin-Brown Commission, observed of this period only that the Agency's "analytical efforts during the Korean War established the Agency as a key player in the defense and foreign policy areas."[28]

Iran I

At first President Dwight D. ("Ike") Eisenhower shared Truman's uneasiness with the wide range of clandestine operations that were being crafted and set in motion by the CIA. Ike seemed more interested in focusing on King George's cavalry—financial support—to win over friends abroad than in attempts to engage in coups to overthrow unreliable foreign governments.[29] Yet, thanks to the persuasive abilities of DCI Allen Dulles and his brother, Secretary of State John Foster Dulles, the president was about to change his mind. A pamphlet at the newly created Eisenhower Memorial in Washington, DC, which opened in September of 2020, notes simply that the president had embraced "aggressive covert action."

The Agency's most famous early success with the Third Option came not in Europe (East or West) or during the Korean War, places where the CIA played a backup role but was still finding its way. Rather, the breakthrough came in the Middle East, just as the war in Korea was winding down. This intervention in an Islamic part of the world gave the still young Agency a substantially elevated status in Washington's community of rival bureaucracies. Seldom again would the CIA's deployment of the Third Option fall so happily into place, one segment after the other. In this instance, the target nation was Iran, in the first of several covert actions aimed at this nation during the coming years (therefore, labeled "Iran I" in this chapter).

Mohammed Mossadegh had been elected prime minister of Iran in 1951 and began to behave far too independently for the tastes of Washington officialdom, not to mention British and American oil executives. The discovery of oil in Iran in 1908 was proving to be both a blessing and a curse for the nation. The aging Iranian leader (Mossadegh was seventy) viscerally despised the British "colonists" in his country, and he nationalized the Anglo-Iranian Oil Company soon after his rise to power—a step unanimously endorsed by the Iranian Parliament. British petroleum executives and their US counterparts reasonably wondered if the access their companies had enjoyed to Iran's "black gold" would be cut off, or at least dramatically reduced—accompanied, no doubt, by painful price increases. An added concern in London was the fact that Iran straddled the UK's trading routes to India. In hopes of winning Washington's support in taming Mossadegh, the British played on the anxieties of the American oil industry, which in turn pressured the Eisenhower administration to oppose Mossadegh's nationalist stance. As well, behind the scenes, the British pushed the theme on Washington officials of possible Soviet expansion into the Middle East—indeed, perhaps even an imminent Red Army invasion of Iran. Downing Street and Whitehall, with Prime Minister Winston Churchill leading the way, hoped this tactic would bring the Eisenhower White House rushing to join London's anti-Mossadegh plotting. It was not a hard sell, especially given Churchill's close ties with Ike during the years of warfare against the Nazis. It was, nonetheless, an odd coalition since for decades the UK had done its best to keep the United States away from Iranian oil, which government officials in London preferred to monopolize for the United Kingdom.

The Truman administration's State Department had already expressed concern during meetings of the National Security Council (NSC) about Iran's "absorption immediately or eventually into the Soviet bloc."[30] Few in America's national security establishment at the time would have denied that a wave of communism washing over Iran would be an unfortunate development for US interests throughout the Middle East. From its first days in office in 1951, the Eisenhower administration had begun to worry as well that Mossadegh might extend a hand of friendship to Russia, which shares a lengthy border with Iran—rarely a happy circumstance for the less powerful country. The Iranian prime minister did have known ties with the Tudeh, the Soviet-backed Iranian Communist Party, but so did he with every other significant group in Tehran. Mossadegh never joined the popular front sponsored by Tudeh. The prime minister was once widely popular in Iran; but, as with most every leader, he had begun to sense that his public backing had eroded. For one thing, Mosaddeq remained a secular liberal democrat while at the same time refusing to abolish the monarchy in favor of a republic.[31] Government decisions can never make everyone happy; there are winners and losers. So he needed to shore up his political standing and could ill-afford to alienate factions, even the local communists. Another mark against Mossadegh in London and Washington was his negotiations with Moscow over oil sales. What country, though, would fail to hawk this valuable commodity—if lucky enough to have it—to another country, especially a well-armed neighbor who might otherwise step in and take over the production fields by force if denied petroleum at a reasonable price?

In a move that accelerated the growing Western resentment toward him, Mossadegh warned officials in Washington and London that they might be forcing him to reach out to Russia in the marketing of his nation's natural resources, especially since British commercial sanctions and oil boycotts were wreaking havoc on the Iranian economy. A Royal Navy cruiser, anchored ominously in the Gulf of Abadan, had already succeeded in frightening away many foreign tankers making port calls in Iran. The British were tightening the screws.

Mossadegh was a wealthy man and hardly a poster boy for Marxism. *Time* magazine selected him as its "Man of the Year" in 1952; moreover, he was clearly on record as anti-communist. Nevertheless, among the panjandrums in the White House, the State Department, and the CIA, national security meetings began to focus on fearful images of Iranian oil being diverted from the West to the USSR—a key Middle East domino falling under Moscow's influence and the rest of the region likely to topple next, in the famous "domino theory" of that era. Mossadegh had to go, doubly so since earlier he had already stymied a major business proposal advanced to Iran by the law firm Sullivan & Cromwell in New York City, for whom in the past Allen and Foster Dulles had been legal consultants and investors. It was time for payback, never mind that many experts on Iran—including the CIA's own chief of station in Tehran—viewed Mossadegh as, yes, deeply anti-British, but essentially a nationalist who sought to protect his country's oil wealth from Western exploitation; plus, he was a man who wanted nothing to do with the heavy hand of Joseph Stalin.[32] Nonetheless, in dealing with Iran, anti-communist instincts became Washington's primary impetus for action, coupled with lobbying pressure from US business interests (as would be the case periodically in the future).

The person who had been President Truman's ambassador to Tehran, George McGhee, described Mossadegh at the time as a "patriotic Iranian nationalist."[33] In contrast, Eisenhower's ambassador, Loy Henderson (hand-picked by Foster Dulles), was on board with the growing sentiment in Washington that Mossadegh was "a madman who would ally himself with the Russians."[34] As McCarthyism swept the nation's capital, the Eisenhower administration also felt a need to demonstrate that it could vigorously stamp out all international Bolshevist threats, whether genuine or manufactured by Western politicians knowing a good campaign slogan when they saw one—in this instance, both. The GOP had already claimed, in staggering oversimplification, that the Truman administration had allowed China to fall into the communist camp. Eisenhower and Foster Dulles had felt the heat from some Republican Party flack for ending the war in Korea instead of seeking an all-out victory. The administration was not going to be blamed for "losing" Iran and endure the deep bruises of political attacks like the ones that had battered Truman and Acheson over communist advances on the Korean Peninsula and in China.

Historian Richard H. Immerman concludes that "Moscow's involvement in Iran was negligible, but [Secretary of State] Dulles could not distinguish between indigenous nationalism and imported communism."[35] Or perhaps the secretary could but preferred not to, since anti-communism (the Red Menace) had become his favored political banner to uncoil—his bugbear and foreign policy *raison d'état*. Even though the anti-religiosity of communism was anathema to the Islamic faith and yet another force inside Iran likely to keep the Soviets at bay, this factor, too, was also largely discounted by the brothers Dulles.[36] Despite the existence of strong counterarguments, the Dulles brothers began to speak persistently at NSC meetings about a likely Soviet takeover in Tehran—a classic illustration from these times of paranoia and politics in high government circles bending officials toward the acceptance of interventions abroad and the adoption of a tough-guy approach to foreign policy. As historian Fredrik Logevall writes, "Opposing the Soviet Union overseas and leftists at home became a way of corralling votes and building electoral strength, or of avoiding being labeled a Red sympathizer."[37] Alan Ladd of *Shane* to the rescue for Western democracy against the rising peril of global communism, while accruing lucrative corporate advantages overseas (cheap oil in the case of Iran, managed starting in October of 1954 mainly by a consortium of US companies) and winning political points at home for foreign policy toughness.

In another joint U.K.-US intelligence endeavor (Operation "TPAjax"), the CIA and MI6 toppled Prime Minister Mossadegh and elevated a more compliant shah (king) of Iran, Mohammed Reza Pahlevi, into the top leadership post. The shah, the *Shahanshah* or King of Kings, had served as Iran's ruler before Mossadegh undercut the authority of the monarchy. At the time, the shah had been compelled to name him prime minister as he rode to prominence on the wave of a nationalist movement. The United States hoped now that a reestablishment of the monarchy by a coup would give Washington and London more leverage over Iran than the unpredictable electoral politics that had brought Mossadegh to power. Never mind that monarchy was hardly in the American tradition, and that Mossadegh had come to high office through Iran's legitimate system of voting.

Some have viewed the coup as the CIA's single greatest achievement, at least to that date, and the beginning of a Golden Age of covert action. The Agency had demonstrated a useful new approach to international affairs: overthrowing governments that dared to resist American (and, in this instance, British) leadership and commercial dominance. The outcome seemed miraculous at the time. The West had managed to establish a reliable Middle East ally—a trusted friend in the shah—without firing a shot, no easy feat as underscored by America's experiences in that part of the world since the end of the Cold War in 1991. Further, from the vantage point of Western business and consumer interests, American and British oil companies continued to profit from Iran's extensive fossil-fuel deposits; and automobile owners in both nations enjoyed a quarter-century of reasonably priced gasoline, complements of the shah's appreciation for their backing.

In the future the Agency's skills in covert action would be called on to assist other US corporations, not just those owned by Texas oil titans, in their exploitation of natural resources overseas. International affairs are complex, though. At the time of the coup in 1953, oil and anti-communism were not the only sources of concern in Washington about the situation in Tehran. Of importance, too, was that Iran presented an excellent platform for spying on the Soviet Union, especially by way of America's latest electronic-eavesdropping antennae positioned along the Russian-Iranian border and aimed at nearby Soviet missile-testing sites near the Black Sea. National security officials in the United States were loath to lose this valuable listening post.

So the outcome seemed a happy one—until fundamentalist theocrats ("mullahs") in Iran toppled the shah in 1979 and replaced him with a Muslim republic led by Ayatollah Khomeini, a man with medieval visions for his people and harsh anti-American sentiments. In Iran, nationalism and Islam had become united into an amalgam of powerful historical forces—a confluence largely misunderstood by CIA analysts and other Middle East experts in the United States at the time. The ayatollah had been in exile in Paris for the previous fifteen years and returned to Tehran triumphantly to initiate an Islamic revolution backed by religious militants opposed to the modern reforms instituted in Iran by the US-backed shah, who had become an increasingly unpopular figure in his own country. With ever darkening consequences that continue to unfold, the anti-American (and anti-communist) Muslim rebels were lifted into power by the shah's missteps. Among other outcomes, the United States immediately lost its signals intelligence sites so conveniently located on the rim of the USSR since the CIA first established a listening post there to monitor Soviet missile-testing in 1957.[38]

The animosity of Iranians toward the shah stemmed from his remote and dictatorial approach to leadership, his failure to include an array of local political groups in the governing process, and a perception that he was essentially a Washington marionette. Resented, as well, was the lavish lifestyle enjoyed by the king and his family, along with the extensive corruption in his regime fed by a deluge of US weapons sales to Iran over the years. There was another, more positive side of the ledger, however: the shah had helped to bring Iran into the twentieth century with progressive land and educational policies; the construction of hospitals and schools, along with modern power grids and highways; the establishment of voting rights for women, a rarity in that part of the world; and the blossoming of an educated middle class. Iranians, though, had a strong conservative element; devout Muslims felt the shah was attempting to turn their nation—an old and distinguished, strongly religious civilization—into a Western, consumer-oriented, secular society. Unrest began to spread. The pear was ripe. As a long-time CIA watcher has concluded, "We picked the wrong guy in Iran—the greatest intelligence failure of the twentieth century."[39]

The long-term repercussions of America's efforts to prop up the shah were, in a word, catastrophic. One of the best of the Agency's senior officers, Deputy Director for Operations John McMahon, has said: "In covert action, you always have to think of the endgame before you start it. And we don't always do that."[40] One reason is quite obvious: a disastrous outcome in 1979 is difficult to predict decades earlier in 1953. History follows a zig-zag path, not a straight line. Still, one can try harder to ponder the long-range possibilities ("downstream," in CIA parlance) before a covert action is undertaken, drawing more widely on outside academic and think-tank experts to supplement the thinking of inhouse Agency analysts. Little of this forecasting and outreach was included in the Iranian coup planning of 1953.

Perhaps the most impressive feature of the sudden alteration of Iranian history that year, led by Kermit "Kim" Roosevelt (the top CIA operative in the Middle

East, and a distant cousin of Franklin Delano Roosevelt), was how smoothly it all proceeded—at least after an initial attempt sputtered and died. The second try, weeks later, proved a charm, leading to success within a fortnight—too easy in fact, giving officials inside the Agency and the White House a false sense that here was an excellent way to conduct US foreign policy.

Colluding with MI6, the thirty-seven-year-old Roosevelt and four Agency colleagues accomplished the coup objectives in Tehran (while the unnerved shah was hiding out in Rome, just in case things failed to go well) simply by way of some judiciously placed covert propaganda, accompanied by a few hastily prepared political and minor PM activities. On the more aggressive non-propaganda side, the coup architecture consisted mainly of aggressive demonstrations in Tehran's city squares as well as some fisticuffs in the streets against supporters of the Iranian government. Enter King George's cavalry to pay for the "volunteer protestors," who were chiefly MI6 assets and thugs from local sports clubs—some of whom were dispatched to intimidate parliamentarians (not unlike the reliance by President Trump on January 6, 2021, on a mob of ruffians to block the congressional confirmation of his Electoral College defeat in the 2020 presidential election). In addition, some funds went toward supporting dissident elements in the Iranian military, including guidance on how they should take over the key radio station in Tehran.

The important imponderable in these calculations, and so vital to the outcome in 1953, was exactly how the Iranian Army would react. No one could tell for sure how many pro-Mossadegh supporters there would be in the streets, or what the "tipping point" was for army loyalty to the prime minister. Anywhere from 100 to 300 people died in the street clashes (reports vary) and another 300 were wounded, though no Agency personnel were among the injured or killed. Into the fray, too, Roosevelt launched an inventive CIA/MI6 rumor campaign—another common ingredient of covert propaganda—that falsely portrayed Mossadegh as nothing but a Soviet puppet. Moreover, luck played a significant role in this rush of events (as usual in human "planning"), when dissidents attached to neither the CIA nor MI6 chose to take advantage of the opportunity presented by the chaos in Tehran by turning against Mossadegh for their own personal reasons.[41]

The Agency had managed to be at the right place at the right time, pushing on an open door to aid indigenous opponents of the Mossadegh government. At the climax of the street demonstrations, the army—at first assuming a posture of neutrality—stuck a finger in the air to check which way the winds were blowing and decided to abandon Mossadegh as a losing proposition. (Similar calculating by the army would occur again in 1979 when its officers abandoned the shah.) The prime minister was arrested and imprisoned for three years in solitary confinement, followed by placement under house arrest at his Ahmadabad home until his death in 1967.

As would be the case in subsequent CIA involvement in coups, the main reasons for action in 1953 were predominantly twofold and mixed together in complicated ways, each viewed as important at the time: anti-communism along with the protection of American business interests. The outcome in Iran, though, proved a lost opportunity for the United States to advance a more benign and well-meaning helping hand in the Middle East. David Wise and Thomas Ross maintain that the coup "bought time" in Iran, as the CIA established what appeared to be an oasis of stability in a rough precinct. They concluded, though, that Washington officials "seemed unable to follow this up with badly needed social and economic reforms."[42]

Further, the shah may well have moved too quickly with his modernization reforms and was too closely affiliated with officials in Washington and London. Nor did his US patrons insist that a portion of Iran's oil revenues be channeled toward alleviating the extensive poverty that plagued the nation. As well, the shah was desperately ill with cancer by the time his government fell in 1979 and was unable to muster the leadership energy he once had. Perhaps most telling, though, the shah had gained a reputation at home for rule by "violence, fear and repression."[43] His terrifying state police—SAVAK, created, named, and trained by the CIA in 1956— seized regime critics off the streets in Tehran and dealt with them in unspeakable ways, eventually sealing the shah's fate.

Guatemala

The next year, 1954, witnessed another success for the Third Option, this one closer to home in Guatemala, a country ruled by another democratically elected government. It would be a further illustration of the CIA standing up against communism while at the same time coming to the aid of an American business interest—in this instance the United Fruit Company. The UFC, known as La Frutera in Central America, was a banana enterprise with the largest landholdings in Guatemala and deep fingers as well into the nation's railway, communications, and shipping industries. La Frutera's profit margin came from keeping this desperately poor republic under its thumb. The US ambassador cabled the State Department, which passed along the message to President Eisenhower, that "large American interests will be forced out completely" unless the current Guatemalan leader was ousted.[44] The cable noted, too, that although the leader, Jacobo Árbenz Guzmán, was "not a Communist, he will do until one comes along." President Eisenhower was happy to help UFC protect its investments in Guatemala, but his administration had a more urgent goal: reducing—and eventually, eliminating altogether—communist influence in the Western Hemisphere.

Here was Iran déjà vu, although this time the targeted leader, Árbenz—who in 1951 had been elected president by two-thirds of the popular vote and brought his nation a decade of democratic government for the first time in its history—was indeed a leftist and viewed himself, during his later years in office, as something of a communist. The clincher in the eyes of many Washington officials was his acceptance in early 1954 of military weapons from Czechoslovakia (a Soviet pawn at the time), smuggled in on the Swedish freighter *Alfhem* and discovered by Agency assets assigned as port watchers. Here was the final straw, and a perfect excuse to depose the Central American president in a coup scheme that was already in advanced stages of planning. From Árbenz's vantage point, he knew he was under siege from the United States, along with some other unfriendly neighbors in the region, so he had sought out weapons—from anywhere he could get them—that might help defend his regime.

While Árbenz was far removed from taking orders from the Kremlin, he was a fervent believer in land reform. For some critics, that sentiment may have given him the aura of being a Bolshevik; but, seen within the context of widespread Guatemalan poverty, it was a policy designed to give the peasant class a chance in life. This posture created an immediate problem for the Eisenhower administration, as land reform would come in part at the expense of La Frutera's vast and largely untilled acreage in the nation. Árbenz confiscated two-thirds of this property, with—at least in UFC's opinion—meager compensation. The country was broke and unable to pay the huge sums the corporation demanded in return for its land. On the political side of things in Guatemala, only four of the nation's fifty-six members of Parliament were communists; and Árbenz never invited a single communist to join his cabinet, unlike a future CIA target (two years hence): President Sukarno of Indonesia. The Communist Party in Guatemala was, at best, a minor partner in the Árbenz government.

Nonetheless, *Time* magazine and other peddlers of overheated Cold War rhetoric echoed talking points from the Dulles brothers and chastised the Guatemalan president for his "pro-communist declarations" whenever he complained about the UFC's monopolistic activities in Guatemala. The Agency's own chief of station in Guatemala City rejected the argument forwarded to him from CIA headquarters that Árbenz's land reform amounted to communism. Lickety-split, the Agency replaced him with a more malleable individual. Even the administration's assistant secretary of state of inter-American affairs, John Moors Cabot, said at the time that Árbenz's was "a leftist, yes, but not Communist."[45] He, too, was dismissed by the administration.

As the CIA's confidence grew in its ability to change world history after the outcome in Iran, the years 1953–54 were turning out to be a heyday for covert action. The Iranian coup had suggested a panacea for foreign policy headaches, a remedy as simple as a magician pulling a rabbit out of a hat: just call in the CIA's Covert Action Staff and Special Operations Group. Guatemala would be the next test of that proposition.

Both Foster and Allen Dulles had performed legal work for UFC at Sullivan & Cromwell before entering the government, and both continued to have significant investments in the company's stock. In law practice before they joined the Eisenhower administration, the Dulles brothers had been aggressive promoters of American commercial interests abroad. It was a convenient relationship that UFC enjoyed with the brothers Dulles—indeed, the envy of any American business in search of insider help from Washington to avoid a diminution of foreign investments, or perhaps even corporate banishment from a country.[46] Lobbied vigorously by the UFC, and already concerned about the possibility of strengthened Árbenz ties with the USSR in the future, President Eisenhower approved—with the encouraging Iranian outcome fresh in mind—the plan for a change of regime in Guatemala. The administration wanted someone in power who would be friendlier toward the United States and, not coincidentally, toward the United Fruit Company.

Ramping up the full panoply of propaganda, political, economic, and paramilitary activities, the CIA—this time operating in its own backyard and driven by an élan that followed the pleasant Iranian results—moved swiftly toward a coup with its Operation "PB/Success." Frank Wisner, a well-regarded deputy director for plans (DDP), was at the controls of the operation as he deployed the Covert Action Staff (CAS) and the Special Operations Group (SOG) to work their clandestine mau-mau. By this stage in its evolution, the Agency's paramilitary wing—now seven years old—had its own small air force and navy. A few vintage P-47 Thunderbolt bombers dropped their ordnance onto Guatemala City, hoping these attacks would cause Árbenz to flee. The bombing did spook some of the population, but the president fought back and his military managed to disable some of the CIA aircraft with return ground fire.

Allen Dulles estimated at the time that the chance for success in Guatemala was about 20 percent; nevertheless, he recommended to the White House that the operation move forward.[47] To improve the odds, the DCI informed the president and Secretary Foster Dulles that the Agency desperately needed additional aircraft. He was singing to the choir, with the Eisenhower administration delighted to adopt a tough stance in Central America as part of its global anti-Red strategy. "Already one-third of the world is dominated by an imperialist brand of communism," Foster Dulles had warned publicly from his high perch in the Department of State; "already the free world has been so shrunk that no further substantial parts of it can be lost without anger to the whole that remains."[48] The administration provided the Agency with three additional B-26 bombers for the cause, requisitioned from US Air Force inventory.

The aircraft were sent first to Nicaragua, then on to the rebels in Guatemala. The costs for the bombers was absorbed, at least in part—and outside the normal appropriations process—by businessman William Pawley, a donor to President Eisenhower's presidential campaign war chest. This secret private funding was entirely inappropriate and foreshadowed an approach adopted again during the Iran-*contra* scandal of the 1980s. The Eisenhower administration also augmented the Agency's propaganda and political funding to support an expanding cadre of anti-Árbenz rebels on the ground in Guatemala, known as the Guatemalan Army of Liberation and led by a pliable, pro-US army officer by the name of Colonel Carlos Castillo-Armas. For its part, the United Fruit Company helped smuggle weapons to the ragtag rebels.

The paramilitary element in the Guatemalan coup was much greater than it had been in Iran; indeed, it was the Agency's first significant PM venture, beyond its nascent and largely lackluster field activities during the Korean War. The most vital feature in this covert action, though, was—as is often the case—the extensive use of propaganda. Agency advisers and the local Army of Liberation set up a makeshift radio station to saturate the airwaves of this small feudal nation with misleading propaganda. The United Fruit Company, at the same time, spent large sums of money to market the intervention to Americans at home. The main theme of the broadcasts and the marketing in Central America, both vastly exaggerated, was that the Guatemalan people were, at that very moment, rising up against Árbenz. His days—indeed, his hours—were numbered.

In perhaps the most important development on the propaganda front, the CIA managed to convince Francis Cardinal Spellman of New York to arrange a meeting between an Agency operative and Archbishop Mariano Rossell y Arellano in Guatemala. The purpose was to lean on the local church leader to have an anti-communist, anti-Árbenz pastoral letter read in all Catholic gatherings in Guatemala, tantamount to practically every church in the country. Warning parishioners of the thorns and dangers posed by their left-leaning president, the letter claimed that communism was stalking the countryside, "masquerading as a movement of social reform for the needy classes."[49]

The CIA's established assets and other local recruits, including some 300 well-armed fighters, filled the streets in Guatemala City, while the Agency's radio broadcasts (from La Voz de la Liberación, the Voice of Liberation) and other sources of propaganda announced the president's demise. Simultaneously, resupplied CIA bombers strafed the capital. Árbenz's courage began to waver as he sank deeper into this stream of the Agency's activities. The propaganda campaign was especially effective in eroding the president's self-confidence;

moreover, the aerial bombardment was beginning to cause dissension among his military leaders. Few people actually died in the skirmishing, but Árbenz began to believe that the noose was fatally tightening around his presidential palace. He resigned on June 25, 1954, and fled to asylum in the Mexican embassy.

First Mossadegh and now Árbenz, yet another of the Kremlin's alleged puppets, had been removed from office. In both cases, whereas nationalism was the true dominant force inside the targeted country, the United States insisted that it was really communism at work. The United Fruit Company, Guatemala, the Panama Canal, Central America, the Western Hemisphere, perhaps a world of collapsing dominoes—all had been breathlessly saved from the Red Peril by a timely CIA intervention. Or so was the view promoted by the Eisenhower administration and the Agency's Directorate of Plans. In both the Iranian and Guatemalan cases, the Agency should have extended a warm hand of appreciation to Kismet, for both Mossadegh and Árbenz had teetering regimes to begin with, and both suffered from unpopularity at home.

The gift of the United States and Guatemala's new leader, Armas, to the people of Guatemala? According to the reflections of two former CIA officers, the end result was a right-wing military dictatorship engaged in "corruption throughout his government and kowtowing to the United Fruit Company more than his own people," as well as killing "hundreds of thousands of its own citizens."[50] The judgment of the *New York Times* journalist Anthony Lewis was equally severe. In his view, the Agency's intervention had pushed Guatemala into "a long national descent into savagery," a decline that would last for over three decades.[51] An unfortunate consequence of paramilitary coups can be the creation of a leadership vacuum in a nation, one that can be filled quickly—as in this case—by a venal autocracy whose citizens must suffer the whip of the calamity. Further, as historian Jeffreys-Jones observes, the covert actions in Iran and Guatemala "would weigh down the reputation of the United States and undermine its authority in the United Nations, ultimately contributing to the decline of the CIA's standing domestically."[52]

However much of a role the element of luck may have played in the outcomes in Iran and Guatemala, and however ill-advised these interventions may have been ultimately, the results yielded a heady sense of euphoria at the CIA, the White House, and the Department of State at the time. Perhaps there really was something to this notion of having the Agency in charge of shaping world affairs. "It was great adventure—and killed less than war," recalls a CIA veteran.[53] The United Fruit Company was pleased to have its land and privileged position back; the Eisenhower administration was happy to assist its business friends and political campaign contributors, while at the same time ridding Central America of an allegedly pro-communist regime and signaling to the GOP its toughness on world communism; and managers inside the Agency's Directorate of Plans were grinning from ear to ear, as if posing for a toothpaste commercial on TV. In the meanwhile, the image of the United States as a dangerous imperial and anti-democracy power spread like a pampas grass fire throughout South America.

Inside the CIA, power and prestige were shifting dramatically from the analysts in the Directorate of Intelligence to the "knuckle-draggers" in the DP, never mind that collection and analysis had been the only intelligence activity mentioned in the Agency's founding charter. The DP's operations officers were on velvet with this acceleration of the "cowboys" past the DI's "librarians." When it came to collection and analysis, the Central Intelligence Agency may not have been all that "central" anyway, since several of America's espionage services were engaged in that side of the intelligence business. The CIA was clearly central, though, when it came to the Third Option. In this exclusive domain, it had become "hyperactive."[54] As for the citizens of Guatemala, like those of Iran they continued to suffer extreme poverty—this time under the thumb of a dictator chosen by *gringos* in Washington, DC.

Egypt

In the mid-1950s the Agency also did its best, in Operation "Omega," to depose the president of Egypt, Gamal Abdel Nasser. He had gotten himself crosswise with the United States by inviting the Soviet Union to build a major dam on the Nile and, generally, for being too cozy with the Kremlin—although Nasser's turn eastward came only after the United States had rejected an opportunity to help him with the dam and with his desire for modern weaponry. Pretty soon, went the logic among CIA leaders and the Eisenhower administration's senior cadre of national security officials, the Soviets would dominate all of the Middle East. It was the same fear that had played an important role in the Agency's interventions in Iran and Guatemala: yet another domino would fall, then another and another. Eventually only the United States—the last domino—would be left standing.

To prevent this disastrous chain of events, money was pumped into the Agency's station in Cairo to sow anti-Nasser propaganda and support opposition politicians. Tentative steps were taken to recruit a mercenary army to attack a pro-Nasser government in Syria. The plan was soon scuttled, however, when the recruits displayed a stronger allegiance to their Muslim brother in Egypt than to their ever-hopeful CIA advisers. Further efforts were abandoned, and Nasser continued on as one of the most prominent Arab leaders in the modern era—and no patsy for the Russians.

Indonesia

Among the more bizarre, and one of the largest, Agency covert actions during the Eisenhower era took place in Indonesia beginning in 1957. Fittingly for this nation of multiple islands, the CA bore the codename Operation "Archipelago." It was another example of a Third Option that has occurred from time to time in which the State Department was carrying out one approach toward the targeted nation while the CIA was engaged in just the opposite—a situation akin to driving a car with the brakes on.

As was so often the case throughout these early Cold War years, the Agency saw in Indonesia's president, Sukarno, a leader who had become too flirtatious with the USSR. He had even been foolish enough to appoint a few communists to his cabinet. Again, Sukarno was in fact less a devotee of communism, let alone a Kremlin puppet, than he was a nationalist who was content to receive foreign aid from Moscow *and* Washington—what appeared on the surface to be a dual allegiance that was unlikely to endear him to the Dulles brothers. On the checklist against him, too, in the reckoning of Eisenhower administration security officials, was Sukarno's hosting of an international conference of non-aligned nations. Hadn't the Indonesia president gotten the White House memo? You were either with the United States or against it.

As usual, the Agency began its clandestine operations in Indonesia with a propaganda campaign, although one with a carnal twist: the production of a pornographic movie with a Sukarno look-alike in the lead role. Rather than glorify his sexual prowess, which might have been admired in Indonesia's male-dominated society, the film instead made him look as though he were a weak man beholden to the wiles of a woman, a stance held in far less esteem by the male species in an Islamic nation. When this risible approach had little effect on deposing Sukarno, the Agency escalated the Third Option into a paramilitary attack against his regime.

First, a plan for "executive action" (an Agency euphemism for assassination) was seriously considered to remove Sukarno from power. That approach was eventually set aside in favor of a full-fledged coup. The COS and his associates in Jakarta recruited, and supplied with weaponry, a gaggle of dissident army colonels and half-hearted rebels rounded up in Sumatra, using durable old King George's cavalry as an inducement. In early 1958, while Sukarno was away on a trip to Japan, the delusional military officers declared themselves the new government of Indonesia. When Sukarno returned and set loose his security forces against the upstarts, the rebellion quickly fizzled.

At that point, and accompanied by a widespread dissemination of anti-Sukarno leaflets and other propaganda materials, the Agency turned to its limited but lethal air force—once more featuring B-26 bombers, as in Guatemala.

The CIA bombardiers dropped their payload on government trucks and planes at a military base—along with, by mistake, a church with its full congregation deep in prayer (a prefiguring of tragic drone errors to come, some forty years later, in Afghanistan and Pakistan). Indonesian anti-aircraft artillery shot down one of the Agency's pilots, Alexander Lawrence Pope, a former Korean War ace. He somehow managed to survive the crash, but was captured, imprisoned for four years, and condemned to death by Indonesian courts. He was released in 1960 as a result of back-channel diplomatic negotiations between Jakarta and Washington.

The Agency soon withdrew from the coup attempt, its hands bruised by defeat as the whole scheme fell apart in the Agency's first truly calamitous—indeed, extravagant—Third Option failure. Sukarno proved to have the patience of Job and the tolerance of Paul. He forgave the United States for what he knew was the CIA's "invisible" hand in these events. Better America as a friend than as an enemy, he apparently calculated. Perhaps he remembered, as well, his warming chat with Marilyn Monroe on a visit to the United States arranged by the State Department in earlier years. Maybe neither marching rebel armies nor marauding CIA aircraft could achieve as much success abroad as public diplomacy involving America's most glamorous movie star. Sukarno put his friendships with the Soviet Union and China on a backburner—relationships that were never more than on low heat from the beginning.

Hungary

During this time of high confidence in the value of the Third Option as a solution to America's foreign policy woes (remembering Iran and Guatemala, with the Egyptian failure and the Indonesian farce conveniently set aside), the Eisenhower administration entered into additional clandestine experimentations, including election manipulations in Lebanon in 1957 and a failed paramilitary attempt in 1959 at sponsoring a quixotic Tibetan revolt against Chinese rule. The president had shied away, though, from continued support to anti-communist rebels in Moscow-dominated Hungary when they boldly, recklessly, rose up against the mighty Red Army that rapidly marched into Budapest and mowed them down in 1956. Further, the CIA's most ambitious targeting of the Third Option during the Cold War—fomenting and supporting revolutions against the Soviets in Eastern Europe—continued to go nowhere. The White House was unwilling to risk World War III by confronting the Russians in Hungary, or anywhere else in Eastern Europe, with overt military force in support of local uprisings— presidential campaign rhetoric by President Eisenhower and Vice President Richard M. Nixon in 1952 and 1956 notwithstanding.

Promises are said to have been made by some in the Directorate of Plans to the pro-democracy dissidents in Hungary, to the effect that the United States would come to their rescue if they took up arms against the communist regime—America's real cavalry, not just the King George variant. These assurances were reinforced by offers from Radio Free Europe to provide tactical guidance during the crisis.[55] Among others at the CIA, former DCI William E. Colby subsequently rejected the notion that the Agency had stimulated the revolt. In apparent contradiction he does acknowledge, however, that top officials in the DP "were fully prepared with arms, communications stocks and air resupply, to come to the aid of the freedom fighters" once the uprising was under way.[56]

Although views on the exact degree of CIA involvement in the uprising diverge, one fact seems clear enough: thanks largely to John Foster Dulles, the Eisenhower administration had made promises to rid communism from Hungary and the rest of Eastern Europe. According to a thorough analysis of the secretary's foreign policy views, he saw a "world dominated by bold strokes of black and white," a zero-sum perspective that pitted communism against Christianity, atheism against spiritualism, Marxist economic doctrine against the free enterprise system.[57] For years Dulles had publicly preached a gospel of "liberation theology" and "rollback" for Eastern Europe, leaving the insurgents in Budapest with a sense that the United States would in fact have their back. The CIA didn't need to communicate any messages of encouragement; the White House, the State Department, and the Republican National Committee (RNC) were already doing that on a regular basis. Under assault from a massive Soviet army that came across the border into Hungary, the trampled rebels would have stared toward the skies in vain for the sight of US bombers delivering salvation.

As the feckless revolution unfolded, Budapest filled with burning struggle. Whatever false hopes may have been raised were soon dashed in a hail of bullets from Soviet machine guns, artillery, and powerful T-54 tank attacks that slashed through the streets of Budapest, leaving over 2,500 mainly young idealists lying in pools of blood with fatal wounds, in city plazas where the bullet holes in pockmarked storefronts can still be seen today.[58] Throughout the countryside Soviet troops slew thousands of other insurgents, leaving them to rot where they fell, as if carrion for the birds.

Journalist and novelist Burton Hersh notes that the liberation of Eastern Europe may have been the primary mission of the early covert action practitioners at the CIA, but this failure to assist the besieged rebels in Hungary proved that "rollback was a bust."[59] According to one of Frank Wisner's sons, the DDP took his own life in 1965 in large part because of "his disappointment—and some would say betrayal—over Hungary. I think he felt betrayed."[60] As one of the most prominent early leaders of covert action in the CIA, Wisner could not come to terms with the fact that the United States had failed to shield the people of Hungary against the Soviet scourge during their quest for democracy.

Twelve years later, in 1968, students in Eastern Europe again rose up against the Soviets, this time in Prague. The life-and-death drama proceeded more slowly than it had in Hungary, stretching over an eight-month period. During this time, some 650,000 Warsaw Pact troops (mainly from the Soviet Union) occupied Czechoslovak and subdued the insurrection, killing an estimated 108 rebels, with thousands more wounded. The CIA used its propaganda channels in limited support of the attempted revolution; but, in this instance, the DP toned down the rhetoric to avoid renewed blame (after Hungary) that it was unrealistically stirring up violence in Eastern Europe, which was tantamount to encouraging the rebels into suicide-by-Soviet-tank.

As the end of the Eisenhower administration approached, the CIA's clandestine arts would take on an even darker hue, as the Directorate of Plans began to focus more on directly snuffing out the lives of foreign leaders who dared to oppose the United States, starting in the heart of Africa.

4
Murder Most Foul, 1960–1975

A Hot Cold War

As the 1950s continued on, the Eisenhower administration authorized the Agency's engagement in several Asian election manipulations, as in Laos during 1960 to ensure the success of local strongman General Phoumi Nosavan, who had been chosen to lead that nation personally by Secretary of State Dulles.[1] Then, upping the ante, the administration acted in utmost secrecy as it skittered up the Ladder of Clandestine Escalation toward the extreme end, namely, a bespoke PM operation against a foreign head of state. In the final months of the Eisenhower presidency, the White House approved—in opaque, circumlocutional language equivalent to a wink and a nod—the use of a CIA assassination plot against a charismatic African leader.

This decision was a drastic step that crossed the long-held, sacrosanct line that violence against foreign sovereign states would be confined to battlefields, not directed against civilian public officials. A murder attempt against a foreign president or prime minister could have the effect of prodding a hornet's nest, out of which might fly a retaliation against America's own chief executive. It was a disturbing turn of events and an unexpected decision from an American president with Eisenhower's renowned sensibilities. A close observer of US intelligence practices, journalist James Risen looks back on the Agency's murder plots as "among the worst things the CIA ever did," illustrating how "covert action plans are roadmaps to perdition. They inevitably lead to terrible actions."[2]

Democratic Republic of the Congo

The assassination target was President Patrice Lumumba, the freely elected leader of the Democratic Republic of the Congo ("Congo," for short), in central Africa. He had displayed the same fatal inclination that placed Mossadegh, Árbenz, Nasser, and Sukarno on America's top-secret list for coups d'état: a friendship with Moscow—however limited and driven by national self-interest the tie may have been viewed by the junior partner. In Lumumba's case, an earlier rejection from the United States had led him (as with Nasser and others) to seek economic and military assistance from Moscow as an alternative. This is a game that some nations continue to play today, as when the leader of a supposed US ally, Mohammed bin Zayed al-Nahyan of the United Arab Emirates (UAE), made it clear in the early 1990s that he would be entirely happy to shop elsewhere if the United States turned down his request for military hardware.[3]

At one point, Lumumba had invited ten small Soviet aircraft to land in his country. Although he was essentially an independent nationalist skillfully playing off the Kremlin against Washington for Congo's betterment and his own advancement, that indiscreet hosting of the Soviet Air Force placed him high on the CIA's roster of enemies. In 1961, DCI Dulles himself sent this cable to the Agency's chief of station in the Congo, all in capital letters:

IN HIGH QUARTERS HERE IT IS THE CLEAR-CUT CONCLUSION THAT IF [LUMUMBA] CONTINUES TO HOLD HIGH OFFICE, THE INEVITABLE RESULT WILL AT BEST BE CHAOS AND AT WORST PAVE THE WAY TO COMMUNIST TAKEOVER OF THE CONGO WITH DISASTROUS CONSEQUENCES FOR THE PRESTIGE OF THE UN AND FOR THE INTERESTS OF THE FREE WORLD GENERALLY. CONSEQUENTLY WE CONCLUDE THAT HIS REMOVAL MUST BE AN URGENT AND PRIME OBJECTIVE AND THAT UNDER EXISTING CONDITIONS THIS SHOULD BE A HIGH PRIORITY OF OUR COVERT ACTION.[4]

The plan was to send from the CIA's labs in the Directorate of Science & Technology (DS&T) to the Agency's COS in Léopoldville (renamed Kinshasa in 1966) an especially toxic poison for use in removing Lumumba from the scene. The slow-acting potion would make it appear as though the Congolese leader had succumbed to a local disease. The accompanying instructions advised the station chief that the material should be injected into food, toothpaste, or whatever else might reach Lumumba's mouth. At the last minute the Agency decided to have its top CIA scientist who had prepared the potion, Dr. Sidney Gottlieb, personally carry the poison to Léopoldville in a locked satchel, handing it off directly to the station chief and double-checking that the plot was developing properly. Accompanying the lethal biological material in the satchel were rubber gloves, a mask, and a syringe. As Kinzer notes, Gottlieb "became the only CIA officer known to have carried poison to a foreign country in order to kill that country's leader."[5]

It proved impossible, however, for the Agency's assassination assets to gain direct access to the well-guarded presidential palace. So the mission was never consummated, at least directly by the CIA. The Agency continued to pour money into the Congo, however, lining the pockets of politicians friendly toward the United States. The favorite was Joseph Mobutu, who agreed to stage a coup against Lumumba.

The promised overthrow succeeded and the United States immediately recognized the Mobutu regime. The new government apprehended Lumumba and placed him under house arrest, which at least brought the coup victim one advantage: it helped avoid another CIA poisoning attempt, since the UN provided Lumumba with layers of security while he was being held captive. Lumumba managed to escape his confinement; but he was soon recaptured, placed in a military prison, and beaten regularly and viciously by Mobutu henchmen. With his own assassination plot going nowhere, the Agency's COS in Léopoldville proved more skillful in working with Sûreté de l'État, the Belgian spy service, which also wanted Lumumba out of the picture.

In tandem and with the help of local assets, the two intelligence services managed to maneuver Lumumba into a countryside meeting with another Congolese faction that also disliked him. The pretext was to seek a negotiated settlement of their disputes. In a succession of deteriorating circumstances, as anticipated by the Agency and its Belgian cohorts as well as by the Mobutu gang, this rival faction apprehend the former president, beat him nearly to death, then placed him and three of his allies before a firing squad in a remote savanna on the outskirts of Elisabethville. The CIA had succeeded in eliminating Lumumba, however indirectly and thanks largely to the Belgian intelligence service. Was his death truly necessary for the security of the United States? The incoming Kennedy administration didn't think so; and, in retrospect, even Allen Dulles viewed the covert action in Congo as superfluous and the danger posed by Lumumba "overrated."[6]

Cuba

In 1961, John F. Kennedy replaced Eisenhower as president and the aura of successful covert actions from the 1950s, especially in Iran and Guatemala, warmly lapped over into his administration. The Third Option had become a go-to instrument of America's foreign policy. This was the time of the "hot Cold War," recalls an early 1960s CIA recruit from Yale who would eventually serve as DCI.[7] Near the end of the Eisenhower administration, which in the euphoria of covert victories in Iran and Guatemala was possessed by vaulting ambitions, the number one target for the Third Option had become Fidel Castro, suspected of dangerous communist leanings. The Cuban leader appeared increasingly reliant on Nikita Khrushchev, the replacement for Stalin as head of the Soviet Union. Despite the pleasant nimbus of memory they imparted, the CIA's archive of experience in Iran and Guatemala would prove a misleading guide for its next major intervention, in the Caribbean.

With the help of Che Guevara and other dedicated revolutionaries, Castro had managed to overthrow a vile dictator in Cuba, Fulgencio Batista y Zaldivar.

Whether or not the new regime could have enjoyed a cordial relationship with the United States, rather than with the USSR, is a matter of ongoing debate. Castro was clearly a fan of US-style baseball and basketball, and he had traveled to this country many times in the past (as did untold numbers of his fellow countrymen over the years). Soon after his victorious revolution in 1959, President Castro visited Washington, DC, but was rebuffed by the Eisenhower administration; the president refused to meet with him, shunting him off to Vice President Richard M. Nixon (whom Castro found repulsive). The new Cuban leader then traveled to Canada, where he was more graciously welcomed by government officials in Ottawa.

Perhaps the United States missed an opportunity to assist Castro with what he most wanted: extraction of his country from crippling poverty. Yet his expropriation of US businesses in Cuba was a bitter pill for the Eisenhower administration and its Wall Street allies to swallow. The Kennedy administration had to consider, as well, the growing political strength of exiled pro-Batista Cubans, a group that included wealthy owners of sugar plantations, an industry controlled by US business interests. They had escaped to Florida, a key Electoral College state. On the one hand, Batista was indisputably a corrupt leader with Mafia connections in the United States as well as a ruthless dictator; yet on the other hand, Castro was no angel either. He had installed his own form of autocratic rule with the requisite secret police, imprisonments, and firing squads. These negatives, coupled with mounting political pressure in Washington from American corporations and Cuban exiles with their endless recriminations that Washington had not done enough to save Batista, meant that the hand of friendship was never extended to the new Cuba by the Eisenhower or the Kennedy administrations. This breach would lead to dire consequences in the immediate future.

At the direction of the Eisenhower White House (urged on, as always, by the Dulles brothers), the CIA had begun to train a Cuban exile invasion team, based in Guatemala. On the eve of Kennedy's inauguration, Ike told the incoming president that it was his responsibility "[to do] whatever is necessary"—whatever it would take—to rid the world of President Castro.[8] Kennedy promised to carry on the anti-Castro expedition, not least because the GOP would have excoriated him as "soft on Communism" had he opted otherwise—even though Castro was not a member of the PSP, the Cuban Communist Party. He belonged instead to the reformist Ortodoxo Party. Besides, both the Eisenhower and the Kennedy administrations reasoned, if the CIA could so easily topple suspect regimes in Iran and Guatemala, why not nearby Cuba? Hubris became the father of delusion, never mind that in 1957 the Agency's involvement in efforts to change regimes in Syria, Egypt, and Indonesia had fallen flat on their faces—what should have been amber-lit warnings that history is not so easily manipulated by mere mortals.[9]

Though far less ruthless in his domestic reprisals against adversaries than Stalin had been, Khrushchev, too, had big ideas (despite his 5'3" stature) when it came to world politics. Like his predecessor, he was determined to lead a communist victory over the corrupt capitalist states. "We will bury you," he declared before an audience of Western ambassadors in 1958.[10] An island nation located just ninety miles from America's Eastern Seaboard, Cuba's ties with the USSR—a source of mounting criticism by Republicans against the Kennedy administration for tolerating this development—caused more distress for the handsome new president from Boston than any other foreign policy issue. From Khrushchev's perspective, however, Cuba had become a showcase for how the Soviet Union could assist a Marxist-oriented Third World nation, even one 6,000 miles away from Moscow and in the backyard of the United States.

Diplomacy between the United States and Cuba—the First Option—had faltered, in large part because Castro's reforms (like those of Árbenz before him) envisioned a diminution of the US business presence in the Cuban economy, including utilities, banking, transportation, mining, ranching and, most visible of all, the sugar industry. None of this sat well, of course, with big business in the United States, with its well-lubricated lobbying machines in the nation's capital. The Eisenhower administration had been prepared to overthrow the Árbenz government for fewer infringements on US commercial interests than those perpetrated by Castro. "The irony," notes Professor Louis A. Perez, director of the Institute for the Study of the Americas at the University of North Carolina, "is that the [Castro-led] reforms of 1959 were all directed by liberal—in other words, not radical or communist—economists, many of them trained in the United States." He adds: "Radicalization did not begin until late 1959, as a tit-for-tat response to US pressure."[11]

As for the Second Option, obviously a full-scale US military invasion of Cuba could have ended the Castro regime within days; but the fighting would have been fierce, and Soviet troops stationed on the island (including a few Red Army generals) would have been killed. Might this have led to a Soviet retaliation against the United States, perhaps in Berlin or—in the worst-case scenario—directly against the American homeland? By 1961, the Soviets had intercontinental ballistic missiles (ICBMs) with nuclear-tipped warheads. The thinking in the White House was that it would be more prudent to rely on the Third Option. President Kennedy, champion of idealism in international affairs with his Peace Corps and liberal trade policies, turned to the dark side of America's government to remove the Castro irritant.

So was born the second most notorious covert action in the Agency's history: Operation "Zapata," the Bay of Pigs disaster of April 1961. (First place is reserved, in this book at least, for the Iran-*contra* debacle of the Reagan administration, examined in Chapter 5.) Richard Bissell, who had entered the Agency during the 1950s, leaving behind a promising academic career as a Yale economist, was deputy director for plans (DDP)—the CIA's top covert action boss—at the time of the Bay of Pigs misadventure. He was widely acclaimed as a brilliant organizer and, in addition, a Georgetown socialite with close ties to President Kennedy. Given this status, Allen Dulles allowed him free rein in the planning of the ill-fated operation. As Bissell's son recalls, his father "was very concerned for his country and very anti-communist and believed that communism had to be stopped at any cost."[12]

The Kennedy and Johnson administrations spent over $1 million on clandestine operations aimed at Cuba from FY1960 to 1964.[13] About half of that amount was for paramilitary activities. These ops included the invasion of Cuba at the Bay of Pigs by a CIA-trained force of some 1,400 Cuban exiles, meant to stimulate an uprising across the island against the Castro government. Instead, the attack immediately collapsed in a fast-moving zigzag of events. Ineffectual planning and an unexpectedly strong resistance from Castro's supporters at the beach landing site spelled doom for the Agency's small but eager invasion force, Brigade 2506.[14] The Directorate of Intelligence (DI), home of the Agency's analysts, had warned of this likely outcome, but neither the Directorate of Plans nor the Agency's leaders were listening. The DP had convinced itself, in a severe bout of wishful thinking, that the people of Cuba did not like Castro any more than they had Batista. The DI knew better, however, realizing from close study and recent intelligence reports from assets on the island that Castro was an immensely popular figure at home. Unfortunately, a cultural chasm existed within the CIA that hindered communications and cooperation between the DI's "thinkers" and the DO's "doers."[15]

Moreover, at a key moment during the coup attempt, the Kennedy administration proved unwilling to provide overt bombing support when the invasion began to falter. That action would have entailed, so Secretary of State Dean Rusk argued to the president in opposition at a critical moment in the invasion, an admission to the world that the White House was complicit in a PM operation prohibited by international law.[16] One of the Agency's veterans who fought with the Agency's Brigade 2506 in this battle on the Cuban beaches argues that "the invasion failed precisely because of President Kennedy's order not to provide air support and to destroy the Cuban Air Force."[17] When the smoke cleared at the Bahía de Cochinos after less than two days of fighting, a swirl of darkened hopes had left 114 of the Agency's PM assets lying dead on the sands, with another 1,189 taken prisoner. Among the many operational errors, the invaders had no escape route: just the ocean behind them and swamps in front. The operation had become a woeful hash—in CIA lingo, a "goat fuck."

President Kennedy was furious over the debacle. Privately, in its aftermath, he threatened to "splinter the CIA into a thousand pieces and throw it to the winds."[18] The Agency had reached a low point in relations with the White House, which would remain unsurpassed until the days of President Trump and his constant bickering with the Intelligence Community. The bad publicity over the failure also gave the CIA a new and unwanted public profile. Prior to the Bay of Pigs (President Kennedy's first major use of covert action), most members of Congress and the American people were largely unaware of its earlier clandestine interventions in Europe, the Middle East, Asia, Africa, and Latin America. Now they realized, in a sobering moment, that the Central Intelligence Agency did more than gather and analyze information from abroad; it possessed a risky war-fighting capability as well.

As with all large-scale covert actions, this one had short- and long-term consequences—the latter in particular often leading toward the unintended. Short term, the Bay of Pigs was an unmitigated fiasco; long term, it almost led to a nuclear war between the United States and the Soviet Union. As strategist and Nobel Laureate in Economics Thomas Schelling observed, the foremost reason that Nikita Khrushchev placed nuclear missiles in Cuba a year after the clandestine invasion was "as a means to protect Cuba against a repeat of the kind of attack that the United States had mounted at the Bay of Pigs."[19] Although the relationship is certainly not a straight line—the United States and Cuba had many grievances against one another, and Castro began to rely on Imperial Uncle Sam as a rhetorical whipping boy to help him keep Cubans united behind him as their leader—the close approach of the United States and the Soviet Union to Armageddon in 1962 during the Cuban missile crisis may have had its origins in the CIA's Bay of Pigs covert action in 1961. One conclusion drawn from the Bay of Pigs experience was more certain: the Third Option could no longer be viewed as an assured panacea for America's foreign policy woes.

John Kennedy soon cooled down after this setback and he again called upon the Agency to try another engineering of regime change in Cuba. A newly created CIA/NSC panel, known awkwardly as the "Special Group (Augmented)" and chaired by the president's brother, Attorney General Robert F. "Bobby" Kennedy, would steer the efforts. Relations with Cuba had now become, in the view of an influential Agency operative, a matter of "personal vendetta" between the Kennedy clan and the Cuban leader.[20] In quick order, the Directorate of Plans cooked up Operation "Mongoose," whose ingredients included the projected use of every possible Third Option against the Castro regime, short of another paramilitary invasion. The schemes included sabotage; funding to anti-Castro exiles in the United States and elsewhere; and the establishment of a special radio station (Radio Martí) to broadcast anti-Castro propaganda from Florida toward the island. According to DCI Helms, the sabotage never amounted to anything more than "pinpricks." He concluded, as well, that the notion popular within the

Directorate of Plans regarding how the people of Cuba would eventually rise up against Castro proved to be nothing more than a "romantic myth."[21]

Outside the Mongoose framework, during the Kennedy administration the CIA crafted an additional scheme to end the Castro regime, an approach that mirrored the modus operandi of the KGB: yet another assassination plot, coming on the heels of the failed stand-alone attempt against Lumumba. Some claim that as many as thirty-two schemes against Castro's life emerged from the CIA; others say that figure is exaggerated and the accurate number is somewhere between five and eight.[22] Whatever the correct number, all of the plots failed, whether the weapon had been an exploding cigar; a walking cane designed to inject a poisonous gas into Castro's leg; Mafia hitmen; a poison dart-gun (in DS&T parlance, an electric "noise-free disseminator" armed with a "nondiscernible microbioinoculator"); fountain pens equipped with saxitoxin-laced needles, for quick jabbing or squirting; curare-coated swizzle sticks; or any of the other ingenious but ineffective devices dreamed up by scientists in the DS&T.

In addition, the CIA's scientists had in their labs multiple vials of potassium cyanide, along with cannisters of deadly powders, as well as Blackleaf 40, strychnine, fungi toxins, potassium cyanide, cobra venom, curare, and—the favorite because of its quick action, bringing death to the victim in seconds—botulinum, an especially lethal form of saxitoxin extracted from diseased shellfish. These activities, all Mongoose derivatives, were known in the Agency and the White House as Operation "ZR/RIFLE," later referred to by President Lyndon B. Johnson in disparagement as "Murder, Inc." Johnson continued some of the more benign aspects of Mongoose, most notably anti-Castro propaganda operations, but brought the assassination attempts to a stop.[23]

These multiple plots to eliminate the Cuban leader raise the troubling question of whether Castro might have decided to retaliate against America's president on November 22, 1963, the day John Kennedy was shot dead in Dallas, Texas. Did Cuban intelligence recruit the killer, Lee Harvey Oswald (an admirer of Castro), as a means for settling the score with Kennedy? Some members of the Warren Commission, which investigated Kennedy's death, privately believed so, based on evidence that Oswald had ties to Cuban intelligence. The commissioners reached this conclusion, even without key information kept from them about the US plots against Castro. Though retired DCI Dulles served on the Commission, astonishingly he never informed his fellow commissioners about Mongoose or, even more importantly, ZR/RIFLE.

Whether or not President Kennedy knew about the CIA's plans to dispatch Castro remains a matter of dispute. His top NSC aides and cabinet members—including Secretary of State Dean Rusk, a man known for his integrity and honesty (even if widely reviled by liberals for advocating war in Vietnam during the Johnson administration)—have denied that President Kennedy, or any of his cabinet secretaries or White House aides, authorized the plots.[24] Many journalists and others, though, discount that testimony as self-serving and have accepted the CIA line that the Directorate for Plans would never have adopted murder as an appropriate covert action without an official blessing, indeed insistence, from the White House.

Richard Helms, DDP at the time of the scheming against Castro, conceded to Church Committee investigators that White House approval came more as an implied nod in the Oval Office than as a clearly expressed order; nevertheless, Helms testified that he understood what President Kennedy wanted, without having to denigrate the nation's highest office by engaging in a conversation about a killing. As he recalled: "No member of the Kennedy Administration.... ever told me that [assassination] was proscribed, [or] even referred to it in that fashion."[25] Journalist Tim Weiner asked Helms in an interview about the decision to end Castro's life. "There is nothing on paper, of course," he replied. "But there is certainly no question in my mind that he [Kennedy] did [want the Cuban leader removed]." The problem with Helms's philosophy of assassination as a form of covert action is that it obliterates all possibilities for accountability. He admitted to another danger this approach presents in world affairs: "If you kill someone else's leaders, why shouldn't they kill yours?"[26] At the time of the attempts against Fidel Castro, however, this reasoning did not stand in Helms's way.

During the Church Committee inquiry in 1975, panel member Senator Charles McC. Mathias Jr. (R, Maryland) engaged in a colloquy with Helms about the plots against Castro:

Senator Mathias. Let me draw an example from history. When Thomas Beckett was proving to be an annoyance, as Castro, the King [Henry II] said, "Who will rid me of this man?" He didn't say, go out and murder him. He said: "Who will rid me of this man," and let it go at that.
Mr. Helms. That is a warming reference to the problem.
Senator Mathias. You feel that spans the generations and the centuries?
Mr. Helms. I think it does, sir.
Senator Mathias. And that is typical of the kind of thing which might be said, which might be taken by the Director or by anybody else as presidential authorization to go forward?
Mr. Helms. That is right. But in answer to that, I realize that one sort of grows up in the tradition of the time and I think that any of us would have found it very difficult to discuss assassinations with a president of the U.S. I just think we all had the feeling that we're hired out to keep those things out of the Oval Office.
Senator Mathias. Yet at the same time you felt that some spark had been transmitted, that that was within the permissible limits.

MR. HELMS. Yes, and if he had disappeared from the scene, they would not have been unhappy.... Nobody ever said that [assassination] was ruled out.[27]

Furthermore, in response to a Church Committee query, John McCone, another former DCI (1961–65), pointed out how the "conditions of the time" lent themselves to a belief that Castro had to be dealt with. In McCone's words:

> Here was a man who for a couple of years would seize every opportunity before a microphone or television to berate and criticize the United States in the most violent and unfair and incredible terms. Here was a man that was doing his utmost to use every channel of communication of every Latin American country to win them away from any of the principles that we stood for and drive them toward Communism. Here was a man that turned over the sacred soil of Cuba in 1962 to the Soviets to plant nuclear warhead shortrange missiles, which could destroy every city east of the Mississippi. This was the climate in which people had to think what to do.[28]

Yet was this form of decision-making process appropriate in a democracy, with its vague language, circumlocutions, winks and nods? Similar to the knights who served Henry II, so, too, did Napoleon's chief of police, René Savary, seem to think he was doing what Napoleon wanted in executing a rival, Prince Louis Antoine duc d' Enghien, in Paris. Napoleon, however, appeared taken aback by this outcome when told about it after the fact.[29] The method by which the CIA arrived at the murder plots against Castro (and others) held significant moral hazard for the proper use of the Third Option in a democratic society, a form of government that depends upon clarity, honesty, frankness, and specificity if public officials are to be held accountable, as they must be for liberty to endure

The findings of the Church Committee on the possible earlier involvement of President Eisenhower in the assassination plots against Lumumba further illustrate the dilemma. "The chain of events revealed by the documents and testimony is strong enough to permit a reasonable inference that the plot to assassinate Lumumba was authorized by President Eisenhower," reported the Church panel, but its report added: "Nevertheless, there is enough countervailing testimony by Eisenhower Administration officials and enough ambiguity and lack of clarity in the records of high-level policy meetings to preclude the Committee from making a finding that the President intended an assassination effort against Lumumba."[30]

The Church Committee investigators were unable to know *for sure* exactly what had happened in the Castro and Lumumba cases. It decided, to the snarky mockery of some journalists who were following its proceedings, that it would be irresponsible to tag Presidents Eisenhower and Kennedy with charges of homicide without hard evidence to that effect. Obviously, though, the covert actions in both administrations were sadly lacking in appropriate procedures, so necessary for national security decisions in a democratic society. A statute known as the Hughes-Ryan Amendment would attempt to redress these shortcomings from 1975 onward (Chapter 5).

Although drawing a line against further assassination plots against Castro, the Johnson administration continued to explore (as expressed in an NSC document dated soon after the death of President Kennedy) "every avenue in order to make life as difficult as possible for Castro and as expensive and unpleasant for the USSR as possible."[31] As National Security Adviser McGeorge ("Mac") Bundy would urge President Johnson, the administration should seek "to take every available means to stop and turn back the spread of Communism in this hemisphere."[32] Among the initiatives undertaken by the Johnson administration against Cuba in late 1963 were several sabotage raids, including destruction of storage tanks at Casilda; mortar attacks against a sulfuric acid plant at Santa Lucia; destruction of a lumbermill at Bahia de Maravi; the sinking of a dredge moored at the La Isabela harbor; and an attack against a Cuban P-6 patrol boat at the Isle of Pines naval base, which resulted in the death of three Cuban naval personnel and the injury of eighteen others in the explosion. In early 1964, the administration conceded that it was unsure about whether or not the Third Option had achieved any basic changes at all in Cuba during the Castro years, but at least the CIA operations had forced the Cuban president "to divert valuable resources for defense against covert activities."[33]

Despite the lack of genuine change in Cuba, the administration persevered with covert actions in 1965, with an emphasis on PM sabotage operations. These included ongoing maritime raids against coastal targets, as well as Cuban merchant vessels in Cuban territorial waters and ships in Cuban ports; and the air bombing of selected targets inside Cuba—all accompanied by a steady propaganda barrage of deception operations meant to give the impression of an imminent invasion of the island by the United States military. Doubts about the usefulness of these activities was beginning to grow, however. As Bundy put it in a memo to President Johnson: "The trouble most of us see in such operations is that their international noise level outweighs their anti-Castro value." He continued: "Most of us do not recommend visible violent actions against Cuba. I believe this is also the opinion of [Secretary of State] Dean Rusk and [Secretary of Defense] Bob McNamara."[34]

Indochina

Another major covert action challenge for the Agency was, as in the Korean War, providing support for US military efforts in Indochina, a region comprised of Burma (now known as Myanmar), Cambodia, Laos, Thailand, and Vietnam.

Those efforts began as a trickle in 1953 and became a torrent from 1965 to 1973. Throughout, the primary objective was to drive communists out of South Vietnam and, ideally, to turn Indochina into a pro-Western—or at least anticommunist—region of the world.

Vietnam. The Agency attempted in 1953 to ruin the aspirations of the North Vietnamese leader, Ho Chi Minh, to unite all of Vietnam under a red banner—although a regime that would simultaneously pursue national independence and even friendship with the United States. Ho had traveled to the United States and was known to be an admirer of the American Revolution.[35]

The stance taken by Ho in the 1950s was common among poor countries, especially those unlucky enough to share a border with one of the communist giants; but this concept of self-interested nationalism in the developing world was lost on the Dulles duo, with their Manichean worldview of communism versus capitalism. And, again, commercial considerations entered the picture. President Eisenhower described the importance of Indochina to the United States in these economic terms: "First of all, you have the specific value of a locality in its production of materials that the world needs." More specifically, the president highlighted "tin and tungsten," as well as "the rubber plantations."[36]

Most important to the Eisenhower administration, though, remained the threat of global communism. Allen and Foster Dulles chose to approach international affairs free of nuances: a nation was either Christian, oriented toward a free-enterprise economy, democratic, and anti-communist, or it was just the opposite. What was important in American foreign policy was the global dynamics of the good guys against the bad guys. None of this "neutralism" or non-alignment nonsense; nationalism and independence among the poor nations was considered a delusional myth. A nation had to decide: the USA or the USSR, God or godlessness. Ho, as with Mossadegh, Árbenz, Nasser, Sukarno, and Castro (among others), failed to choose clearly enough and, therefore, both Eisenhower's DCI and his secretary of state concluded that the popular North Vietnam leader could not be trusted.

The first step was to give South Vietnam an inspiring champion who could outdo Ho Chi Minh. As a former Agency operations officer has written, the CIA became the "midwife" in the rebirth of South Vietnam.[37] As the US presence in South Vietnam further gelled in the 1960s and early 1970s, the number of Agency personnel in Indochina expanded dramatically, accompanied by another rise in funding for the Third Option. Soon after the Bay of Pigs episode, the Directorate of Plans had moved with the rest of the CIA to a new Headquarters Building in Northern Virginia, in a bucolic region known locally as Langley, near the township of McLean. Pushing the Cuban embarrassment aside and taking on its newest challenge in Indochina, the DP was once again in high clover.

The man selected by the Agency—that is to say, by DCI Allen Dulles—to lead the people of South Vietnam, who were Buddhist, poor, and fed up with corruption, was Ngo Dinh Diem, who was Catholic, wealthy, and corrupt. It was not a great match. All the psy warfare, bribing, and bombing the CIA could bring to bear were of no avail in achieving success for Diem and avoiding what became in 1964 an overt US war in Vietnam against Ho and his regime. The North Vietnamese leader and his determined, experienced jungle fighters had already defeated a well-armed and well-funded French army of occupation in 1954, at the famous battle of Dien Bien Phu in the far northwest corner of North Vietnam.

Within a few years of Diem's rule, a cadre of local generals in Saigon—coup plotters—assassinated him and his brother on November 2, 1963, just twenty days before President Kennedy was struck down in Dallas. The National Security Archive, an independent research group in Washington, DC, has posted documents (notably a White House tape and transcripts) that indicate Kennedy "was more disposed to support the removal of [Diem] than previously appeared to be the case."[38] At any rate, the administration and the CIA did nothing to stop the coup, perhaps hoping against hope that removal of Diem, and a new start that would allow, might improve the prospects for American success in Indochina. It did not.

Aiding the Department of Defense in the hunt for an elusive military victory in Vietnam, the CIA deployed all of its covert action arts, including a controversial program known as Operation "Phoenix" that ran from 1967 to 1971. The objective of Phoenix was to help destroy the pro-Ho presence in South Vietnam by gathering intelligence about likely North Vietnam sympathizers, whether organizations or individuals, then "neutralizing" them—yet another Agency euphemism meaning to kill the suspected communists. During the stew and ferment of civil war in Vietnam, the Phoenix program did away with 20,587 individuals thought to be North Vietnamese agents operating under the command of the Viet Cong (VC), the North's communist ally in the South. The killings usually occurred—about 85 percent of the time, according to CIA estimates—in paramilitary operations on battlefields throughout South Vietnam. Moreover, those who died were suspected enemies within the setting of an overt war against North Vietnam and its VC partners. Another 12 percent were executed by South Vietnamese security forces. William E. Colby, who directed the operation before becoming DCI, concedes, though, that some of the assassinations were inappropriate, carried out by overzealous South Vietnamese or occasionally even US personnel.[39]

Laos. An important part of the war efforts in Indochina was the CIA's program to subdue communist guerillas in Laos from 1962 to 1968. This was a country through which the North Vietnamese military moved supplies, along the Ho Chi Minh Trail, to its army fighting the United States in South Vietnam. The paramilitary undertaking in Laos, known by the CIA as Operation "Momentum," was the first major, long-lasting war run by the Agency on its own. As former DCI Helms has written, the mission had two purposes: first, to sustain the independence of the Royal Lao Government from communist domination; and second, to support the American war effort in neighboring South Vietnam. Because of the Agency's involvement in Laos, North Vietnam (NVN) was forced to allocate three combat divisions there. "Every NVN soldier in Laos," recalled Helms, "was one less enemy in South Vietnam."[40] No covert action would cost more CIA lives than this one, or save more lives of American soldiers across the Laotian border in Vietnam.

In the Korean War, the CIA had been assigned a limited support role for the US military; and the Cuban invasion in 1961, too, was a modest foray compared to this massive venture in Laos. The PM section of the Directorate of Plans now came into its own and, henceforth, violent forms of covert action would be viewed at Langley as a central part of its clandestine mission. Killing and warfighting were replacing analysis as the Agency's *raison d'état*.[41] The advent of the CIA's use of drone warfare against terrorists after the 9/11 attacks would reinforce this trend, in spades.

In one of the proudest periods for SOG paramilitary personnel and other DP officers, the Agency and its local guerrilla army, the Hmong (pronounced "mung," and also known as the Meo), were able in Laos—through courageous and tenacious fighting by CIA paramilitary officers and these local allies—to keep that nation's communist regulars, the Pathet Lao in North Laos, puppets of the North Vietnamese, away from the South Vietnam battlefields and the slaying of US troops.

The war in Korea had not been the first time the Agency performed the important task of diverting enemy soldiers away from shooting at US troops and their allies. In 1950, for instance, the Chinese Nationalist Army, defeated in the Second World War by the Communist Chinese, was still in the jungles of northwest Burma. The Directorate of Plans helped the Nationalists in raids against the communists within the southwest region of China. From the Agency's perspective, these harassing activities had kept part of the Chinese Army pinned down and away from US warfighters engaged in battle on the Korean Peninsula. Critics have been less generous, with the *New York Times* referring to the covert action in Burma as "a troublesome and costly burden," resulting in (among other outcomes) the alienation of modern-day Myanmar toward the United States.[42]

Fifteen years later, in 1965, American troops had their hands full in the form of North Vietnam regulars and the Viet Cong in South Vietnam. Tangled human causes had brought the Hmung and the DP together, now both bound by the terrible rope of circumstance; both united in warfare against a common enemy, the Pathet Lao. The US Air Force backed up the Agency's efforts on the ground in Laos, making an astonishing 580,000 bombing runs against the country during the six-year period from 1962 to 1968—more than in Vietnam at the time.[43] According to Helms in his 2003 memoir, the paramilitary operations in Laos were the war the CIA "had won."[44] As he similarly recalled in an earlier interview, "We really won that war in Laos, you know. We kept viable an anti-communist government in that nation. In other words, we did what the President [Lyndon B. Johnson] asked us to do, and we achieved the objective that he asked us to achieve. I don't know what more you can do."[45] The Agency had left the Bay of Pigs behind and was now demonstrating its mettle in faraway Asia.

Yet ultimately the cards would fall badly for the Agency's battleground surrogates in Laos, the Hmong. This intervention proved to be a short-term success (as in Iran in 1953) but again proved deeply flawed over the longer run—in this instance by the CIA's abandonment of its local allies in 1968, so much spindrift left behind in a storm. Only a fortunate few from the tribe's top leadership echelons were whisked out of the country and resettled in the United States (chiefly in Minnesota). The long-suffering Hmung, once inextricably braided with officers of the Directorate of Plans, had drawn in the end a busted flush.

The communist Pathet Lao regrouped and, following the American departure from Laos, the CIA's "undoubted moral obligation" (in the elegiac remembrance of an Agency officer involved in Operation "Momentum") to protect its surrogate warriors crumbled. For the courageous Hmong, the candle began to burn low. The communists marched through the jungles of Laos, insidiously, by degree, and overwhelmed the vulnerable Hmung who had been left behind. Their clandestine sheet anchor, the CIA, was no longer at their side and American bombers were no longer in the skies, just as decades later during the Clinton and the Trump administrations the candle would burn low for the Agency's Kurdish allies in Iraq and Syria, respectively, who had supported its operations in the Middle East only to be abandoned.[46]

Author Joshua Kurlantzick quotes a US Air Force General, Heinie Aderholt, who aided the Agency in this secret war, to the effect that the Hmung did suffer greatly, but that the PM op probably saved the lives of some 10,000 American warfighters across the border in Vietnam. "It's easier to lose your Hmong people than to lose Americans," the general concluded matter-of-factly. "It doesn't make as bad publicity at home."[47] In some parts of the military and the CIA, there appears to be a disquieting indifference to the use of indigenous people overseas as instruments of US foreign policy, at whatever cost these erstwhile partners may incur. And on Capitol Hill, blindness was the prevailing affliction; throughout these events in Laos, members of Congress knew few details about this major operation.

Chile

Without a clear victory emerging in Vietnam, the overt war became unpopular in the United States during the late 1960s and, in the early 1970s, the Nixon administration wound it down (all too slowly), along with its CIA paramilitary component. Richard M. Nixon was no fan of the Central Intelligence Agency, which he viewed as a bastion of liberalism (somewhat true then, less so today). The president turned away from most other covert action proposals as well, especially in Asia, as he became ensnared in Watergate. Before this scandal became his obsession, though, Nixon did approve—with unalloyed enthusiasm—the extensive use of the Third Option against Chile, continuing a progression of clandestine activities against that country that had been initiated by John Kennedy and passed along to his successor, Lyndon Johnson. Both failed to halt the edging of Chile toward socialism and the expropriation of US businesses in that country, even though beginning in 1962 these Democratic administrations had secretly funneled thousands of dollars into Chile in hopes of strengthening the pro-American Christian Democratic Party (PDC).[48]

Following the established pattern of American foreign policy, the fear of communist influence in a developing country became the preoccupation of the Nixon National Security Council, as well, with respect to Chile. When the plans to depose that nation's president, Salvador Allende, were in their early stages, the US ambassador objected to a coup, to which the Agency's COS in Santiago replied rhetorically: Do you want to be responsible for seeing a communist come to power in Chile?[49] The ambassador was won over. Further, as in Iran, Guatemala, and Cuba, US commercial interests became part of the calculus. The theme of global anti-communism and the fate of US business prosperity were once again on the same string.[50]

The telecommunications giant International Telephone and Telegraph (ITT) quietly went to the White House to seek presidential assistance in preventing Allende, who was not shy about admitting his Marxist leanings, from being elected president in Chile; and, if he were elected anyway despite the CIA's earlier and unsuccessful clandestine efforts to block his victory, to destroy his government through a stepped-up use of the Third Option. Executives at ITT feared, with good reason, that Allende would nationalize its 60 percent interest in the Chilean telephone company, costing the corporation millions of dollars in revenue. Another US company, Anaconda, which ran a huge copper industry in Chile, also expressed an interest in secretly funding the CIA's efforts to prevent Allende's rise to the presidency and, if that failed, to undermine the continuation of his regime. Both corporations were joined by Pepsi-Cola executives, who also expressed their concern to the Nixon White House.

These companies were right to be worried. Presidential candidate Allende had often threatened to confiscate US property in Chile and nationalize industries owned by American entrepreneurs. Frank Church (D, Idaho), a senator who had spent years investigating U.S. involvement in Chilean affairs, concluded that the CIA's intervention in that country had more to do with guarding "American business investments" than with confronting a foreign threat to the United States.[51]

A well-regarded senior officer with the Directorate of Operations (DO) agrees. "There was really no heavy US interest except business interest," notes Burton Gerber. "That's what was driving us."[52]

The ITT executives, who had hired the door-opening skills of lobbyist and former DCI John McCone (1961–65), a successful businessman himself, went so far as to bring with them to the White House a suitcase filled with a million dollars in cash, as means of facilitating the CIA's hidden activities in Chile. Nixon turned down the money but promised to do something about Allende. He kept this vow with a vengeance, becoming more involved in a covert action than has been the case with any other president, until George W. Bush and Barack Obama during the Age of Terrorism that followed the 9/11 attacks on the United States (Chapter 6). When DCI Helms dragged his feet on the plan to topple Allende, President Nixon said in an emotional outburst: "The CIA isn't worth a damn."[53]

Concerned more with the Cold War contest against the Soviet communists than with US business machinations, Secretary of State Henry Kissinger—America's premier Grand Strategist—urged Nixon not only to assist ITT and other US businesses but also to obliterate Allende and his socialist party. Reflecting back on this episode in 2001, Kissinger stressed that the United States had been in a "life and death struggle with the Soviet Union."[54] In this frame of mind, Kissinger told top-level officials at a White House meeting held on June 27, 1970, "I don't see why we need to stand by and watch a country go communist because of the irresponsibility of its own people."[55] This remark soon made the rounds in Washington. On the Hill, it was sometimes simplified as in the kid's game of "telephone," wherein one child whispers a message that is passed along in a chain of friends with the final version often altered from the original. One variation in the mid-1970s was: "According to Kissinger, the people of Chile are too stupid to pick their own leader; we must do it for them."[56]

In public, when word seeped out about his fear of events in distant Patagonia, Kissinger quipped in a rare moment of self-deprecating humor: "Chile is like a dagger . . . pointing to the heart of Antarctica." Yet, inside top-secret NSC meetings, he insisted that an Allende government posed an unacceptable danger to democracy in the Western Hemisphere—a dagger actually pointed, in his view, directly at the heart of the United States. This bleak outlook reminded some in Washington of the searing remark made by George F. Kennan in 1966 about LBJ's response to North Vietnam. The Johnson administration had acted, concluded the renowned diplomat, like "an elephant frightened by a mouse."[57]

Nevertheless, the Kissinger School of realpolitik was persistent and influential in the nation's Capital. The secretary of state had nothing but disdain for the likes of Frank Church and other internationalists on the Senate Foreign

Relations Committee, and his views were parroted by conservative journalists. Washington columnist James Kilpatrick, for instance, declared that Church and his allies on Capitol Hill were intent on having the United States "go abroad in a dangerous world, accoutered like Little Lord Fauntleroy, to play pattycake with gangs who fight with switchblade knives."[58]

Who could say, reasoned Kissinger and his acolytes, including President Nixon: perhaps Allende would be another Fidel Castro, cozying up to the Kremlin and possibly even inviting a military presence into his country, just as Castro had allowed nuclear missiles into Cuba. Widespread skepticism was evident at the time throughout the Intelligence Community that Allende truly presented a national security risk to the United States. An interagency intelligence report at the time concluded that the United States had no vital interests in Chile.[59] Nonetheless, Kissinger's arguments were taken seriously in GOP and conservative Democratic circles. Never mind that the Soviet Union had already burned itself twice in the Western Hemisphere: initially with the Cuban missile crisis in 1962, and then with its failed efforts to establish a submarine base on that island in 1970. If anything, the Kremlin was recoiling from any major commitments in the Western Hemisphere.

Despite this history, the Kissinger School insisted that the United States had to demonstrate resolve against socialist and communist influence—the two were usually conflated—wherever they arose and however minimal their manifestation. Cuba, Guatemala, and Chile may not have been of enormous strategic value to the United States in themselves, but Japan, Germany, and others were watching to see whether these "dominoes" would fall. If America failed to stand tall even in its own neighborhood, why would these other countries believe that Washington would come to their aid if they found themselves jeopardized by an aggressive Soviet Union or China? This perverted reasoning had raised its ugly head before during the Johnson and early Nixon administrations: America's friends would supposedly lose confidence in the Western coalition unless Washington sent troops to Vietnam, never mind that the other top members of NATO—America's close allies—opposed the war.

So went the Cold War argument pushed to an extreme by Kissinger and the rest of the Nixon administration's national security apparatus. As Thomas Meaney has observed, it was a perspective on global affairs that "made every pawn appear to be a threatened queen."[60] In one form or another, this dire *Weltanschauung* led the United States to launch a seemingly endless number of covert actions—large and small—in most every part of the world. Chile is a thin reed of a country, as long vertically as the United States is wide and averaging only a couple of hundred miles in width—not exactly a fearful presence. Plus, it lies thousands of miles away from the United States. Yet the Nixon administration saw fit to unleash against the people of Chile one of the largest and most ambitious covert actions to that date.

The CIA began, as usual, by reviving up its Mighty Wurlitzer to blast away at Allende through multiple media outlets, secretly opposing his election in 1970. When he won the presidency anyway, the Nixon administration set out to undermine his rule. The overall propaganda message: Allende would bring down the curtain on democracy, religion, and the family throughout Chile. Further, the CIA resorted to powerful economic weapons of clandestine intervention, including what Langley and the White House considered the gem of this hidden campaign: indirect assistance to anti-Allende groups in Chile who were planning a major truckers strike.[61] The objective was to paralyze commerce throughout the nation, bringing about a financial crisis and convincing citizens that President Allende was too incompetent to govern, at which point the Chilean military would have to intervene against his socialist government. The evidence concerning the Agency's involvement in these paralyzing strikes remains spotty, but intelligence scholar Gregory F. Treverton concludes that "the truckers got money from somewhere. Their strikes were actively supported by several of the private-sector groups that did receive CIA money, and some CIA money surely found its way through them to the strikers."[62]

The notes of DCI Helms, taken during an NSC meeting in the White House, captured the administration's fervor for the use of economic covert action in Chile. "Make the economy scream," he jotted down into a notepad.[63] By now, the American ambassador in Chile was fully onboard. He pleaded with his boss, Secretary Kissinger, who didn't require much convincing, to help ensure that "not a nut or bolt will be allowed to reach Chile under Allende." For his part, the ambassador abandoned all viestiges of a moral foreign policy and vowed:: "We shall do all within our power to condemn Chile and the Chileans to utmost deprivation and poverty."[64] He later changed his mind about the likelihood of a coup succeeding, but it was too late to shut down the "drastic action" that Kissinger said was necessary.

President Allende managed to survive these early efforts to destroy his reputation and his administration. Eventually, though, the economic, political, and propaganda pressures proved too great and his government fell. He took his own life with a machine gun, as the Chilean military—cheered on (and funded) behind the scenes by the CIA and the Nixon administration—surrounded the presidential palace, La Moneda.[65] During these events, in a Mafia-like hit, an anti-Allende faction murdered the government's military commander General René Schneider, surrounding his car, knocking out the rear window with a sledgehammer, and gunning him down. The Agency claimed to the Church Committee that it had not intended the general's death, and it was true that the killers were only indirectly affiliated with the CIA's plot against the Allende government; nonetheless, the faction had received arms from the Agency, and Langley officials were fully aware of the group's plan to kidnap Schneider—a risky operation that clearly might have resulted in the general's death. Moreover, the National Security Archive discovered that "in the aftermath of the assassination the CIA went to great lengths to cover up all evidence of its involvement." The Archive's researchers cited a HPSCI finding that the Agency had paid "hush money to representatives of the assassination team."[66] Langley, therefore, cannot evade complicity in the general's murder—another assassination in which it had a hand, however light the grip may have been in this instance.

Anti-communist crusaders, Business America, the Nixon administration, and the CIA had won, ensuring that an unscrupulous autocrat, General Augusto Pinochet, came to power in Chile. For the first time in its history, this proud, highly cultured nation became a dictatorship; and, again (as in Iran and Guatemala) the Agency had helped to overthrow a democratically elected government. A reign of terror began in Chile that would last seventeen years and cost the lives of untold numbers of individuals who sought to restore freedom to their nation, but instead "disappeared" from the face of the earth at Pinochet's orders. Torture and killing became a commonplace tactic against his critics during this reign of terror. How necessary was the CIA intervention in the first place? An objective, authoritative study by Treverton published in 2007 concluded that without all of this subterfuge and sorrow, "Allende's experiment in Chile would have failed on its own terms."[67]

~~~

In 1975, on the heels of this dismal episode in Chile, the Senate and the House investigated the CIA and its companion intelligence services, spearheaded by the Church and the Pike Committees, with Senator Church and Representative Otis Pike (D, New York) at the helms. These inquiries led to widespread public criticism of covert action. The DCI at the time when the Committees reported their findings was George H. W. Bush, who had replaced William E. Colby in that position and would go on to serve as president later in his career (America's only chief executive to have been a CIA director). Reacting to the general lack of enthusiasm for covert action in the wake of the Nixon and Ford administrations (although the latter had backed a lively pursuit of this approach in Angola, discussed in Chapter 5), plus—above all—reeling from the Church Committee's exposure of covert actions in Chile, DCI Bush spent little time pushing the Agency into clandestine operations around the world.

As one senior Agency official recalls, covert action came "to a screeching halt" in 1975–76, while a colleague of his predicted bleakly that it would be "nearly impossible to conduct future CA operations."[68] The Third Option had plummeted to its Cold War nadir, as Langley officials and the White House focused on dealing with the congressional intelligence inquiries and regrouped to concentrate mainly—at least for the time being—on the CIA's original mission: the assessment of information gathered from the four corners of the planet.[69] This lull in aggressive covert actions would not last long, though, regardless of predictions that suggested otherwise.

PART III
PRACTICE, 1975–2020

5
A New Approach to Covert Action, 1975–2000

Democracy Comes to the Third Option

With the enactment of the Hughes-Ryan Act on December 30, 1974, whose passage was directly stimulated by revelations in the *New York Times* about CIA operations to overthrow Allende in Chile, the Third Option moved into a much more complicated world at home. Stringent new rules would henceforth govern the approval, conduct, and accountability of covert actions. Formal presidential authority and reporting to Congress would be required for any adoption of this approach to foreign policy—a pathbreaking legal dimension of America's secret power (examined with more detail in Part IV of this book). This chapter and Chapter 6 explore some of the more prominent examples of covert action under this new legal regime, beginning with a short-lived covert action in Angola during 1975 (see Figure 5.1).

Angola

In 1975, the CIA conducted its first covert action under the new Hughes-Ryan regime of tighter accountability. The objective of the clandestine intervention was to prevent the MPLA (Popular Movement for the Liberation of Angola), a faction supported by the USSR and Cuba, from seizing power in Angola, located in southwest Africa. Secretary of State Henry Kissinger argued at the time that the Soviet presence there represented the most significant attempt at Russian military influence anywhere outside the Middle East since 1960. During the Church Committee hearings on covert action, Senator Walter F. "Fritz" Mondale (D, Minnesota), the second-ranking Democrat on the panel, asked Kissinger: "Is it the spectical of the Russians coming in and dictating the course of the government through force that worries?" The Secretary's response: "That is it." He expressed his fear that subsequently other Africa states would feel pressure to tilt toward Moscow in the Cold War superpower competition. Neither Mondale nor Church bought into this argument. As we walked through the corridors of the Senate Russell Building a few days prior to Kissinger's appearance before

118 THE THIRD OPTION

ANGOLA, Portugal
Afghanistan, Nicaragua, El Salvador, Grenada, Jamaica
South Yemen, Egypt
USSR, Poland, **IRAN**
Ethiopia, Chad, Grenada, Lebanon
AFGHANISTAN, USSR
NICARAGUA, El Salvador
POLAND, Libya, Sudan
Cambodia, Philippines
Mauritius, Angola
Panama
Somalia
SERBIA, IRAQ

1975 1981   1982-88   1990-91   2001-2003   2005   2010-2011   2020

AFGHANISTAN, PAKISTAN
TERRORISM
IRAQ
CHINA, N. KOREA, RUSSIA
CYBERTERRORISM
Somalia, Yemen
Libya, Mali, Maghreb
SYRIA, Pakistan
TERRORISM
IRAN

---

*The cases examined more closely in this chapter and the next are in bold capital letters. The "Terrorism" and "Cyberterrorism" cases in the figure are examples of a global phenomenon.

Figure 5.1 Key Targeting in the Evolution of Covert Action, 1975–2020

the Committee, Church said to the author in disgust: "When will this country stop being so uptight about the world? The foundations of the Republic will not crumble away if someone we don't like takes over in Chad." Yet Kissinger remained convinced that a call to covert arms was necessary to reestablish the balance of internal forces in Angola and globally. That task, he maintained, had passed beyond the capacity of diplomacy to resolve, ever since the introduction of sophisticated Soviet arms on the MPLA side. In response to this Russian intervention, the United States came to the aid of two pro-Western groups: UNITA and FNLA in the local acronyms for, respectively, the National Union for the Total Independence of Angola and the National Front for the Liberation of Angola.

The Soviets and the Cubans, who sent troops from Havana to fight alongside the MPLA, placed far more resources into this struggle than the United States was willing to invest. The CIA-backed groups began to falter, even though the Agency had gone so far as to provide UNITA with sophisticated weaponry, including high-powered Stinger missiles: a shoulder-held weapon capable of bringing down enemy bomber aircraft from five miles away. With these resources in hand, CIA/SOG "advisers" and their African partners had fought with determination and, in the process, had substantially raised the costs of winning for the communist forces. The goal of statis became the tactical fallback position of the Ford administration when outright victory over the communists proved unlikely in Angola. The administration adopted the same strategy of settling for an equilibrium of communist and Western forces in a number of other clandestine battleground states in Africa, including Rhodesia, South West Africa, and Mozambique.

Paramilitary challenges in Africa aside, President Ford had an even greater covert action problem at home: recalcitrant lawmakers who didn't like what they had read in the *Times* about Allende's demise. In the heat generated by news reports on the CIA's overzealous operations in Chile, members of Congress were up in arms against the Third Option across the board and, in the form of the Tunney-Clark Amendment, they voted against further funding for CIA operations in Angola.[1] It was the first time Congress had shut off the money spigots for a covert action already under way. In response to these predicaments at home and abroad, the Ford administration simply declared victory in Angola—however hollow the claim—and ordered the Agency home from that contested nation.

The first DCI who had to deal with the Church Committee inquiry in 1975 was William E. Colby, a well-known enthusiast for the Third Option, inspired by his OSS days when he was an able and daring saboteur against the Nazis in Norway and France. The Directorate of Plans had been renamed the Directorate of Operations (DO) in 1973 and Colby became the deputy director for Operations (DDO). He soon won promotion to the top CIA slot, the DCI, yet he was immediately caught in the rapidly spinning downward spiral of America's disengagement from the Third Option as a foreign policy tool, as exemplified by the political ruckus on Capitol Hill over the Agency's presence in Angola. Just a few years earlier, Richard Helms had moved from DDP to the DCI position, preceding Colby. Ironically, Helms had been wary of clandestine operations and yet found himself "up to his scuppers" (as he might put it in a favorite expression of his) in the full range of the Third Option being carried out in Indochina. Colby, the covert action advocate, had arrived on Langley's Seventh Floor a little late for an enthusiastic pursuit of his favorite intelligence activity and had to preside over its decline.

A further irony pertaining to covert action had cropped up in Angola. The Ford administration, with Kissinger continuing on as secretary of state, was predictably driven by the anti-communist outlook on world affairs that still held Washington in its grips. This time, though, America's business interests favored the communist MPLA faction! The US petroleum industry opposed the CIA's anti-MPLA activities for a simple reason: corporate profit. The Marxist party in Angola controlled that nation's oil fields and Texas oil tycoons did not want to lose access to this wellspring of African riches. The outcome was a situation of strange bedfellows, with US oil execs and Marxist revolutionaries lined up on the same side.[2]

Iran II

Jimmy Carter of Georgia ran successfully for the White House against President Ford in 1976 on a campaign platform that strongly opposed US involvement in covert actions—a subject unprecedented for a candidate to feature in a bid for national office. Carter had been influenced by the Church Committee hearings of the previous year, which uncovered the Third Option excesses employed by the Nixon administration in its efforts to bring down the Allende regime. Two of the five people Carter considered as possible vice-presidential running mates had served on the Church Committee: its chair, Frank Church, and the person Carter finally chose, Senator Mondale (D, Minnesota), the second-ranking Democrat on the panel.

With the CIA domestic spy scandal of 1974 fresh in the public mind, as well as the disclosures from the Church Committee the next year about the Agency's assassination plots and its attacks against Chile, Carter and Mondale spoke in public often during the election about how intelligence reform was needed at Langley and elsewhere in the Intelligence Community. They emphasized the necessity of lowering the temperature in the Agency's Operations Directorate. It appeared at the time that America's clandestine involvement in the Angolan civil war during the Ford years might be a last hurrah for the Third Option, at least during the duration of the Carter presidency.

Once in office, though, President Carter discovered that the Third Option could be useful, and, rare for a president, he even crafted a proposal himself aimed at improving human rights in a small country. Another illustration of President Carter's engagement in this hidden domain of foreign affairs was his administration's secret funding to a group of Afghan moderates, an early, still modest beginning to a much larger paramilitary commitment the Reagan presidency would pursue in that troubled part of Southwest Asia.[3] Things can look one way on the campaign trail and quite another in the Oval Office. By the end of his single term, Carter had chalked up almost as many covert actions as Presidents Nixon and Ford combined. Nixon had been distracted by Watergate, though, and Ford by the Church panel inquiry. Moreover, the Nixon involvement in Chile had far surpassed any Carter covert action, in cost, scale, and moral turpitude.

Despite turning to the Third Option more than one might have guessed based on their presidential campaign rhetoric, Carter and Mondale (the most active vice president to that date on national security issues) kept America's secret interventions overseas at a relatively low level of frequency and scope, certainly when compared to the next administration led by Ronald Reagan. President Carter, a devoutly religious man, set a high moral tone that pervaded his administration and kept national security officials at arms-length from most covert "dirty tricks." By 1980, the number of "special activities" had risen somewhat from their low point in 1975–76 during the Church Committee inquiry, but they still accounted for less than 5 percent of Langley's total spending.

The exception to this coolness toward the Third Option among key officials in the Carter administration came from the office of its national security adviser, Zbigniew Brzezinski, a fervent anti-Russian and a devotee to whatever instruments of foreign policy might set back the USSR. "Zbig" waged many a battle within the NSC over the value of covert action against the more skeptical DCI Admiral Stansfield Turner.[4] The national security adviser did his best to push the envelope as far as President Carter would allow in the realm of covert action, which was not far—although Zbig was able to draw the president into limited covert support for the pro-democracy movement in Poland, led by the labor group Solidarity. This hidden East European battlefield in the Cold War became one of Brzezinski's top priorities, as a way of tweaking his nemesis, the Kremlin, and weakening its bear-like grip on Poland. He even managed to convince Pope John Paul II, who was born in Wadowice, Poland, to assist in these behind-the-scenes, anti-Soviet intrigues.[5] Soon the Reagan administration would nurture these, and many other, covert operations into full flower.

As mentioned in Chapter 2, the top form of covert action adopted by DCI Turner was, as its value slowly grew on him, the infiltration of anti-communist books and magazines into the USSR, including Bibles and Korans, as well as desktop publishing capabilities so that the pro-Western underground in the Soviet empire could write and disseminate its criticism (*samizdat*, in Russian) of communist society.[6] Plus, as one would expect for the Carter administration in light of the president's well-known devotion to human rights, the condemnation of those nations guilty of violating these basic liberties became a central theme in the DO's propaganda activities.

The Carter administration's most dramatic use of the Third Option came, though, as part of an attempt to rescue fifty-two US diplomatic personnel taken hostage in Iran on November 4, 1979, by fervent disciples of the Ayatollah Ruhollah Khomeni, the Iranian leader. An intricate plan, Operation "Eagle Claw," relied on close coordination between the Pentagon and the CIA, with the Agency playing a support role with respect to rescuing hostages in the US Embassy, as well as assuming responsibility for guiding some other Americans in Iran to a successful escape with the help of the Canadian Embassy in Tehran.

The initial objective was to aid the evacuation of a small group of Americans in Tehran located outside the US Embassy. Through use of covert action, and thanks to extraordinary and risky cooperation from Canadian diplomats in Tehran, the CIA managed in January of 1980 to sneak out of Iran ("exfiltrate," in Agency lingo) these US citizens who had been visiting at the Canadian Embassy at the time of the American Embassy hostage-taking across town. The DO quickly prepared counterfeit Canadian passports for these few lucky individuals, then smuggled the documents to the Canadian Ambassador in Tehran. The Canadians hustled the Americans to the airport in the capital city, and they were homeward bound before the local authorities grew suspicious.

The effort to rescue the remaining Americans held in the US Embassy was a much greater challenge. In frustration over the unwillingness of the Islamic Republic to return the US Embassy hostages, President Carter turned up the heat in his administration's earlier covert action attempts to oust the mullahs and their fourteenth-century theocracy in Tehran. In December of 1979, he signed another, stepped-up presidential order (a "finding") that authorized the CIA to "conduct propaganda and political and economic action operations to encourage the establishment of a responsible and democratic regime in Iran; [and] make contacts with Iranian opposition leaders and interested governments in order to encourage interactions that could lead to a broad, pro-Western front capable of forming an alternative government."[7]

These attempts also went nowhere and, in April of 1980, the frustrated American president dispatched a covert military rescue team to an isolated location in the desert not far from Tehran. Beforehand, the CIA had tested the density of the sand in the proposed landing area to ensure it was firm enough to support US aircraft—a dangerous preliminary intelligence-collection operation vital to the planning of the mission. The Agency also installed navigation systems in the rescue aircraft, and infiltrated a DO asset into Tehran to assist in the exfiltration mission.

The idea was to fly combat helicopters from the desert landing zone to a soccer field near the American Embassy in Tehran. Special Forces would storm the compound, throwing concussion grenades inside the embassy to stun the Iranian guards. They would then scoop up the captive embassy personnel and make a fast getaway back to the choppers. Unfortunately, though, a series of communications snafus, equipment breakdowns, and a trick played by Nature—a sandstorm at the desert landing zone—foiled the rescue attempt on April 24 before the aircraft could even lift off from the hideaway site and head for Tehran. In the poor visibility, one helicopter crashed into another, killing eight of the Special Forces personnel and forcing commanders to abort the mission, in a cruel reminder of history's packet of tricks.

On the day of President Ronald Reagan's inauguration, the government in Tehran finally returned the beleaguered Embassy hostages to US custody after their 444 days in captivity. It was a final poke in the eye by the mullahs to the defeated Carter administration.

Iran III and Nicaragua: The Iran-*Contra* Affair

When President Reagan arrived at the White House in 1981, the contrast between him and Carter was stark, including an infinitely greater attraction to the Third Option among members of the incoming administration. Many DO officers at Langley had been resentful toward the Carter national security team for its criticism of Agency activities in the past (especially the domestic spying, the assassination plots, and the coup in Chile). Nor did they appreciate Carter's campaign rhetoric specifically critical of covert action; his overly cautious approach to international affairs; or how he had stuck the Agency with an "outsider" as DCI, Stansfield Turner—an aloof admiral (in the Langley perspective) who would soon dismiss a large number of veteran DO operatives on grounds of trimming down the Agency and making it more agile.

In contrast, DO officers displayed an enthusiastic, almost Pavlovian reaction to the arrival of William J. Casey, a prosperous investor and corporate law professor, on their doorstep as the new DCI. He seemed ready to emancipate the Agency so it could continue its hallowed tradition of fighting commies around the world. President Reagan's rhetoric during the presidential campaign of 1980 about "peoples enslaved by the Soviet colonies in the satellite nations"—a virulent anti-Russian philosophy that he would continue to promote against the "Evil Empire" (as the president described the USSR in 1983)—hit a sweet spot within the Operations Directorate at Langley.[8] "Abroad the Soviet Union was engaged in a brutal war in Afghanistan," candidate Reagan had warned on the campaign trail, "and Communism was extending its tentacles deep into Central America and Africa."[9]

William Casey was known at Langley as someone who endorsed a no-holds-barred approach to American foreign policy. According to Robert M. Gates, a former DCI and Agency analyst far less impressed by covert action, for Casey it was a matter of "life and death.... We will do whatever it takes to win." Another senior Agency officer recalls that in this envisioned clandestine war against the KGB and the GRU, Casey "was a little short on morals."[10] Casey had been involved in covert actions during his youthful days in the OSS; as he would later write, that organization and its British paramilitary counterpart, the Special Operations Executive (SOE), had significantly aided the war against Hitler by way of "deception, clandestine intelligence and covert action."[11]

Planners in the DO must have visualized impending covert actions sprouting like vast fields of Shasta daisies across the globe. They were right, as new monies poured into the Directorate's coffers and the DDO set about hiring over 2,000 new officers. In addition to a zeal for mixing it up with the Soviets—the "Sovs"—on the global chessboard, Casey held out strong promise for what the CIA values above all else: easy access to the Oval Office. As Reagan's former national campaign manager, the new DCI had a lock on this important advantage, perhaps more so than any other Agency director had ever enjoyed.

The exuberance of the pro-Casey faction at Langley, especially inside the DO, was well placed. Some may view the 1950s as the prime years for covert action during the Cold War, but those who have studied the record closely would reserve that approbation for the Reagan presidency during the 1980s. No administration to date had been as devoted to a large-scale, worldwide use of the Third Option as the Reagan White House: back into Angola, as well as fresh secret forays into Chad, Ethiopia, Lebanon, Poland, and beyond. The planets were well aligned for a revival of the superpower rivalry—Cold War II—with two arch anti-communists, Reagan and Casey, teamed up and with no instrument of foreign policy more attractive to them than "special activities." These two men shared a deep belief that clandestine ploys carried out against America's adversaries could turn the tide in the direction of a US victory in the international contest between communism and capitalism.

It was the best of times for special activities, with remarkable successes in Poland and Afghanistan. Here were the makings of a Second Golden Age of Covert Action (the first coming with Iran and Guatemala during the Eisenhower administration)—at least over the short term. Yet it was also the worst of times, soon blotted by the stain of the Iran-*contra* scandal. This affair began when Casey went to the White House in 1984 with an emotionally charged intelligence report for the president. The Agency's chief of station in Lebanon, Bill Buckley, had been taken hostage by pro-Iranian terrorists and was being slowly tortured to death in an unknown location somewhere in Beirut.

Casey knew Buckley personally and was understandably shaken by his friend's plight. Immediately and with heartfelt concern, the president approved the DCI's request that the United States offer to sell missiles to Iran at a reduced price in exchange for its help in gaining Buckley's release. Israel, which enjoyed good contacts in Tehran at the time despite the public animosity between the two nations, would serve as an interlocutor for the deal. A further enticement for Iran: its Shiite government was at war with the Sunni government in Iraq, with whom it shared a long border, and Tehran had an appetite for missiles and other arms to fight this war.

It may have been a worthy plan, except for a couple of highly significant flaws. First, since passage of the Hughes-Ryan Act, the law required that Congress be informed of covert actions, which would include the secret sale of weaponry abroad in exchange for influence. The staff on the NSC chose to ignore this requirement, however. It went ahead with the operation in 1985, and only the next year requesting formal approval from President Reagan. Even then, the belated formal White House authorization was never reported to Congress—another violation of Hughes-Ryan.

Second, the Arms Export Control Act of 1976 banned the sale of US weapons to nations, such as revolutionary Iran, which had been deemed guilty by the Department of State of sponsoring terrorist organizations. Moreover, the arms sale exceeded the law's requirement that any shipment of weapons to another nation valued at $14 million or more had to be reported to Congress—another provision ignored. The law was brushed off by NSC staff. In response to the administration's secret offer, officials in Tehran happily purchased the missiles, but did little to help free Buckley. The talented COS died in 1985 of torture injuries inflicted by his terrorist captors.

Then DCI Casey, in cahoots with the senior staff of the NSC, came up with yet another illicit Third Option proposal, this one also kept from Congress at Casey's urging.[12] The plan: money gained from the missile sales in Iran would be shifted over to the administration's budding paramilitary operations in Nicaragua. These envisioned clandestine activities were crafted to dislodge Daniel Ortega, the leader of the Sandinista Party, from the presidency of that country because of his alleged Marxist leanings. The Carter administration had rejected the notion that Ortega was a dangerous ideologue who presented a grave threat to the United States, and the Department of State fully recognized the Ortega government. President Reagan's view, though, was quite different. As he put it, Soviet proxies—the Sandinistas—were "just two days driving time from Harlingen, Texas. . . . [I]f we don't want to see the map of Central America covered in a sea of red, eventually lapping at our own borders, we must act now."[13] The administration respectively labeled these schemes aimed at Iran and Nicaragua as Operations "Staunch" and "Toys."

The same problem existed for the administration with respect to these covert action plans in Nicaragua as occurred with the Buckley-driven operations in Iran: the secret intervention aimed at Ortega had to be reported to Congress, by law, yet it never was. Further, the renegade nature of this clandestine activity stood in direct violation of a series of specific laws related to Nicaragua: the Boland Amendments, seven statutes passed from 1982 to 1984, each signed by President Reagan, that increasingly restricted funding for coup attempts against the Sandinista regime.[14] Representative Edward P. "Eddie" Boland (D, Massachusetts), the first chairman of the House Permanent Select Committee on Intelligence (HPSCI), sponsored the laws and a Democratic majority in Congress passed each measure by veto-proof margins (and, therefore, were reluctantly signed by President Reagan). That, according to the Constitution, should have shut down covert actions in Nicaragua. Or so lawmakers thought.

Again, though, the Reagan administration simply disregarded legal barriers that it found inconvenient and wrong-minded. The Hughes-Ryan Act? Formal presidential approval of covert actions and reports to Congress? Ridiculous! The attitude on the NSC staff was that the Third Option was the president's prerogative under Article II of the Constitution. The Council's staff attorney prepared an internal legal opinion that reached an exotic conclusion: despite their language to the contrary, the intelligence laws—including the Boland Amendments—may have applied to the Intelligence Community, but not to NSC staff. The weakness of this argument is dissected in Chapter 7. Nevertheless, DCI William Webster has suggested that "the Congress deserves some blame. The Boland Amendments were ambiguous; lawmakers needed to come up with clearer guidelines."[15] Yet the language in the law explicitly banned US support "for the purpose of overthrowing the Government of Nicaragua"—not exactly an ambiguous prohibition.

To manage these renegade operations, the Reagan administration created a special rogue organization known as "The Enterprise." William Casey knew that several of his top-level colleagues at Langley viewed his Iran-*contra* activities with suspicion and concern that he was dragging the Agency into perilous legal waters, but none of them wanted to take on the irascible CIA chief. So they kept a low profile; and Casey, realizing this lack of support among several Agency elites, found more attractive the options of using the NSC staff and The Enterprise for his objectives, with only a few key people at Langley—including the sympathetic DDO—brought into the controversial plan to bypass the Congress.[16]

At the time, Lieutenant Colonel Oliver L. North, a Naval Academy graduate and first-rate military officer during the Vietnam War, was the deputy national security adviser and one of the Iran-*contra* conspirators. He described The Enterprise as "an off-the-shelf, stand-alone, self-sustaining secret entity."[17] It was one of the most chilling chapters in the annals of America's democracy. The

Congress and its constitutionally based appropriations process be damned; the administration would make an end run around the law and the Constitution, by creating an invisible clandestine organization of its own that would raise money for covert actions from private sources. To hell with the Hughes-Ryan Act, the Intelligence Oversight Act of 1980 (which required prior notice to Congress on covert actions, examined in Chapter 7), the Arms Export Control Act, and the Boland Amendments. To hell with the Constitution.

The donors who supported The Enterprise included foreign potentates, such as the royal family of Saudi Arabia (which put up $32 million) and the Sultan of Brunei (good for another $7 million), along with wealthy Americans who had helped finance the Reagan campaign for president. Joseph Coors, the Colorado beer magnate, for one. Creation of The Enterprise was the most shocking feature of the scandal, but it had several close competitors. Working hand in glove with The Enterprise, the CIA contributed in several ways to the illegal covert actions in Nicaragua, such as preparing an operational field manual for the *contras* ("counter-revolutionaries," the anti-Ortega, anti-Sandinista faction backed by The Enterprise and the Agency). Entitled *Psychological Operations in Guerrilla Warfare*, the manual advocated the selective assassination of leaders associated with the Sandinistas, even though just a few years earlier (1976) the Ford administration had banned assassinations by way of an executive order—an E.O. (No. 11905) endorsed by subsequent presidents, until Trump. When the media exposed the manual, DCI Casey apologized publicly and slapped on the wrist five low-level officers involved in authorship and distribution.

Harvard University professor of constitutional law Laurence H. Tribe reached an apt conclusion about the methods of governance chosen by the Iran-*contra* conspirators. "Congress's control over the purse [Article I, Section 9 of the Constitution] would be rendered a nullity," he wrote, "if the President's pocket could conceal a slush fund dedicated to purposes and projects prohibited by the laws of the United States."[18] For social commentator Bill Moyers, The Enterprise was an organization dreamed of by zealots: "no watchman to check the door, no accountant to check the books, no judge to check the law . . . no Constitution . . . permanent and wholly unaccountable."[19] In sharp contrast to the Carter presidency, the Reagan administration had adopted an anything-goes attitude. As recollected by a seasoned Washington staffer on Capitol Hill known for his bipartisanship, several of President Reagan's top national security aides were "people who were always trying to get around the roadblocks of institutional and statutory limitations, who were looking for a way to get it done."[20]

In 1987, the sordid affair leaked out in a Beirut newspaper, *Al Shiraa*, and the bombshell exposé quickly made its way back to the United States. For the Iran-*contra* conspirators, the knell had knolled. Congress was not pleased and held extensive investigative hearings that brought to light the twin illegal operations in Iran and Nicaragua. Lawmakers on the investigative panel asked National Security Adviser Admiral John M. Poindexter, who had graduated first in his class at Annapolis and was now in his middle years, why he had failed to inform HPSCI and the Senate Select Committee on Intelligence (SSCI) about the covert actions, as required by law. His response: "I simply did not want any outside interference."[21] In other words, Congress was a non-entity and the law could be ignored.

Fawn Hall, secretary to Lieutenant Colonel North, explained in her testimony before the committee that "sometimes you have to go above the written law."[22] What law stood above the Boland Amendments and the intelligence oversight acts? For North, honoring the requirement to keep Congress informed of covert actions failed to come even come close to what he saw as a higher duty: to serve the commander in chief, the president.[23] For some others among the conspirators, including Ms. Hall, the law of God also far surpassed the law of the land when it came to dealing with America's archenemy: the godless communists in Moscow and Managua.

On the Hill, a majority of Republicans and Democrats alike rejected this astonishing resurrection from the Nixon years of unfettered executive power, what historian Arthur M. Schlesinger Jr. had famously labeled the "Imperial Presidency." A respected GOP senator from New Hampshire, Warren B. Rudman, a tough-minded Korean War veteran, concluded that the Iran-*contra* conspirators had "wrapped themselves in the flag and go around spitting on the Constitution."[24] Those involved in the scandal would likely have gone to prison as a result of their blatant disregard for the law, except for a lucky break: by 1989, George H. W. Bush, the former DCI and Reagan administration vice president, had become president and, in 1992, he granted a pardon to the participants in the Iran-*contra* affair. Critics saw it as a cynical move by President Bush to prevent disclosures that might have emerged in further court trials, implicating him in the affair. (Vice President Bush's national security aide during the Iran-*contra* operations was Donald Gregg, a former CIA operative and as closely tied into Agency activities as anyone could be.) "Where was Bush?" became a popular lapel button in Washington at the time, at least among Democrats.

As for the incumbent president, Ronald Reagan denied knowledge of the whole affair. In the spirit of plausible deniability (a doctrine of keeping the US president above covert action scandals), Poindexter backed him up—at first. After the congressional inquiry was over, though, the admiral recanted as he began to resent his role as scapegoat, and the unwillingness of the president to share blame for the illegal operations. The initial shield provided by Poindexter—along with Reagan's own public denial in his popular, avuncular manner—saved the president from House impeachment proceedings and a Senate trial, both before large Democratic majorities. Nonetheless, Reagan's once robust standing in the public-opinion polls plummeted by twenty-one points during the congressional inquiry into the affair. His presidency had survived, however, and indeed President Reagan began to flourish again as he turned—cheerfully and unexpectedly, urged on by his wife, Nancy Reagan—toward the more constructive goal of arms control negotiations and the reduction of global tensions between the United States and the Soviet Union. Diplomacy now seemed a safer foreign policy route than covert action.

No wonder Reagan was known as the "Teflon President". Like the kitchen dishpans coated with the Teflon chemical, everything untoward just seemed to slide off him. Whatever the president's true awareness of the Iran-*contra* affair, his chief of staff, James A. Baker (later an exceptionally able secretary of state in the first Bush administration) had understood the gravity of raising private funds from foreign countries to skirt the Boland Amendments. Early in the planning, he warned the NSC staff that such action would be an "impeachable offense."[25]

Long before the scandal broke into the public domain, HPSCI and SSCI had been concerned about rumors floating around Washington suggesting the administration was neck-deep in unlawful activities in Nicaragua. The HPSCI chairman, Lee H. Hamilton (D, Indiana), directed staff inquiries into the allegation; and he solicited, as well, a formal reply from then-national security adviser, Robert C. "Bud" McFarlane, who preceded Admiral Poindexter in that position—both men with shared seating in the lee scuppers during the scandal.

McFarlane was an experienced national security official, a troubled man known for agonizing over decisions that skated along ethical boundaries. Yet, in 1985, two years before the affair came to light, he had replied to Hamilton in a letter with a bald-faced lie. "I can state with deep personal conviction," he wrote, "that at no time did I or any other member of the National Security Council staff violate the letter or spirit of Congressional restrictions on aid to the Contras."[26] A core McFarlane strategy was to deceive overseers on Capitol Hill, including as part of the effort the placement of a CIA propaganda specialist on the NSC staff to advance the administration's goals in Nicaragua.[27]

McFarlane sent five additional letters like this one to inquiring lawmakers, each drafted by Lieutenant Colonel North for his signature—that is, when North wasn't busy shredding documents that might incriminate him if these activities became public. North, who had returned from a tour in Vietnam with an exemplary record of bravery and effectiveness, was now in a different milieu where the law, accountability, and the Constitution were far more important than they had been to him in the war-torn jungles of Vietnam. In the White House, he was out of his element. He had never taken a class on constitutional law or even American government while a cadet at the US Naval Academy, which might have provided him with some orientation to the basics of America's legal system and form of government. (After the Iran-*contra* affair, the Academy made a basic course in American government mandatory for all cadets, as it has long been at many public universities around the country.)

At least, though, North must have been heartened during the subsequent formal inquiry into the scandal to have several members on the congressional investigative panel cheering him on, namely, some among the committee's GOP minority and—above all—the ranking Republican on the panel, Representative (and later vice president for George W. Bush) Dick Cheney of Wyoming. North's record of military service and his Marine Corps bearing made him an attractive witness for many viewers during the televised hearings—unless one was attentive to the details of the colonel's testimony and understood his casual acquaintance with, or respect for, the law. After this moment of publicity, North was inspired to run for the US Senate from Virginia but he lost the election.

Meanwhile, an additional Reagan administration schemer against the Boland Amendments, Elliott Abrams, testified before Congress with yet another blatant falsehood. He said: "While I have been Assistant Secretary [for Inter-American Affairs in the State Department], which is about fifteen months, we have not received a dime from a foreign government, not a dime, from any foreign government."[28] With the exception, he failed to note, of the money he had personally asked a Brunei official to contribute to The Enterprise's secret cause in Nicaragua. Abrams subsequently claimed that he had been technically truthful, because the funds had not yet arrived in his hands. As two prominent members of the investigative panel, Senator William S. Cohen (R, Maine) and Senator George J. Mitchell (D, Maine) concluded in reaction to this and additional examples: "Abrams used his verbal skills to obscure and deceive."[29] Why did Abrams lie? In a memoir, he recalled: "We were at war, we and the Democrats in Congress."[30]

Falsehoods came from the very top of the CIA as well, with DCI Casey misleading HPSCI members in 1985 by claiming (for example) that instead of Agency missiles going to Israel by airplane on their way to Iran, the cargo was merely oil-drilling equipment.[31] The president repeated these lies in a public press conference, although he genuinely may have thought them to be true, as lower policy officers had periodically kept him out of the decision loop in the spirit of plausible deniability (or simply wanting to have their way without hassle from the Oval Office). Casey passed away one day before the Congress began its hearings into the scandal (May 6, 1987); but justice caught up with the Agency's DDO, Claire George, who in 1992 was found guilty of perjury before the congressional investigative committee (and was later among those pardoned by President Bush).

Congressional investigators summed up the meaning of these improper covert actions. With respect to the arms-for-hostages scheme, "there was no improved relationship with Iran, no lessening of its commitment to terrorism, and no fewer American hostages." More broadly, the committee's report concluded that the affair succeeded only in "leading certain NSC and CIA personnel to deceive representatives of their own government, undermining U.S. credibility in the eyes of the world, damaging relations between the Executive and the Congress, and engaging the President in one of the worst credibility crises of any administration in U.S. history."[32]

Former DCI Admiral Turner has reflected on the meaning of the Iran-*contra* affair. "What bothers me," he told an interviewer, "is that the public and the Congress were not more enraged at the CIA's role in Iran-*contra*. The public and the Congress did not send the right message to the Agency after that." He continued: "There is no question in my mind that the Agency broke the law; there is no question that a couple of people involved ought to have gone to trial; there's no question they destroyed messages that they shouldn't have; and so on. The fact that the scandal was pushed under the rug is a bad signal to the Agency, because legality is not something you tamper with."[33] The undertow of the Iran-*contra* affair would be felt long after by those dedicated to the rule of law in the intelligence domain.

Afghanistan I

Running simultaneously with the Iran-*contra* disgrace, a second major front for covert action opened during the Reagan years in Afghanistan, the notorious graveyard of empires. In this case, the results were dramatically different from the Iran-*contra* affair; the administration obeyed the law and achieved significant accomplishments, in the most elaborate paramilitary undertaking since Laos. This operation reached its apex in the late 1980s, at which point it was consuming some 70 percent of the DO's annual budget.[34] With Iran-*contra* and this intervention in Afghanistan, the Third Option had sputtered back to life in a big way, following its low points under DCIs George H. W. Bush during the Ford administration and Admiral Stansfield Turner during the Carter years.

Even with its lack of zeal for the Third Option, the Carter national security team had been unwilling to sit by idly as the Soviet Army invaded Afghanistan in 1979, murdered its leader Hafizullah Amin, and took over Kabul, where it installed a puppet regime. President Carter took this personally, as a direct rebuff from Moscow just as he was trying to improve US-Soviet relations. With DCI Turner at the helm, the Agency began to ease the United States into a relationship with the *mujahideen*, the local anti-Soviet tribesmen and fiercely proud Afghan nationalists known today as the "Taliban." With approval from the White House, the CIA began to slowly open the budget sluices for a flow of weaponry toward these mountain fighters—chiefly batches of small arms, clothing, and, important for logistics, thousands of mules brought to Afghanistan by the CIA from around the world (mainly China).

Subsequently the Reagan administration eventually went all-out—dragging its feet at first, though, with misgivings about committing itself to a major paramilitary operation in Southwest Asia at the same time the Iran-*contra* activities were demanding time and attention in Central America; and with a feeling of skepticism among some officials in the administration about the chances for the Third Option to bring about a defeat of the Red Army in its own backyard. To compress a long and complicated story, the administration was urged toward covert action in Afghanistan more than ever before by a few members of Congress, most prominently an influential, hard-drinking, womanizing, swashbuckling Democratic lawmaker from Texas, Representative Charlie Wilson, a senior member of both HPSCI and the Appropriations Subcommittee on Defense—two key posts on the Hill that provided him with rare leverage over Third Option funding.

Initially, officials in both the White House and even the DO expressed little faith that the muscular Soviet war machine could be ousted from Afghanistan by a modestly armed assortment of bickering tribesmen from that nation's countryside, any more than a rhino would be much affected by a swarm of tsetse flies. Congressman Wilson, though, was possessed by a feverish belief in the idea of driving the Soviets out of Afghanistan. He pushed hard to win over converts within the DO and the NSC staff, as well as on Langley's Seventh Floor where William Casey seemed a naturally ally. With Wilson earmarking secret funds in DoD appropriation bills for this proposed CIA intervention—entirely legally from his perch on HPSCI and the Defense Subcommittee for Appropriations—the *mujahideen* were about to be showered with weaponry and logistical support.[35]

The main attraction for Representative Wilson, as well as (after a brief lag) for Casey and the White House, was that the Taliban were already engaged resolutely in a holy *jihad* against the Soviet military intruders, despised violators of their sovereign homeland. Killing commies—that notion had a nice ring to it for Wilson, as it did for Agency veterans of the long struggle against the USSR, not to mention the scores of unreconstructed Cold Warriors in the Reagan administration. Wilson convinced Casey, although the DCI was initially slow to believe in the possibility that the Third Option just might succeed in Southwest Asia. He finally issued an order to officers in the Operations Directorate: "I want you to get out there and win."[36]

President Reagan officially authorized the Afghan intervention as soon as Casey sent over a formal request to the White House; and, unlike the Iran-*contra* operations, the presidential approval was duly reported to Congress as well—all in harmony with the Hughes-Ryan stipulations. Members of SSCI and HPSCI reacted favorably to the proposal. Here was an opportunity to teach the Soviets a lesson about sovereignty and the importance of keeping the Red Army inside its own borders. As a result of their strong commitment to the PM operation, the CIA kept lawmakers closely apprised of its activities in Afghanistan. This allowed SSCI and HPSCI members to conduct more serious oversight than with any other Third Option during the Reagan years—with the exception of the Iran-*contra* scandal, but in that case their duties of policy scrutiny were belated thrust upon them by public reaction to the scandal after it leaked to the media.

The military supplies smuggled to the *mujahideen* by the Agency's assets in Afghanistan quickly reversed the fortunes of the Soviet 40th Army. Possession of Stinger missiles, a state-of-the-art weapon provided to them by the Agency, was a game-changer for the *mujahideen*. Soviet MI-24D attack helicopters, which had previously controlled the airspace over the battlefield, were now suddenly falling like helpless quail from the skies above Afghanistan, struck down by the Stingers. According to one authoritative report, 70 percent of the time the *mujahideen* fired a Stinger missile during this "covert" warfare (widely reported in the newspapers) a Soviet helicopter or airplane paid the price. The worm had turned and the Kremlin soon started to reconsider the rising costs of this Vietnam-like venture of its own making. Eventually, 15,000 to 28,000 Soviets would perish in the conflict (estimates vary).[37]

Important to the success of the *mujahideen* as well were crates of additional Agency supplies. High on the list of this weaponry: anti-armor, French-made Milan missiles that stopped Soviet tanks dead in their tracks, as their support helicopters were crashing down around them, when stung by Stingers. Significant, too, were SPG-9s 73 mm. recoilless rifles (a Soviet-designed weapon); small arms manufactured in China and Egypt; thousands of Datsun pickup trucks; and an endless caravan of Chinese mules for hauling food and equipment over the Agency's 300-plus infiltration routes from Pakistan into Afghanistan.[38] On average, the CIA and a few allied intelligence services gave some 60,000 tons of weapons and other supplies to the *mujahideen* each year of this covert action (1982–88). Other nations secretly joining the Agency's efforts included, for instance, Egypt, which provided tons of small arms (designed, ironically, by the Soviets).[39] Further, the Pakistani intelligence service, ISI, played a significant role in protecting the CIA's supply routes, which wended their way northward from Pakistan toward *mujahideen* encampments.

In light of these developments and the upward spiral of Red Army casualties, the Kremlin—fiercely lobbied in Moscow by the mothers of young Soviet soldiers under fire—decided to cut bait. Had the Pentagon attempted such activities openly against the Soviet military, the Kremlin may well have felt compelled to retaliate against the Agency's presence inside Afghanistan and perhaps elsewhere against the United States, with the conflict possibly escalating to unpredictable but dangerous levels. Again, some degree of plausible denial—even though the CIA's low-profile presence in Afghanistan was well known by

Moscow (and most everyone else)—dampened down the risks of a superpower confrontation.

To a large extent, the Hughes-Ryan Act had erased the potentially mischievous doctrine of plausible denial when it came to decision pathways inside the United States for the Third Option; now, within the US government, presidential approval was explicitly required, recorded, and reported to Congress. Still, plausible denial had some life left; America's clandestine interventions would allow the Soviets to assume the public posture that the military of the United States had not been at war with the Red Army. The remnants of the doctrine were useful in this situation, though appalling when adopted to violate US law during the Iran-*contra* affair.

It was a stunning victory for the determined, if outnumbered and initially outgunned, *mujahideen* forces; and it was an extraordinary outcome for the Agency and its Near East Division in the Operations Directorate, too, against America's primary Cold War foe. One study has referred to this covert action as "the biggest, meanest, and far and away most successful CIA campaign in history."[40] The costs were high, though, for the people of Afghanistan, with a million perishing as a result of the fighting. That number would have been high even without a CIA presence.

If victory could be fairly claimed by the Agency in the short term, the long-term results were less clear-cut. Like a stone thrown into a pond, the consequences of this secret intervention rippled outward. Several of the Stinger and Milan missiles were never returned to the CIA; some were sold on the open market and no doubt purchased by one terrorist faction or another. Moreover, civil war erupted in Afghanistan after the Soviet withdrawal, killing yet thousands more Afghans. The Taliban took over the country and, fatefully for the United States, welcomed Al Qaeda to settle within its territory. The terrorist group used this haven as a home base for global operations, including the 9/11 attacks against New York City and Washington, DC. Once an ally of the Carter and Reagan administrations, in the shifting currents of world affairs the *mujahideen* had become—along with Al Qaeda—America's Enemy No. One.

McGeorge Bundy, national security adviser in the Kennedy administration, once remarked: "You get all steamed up backing a rebel group for reasons that are yours and not theirs. Your reasons run out of steam and theirs do not."[41] At one time following parallel lines that had intersected for a moment in the anti-Soviet operations, the United States and the Taliban by the early 1990s were on courses that were far apart. Former DCI Richard Helms observed that the initial US policy of opposing a communist government in Afghanistan had led, through the "law of unintended consequences," to the even worse condition of a repressive Taliban regime harboring international terrorists.[42] In August of 2021, the Taliban would ride victoriously in Kabul, after quickly taking over Afghanistan in the wake of a US withdrawal from that nation after twenty years of trying to build up an indigenous pro-US military force that could stand up to the repressive insurgents.

The lessons from the Reagan administration's experiences with the Third Option in Afghanistan? First, US-supported factions abroad will always have their own goals, which may or may not coincide with America's best interests; and, second, the Third Option can have long-term outcomes that can end up harming the United States. No one has a crystal ball, obviously, so a determination of a covert action's long-range implications will always remain to some degree an insoluble dilemma. Nevertheless, officials can engage in more imaginative consideration at the time of the original planning; and they can stay closely attuned to how the operation is developing as time moves forward, making midcourse corrections as indicated.

Just how wise was it to assist the *mujahideen*/Taliban, with their seventh-century beliefs about the limited place of girls and women in society and other archaic ideas? The United States and the Taliban shared an interest in halting Soviet expansion in the Near East during the 1980s, but on little else. Was that enough for the Agency to provide them with Stinger missiles and other equipment that could be used at a later date by—who knows whom, where, when, or against whom? Aligning the United States with sects that fail to respect even the most basic democratic values can be a sure road to buyer's remorse. The 1953 Iranian intervention is another illustration: how well did the Agency—and, more broadly, the US government—track the shah's performance inside his country over the ensuing years, helping as a friend to guide him toward more popular decisions and a less vicious style of governing? The sad answer: poorly.

Poland

In Washington, the Iran-*contra* affair dealt a devastating blow to the legitimacy of the Third Option. Despite the impressive results in Afghanistan, this subterranean side of American foreign policy went into a tailspin again in the aftermath of the scandal (as it had when the CIA was being investigated in 1975 by Congress and a presidential commission for domestic spying). Before the downslide in the use of covert action, though, the Reagan administration managed to chalk up another stunning clandestine victory abroad, this time in Poland from 1983 and extending through the Bush I years in 1991. The operation was known as "QR/HELPFUL"—what James Scott and Jerel Rosati have referred to as "perhaps the most successful political action program ever," and Seth Jones as "one of the nation's greatest covert action programs."[43]

In Poland, the objectives of the Reagan administration were threefold: first, to discredit the pro-Soviet military government that had taken over Warsaw in

1980, led by General Wojciech Jaruzelski, a dedicated Marxist; second, to support and boost the morale of the labor movement in Poland known as Solidarity, a pro-democracy organization founded in 1980 and strongly opposed by the Kremlin and its handmaiden Jaruzelski; and, third, to discourage a Soviet invasion of Poland that would shatter Solidarity and all possibilities for liberalizing trends in the country, comparable to when the Red Army rolled into Hungary in 1956 and Czechoslovakia in 1968 to crush incipient anti-communist revolutions. As in the Afghanistan example, this covert action was also accorded formal presidential approval, signed by Reagan on April 11, 1982, with subsequent reporting to SSCI and HPSCI—the system working as it should.

The White House directed the CIA to use non-lethal operations—the secret arts of propaganda, as well as political and economic interventions—in pursuit of these objectives, with a special focus on help for Solidarity. Unlike the across-the-board clandestine assistance provided to the *contras* and to the *mujahideen*, under the president's rules for QR/HELPFUL, high-rung PM operations or even economic CAs would be eschewed. Poland, after all, was located within the geographical space of Eastern Europe, a sphere of influence claimed by the USSR since the Yalta accords of 1944. Resorting to the Third Option behind the Iron Curtain even at the lower rungs of covert action was provocative enough, without kicking the Russia bear in the shins near its own border with more extreme forms of covert action that might trigger a Soviet invasion into Poland.

On the one hand, the Agency would concentrate on its full panoply of propaganda activities—newspaper articles, TV, radio, banners, newsletters—and, on the other hand, it would pursue a host of limited political and economic ploys, such as supporting Solidarity rallies and labor strikes. The mother's milk of covert action—the secret distribution of funds to the anti-communist underground in Poland—was considered vital to success. Still, whether any of this was going to work and lead to a free Poland was debatable, with both skeptics and true believers watching closely from Langley and the White House, as well as inside the confines of SSCI and HPSCI on Capitol Hill.

Solidarity was sufficiently well organized by 1981 to air its criticisms publicly, using mass protests against the incompetence of the Jaruzelski administration. The general had proven unwilling to improve labor wages, as well as unable to keep down the cost of bread, butter, and other household staples. In 1980, the price of meat climbed as much as 90 percent. The regime responded to the protests by imposing martial law, accompanied by the beating and jailing of Solidarity members. Foremost among the rebels was Lech Walésa, an electrician in the shipyards at Gdańsk on the Baltic Sea and a stirring public speaker at labor rallies. On occasion, the Polish security apparatus resorted to the murder of selected outspoken figures in the movement, including a popular priest, Father Jerzy Popieluszko. Walésa, though, was becoming too famous internationally for the government to attack him physically without suffering a severe global backlash. (In 1983, Walésa would be awarded the Nobel Prize for Peace.)

In October of 1982, seven months after the birth of QR/HELPFUL, Jaruzelski upped the ante by banning the very existence of Solidarity. During this struggle between workers and the Polish communist government, the Agency excelled in its clandestine media, political, and economic activities, maintaining a profile low enough to avoid being caught red-handed by the Polish government or Soviet counterintelligence while at the same time contributing to the ability of the labor movement to stay above water. Solidarity was in a revolution mode against the Polish regime, although its members wisely pursued a Gandhi-like, non-violent, largely behind-the-scenes approach meant to dissuade the Russian Army from rolling into Warsaw from the east.

Revolutions, even of the peaceful variety, require support, though: funding, a means of communication (printing capabilities were limited in Poland), and other organizational assistance—all, by the 1980s, well-practiced Agency skills. The DO's clandestine cornucopia opened up for Solidarity and tumbling out came modern communications equipment; fax machines; photocopiers (Xerox equipment was in high demand); typewriters; reams of printing paper; ink by the barrel; thousands of postcards; silk-screening frames; video devices (including a capability for hacking Polish government TV stations and inserting Solidarity themes); anti-communist movies; computers; "Solidarity" buttons, stickers, tee-shirts, and banners, as well as posters large and small; leaflets; and even old-fashioned duplicating machines. The CIA's propaganda program in Poland had become Madison Avenue on steroids.

Since their exposure in 1972, Radio Free Europe and Radio Liberty were no longer arms of the CIA, but they continued to play an open propaganda role in advancing the American viewpoint around the globe, including backup for the pro-Solidarity covert actions through broadcasts that featured details of the Jaruzelski government's brutal crackdown on labor protests and ensuing riots in Poland.[44] Their companions included the Voice of America (also run by the State Department) and the BBC, which was especially popular around the world in part because it was widely viewed as more objective than the American stations. On the covert side of radio broadcasts, an Agency-funded "Radio Solidarity" began transmitting programs in 1982 from shifting locations inside Poland.

Not only did the CIA help to sully the standing of the Jaruzelski regime and buttress the Solidarity movement, but behind the scenes, Langley and the White House worked toward deterring Moscow's use of military force to stabilize the shaky communist satellite. The Reagan administration professed publicly that it would not tolerate Soviet intervention, which was a bluff, of course, but one that hit home as the Red Army was already beginning to reel from setbacks in Afghanistan. Further, the positive outcomes for the democracy movement in

Poland were stimulating other US-sponsored secret interventions on a more modest scale in other East European countries that, when combined, may well have weakened the Kremlin's hold over its satellite nations in that part of the world and contributed to the eventual erosion and collapse of the Soviet Empire.

By 1989, Solidarity had become a legal organization in Poland. Even more important, the nation held its first free elections that year. Solidarity overwhelmingly won at the ballot box and, in 1991, General Jaruzelski resigned from office. In the subsequent presidential election, Walésa became president of Poland; and, in 1999, eight years after the end of the Cold War, Poland joined NATO. The CIA had aided the pro-democracy movement, at least at the margins; and its activities underscored, as Jones writes, that "covert action remains critical in such areas as political action"—not just with the use of PM operations.[45]

The most important reasons for Solidarity's victory over the repressive Jaruzelski regime, though, were no doubt the charisma of Walésa and the great courage of Polish workers and their trade unions. Key, as well, were a number of other circumstances: the declining economy in Poland that undermined the communist government; public words of encouragement for Solidarity delivered publicly by Pope John Paul II; Jaruzelski's vacillation, as he found himself torn between Solidarity, on the one hand, and his fearsome puppet-masters in the Kremlin, on the other hand; and, finally—of enormous significance—the rise of a new Russian leader, President Mikhail Gorbachev, who had turned out to be something of a peacenik, willing to relax Moscow's chokehold over its satellite nations.

When elected in 1988, President George H. W. Bush continued on with a few of the Reagan administration's Third Option initiatives in Eastern Europe. More of an analysis-oriented than an operations person, though, the former spymaster and Texas politician was inclined to ask the CIA for its latest intel report on, say, unrest on the Horn of Africa rather than to urge a major clandestine intervention in some corner of the globe. Besides, it was a time for winding down the Cold War (1989–91), not for provoking the Russians and the Chinese. Perhaps, too, this president had seen enough of covert action for a while, having just tiptoed his way through the mine field of Iran-*contra*. Under President Bush I, funding for the Third Option plunged dramatically to just below 1 percent of the US intelligence budget, close to the near-dormancy levels recorded during the Church Committee days in the mid-1970s.[46] A prominent retired DO officer, Charles Cogan, wrung his hands at the end of the Bush administration; covert action would now be "largely a thing of the past," he predicted.[47]

Looking back at this period, another senior DO officer also regretted Washington's shift away from the Third Option:

> I feel that a lot more could be done in the broad area of covert action in support of policy with the proper resources allocated to the mission. I am not thinking

in terms of going back to the days when CA was 60 percent of the CIA budget; but I do feel that less than 1 percent is below minimum. It is a mission that is legally and properly assigned to the Agency and, once we can get better understanding of it and clear up some of the controversies that surround it, I think it should have additional people if we are to carry out effectively what is the mission assigned to us by the President.[48]

The Third Option Rises Again

Little did DO officers or anyone else know that, as the Third Option hiatus under the first President Bush drifted along, the United States was about to commit more resources toward clandestine interventions abroad than ever before. Another global threat—one that would prove even more immediately dangerous to Americans than Russia or China—was stirring, though still on a distant horizon and poorly understood in the United States: global terrorism. Prior to the upsurge of counterterrorist covert actions, though, the United States found itself faced with a horrific outbreak of anti-Muslim genocide in Serbia.

Serbia

The first president to serve in the White House for an extended period of time during the new post–Cold War era, Bill Clinton (1993–2001) devoted little attention to intelligence activities of any sort. Nevertheless, compared to the trough of the George H. W. Bush years, the Third Option made something of a modest comeback. Unlike Bush with his deep appreciation for intelligence, Clinton was never that interested in this subject, whether collection and analysis, counterintelligence, or covert action.[49] Part of the reason was that he had failed to connect well on a personal level with his first choice as DCI: R. James Woolsey, a fellow Yale Law School and Rhodes Scholar alumnus.

Moreover, a mood of *détente*, however temporary, had settled over superpower relations in the aftermath of the Cold War. The United States could now reduce its spending on intelligence and, especially, defense; the time for a post–Cold War budgetary "Peace Dividend" had arrived. Instead of covert operations, President Clinton's mind was laser-focused on the US economy, where he performed with high marks. America's budget was balanced during his administration for the first time since the Eisenhower years (and it hasn't been balanced since Clinton's tenure in the White House). Further, President Clinton put the final touches on the North American Free Trade Agreement (NAFTA), initiated by Bush; and he helped boost the nation's tech industries to new heights.

Even with this relative inattention to the CIA from the White House, as the 1990s progressed, the Directorate of Operations enjoyed ample funding. Former DCI Helms advised the Aspin-Brown Commission on Intelligence in 1995 that the DO "could be easily cut by 25 percent."[50] Not money but rather the lingering bad taste that covert action had left in the mouths of government officials, as a result of the Iran-*contra* scandal, was the real problem behind the temporary decline of the Third Option. While serving as President Clinton's first DCI, R. James Woolsey (1993-95) noted that "covert action is such a tiny share of the Intelligence Community these days." When asked if he thought there should be a larger role for the Third Option, his view was that this approach to foreign policy was "kinda the last arrow in the quiver you reach for. There are some cases in which there is nothing else that can be done." His examples: terrorists and WMD proliferators.[51] President Clinton's second DCI, John Deutch (1996-97) further noted, "Since the public controversies of the eighties over Iran-*contra* and activities in Central America, we have greatly reduced our capabilities to engage in covert action."[52] He vowed to "change the culture [of the DO] down to the bare bones," yet he believed as well that the United States needed "to maintain, and perhaps even expand, covert action as a policy tool."[53] In other words, he was torn on the best way to handle the Third Option. Deutch eventually became thoroughly disliked in the Operations Directorate for what its officers perceived as his lack of interest and support for their activities.

Even though the president was relatively detached from the Intelligence Community and its functions, the Clinton administration did provide authority for a few significant secret initiatives related to war fighting in the Balkans, a troubled area in Southeast Europe comprising Bosnia, Croatia, Kosovo (a tiny corner of Serbia), Macedonia, the highly militant and aggressive Serbia-Montenegro, and Slovenia. The CIA deployed PM officers to train and arm Bosnians; and, on the collection side of the intelligence mission, a high priority was US intelligence surveillance support for NATO bombing missions, designed to dissuade Serbia from committing further atrocities against its neighbors, which had been going on since 1995.[54] Cameras mounted on Agency drones (unmanned aerial vehicles or UAVs, a new initiative now in the hands of the DoD and the Agency) served several purposes, from monitoring battleground developments in Serbia to using aerial imagery as a means for accumulating irrefutable proof that the Serbs had committed genocidal assaults against Bosnian Muslims, Kosovars (a people chiefly of Albanian descent), and others who got in the way of their designs on regional expansion spearheaded by a vicious policy of "ethnic cleansing."

The Serbian methods of paramilitary warfare included mass executions of men, women, and children by firing squads, as well as the additionally subhuman war tactic of mass rape. Their leader, President Slobodan Milosevic, informed US General Wesley Clark that Serbia didn't need NATO involvement to bring peace to the Balkans. He knew the best way to deal with the Kosovars and other enemies in the region: "We kill them. We kill them all!"[55]

By 1999, NATO had resigned itself to the reality that diplomacy was not going to resolve Serbian aggression. The extensive bombing of Serbia began, with standby plans for a ground invasion if necessary. As a complement to the bombing, Clark turned as well to international law as a tool and the UN's International Criminal Tribunal on Yugoslavia indicted Milosevic in the midst of the bombing campaign, bringing the war to an uneasy end. Throughout this fighting, the Serbs had used propaganda broadcasts extensively. Clinton's DCIs, Woolsey and Deutch, were both "techies," fascinated by techint or technical intelligence, what the Agency refers to in slang as "toys"—such as fancy surveillance satellites with high-resolution cameras. Of less interest to them was the DO's specialty of "humint" or human intelligence, that is, the use of agents to gather intelligence as well as engage in covert actions. Nevertheless, during the Clinton years the CIA did pursue some forms of the Third Option in the Balkans, with an emphasis on propaganda and political operations in support of anti-Serbian opposition groups engaged in the struggle against Milosevic and his military thugs.

Iraq

As well, the Clinton administration tried its hand at eliminating Saddam Hussein. The Iraqi leader had sent an assassination team to Kuwait with orders to kill visiting former US president George H.W. Bush and his wife, Barbara, in April of 1993—an act of retaliation for Bush I's initiation of the First Persian Gulf War against Saddam in 1990–91. The Iraqi leader was a target for another reason as well. He had ordered his anti-aircraft sites to fire at American aircraft assigned in the aftermath of the First Gulf War to enforce a no-fly zone over Iraq. Given the fact that the United States remained at military odds with Iraq during this period, the executive order against assassinations was waived by the White House when it came to Saddam, and the operations were properly reported to SSCI and HPSCI. The paranoid and elusive leader managed to foil the coup schemes for the time being, however, and he avoided DO hit squads by constantly moving around the countryside in disguise.

~~~

While covert action remained in a relatively lethargic stage during the Clinton years, the United States was unknowingly approaching the rim of a vortex. The Age of Terrorism was at hand. The presence of this threat would exert a strong sense in Washington that a rapid and expansive revival of the Third Option was necessary as a shield and sword against this new threat. In the Clinton years, the Agency's initial concerns about various terrorist organizations turned mainly toward Al Qaeda. Led by Saudi-born Osama bin Laden, this *jihadist* faction was considered the likely culprit behind simultaneous bombings in 1998 of US embassies in Kenya and Tanzania, and two years later against the US naval vessel USS *Cole*, a guided missile destroyer anchored off the port city of Aden in Yemen. Over 200 Africans and a dozen Americans perished in the embassy attacks, along with another seventeen American sailors on the *Cole* in the Gulf of Aden.

As events in Serbia and Iraq played out, with the United States and other members of NATO pounding the Milosevic regime with overt aerial bombardments and the hunt for Saddam ongoing, the terrorist organization Al Qaeda, now based in Afghanistan after a period of residence in Sudan, had clearly escalated its plans for attacks overseas against the United States. America was about to learn that its homeland was going to be a target as well, as terrorism began to spread like a deadly virus across the continents. In pace with this new challenge, the CIA was on the verge of a third Golden Age of covert action.

6

The Third Option in an Age of Terror, 2000–2020

Covert Action and Counterterrorism

The US posture of taking the foot off the covert action pedal, to a considerable extent, during the 1990s would change dramatically with the next administration, led by George W. Bush. The reason was a single tragic event: the 9/11 strikes against the American homeland, one year after the *Cole* attack in Yemen had further emboldened Al Qaeda.

Terrorism I: 9/11

President Bush II initially placed an emphasis on use of the Third Option that was barely higher than that of the Clinton administration—until September 11, 2001. Prior to that fateful day, the second Bush administration was more likely in this post–Cold War era to fund friendly groups overseas through the State Department by way of *overt* stipends, as with his public support to Iranian opposition groups; or through the National Endowment for Democracy (NED), a bipartisan non-governmental organization that openly supports democracy movements around the world (as it did in Egypt during the Arab Spring, for example). These approaches were a dramatic departure from the Cold War days of secret operations carried out by the CIA around the world, in the manner of Iran, Guatemala, and Chile. After 9/11, though, counterterrorism became the centerpiece of US foreign policy activities and, as a result, the primary mission of Third Option specialists at Langley as well. The marching orders from the White House and Capitol Hill were clear: no more 9/11s—or perhaps even worse forms of mayhem against the United States using weapons of mass destruction (WMD).

Presidents Bush II and Barack Obama relied on Langley for leadership against the likes of Al Qaeda and other *jihadist* organizations that had vowed to destroy Israel and its close ally, the United States. The Agency, along with the Intelligence Community as a whole, had failed in their lack of specific warning to Washington officials and US citizens about the impending 9/11 attacks. Moreover, the few general warnings that were provided, including a blinking red light from the CIA in 1995 that "aerial terrorism seems likely at some point" and would be aimed at American skyscrapers, had yielded no serious responses by the Clinton or the Bush II administrations to strength the American counterterrorism shield, such as tightening airport security across the nation.[1]

Still, the Intelligence Community knew more about terrorism and counterterrorism than any other segment of the government and had even infiltrated a few assets into *jihadist* factions; so this Bush administration turned to the CIA and its companion agencies, if only by default. The exploration that follows of this latest phase in covert action is shorter than in earlier chapters, because so much of the Agency's recent activities remains classified. Still, a fair amount can be found in the public record about America's immediate Third Option responses to the 9/11 treachery.

Afghanistan II

The most important use of the Third Option by President Bush II was Operation "Enduring Freedom": the immediate steps taken after 9/11 to deploy the CIA's paramilitary components and the Pentagon's Special Forces, as well as US Air Force bombers, in a combined overt/covert counterattack against Al Qaeda and its Taliban hosts in Afghanistan. George Tenet, the DCI at the time, refers to this covert action as "one of the great successes in Agency history."[2] He is not alone in that judgment.

A spearhead force of 110 paramilitary officers from the Operations Directorate were the first US armed contingent to enter Afghanistan after 9/11, in search of bin Laden and other members of Al Qaeda. Wisely, their opening gambit was to recruit an important local ally: the Northern Alliance, a hardened tribe of warriors who opposed the Taliban's draconian rule in their country. Organized into "Jawbreaker" teams, some Special Operations Group officers from the DO rode on horseback across the Afghan countryside with King George largess stuffed into their saddlebags—some $10 million in cash—for delivery to assets in the Northern Alliance, which had been led by a former *mujahideen* commander, the charismatic Ahmad Shah Masoud, until his murder by Taliban operatives a few days prior to the 9/11 attacks against the United States. These Agency officers "handed out bundles [of money] like candy on Halloween," reports Steve Coll.[3] They also engaged in direct fighting, with one young PM officer—Johnny Michael "Mike" Spann, from Alabama and a graduate of Auburn University—being the first US casualty in this vital but dangerous mission.[4]

The combined force of the SOG officers, plus 316 additional Pentagon Special Forces personnel, was never able to track down bin Laden; that gratifying day would have to wait a decade's worth of further searching, as he shifted location from a hideout in the mountains of Afghanistan to a concealed sanctuary in Pakistan. Moreover, the Bush White House ended this stellar paramilitary campaign in Afghanistan prematurely, as the president and his aides diverted US resources toward an ill-timed and misguided invasion of Iraq in 2003—a country that had played no role in the 9/11 attacks and (although alleged by the Bush administration to the contrary) had no WMD ready for use against the United States. Nevertheless, the covert action in Afghanistan, along with some critical overt elements—the Special Forces contingent and the B-52 bombing—quickly routed the Taliban regime. Operation "Enduring Freedom," and its 2002 spinoff in eastern Afghanistan, Operation "Anaconda," had earned a high place in any evaluation of America's most successful covert actions.

After this exceptionally efficient overthrow of the Taliban regime—an operation which, according to one keen observer, "exceeded expectations" with victory secured within five weeks[5]—the CIA turned to the Third Option over and over again in the struggle against global terrorists. Never before in the nation's history had covert action been relied on so frequently. These clandestine interventions, driven by the fear of additional terrorist attacks against the United States or its armies in the field, coupled with America's determination to avenge the death toll from 9/11, had flowered into yet another Golden Age for the Third Option, surpassing the earlier peaks reached during the Eisenhower and Reagan administrations in the frequency of clandestine operations, as well as their magnitude and deadliness.

As Treverton has observed, "Covert action has become, post-9-11, primarily paramilitary, with the CIA operating either independently or, more often, with military operators."[6] The *New York Times* reported that, following the Bush II presidency, the Obama administration further revved up counterterrorism-oriented covert action (CT/CA) operations early in the president's tenure, with the result that the Agency "became a paramilitary organization as much as a spying agency."[7]

From the vantage point of a seasoned CIA expert on clandestine operations, "Barack Obama was the Covert Action President"—a conclusion that stemmed chiefly from the growing importance of CIA drone attacks during this president's tenure. Having begun during the Bush II years, the robotic conduct of aerial covert action increased tenfold under Obama. As well, the Obama administration vigorously pursued other, more traditional PM activities directed against terrorist cells. The most persistent target was Afghanistan, in support of US combat troops stationed there, but also in Libya and several other locations around the world. Syria became a country of special interest, because of the harboring by its government of terrorists and its engagement in acts of barbarism against dissenters among its own citizens.[8]

Syria

Despite America's growing reliance on PM drone operations, which had become the new bone and sinew of covert action, the DO's older bags of tricks had not been forgotten in the wake of the 9/11 tragedy. An example is President Obama's resort to Operation "Timber Sycamore" during the ongoing civil war in Syria. A hybrid secret intervention with both CIA and Pentagon participation, Sycamore drew down the Agency's operating budget by more than $1 billion, making it "one of the costliest covert action programs in the history of the CIA."[9] The Obama national security team vowed to take a stand "secretly"—although, in fact, this was another "overt-covert action" as it turned out, widely reported on by the media—against the Syrian government in the central and northern expanses of that Middle East nation.

A simultaneous target in Syria was a vicious terrorist organization with the name Islamic State in Iraq and Syria (ISIS, known as well as ISIL, the Islamic State of Iraq and the Levant, or simply the Islamic State, and, in Arabic, *Dalat*—"the State"). Members of ISIS relished burning its captured adversaries to death, filming the execution and distributing the images worldwide. In opposition to these Sunni extremists, as well as the Syrian government, the CIA recruited and trained local men—chiefly indigenous rebels—to form a paramilitary band of war-fighters. The Agency trainees included members of the group Nusra Front, which was affiliated with Al Qaeda no less. Al-Nusra was supposedly willing to fight alongside the United States to counter Syria's authoritarian ruler, Bashar al-Assad. The Nusra Front hoped to establish a new regime in Damascus under which it might survive and prosper.

It is said that politics makes for strange bedfellows; obviously the Third Option can, too. In this instance, the United States found itself in loose partnership with several groups and individuals who were often poorly aligned with the objectives of the Obama administration. The context of the Syrian covert action was the series of revolutions that began, in late 2010, in the Middle East and North Africa and is known as the "Arab Spring." The fever of revolution spread to Syria and an indigenous faction of rebels rose up against that country's dictator, Assad. The surrounding nations of Turkey, Saudi Arabia, Qatar, and Jordan jumped at the opportunity presented by unrest in Syria to advance their own grievances against the regime in Damascus. Also seeing an opportunity to rid the Middle East of Assad, a ruthless tyrant who had used nerve gas against the rebels (the Free Syrian Army or FSA), the Obama administration joined this diverse coalition in 2012 and, the next year, launched a covert action designed to arm and train the Syrian insurrectionists.

Preparing these paramilitary troops for war fell mainly on the shoulders of the CIA in 2013, with much of the funding and arms for the rebels coming from oil-rich Saudi Arabia. Jordan and Turkey provided secret bases for these preparations and, when the training was completed, the Agency's small army enjoyed some initial victories on the Syrian battlefield. Throughout these months, though, the coalition partners communicated with one another ineffectively and moved forward uneasily, with disparate—often conflicting—objectives. Further complicating matters was the fact that the anti-Assad rebels were made up of some fifty different groups inside Syria, ranging from moderates who sought to bring democracy to Damascus to rabid *jihadists* (like al-Nusra) who often sided with ISIS, one of the enemies—along with Assad—the Obama administration was trying to subdue. A study of this uprising reported that *jihadists* accounted for some 60 percent of the men recruited by the CIA.[10] Efforts at coordination among these nations and factions began to fray apart like a rope under too great a strain.

As if that situation were insufficiently complex, the civil war offered another, even more daunting, feature: an alliance between the Russian Federation and Iran with Assad. Russian bombers and jet aircraft soon pounded the CIA's recruits on Syrian battlefields and the original Third Option cadre of some 5,000 warriors shrank to just a handful of pro-US paramilitary soldiers willing to continue the fight. According to some reports, the Agency's "army" had dwindled to only four or five men![11] Moreover, the Nusra Front (today known as Hayat Tahrir al-Sham, and still linked to Al Qaeda) absconded with some of the weaponry supplied by the Saudis and the CIA, including tank-destroying missiles. Plus, America's Saudi, Turkish, and Qatari "allies" backed ISIS from time to time as another possible means of eliminating the Assad regime, even as the United States was attempting to destroy that terrorist organization.

An added layer of confusion stemmed from the high desertion rates among the anti-Assad rebels, including many of the best warriors picked by the CIA who were now rejoining *jihadist* elements taking with them their Saudi-CIA weaponry and equipment. Further, combat between and among the fifty factions proved commonplace—these same men who were supposed to be devoting their energies, and all that Agency training, toward overthrowing the Assad regime. As political scientist Krishnan puts it, the various groups spent "almost as much effort fighting each other [as] fighting the Syrian Army."[12] By 2015, the United States resorted to another possibility: providing support to Kurdish fighters in Syria, who were also fighting Assad; but the Kurds were at war already with one of America's covert action partners, Turkey, and further, they were in secret cahoots with none other than the Russians as both engaged in ongoing warfare against the CIA-trained rebels. If these shifting sands of alliance leave the reader's head spinning, that is how national security officials in the Obama administration must have felt, too.

The whole Timber Sycamore operation had to be scrapped after a four-year effort of planning, training, and disjointed fighting, in what turned out to be a Bay of Pigs in slow motion. President Trump brought the covert action to an end in July of 2017. Adding insult to injury, corruption had tangled these events as well. Weapons provided by the CIA for dispersal to the rebels were stolen by members of the Jordanian intelligence service, the General Intelligence Directorate or GID (known also as the Mukhabarat), including thousands of Kalashnikov (AK-47) assault rifles, mortars, rocket-propelled grenades, and anti-tank guided missiles. The Jordanian intelligence officers reportedly pawned these weapons and equipment on the black market and pocketed the profits for themselves.[13] So much for "friendly intelligence liaison" (although Jordan had worked well with Agency officers in some previous, small-scale counterterrorism activities).[14]

Before the United States stumbled into the Syria fiasco, the CIA should have learned a clear lesson from its experiences with paramilitary operations in other countries—mainly, to succeed, the CIA needs to have at least one major trustworthy and dedicated ally on the ground in the targeted nation. This was not exactly the profile presented by the kaleidoscopic and dubious alliances in Syria during the Obama years. Nor did the Obama administration manage to secure a reliable local ally in 2011 when the CIA provided PM assistance to rebels in Libya who were attempting a coup against Muammar al-Qaddafi. He was murdered in the chaos that descended on this oil-rich, but star-crossed, nation.[15]

In Laos from 1962 to 1968, the Hmong tribesmen had served in the role of battle-ready soldiers loyal to their CIA advisers, allowing the Operations Directorate to mount a six-year war against communists in that nation and thwarting their movement into Vietnam to fight against US troops. In another example, one of the reasons the PM action in Afghanistan succeeded so well immediately after the 9/11 attacks was the presence of the Northern Alliance, a tortoise-shell tough cadre of Afghan anti-Taliban guerrillas wedded in a marriage of convenience to the CIA, the US military, and King George's cavalry. No such ingredient was at hand for the Syrian venture. Moreover, as Stephen Weissman notes: "There is no evidence that the intelligence committees [SSCI and HPSCI] ever used their powers to prevent, seriously modify, or terminate this fatally flawed operation."[16]

Terrorism II

Inside the Special Activities Division that is housed within the DO at Agency Headquarters, one approach was racing to the top of the CIA's most favorite instruments of clandestine intervention: the use of drones to hunt down, spy on, and "neutralize" known and suspected terrorists, drawing on White House, Pentagon, and Agency target lists. The drone had become the King of Covert Action.

Assassination as a CIA practice had not been entirely dormant since the Kennedy years. For instance, the Clinton administration targeted anti-Amerian warlords in Somalia, sometimes successfully, in another quasi-battlefield waiver of the Ford Executive order against assassinations. These operations were in response to assaults against US Special Forces on the Horn of Africa, memorably captured by the *Black Hawk Down* book and film.[17] Further, recall how Saddam Hussein entered the CIA's crosshairs during and after the First Persian Gulf War (1990–91). The Iraq leader proved as elusive—and as lucky—as Fidel Castro, until finally captured by US troops in 2003 during the Second Persian Gulf War. He was tried in Iraq by a US military tribunal and hanged.

Now, though, this extreme form of covert action had been resuscitated to advance America's US foreign policy agenda with a vengeance. Especially controversial were "signature strikes" by drones, aimed at broad categories of suspected terrorists in the Middle East and elsewhere—nameless individuals killed because they were in questionable locations or had the superficial markings of a terrorist, say, someone in or near a building thought to be a *jihadist* haven. In one instance, a man in Afghanistan was reportedly killed by a US drone because he was roughly 6'5". Maybe it was bin Laden, who stood at that height. As it turned out, he was not.

Osama bin Ladin

On a graph, the incidents of drone attacks against suspected terrorists in the Middle East and Southwest Asia, along with northern and central Africa, would be represented by a line drawn steadily upward from the Bush II through the Obama and Trump presidencies. The killing of a high-profile target provided President Obama with his administration's most prized use of covert action. This operation involved a paramilitary hit in 2011 against Osama bin Laden (OBL, in spy shorthand). He had finally been tracked down, as a result of skillful intelligence work by the CIA and the NSA, at a compound near Pakistan's "West Point" military academy in Abbottabad, a city north of Islamabad, the nation's capital.

In an internal debate over whether to use a CIA or DoD drone to take out OBL or to send in military commandos, the latter won out on grounds that a small Special Forces team might be able to enter Pakistani airspace more effectively, then capture rather than kill the Qaeda leader—even though the inclination among leading DO operatives was to murder the arch-terrorist. "I want his head shipped back in a box filled with dry ice," declared Cofer Black, head of the CIA's Counterterrorism Center, to fellow DO officers.[18] Plus, US boots on the ground—in contrast to a CIA drone strike—might enable the commandos to sweep up a bonanza of important intelligence documents in OBL's residence. The team could confirm, too, beyond the shadow of a doubt, that the target truly was the elusive mastermind behind the 9/11 attacks.

The debate over whether Operation "Geronimo" (later renamed Operation "Neptune Spear," when criticism arose after the event about adopting the name of a Native American hero for a secret government activity) should be carried out by the DoD or the CIA took decision-makers into the arcane legal terrain of Title 10 versus Title 50 of the US Military Code. Title 10 covers DoD operations, which are meant to take place in battleground situations; Title 50 covers CIA paramilitary operations, which can extend outside formal battlefields and are designed to be deniable intelligence operations. Neptune Spear could have fallen under either title, since it was a hybrid intrusion relying on information acquired by the Intelligence Community, but with the possibility of turning in the direction of a guns-on-the-ground foray by the military's Joint Special Operations Command (JSOC). The administration chose Title 50 for the operation's basic legal authority, in a nod to the CIA's leadership role in planning the raid, along with the deniability advantage under this article that comes with intelligence activities. Nonetheless, JSOC would field the team actually going into Pakistan with responsibility for the capture-or-kill mission.

The Agency's paramilitary contingent had been eager to show its stuff and was disappointed when the administration settled on the Pentagon for this important boots-on-the-ground assignment that SOG officers (most of whom had a DoD background) thought they could handle just as well. As Obama's DCI Leon E. Panetta recounts, he considered a CIA-led raid, but concluded that an operation of this kind would be better conducted by Defense Department's special operations forces. "The biggest problem was that it would be very difficult to deploy [CIA personnel] as a unit," he has written. "Each of them would have to sneak into Pakistan under a different guise and somehow put the logistics together. It was asking too much." Panetta further recalled the chief reason for a hybrid CIA/DoD combination: "The unique aspect of Title 50 operations—covert action—is that you don't acknowledge them."[19] The concepts of secrecy and deniability didn't last long, though, with Operation "Neptune Spear" soon to become one of the most public and celebrated joint DoD/CIA Third Options in American history. The result was neither caterpillar nor butterfly—a complicated and lethal blend of JSOC military and Agency intelligence capabilities.

Since enactment of the Hughes-Ryan Act in 1974, Title 50 operations require reporting to SSCI and HPSCI on Capitol Hill—an added step that concerned President Obama with respect to the high sensitivity of this plan. Panetta, a former member of Congress, thought it was not only in accordance with the law (the Intelligence Oversight Act of 1980 required *prior* reporting on covert actions, that is, before their implementation), but politic as well to inform at least the top lawmakers on the Hill. And he did so; and they, of course, maintained the strict secrecy requirements necessary to protect the lives of the commandos. The president was upset by this outreach to Congress; but Panetta had made the right call—legally, and in the spirit of the post–Church Committee intelligence oversight expectations, not to mention the Constitution's devotion to shared powers between the executive and the legislative branches of government.

The daring forty-minute raid into Abbottabad was carried out by Navy SEALS who fast-roped down from the Blackhawk helicopters into the suspected bin Laden compound. They were surrounded by darkness and, almost immediately, an exchange of gunfire erupted with OBL's security guards. The scene was made all the more chaotic by the crash of one of the aircraft. In this dangerous and confusing setting, the capture of OBL alive proved unfeasible. Under fire as they entered bin Laden's two-story home and climbed the stairs to his study, the commandos shot him to death, along with one of his sons and some bodyguards. The raiding team fled the compound intact in a second rescue helicopter, taking with them bin Laden's body and a rich lode of intelligence documents. Out of respect for the Muslim faith, bin Laden's remains were scrupulously honored with customary Islamic practices and buried at sea within twenty-four hours.

In this joint military-and-intelligence mission, Special Forces had done the heavy lifting; nevertheless, the CIA and other US spy agencies had played an important part in the success of the operation, too, by providing intelligence about bin Laden's whereabouts, along with recommendations on logistics that aided the attack and the useful cloak of deniability that accompanies Title 50. In retrospect, given the DoD helicopter crashes in both this case and during the Carter administration hostage rescue attempt, the Agency's SOG officers might warrant a try next time.

Despite concern by the president and his aides that it would fail, Operation "Neptune Spear" was an almost flawless maneuver—with some luck involved, when the dragon of Chance entered the picture and no one was injured in the helicopter crash. Although they have been few in number (and the hybrid rescue operation was a disaster during the Carter presidency), Neptune Spear demonstrated that joint CIA/Special Forces operations can lead to covert victories. Indeed, this one earned high marks in the modern history of covert actions (a ranking discussed further in Chapter 9).[20]

Terrorism III

The most significant recent change in the conduct of covert actions, then, has been the adoption of CIA drone attacks against suspected terrorists, leading to the largest paramilitary program in the Agency's history, mostly directed toward Afghanistan and often concentrated for staging purposes in the North West Frontier region of Pakistan.[21] These UAVs—including the Predator and the Reaper, among a fleet of other quiet, low-flying aircraft, large and small—feature Hellfire missiles nestled beneath their fuselage that can release fiery thunderbolts of havoc on targets below, making this the Agency's most deadly form of covert action ever.

The latest version of drone missilery—the "Ninja" or R9X—has been used near Idlib in northwest Syria against a Qaeda affiliate known as Hurras al-Din, formerly the Nusra Front group armed by the CIA in its earlier Syrian covert action.[22] (Alliances can shift as quickly as sand dunes in the Middle and Near East.) In place of an explosive warhead, the R9X features six long blades that deploy a moment before slicing the targeted victim to death—however gruesome, supposedly a more surgical weapon that will reduce civilian casualties and property damage.

Following the introduction of US drone warfare by the second Bush administration, President Obama stepped up the use of this approach and other forms of PM activity, not only on explicitly authorized battlefields in Iraq and Afghanistan but in Pakistan, Somalia, Yemen, Mali, and Syria as well. Indeed, more US drone strikes occurred in Pakistan alone during Obama's first year in office than in the full eight years of the preceding Bush II administration. In Obama's second term, the frequency of Agency drone attacks diminished as the president recoiled from the rising number of accidental civilian deaths overseas among the targeted victims. The Trump administration less vigorously monitored the use of drones while simultaneously further reducing the number of strikes outside of war zones like Afghanistan and Syria. Despite this slight decline in drone attacks near the end of the Trump years, the number of CIA bases in the Sahara expanded to include the Sahel region of Niger and the nation of Chad. In the first year of the Biden administration, drone targeting outside of war zones continued to taper downward.[23]

In 2006, *New York Times* journalist James Risen warned of "the militarization of American intelligence."[24] Despite some falloff in the use of drone attacks in recent years, this judgment appeared true, not only with respect to CIA drone warfare and other PM operations but in the intelligence-collection domain as well—a result of the Agency's new capacities for rapidly downloading high-resolution battlefield photography, which is an invaluable gift to field commanders on the eve or in the heat of battle.

Some officers within the Operations Directorate applaud the development of drones as the most effective form of covert action yet devised, the key element in the Third Golden Age of Covert Action. A consideration in their praise, too, is the fact that this latest approach to the Third Option has breathed life back into the Agency at a time when it had stumbled badly and lost its luster in national security circles after the intelligence failures of 9/11 and its erroneous prediction in 2002 that Iraq possessed WMDs. Others, though, including former senior Agency analyst and D/CIA John O. Brennan (2013–17), view Langley's embrace of drone warfare as a disquieting diversion from the CIA's basic mandate as an analytic organization, not a combat unit.[25] In Brennan's view, the Agency had been created to gather information from around the world and make sense of it for US leaders; it was not meant to serve as a worldwide killing machine for the United States.[26]

Some fifty years ago, DCI Helms worried about this trend toward militarizing the CIA, cautioning against "an ominous drift" of Langley toward becoming just an auxiliary unit of the Pentagon at the expense of its broader collection-and-analysis responsibilities.[27] Unsettling, too, have been the accidental deaths caused by Agency and Pentagon drones. A *Times* journalist tells of a drone strike in Pakistan that killed tribal elders who had convened merely to discuss a dispute over chromite mining.[28] The Bureau of Investigative Journalism reported that, in 2008, one-third of all Agency drone strikes killed at least one child.[29] Another controversy revolves around whether suspected terrorists should be assassinated by drone missiles or only identified by the aircraft's cameras for capture by US Special Forces or CIA/SOG operatives, then brought to trial. One suspect successfully targeted for death in 2011 was Anwar al-Awlaki, an American citizen and Muslim cleric who fled this country for Yemen, where he became a popular internet personality spouting anti-American rhetoric throughout the Middle East and Southwest Asia. He was perhaps driven away from his more benign stance of traditional preaching in Virginia to a posture of radicalism by ham-handed FBI surveillance methods used against him when he lived in the United States.[30]

Disputes have arisen as well over the procedures for establishing a drone target. In 2013, the Obama administration established rules for this important step, codified in a Presidential Policy Guidance or PPG. Potential targets are reportedly based on recommendations primarily from attorneys in the CIA and occasionally other agencies in the Intelligence Community, the Department of Defense, and the Department of Justice. A couple of additional lawyers on the NSC staff are assigned to check and collate the hit list. The NSC Deputies Committee, which consists of the second-in-command at the recommending departments, reviews the request before it travels along to the D/CIA and the DNI for their final approval. The next step is a review by the SecDef and the SecState on the NSC Principals Committee, which gives a thumbs-up or thumbs-down decision on a case-by-case basis for the targets "nominated" for this sardonically named "goodbye list," who could then be "lawfully incinerated" (according to the language of the authorizing documents).

If the target selection is controversial—say, an American citizen living abroad—the president is brought into the decision loop and must approve the strike before it can be implemented. The congressional oversight committees, SSCI and HPSCI, are kept informed of the targeting decisions as well; but sometimes the rules of prior notice and an opportunity for lawmakers to weigh in have been given short shrift. In times of a fast-moving emergency, the president alone has the authority to approve a hit, followed by reports to HPSCI and SCCI "in a timely manner." Under the Biden presidency, the rules for CIA drone attacks have tightened—especially with respect to assurances that women and children are nowhere near the strike zone.

Still, critics insist that the decision to kill someone overseas is too important for even the improved Biden administration's internal reviews of targeting. As a supplement, they argue, the United States ought to have an assassination warrant process, as required for national-security wiretaps by the Foreign Intelligence Surveillance Court (created in 1978 by the Foreign Intelligence Surveillance Act or FISA). It seems strangely incongruous to critics that a judicial warrant is required for a national security wiretap but not for a national security assassination. Moreover, critics add, this extreme form of the Third Option ought to be more formally reported to SSCI and HPSCI members in every instance *before* the drones take flight on their existential, remote-controlled missions, allowing designated lawmakers a chance to offer their viewpoint on the targeting in advance of its implementation. Discord has surfaced, further, over the periodic lack of coordination between DoD and CIA drone attacks. Sometimes they are undertaken against the same, or nearby, targets without Pentagon or DO officers knowing about one another's flight paths and precise targeting intentions.[31]

As with every other undertaking by the government (or any other large organization), management challenges and occasional snafus occur—only in this instance with lives at stake. Disagreements abound, as well, over whether accountability is maintained more effectively over DoD or CIA drone activity—back to the tensions between Title 10 and Title 50, respectively. Some say accountability is better with DoD, since it engages in overt warfare and this is just one of its weapons on the battlefield, whereas the CIA is all stealth and deception around the world. Drone attacks carried out by the Agency, though, are subject to both White House approval and HPSCI/SSCI review procedures. In contrast, military drone attacks—however "overt" they may be compared to the Agency's furtive profile—are far less transparent to members of Congress and elide the important layer of accountability that SSCI and HPSCI can provide.

Thus, CIA drone operations seem to many observers more carefully examined by lawmakers on this legislative review panels, and in advance, than those launched by the Department of Defense.

Although these arguments remain tangled and often unclear, one thing is certain: the drone form of PM ops is rife with controversy. This manifestation of the Third Option is far distant from the Agency's original analytic charge in the National Security Act of 1947, and policy in this domain continues to suffer from procedural and oversight inexactitudes—chief among them, precise and fair steps for establishing the drone kill list. There are larger questions. Should the CIA even be engaged in drone assassinations—"targeted killings" or "hits," in the terms preferred by intelligence and military officers? Indeed, should the United States pursue any forms of assassination at all, except in the most dire emergencies of self-defense?

The founding National Security Act of 1947 never envisioned CIA officers engaged in the fiery killing of America's adversaries with Hellfire missiles. The Agency's job was primarily to inform—educate—Washington decision makers about the latest developments in world affairs. It would appear more logical to leave such "kinetic" activities as drone hunting to the military, although with dramatically improved accountability procedures that match the current approval and reporting process for the Third Option (examined in Chapters 7 and 8)—and only when used on authorized battlefields. The phrase "authorized battlefields" should mean actions taken only with the prior approval of both chambers of Congress and based on some reasonable degree of specificity—as opposed to such broad and meaningless grants of authority from lawmakers as an order to "fight global terrorism."

President Trump and the CIA

The funnel of covert action since 1947 reviewed in this book comes to an end with the Donald J. Trump administration. Although the Third Option reportedly expanded in the frequency of its use during the Trump years (despite somewhat fewer drone attacks against suspected terrorists outside of authorized battlefields), the handling of the topic here is comparative thin because less is known about the activities of the CIA the closer one comes to the present. What has gone on recently remains largely classified. Some aspects of the relationship between the Trump presidency and the CIA have made their way into the public sphere, though, and are summarized here.

The four years from 2017 through 2020 make for a peculiar interlude in relationships between the White House and the CIA, in what journalist David Ignatius has referred to as the Trump administration's "four-year battle with the intelligence community."[32] In the first place, Trump played fast and loose with all of the nation's intelligence agencies to a degree that has exceeded the action of any other president. The first dubious move came during the presidential campaign in 2016, when candidate Trump refused to accept the traditional daily briefings on world affairs that the Agency has traditionally provided to leading presidential contenders since the 1950s, as a way of preparing them with up-to-date information on world affairs for immediately more effective leadership in the White House under a new president.[33]

Once in office, President Trump rejected receiving the most important US intelligence report: the *President's Daily Brief*. He later changed his mind, but insisted on being given only an oral briefing on the document rather than having to wade through the written version. As a result, the president lost much of the detail and texture reported in its pages, which are not really a burden to read; indeed, the *PDB* is attractively presented (glossy and in four colors, in the manner of an expensive fashion magazine), lively to read, and certainly informative.[34] The loss in ignoring its detailed contents? A more complex truth about world events and conditions is far more likely to emerge from a study of its pages than from just a selective oral briefing, although a prudent president will request both. Trump stated that when it came to international affairs, "my primary consultant is myself, and I have good instincts for this stuff."[35] It was an approach to leadership reminiscent of the ancient Roman emperors who read animal entrails to predict the future.

The president also said early in his single term that neither the chair of the Joint Chiefs of State (C/JCS), the director of Central Intelligence (D/CIA), or the director of National Intelligence (DNI) would be welcome at most of his NSC meetings, whereas their presence had been routinely expected and valued by previous administrations. He later changed his mind about this prohibition as well; however, he still paid only marginal attention to these officials, except for D/CIA Mike Pompeo, a former member of Congress from Kansas who had become his Polonius. On the eve of his failed re-election bid, Trump—in a constantly huffy mood—cancelled all meetings in the Oval Office with top CIA briefers, favoring instead a reliance on intelligence reporting from his political appointees, none of whom had any significant intelligence experience.

Moreover, the president bizarrely continued to insist that he had won the presidential election even though all the facts indicated a resounding defeat for him in the popular and Electoral College balloting. In this state of denial—a great danger to America's democracy, which depends on a peaceful transition from one administration to another (a point of catastrophic failure for many nations in the past)—the president blocked CIA intelligence briefings for his victorious opponent, former vice president Joe Biden of the Obama administration, even though these informational sessions have been the norm in past transitions.

During the Chinese fire drill that intelligence had become, the president pardoned his first National Security Adviser, General Michael Flynn, a former director of the Defense Intelligence Agency (DIA), who had been found guilty after only twenty-four days in office of lying to FBI officers who were investigating his ties during the presidential campaign to Russian intelligence officers. Once pardoned by Trump and free from prison, Flynn (in a prelude to the January 6, 2021 insurgency) "called for a military coup and the imposition of martial law to overturn the elections" that had been fairly won by Biden.[36] It was as though the United States had turned back the clock to 1860 when pro-Confederate would-be assassins vowed to prevent Abraham Lincoln's inauguration, because the Rail Splitter had defeated their pro-South, pro-slavery candidate.

Early in his administration Trump had selected Pompeo to serve as D/CIA even though (or perhaps because) the congressman had been a leader of the ideologically far-right Tea Party faction in the House of Representatives. At the Agency, Pompeo often appeared to be more of a White House aide and policymaker than an unbiased intelligence chief. He even publicly called for regime change in North Korea. Soon the president would appoint him secretary of state, where his policy pronouncements were more suitable. Former DCI Richard Helms once advised that in high-level meetings at the White House, what was needed was someone in the room "who was not trying to formulate a policy, carry a policy, or defend a policy; someone who could say: 'Now listen, this isn't my understanding of the facts.'"[37] While serving as D/CIA, Pompeo's extreme political views—coupled with his policy pronouncements—disqualified him as the trustworthy fact-provider in the room.

Soon after Trump settled into office, he often lashed out at the CIA and the FBI—savagely so at times. Among his accusations:

- that President Obama and the FBI had carried out an illegal surveillance against him during the 2016 presidential campaign. The Department of Justice and the FBI, in fact, had initiated an inquiry to examine the validity and implications of widely reported ties between Trump's senior election staff (including Flynn) and Russian intelligence officers. To have ignored these relationships would have been a gross negligence of the FBI's counterintelligence responsibilities.
- President Trump was over the top as well in his scathing, ongoing denigration of the CIA. While visiting Langley Headquarters in 2017, he claimed that the Agency was involved in behind-the-scenes plotting against him that reminded the president of approaches used by Hitler to defame adversaries during the Third Reich. This comparison stunned and deeply demoralized CIA officers. They had been called nasty things before, but never Nazis.

- President Trump also periodically expressed his belief that America's spy agencies comprised a nefarious "deep state" opposed to his administration and committed to its own agenda. He publicly attacked former D/CIA John Brennan and DNI James R. Clapper, angry that they had acknowledged in the media that Russia had placed its thumb on the presidential election scale in 2016 in Trump's favor. Despite the proof that Brennan and Clapper had at hand to support their statements, the president denied Russian interference in the election, preferring to believe that he had won purely on his own merits. Trump also blasted the incumbent D/CIA Gina Haspel, supposedly because she was insufficiently deferential to him, even though some Agency people complained that she had been just the opposite.

Further, Trump routinely expressed a cavalier attitude toward the usefulness of intelligence, preferring to rely on his own gut feelings. The end result: a presidential waste of America's $80 billion a year investment in intelligence activities, meant to provide the nation's leaders with up-to-date, reliable information about world affairs.

Though not exactly an Agency fan, Trump's use of drone warfare nonetheless turned out to be more frequent throughout his administration than had been the case even during the Obama years, although with a slight decline during Trump's his waning weeks in office. According to one account, this White House change in direction represented "a last attempt by President Trump, who has long reviled the intelligence agencies over their assessment that Russia interfered to his 2016 presidential campaign, to diminish the C.I.A."[38] In light of this decision, as well as incoming President Biden's adoption of at least a temporary decline in drone strikes, Figure 6.1 displays a gradual downturn in Third Option UAV attacks at the end of the Trump administration, and, therefore, in the frequency of covert actions.[39]

Despite this modest reversal in 2020, drone attacks were the key means for covert action from the second Bush administration forward, accounting for the widening role of the Third Option in recent decades (as depicted in Figure 6.1). Trump's aggressive attitude toward a robust use of secret power was revealed in a comment he made during the 2016 election. While the CIA had sworn off waterboarding against suspected terrorists after being sharply criticized for its use, President Trump sang the praises of this odious procedure. "I would bring back waterboarding, and I'd bring back a hell of a lot worse than waterboarding," he declared.[40]

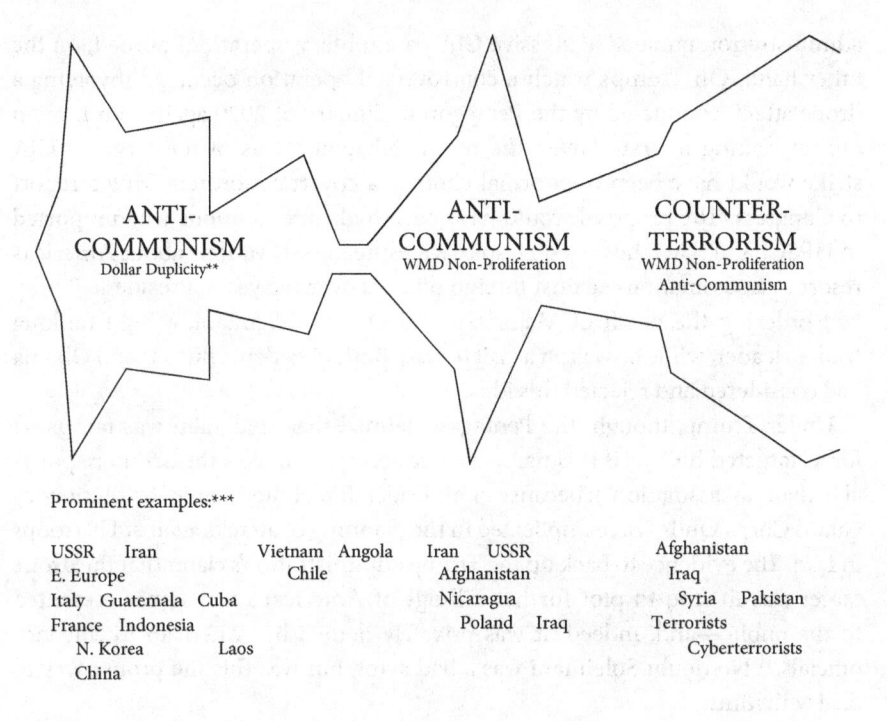

THE THIRD OPTION IN AN AGE OF TERROR   159

ANTI-
COMMUNISM
Dollar Duplicity**

ANTI-
COMMUNISM
WMD Non-Proliferation

COUNTER-
TERRORISM
WMD Non-Proliferation
Anti-Communism

Prominent examples:***

USSR Iran	Vietnam Angola	Iran USSR	Afghanistan
E. Europe	Chile	Afghanistan	Iraq
Italy Guatemala Cuba		Nicaragua	Syria Pakistan
France Indonesia		Poland Iraq	Terrorists
N. Korea	Laos		Cyberterrorists
China			

'47–'52 '53–'60 '61–'63 '64–'68 '69–'76 '77–'80 '81–'88 '89–'92 '93–'00 '01–'08 '09–'16 '17–'20

*The Figure provides an approximation of the emphasis placed by administrations on the Third Option in the modern era, as discerned by the public literature and the author's interviews. The wider the "river" in the drawing, the greater the emphasis. It also depicts the major motivations or "currents" driving the river: chiefly anti-communism (especially during the early years of the Cold War, as well as with "Cold War II" under the Reagan administration). Other motivations have included "dollar duplicity" and WMD non-proliferation (see below); and, more recently, counterterrorism.

**Suggested here as the CIA analog of "dollar diplomacy," an approach to foreign policy based on advancing private US business interests overseas [see Loch K. Johnson, *American Foreign Policy and the Challenges of World Leadership: Power, Principle, and the Constitution* (New York: Oxford University Press, 2015): 119].

***Discussed in Chapters 3 through 6.

Figure 6.1 Fluctuating Flows and Main Currents in the "River" of Covert Actions, Since 1947*

Iran IV

While Trump's cordial—and odd—ties with Russia's Putin suggested that he would refrain from directing covert actions against Russia, the president otherwise seemed to like the idea of unleashing tough clandestine operations. While he was routinely trashing the Intelligence Community, on the one hand, Trump's administration pursued aggressive CIA paramilitary operations abroad, on the other hand. On Trump's watch a controversial operation occurred involving a drone attack conducted by the Pentagon in January of 2020 against an Iranian official visiting in Iraq. Given the non-combatant status of the target, a CIA strike would have been the normal choice—a covert action requiring a report to Congress. The proposal would have been highly contentious when reported to HPSCI and SSCI, however. Despite widespread reservations about America's resort to assassinations against foreign officials over the years, President Trump had ordering the death of Major General Qasem Soleimani, a high-ranking Iranian leader, while he was on a visit to Iraq. Both Presidents Bush II and Obama had considered and rejected this idea.

Under Trump, though, the Pentagon claimed that Soleimani was fair game for a "targeted hit" (as if this name change somehow makes the act more palatable than "assassination"), because of his leadership of the Islamic Revolutionary Guard Corps Quds Force implicated in the planning of attacks against US troops in Iraq. The evidence to back up the Trump administration's claim that the drone target was in Iraq to plot further killings of Americans was never presented to the public—and, indeed, it was privately denied by American intelligence officials.[41] No doubt Soleimani was a bad actor, but was this the proper way to deal with him?

Critics viewed the assassination as an unfortunate use of a military MQ-9 Reaper drone under Title 10, which required no congressional review. They looked with alarm on the fact that the operation extended the UAV method of assassination to a *foreign government official*, inviting similar retaliations against US government personnel by Tehran's secret agents—or perhaps one day by intercontinental drones. Yale University law professor W. Michael Reisman has commented on murder plots as a US foreign policy tactic. "Assassination in any form," he argues, "presents a cascading threat to world order."[42] Professor Karen J. Greenberg of Fordham Law School called out the president for this "expansion of executive authority without congressional approval."[43] Outside of official battlefields, killing is ipso facto immoral, with the exceptions of immediate self-defense or the careful targeting of terrorist groups proven to have murdered US citizens. As Adam Entous and Evan Osnos write: "Since the Hague Convention of 1907, killing a foreign government official outside wartime has generally been barred by the Law of Armed Conflict."[44]

The United States was not at war with Iran when Soleimani met his death, along with his staff aides and Iraqi hosts—the latter, American allies—meeting him at the Baghdad airport. The Trump-ordered strike invited an international donnybrook of state and non-state assassins, whether at the controls of a drone, wielding a poison-tipped umbrella, or detonating a suicide vest. The end result of such dynamics is international chaos, a crumbling world order that would surely endanger America's own leaders who live in an open society. A majority of Americans (52 percent) polled on this subject by *USA Today*/Ipsos believed that the killing of Soleimani had made the United States less safe.[45]

What could have been done instead? Shaming is an important and underrated method in international affairs. If true, Soleimani's unsavory support of Iranian covert actions against US troops in Iraq could have been thoroughly profiled and denounced in a host of US and allied news reports, both overt and covert. Electronic attacks against his banking assets, along with those of his travel hosts, could have been pursued, too—ideally, with assistance from fellow democracies. Economic sanctions aimed directly at someone like Soleimani, not just against the government of Iran (which is about sanctioned-out), can hurt individual bad actors. Above all, JSOC and SOG personnel could have raised the stakes overseas for the Islamic Revolutionary Guard. But the murder of a leading political figure from a sovereign nation not at war with the United States? In that direction lies global anarchy.

Cyberterrorism

Secret cyberwarfare and intelligence hacking have become, regrettably, a common practice among nations. This form of PM ops—electronic covert action—is in its nascent stages; but, as Russian attempts at the manipulation of US presidential elections remind us, its potential should be cause for alarm. Former DNI Clapper is convinced that Moscow's intervention in the 2016 election shifted victory toward Trump over his opponent, Democrat Hillary Clinton.[46] A pattern of Russian cyberattacks against the Western nations is emerging. As the COVID-ridden year of 2020 came to an end, US authorities discovered that Russian intelligence had mounted its most aggressive cyber-espionage hit against America's government in over a decade—a sophisticated hacking that would take much of 2021 to unravel and build defenses against. The objective of the Kremlin is clear: through the use of active measures, to foment widespread disbelief in the value and the future of democracy. And, on the espionage side, to steal as many industrial and defense secrets from the United States as possible.

Lurking in the near future is the threat of massive electronic assaults against the United States: perhaps even a surprise, Pearl Harbor-like disintegration of energy grids, as well as the electronic infrastructure of the stock exchange, schools, hospitals, air-traffic control, nuclear reactors, and scores of other targets. Suffice it to say that quite properly the government in Washington is ramping up America's cyber-defenses, as well as its ability to attack the electronic vulnerabilities of other nations that continue to harass this nation's open society.

Gazing into the crystal ball as best one can, it is easy to see how this threat will be a top-tier focus for future uses of the Third Option. General Clapper takes an aggressive stance on the pursuit of cyber covert actions, advocating a strong response to Russian electronic attacks and meddling against the United States. "You could do a lot of damage to the Russian economy if you essentially cut them off from the world financial system," he has remarked.[47] Further, Paul R. Kolbe, a career DO officer, suggests that in response to cyberattacks from Russia and elsewhere, the United States should "when needed, quietly bloody a few noses."[48] The Intelligence Community already engages in its share of cyberattacks against Russia and other adversaries, but in a more discriminating manner by focusing on military and economic institutions, and certainly never hospitals—which says something about the difference in values between the authoritarian and the democratic societies.

The United States and Russia decided long ago to embrace arms control accords before an arms race spent them dry—or blew them to oblivion in a global nuclear witch fire. Similarly, all nations should now work collectively toward bringing a stop to the cyber assaults that are currently so pervasive around the world. The United States can play the cyberattack game as well as any other nation, but it behooves no one to allow this trend to continue. Ultimately, it is a game without winners. Negotiations leading to an international cyber-peace treaty are imperative, or else the major powers will be facing the near certainty one day of an electronic war that sweeps across the planet.

In 2015, the United States agreed with China to cease cyber-based robbery of intellectual property. The emphasis was on protecting the commercial interests of both nations. Regrettably, the pact remained mute on the question of purloined government data. Nations will have to move quickly to broaden the curbs on cyberattacks, based on President Reagan's sound principle for international negotiations: trust but verify. While some scoff at the possibilities for cyber "arms control," the proposition is worth seriously testing. Even Koble, who admits to skepticism that it would work, recommends that those nations involved in cyberattacks should take "small steps" toward building "some degree of cooperation and, in time, a foundation for eventually regulating norms and behavior."[49] The alternative is clear: we will all witness, firsthand, the disintegration of the civilized world.

~~~

The history of CIA covert actions reveals an on-again, off-again emphasis on this phantom approach to US foreign policy. Interviews with Agency insiders and their congressional overseers suggest that the Korean War was an early high point in America's use of the Third Option, as the CIA attempted to earn its bones by way of aggressive PM activities in support of the US military in that war.

The Vietnam War era was another period when the Third Option experienced a burst of activity, in Laos and in South Vietnam. The next period of marked enthusiasm for covert action, even higher than for Korea or Vietnam, came during the 1980s, the Reagan years, and not in "hot" wars fought by the American military but with secret paramilitary operations spearheaded by the CIA, especially in Afghanistan and Nicaragua (see Figure 6.1).

The Iran-*contra* scandal discredited the Third Option as a tool of foreign policy until 9/11 when America's struggle against global terrorism significantly expanded, and covert action again became an important instrument for protecting and advancing US global interests. The most recent Golden Age of Covert Action has proven to be the longest lasting in US history, the most expensive, and the most oriented toward paramilitary activities, led by Langley's involvement in major drone strikes in the Middle East, the Near East, and North Africa (the main locations—so far).

Wars have been the hallmark of the periods that exhibit Washington's strongest devotion to covert action, whether these are conflicts engaged in openly by US forces with the CIA in support, as in Korea, Vietnam, Grenada (1983), Iraq, and Afghanistan, or Agency-led paramilitary activities, as in Laos (though in support of the Vietnam War) and in Nicaragua. These open warfare and paramilitary operations have taken place mainly in developing nations around the world, which is true as well for the smaller, less expensive covert actions. As shown throughout this book, though, and with detailed data presented in Chapter 10, the more industrialized, developed world has sometimes been an arena for covert operations as well, most notably with propaganda campaigns aimed at the Soviet Union and its East Europe satellites during the Cold War. In the case of America's most powerful adversaries, Russia and China, the Third Option has failed to make made much of a dent directly against them because they are so large and well defended by experienced counterintelligence services.

The outcomes of the Agency's clandestine interventions have been a mixture of success and failure—legally, practically, and morally. The second part of this volume explores the legal aspects of covert action, as well as its decision pathway, degree of accountability, and ethical ramifications. The final two chapters offer an evaluation of America's best and worst experiences with the Third Option since the creation of the CIA in 1947.

PART IV
LAW AND ACCOUNTABILITY

7
Legal Foundations

The National Security Act of 1947

Not until 1947, with enactment of the National Security Act that created the CIA, did covert action enjoy a lawful underpinning. Legal analyst James E. Baker has referred to that statute, signed by President Truman on July 26, as "the bedrock of U.S. intelligence laws"—despite its brief and vague language (see Chapter 1).[1] The leader of the Intelligence Community created by this law, the DCI, would have little formal authority over America's other secret services that lie beyond the CIA. In 1969, deputy DCI Admiral Rufus Taylor referred to these various spy agencies (they are illustrated in Figure 1.3) as little more than a "tribal federation," with no meaningful leadership from a *Central* Intelligence Agency.[2]

Almost three decades later, HPSCI Chairman Lee H. Hamilton would describe the Office of the DCI in a similar fashion, highlighting the paucity of Community-wide authority in the hands of the nation's "spymaster." "We don't really have a Director of Central Intelligence," he said. "There is no such thing."[3] In 2004, the government abandoned the DCI position in the wake of America's worst intelligence failure, the surprise 9/11 attacks. With enactment of the Intelligence Reform and Terrorism Prevention Act of 2004 (IRTPA), that office was replaced with what was supposed to be, at long last, a director of National Intelligence or DNI who could serve as a true leader for the espionage services, with budget and personnel authority over the entire Intelligence Community.

Again, though, as in 1947, the Pentagon managed to emasculate the concept of a genuine national intelligence leader for fear the Office of the DNI (ODNI) would have too much sway over military intelligence—the military's turf.[4] Former DCI Stansfield Turner has written that the United States had ended up with "the worst of all worlds, that is, a DNI without direct control of the CIA and not enough control of the Intelligence Community to compensate."[5] Yet throughout this history, the director of Central Intelligence was at least the boss at the CIA. So was the DCI successor office, the director of the Central Intelligence Agency or D/CIA, also established in 2004 by the IRTPA legislation. And within the Agency, the DCI, and then the D/CIA steadfastly held control over the Third Option. Recall how the elastic language tacked onto the intelligence section of the National Security Act provided the DCI and the CIA with authority over "*such other functions and duties*" as might be assigned by the White House. With these airy words from 1947, the CIA was suddenly in the covert action business. Here was the initial legal authority, such as it was, for the Third Option.

The Agency's top attorney at the time, Lawrence R. Houston, expressed surprise that such ethereal language could become a basis for clandestine interventions overseas. "All during this drafting of the act, all during the presentations to congressional committees and debates, and all during the consideration in Congress, there was no mention of covert action," he recalled. In September 1947, Houston warned DCI and Rear Admiral Roscoe H. Hillenkoetter (1947–50) that covert action "would be an unwarranted extension" of the CIA's authority.[6]

The notion of a modern-day Third Option capability had originated with senior officials in the Departments of State and Defense, not inside the CIA.[7] As the Truman administration began to grapple with the global communist threat, the White House told Houston to prepare a legal document that would allow the CIA to engage in subversive activities against the Soviet Union. In response, Houston wrote an opinion that said the president could move forward with covert action based on that misty clause in the 1947 act, as long as the White House backed it up with internal directives and Congress provided the funding. The Agency remained lukewarm, though, about this new, ill-defined, and potentially high-risk burden. As one of its top analysts has remembered, the Third Option "was not [a mission] sought by the agency. CIA entered into covert action operations under pressure from leading U.S. officials of the day to support basic U.S. foreign policy."[8]

An attractive feature for involving the CIA in clandestine ventures was its access to unvouchered funds, a rare privilege associated with its sensitive work. This capacity to spend without the need for clear justifications to Congress permitted the CIA to pursue heavily veiled activities around the world, free of annoying questions from lawmakers.[9] In a follow-up to the initial National Security Act, the Central Intelligence Agency Act of 1949 made it clear that the DCI would only have to certify that the funds appropriated by Congress for the Agency were indeed spent, without accounting for details since that would require an inappropriate disclosure of specific, highly classified intelligence "sources and methods."[10] Furthermore, the CIA had already begun to spin out a worldwide web of officers who were busily gathering intelligence and recruiting foreigners as espionage assets—a ready-made network that could take on covert actions as well. "The fit between the CIA and covert operations was irresistible," conclude two prominent intelligence scholars, Bruce D. Berkowistz and Allen E. Goodman.[11]

LEGAL FOUNDATIONS   169

Covert Action by Executive Order

A DCI from the 1970s would note that intelligence "ethics or propriety are things that are subjective; but unless you insist that a government organization adheres to the law, it's pretty hard to set some ethical standards for it."[12] Yet in these start-up years, the CIA enjoyed broad discretionary authority to pursue the Third Option largely as it saw fit, a leeway enhanced by Stalin's alarming rhetoric and global aggressiveness. The Church Committee described the Agency's covert action mandate as "somewhat cloudy" and based largely on the opinions of the DCI.[13] These opinions reflected the core objective of the United States, which was (according to Church Committee historian Anne Karalekas) to "frustrate Soviet ambitions without provoking open conflict."[14] As the Agency faced this daunting assignment, legal clarity was not always a sine qua non.

Rule by NSC Directives

In these circumstances of an embryonic Cold War, it is easy to see why the Truman administration wasted no time in developing America's capabilities for a covert contest of wills with the communist world. What seemed to be an existential struggle was under way, fought primarily at a subterranean level by Soviet and US spies—a means of avoiding outright overt military confrontations between the superpowers. For the next twenty-seven years (until the end of 1974), the CIA would pursue its clandestine interventions with no further statutory guidance from Congress beyond the initial vague wording of the National Security Act. The Agency would rely on executive guidelines, usually loosely worded and lenient, from the president, the NSC (also established by the 1947 Act), and, most commonly, the organization's immediate boss, the DCI.[15]

During these early years, the Agency was housed in provisional and run-down barracks, known as the E Street Complex in the Foggy Bottom district of Washington, with additional quarters on the Mall near the Lincoln Memorial and the Reflecting Pool. The E Street buildings, previously occupied by the OSS, lacked ideal security or even efficient air-conditioning and blinds. Not for nothing was a building in the complex known as the Rat Palace. Officers in one facility could easily peer through their windows into adjacent offices. On one occasion, this led a CIA operative to observe a colleague removing the clothing of a charming secretary, with the intention "of committing a bit of unauthorized covert action."[16]

These quarters were deemed far too crowded and insecure by the mid-1950s; a new location had to be found. Allen Dulles, DCI at the time and known by Agency insiders as "the old master" because of his extensive intelligence experience in the OSS, supervised the selection of a prime parcel of real estate for the CIA's new quarters. The Headquarters Building would be located on a site known as Langley, near the township of McLean, seven miles northwest of the White House on the Virginia side of the Potomac River. The tract boasted a leafy, campus-like setting of 219 acres, with deer prancing through willow oaks and magnolias, the Potomac River sunlit and sparkling nearby, and views of the Georgetown University steeple and the Washington Monument reaching into the sky above the District of Columbia.

As soon as construction was completed on the seven-story modern structure (known by some wags as the "Allen Dulles Memorial Mausoleum"), barbed-wire barriers were erected around the property, guard houses staffed, and armed patrols assigned to protect "the campus" perimeter. The CIA opened its Langley doors to greet employees on September 20, 1961, just five months after the Bay of Pigs. Some of the Old Guard were less than impressed. "We ought to be lurking in scrabbly old hideouts, with the plaster peeling and stopped-up toilets," carped one. "There's something about the atmosphere of this building that leads to too many memos, too many meetings, and not enough dirty work."[17] These Old Boys would have preferred to stay in DC, shoulder to shoulder with other government agencies with whom they needed to coordinate on a daily basis, not isolated way off in the Virginia countryside. In later years, though, the move would prove to have advantages, not least the fact that the Langley site had abundant parking space—a nearly non-existent luxury for most government office buildings "downtown."

When the Agency was still located in the District, its clandestine side—the Directorate of Plans—was hard at work trying to construct an organizational infrastructure while at the same time jockeying for funds from the CIA's leadership cadre. There was much to do, with the Soviets probing Western weaknesses around the world. In December 1947, five months after the enactment of the National Security Act, the National Security Council issued NSC4/A, a directive that gave the CIA responsibilities for psy ops (psychological operations). The Agency was a natural for this duty, since fully a third of its start-up staff had served in the OSS, which had regularly carried out these kinds of propaganda activities against the Nazis. Moreover, the unwillingness of State or Defense to risk their reputations by engaging in such sneaky and controversial practices pointed in the direction of reliance on the CIA—the less visible side of government.

The Agency hired a number of bored, well-educated New York City admen who found it more adventurous and noble to take on Joe Stalin than to spend their time conning US consumers. The entity within the CIA selected to guide this Madison Avenue approach to world affairs was the Special Procedures Group (SPG, sometimes referred to as the Special Projects Group). Its initial approach was to smuggle publications behind the Iron Curtain (a fleet of balloons floating across Eastern Europe with anti-communist leaflets was one method), as well as to beam pro-West radio broadcasts into the Soviet empire.

The man who would become America's most famous diplomat, George F. Kennan, was head of the Policy Planning Staff in the State Department at the time. Although most of his colleagues at State may have considered clandestine activities uncouth and anathema to America's motherhood-and-apple-pie values, he proposed nonetheless that the government turn to political covert actions as a supplement to overt diplomatic practices—including direct intervention into the electoral processes of other nations when necessary, not just smuggling propaganda tracts behind the Iron Curtain. Kennan viewed his Department as the best place to administer this form of concealed intervention abroad, as a means for ensuring that the CIA's propaganda themes and political activities were in harmony with the State Department's policy objectives.[18]

Office of Policy Coordination

The NSC accepted Kennan's proposal and in June 1948 it further expanded this initiative by way of Directive NSC 10/2, so that henceforth America's secret approach to foreign policy would include the full gambit of Third Option activities. Who, though, would be in charge of this widened portfolio? The State Department and the Central Intelligence Agency were now pitted against each other in a bureaucratic wrestling match.

State had the edge. Like DoD, it had been a part of the government since 1789—not just for one year, the Agency's record of longevity. Moreover, State enjoyed much stronger ties to key players throughout the government than did the newfangled CIA. Directive NSC 10/2 changed the name of the SPG to the Office of Policy Coordination. The OPC would be in charge of the Agency's growing covert action portfolio to counter global communism; however—and oddly, to say the least—its director would be designated by the secretary of state, and its tasks would be crafted and assigned by both the State and Defense Departments, bypassing the DCI altogether. The job of the CIA was simply to carry out assignments given to it by the Big Boys at State and Defense.

A further complication was the existence of the Agency's Office of Special Operations (OSO), a classic espionage shop that now led the new CIA responsibilities for recruiting intelligence-gathering assets overseas (human intelligence or "humint," in Agency terminology). Former CIA Inspector General Fred Hitz writes that the OSO "was often stumbling over or wandering into operations conducted by the OPC, because the foreign actors who stole the secrets were often the same ones who could manage the propaganda or organize the political meetings for the OPC."[19] The OPC's propaganda activities soon mushroomed inside the Agency's nascent covert action infrastructure, boosted by the war in Korea. Its staff grew from 302 people in 1949 to 5,954 by 1952, with roughly one half at the E Street Complex and the other half overseas.

Congress had nothing to do with these developments; lawmakers may as well have been bivouacked on the dark side of the moon. The Agency and its activities were being shaped by executive orders (E.O.s), drafted by NSC staff members on behalf of the president, the secretaries of State and Defense, and the DCI. These key documents are known variously as Presidential Decision Directives or PDDs ("peds"); National Security Council Intelligence Directives or NSCIDs ("n-skids"); National Security Decision Memoranda or NSDMs ('niz-dems"); National Security Study Memoranda or NSSMs (niz-sims"); National Security Action Memoranda or NSAMs ("niz-ams"), and Intelligence Community Directives (ICDs), among a blizzard of other labels whose names change from time to time. An illustration: during the Reagan administration, National Security Decision Memorandum (NSDM)-75 outlined a new foreign policy initiative that rejected the cautious notion of a superpower co-existence, in favor of *changing* the entire Soviet system—a bold form of "rollback" borrowed from the Eisenhower days that set the stage for significant covert actions in Poland and elsewhere in Eastern Europe in hopes of unraveling the Kremlin's control over this vast expanse.

The purpose of the NSC documents was, according to the Church Committee, to bring about "an intensification of [Third Option] activities . . . without establishing firm guidelines for approval."[20] The directives were, and still are, periodically supplemented by attorney general guidelines (which, for example, were the source for the CIA's involvement in torture after the 9/11 attacks). Underscoring the importance of E.O.s, recall how the Ford administration established through this method a ban against the assassination of foreign leaders.[21] Executive orders are legally binding, unless firmly objected to by Congress—assuming that lawmakers even know about them, which is sometimes a large assumption in an intelligence apparatus that is shrouded in darkness. Phillip J. Cooper notes that E.O.s "have occasionally tempted Presidents to abuse powers conferred by statute or to claim constitutional powers they do not rightly possess."[22] Moreover, they can be altered by secret codicil, without congressional awareness. For instance, using internal directives, both DCIs Stansfield Turner and John Deutch bypassed a congressional understanding with the Agency that its congressional liaison office would inform SSCI and HPSCI any time the CIA employed the services of an American journalist for an intelligence operation.[23]

The use of directives continued with NSC 68, issued in March 1950. This famous document, which outlined the containment doctrine, was a covert action call to arms that significantly broadened the OPC's mission. The Directive encouraged the CIA to instigate unrest and rebellion throughout Eastern Europe (a foreshadowing of sideline cheering for the ill-fated Hungarian rebels in 1956). The following year, in 1951, NSC 10/5 replaced NSC 10/2 as the government's basis of authority for a rapidly expanding use of the Third Option across the world's meridians. This document, though rather vague like its antecedents, placed an inflection point on the importance of establishing resistance groups inside the Soviet bloc.

The concept that the CIA should send émigré volunteers into Eastern Europe to establish a "stay-behind" program began to grow legs. The goal was to have a network of anti-communist guerrillas hide caches of weaponry in remote farm buildings, grain silos, and other locations, secretly readying themselves to rise up against the Soviets if war broke out between the superpowers. As a distant hope and an immediate morale booster, the rebels were encouraged to believe that before long the despised communist regimes would be overthrown and they could gain back their homeland—an early version of the "rollback" doctrine. In light of ubiquitous internal security personnel behind the Iron Curtain, the likelihood that the stay-behind plans would actually work—let alone bring the "liberation theology" to reality—was another matter, pushed aside for the moment in the enthusiasm to *do something*. A similar approach was launched against North Korea in early 1951, with hundreds of intrepid South Korean commandos slipping past the DMZ in hopes of stimulating insurrection. In both parts of the world, the failure rate was horrendous (Chapter 3). Almost all of the infiltrators were captured and executed in Eastern Europe and North Korea. Moreover, often their relatives were targeted for revenge. The Truman administration decided that these operations were basically suicide missions and halted them, but they would be revived with zeal when the Eisenhower team came to Washington—until this administration, too, backed away after a sobering run of losses.

The OPC found itself pulled in opposing directions, like a mule between two haystacks. On one side, State demanded help with propaganda and political operations; on the other side, Defense insisted on using the CIA for paramilitary purposes in support of its overt operations. As the Agency attempted to accommodate both external masters, its personnel roster for covert action expanded exponentially, as did the number of Agency stations abroad, both developments driven by the increasing dominance of the Third Option in the conduct of America's foreign policy—including in the Far East, where DoD's Joint Chiefs of Staff had finally overruled General Douglas MacArthur's prohibition against a CIA presence in that part of the world. In the early 1950s, the CIA's stations began to take the lead in shaping the forms covert action would assume, as well as where and when this approach would be used. The Church Committee discovered that although the Agency had been established for the purposes of the collection and analysis of intelligence, *"within three years clandestine operations became and continued to be the Agency's preeminent activity."*[24]

With other and seemingly bigger fish to fry, the attention paid to OPC by Kennan and the State Department, as well as by the Defense Department, dwindled over the coming years, especially when CIA operations officer Frank G. "Wis" Wisner took over OPC's reins. A dynamic attorney from a socially prominent Southern family, Wisner pulled command and control of the Third Option increasingly into the Agency's exclusive orbit, with little supervision or guidance from either one of the government's giant foreign affairs departments, State or Defense. In an internal research publication, the CIA's Center for the Study of Intelligence concludes that during this period Agency officials "made the rules as they went along, and were much more inclined to ask forgiveness than permission."[25] Under Wisner, OPC had become the largest and most lavishly funded branch of the CIA and, at last, clearly under the DCI's command. "The Wis" was on a high cloud.

The incoming DCI in 1950 was the popular, decisive, hard-working, and well-connected, if gruff, General Walter Bedell Smith. "Beetle" (a childhood nickname) worried about the legal ambiguities surrounding the uses of covert action, particularly its cryptic approval procedures. He asked the NSC to provide more detailed guidance. The result was the Council's adoption of a Psychological Strategy Board (PSB) to help DCI Smith administer the Third Option and, most of all, to provide more clear-cut guidelines for the approval of the Agency's clandestine activities. Any new rules, though, were to be drafted by way of additional NSC directives, not by statute. Whatever the Constitution may have had in mind as the proper form of government for the United States, from the Agency's viewpoint lawmakers could stay out of the intelligence business.

In 1951, an improved degree of management began to evolve for covert action inside the CIA. Under Smith's leadership, the two intelligence tasks of spying and covert action—finding out about things and doing things, gathering and hunting—would be housed in the same unit, the Directorate of Plans (DP). Tensions between these clandestine activities would continue to flare occasionally, but the friction was less heated now that both answered to the same boss: a deputy director for Plans (DDP).

Directorate of Plans (DP)

One of General Smith's more astute moves was the establishment of the DP, known by insiders at the time by a less euphemistic, non-official name: the "Clandestine Service." Its purpose was to manage covert actions across the board, including oversight for Wisner's sometimes overheated operational aspirations. Allen Dulles, whom Smith had brought into the CIA from the New York law firm of Sullivan & Cromwell, would head the new Directorate. Smith gave him the title of DDP, which disappointed Frank Wisner, who had hoped for the job. Dulles was an old friend of Wisner's, however, and was obviously qualified for the spot, so Wis kept his hurt feelings to himself and bided his time.[26] By autumn of 1952, OPC and OSO were integrated at last—no dovecote by any means, but at least now woven more closely together within the DP's organizational fabric, with about a third of the Directorate's resources devoted to covert action and two-thirds to espionage activities.

Dulles continued his rapid climb through the Agency's ranks and, within three months, he had ascended to the position of deputy director for Central Intelligence or DDCI—the number two slot in the organization. Wisner happily followed him into the DDP opening. In the next year, 1953, Smith retired and Dulles became DCI. It was an unmatched meteoric rise through the Agency's top ranks, fueled by Dulles's extensive OSS experience, his nonpareil Georgetown social contacts, Smith's readiness for green pastures, and, not coincidentally, the influence of Allen Dulles's older brother, John Foster Dulles, secretary of state in the Eisenhower administration.

Diving further into the Agency's bewildering alphabet soup for a moment, the DP had become the largest of the Agency's three Directorates at the time. The other two were the Directorate of Intelligence or DI (intelligence technical collection, plus analysis), and today known as the Directorate of Analysis or DA; and the Directorate of Administration or DA (the chief management unit), known today as the Directorate of Support or DS. Under the leadership of General Smith as DCI and Dulles as DDCI, the Directorate of Plans had managed to corrall fully 74 percent of the CIA's total annual budget.[27]

As DCI, Dulles inherited an organization that had grown six-fold in size since its founding in 1947, primarily as a result of Smith's wily and energetic influence in high government circles. Now with Dulles at the helm, the Agency would continue to swell and take on a shape that would last for the next twenty years. During the Dulles era (1953–61), the "ops" officers were able to establish the Plans Directorate as the dominant force in the Agency, both at Headquarters and overseas. Tails at the DP were up and wagging. Several operational types would follow in Dulles's footsteps into the office of the DCI. After him, they included Richard Helms, William E. Colby, William J. Casey, and Porter J. Goss—a total of five altogether (counting Dulles), compared to only one analyst, Robert M. Gates. The other individuals selected for this top position were mostly military men—"outsiders," in the suspicious, turf-conscious opinion of the intelligence careerists at Langley.

Congress rarely weighed in on these institutional ebbs and flows. Lawmakers did help, though, to create in 1952 a Contingency Reserve Release Fund for covert actions and other intelligence activities. The CRF (in its shortened acronym) was a pot of money separate from the usual CIA annual budget. These resources were hidden inside Defense Department appropriations bills and could be tapped into quickly in times of emergency or for an unexpectedly large and fast-moving clandestine activity.

When Dulles was in charge of the CIA, the Directorate of Plans could not have had a better friend in high councils. He had been involved earlier in his career in the recruitment and handling of foreign espionage agents for both the OSS and the Directorate of Plans—what had evolved into half of that Directorate's responsibility, the other half being covert action. Dulles was partial toward this "ground truth" side of the CIA, where information was gathered directly by Agency officers and their local assets in the Gasthauses of Berlin and the Naitokurabus of Tokyo, then acted on by the operatives.

Besides, the Third Option was something special. Around the Intelligence Community, one could find a surfeit of collectors and analysts. But only the DP had operatives; only the DP could secretly transform the world, whether by way of propaganda, assassinations, or something in between; only the DP had officers who stalked the midnight alleys of Cairo and Budapest with a .45 strapped to their ribcage (chiefly in the mythology, although sometimes in reality); only the DP had officers as comfortable at the bar of the Palace Hotel in Guatemala City as a local cop might be in a Milwaukee or Boston tavern. Personnel in the DP read Ian Fleming, one of Dulles's favorite writers (and a former British intelligence officer), and admired his dashing James Bond protagonist. As former DDP and DCI Richard Helms recalls, Allen Dulles "believed covert action to be the prime function of the CIA."[28]

Dulles did not ignore analysis and in fact recorded a high production level for National Intelligence Estimates (NIEs)—the magnum opus in the world of US in-depth intelligence reporting to Washington decision makers (as opposed to the *President's Daily Brief*, a "current intelligence" product).[29] Ops were his passion, however, and he spent most of his time chatting up DP officers, discussing with them everything from recruitment challenges to clandestine tradecraft. He would recommend covert actions and routinely visit the Directorate's suite of offices at Langley. He also frequently traveled to Agency stations overseas, the largest of which was located in Frankfort, West Germany—a country that, along with West Berlin, was as thick with international spies as the Okefenokee Swamp is with gators.

As the Agency's collection-and-analysis duties expanded in pace with the widening role of the United States in world affairs, the DP budget nevertheless remained high under Dulles. It did not reach the summit of 74 percent of the total achieved during the heydays of Iran and Guatemala in the mid-1950s; but this budget still accounted for a majority of the CIA's spending from 1955 to 1961, in support of fifty or so significant clandestine operations within forty-eight nations.[30] The DP was, and would remain, a "pocket of privilege."[31]

When he became DDP, Wisner pushed the advantage. The Agency's Comptroller's Office, responsible for reviewing the budgets of each Agency Directorate, found the Plans shop closed to its auditors, at Wisner's insistence. This was private territory, he argued, with sources and methods far too sensitive for normal procedures. Likewise, the Agency's Inspector General was kept at arm's length. "Accountability"—even inside the CIA, let alone from the Congress or even the NSC—may as well have been an ancient Greek word that no one in the Directorate wanted to look up in the Oxford English Dictionary. Secrecy, speed, flexibility: that was the ticket for the DP, according to Wis and his colleagues, not budget audits, drug tests, personnel reviews, and periodic inspections—the norm in other parts of the government.

The reigning philosophy inside the Directorate of Plans was one of laissez-faire. From 1947 to 1955, it had no formal procedures for the approval of covert action, regardless of DCI Smith's best efforts. Not laws but occasional NSC directive would prevail. Mostly, the DDP ran things in a loosey-goosey style that had become the modus operandi for the Third Option. The men and women of the Directorate considered themselves "honorable," as in fact almost all of them were; they were fighting communists and, in their view, they had to be trusted to get the job done—not "micromanaged" by NSC staffers or, worse still, lawmakers and their aides.[32] Yet this made for a DP dangerously isolated from the policymakers it was meant to serve, and even from their colleagues in the Directorate of Intelligence—experts on the very countries DP officers were carrying out operations against. (Recall the virtually non-existent relationship between the two Directorates during the Bay of Pigs episode, examined in Chapter 4.)

White House Review Panels for Covert Action

Hearing a grumbling through the government grapevine about the freewheeling nature of DP operations, the NSC issued two fresh directives in 1955—NSC 5412/1 and NSC 5412/2—meant to achieve better order. These documents set up the so-called 5412 Committee, based on either the room number where the group met in the Old Executive Office Building (OEOB, next to the White House) or the number of the directive that created the panel—accounts differ. Its membership consisted of aides to the government's top four officials in the national security arena: the president, vice president, secdef, and secstate. The panel's meetings were infrequent during its first three years, however, and its rules for approving covert actions entirely ad hoc. In 1959, the members of the 5412 Committee began to convene weekly but soon decided that the DDP knew better than they did what Third Options might work. The air in Room 5412 grew thick with deference.

The 5412 Committee took on the nondescript name of "Special Group" (SG) during the Kennedy years (1961–63) and boosted its membership to include the chairman of the Joint Chiefs of Staff, the DCI, the deputy secstate, the deputy secdef, and the national security adviser. It had another name change to the 303 Committee in 1964 (the O.E.O.B. room number). According to the Church Committee, between January of 1961 and autumn of 1962, the SG approved 550 covert operations, mostly minor in scope.

At first, the meetings of the 5412 panel had been largely desultory, in the manner of its predecessors—until the Bay of Pigs wakeup call in 1961. Then the ire of President Kennedy turned the Special Group into a more meaningful review and approval board for covert actions—with, understandably, an especially sharp eye focused on any paramilitary proposals recommended by the Agency. The new 303 Committee adopted the use of subcommittees for a somewhat deeper examination of Third Option proposals: a Special Group on Counterinsurgency for PM operations, and a stygian council named the Special Group (Augmented) to supervise Operation "Mongoose" aimed at displacing the Castro regime in Cuba.

The Church Committee learned that only 14 percent of the covert actions from 1961 to 1975 were reviewed by the SG and the 303 Committees. The State Department claims that those activities that escaped review were merely "low-risk and low-cost operations." This is questionable, though, in light of the Church panel revelations about the many important intelligence activities never seen by the NSC staff or principals. The Department concedes that "not all major operations" were brought to President Nixon's 40 Committee (the next iteration of the 303 Committee), including the controversial covert attacks against Allende.[33] Research by John Prado and Arturo Jimenez-Bacardi found that from 1972 to 1974, the 40 Committee met no more than once each year. "The standard became project approval by telephone," they report, "which made reviews pretty much impossible."[34]

A Drift of Authority into the Field

After the Bay of Pigs debacle, the footlights would soon go out for Allen Dulles. After President Kennedy showed him the stage exit, the next two DCIs were outsiders: John A. McCone, a Republican from the business world, and Vice-Admiral William F. Raborn Jr. from Naval Operations. Then another DP leader took over as DCI in 1966, the suave Richard Helms, a twenty-five-year operations veteran. Under his tutelage, the Directorate returned to its preeminence within the Agency. The hallmark of Helms's tenure turned out to be the dominant role played by paramilitary operations, even though he was not personally enthusiastic about any form of covert action—let alone the most extreme.[35] President Johnson also displayed little ardor for this approach to foreign affairs, even the long-standing secret funding of the Christian Democratic Party in Italy. Yet, PM ops would race forward during the 1960s nonetheless, thanks to stepped up CIA counterinsurgency activities around the world, most notably in Africa and Indochina.

Given Helms's lack of zeal for the Third Option, much of the authority for specific operations devolved to lower managers in the DP and even station chiefs overseas, with a premium placed on self-initiative and agility in the field— certainly not review and approvals from the Congress or, most of the time, even by the NSC. Legal constraints were, at best, a distant consideration, with no US statutory boundaries in play for covert actions. International law did speak to the question of secret interventions by one nation against another. Such activities were considered harmful to world peace. These non-interventionist norms were, however, routinely ignored. The looseness in the chain of command in the United States throughout this evolution of the Third Option can be seen in the practice of plausible denial. Under this "doctrine," which protected the White House from blame if a covert action ran awry by allowing the president to deny he had given authority for the operation, the pinning down of higher responsibility for any particular covert action became a mug's game.[36]

During these years, only the most costly interventions were considered worthy of a report in advance to the NSC panel that dealt with covert actions, whether the 5412, SG, 303, or 40 Committees—the succession of panels that Prados and Jimenez-Bacardi refer to as "the high command of the secret war."[37] This left the overwhelming majority of clandestine interventions subject to no, or minimal, NSC review. Nor were the Agency's chiefs of station consistent in their coordination with the US ambassador in their assigned country. Historian Arthur M. Schlesinger Jr., a special assistant to President Kennedy, concluded that "CIA operations have not been held effectively subordinate to U.S. foreign policy."[38]

Directorate of Operations (DO)

In 1973, with James R. Schlesinger as DCI, the DP underwent a name change to the Directorate of Operations or DO. In the mid-1970s, use of the Third Option was winding down, a result of their uneven performance in Vietnam; the controversy they had stirred with respect to *New York Times* reporting on CIA operations in Chile; the ethos in the Nixon administration that government budgets needed to be reduced; the absorption of President Nixon with the Watergate scandal; and, in 1975, the advent of the Church Committee investigation.

The Nixon national security team occasionally backed secret disbursements to friends abroad (such as to Jean-Bedel Bokassa, dictator of the Central African Republic[39]) and, most importantly, backed the military coup in Chile. Nevertheless, the Third Option was headed toward its steepest decline, one that would reach rock bottom during the Ford administration, as a result of the CIA domestic spy scandal known as Operation "CHAOS" (disclosed by the *Times* in 1974) and the Church Committee probe.

DCI James Schlesinger was only at Langley for six months before becoming secdef for President Nixon. His replacements were, first, William E. Colby (1973–76) and then George H. W. Bush (1976–77), both at the Agency's helm consecutively during the firestorm of the Senate and House intelligence investigations. An operations veteran, Colby was only the second attorney to become DCI (after Dulles) and he vowed to ensure that the initials CIA henceforth would stand for "Constitutional Intelligence in America." (As an undergraduate at Princeton, one of Colby's professors had been the famed authority on the Constitution, Edward S. Corwin.) At the time of the intelligence investigations, historian Henry Steele Commager wrote that "perhaps the most threatening of all the evidence that [arose] from the findings of the Church Committee [was] the indifference of the intelligence agencies to constitutional restraint."[40] Colby and many of his Agency colleagues were embarrassed by some of the discoveries made during the Senate inquiry into unlawful Agency spying at home and morally questionable activities abroad; they, too, wanted an Agency that honored the rule of law and American values.

In this interval of acute controversy for the Agency (the "Intelligence Wars," or the "time of troubles," is how intelligence professionals remember the turbulent year of 1975), Colby could see the writing on the wall and tried to prepare the CIA and the broader IC for a new set of intelligence regulations—perhaps even binding laws for the first time since the National Security Act of the Truman era. Colby's philosophy: America's spies had to cooperate with Congress and brace themselves for a new attitude in Washington toward the intelligence mission, which the Agency had itself to blame for involvement in CHAOS, the Allende intervention, and the murder plots against Castro and other foreign heads of state. Otherwise, if the Agency's Seventh Floor failed to cooperate, lawmakers might just slam closed the doors at Langley and throw away the keys.

While the CIA's very survival was not really at stake—it had many well-placed defenders in the White House, on the Hill, and elsewhere in Washington—its leadership clearly was under heavy fire, and Langley could have taken some serious budget hits. Probably about half of the Agency's employees thought Colby had the right strategy; the other half believed, along with his predecessor Helms, that he had sold the CIA down the river.

The Ford White House agreed with the sell-out argument, finding Colby far too cooperative with the Church Committee. The president fired him and picked George H. W. Bush (America's diplomatic envoy to China at the time) to nurture the Agency through the end game of the Church and Pike inquiries, which he did in an adroit balancing act among the views of Colby, Helms, Congress, and the White House. Bush's status as a member of the congressional Old Boys club (as a former member of the House from Texas), along with the fact that his father had been a popular US senator from Connecticut, helped his cause considerably on the Hill. These efforts to step in and save the Agency from the wrath of Congress made Bush a hero at Langley; when he became president, the CIA would name its Headquarters Building after him.

The Ford administration and the CIA knew what was coming, though, despite Bush's skill in slow-rolling congressional reform. There would be a new day of legal accountability throughout the Intelligence Community. From 1947 to 1974, the CIA's Clandestine Service in its various incarnations (SPG, OPC, OSO, PSB, DP, DO) had experienced a high level of autonomy. Formal laws were non-existent other than the amorphous founding language in 1947; NSC directives were vague; White House review was either cursory or, because of plausible deniability, non-existent; congressional accountability was either casual or AWOL; constitutional and moral boundaries remained bleary. In a nutshell, CA operations were carried out absent rigorous internal review in the executive branch, while similarly the Congress indulged in "twenty-nine years of acquiescence."[41] Things were about to change.

The Hughes-Ryan Watershed

The Hughes-Ryan Act has been referred to in early chapters. Here is why this law is so important: in 1974, as the CIA was in the throes of controversy over domestic spying and the Agency's secret manipulation of democratic elections in Chile, and with the backdrop of the Watergate scandal and the soured war in Vietnam, Congress finally addressed the subject of covert action specifically in a statute. Before this time, former DCI Colby has recollected, the Agency had based its paramilitary operations on three rationales:

- the Agency bent toward Article II of the Constitution, which names the president as commander in chief;
- members of Congress were (supposedly) kept informed of Third Option activities;
- the congressional Appropriations Committees paid the bills and, thereby, gave further legitimacy to these operations.[42]

These arguments were not good enough, however, for post-Watergate, reform-minded members of Congress, who were keenly aware of President Johnson's excesses in Indochina and President Nixon's Watergate cover-up at home and legerdemain abroad. They understood the constitutional principle that the United States had to be a nation of laws, not men (as John Adams had memorably put it while serving in the Massachusetts state assembly).

The first serious reform measure on the Hill related to covert action was the Abourezk Amendment of October 1974. This proposal would have done away with the Third Option altogether—an idea that proved too radical to muster majorities in either chamber of Congress, despite the unusually high interest in intelligence reform at the time.[43] Two months later, the Hughes-Ryan Act proved more palatable to lawmakers.[44] Sponsored by Representative Leo Ryan (D, California) and Senator Harold Hughes (D, Iowa), this measure passed on December 30, 1974. The new law lacked a robust definition of covert action and was briefly worded; nonetheless, it was nothing less than revolutionary in its reach.[45] From now on, the CIA had to seek formal White House authority to conduct a covert action, with the president required to "find" that a proposed initiative was important to the national interest and should be implemented. Gone were the days of plausible deniability; now the paper trail for CA approvals led directly to the Oval Office at 1600 Pennsylvania Avenue. More sweeping still, the president had to report all presidential approvals ("findings") to the appropriate intelligence oversight committees on Capitol Hill. Suddenly Congress was explicitly in the Third Option loop.

The Hughes-Ryan law was majestic in its departure from previous practices that had been reliant on secret, and shifting, executive directives. Historian Anne Karalekis has commented on a particularly significant dimension of the statute. "Until 1974, 40 Committee decisions on covert action were not always referred to the President," she writes. "Only if there was a disagreement within the Committee or if a member of the Committee thought the proposed operation was important enough or sensitive enough would the President become involved. Once again, these ambiguous arrangements were intentional, designed to protect the President and to blur accountability."[46]

In contrast, here is the language of Hughes-Ryan (in its entirety):

> *No funds appropriated under the authority of this or any other Act may be expended by or on behalf of the [CIA] for operations in foreign countries, other than activities intended solely for obtaining necessary intelligence, unless and until the President finds that each such operation is important to the national security of the United States and reports, in a timely fashion, a description and scope of such operations to the appropriate committees of Congress.*[47]

Good-bye, plausible denial; hello, presidential accountability. As DCI Woolsey said while in office during the Clinton years, "We made it absolutely clear that nobody will come within a country mile of anything that could be regarded as covert action without having a finding; nobody will do a thing unless and until it is clear the NSC wants us to start putting together a finding document. We'll prepare the finding in a very restricted circle, and let each agency that might be involved in the operation have a chop."[48]

And hello, as well, to a group of elected representatives who now had the opportunity—indeed, the legal requirement—to consider America's uses of the Third Option. This reporting stipulation did not include all 435 members of Congress, of course, with the absurd security implications that would carry, but rather a small number of their colleagues on the Senate Select Committee on Intelligence (SSCI) and the House Permanent Select Committee on Intelligence (HPSCI) who would act as surrogates for their colleagues in the broader legislative branch.

How wise was it to bring some degree of democracy into the dark corners of covert ops—an experiment unprecedented at home, in other nations, or throughout history? From the vantage point of decreasing ill-considered covert actions, it was prudent; the reigning Langley point-of-view, though, was that lawmakers would merely "micromanage" their affairs and paralyze the Operations Directorate. Some in the Agency considered the decline in the use of the Third Option around this time a product of the CIA now having to report to Congress on these activities.[49] The decline was much more a function, though, of the churning effects resulting from the *Times* reporting on CIA operations in Chile, along with the Church Committee inquiry and the sheer exhaustion in Washington that stemmed from foreign policy setbacks summed up in the word "Vietnam." It is true, though, that the rules delivered a shock to the clandestine professionals in the DO. "It was as if," recalls a tongue-in-cheek British observer of the CIA, "they were in the position of the medical staff in a hospital waking up one morning to find their board of governors consisted of Christian Scientists and herbalists."[50]

The provisions of Hughes-Ryan are sufficiently important to an understanding of the law for covert action to warrant further dissection:

No funds . . . may be expended by or on the behalf of the Central Intelligence Agency for operations in foreign countries . . .

This clause announced that the government's money spigots would remain in the "off" position for the Third Option unless the rest of the Hughes-Ryan law was honored.

. . . other than activities intended solely for obtaining necessary intelligence . . .

The language here underlines the fact that the Hughes-Ryan statute is not about intelligence collection and analysis—or, for that matter, counterintelligence. It is about covert action.

> ... unless and until the President finds that each such operation is important to the national security of the United States.

The far-reaching requirement stated in this part of the law is that the president must put his or her good name on any important Third Option about to go forward in the field. This is the first revolutionary aspect of Hughes-Ryan: the clause that banished the doctrine of plausible denial.

> .... and reports, in a timely fashion, a description and scope of each operation. .

Here is the second revolutionary feature: the Congress—that is, its intelligence oversight panels—*must* be told about all presidential findings. What would constitute "timely," however, or "description and scope"? These ambiguities set the stage for inevitable wrangling among the White House, the NSC, and the nation's spies, on the one hand, and lawmakers and their aides, on the other hand (a political dimension of covert action taken up in Chapter 8). Two rare examples of declassified findings are presented in Figure 7.1, both declassified during the Iran-*contra* investigation. The difference in specificity between the Nicaraguan and the Iranian findings is notable, with the "Purpose" section of the former overly brief, allowing the CIA wide leeway—with all the mischief that can invite.

> ... to the appropriate committees of Congress.

Today these panels include SSCI and HPSCI, plus small twin subcommittees dealing with intelligence budgets on the Senate and House Appropriations Committees, as well as periodic briefings to the Armed Services committees on topics dealing directly with their concern for military intelligence. With passage of the Hughes-Ryan Act, the White House and the Congress were now very much in the Third Option action game.[51]

An Intelligence Charter

Following the Church Committee inquiry, some reformers on the Hill believed the time had come for even more far-reaching changes in America's use of its intelligence services. A coalition of reformers led by Senator Walter "Dee" Huddleston (D, Kentucky, a former member of the Church Committee and, at the time, a member of SSCI), attempted to pass a comprehensive oversight

Example No. 1: Central America

> Finding Pursuant to Section 662 of the Foreign Assistance Act of 1961, As Amended. Concerning Operations Undertaken by the Central Intelligence Agency in Foreing Countries. Other Than Those Imended Solcly ot the Purpoge of Intelligence Collection

I hereby find that the following operations in foreign countries (including all support necessary to such operations) are important to the nationl security of the United States, and direct the Director of Central Intelligence, or his lesignee, to report this Finding to the concerned conmmitees of the Congress pursuant to Law, and to provide such briefing as necessary.

SCOPE	PURPOSE
Central America	Provide all forms of training, equipment and related assistance to cooperating governments throughout Central America in order to counter foreign-sponsored subversion and terrorism. [still-classified section missing here] Encourage and influence foreign governments around the world to support all of the above objectives.

Example No. 2: Iran

> Finding Pursuant to Section 662 of The Foreign Assistance Act of 1961 As amended. Concerning Operations Undertaken by the Central Intelligence Agency in Foreign Countries. Other Than Those Intended Solely for the Purpose of Intelligence Collection

I hereby find that the following operation in a foreign country (includeing all support necessary to such operation) is important to the national security of the United States, and due to its extreme sensitivity and security risks. I determine it is essential to limit prior notice, and direct the Director of Central Intell gence to refrain from reporting this Finding to the Congress as provided in Section 501 of the National Security Act of 1947, as ameneded, unit I otherwise direct.

SCOPE	DESCRIPTION
Iran	Assist selected friendly foreign liaison services, third countries and third parties which have established relationships with Iranish elements, groups, and individuals sympathetic to U.S. Government interests and which do not conduct or support terrorist actions directed against U.S. persons, property or interests, for the purpose of : (1) establishing a more moderate government in Iran, (2) obtaining from them significant intelligence not otherwise obtainable, determine the current Iranian Government's methods with respect to its neighbors and with respect to terrorist acts, and (3) furthering the release of the American hostages held in Beiruz and preventing additional rerrorist acts by these groups. Provide funds, intelligence, counter-intelliegence, training, guidance and communications and other necessary assistance to these elements, groups, individuals, Iiaison services and third countries in support of these activities.
	The USG will act to facilitate efforts by third parties and third countries to establish contact with moderate elements within and outside the Government of Iran by providing these elements with arms, equipment and related material in order to enhance the credibility of these elements in their effort to achieve a more pro-U.S. government in Iran by demonstrating their ability to obtain requisite resources to defend their country against Iraq and intervention by the Soviet Union. This support will be discontinued if the U.S. Government learns that these elements have abandoned their goals of moderating their government and appropriated the material for puposes other than that provided by this finding.

Sources: *Public Papers of the President: Ronald Reagan* (Washington, DC: U.S. Government Printing Office, 1986); Presidential Finding on Central America, N16534: Iran Finding, 1/17/86. Hearings, Ex. JMP-29-D. Report of the Congressional Commitees Investigating the Iran-Contra Affair S. Rept. No. 100-216 and H. Rept. No. 100-433, 100th Cong., 1st Sess, U.S. Senate Slecet Committee on Secret Military Assistance to Iran and the Nicaraguan Opposition and U.S. House of Representatives Select Committee to Investigate Covert Arms Transactions with Iran (the Inouye/Hamilton Committee), November 1987.

Figure 7.1 Examples of Presidential Findings on Covert Actions, 1981

law, known informally as the "Grand Intelligence Charter" or officially as the National Intelligence Reorganization and Reform Act of 1978.[52] The proposal was introduced on the Senate floor in February 1978. The initiative addressed the entire scope of US intelligence, with a seaweed intricacy, in the advocacy of more than 270 pages of legal regulations. The goal was to eradicate as many ambiguities in intelligence law and practice as possible, once and for all.

The Carter and the Reagan administrations, unusual allies normally at opposite ends of the political spectrum, both considered the proposal too all-encompassing and restrictive. Among the details on covert action, the Charter proposed a ban on

- the mass destruction of property;
- the creation of food or water shortages or floods;
- the creation of epidemics or diseases;
- the use of chemical or biological (CB) weapons;
- the violent overthrow of the democratic government of any country;
- the torture of individuals; and,
- the support of any action which violated human rights, whether conducted by the police, foreign intelligence, or internal security forces of any foreign country.[53]

The proposed law managed to rile up the entire Intelligence Community and its extensive network of supporters, as America's secret agencies pulled out all the lobbying stops to halt the initiative. Congress seemed to take on the configuration of an adversarial foreign country, and the Agency knew a thing or two about maneuvering against hostile regimes.[54] Its legislative liaison staff, which included a sizable component of DO officers, fanned out across the Hill to work their skills of persuasion. The theme of their counterattack: with its detailed prohibitions, the Charter would be devastating to operational flexibiliuty and place the CIA at a great disadvantage in confrontations with the KGB and other hostile spy services. When the dust settled, the Charter had nowhere near the number of votes necessary for passage and it vanished into the dustbin of history. This did not mean, of course, that critics of the proposal endorsed the horrific CA examples cited above. Almost all would have agreed with those taboos. It was a massive document, however, and critics had remonstrated chiefly against its vast number of tentacles that reached into every corner of intelligence.

This burst of energy by Charter reformers was not without effect, however. Their efforts would turn defeat into victory as they shifted adroitly to a more manageable and acceptable law governing intelligence accountability. Indeed, the most significant statutory guidance for the Agency since its creation twenty-eight years earlier.

The Intelligence Oversight Act of 1980

In lieu of the sprawling measures presented in the Intelligence Charter, reformers retreated to a two-and-a-half-page bill—a 99 percent reduction in the number of pages from the Charter. This alternative proposal was known as the Intelligence Oversight Act of 1980.[55] It appeared, at first glance, that intelligence reformers had lost the day. In fact, though, within this brief Charter spinoff was packed a powerful set of oversight requirements, including corrections to glaring omissions and obscurities in the Hughes-Ryan Act. Treverton has referred to this statute as "the most important law passed by Congress in the realm of covert action."[56] Its full wording can be found in Appendix B, but key provisions are succinctly reviewed here:

> *To the extent consistent with all applicable authorities and duties, including those conferred by the Constitution upon the executive and legislative branches . . .*

This preamble to the law exhibits an amusing dance of legislation, wherein both branches mollified one another by suggesting that none of the legal language to follow would jeopardize either's constitutional rights—for purists of legislative accountability, an alarming concession that might allow nimble-footed presidents in the future to ignore the law's provisions, on grounds that his or her constitutional duties as chief executive must come first (Article II). Despite this ambiguous beginning, the subsequent language bared not just teeth but fangs when it came to a determination by Congress to exercise a meaningful role in the monitoring of the nation's secret agencies, including—above all—the Third Option. The goal: no more Chiles and no more assassination plots, at least not unless examined in advance by HPSCI and SSCI lawmakers.

> *(1)   ". . . fully and currently informed . . ."*

For Congress to play a role in the shaping of intelligence operations, its members first had to know what the nation's spy agencies were doing. Toward that end, some of the most powerful language in this law underscores the insistence of lawmakers that SSCI, HPSCI, and the Appropriations Committees must be included in the witting circle when it came to spy activities, not least the Third Option. This requirement included "any significant *anticipated* intelligence activity"; and later in this section, the momentous word "*prior*" is inserted for emphasis. Congress had further tightened the legal screws on clandestine interventions, mandating *prior notice* to SSCI and HPSCI on *all* covert action of importance approved by the president. No more *ex post facto*—after the fact—reporting to lawmakers. These new rules required *ante facto* briefings, that is, *in advance*. No more two-day delays as under Hughes-Ryan (except in emergencies; see below), which often made it too late for lawmakers to register whatever objections they might have.

This concept of prior notice is as important to the examination of covert actions by SSCI and HPSCI as the long-held possession of subpoena powers by the Congress to call witnesses for hearings—both rare procedures absent from most every other legislative or parliamentary chamber in the world. From now on, members of SSCI and HPSCI had an opportunity to offer their critiques *before* clandestine operations were under way, perhaps managing to close the barnyard door (if necessary) before the horse bolted out. By virtue of this chance for genuine debate, two groups of surrogates for all of Congress—one in the House (HPSCI) and one in the Senate (SSCI)—could rebuke untoward proposals, even threaten budgetary retaliation should the executive branch choose to ignore guidance from the congressional oversight committees.

(1)(B) "... if the President determines it is essential to limit prior notice to meet extraordinary circumstances..."

Prudently, the statute permitted some delay in reporting in times of dire emergency. Even then, however, the law required reports in advance to a small group of eight congressional leaders who became known as the "Gang of Eight." These individuals included the House Speaker, the House Minority Leader, the HPSCI Chair, the HPSCI Ranking Minority member, along with their counterpart leaders in the Senate.

(3)(b) "...fully inform... in a timely fashion..."

This prescription, the same language that appeared in Hughes-Ryan, was a follow-on to the Gang of Eight provision, making it clear that the other members of SSCI and HPSCI would have to be informed—and before long—about the operation that had been too sensitive to discuss in advance during the time of emergency. "Timely manner" is, of course, an amorphous concept with some wiggle room; but the colloquy during the passage of this law pointed to forty-eight hours as the proper benchmark, a standard that would be made more transparent in a letter from President George H. W. Bush to Congress in 1991 (along with another landmark oversight law passed that year, discussed below).

In short, as insisted on by the Constitution, Congress would be an equal partner in the affairs of state—now including the hidden side of government, too, by joining the White House as a partner in the sharing of information about spy operations. The exception: emergency circumstances, and even then the leadership on Capitol Hill and the intelligence oversight panels (the Gang of Eight) would be on an equal footing with the president. Afterward, in a maximum of two days, so would the remaining members of SSCI and HPSCI.

(1)   "... *shall not require approval of the intelligence committees*..."

The 1980 statute did not expressly require congressional *approval* of covert actions; that would have drawn the debate over the legislation into a constitutional thicket regarding the president's control of the executive bureaucracy. It did, however, establish a setting—the required briefing on a finding—that permitted lawmakers on SSCI and HPSCI to weigh in. Given the congressional power of the purse, opposition among these members of Congress to a specific covert action could not be taken lightly, either in the Oval Office or on Langley's Seventh Floor.

(1)   "... all *intelligence activities which are the responsibility of, are engaged in by, or are carried out for or on behalf of, any department, agency, or* entity *of the united States*... [underscoring added]

This clause's short but muscular language went far beyond Hughes-Ryan, which was strictly a covert action statute, to clarify that SSCI and HPSCI had to be told about *all* significant operations within the three intelligence missions: collection and analysis, counterintelligence, and covert action. "All" is a small but powerfully encompassing word. Further, the 1980 Oversight Act closed a Hughes-Ryan loophole by insisting that covert action, or any of the other significant intelligence activities, had to be reported to Congress, *regardless of which agency was carrying them out*—as captured unequivocally by another all-encompassing word: "entity."

The president might decide—though one would hope not—to assign a covert action mission to the Department of Agriculture, instead of the CIA; say, a Third Option dealing with the destruction of crops or livestock in an adversarial country. Under this provision, however, the Department—a government entity—would still be subject to *ante facto* reporting to SSCI and HPSCI. This language became important during the Iran-*contra* investigation, when NSC staff members claimed that the 1980 Oversight Act did not pertain to them because they were not within the CIA or any other agency of the Intelligence Community. As congressional investigators pointed out, though, the NSC is a government *entity*, and they were engaged in covert actions. Full stop.

Two other significant intelligence laws emerged from the deliberation of lawmakers in reaction to their shock over the Iran-*contra* scandal: a CIA Inspector General Act, and a follow-on to the 1980 Intelligence Oversight Act.

CIA Inspector General Act

The Iran-*contra* affair was the greatest setback in the experiment to bring democracy into the closed world of covert actions. Once the congressional and executive branch investigations were over (the Inouye-Hamilton Committee and the Tower Commission, respectively),[57] members of Congress enacted a CIA Inspector General Act to help avoid another illegal intelligence fiasco. This measure made the Office of the IG more effective within the CIA— and answerable to Congress.[58] The language of the statute gave the IG enhanced authority to conduct internal inquiries (the Church Committee had found that the Agency's IG from 1947 to 1974 was basically clueless about most of the CIA's controversial Agency operations, including its covert actions in Cuba and Chile, as well as the assassination plots). Further, the law required the new IG to report to SSCI and HPSCI at least twice a year, as well as whenever any instance of malfeasance came to light at Langley.

The Intelligence Oversight Act of 1991

A second Iran-*contra* inspired law was the Intelligence Authorization Act of 1991, known less formally as the Intelligence Oversight Act of that year and a follow-on to the Intelligence Oversight Act of 1980. At long last, this law formally defined covert action. The definition states that CA is "*an activity or activities of the United States Government to influence political, economic, or military conditions abroad, where it is intended that the role of the United States Government will not be apparent or acknowledged publicly.*"[59]

The initial draft of this proposal had emphasized that, in those rare emergency "Gang of Eight" circumstances, the rest of SSCI and HPSCI indeed would be informed within forty-eight hours, as set forth in the 1980 Oversight Act. President George H. W. Bush balked, however, at what he thought was an inappropriately mandatory timeclock for reporting to Congress. He exercised the presidential prerogative of a pocket-veto, which stopped the entire proposal dead in its tracks—the only time a proposed intelligence law has been vetoed by the White House. Soon afterward, though, President Bush offered a conciliatory letter addressed to chairmen of SSCI and HPSCI. "I anticipate that in almost all instances where prior notice is not provided, notice will be provided within a few days," he wrote. "Any withholding beyond this period will be based upon my assertion of authorities granted to this office by the Constitution."[60]

In light of this laudable (if still somewhat obscure) effort by President Bush to pass the peace pipe to SSCI and HPSCI so that the new oversight law could be enacted, Congress took up the legislative proposal once more. Again the legislation passed and this time the president signed it into law. At the signing ceremony, he reiterated the point he made in his letter, namely, that he had the constitutional authority to ignore prior reporting to HPSCI and SSCI if necessary—though presumably strictly in situations of utmost emergency. This ongoing ambiguity was the price paid by Congress for the bill's enactment. (The reactions of lawmakers to presidential reporting on findings are examined in Chapter 8.)

The 9/11 Statutes

In the wake of the 9/11 attacks, new laws emerged to guide America's spy agencies. Among them was the Intelligence Reform and Terrorism Prevention Act (IRTPA) of 2004 (Chapter 6), which started out as an attempt to strengthen the DCI office and instead ended up creating an isolated and weak Office of the DNI. The only time that office has worked well so far was under the leadership of James R. Clapper Jr., who enjoyed a long-time working relationship with several of the intelligence agency heads and could make things happen within the IC. The other DNIs lasted only a short time—about a year on average, compared to Clapper's six years in that office. Also, in disgust over the use of torture by the CIA to elicit intelligence from suspected terrorists, the Congress enacted a measure in 2005—the Detainee Treatment Act (DTA)—that made such practices illegal.[61]

Legal and Constitutional Ramifications

Executive branch directives have provided some authority for the Third Option since 1947, although they have tended to be broadly worded. This watery language has allowed the Agency considerable discretionary leeway in carrying out its operations. Anyone with even an ounce of managerial experience understands the importance of flexibility and agility for an organization's field units that must implement policy, as opposed to the more ponderous bureaucracy at headquarters. Yet specificity is also important to ensure that a policy is being carried out as headquarters and overseers intended. This is a balancing act, and for covert action it has sometimes tipped toward excessive ambiguity at lower levels.

As Clark Clifford, the chief author of the National Security Act of 1947, testified before the Church Committee, slippage in the Third Option's chain of command has sometimes gone "from point A to point B. . . . When point B is reached, the persons in charge feel it is necessary to go to point C, and they assume that the original authorization gives them such a right. From point C, they go to D and possibly E, and even further."[62] McGeorge Bundy, National Security Adviser during the Kennedy and Johnson administrations, recalled, too, that an operation might have been "presented in one way to [the 40] committee and executed in a way that is different from what the committee thought it had considered."[63] Open-ended directives, coupled with the lack of clear legal guidelines and accountability, led to mistakes and, in the case of Iran-*contra*, stunning lawlessness.

In response to these experiences, and jarred by the revelation of the operations directed against Chile, Hughes-Ryan was born, the Church Committee established, SSCI and HPSCI created (with their access to mandatory briefings on CA findings), and a new premium placed on Colby's notion of "Constitutional Intelligence in America." Tone is vital with respect to governmental leadership within a democracy. The chief counsel of the Iran-*contra* investigation on the Hill, Arthur L. Liman, remarked that the scandal "wasn't just a series of improper actions, it was a mentality." He observed that during the Reagan years it became "patriotic to lie to Congress, to circumvent checks and balances through covert actions, and to create the Enterprise to do what the CIA was not permitted to do."[64]

The Oversight Acts of 1980 and 1991, plus the few additional statutes enacted and executive orders written in this new era of intelligence accountability, established clearer boundaries for the Third Option. This historically unprecedented attempt to bring America's secret agencies into the full workings of a democratic society, against significant opposition—including from the intelligence agencies themselves—was remarkable. One result was to inspire other democracies around the world to take steps in this direction, from the United Kingdom and Canada to Australia and New Zealand (among many other countries, including France, Germany, and Holland). In the United States, this experiment fell flat on its face after only five years when the Iran-*contra* conspirators shredded the Hughes-Ryan Act, the 1980 Intelligence Oversight Act, the Boland Amendments, and the Constitution. The ship of state righted itself, though, after thorough probes into the abuses and a reaffirmation of constitutional principles now applied to the dark side of government, as urged by the Church Committee and DCI Colby (among many others).

These efforts at intelligence reform have continued to have their ups and downs. They are often dependent on the views of, and the commitment of time to oversight by, individual SSCI and HPSCI leaders and members, presidents and their advisers, agency directors, and rank-and-file intelligence officers. Their degree of involvement has ranged from a belief that the proper degree of commitment to these duties is "none at all," to a robust understanding that the genius of the Constitution was its insistence on shared government and congressional checks and balances as a guard against the abuse of power—and, most dangerous of all, secret power.

There is no finality to this debate. The Constitution remains, as Professor Corwin famously put it, "an invitation to struggle" among the branches of government.[65] One can hope, though, that the framework of balanced government—a government with all its cylinders firing, not least the Congress—is seriously considered and appreciated by all parties, and that laws designed to encourage a constitutional balance within the secret realm of intelligence remain on the books, and in the hearts and minds of the nation's leaders and citizens.

8
Decision Paths and Accountability

Covert Action, Democracy, and the Constitution

When it comes to decision making for the Third Option as well as its accountability, one feature stands out in the twenty-seven years that separate the National Security Act of 1947 from the Hughes-Ryan Act of 1974: the CIA was only loosely part of America's government. The result was predictable. As a former DNI James R. Clapper has put it, "The history of the Intelligence Community is replete with abuses."[1] The foolish embrace of "intelligence exceptionalism" at the very beginning of the nation's history was finally addressed, for covert action at any rate, by the Hughes-Ryan Act, the Church Committee inquiry, and the Intelligence Oversight Acts of 1980 and 1991. Today, as former DCI Robert M. Gates has written, intelligence serves the president and lawmakers equally, which is exactly how the Constitution envisioned the way a democracy should work.[2]

Nevertheless, some in America's society continue to resist efforts at keeping proper checks and balances over the hidden side of government, preferring to return to the days when the CIA and its companion intelligence agencies enjoyed wide discretionary authority. These nostalgists either forget or choose to ignore the disasters that arose as a result of unbridled secret power. Among them: the Bay of Pigs, assassination plots against leaders in the developing world, and the Iran-*contra* scandal (not to mention, on the collection side, Operation "CHAOS" and its program of domestic spying against anti-Vietnam War protestors).

Allen W. Dulles, the most famous of the DCIs, preferred to tell the truth about the CIA's activities only to one person: the president.[3] Conveniently for him, presidents seldom asked questions. Nor did members of Congress in that era. Almost always, the White House and the NSC were content to let the CIA duke it out with the KGB, leaving the details to officers in the DP and later the DO. Former Secretary of State Rusk, for example, recalled that he "never saw a budget of the CIA," even though he was a statutory member of the National Security Council, the hub of the wheel for US national security policy.[4]

As for Congress, "the old tradition was that [lawmakers] didn't ask," remembered former DCI Colby. "It was a consensus that intelligence was apart from the rules . . . that was the reason we did step over the line in a few cases, largely because no one was watching. No one was there to say don't do that."[5] On the Hill, Senator Church also reflected on these earlier years, noting that "some of those senior senators who did have this so-called [intelligence] watchdog committee were known to say in effect: 'We don't watch the dog. We don't know what's going on, and furthermore, we don't want to know.' "[6] The result, which James Madison would have predicted, was a collapse of democratic principles and institutions within the hidden side of government, as manifested most shockingly in illegal spying at home and the Iran-*contra* scandal overseas.

The Third Option Approval Process

With the advent of the Hughes-Ryan statute, the procedures for approving covert actions went from simple to complex, from a short sprint to the 400-meter hurdles. For those who opposed bringing accountability into the world of intelligence, the new rules were a catastrophe. Too many players would now gum up the works and leak sensitive information, ruining one of the best instruments for foiling the machinations of communists and other enemies of the United States. In contrast, for proponents of accountability—the establishment of debate and the serious review of intelligence operations by executive and legislative authorities outside the CIA—Hughes-Ryan was a wise compromise for bringing some degree of democracy into the remotest part of the government without harming national security.

Opponents of accountability were correct in their belief that the procedures for the Third Option had become more complex. The diagram in Figure 8.1 depicts the process mandated by the Hughes-Ryan rules, beginning with the first day of the New Year in 1975. This decision pathway remains essentially the same today, with a few name changes here and there for the NSC review panels. The most significant difference between now and then has been the entry of the DNI into the decision loop, even though the Intelligence Reform and Terrorism Prevention Act (IRTPA) of 2004 that created that office said nothing at all about the DNI having a say over covert actions.

Actual policymaking can be quite different from formal law, however, and the DNI has become "deeply involved" in Third Option decisions.[7] In the first place, the DNI is the chief representative of the entire Intelligence Community. This means that a covert action proposal must be included in the DNI's National Intelligence Program, or NIP—the annual spy budget (*sans* military intelligence, which is located in a separate appropriations compartment).

Moreover, in a document sent to lawmakers each year, known as the Congressional Budget Justification Book (CBJC, which has a classified annex on intelligence activities), the reasons that a particular covert action appears in the NIP and deserves funding are spelled out. These reasons must be defended by both the D/CIA and the DNI. As a result, it becomes important for the Agency

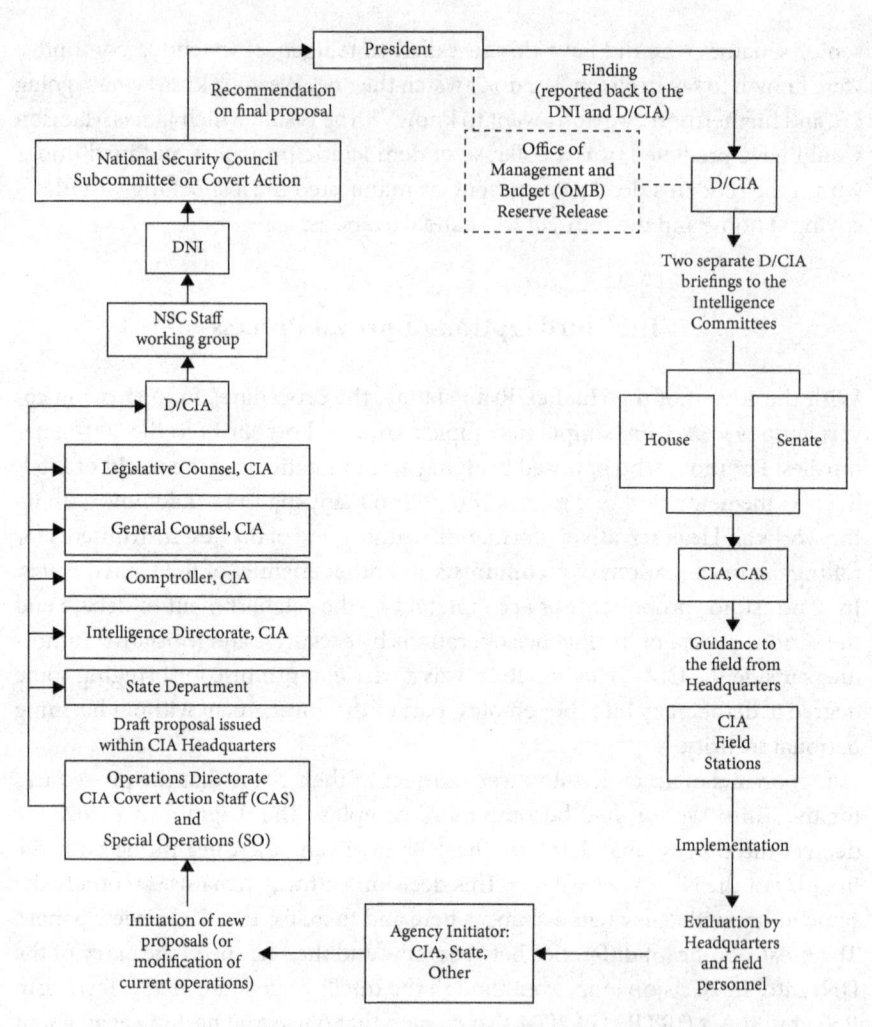

Figure 8.1 Decision and Reporting Paths for Covert Action, Established in 1975.
Source: Loch K. Johnson, *American Foreign Policy and the Challenges of World Leadership: Power, Principle, and the Constitution* (New York: Oxford University Press, 2015): 392.

to bring the DNI on board in support of a clandestine intervention, since he—and with the Biden administration, she: Avril Haines—may well be queried by lawmakers about the operation. Two voices, the D/CIA and the DNI, both visiting SSCI and HPSCI (as well as the Appropriations Committees), are able to provide a stronger case than one person alone. The reality is that without the DNI as an advocate, a Third Option proposal might well stall out in Congress. Finally, D/CIAs have found it politically wise to have the weight of the DNI—a senior professional colleague—included in the vetting process, as a CA proposal initially wends its way upward within the executive branch hierarchy from Langley to the Oval Office.

On the post-decision side of covert action, having the DNI aboard also gives the Agency an opportunity to have an ally in shouldering the blame, should things go wrong. Former Air Force three-star general and DNI Clapper has said that he routinely told each of the four D/CIAs with whom he served during his six-years-plus on the job as DNI (2010–17): "If you want me around when the plane crashes, have me around when the plane takes off."[8] Each of the Agency's directors abided by this old Air Force saw and embraced a policy of transparency toward Clapper on all Third Option initiatives. Referring back to Figure 8.1, the DNI now stands between the DCI (renamed the D/CIA in 2004) and the NSC, as the final senior intelligence official to sign off on a proposal for a clandestine intervention before the Council's staff, then the president and the other top three members of the NSC, evaluate its merits.

As one might suppose, the Agency's stations overseas—on the front lines of America's secret foreign policy—are significant germinators of new Third Option ideas. In 1980, for instance, many proposals bubbled up to Headquarters from COSs around the world, usually in response to directives from Headquarters that seek recommendations on how to solve various global challenges.[9] Occasionally, clandestine schemes are concocted by CIA assets, too, although the DO has learned to be cautious about these individuals who sometimes simply try "to make themselves appear busy and worth their keep."[10] Plus, recall the risks of dealing with wild-cat operatives like WI/ROGUE (Chapter 1). A high-ranking DP operative, Desmond "Des" FitzGerald, sensitive to the question of whether the Agency was creating too many CA proposals without proper alignment with America's overt foreign policy, reminded National Security Adviser McGeorge Bundy in 1964 that "although the Agency appears as the proposer of most covert action programs at the Special Group and elsewhere, we do this only in response to what we understand to be policy requirements and have no interest in either commencing or perpetuating any programs which are not demanded by policy and which are not geared to the accomplishment of a specific objective."[11]

From year to year, the pattern of having most CA proposals arise from the field has remained fairly constant, though with occasional ideas seeping up from elsewhere in the Agency bureaucracy and in other parts of the national security apparatus. For example, as one would expect, the DO's Covert Action Staff (CAS) will periodically offer suggestions, driven in part by a bureaucratic imperative to be creative and productive as a way to impress the boss at promotion time—the Agency's version of the "publish or perish" syndrome found in the nation's universities. As a former CAS operative recalls, once the US government established a capacity for covert action, the White House and other senior authorities sometimes failed to realize "that we would *seek* fires to put out, even if we had to light them ourselves"[12] Or as Scott Anderson writes: "Covert Action specialists get noticed for conducting operations, not for canceling them."[13]

Moreover, the Counterintelligence Staff (CIS)—an even deeper and darker cavern at Langley under the leadership of James Angleton from 1954 to 1974 than the CAS—has pushed forward a Third Option idea or two over the years, such as spreading around Eastern Europe altered copies of Khrushchev's anti-Stalin speech to the Twentieth Congress of the Communist Party of the Soviet Union (CPSU) in 1956. Angleton was no stranger to clandestine activities and enjoyed a coign of vantage in this domain, having served as special assistant to the DDP until tapped to lead the CIS in 1954. The Agency's Nonproliferation Center (NPC) has also advanced some covert action proposals now and again before that intelligence mission shifted in 2005 over to the Office of the DNI. The NPC was renamed the National Counterproliferation Center (NCPC) and expanded. This Center has become an important source of CA proposals aimed at the possible spread of WMD around the globe. As well, the Agency's Center for Counterterrorism (CTC) puts in an occasional oar, as when assisting DO operatives to destroy suspected chemical or biological facilities held by terrorist organizations in different parts of the world.[14] The creation of the CTC in 1986 was a significant boost to the Agency's covert action capabilities. As former DCI Gates writes: "Before, we issued analyses to policymakers about terrorist organizations. Now we were operational."[15] Planners in the DO began to employ the Third Option far more often against terrorism, illegal drugs, human trafficking, and the proliferation of WMD, rather than just against specific countries and regimes—a trend that has accelerated in recent years.[16]

Other organizations outside the Agency sometimes offer covert action recommendations to the Operations Directorate, such as DoD and DoS (at the secretary level), ambassadors in the field, and (though rarely) from individual lawmakers and presidents. Only once has a member of Congress, HPSCI's Charlie Wilson, sustained a truly gung-ho involvement in covert action planning from A to Z, in his case in support of the Agency's operations against the Soviet military in Afghanistan (Chapter 5). Every once in a while, though, an influential lawmaker will jump in, as did Speaker of the House Newt Gingrich (R, Georgia) in 1995, when he insisted on adding $18 million from Congress for a secret fund aimed at overthrowing the Iranian regime. As noted earlier in this book, the Carter administration offers an unusual example of a president personally recommending a covert action (still classified), one designed to advance human rights—his favorite policy subject—in a developing nation.[17]

Here is an illustration of the decision process for covert actions since Hughes-Ryan. After a COS's initiation of a proposal, let us say, it is scrubbed by the Covert Action Staff (CAS) or, for paramilitary operations, by the Special Operations Group (SOG, nicknamed the "Ground Branch" by insiders), both located within the Agency's Directorate of Operations. Since the advent of Hughes-Ryan and the demise of plausible deniability (what Chris Whipple has referred to as "a tectonic shift in the landscape of intelligence, signaling a new world"),[18] the CIA has taken great pains to forward to the White House only those Third Option proposals that have been prepared with great care and coordinated with other relevant entities at Langley—such as the Analysis Directorate. The Agency's reputation was now more directly on the line with the president and top White House advisers.

After emerging from these DO scrubs, a CA initiative is subject to much greater inhouse discussion and coordination than before Hughes-Ryan, to the dismay of operations officers. Former DCI Gates remembers how the DO "was neither comfortable nor happy" with the involvement of other parts of the Agency in its activities.[19] Nevertheless, such was the reality of the new scene. As traced in Figure 8.1, the DO was expected in the post-Hughes-Ryan era to touch base with several units within the Agency:

Legislative Counsel: how would the proposal play on Capitol Hill?
General Counsel: how did the proposal come across from a legal point of view?
Comptroller: what would the operation cost, and was that funding available?
Intelligence Directorate (today, Analysis Directorate): Did the CIA's analysts have any guidance that might improve, or perhaps discourage, moving forward with a covert action?

As Figure 8.1 depicts as well, the CIA now makes more of an effort to coordinate its clandestine interventions with the State Department, especially when it comes to planting propaganda overseas. As former DCI Leon Panetta has said: "Even though we were operating on a covert basis, you had to make sure that the overt methods that were being used at least delivered the same message."[20]

In the propaganda domain, first the CAS develops a concept ("perspective"), say, on the merits of stationing US troops in Estonia, or of building sophisticated anti-ballistic-missile shields in South Korea and Japan. A theme, once drafted, is sent under these new procedures to the State Department's intelligence agency (the Bureau of Intelligence and Research or INR) for review, modification, or even a veto. The intelligence professionals in INR check with relevant members of State's diplomatic corps for their opinions and, if necessary in particularly sensitive cases, with managers up the Department's hierarchy, all the way to the secretary's office for especially delicate proposals. This coordination became doubly important once the United States created overt organizations to fund political activities abroad, such as the National Endowment for Democracy (created in 1983), to ensure that the Agency's activities dovetailed with the State Department's programs.

At the time of the Carter administration, about a quarter of the CAS-generated propaganda themes would be deep-sixed by State. Those that survived were then forwarded to the DCI—or, today, to the D/CIA and the DNI—for review, where the proposals are sometimes sent back to lower levels for revision. If approved, the themes move on through the rest of the decision points displayed in Figure 8.1. If the propaganda theme is merely a slight variation of one already covered under a previous presidential finding, the CAS can then contact the Agency's station to allow dissemination of the message—although, even in these instances, only after running the modification by the State Department. In some instances, findings from a previous administration can continue under a new presidency, but the incoming president and the congressional oversight committees must be informed about these extensions (which were more plentiful during the Obama years than is usually the case).

As further shown in Figure 8.1, in addition to State for propaganda themes, the Agency has another—and even more daunting—outside entity to deal with as it seeks Third Option approvals: an NSC staff "covert action working group," which has had various names over the years. The DCI (and now the D/CIA and the DNI) must interact with this White House sentinel to advance a clandestine initiative.

The NSC staff working group (senior deputies who represented the president, the vice president, the secdef, and the secstate, on the Deputies Committee) is expected to give the Third Option an acid bath of criticism, and a high percentage of proposals are cancelled at this stage. Those that pass muster move forward to the NSC "principals" themselves on the Principals Committee: the president, vice president, secdef, and secstate, known formally as the NSC Subcommittee on Covert Action—the center piece in the executive branch for Third Option approvals. In the tradition of Council panels, this one has undergone a number of name changes from administration to administration, such as the Special Coordination Committee (SCC) during the Carter administration and the National Security Planning Group (NSPG) during the Reagan administration (for precursors, see Chapter 7). As the last step, the president decides whether to bless the operation by issuing or rejecting a "finding," as required by Hughes-Ryan. If the covert action is a response to a foreign policy emergency, the White House has access to the CIA Contingency Reserve Release Fund. This reservoir of money consists of several million dollars, on hand for use in fast-moving circumstances. Access to this funding is subject to presidential approval, followed by immediate reporting to SSCI and HPSCI. An example of its use: $1 million released for timely assistance to the Polish workers movement, Solidarity, in 1983.

These Hughes-Ryan procedures are strikingly different from the earlier days of brief telephone conversations between a DCI and a national security advisor—or, often, no higher clearance at all outside the confines of the Agency's leadership pod at Langley. In each of these new steps, officials have an eye out for several features in a proposal. What is the justification for it? How important is the operation for America's global interests? What has been the history of activities against the target? How much will the operation cost? What are the risks? How will it be coordinated with State and Defense, or other relevant US departments and agencies? What are the odds of success? What are the alternatives? How are HPSCI and SSCI likely to react?

These questions have always been present for Third Option planning with the exception of the lack of concern about the views of lawmakers in the pre-Church Committee era. What was new about the Hughes-Ryan procedures was the number of individuals now scrutinizing the proposal and addressing these questions, including—in the most dramatic change—members of SSCI and HPSCI.

Speed of Action and the Hughes-Ryan Rules

Some have criticized this decision sequence for being too complicated, taking too long, and, as a result, robbing the United States of advantages once accrued to the Agency by virtue of its ability to engage quickly and nimbly in secret interventions. "What we have is covert action by national consensus!" bemoaned a senior DO official after adoption of the new rules.[21] In a comparison between reliance on a telephone call to the national security adviser in the old days versus the various steps outlined in Figure 8.1, obviously the former is quicker. Yet, when it counts, not by much. In times of urgency, a proposal can race through this flow chart. The key personnel—the DDO, the D/CIA, the DNI, the four NSC principals (including the president), and the "Gang of Eight"—can all be patched together quickly on a secure phone or internet connection, when fast-moving authority is necessary. Even when Congress is in recess and key members are traveling in their home districts, away from secure telephones, they can be reached with a little bit of persistence, as when the CIA speedily contacted the Gang of Eight about Russian interference in the 2016 presidential election.[22]

In normal times, democracy is—to its credit—slower than the decision process for the world's autocrats. Slowness can be a good thing, as the nation debates and deliberates over the best way to proceed, all the while keeping the likely reaction of citizens to the operation in mind, should the covert action become public. Moreover, in almost all cases, the development of a Third Option is not acutely time-sensitive. Thus, the criticism of these new procedures as a hopeless, time-consuming labyrinth is unfounded. In addition, much is gained by including others in the shaping of covert actions beyond bureaucrats and specialists in the DO, such as a few elected officials on Capitol Hill (SSCI and HPSCI members) or foreign policy experts in the Department of State. At least some degree of debate, the linchpin of democracy, can take place even in this sheltered and sensitive realm of government.

One worthy Third Option proposal, which remains classified, took six months to travel through the steps in the Hughes-Ryan circuit. At the beginning, the initiative received close scrutiny inside the DO for two months, going through a series of drafts as experts worked out the kinks, tightened the language, and anticipated possible questions from the NSC's staff and principals, as well as from SSCI and HPSCI. During this period, the proposal was vetted by the other Agency entities presented in Figure 8.1, as well as by the State Department. The next month was devoted to a gimlet-eyed review by the NSC staff working group, followed by another month for review by the NSC Subcommittee on Covert Action—the principals in the executive branch. Finally, during a fifth month, the proposal gained presidential authority by way of a finding. The journey took time, but the end result was a first-rate operation that easily sailed through HSPCI and SSCI review over the final month, then succeeded admirably in the field. Had a faster approval period been necessary, that would have happened, too—although the end product would have been less thoroughly studied, thereby increasing the odds of error or outright failure.

Generic or "Worldwide" Findings

A controversy has evolved regarding the presidential use of so-called generic or worldwide findings: White House approvals so broad and open-ended ("thwart Qaeda operations in North Africa") as to invite forms of tradecraft in their pursuit that were never anticipated by a president or legislative overseers. This type of finding takes advantage of the law's silence on how detailed a finding should be, occasionally sending a Third Option cascading down the unpredictable slide that Clark Clifford warned against, from Points A to B to C, and perhaps even further.

Naturally, it should not be the purpose of a finding to put the CIA and its officers into a straitjacket. As argued in Chapter 7, flexibility in the field can be a necessity. A long-toothed DO veteran has stressed. "Covert action teams often could respond more quickly and effectively [during America's recent long war in Afghanistan], sometimes before we at HQS [Headquarters at Langley] even knew what action they were taking," he writes. "This was more than OK—it was what I wanted. The field leaders demonstrated flat, networked intelligence collaboration and covert action at its best."[23]

Yes, "OK"—until it isn't.

Findings should be a carefully calibrated balancing act that takes into account the need for agility in the field but that also honors the original intent of the covert action. Too often, instead, findings have been so vague as to permit almost any approach during the implementation phase overseas. A highly placed insider reports that "post-9/11 findings have been extremely broad"—a worrisome drift back to open-ended authority for covert actions.[24] Historian Arthur M. Schlesinger Jr. observed after the Bay of Pigs that "one of the most shocking things which emerged after the last Cuban episode was the weakness of top-level CIA control—the discrepancy between what high CIA officials thought their operatives were saying and doing in the field, and what these operatives were actually saying and doing."[25] An experienced operations officer in the Agency has pointed to yet another potential trap that can accompany a lack of accountability over field activities. "When you're in the field, it's very easy to fall in love with your operations and your agents," recalls Peter Sichel, who was engaged in Agency clandestine activities in Berlin after the Second World War. "And just as with love, you can become blind to their faults. This is why you must have outside oversight—the field officers can't do it—but it's also why completely worthless operations can continue on for years."[26]

Obviously, it would be unreasonably taxing on a president and the oversight committees in Congress to have hundreds of mini-findings that deal with every possible clandestine move against America's adversaries. Some broadness of scope makes sense, but not so much that the finding becomes a blank check. Former DCI Stansfield Turner pondered this dilemma, although his remedy has proven (at times) overly optimistic:

> Under a broad finding, an operation can be expanded considerably; with a narrow one, the CIA has to go back to the President to obtain a revised finding if there is any change of scope. The Congress is wary of broad findings; they can easily be abused. The CIA is afraid of narrow findings; they can be a nuisance. What has evolved is a working understanding that whenever the activity being carried out under a finding is widened past the original description to the Congress, the CIA will advise the committees.[27]

Changes are reported to the NSC, SSCI, and HPSCI via Memoranda of Notification or MONs. A "significant" change that warrants the MON procedure includes any mid-course correction that increases the risks of exposure or raises the chances of a substantial political repercussion, if exposed. A MON tripwire, too, is any modification that involves a distinct change in operational direction; or a sizable increase in spending. A 20 percent budget increase is a standard threshold figure for triggering MON reporting.

Admiral Turner was conscientious about keeping SSCI and HPSCI informed about alterations in the original scope of a covert action. To rely today on the good intentions of every D/CIA and DNI, though, would run contrary to best practices for reliable accountability. In that world, witnesses are sworn in under oath; interviews are crossed-checked with official documents; and facts overrule conjecture and supposition—all in the spirit of the venerable saying, "Even when you're playing poker with your Grandma, you should cut the cards." The bottom line: findings can, and have been, misused—twisted out of shape from their original intention. The congressional Iran-*contra* investigative committee reported in 1987 that "while [William J.] Casey was Director of Central Intelligence, CIA personnel attempted to craft Findings in terms so broad that they would not limit the CIA's freedom to act."[28]

~~~

Within the executive branch, then, Hughes-Ryan has made a major difference in the nation's approach to covert action. Since 1974, Third Option initiatives—drone assassinations aside (a big exception; see Chapter 6)—have been subject to exhaustive executive reviews, with proposals scrutinized within the Agency, the NSC, and the White House. Checks on ill-considered proposals now exist throughout the top-level national security apparatus, to include a State Department and CIA coordination of propaganda themes; NSC reviews at the staff and principal levels; and, above all, the knowledge that presidents will hold the proposals in their hands and take a close look. So will members of SSCI and HPSCI. Beginning with Jimmy Carter, some chief executives have invited the attorney general to sit in on the NSC Subcommittee review, as well—a way of ensuring that the legal aspects of any proposal are seriously weighed.

The new rules of CA accountability have carried the United States a long way toward bringing democracy into the inner recesses of the government. It was a heartening development for an open society—until the Iran-*contra* scandal. The most elaborate rules for covert action proved to be of no avail in stopping an administration hell-bent on having its way in that instance, regardless of the law. It was a lesson from antiquity—the writings of Plato and Aristotle, among others—that officials of good character in high office are an essential ingredient for constitutional government to work. Even when the process is entirely honorable and the rules are obeyed, there is no guarantee that the operation will be wise or successful, as demonstrated by the Obama administration's major covert action snafus in Syria (Chapter 6). Still, democratic procedures are more likely to produce good policy than is the whim of an autocrat or a power-drunk American president acting unilaterally.

How did SSCI and HPSCI fail the nation in preventing a rogue NSC staff from bypassing Hughes-Ryan and the Intelligence Oversight Act of 1980 during the Iran-*contra* affair? That key matter of CA accountability is taken up next, with a look at the other half of the Hughes-Ryan Act: reporting to Congress on presidentially approved covert actions. This requirement sounds simple enough, but it has been plagued by ambiguities and failures.

Congress Is Invited to the Party

Chapter 7 illustrated how the new oversight laws brought the Congress into the Third Option decision circuit in a major way, more in tune with the intent of the Constitution. Under the new procedures, a handful of senators and representatives, supported by expert aides, would review CA findings. Accountability in this dimly lit space shifted intelligence toward a higher ethical posture, because the United States finally had in place significant checks on secret executive power. The shaping and authorization of the Third Option had gone from the hidden hands of bureaucrats in the inner recesses of the CIA, with occasional course corrections from the White House, to a requirement for formal presidential approval, followed by serious Q-and-A sessions within the inner sanctums of SSCI and HPSCI on the merits of specific findings. In addition to providing this vital forum for closed door hearings into proposed covert actions, these committees draft legislation related to intelligence activities, conduct investigations and reviews, and engage in day-to-day checking up on the activities of the eighteen major spy agencies. Further, SSCI is responsible for the confirmation process whereby presidential nominees for top intelligence posts are subject to close scrutiny.

This strengthening of democratic procedure inside the dusky world of America's spies must honor, of course, the protection of bona fide national security secrets. The two Intelligence Committees have proven themselves responsible in dealing with the classified information shared with them by the secret agencies. Only once has one of the Committees, HPSCI, had a member in the mid-1990s who violated this trust: Representative Robert G. Torricelli (D, New Jersey). He became so agitated about the CIA having a thug on its payroll in Guatemala that he held a public press conference to complain about this asset, even though the matter was classified at the time. He was castigated by his colleagues on the Committee for this inappropriate disclosure.[29] This unfortunate case aside, HPSCI and SSCI have earned high marks from intelligence officials for their reliable partnership in honoring the nation's legitimate secrets, such as the names of assets overseas. (On the matter of the unsavory Guatemalan asset, HPSCI and SCCI complained about this privately to the DCI and the president, with the result that the asset was fired—the proper way to deal with improprieties, not by calling a vagrant press conference.)

So with respect to the canard that the value of the Third Option has been ruined by the new laws and procedures because lawmakers are unable to keep a secret, the evidence since the creation of SSCI and HPSCI simply does not support that claim. Such allegations are expressed by those who long for a return to the supposedly halcyon days of Article II supremacy, when the Agency operated almost solely within the auspices of the executive branch and with minimal supervision even from the White House, let alone Capitol Hill. During the regular briefings that take place on findings, HPSCI and SSCI members act as eyes and ears for the broader membership of their parent chambers, debating (when warranted) the pros and cons of a particular covert action proposal. Now and then these lawmakers reject a covert action idea out of hand, or request that it be revised and resubmitted to the panels. All but one of the nation's DCIs has endorsed this new and more rigorous form of intelligence accountability, with William J. Casey, architect of the Iran-*contra* affair, the outlier—and, as it turned out, the outlaw.

Covert Action and the Centrality of Process

Process, that is, the procedures established by the Constitution and law for decision making and accountability in the United States, resides at the heart of democratic government. As Treverton has observed with respect to the Iran-*contra* scandal, "Excluding the designated congressional overseers also excluded one more 'political scrub,' one more source of advice about what the American people would find acceptable."[30] Ethical covert actions depend on an ethical findings process, which is based in turn upon honoring the shared-powers prescription embedded in the Constitution. The intelligence oversight laws reflect this understanding of the nation's founding document. Senator Church and DCI Colby, both with law degrees but otherwise unlikely associates, got their wish for "Constitutional Intelligence in America" (in Colby's awkward use of the "C.I.A" acronym).

The quest for a spy system based on constitutional principles has been far from perfect. This fact was underscored by the ease with which the Iran-*contra* conspirators bypassed the intelligence oversight rules. Unsettling, as well, is the reality that the scandal was brought to light not by congressional overseers on HPSCI and SSCI, but by a leak to a newspaper in the Middle East. As the following section illuminates, that affair has not been the only flaw in the efforts since 1975 to bring intelligence under the law and constitutional safeguards.

Intelligence Oversight Leadership

The CIA and the executive branch have displayed an unevenness in the quality of their intelligence leadership under the new rules. Compare DCI Robert Gates, on the one hand, who understood the importance of congressional checks on executive branch activities and cooperated closely with Congress, with William Casey, on the other hand, who would like to have taken a giant saw, cut around the Capitol, and shoved the legislative branch into the Potomac River, waving bye-bye as it floated off into the Chesapeake Bay and disappeared forever in the waves of the Atlantic Ocean.[31]

Or contrast Presidents Dwight D. Eisenhower and George H. W. Bush, both of whom spent hours studying reports from their intelligence agencies, seeking to be better informed as they made fateful decisions on behalf of the United States, with President Donald J. Trump, who often ignored the value of intelligence—including early warnings in the *President's Daily Brief* from the Intelligence Community that COVID-19 presented a significant threat to the United States.[32] As summarized in Chapter 6, beyond casting aside the reporting of the spy agencies on world affairs, Trump also spent a considerable amount of time fighting with these organizations, turning covert action and other forms of intelligence—meant to be above the partisan fray—into a political football.[33]

So, too, has the Congress revealed a range of responses from SSCI and HPSCI members toward their duties as watchdogs over the Third Option. A few lawmakers have been dedicated—dogged even—in their attempts to monitor covert action and other intelligence activities, attending every meeting of SSCI and HPSCI, seriously engaged in the proceedings. They have come to hearings, whether closed (the usual case, with sensitive intelligence briefings) or open, armed with probing questions meant to improve clandestine interventions whenever necessary, and to guard the nation's purse-strings against cavalier spending.

Moreover, dedicated congressional overseers have routinely traveled to Langley for powwows with the D/CIA and his or her top staff; and to the DNI's offices at Liberty Crossing in North Arlington, Virginia. They have met periodically with the NSC's intelligence staff, and with the secdef on PM activities that might affect the US military posture abroad; or with the secstate on public diplomacy and its coordination with clandestine Agency propaganda. In addition, the conscientious lawmakers on HPSCI or SSCI (and their staffs) have toured CIA stations overseas, courteously but firmly posing questions to the COS about the details of covert actions that might be taking place within their part of the world, comparing this "ground truth" perspective with the wording of the findings and the congressional briefings that have followed the president's approval. When not engaged in discussing the Third Option face to face with practitioners, responsible overseers have spent a fair amount if time on secure telephone or internet connections with intelligence officials, routinely requesting updates and clarifications.

If anything seems questionable, the best of the overseers will arrange committee hearings in closed session to ask Agency witnesses—under oath, when a matter is particularly controversial—about worries the Congress might have with respect to an ongoing operation. One of the unfortunate omissions of rigorous accountability when SSCI and HPSCI looked into rumors about the Iran-*contra* activities before the scandal broke was to take NSC officials McFarlane, Poindexter, and North at their word. Here were the leading NSC conspirators behind the affair: McFarlane, morally the most conflicted; Poindexter, intellectually the most gifted; North, as a decorated warrior, the most noble. Out of their zeal and secrecy the scandal was born, without morality, without intellect, without nobility.

Eventually, it was discovered that these officials had lied to Committee members, including panel chairs Daniel K. Inouye (D, Hawaii) of SSCI and Lee H. Hamilton (D, Indiana) of HPSCI, about the administration's failure to honor the Boland Amendments and the other intelligence oversight laws. Had this Reagan administration trio, among other dramatis personae in the affair, been placed under oath and queried about the rumors, lawmakers might have unraveled the truth much earlier. At least, though, the Committees conducted a thorough inquiry after the Mideast newspaper leak revealed the affair. There is no guarantee that the truth would have emerged at an earlier stage, even under oath; but that would have been the correct procedure. Swearing an oath before a congressional committee to "tell the truth, the whole truth, and nothing but the truth" can have a sobering effect, even on highly placed ideologues in the executive branch. Few individuals relish the notion of a prison term for perjuring themselves before Congress.

Oversight Cheerleaders and Champions

SSCI and HPSCI leadership over the years is listed in Appendix A. These men and one woman (SSCI's Dianne Feinstein, D, California) have included champions of accountability who understood that oversight is about both praise for the spy agencies and, when warranted, criticism; but the list also includes cheerleaders—lawmakers who have interpreted their job as merely one of supporting the intelligence agencies no matter what, laws or no laws, bungles or no bungles, disciplined or undisciplined spending. Despite all the intelligence oversight reforms, the cheerleaders have had a greater presence in numbers on Capitol Hill than the champions of genuine accountability. "We really don't have, still don't have, meaningful congressional oversight [of the intelligence agencies]," concluded GOP leader Senator John McCain (Arizona) in 2004.[34] That same year, the 9/11 Commission agreed. In the words of its final report, "Congressional oversight for intelligence—and counterterrorism—is now dysfunctional."[35]

Yet, despite the prevalence of institutional fawning, there have been notable exceptions to the supine posture of cheerleading since the watershed year of the Church Committee inquiry. On the Senate side, for instance, the inaugural SSCI Chairman Daniel Inouye—although failing to pursue the Iran-*contra* rumors more determinedly in their early stages—generally shined as someone who launched the new Committee well (starting in 1976), and who spent long hours trying to carry out the challenging and time-consuming task of policy review for the many spy agencies.

Joining Inouye in SSCI's ranks of stellar overseers has been Birch Bayh (D, Indiana), who carried on Inouye's tradition of regular hearings and serious questioning; David L. Boren (D, Oklahoma), who joined with DCI Gates in a model working relationship—one of the very best so far—between the CIA and the Congress; Dennis DeConcini (D, Arizona), who stood up to DCIs who failed to treat SSCI fairly and with respect; Dianne Feinstein, who had the guts to probe into rumors about CIA torture practices, and who became publicly outraged by Agency attempts to curb this legitimate inquiry; Bob Graham (D, Florida), who raised red flags about possible Saudi complicity in the 9/11 attacks, in the face of all manner of expedients by DCI George Tenet to ignore or delay responses to SSCI on this important question; Kamala Harris (D, California), known for her thorough preparation and insightful questioning of panel witnesses during hearings; John D. Rockefeller IV (D, West Virginia), who had the courage to say openly that the CIA's response to the torture revelations was an "active subversion of meaningful congressional oversight";[36] Arlen Spector (R, Pennsylvania), a hard-nosed former prosecutor interested in coming to the facts related to intelligence activities; and Mark Warner (D, Virginia), the current SSCI chair who consistently displays a laudable ability and willingness to encourage bipartisan cooperation on today's SSCI.

Even Barry Goldwater (R, Arizona)—an unalloyed defender of the CIA while serving on the Church Committee, as well as an advocate of an unfettered (that is, king-like) president in foreign affairs—had a come-to-Jesus moment as SSCI chair when DCI Casey misled him about the details of covert action in Nicaragua. The rumor mill in DC hinted that the Agency was mining harbors in the ports of that nation. Casey seemed to deny this in closed hearings, or at least quickly slid by the topic with a mumbled, one-sentence mention in an eighty-four-page testimony (memories differ on which of the two inadequate approaches—denying or sliding by—happened). When SSCI members queried the DCI further about the topic subsequent to these hearings, Casey tried to evade the truth by claiming that he had already provided an accurate statement to the Committee: the Agency had not mined *harbors* in such ports as Corinto, but rather *piers* within those harbors.[37]

This game-playing angered SSCI members, including even Goldwater, the erstwhile unbending defender of Casey and the CIA. When the senator realized that the DCI had failed to make the scope of the clandestine operations in Central America clear to his Committee, his institutional and personal pride kicked in and, for a time at least, Goldwater became just the opposite of his former self. He turned into an arch-advocate of intelligence accountability, dedicated to ensuring that SSCI (and, therefore, the Senate) was dealt with in an honest and forthright manner by the DCI. No more lies, or even inaudible responses. Goldwater sent a letter to Casey, with a copy to the *Washington Post*, that read in part: "It gets down to one little, simple phrase: I am pissed off!"[38] It took Casey many months to repair the damage he had inflicted on his relationship with SSCI and its chair.

On the House side, HPSCI's inaugural chair, Edward P. Boland, also stands out as an exceptionally good overseer, although his experience is more nuanced than that of Inouye or Goldwater, and eventually he became an even better guardian of his panel's prerogatives than they were for SSCI. At first Boland chose to waltz politely with DCI Stansfield Turner, who treated HPSCI with respect; but when Casey came on the scene as President Reagan's intelligence chief, Boland found the new DCI arrogant and disdainful toward the entire notion of congressional accountability for intelligence. When Casey proved uncooperative in HPSCI's efforts to find out about covert actions in Nicaragua, Boland resorted to his well-known amendments to shut down these activities. Unbeknownst to Boland, DCI Casey and Colonel North responded by inventing The Enterprise, taking their prohibited Nicaraguan Third Option underground (Chapter 5). During this period, the mild-mannered Boland went from being a reliable friend for the Agency, in hopes of calming down what had been a turbulent relationship between the House and the CIA during the "Year of the Intelligence Wars" in 1975, to becoming an angry critic of Casey.

Lee Hamilton followed Boland as HPSCI's chair and blossomed into one of the best intelligence overseers in congressional history—although, again, after being fooled at first by McFarlane, Poindexter, North, and Company. Hamilton displayed an unyielding belief in the value of a constitutional balance between the branches; and, especially after being burned by the Iran-*contra* conspirators, he proved indefatigable in his pursuit of information about the nation's intelligence activities, through all the proper methods of hearings, visits to the agencies and their overseas stations, one-on-one conversations with IC leaders, and thoughtful probes and recommendations during CA briefings. Larry Combest

(R, Texas), Porter J. Goss (R, Florida), Peter Hoekstra (R, Michigan), and Dave McCurdy (D, Oklahoma) also recorded tenures of serious intent while at HPSCI's helm, although the chair who has proven to be another indefatigable Lee Hamilton is its current leader, Adam Schiff (D, California). He has proven relentless in his dedication to maintaining proper intelligence accountability.

Below the top positions of chair, several other members of SSCI and HPSCI have displayed backbone, hard work, and a strong interest in making sure the nation's covert actions are well-planned, legal, and thoroughly debated within the confines of these committees. Among other examples, such individuals on SSCI included Wyche Fowler (D, Georgia), who sharpened his accountability skills earlier as a HPSCI member; Angus King (I, Maine), an independent and deep thinker known for calling it how it is; Mark Warner (D, Virginia), with his ability to reach across the aisle on oversight duties; and Ron Wyden (D, Oregon), another contemporary whose tenacious attention to detail in briefings—with tough follow-up questions—has been admirable.

On HPSCI: Les Aspin (D, Wisconsin), the inaugural chair of that panel's Oversight Subcommittee, who devoted long days and often stayed into the night to help guide the nation's intelligence activities; again, Wyche Fowler in an earlier incarnation when he served in the House as a sensible critic of PM ops; Roman Mazzoli (D, Kentucky), a fire-brand inquisitor during CA briefings; Keith Robinson (R, Virginia), who probably knew the CIA's budget better than any DCI ever did and was not shy about recommending spending economies; and, a young contemporary member, Eric Swalwell (D, California), who has a knack for asking just the right questions to untangle a complicated intelligence issue and, in addition, a fine-tuned moral radar.

Moreover, the staffs on both oversight committees have been diligent and, almost always, unbiased professionals driven by a single aspiration: to improve the quality of America's intelligence activities in all three primary missions, while at the same time keeping the spy agencies within the boundaries of law and propriety. At this level, oversight has tended to work reasonably well—with the caveat that staff, too, failed to catch the Iran-*contra* activities in their early stages. It is at the member level, though, that the greatest disappointments have occurred on SSCI and HPSCI.

The worst performances at the helms of these Committees? The former HPSCI chair and current ranking minority member, Devin Nunes (R, California) comes immediately to mind. He was little more than a poodle in the lap of President Trump. He dishonored the history of HPSCI by his unwillingness to take congressional oversight seriously, as well as by his attempt to turn his important position into a source of pork-barrel aggrandizement for his own constituents, leaning on the leaders of the Intelligence Community to push projects toward his friends and constituents.[39]

Just as Iran-*contra* highlighted the necessity of having men and women of high integrity in the executive branch, as reflected by a willingness to take seriously the responsibilities of constitutional government and obedience to the law, so do the records of HPSCI and SSCI highlight the importance of these same principles on Capitol Hill. Ultimately it is incumbent upon voters to select individuals for high office like Aspin, Boland, Feinstein, Fowler, Hamilton, Hoekstra, Inouye, and Robinson (to name again a few of the intelligence oversight heroes in Congress). Only in this manner can we ensure the proper workings of the people's government—with the invisible side of America's democracy, the spy agencies, presenting the most difficult oversight challenge of all.

The Quality of Covert Action Reporting to Congress

Beyond the often missing, though fundamental, requirement of personal devotion by lawmakers to a thorough examination of Third Option proposals, additional points of friction have led to sparks in the conduct of intelligence accountability on the Hill.[40]

Reporting to Congress

An important question has always been, Who in Congress should be the recipient of covert action briefings? It is now established practice that the answer is members of SSCI and HPSCI, along with a few senior staff experts assigned to this topic, plus a couple of members and staff on the Senate and House Appropriations Committees who review the annual intelligence spending requests. Things have become complicated, though, as a result of the "emergency" provision laid out in the Intelligence Oversight Act of 1980. Too often CIA officials have jumped at the chance to inform only the Gang of Eight. As Kathleen Clark has reported, the Agency will then often claim that it has the support of the entire Congress after these briefings—as if these eight lawmakers represented all of SSCI and HPSCI, along with the full chambers of Congress.[41]

A further problem is that officials in the executive branch sometimes never follow up on the rest of that law, which requires briefings to the *full* memberships of SSCI and HPSCI within a couple of days. The temptation is strong, and periodically irresistible, to stick with only the Gang of Eight—senior lawmakers who may not have the time or the determination of younger members to probe into the details of a Third Option initiative. Moreover, a habit of reporting on findings just to a Gang of Four has evolved—an invention of the executive branch in the last few administrations as an attempt to shrink the list of witting members to only the top two leaders (one for each party) in the House and the Senate. This was the approach used by the Bush II administration to limit the number of lawmakers who would know about the use of torture against suspected terrorists. Or, in a variation, to just the top two leaders on SSCI and HPSCI. Going a step further, the DCI and now the D/CIA have attempted periodically to reserve Third Option briefings to only a Gang of Two: just the SSCI and HPSCI chairs, especially if those lawmakers are predisposed to act as cheerleaders for whatever activities Langley may wish to pursue.

Prior to the Hughes-Ryan Act, reporting to a "Gang of None" was commonplace. During Iran-*contra*, for example, Congress was simply never told about the operations in Nicaragua that were under way, compliments of the CIA and the Enterprise. When a finding was retroactively sought for the Iranian portion of the affair, the administration decided not to report on the president's approval to SSCI or HPSCI at all. As well, earlier during the Kennedy administration, the assassination plots against Castro and other foreign leaders remained unknown to anyone in Congress, or even to the Agency's IG, until the Church Committee inquiry. As Allen Dulles once conceded, "I'll fudge the truth to the oversight committee, but I'll tell the chairman the truth—that is, if he wants to know."[42] The Gang of One . . . maybe.

The SSCI chair David Durenberger (R, Minnesota) concluded in frustration during the Iran-*contra* affair that his committee's biggest problem was "what they don't tell us."[43] During the Trump administration, the CIA's leadership cadre was widely accused of keeping information from Congress for fear that a more cooperative stance with lawmakers—especially Democrats—would anger the White House. In 2020, for example, HPSCI chair Schiff reported that "the intelligence community is reluctant to have an open hearing [on global threats to the United States], something that we had done every year prior to the Trump administration, because they're worried about angering the president."[44] The end result: Congress and the American people were kept in the dark about the state of world affairs, as seen from the well-informed vantage point of the nation's top intelligence officials.[45]

Game-playing in this manner has occurred periodically even under the new, post-Church Committee, post-Hughes-Ryan rules. During the Iran-*contra* investigation, for example, prominent lawmakers on the Inouye-Hamilton Committee recalled that the Agency displayed a "contemptuous disregard of our requests." They said further: "It was evident that the CIA had concluded that it had little to fear from our Committee and decided to adopt a narrow and conservative view of what information it had to produce."[46]

This has been a common experience for lawmakers. When HPSCI and SSCI attempted to find out from the Trump administration more about the reasons for the murder of the Iranian government official Qasam Soleimani, Representative

Gerald E. Connolly (D, Virginia) recalls the reaction of the executive branch. "What really came across was a sense of disdain and contempt for the legislative branch," he said. "They didn't even pretend to be engaged in information sharing and consultation." On the Senate side, Mike Lee (R, Utah) told reporters that it was "probably the worst briefing" he had ever experienced since becoming a member of SSCI. "We never got to the details," he commented. "Every time we got close, they said, 'Well, we can't discuss that here because it's sensitive.'"[47] The well-worn excuse of "sources and methods" again. The Speaker of the House, Nancy Pelosi (D, California), drew this obvious conclusion: despite the outstanding records of SSCI and HPSCI for keeping secrets over the years, the Trump administration was unwilling to "trust the Congress of the United States with sources and methods and timing."[48]

Even worse than failing to report to Congress on Third Option approvals made by the president is a close relative of this silent-Sam approach: the evil cousin of misleading lawmakers. During the Iran-*contra* inquiry, national security adviser McFarlane admitted to investigators on Capitol Hill that he had tried "to use some tortured language" in evading congressional queries about the rumored events that made up the affair.[49] A decade earlier during the Church Committee probes, investigators questioned former DCI Helms about various intelligence activities that took place during his watch, including assassination plots against Castro. This bright, sophisticated individual suddenly began to suffer terrible bouts of amnesia. His answer to question after question posed by lawmakers and their staff was "I can't remember," even when the events being asked about were among the most salient of his career.[50] Richard Helms had many skills; among them was proficiency in the Dance of the Seven Veils.

Beyond misleading overseers, national security officials have resorted to the most regrettable act of all: flat-out lying. Officials on the NSC during the Reagan administration gave denial after denial to HPSCI and SSCI members when asked about the Iranian and Nicaraguan covert actions, long before the full implications of the scandal broke in the Lebanese newspaper. Their passports for travel into the Republic of Mendacity were heavily stamped. "They lied to me," remembers HPSCI chair Hamilton, in reference to his conversations with McFarlane and North. "So did Elliott Abrams," he added—another Iran-*contra* figure on the NSC staff.[51] In a further illustration, the CIA's chief of the Central American Task Force gave members of Congress a twisted explanation when they asked him why he had misled lawmakers during their probes into the affair, maintaining that he had been "technically correct, [if] specifically evasive."[52] This kind of gibberish makes accountability next to impossible. What is necessary instead are intelligence leaders with the attitude of Leon Panetta, D/CIA under President Obama. "The Intelligence Community didn't always tell the whole truth," he recollects, "I said to them: Do the right thing. Tell the truth!"[53]

Another form of gamesmanship is for the Agency to demand that the hearing room where briefings take place be cleared of all staff, on grounds that the subject is much too sensitive for any ears but those attached to a few elected members of Congress. This undermines the reality that often only the staff has had the time to closely study a covert action proposal and, as a result, is in a position to provide the lawmakers with details about its merits or demerits. The absence of staff robs members of a vital information resource; that's why Congress employs staff in the first place. "The staff has to take the lead," acknowledges an experienced former Agency officer who served as a liaison to SSCI and HPSCI.[54] A journalist with expertise on intelligence oversight put it this way when officials at the NSA pulled the "no staff" stunt: "By giving the lawmakers secret briefings with no staff present and then demanding that they never discuss the matter with anyone, the congressional leaders were paralyzed."[55]

The "When" of Reporting

A closely related matter is the question of when Third Option reporting should occur. "Never" is the answer that some at Langley and the White House have proffered; but the 1980 and 1991 Intelligence Oversight Acts, along with the letter from President Bush accompanying passage of the latter, resolved that issue. Normally, the timing would be *in advance*, or, when the emergency provision had to be used (a rare occurrence), at least soon thereafter—two days, or close to it. The objective is to give representatives a chance to consider the worthiness of a covert action *before* it moves forward in the field. Otherwise, accountability would have little meaning.

Several countries around the world, including the United Kingdom, are content to provide their intelligence oversight panels with only *ex post facto* review powers. *Ante facto* reporting, however, puts real teeth into the oversight process, allowing lawmakers to spot and fix dubious—that is, insufficiently considered, wasteful, overly risky, unlikely to succeed, or just plain silly—covert actions. Understanding the importance of legislative participation in foreign policy, overt and covert, DCI Gates testified during his confirmation hearings that he would consider resigning from his post if the executive branch failed to report on a covert action within the time periods designated by the oversight laws.[56]

In some instances, both SSCI and HPSCI have balked at a presidential finding for a covert action. For instance, Representative Hoekstra convinced President George W. Bush to revise a proposal, after HPSCI members strenuously objected to the finding.[57] "Should committee members or the staffers raise serious questions," writes former HPSCI staff director Mark M. Lowenthal, "a prudent covert action briefing team reports that fact to the executive branch. This should be enough to cause the operation to be reviewed."[58]

The "What" of Reporting

As to the matter of what needs to be reported, the Intelligence Oversight Act of 1980 made that clear with a simple three-letter word: "all" significant intelligence activities: covert action and counterintelligence, as well as collection and analysis. As an equal partner in government, Congress—through its surrogates, SSCI and HPSCI—seeks to know about every important intelligence activity. Otherwise what is the point of having panels for intelligence accountability on the Hill in the first place?

Which Agencies Are Expected to Report?

Prior to 1975, only the CIA reported to Congress on covert actions—when and to whom it wanted on Capitol Hill, if anyone at all. Hughes-Ryan *required* reports to lawmakers on the intelligence oversight panels; and then, just to be safe, the 1980 Oversight Act made it clear that "any department, agency, or entity" given a Third Option assignment would have to inform SSCI and HPSCI under the prior-notice provision—including the NSC staff, which is indisputably a government "entity."

The Importance of Specificity

For the reporting to Congress on covert actions to be meaningful, the quality of the finding, the briefing, and the ensuing question-and-answer period is critical. Here is where democracy faces a major test when it comes to the Third Option. To qualify as "high quality," the finding must have a degree of specificity that allows lawmakers to judge its value and likelihood of success. Only from details does the truth arise. A good example of appropriate specificity was the finding that permitted the CIA to participate with Mossad in the killing of the terrorist Imad Mughniyah. As a former senior government official told a journalist, "The finding was very specific." For example, "[Mughniyah] had to be alone, so there couldn't be anybody else killed."[59]

Once the specificity criterion is satisfied, which is not the case when the CIA and the White House resort to broadly worded "generic" or "worldwide" findings, the success of accountability relies on an engaged set of SSCI and HPSCI members who attend the briefing on the presidential finding well-prepared to pose meaningful questions and suggestions.[60] A briefing on a finding is considered a big deal on the oversight panels, with membership participation rates higher than usual at these meetings, and certainly more robust than when the subject matter has to do with the specification of surveillance satellites, or the accuracy of Agency predictions on wheat production in Russia (although, commendably, hard-core overseers like the late Les Aspin have waded through even these more esoteric, if often useful, reports from the Intelligence Community).

Once SSCI and HPSCI were established, the briefing on a finding initially became an exercise in DCI efforts to wiggle away from extensive questioning by lawmakers on the nuances of a finding. President Carter kept the findings short, and sometimes excessively open-ended. His DCI, Admiral Turner, similarly attempted to keep answers as terse as he could get away with during the subsequent briefing; and then to make a beeline for the exit doors of the SSCI and HPSCI hearing rooms as soon as possible.

On HPSCI, Eddie Boland—still in his phase of marked deference toward Agency officials—initially allowed Turner to use these Houdini briefing methods. This Carter administration strategy was not long tolerated, however, as more aggressive younger members (most notably Representatives Aspin and Mazzoli) insisted on asking a series of rigorous, detailed questions during the briefings, much to Turner's annoyance at first. Boland tried to head off the young Turks, but they would not be silenced. Aspin, a junior member of the Committee, even had the gall—or courage—to call for a roll-call vote on whether a stenographer (cleared for top-secret material) could be present during the meetings, to ensure that a verbatim record of the Q-and-A with the DCI would be available for later review by HPSCI members. With Aspin leading the way, the young Turks succeeded in overturning the powerful chair's decision to dismiss the stenographer from the hearing room.[61]

Turner, an individual with a strong sense of integrity and ethics, rapidly adapted to this demand from the younger HPSCI members for a thorough discussion of a finding. For the remaining years of the Carter administration, relations between the executive branch and the Congress on intelligence subjects were usually a paragon of what Church Committee reformers had envisioned for intelligence accountability: sharing information, debating policy in a spirit of comity, and moving forward with a strengthened operational plan. On the Senate side, SSCI went through a similar evolution. The Carter administration could have chosen a different direction, as the Ford administration often did in its dealing with the Church Committee. The Ford-Kissinger method was to slow-roll and stonewall Congress as much as possible, battening down the hatches and refusing to provide covert action (and other) details to lawmakers. Congressional panels, though, are not without an ability to retaliate. The Boland

Amendments—taking the case for halting covert actions in Nicaragua to the full Congress in a "secret" session—represented one possible response, born of extreme frustration. This approach to accountability is generally too blunt and unwieldy a tool, though, with the possibility of leaks too high, for use except in the most extraordinary circumstances.

At less extreme levels of response to executive non-cooperation, the oversight panels can demand an audience in the Oval Office with the president to explain why a certain Third Option is wrong-minded. Moreover, members of SSCI and HPSCI can threaten to shut off funds for programs dear to the CIA; or drain the Agency's Contingency Reserve Release Fund. Such political jockeying usually produces a change of heart at Langley and the White House, resulting in a withdrawal or revision of an objectionable finding. As William Casey found out in his relations with Senator Goldwater and SSCI, prudent executive officials understand that it is risky to pull on the tail of a tiger, even if the beast seems to be asleep. The belligerent attitude toward SSCI and HPSCI exhibited by Casey eventually drove Boland toward the Aspin-Mazzoli School of Rigorous Accountability and his series of amendments to curb covert actions in Nicaragua. The once benign chair became one of the most demanding interrogators on Capitol Hill, as unsatisfactory—even hostile—responses from DCI Casey led Boland down a road of last resort: a full congressional secret session on Casey's clandestine operations in Central America.

The Ingredients for Success

The broader ingredients for making intelligence accountability succeed are simple to list, but they can be hard to achieve. They are simple in this sense: all that is required is, first, executive branch cooperation in providing thorough and timely Third Option briefings and progress reports to lawmakers, who are mandated by the Constitution to have a meaningful role in the shaping of US foreign policy. "Controlling covert actions must start with knowledge on the part of the Congress," emphasized two leading members of the Iran-*contra* investigation, Senators William S. Cohen (R, Maine) and George J. Mitchell (D, Maine).[62]

Second, members of Congress must be sufficiently motivated to carry out their duties: attending SSCI and HPSCI meetings to receive the briefing on a finding, asking thoughtful questions, and insisting on compliance with the provisions of the intelligence laws and traditional standards of morality (an aspect of covert action explored in the next chapter). One recent HPSCI member, John Ratcliffe (R, Texas), reportedly had an abysmal record of attendance at briefings, present only about half of the sessions. He was less an intelligence cheerleader than an ostrich with his head in the sand.[63] Yet, in 2020, President Trump named Ratcliffe as his DNI. One of new director's first moves was to limit briefings to Congress about Russian interference in the 2020 presidential election.[64]

During the Reagan administration, Secretary of Defense Casper Weinberger testified in hearings before the Inouye-Hamilton Committee. "We can't fight with the enemy, whoever that may be, and we can't fight with the Congress at the same time," he said. "We need to have the United States government unified if any kind of activity is going to succeed over the long run."[65] That is exactly right, and this approach requires what the Constitution set forth: the executive and legislative branches working together, and across party lines, to decide the best options for American foreign policy. In the executive branch, President Trump's vindictive retaliation against any intelligence agency or officer who dared to bring up truthful information that ran counter to his own views cast a pall over the Agency's relationships with the White House and the Hill. "It's affecting the work product of the Intelligence Community," said HPSCI chair Schiff in 2020. "There's less reporting to Congress, with fewer details, on issues that might embarrass Trump, such as [weaknesses in US] election security."[66] Further, the example set by Senate majority leader Mitch McConnell (R, Kentucky), who studiously avoided intelligence briefings on possible Russian influence in the 2016 presidential elections and dodged Agency experts for weeks on end, is just the opposite of how a serious overseer should behave.[67]

Executive cooperation and *legislative motivation*—here are the keys to furthering the noble aspiration of the nation's founders to protect and advance their newly created democratic society. With respect to the opaque agencies of America's government, both the Congress and the president are capable of honoring these bedrock obligations. All they need is the will.

PART V
ETHICS AND ASSESSMENTS

9

Drawing Bright Lines

Ethics and Covert Action

The Morality of Secret Interventions Abroad

On the question of whether ethical considerations should enter into the wilderness of clandestine operations, opinions range widely. Leading intelligence scholars David Omand and Mark Phythian insist that "ethical issues should not be left to the intelligence community to assess alone within that secret world."[1] Commenting specifically on the Third Option, a well-regarded former operations officer, B. Hugh Tovar, observes that "fundamental decency, legalities, and proprieties must be observed in covert action."[2]

Yet one can easily become the object of ridicule by advocating a moral approach to intelligence activities, especially when it comes to covert action. On the Aspin-Brown Commission in 1995, for example, Commissioner (as well as former SSCI and HPSCI member) Wyche Fowler was referred to as "Reverend Fowler" behind his back by some staff members, because he often raised ethical objections to the harsher forms of the Third Option. "Is there any way we can talk about covert action when Senator Fowler isn't present?" complained a senior staffer to his colleagues.[3]

Some scoff at the very notion of placing the word "ethics" in the same sentence as the word "intelligence"—an oxymoron if there ever was one, they claim, if not just plain moron. For example, Roger Bradbury, an Australian professor of complex systems science, stresses that an intelligence community "is not a moral or ethical machine, it's just a survival machine. It will be ethical enough to survive in its environment but not more, since that is a cost."[4] In this vein, journalist Steve Coll cites CIA career officers to the effect that among the "essential functions" of those who serve on Langley's Seventh Floor is less about obeying ethical constraints than it is "protecting the C.I.A. at the White House and in Congress."[5] Harry Rositzke, a hardnosed DO officer has noted as well that "the world we live in is not a moral world. It is a world of more power and less power, of more goods and less goods, of greater security and lesser security. . . . Nations are inevitably committed to the motto: Better bad than dead."[6]

Although recognizing the morally mottled nature of some intelligence activities, this book is in sympathy with the outlook of Omand and Phythian. There is indeed a place for ethical considerations in the conduct of covert actions. An important distinction between the Western democracies and autocratic regimes, like Russia and China, is the more honorable approach to intelligence operations the West has normally—though by no means always—adopted.

A Constitutional Standard for Evaluating Covert Action

An important aspect of any ethical standard in a democracy is the extent to which government officials and agencies act in a manner faithful to a nation's constitutional and legal framework (or just the body of laws, in those nations without a formal constitution). From this vantage point, an ethical evaluation of America's uses of the Third Option rests heavily on one's interpretation of the Constitution and related statutes.

Most American political scientists and legal scholars understand the US Constitution to have established executive and legislative branches of government that were meant to have equal powers. Recall the prescription, "Ambition would be made to counter ambition," advanced in *Federalist Paper* No. 51 by James Madison, the leading light in the drafting of this nation's founding document.[7] Those who joined him in writing the Constitution in 1787 gave to Congress duties outlined in Article I of that document. The legislative branch of government was addressed first for a reason: lawmakers would be the primary guardians of freedom in the United States, with strong authority to curb what could be the aggrandizement of dangerous executive powers.

Viewed through this important lens, intelligence laws in the United States specifically related to covert action—statutes that had a late beginning with the Hughes-Ryan Act in 1974—are invested with a moral goodness, because they have established for the first time in world history legislative authority to monitor and, if necessary, discipline a president who has spiraled out of control toward authoritarian inclinations. However belatedly, with Hughes-Ryan, the Church Committee, and subsequent intelligence laws, the most fundamental principle of democracy—unyielding anti-authoritarianism—was at last carried into the hidden recesses of government.

If, however, one believes that Article II of the Constitution, which addresses presidential authority, holds a superior status over Article I and grants boundless powers to the White House when it comes to covert action (and other instruments of national security and foreign policy), then the oversight laws enacted from 1974 onward in the United States that address the Third Option are nothing less than morally bankrupt and a danger in themselves to the nation's security. From this viewpoint, the legal evolution toward a balance of power between Congress and the presidency has perilously hobbled the ability of the nation's chief executive to protect Americans from foreign threats and internal subversion. When applied to the sensitive domain of intelligence (this argument continues), democratic checks-and-balances place an undue burden on the executive in its struggle against the nation's adversaries, whether global communists, terrorists, drug cartels, or some other risk to the nation's security. The survival of democracy—the ultimate moral good—is held hostage to a perverted doctrine of "separation of powers" in the federal government. Giving Congress a role in domestic affairs, say, agriculture, is reasonable, but not in the realm of national security, where the survival of the nation is at stake in a hostile and uncertain world bristling with terrorists and WMD. So goes the philosophy of Article II devotees.

Yet an unrestrained pro-presidency stance was roundly rejected at the Constitutional Convention in Philadelphia in 1787; and, in the modern era, it was crushed again following America's painful experiences with presidential supremacy during the 1960s and 1970s, with the Vietnam War and the Watergate scandal. Then came the domestic spying disclosures revealing that the CIA had spied at home against anti-war protestors, followed by the Iran-*contra* affair and the slight-of-hand intelligence rationales for invading Iraq in 2003. John Locke, Montesquieu, James Madison, George Washington, Lord Acton, Justice Louis Brandeis—this is only the beginning of a long list of wise counsels over the decades who have warned against the accumulation of power within the hands of a chief executive—one person, with all the resources of the intelligence agencies, the military, attorneys in the Department of Justice, and the bully pulpit at his or her disposal.

In contrast, Richard Nixon, Henry Kissinger, Dick Cheney, Admiral John Poindexter, as well as more recently Donald J. Trump and his attorney general William "Bill" Barr (to mention only few), reject the notion that a moral imperative to oppose concentrated power lies at the core of the American Republic.[8] Indeed, they have wholeheartedly embraced the imperial presidency. As a result, they have contributed to the subversion of the most basic moral principle that undergirds democracy: freedom from the wiles of an autocrat. They have routinely pushed aside a role for Congress in international affairs, as though the value of executive efficiency surpasses the need for legislative restraints on power. As well, they overlook the experienced counsel that lawmakers often possess and can contribute to America's security and foreign policy decisions. Then, on that horrendous day of January 6, 2021, a president even whipped up into a frenzy a gang of insurrectionists who attacked the Capitol, terrorized its members and staff, trashed its historic hallways and chambers, and engaged in hand-to-hand combat against its small and overwhelmed police force.

"Our country has, quite self-consciously, given one person, the President, an enormous sprawling military and enormous discretion to use it in ways that can easily lead to a massive war," Harvard University law professor and former Justice Department official Jack Goldsmith has written on Twitter, commenting on President Trump's decision to assassinate Iran's Major General Qasem Soleimani in January 2020. "That is our system: one person decides."[9] Yet that one-person "system" is distinctly alien to how the founders conceived of America's future government as they wrote the Constitution. Nor do most Americans want too much power in the hands of a president, or anyone else in the government. Indeed, citizens of this nation tend to be properly suspicious of governmental powers; most know better than to let one person, or a small cabal, decide the fate of the nation.

Sometimes at the CIA, intelligence officers have been all too quick and compliant in their response to orders from the White House, as when personnel in the Operations Directorate readily turned to the use of torture for interrogation purposes in the aftermath of the 9/11 attacks, based on flimsy legal arguments from the office of the vice president and the Department of Justice during the second Bush administration. "It is a core aspect of CIA culture," candidly remarks a senior DO officer, Robert L. Grenier, "that it responds to the needs of the moment. Given direction from the president, it quickly becomes whatever its masters need it to be."[10] Of course, some forms of discipline in government can be vital; America's military services, for instance, would be useless in wartime without discipline in its chain of command. Nevertheless, in a constitutional form of democracy, blind obedience to authority when the orders from above are questionable and devoid of legal standing is anathema to the nation's basic freedoms. The Nürnberg defense fits poorly into the traditions of the United States.

The history of intelligence law and covert action is, then, from the perspective offered in this book, an impressive—though relatively recent—embrace of measures to improve the chances that the United States will test and temper "special activities" turned to by the executive, with meaningful debate inside the Congress as represented by SSCI and HPSCI. The unacceptable alternative is to rely solely on intelligence bureaucrats and just two elected officials, the president and vice president, to make important judgments on behalf of the American people about the uses of secret power—and sometimes without even involvement of the White House.

It bears remembering that a sole reliance on executive authority has led to, among other unfortunate illustrations, the Bay of Pigs fiasco, the assassination plots against Fidel Castro and others, and the Iran-*contra* affair. Further, on the espionage side of the Intelligence Community, arrant behavior yielded for the CIA: Operation "CHAOS" (domestic spying); for the FBI, COINTELPRO (spying against and harassment of anti-war protestors and civil rights activists—covert action by the Bureau against America's own citizens); and for the NSA, Operations SHAMROCK and MINARET (only two of several examples of the improper interception of US citizen communications by this massive agency).[11]

Ethics, Decision Making, and Accountability for Covert Action

Prior to passage of the Hughes-Ryan Act, the principles of representative government—the soul of moral goodness in an open society—had been largely abandoned in the world of America's clandestine operations. On those occasions when the president and vice president were in the know ("witting") about Third Option activities, seldom were members of Congress informed— even those who served on the small subcommittees in both chambers that were supposed to review the Agency's programs. Since 1975 and the Church Committee reforms, however, decision making for covert actions has been more in harmony with the intent of the Constitution. As related in Chapter 8, now a handful of senators and representatives on SSCI and HPSCI, supported by expert aides, deliberate on key intelligence initiatives within the well-guarded walls of these oversight committees. As intelligence law has further matured since Hughes-Ryan toward strengthening democratic procedures within the veiled side of government—while always carefully protecting legitimate national security secrets—so have covert action choices become more subject to both presidential *and legislative* evaluations and, therefore, more ethically defensible in a democratic society.

Not only the decision pathways for covert actions but their accountability as well have moved in a direction of higher ethical goodness, as the shaping and review of Third Options migrated from the solitary jurisdiction of bureaucratic specialists at Langley, with occasional modifications by the White House, to regular and serious scrubs within the inner sanctums of the NSC and the Congress (SSCI and HPSCI). The formula for proper governance in the screened-off world of the Operations Directorate is straightforward: legitimate clandestine interventions abroad depend on an ethical process of decision making and accountability, which in turn rests on honoring the institutional power-sharing prescriptions of the Constitution.

In appraising the moral acceptability of any given Third Option, this hidden approach to foreign policy may be thought of as a set of activities that lie along a continuum marked by Red Zones at either end, in the manner of a football field. Covert action proposals with a potential for acceptable moral standing are located within the green expanse between the two forbidden zones.

The Red Zone of the Absurd

One can envision a Red Zone on one end of the field that encompasses proposed covert action initiatives that can only be described as vaudevillian, so comical are they—were it not for the fact they had been seriously proposed. These initiatives are worthy of only a quick dismissal by any official with an ounce of good sense. An example is the CIA's plan to rid Cuba of Fidel Castro by way of Operation "Elimination by Illumination." The idea behind this bizarre Agency recommendation was to spread the word through media assets in Cuba, clandestine radio broadcasts from Florida, and leaflets dropped over the island from high-flying Agency aircraft under the cover of night, that the Second Coming of Christ—communism's archenemy—was imminent and spelled the end of Señor Castro. Simultaneously, an American submarine was to surface off the island's coast, firing star-shells into the dark skies: a manifestation of the Lord's long-awaited return.

The hope was that the Cuban people would witness this miraculous epiphany and rise up against Fidel, the anti-Christ. When this sequence of anticipated events was presented to the Kennedy administration at an NSC meeting, a chorus of snickers immediately quashed the madcap scheme. "Elimination by Illumination" had failed, among other standards, the Smell Test.[12]

Into this Are-You-Kidding-Me Zone should have fallen, as well, a number of other embarrassing Agency initiatives designed first to discredit, then to topple Castro.[13] They included dispersing an aerosol spray into a radio broadcast booth where Castro was speaking; the particles contained a disorienting chemical that would supposedly cause him to hallucinate during the program. Such odd behavior by *El presidente* might cause the Cuban public to lose confidence in their leader. Another bright idea was to sprinkle thallium salts, a depilatory powder, in Castro's boots at night when he placed them outside his hotel room in Europe. The intention was to make his charismatic beard fall out. Without this beard, grown during the Cuban revolution of 1959, how could he possibly inspire the people of Cuba? It proved impossible, however, to gain access to the broadcast booth; and Castro never place his cherished boots (also from the Revolution) into the hotel hallway.

An additional illustration of looney approaches to covert action: in the lead-up to the war in Vietnam, Agency propaganda distributed in the northern regions of that country was meant to encourage Catholic residents to rush to the south before they were (supposedly) going to be annihilated by communists. The propaganda breathlessly advised recipients that already "the Virgin Mary has fled to the south."[14] Such initiatives bring to mind Compton Mackenzie's spy spoof, *Water on the Brain*. He wrote in the preface: "It has indeed become impossible for me to devise any ludicrous situation the absurdity of which will not soon be surpassed by officialdom."[15]

The Red Zone of the Extreme

Within the other Red Zone on this Third Option "football field" are a set of operations so repugnant and contrary to American values that they should be automatically denied as well. Here are the most extreme forms of covert action on the Ladder of Clandestine Escalation that, one would hope, the United States would reject reflexively on moral grounds. For instance, one can envision the possibility of using Third Option methods to disperse lethal chemical and biological agents into an adversary's environment; to flood the countryside by destroying dams; or to engage in devastating economic dislocations incurred by crop and livestock destruction (*Rungs 42* and *43* on the ladder). Even higher up the rungs is the dread of using NBC weapons; violence against civilians (non-combatants); a gross pattern of assault against human rights; torture against anyone; and dismissal of the law and the Constitution (*Rungs 52* through *55*). Any nation with an advanced covert action capability could carry out these operations—and have on some occasions. Witness the lawlessness of Iran-*contra* and the adoption of medieval torture practices in the aftermath of the 9/11 attacks.

Intelligence officials in Washington proposed some extreme measures during the Kennedy years; but, in all but one known instance (discussed below), the administration backed away at the last minute. In one operation, almost implemented, the CIA's special Miami Station (a Mongoose coordinating unit) proposed undermining Cuban-Russian relations by lacing sugar exported from Havana to the Soviet Union with a bitter, though harmless, chemical substance. Cuba's Number One export would be rendered unpalatable—an economic covert action. Soviet consumers would presumably turn against further Cuban sugar purchases and thereby undermine not only the Cuban economy but relations between the governments in Havana and Moscow as well. One version of this history has the Kennedy administration finding out about the scheme in its early stages and ordering the 14,125 bags of contaminated sugar destroyed before they were shipped to the Soviet Union. According to a second account, though, "the ship had sailed by the time the Special Group (Augmented) got wind of this."[16]

Yet a third account, one given the most credence, holds that the ship carrying the Cuban sugar suffered a mechanical problem soon after departing from Havana and was waylaid for a few weeks in San Juan harbor, Puerto Rico.[17] (This version could be compatible with the second one, if "the ship had sailed" phrase referred to the vessel's passage from from Havana to San Juan.) The ship's mooring in San Juan presented a golden opportunity for the Mongoose team to carry out the operation. According to this account, Agency assets slipped on board the ship late at night and sprayed noxious chemicals into the bags of sugar in the hold. Shortly before the vessel's departure for the Soviet Union, President Kennedy met with NSC and Mongoose personnel in three meetings to discuss the operation, going round and round in circles—like a goat with one eye—on the merits of the plan. At the last minute, the president ordered the contaminated sugar to be trashed. As this account has it, President Kennedy's belated misgivings were based not on ethical grounds, but rather arose from concern that the United States might be caught red-handed in an assault against food products intended for the Soviet people. The president worried not about the immorality of contaminating food but rather about the "What if we get caught?" problem. At any rate, all of the bags of sugar were removed just before the ship set sail.

Less squeamish later in his administration, President Kennedy approved a DoD plan (the military again creeping into the realm of covert action) to join with the South Vietnamese military in poisoning rice fields in South Vietnam controlled by the Viet Cong—even though there was no such thing as an exclusive "VC rich paddy," just rice fields throughout South Vietnam that peasants seeded to nourish their families and from which the VC stole food now and then. This operation was a stunning departure from America's championship of humane values in the world—an apparent singular, and deeply shameful, exception to this country's normally honorable behavior in the conduct of its foreign affairs. In this rice-paddy incident, SecDef Robert S. McNamara argued in his usual forceful manner that the Pentagon and the Army of the Republic of Vietnam (ARVN, America's ally in the war) favored the idea, as did the US Ambassador in Saigon. So why not do it? Another Kennedy adviser, the wealthy and influential Averell Harriman, vehemently opposed the initiative, pointing out that poisoning crops would turn the populace of South Vietnam against the United States, driving them into the arms of the Viet Cong. He noted further, to no avail, the chilling central fact that, even though the VC would be the ostensible target, innocent South Vietnamese civilians would be the ones directly affected.

Again, as with the contaminated sugar misadventure, it turned out that moral considerations were of little consequence in the deliberations of the Kennedy NSC. The Council was riveted on questions of effective war-fighting, along with calculations about South Vietnamese politics, not the morality of manipulating food. President Kennedy approved the proposal, although he expressed his concern that the ploy might leak. Again the risk of getting caught was much on his mind, more so than the ethics of killing civilians in a war zone. The president asked: "What can we do about keeping it from becoming an American enterprise, which could be surfaced as [the United States] poisoning food?"[18]

In another case from 2002, reminiscent of the French intelligence excesses during the *Rainbow Warrior* misadventure in New Zealand, some officers within the CIA (including a youthful COS) argued in favor of sinking a Persian Gulf ferry carrying cash and goods bound for Iraq's leader, Saddam Hussein, as a way of fueling his paranoia. Never mind that many innocent passengers on board would have died in the process. Wiser heads prevailed and Langley officials shelved the proposal.[19]

Shocking, too—arguably even more than the CIA's assassination plots—was Operation "Square Dance," touched on in Chapter 2. The product of overheated imaginations in the Defense Department, Square Dance was meant to edge the military into the CA game during the early 1960s by joining the Agency in efforts to put the kibosh on Castro. The plan, recall, envisioned the ruination of the Cuban economy by dropping Bunga from aircraft onto the island late at night. This rapacious, sweet-toothed, plant parasite would supposedly feast its way through all of the island's sugarcane fields. According to a memo prepared in the Office of the Joint Chiefs of Staff (O/JCS), it appeared "feasible to introduce gradually Bunga into Cuba and maintain a basis for plausibly disavowing US involvement." The covert action would start off with a 30 percent elimination of the anticipated 1966 Cuban sugar yield; within three to six years, the Cuban economy would be in ruin. The memo went on to argue that the "covert introduction of Bunga into Cuba merited serious consideration," despite "disadvantages" that included the insertion of "a new dimension into cold war methods." Also, if the plan were discovered, "the influence of the United States in international organizations such as the United Nations and the Organization of American States (OAS) would be impaired."[20]

When presented with this proposal, National Security Adviser McGeorge Bundy and his staff aide R. C. Bowman agreed that the president should "remain aloof from formal consideration of 'Square Dance' at this stage."[21] The contemptible proposal had run into the formidable Mac Bundy barrier in the West Wing of the White House. The DoD/JCS planning group suggested further that the Bunga attack could be "exacerbated and exploited by such measures as spreading hoof-and-mouth disease among draft animals, controlling rainfall by cloud seeding, mining cane fields, burning cane, and directing other acts of conventional sabotage against the cane milling and transportation system."[22] Bundy axed these proposals, too.

By spring of 1965 in the Directorate of Plans at Langley Headquarters, the CIA began to display a marked ambivalence about Third Option possibilities against Cuba. Some within the DP continued to be willing to throw aside moral considerations, such as pursuing a scheme to dilute pesticides given to Cuba in a prisoner exchange deal—never mind, as proponents admitted, that "it would be highly embarrassing if this one ever leaked out."[23] Yet by March 1965, the CIA had arrived at a position in favor of abandoning its paramilitary capabilities altogether—over the opposition of State and DoD.[24] While unwilling to go that far, John McCone, the Agency's director at the time, understood the inadvisability of adopting extreme measures against Cuba. The DCI noted that he was against them "on humane and moral grounds." He wrote further in a memo, a few days before his retirement in April 1963, that such initiatives "would stand as a black mark on our record for all time. They would cause untold hardship to thousands, perhaps millions, of individuals who are not responsible for Castro and can do nothing about him."[25]

Another official in the Kennedy and Johnson administration dubious about extreme CA activities was Secretary of State Rusk. Normally a mild-mannered individual, he became overwrought at an NSC meeting during the Kennedy years. The cause was a recommendation brought before the panel in early 1962 for a large-scale PM operation against mainland China—a plan advocated by the Agency's COS in Taiwan. The station chief argued that this would lead to a spontaneous uprising of people against the communist regime on the mainland. Rusk had heard arguments like this one before; that was also supposed to have happened when the brigade of Cuban exiles landed at the Bay of Pigs the previous year. He was having none of it. In the secretary's view, an uprising was highly unlikely (he knew China well, having served as the State Department's assistant secretary for that part of the world, as well as a US Army officer stationed there during the Second World War). Moreover, the United States would be immediately implicated, Rusk pointed out; the venture was too large for a credible denial of America's involvement. The NSC dismissed the proposal.[26]

Even the very acquisition of weaponry, as well as chemical and biological substances of an extreme nature, should raise serious moral concerns. Recall from Chapter 4, for example, how the Church Committee discovered that the CIA had a dart gun in its inventory. The weapon was designed to silently fire a sewing-sized needle that was hollowed out to carry poison and would dissolve once entering the target's body. When Army Intelligence originally invented the macabre weapon, it was meant to eliminate enemy guard dogs in wartime.[27] The CIA had a rather different purpose in mind, although there is no record that this particular handgun ever playing a part in any of the Agency's assassination plots. The Church Committee found, too, that the CIA had sequestered away in its labs enough exotic poisons to eradicate the population of a small city.[28] Some of these substances, including highly potent shellfish toxins, were incorporated into plots against Castro that proved unsuccessful.

Moral Guidelines for the Mid-Field

In between the Red Zones of the risible, on the one hand, and the appalling, on the other hand, are additional Third Option initiatives pursued by the United States since 1947: a mid-field of secret interventions whose moral attributes may not be immediately self-evident and, therefore, warrant closer inspection at Langley, the White House, SSCI, and HPSCI. The historical case studies presented in earlier chapters (3 through 6) can be appraised through an ethical lens, with both the Ladder of Clandestine Escalation in mind and some additional considerations that help to orient normative judgments about America's secret foreign policy. How is one to evaluate which of the various "rungs" on the escalation ladder could be adopted without inflicting moral harm on the reputation of the United States? The future is too unpredictable to construct precise and binding rules in perpetuity regarding the proper use of secret initiatives abroad; still, some reasonable rules of the road have emerged as the United States accrued experience with the Third Option since the end of the Second World War.

A good place to begin in an ethical evaluation of covert actions is with an acknowledgment that the use of PM operations in support of properly authorized US overt wars against the enemies of democratic societies is a rational and proper use of the Third Option, as long as the CIA remains outside the Red Zones—especially at the extreme end of the field. Helpful, as well, are some reasonable rules for judging covert action, as espoused by three directors of Central Intelligence: Admiral Stansfield Turner (1977–81), Judge William H. Webster (1987–91), and Professor John Deutch (1995–97).[29]

"There is one overall test of the ethics of human intelligence activities," Turner suggested. "That is whether those approving them feel they could defend their decisions before the public if their actions became public."[30] This is sometimes known as the *New York Times* test.[31] How would the covert action story play on the front page of the nation's newspapers?

Serving six years later at Langley Langley in the wake of the Iran-*contra* affair, Judge Webster crafted his own set of criteria for grading Third Option proposals. He requested answers before he would grant approval:[32]

Is it legal—that is, does it follow the approval and reporting rules laid out by Hughes-Ryan and the Intelligence Oversight Act of 1980 (not whether it passes the test of international law, which few would)?[33]
Is it consistent with American foreign policy and, if not, why not?
Is it consistent with American values?
If it becomes public, will it make sense to the American people? The "front page of the newspapers" standard again.

Webster said in an interview that this set of questions requires "people to think about it [the covert action proposal] and they ask themselves: "Do I really want to do this?" The DCI stressed the importance of the newspaper consideration. When a staff aide observed to him that the public would have "a tough time understanding" a particular Third Option initiative he was reviewing before approval, Webster remembered that he replied: "Well, maybe we better think twice before we do it that way." This question in his set was a particularly important check. For each covert action candidate for a finding, Webster presented his questions and the Agency's answers in the NSC decision forum, too, as a way of demonstrating to the White House that the CIA was "not following a pattern that's inconsistent with what our country stands for." Another advantage, Webster continued: "This procedure, too, I think, tends to keep the executive branch from wanting us to do things on the spur of the moment that will not serve the national interest, and may weaken the intelligence structure as a result of doing something."[34]

During this interview, William Webster grinned at the comparison sometimes made in the media between him as "Mild Bill" and William J. Casey of Iran-*contra* notoriety as "Wild Bill." He noted that, as FBI Director prior to his service at Langley, he was known for taking risks—"as long as I know they are lawful," he emphasized. "That's very, very important. You lose that, then you lose trust; and, then, you have another congressional investigation like the Church and Pike inquires [led in the House by Otis Pike, D, New York) and things don't happen. You don't get the money, you get restrictions."

On the "*New York Times* test," HPSCI overseer and later SecDef Les Aspin had offered a comparable suggestion several years earlier, in the 1970s. "Covert action should be as consistent as possible with the moral character of the American public," he advised, "so that if some action becomes public, it would not be terribly embarrassing to the government of the United States because it is not something most Americans would consider immoral."[35]

While brainstorming with retired DCI Helms on the subject of the Third Option, John Deutch developed a two-item set of queries he would pose to the DDO before green-lighting a covert action:

"Will the American people support you if it shows up on the front page of the paper?" Once more, the litmus test of potential public embarrassment.
"Do you have some confidence that you can do it effectively and completely?" Here is an added wrinkle to the advice of Turner and Webster: a will-it-actually-work criterion.[36]

As Operation "Neptune Spear" to capture or kill Bin Laden unfolded in 2011, President Obama estimated that the chances for success were about fifty-fifty—and these odds were higher than those of some of his professional aides planning the operation.[37] Such statistics (remember Allen Dulles's estimate of a 20 percent chance for success in Guatemala during the 1954 anti-Árbenz operation, examined in Chapter 3) underscore the iffy chances for a positive outcome that often accompany a covert action, even over the short haul. Still, Deutch is right: responsible planners must do their best to estimate the chances of success, and (one might add) adopt a skeptical posture when the odds are low.

In addition to what we might refer to as the "DCI Covert Action Checklist" outlined above, this book stresses as well (in an elaboration of the judge's "values" point) that the core value for governance in America's democratic society is the constitutionally based *process* by which decisions are made. A central ethical question to guide America's use of covert action, therefore, is this: Has a proposed Third Option been carefully reviewed by lawmakers, *as required by the Constitution and since 1975 explicitly by law as well*, and not just by officials in the executive branch?

America's Covert Actions Seen Through a Moral Prism

In light of the moral risks displayed on the rungs of the escalation ladder, and taking into account the Turner-Webster-Deutch guidelines as well as the fundamental constitutional requirement for executive *and legislative* review of policy initiatives before they proceed, how well do the most prominent covert actions since 1947 fare? What follows is an exploration of the author's estimation of the best and the worst outcomes in America's modern experiences with this hidden side of foreign policy, drawing on examples presented earlier in this book.

First, a caveat: in retrospect, one may wish that the nation's intelligence agencies had always been part of the normal framework of American government, with the same checks and balances applied to the CIA in the modern era as to the Departments of Agriculture, Commerce, and the rest of the executive bureaucracy. In fact, though, other than the vague last-minute reference to "such other action" in the National Security Act of 1947, there simply was no statutory law in the realm of covert action until Hughes-Ryan in 1974. Moreover, although the Constitution has been in effect since ratification by the states in 1788, spy activities were sheltered from the usual expectations for government accountability by the widely accepted norm of "intelligence exceptionalism"—the notion that intelligence activities were too sensitive to be governed by normal constitutional expectations.

After Hughes-Ryan and the Intelligence Oversight Act of 1980, though, the sense was that America's intelligence services would now join the rest of the government in adherence to the new accountability laws. Moreover, since the idea of intelligence exceptionalism had been properly jettisoned, the expectations now included adherence to constitutional procedures, as well, even within the hidden side of government—that is, the process that involves formal presidential approval of covert actions and their consideration by Congress prior to implementation, with the executive and legislative branches sharing authority in this concealed domain.

In the evaluations to follow, then, some Third Options are given high ratings in the pre-Hughes-Ryan era even though these operations lacked full legitimacy, as defined by an adherence to constitutional principles and the rule of law. Since neither of these important guardrails were formally part of the covert action procedural sequence during these early years, it would be unfair to weigh these CAs solely on the post-Hughes-Ryan scales. It is unfortunate, though, that the Agency did not take it upon itself to consult regularly with legislative overseers about uses of the Third Option without awaiting for the passage of Hughes-Ryan.

With this adjustment for process and legal considerations in mind during the pre-1975 period, this chapter turns to an appraisal of America's modern-day clandestine interventions. The specific criteria guiding these judgments include:

- the level of covert action on the rungs of the Ladder of Clandestine Escalation;
- Judge Webster's standards (designated here as "Webster's Writs"), which include the emphasis of Admiral Turner and Les Aspin on the *New York Times* test;
- Deutch's "odds of success" benchmark; and,
- the constitutional and legal expectations central to this book, with the adjustment made in fairness for the pre- and post-Hughes-Ryan and Church Committee standards present in the United States before and after 1975.

This is a subjective exercise to be sure, presented here with full acknowledgment that thoughtful people may disagree on exactly which Third Options should be listed below as either the "best" or the "worst."[38]

~ ~ ~

The Best of America's Covert Actions

1. Afghanistan II (2001–2011): The Taliban, Al Qaeda, and Bin Laden

The Ladder of Clandestine Escalation: In the wake of 9/11, the terrorist perpetrators became CA target Number One, namely, Osama bin Laden (OBL) and his terrorist organization Al Qaeda, along with their host Taliban regime in Afghanistan. Here was a major *Rung 49* paramilitary intervention against an autocratic regime, with direct involvement of DoD personnel as well, and accompanied by aggressive covert political operations (most notably funding for the Northern Alliance). Following the 9/11 attacks and the US invasion of Afghanistan in response, it took another ten years to locate Bin Laden. When he was finally found in Pakistan, thanks in part to CIA and NSA intelligence and logistical assistance, he was killed by US Special Forces while resisting capture (*Rung 46*).

Webster's Writs:
1. Legality. For both the Afghan invasion and the OBL take-down, the laws for the Third Option were honored, with a report in advance to the Gang of Eight and full briefs to SSCI and HPSCI soon thereafter.
2. Foreign Policy Consistency. These covert actions were in harmony with—and in fact conducted hand in glove with—US military operations to rout the Taliban regime in Afghanistan, destroy Al Qaeda, and capture or kill Osama Bin Laden.
3. Values. Few would dispute the importance of defending the United States and its values against terrorists and their state sponsors in Afghanistan, responsible for the craven attacks against New York City and Washington, DC, that killed almost 3,000 Americans.
4. Public Awareness. The American public, with the horrors of 9/11 always in mind, were fully supportive of these anti-Taliban, anti-Qaeda, and anti-Bin Laden operations.

The Chances of Full Success. The United States mobilized its military and CIA might to topple the Taliban government for its role in the 9/11 attacks. Success against the Taliban was likely, and came quickly (five weeks). Tracking down OBL proved a more difficult task (ten years), and the chances of apprehending him in Pakistan were still considered low but worth the risk in 2011.

Constitutional Expectations: Process. The post-1975 system of accountability worked—a big plus in the moral evaluation of a Third Option.

2. Afghanistan I (1979–1989): The Soviets and the *Mujahideen*

The Ladder. Here was another ambitious clandestine intervention, this time assisting the *mujahideen*—when they were not yet a haven for Qaeda terrorists (*Rung 34*)—with the provision of Stinger missiles and other assistance in their fight to rid Afghanistan of the Soviet Red Army. The effort, known as Operation "Cyclone," began under President Carter and took flight under President Reagan, becoming the longest run and most costly of the CIA's covert actions.

Webster's Writs:
1. Legality. Ironically, at the same time the Reagan administration was ignoring the Constitution and the law in its simultaneous conduct of the Iran-*contra* affair, some of the Agency's operations personnel were working closely with the Congress and in full compliance with constitutional and legal procedure when it came to helping the *mujahideen* in

Afghanistan. Indeed, the Agency was being pushed into action by influential HPSCI member Charlie Wilson of Texas. Initially, the administration, and even DCI Casey, who was normally gung-ho for covert actions on most occasions, was skeptical that the CIA could drive the Red Army from Afghanistan. The operation succeeded, however, and it, too, stands in the front ranks of the DO's Third Option Trophy Case. Unfortunately, though, the *mujahideen* subsequently transmogrified into the Taliban, which befriended Al Qaeda in the aftermath of America's departure from Afghanistan in the late 1980s.

2. Foreign Policy Consistency. This Third Option fit well into the anti-communist resistance mounted by the Reagan administration worldwide—even if there wasn't much to resist, since communism had failed most everywhere and Russia remained a fourth-rate economic power. The question arises, though, about whether the United States should conduct PM activities on the border of a major, well-armed adversary, any more than Americans were willing to tolerate the presence of Soviet missiles in Cuba in 1962, or (hypothetically) Russian paramilitary operation in Mexico today.

3. Values. One could argue that CA support for the *mujahideen* against the Soviets was a blow against autocracy, an objective in harmony with US values; yet, the Afghan fighters morphed into the Taliban, a coalition of tribes hardly known as a regime that favors freedom and democracy. This PM was a means to give the Soviet Union a black eye—and it worked, bringing great satisfaction to the DO, the Reagan administration, and others who looked at the world through a narrow Cold War aperture. In the grand scheme of things, though, Afghanistan then became a hideout for terrorists—including those responsible for the 9/11 attacks. That country remains a basket case of civil unrest today, after claiming the lives of over 2,300 US troops before a US troop withdrawal from that troubled part of the world in 2021.

4. Public Awareness. Americans may have been pleased to see the Soviets suffer their own Vietnam in their war with the *mujahideen*, but today the very word "Afghanistan" invokes an image of chaos, lawlessness, and endless strife—compounded wreckage added to the US covert action record during the Reagan years that, it turns out, resulted in long-term disastrous consequences in this distant land.

The Chances of Full Success. This was a long shot, it seemed at first; but as the operation moved forward, the *mujahideen* demonstrated their mettle and the Stinger missiles their malice.

Constitutional Expectations: Process. Surprisingly, given the Reagan administration's simultaneous Iran-*contra* operations, the CIA's PM activities in Afghanistan demonstrated that the procedures of the Hughes-Ryan and 1980 Oversight Act could function as intended, yielding clear presidential authority, robust congressional review, and at least a short-term CIA success in the field. The Constitution and the law worked in this case during the Reagan administration, because in this instance key officials respected and honored constitutional intent and contemporary legal procedures.

3. Laos (1962–1968): Protecting the Western Flank of US Soldiers in Vietnam

The Ladder: As in Korea in 1950, the CIA found itself in the 1960s shoulder deep in PM operations to support US warfare in Indochina, especially in Laos and South Vietnam—*Rung 36*. As usual with major covert interventions during times of US open warfare, the other forms of the Third Option were interwoven with the Agency's PM operations.

Webster's Writs:
1. Legality. No covert action law existed at this time, beyond the brief mention in the National Security Act, so this paramilitary endeavor lacked congressional authority and, therefore, full constitutional and moral standing. The operation was in support of the war in Vietnam, though, which was openly funded by Congress, and it saved the lives of thousands of GIs in that conflict; therefore, the PM enjoyed a definite color of good—especially in light of the widespread acceptance of "intelligence exceptionalism" as a way of government in the United States that existed during those years.
2. Foreign Policy Consistency. American foreign policy was riveted on defeating communism in Vietnam, and the CIA fought in harness with that objective.
3. Values. As with most of America's covert actions during the Cold War, the Agency's efforts in Vietnam sought to advance anti-communism and democracy. Ironically, though, the United States might have had an ally in the North Vietnamese leader Ho Chi Minh, who counted George Washington among his heroes and basically sought (in the manner of Mossadegh in Iran) to establish a strong and independent homeland for his people, at arm's length from China and the Soviet Union (despite his own commitment to a Vietnamese version of communism—a country that now makes beautiful yellow raingear and other clothing for Brooks Brothers).

4. <u>Public Awareness</u>. The American people began to turn against the war in Vietnam in 1968, after four years of killing in Indochina and no military victory in sight. Had they known about the full extent of Agency activities in Laos, they would have been pleased that these operations were saving the lives of US troops by diverting Laotian communist forces away from the war in Vietnam. Some would have felt their stomachs churn, though, when considering the CIA's abrupt abandonment of the Hmong in 1968.

The Chances of Full Success. No one could tell how successful the Agency's involvement in Laos could be in helping to protect the western flank of US troop activities in South Vietnam. It was a gamble that worked, though, at least for an important six years; then disaster struck the Agency's local allies, the ever-hapless Hmong. No full success here, but some valuable partial successes—all unpredictable at the outset.

Constitutional Expectations: Process. In this pre–Hughes-Ryan era, congressional review of the Agency's CAs never occurred, another stain (along with the sad plight of the Hmong) on this otherwise commendable diversionary operation that helped to save the lives of American war-fighters in Vietnam.

4. Italy and Covert Containment (1947–1950): Thwarting Red Takeovers in Europe

The Ladder: The earliest of the postwar covert actions focused chiefly on propaganda and political activities at the lower end of the escalation ladder, ranging from *Rungs 1* through *3* aimed at the communist nations; and *Rungs 4* through *5* at independent or "neutral" (non-aligned) nations. Some escalation occurred, as the CIA armed resistance fighters in Greece and elsewhere, but the level of weaponry provided remained at a lower level of sophistication. The showcase success for the Third Option in these days was Italy. Thanks to the Agency's secret assistance with elections against the Italian Communist Party, Italy remained a trustworthy member of NATO, and its allegiance with the United States grew stronger over the years as the Agency's propaganda and financial aid helped to sustain this European democracy. As Senator Church observed during a press conference in Washington on January 15, 1976, the United States was "trying to resurrect democracy from the ashes" of the Second World War.

Webster's Writs:
1. <u>Legality</u>. Meaningful law related to the Third Option was non-existent at this time.

2. Foreign Policy Consistency. In these early cases in Europe and around the world, the Agency's covert actions were consistent with, and designed to support, an anti-communist containment doctrine—the linchpin of America's external relations throughout the Cold War and beyond.
3. Values. American values supported democratic principles and free societies (the very flipside of communism), and the CIA pursued these worthy objectives in Italy.
4. Public Awareness. The American public would probably have supported these activities had citizens known about them, in the same way that their representatives in Congress voted for overt assistance to the democracies around the world, by way of the Marshall Plan, Point Four, the Truman Doctrine, and a variety of other programs.

The Chances for Full Success. The Cold War in all of its phases, but especially these beginning years, was fraught with doubt and angst about the eventual outcome. Whether the open societies would succeed in thwarting the global appetites of the communists was unknown and unknowable; however, the betting odds favored the idea that the people of this planet would be happier with self-governance, freedom of expression, fair justice, and economic prosperity than they would the communist alternatives.

Constitutional Expectations: Process. As with every covert action until 1975, no serious debate or accountability occurred in Congress. As a result, all covert actions before this watershed year must be judged as flawed with respect to this important dimension, however laudable the forms of clandestine assistance were to struggling democracies around the globe.

5. Poland (1978–1991): Support for Solidarity

The Ladder. This *Rung 30* operation—a "High Risk" political intervention—remains mostly classified and cannot be fully appraised yet; preliminary histories indicate, though, that this intervention was helpful to the cause of nurturing freedom in Eastern Europe.

Webster's Writs:
1. Legality. Once again the Reagan administration demonstrated that it was capable of conducting lawful covert actions, Iran-*contra* notwithstanding.
2. Foreign Policy Consistency. This intervention was compatible with the twin US foreign policy goals of containing communism and advancing democratic principles around the world.

3. <u>Values</u>. American values are in favor of freedom for others—in this case, the Solidarity movement.
4. <u>Public Awareness</u>. The US public would probably have supported the idea of assisting the working men and women of Poland behind the scenes in their resistance against a repressive, pro-Moscow regime in Warsaw—although some may have worried about a Soviet military response against Poland and America's clandestine partners in that nation.

The Chances of Full Success. The Reagan administration and the CIA were careful not to provoke a Soviet military entry into Poland; thus, given this caution, the Agency had a good chance of succeeding with its lower-rung covert support to Solidarity—although with no guarantees that it had properly judged the likely reaction in Moscow.

Constitutional Expectations: Process. The CA finding and reporting procedures were honored.

The Worst of America's Covert Actions

1. Iran III and Nicaragua (1984–1987): Above the Constitution and the Rule of Law

The Ladder of Clandestine Escalation: Had these twin covert actions of the Iran-*contra* affair been properly approved by President Reagan and reported to Congress, as required by Hughes-Ryan and the Intelligence Oversight Act of 1980, and had not the Boland Amendments been enacted beforehand to draw down the CIA's interventions in Nicaragua, the rungs would have been 26 (Iran), then 45 (Nicaragua)—the latter an "Extreme" operation on Threshold Four, but one that can be morally acceptable if the regime target is reprehensible. This is a series of big "ifs," however. In fact, these uses of the Third Option amounted to—in the new era of Hughes-Ryan and the Intelligence Oversight Acts—an illegal, unconstitutional, failed, and arrogant misuse of America's secret power, against a regime that the Carter administration had fully recognized and had worked with successfully, and with the Agency itself going along with the wishes of the White House, never mind the law.

This recklessness lands the Nicaraguan segment of the Iran-*contra* activities on *Rung 53*, reserved for assaults by the secret agencies on the US Constitution, as the Reagan administration resorted to creation of "The Enterprise" as a way of bypassing Congress altogether. The violations of US law that occurred during both segments of this affair fall just one rung below. These attempts to cast aside the important shield of the Constitution's First Article that stands between the American people and tyranny, coupled with the multiple violations of statutes, as well as endless lies told to congressional overseers, warrant the strongest condemnation.

Iran-*contra* conspirators and their defenders charged during the congressional investigation into the affair that critics were "criminalizing" what was really just a policy disagreement between Republicans and Democrats. On the contrary, this unsettling episode was about the law and the Constitution, both of which the Reagan administration blatantly ignored and dishonored in this instance. On the ladder of escalation, only the covert use of WMD, along with involvement in a gross violation of human rights, surpass in immorality this alarming assault on the nation's founding principles.

Webster's Writs:
1. Legality. Shockingly, after all the investigations by the Church Committee and other panels into the CIA's misuse of power, the Agency again allowed itself to be pulled into illegal—indeed, unconstitutional—activities. Never has Webster's first writ for covert action been so callously and sweepingly disregarded.
2. Foreign Policy Consistency. Was US interference in the affairs of Nicaragua really compatible with acceptable uses of American foreign policy? Recall the Carter administration's good diplomatic relations with President Ortega; moreover, the people of Nicaragua were entirely capable of voting Ortega out of office, if they so wished (and which they did soon after the Iran-*contra* episode, then voted him back in again several years later). These were affairs of state for the people of Nicaragua to resolve, not matters meant to be settled by remote US officials in their air-conditioned offices in the West Wing, the OEOB, and Langley.
3. Values. The values of the American people do not include breaking the law and undermining the Constitution—or, for that matter, intervening needlessly in the affairs of other nations that have open electoral processes.
4. Public Awareness. When the Reagan administration's illegal covert actions came to light, the president's popularity experienced an elevator drop in the public opinion polls—some 21 points.

The Chances of Full Success. Since 1979, Iran has never been a trustworthy partner of the United States, so relying on its leaders to gain William Buckley's release was wishful thinking. As for Ortega, he had been freely elected by the people of Nicaragua—not a commendable circumstance for launching a coup against the Sandinistas.

Constitutional Expectations: Process. Iran-*contra* tossed Article I of the Constitution onto the compost heap. Laws were broken, and congressional overseers on HPSCI and SSCI were misled, including by witnesses under oath. At one point, the CIA even buried beneath the earth in Honduras its aircraft used during the *contra* side of the affair, to avoid their discovery by congressional investigators. Lieutenant Colonel North has described this bizarre aspect of the *contra* operations. "An enormous crater was dug with bulldozers," he recollected. "The planes were pushed into the pit, covered with explosives, and blown up. The remaining wreckage was saturated with fuel and then cremated."[39]

The Iran-*contra* scandal reminds us anew of a basic principle of democracy. One may have good laws and a revered Constitution, but good government ultimately depends on the presence of honest, law-abiding, principled men and women serving in high office.

2. Cuba (1960–1964): Caribbean Obsession

The Ladder: The covert actions against the Castro regime moved quickly to Rungs 45 and 47 within Threshold Four—a rash escalation for the Kennedy administration, involving a violent coup attempt and multiple assassination plots against Fidel Castro.

Webster's Writs:
1. Legality. Hughes-Ryan did not yet exist and so there were no meaningful laws dealing with covert action against Cuba—an unfortunate lack of brakes on the "Mongoose" race car.
2. Foreign Policy Consistency. Once Castro began to wed Cuba to the Soviet Union, the die was cast and his regime painted itself in crimson hues, in the view of Washington officials. The narrow window of opportunity for a *modus vivendi* with Castro soon after the Cuban revolution rapidly closed to the United States, with fault on both sides, and Cuba became another adversary in the East-West Cold War.
3. Values. The values of the American people were certainly not in favor of a pro-Moscow Cuba, as Castro's regime became; but the Agency's intensive covert actions aimed at the island fed the Cuba leader's paranoia about US objectives, to the point where he was further pushed toward seeking not just Soviet economic aid but security assistance as well—even the placement of nuclear missiles on Cuban soil as a deterrent against an expected overt US invasion of Cuba on a larger scale than the Bay of Pigs. The blinkered Cold War outlook that gripped the United States stood in the way of a *détente* with Cuba (as President Truman had successfully pursued with Tito in Yugoslavia), and brought the superpowers to the brink of mutual destruction during the missile crisis of 1962.

4. Public Awareness. If the evils of the Batista regime had been thoroughly laid out for the American people, along with the reasons that Castro had led a rebellion and now needed a helping hand from the United States, Americans might have been willing to come to the aid of nearby neighbor (as was Canada).

The Chances of Full Success. The CIA's own Intelligence Directorate had warned about the likely failure that would accompany a paramilitary invasion of Cuba; moreover, the early missteps of the Mongoose operations should have indicated the fecklessness of directing CAs against this entrenched island regime with its effective Soviet-trained (and often KGB-staffed) counterintelligence shield.

Constitutional Expectations: Process. The DO misled President Kennedy into believing the coup would be a cakewalk; and, as usual at the time, lawmakers were excluded from deliberations. In addition, although Mongoose was administered by a CIA Headquarters Task Force, even this tight control failed to curb some excessive operations in Cuba. An example is when the assassination plots against Castro continued throughout the Cuban missile crisis—even though the White House had expressly ordered a stop to *any* use of the Third Option on the island during this perilous moment, let alone attempts to murder the Cuban leader. The DO officer in charge, William Harvey, told Attorney General Robert Kennedy during the crisis that he was unable to contact the Agency's assets on the island engaged in these activities.[40] This was not Article I of the Constitution, or Article II. This was Article CIA—Agency operatives acting on their own.

3. Congo (1960–1961): Murder in the Heart of Africa

The Ladder: The objective here was nothing less than the murder of a foreign head of state, President Patrice Lumumba of the Congo—a *Rung 47* assassination plot, high on the Ladder of Clandestine Escalation.

Webster's Writs:
1. Legality. There was no meaningful law for covert action yet.
2. Foreign Policy Consistency. Was American foreign policy based on a doctrine of killing foreign leaders who disagreed with Washington officials? Not from the viewpoint of the State Department or the Pentagon—and adamantly denied under oath, in closed sessions, by top officials from the Eisenhower and Kennedy administrations when cross-examined by the Church Committee. Whatever the truth about the origins of authority for this murder plot (which may never be known with certainty), one thing is

widely accepted as true: international assassinations are a prescription for global chaos, leading to a world plagued by vendetta and awash in blood.
3. <u>Values</u>. Murdering foreign heads of state and other civilian political leaders is not a value endorsed by most Americans, outside of a formally authorized war against a targeted country.
4. <u>Public Awareness</u>. Most Americans would probably have been appalled to read the details of the Lumumba assassination planning by the CIA, as they and their representatives in Congress finally were when the Church Committee disclosed these macabre facts.

The Chances of Full Success. At least two conditions should have given the CIA pause about dispatching Lumumba. First, as with the planning against Castro, the very nature of murdering foreign political leaders should have raised plot-ending reservations—if not on moral grounds, then at least regarding the dangers of a retaliation against America's presidents of this era, Eisenhower and Kennedy. Second, on practical grounds, the difficulty of gaining access to the Congo leader was a consequential barrier to success, as it had been for Castro.

Constitutional Expectations: Process. Expectations should always be high when it comes to honoring the intent of the US Constitution; but they were completely unmet here, in these pre–Hughes-Ryan days. Article II and Article CIA blended into a perfect storm of inappropriate involvement in African affairs, leading to the sordid death of Lumumba, aided and abetted by the Agency and the Belgian foreign intelligence agency.

4. Chile (1962–1973): A Clandestine Assault on a Fellow Democracy

The Ladder. In efforts to topple the Allende regime, the CIA leaped from lower-rung propaganda operations to a full-fledged devotion to political, economic, and paramilitary attacks. No direct shooting was involved, or even a plan to have the CIA use its armed paramilitary forces; but the Agency's PM officers were in touch with the Chilean military to coordinate internal army opposition to Allende, and the CIA provided weaponry and encouragement to additional anti-Allende groups in Chile. As a result, the Agency bears some culpability for the military coup and the murder of Chile's top general, Rene Schneider. It vigorously rolled out all of its forms of covert action against the Allende regime (*Rung 50*), but with a special focus on wrecking that nation's economy by supporting the truckers strike and through other means of commercial disruption.

Webster's Writs:
1. <u>Legality</u>. These operations took place a few years before Hughes-Ryan; therefore, no CA law existed yet.
2. <u>Foreign Policy Consistency</u>. As set by Nixon and Kissinger, American foreign policy in Latin America (like everywhere else around the world) was to resist any government that seemed flirtatious with communism, or even hinted at socialist learning—no matter if that meant bedding down with the most opprobrious right-wing military dictators. The covert actions against Chile were in sync with that particular objective, however odious the outcome. Yet Americans value democratic elections and open societies, exactly what Chile boasted before and during the Allende years; thus, this clandestine intervention runs contrary to the idea of support for fellow democratic governments.[41] The exceptions to this embrace of fellow democracies by the United States have been the misguided intrusions by the Agency against freely elected regimes in small nations, as with Guatemala and Nicaragua within the Western Hemisphere during the Cold War. These are embarrassments, surely; but they represent a small percentage of America's full array of covert actions. Further, they have been repudiated by many subsequent leaders in Washington and by most experts in the community of scholars.
3. <u>Values</u>. Had the democratic aspect of Allende's election to the presidency been properly explained to citizens of the United States, they may well have respected the will of the Chilean electorate, who had made their choice in a fair and open election.
4. <u>Public Awareness</u>. It is doubtful that the American public would have been proud of the excesses engaged in by the CIA against a fellow democracy—unless they had bought into the Kissinger myth that the Allende regime was a dagger pointed at the United States.

The Chances for Full Success. Given the sizable resources the United States was prepared to spend behind the scenes to topple Allende, the chances of success were reasonably good—setting aside the lofty price paid in the moral standing of the United States, as well as the fate of Chileans sentenced to years of repression and, in the case of many dissenters, a torturous death inflicted by the successional Pinochet regime.

Constitutional Expectations: Process. The Third Option continued to operate without statutory guidance at this time, as well as no congressional review worth mentioning. Further, wrong-minded White House officials (chiefly Kissinger) provoked a series of unsavory clandestine activities—all with no objections from a CIA that appeared more interested in keeping good relations with the Nixon administration than in raising questions about the probity of deposing a freely elected president in a democratic society.

5. Syria (2013–2017): Arab Fling

The Ladder. This coup aspiration against the Syrian regime of Bashar al-Assad, an "Extreme Operation" against a strong, autocratic regime (*Rung 49*), caved in with no positive results—indeed, with a major deterioration in relations between the United States and Turkey, both NATO members.

Webster's Writs:
1. <u>Legality</u>. The new rules for the Third Option were honored, although SSCI and HPSCI allowed a poorly designed CA to slip through their fingers.
2. <u>Foreign Policy Consistency</u>. American foreign policy toward Syria, a dictatorship allied closely with Russia, was ambiguous, jumbled, and unsuccessful in opposing Assad—traits that were mirrored in the covert action directed against the country.
3. <u>Values</u>. The broadly accepted anti-authoritarian philosophy of the United States encouraged opposition to the Assad regime, although these good instincts should have been tempered by the impracticality of dislodging a Russian-backed Syrian government.
4. <u>Public Awareness</u>. The American people have been thoroughly unimpressed by the disjointed and ineffectual US presence in Syria; and any sane person would be bowled over by the colossal waste of time and money absorbed by this pitiful CIA paramilitary operation—a near rival with the Bay of Pigs in weak conception and dismal outcome.

The Chances for Full Success. The possibilities for achieving a coup against a long-surviving authoritarian in the Middle East, with Russia and Iran as partners and providing sophisticated military support to Assad, should have raised serious reservations in the White House, on the Hill, and at Langley. This is especially true, given the plethora of alliances the CIA was attempting to work with on the ground. As Krishnan, observes: "The inability of the US to restrain problematic partners turned the covert action in Syria into a policy quagmire."[42]

Constitutional Expectations: Process. The procedures worked, but they demonstrate that congressional involvement is no guarantee the United States will enjoy wiser and more successful covert actions. After all, it is not that members of Congress are more democratic or necessarily wiser than presidents; both lawmakers and the nation's chief executives are popularly elected and, as human beings, are susceptible to the foibles of the species. Nevertheless, the constitutional model of decision making advocated by America's founders, and embraced in this book, defeats all other alternatives in terms of both democratic principles and the possibilities for sound policy outcomes.

Congress can actually count among its ranks many more scoundrels than the number elected to the White House, simply because there are thousands more lawmakers who have been chosen by voters over the decades than presidents (Joe Biden is only president No. 46). Just as there has been a James Buchanan, an Andrew Johnson, a Richard M. Nixon, and a Donald J. Trump in the White House, so, too, has there been a Joe McCArthy and Huey Long on Capitol Hill. Both institutions, though, have been led more often than not by individuals of outstanding character, intelligence, and moral judgment, among them George Washington, Abraham Lincoln, and FDR in the White House, and Senators Everett Dirksen (R, Illinois) and Philip Hart (D, Michigan) in the Congress. The important point is that the two institutions, working together, have a better chance of achieving wisdom and success than they do working alone—at least that is thought to be the case, or else the bedrock principles of American democracy and the Constitution are mere chimeras.

~~~

An Ethical Profile of America's Covert Actions since 1947

As summarized in Figure 9.1, the covert actions explored in this book have often risen to the highest set of rungs on the escalation ladder: the "Extreme Operations" of Threshold Four. Sixteen of the twenty-three nations targeted for the major interventions examined in Chapters 3 through 6 were the targets of operations carried out at this top threshold: *Rungs 37–54*. This number amounts to 70 per cent of the total among nations listed in bold in Figures 3.1 and 5.1 (with some of them targeted more than once and, therefore, counted more than once). Five additional nations were targeted at Threshold Three levels: *Rungs 13–36*. Thus, in almost all cases—twenty-one out of twenty-three major covert interventions highlighted in this book, or 91 percent—US covert actions escalated to the top thresholds on the ladder. Over the years, every rung from *1* to *54* has been used by the Agency at one time or another (especially the propaganda rungs), with torture ranked as the highest step among those that have been adopted because of its intrinsic barbarity—so easily embraced by dictators in repressive regimes and so far removed from the traditional values of the United States. Looking at the non-state categories of drone warfare against terrorists, as well as America's responses to cyberattacks, again the Agency reaches high rungs: *47* and *51*, respectively.

As shown in Figure 9.1 as well, despite the existence of the Hughes-Ryan Act and the experiences of the Church Committee inquiry, the executive branch still

				Honoring Webster's Writs			
Target/Date*	Threshold/Rungs	Form	1	2	3	4	Constitutional Process
Italy, et al. (1947)	1-6, 25	All	N/A	Yes	Yes	Yes	No
Korea (1950)	9, 36	All	N/A	Yes	Yes	Yes	No
Iran I (1953)	1-5, 10, 14, 46	P, POL, PM	N/A	Yes	No	A	No
Guatemala (1954)	1-5, 45	P, POL, PM	N/A	Yes	No	No	No
Hungary (1956)	10	P	N/A	Yes	Yes	Yes	No
Egypt (1958)	3, 5, 35, 49	P, PM	N/A	Yes	No	No	No
Indonesia (1958)	9, 49	P, PM	N/A	Yes	No	No	No
Congo (1960)	47	PM	N/A	Yes	No	No	No
Cuba (1960)	1-6, 47, 49	All	N/A	Yes	A	No	No
Indochina (1965) Vietnam Laos	9, 43, 49	All	N/A	Yes	A	No	No
Chile (1970)	9, 50	All	N/A	Yes	A	No	No

---------------------------------- The Hughes-Ryan Divide ----------------------------------

Angola (1975)	9, 49	P, PM	Yes	Yes	Yes	Yes	Yes
Iran II (1977)	3, 37	PM	No	A	Yes	No	No
Iran III-contra (1985) Iran Nicaragua	26, 50, 52, 53	PM	No	A	Yes	No	No
Afghanistan I (1983)	3, 34	PM	Yes	Yes	A	A	Yes
Poland (1987)	4, 31	P, POL	Yes	Yes	Yes	Yes	Yes
Serbia (2000)	5, 30	P	Yes	Yes	Yes	Yes	Yes
Afghan II/OSB (2001) Taliban Bin Laden	5, 46, 49	P, POL, PM	Yes	Yes	Yes	Yes	Yes
Drone Wars (2002) Counterterrorism	5, 46, 47	PM	Yes	A	A	A	Yes
Syria (2013)	4, 49	PM	Yes	A	A	A	Yes
Iran IV (2020) Soleimani	47	PM	No	No	No	A	No**
Cyberattacks (2002)	5, 51	PM	Yes	Yes	Yes	A	?***

*Beginning date for the covert action (see text for details).
** The Trump administration chose to bypass the Hughes-Ryan reporting procedures by relying on a Pentagon rather than a CIA drone attack, even though the target was a visiting Iranian public official and not a battlefield combatant in Iraq (where the strike took place).
***The text (Chapter Two) provides an example of a joint U.S./U.K. cyberattack as early as 1991, but this form of covert action became more prevalent in 2002 and after.

Key: N/A = not applicable (i.e., predating the Hughes-Ryan Act)
 A = ambiguous
 ? = procedures in flux
 OBL = Osama bin Laden
 P = propaganda
 POL = covert political activities
 E = covert economic activities
 PM = paramilitary activities

Figure 9.1 An Ethical Profile of America's Covert Actions Since 1947

failed on two important occasions to report on key covert actions to Congress in a timely manner. The first was with the Iran rescue mission during the Carter administration, although the reporting procedures were still in flux during the 1970s, with some lingering ambiguities about the new procedures and no established track record to rely on. The second was the Iran-*contra* affair during the Reagan administration, when the procedures were well in place and clear. After Iran-*contra*, though, the executive and legislative branches settled into the expected legal and constitutional pattern of approval for, and reporting on, the Third Option. There is one disturbing exception in recent years. In 2020, the Trump administration skirted reporting to, and review by, lawmakers when the president ordered a Pentagon assassination against the non-combatant public official from Iran, Qasem Soleimani.[43]

On the ladder of escalation, America's covert actions have recorded both moral highs, as with Afghanistan II (the post-9/11 paramilitary operations against the Taliban and Al Qaeda), and moral lows, as with the Iran-*contra* affair. Further, the Third Option has sometimes been adopted prematurely, as when continued diplomacy may have been eventually successful during President Carter's Iranian hostage situation. Or when the forging of an overt international peace coalition aimed at quelling hostilities in Syria—diplomacy again—would have been worth further pursuit instead of the resort to a covert action that posed long odds of success—and failed miserably. Webster's guidelines have been frequently breached, too, although less so in recent years. On the Deutch dimension, the guesswork required on the possibilities for success will continue to haunt Third Option planners; such is the nature of the human mind, which is made of flesh and blood, not magic crystals. When the odds of success appear bleak, though, prudence will suggest backing away from a proposed covert action—unless the resort to clandestine intervention is absolutely necessary for the safety of the United States.

America's cumulative experience with the Third Option has led to the formulation of Webster's writs and other useful guidelines. Honoring these prescriptions, one can hope for wiser decisions. As for constitutional expectations regarding covert action approvals and congressional review, prior to passage of Hughes-Ryan they were invariably dashed; since 1975, however, these principles of power sharing and accountability have been largely honored, with the disquieting exceptions of the Iran-*contra* scandal and the Soleimani murder. The goal of "Constitutional Intelligence in America" will be all the stronger when procedures related to drone warfare, cyberattacks, and the assassination of foreign leaders have been clarified and firmly embedded into the post-1975 rules of presidential findings for the Third Option, along with prior reporting to Congress. The central moral problem, as former DCI Stansfield Turner once stated it with reference to killings outside of a formally acknowledged war zone, is "what it does to your societal values when you break your concept of taking lives without due process."[44]

10
The Third Option Reconsidered

The Covert Action Record

The preceding chapter offered one way of looking at the pluses and minuses of America's covert action. How do practitioners of the Third Option themselves evaluate this history? In interviews with CIA officers, professionals in the business of clandestine operations have pointed with pride to a number of "special activities."[1]

Agency Favorites

High on their list of successes, from the CIA's own point of view, were the Agency's efforts to oppose communist party takeovers during the early stages of the Cold War in Italy, France, West Germany, Greece, and Turkey as well as several other nations in Western Europe, Asia, Latin America, and Africa. Paramilitary support to US troops during the Korean War is another admired time, however roughhewn the CIA still was in its evolution toward becoming a full-service global intelligence agency. The operational pros also view the Iranian coup of 1953 and the Guatemalan coup the following year as solid successes. They then skip forward, quickly over the Bay of Pigs fiasco in 1961, to the CIA's secret war in Laos, which lasted from 1962 to 1968. As discussed earlier in this book, the Agency played an important role in keeping Laotian communist guerrillas and North Vietnamese soldiers preoccupied with civil war in Laos rather than freeing them up to cross the border into Vietnam and join in the targeting of US troops. Senior DO officers are understandably pleased with their efforts to shield America's uniformed war-fighters.

Another highlight, from the vantage point at Langley, was support for the *mujahideen* during the Reagan years, aiding them in repelling the Soviet Army from Afghanistan. These years, too, witnessed gratifying Agency encouragement to dissenters behind the Iron Curtain and inside China, bringing some succor to those who longed for democracy and freedom from authoritarian control. This assistance extended from the CIA "book program" and other initiatives under the "propaganda" heading to the secret funding of various pro-democracy parties and factions around the world (as in Poland). With respect to the Agency's propaganda activities, some Langley officials stress, too, how these operations kept hope alive inside the Russian underground and in other repressive regimes throughout the Cold War—hope that one day freedom would finally prevail over the world's totalitarian communist leaders. An additional high mark for the Third Option, as virtually everyone acknowledges, was the CIA's response to 9/11, when DO officers joined—and, on several occasions, led—the US military campaign to drive the Taliban out of power in Afghanistan after their backing of the cowardly Qaeda attacks against New York and DC.

More recent on the list of positive outcomes, from Langley's perspective (and others—certainly this book), is the elimination of Osama Bin Laden in 2011. After a decade of evading attempts to capture or kill him, the arch-terrorist leader was found in Pakistan and dispatched by US Special Forces. After a five-year manhunt, the Agency dealt a similar fate in 2019 to Abu Bakr al-Baghdadi, the leader of the ISIS terrorist organization based in Syria. On the assassination front more generally, some in the CIA and elsewhere look on the capacity of drones to strike down would-be perpetrators of future 9/11s as an important new form of covert action. Even before the era of drone assassinations, a key witness before the Aspin-Brown Commission in 1996, foreign policy expert Richard N. Haass, director of national security programs at the influential Council on Foreign Relations at the time and later its president, recommended the vigorous resumption of US assassination plots. He proposed abolishing the Ford administration executive order that prohibited that activity, and he promoted, as well, a lively pursuit of coups aimed at regimes around the world deemed unfriendly toward the United States.[2]

The Critics Demur

Critics of the Third Option are quick to respond to these bouquets of praise, however, with the observation that the Marshall Plan, the Truman Doctrine, the Point Four Program, and the stationing of American soldiers permanently in Europe and Japan, along with the overt military defense of South Korea against the spread of communism in Asia, were much more influential in countering the Soviet and Chinese threats during the early Cold War years than anything accomplished by the Third Option. From this angle, the Directorate of Plans and subsequently the Directorate of Operations labored only at the margins of American foreign policy.

The Iranian coup, they note further, eventually led to an uprising in Tehran against America's puppet, the shah—a rebellion that brought a lasting revulsion toward the United States in that country, steadily inflamed by the uprising of nationalist impulses and devotion to a theocracy that swept away the shah's rule. Moreover, those skeptical of covert action point out that Guatemala has endured extreme poverty in all the years since the CIA intervened. The Agency may have aided the United Fruit Company in its desire to extract bananas from Central American jungles, but the United States did nothing to help the people of that nation lift themselves out of poverty.

As for Laos, when the CIA ended its paramilitary operations in 1968, communist forces decimated the Agency's in-country allies—the Hmong—as soon as the CIA "advisers" departed with their weapons in tow and the United States ended its bombing support. The Pathet Lao were then able to turn their attention fully toward combat against America's soldiers in South Vietnam. Further, although the warriors associated with the *mujahideen* were successful in defeating the Soviet Army in Afghanistan in the 1980s (thanks in large part to CIA-provided Stinger missiles and other sophisticated armaments), the *mujahideen* became the Taliban government that soon turned against the United States and embraced Al Qaeda. And even though critics of covert action usually grant a nod of approval to the Agency's role in routing the Taliban in Afghanistan after 9/11, they also point to Bin Laden's escape and evasion for a decade and, more significantly, the Taliban's ongoing—and expanding—military operations in Afghanistan today that have cost the lives of many American soldiers and contractors, recaptured control of Afghanistan, and threatened to turn this part of the world again into a haven for global terrorists.

A Mixed Bag

With respect to the deaths of Bin Laden and al-Baghdadi, most Americans were pleased with those operations, although some would have preferred to see these terrorists captured and tried in an American—or, ideally, international—court of law. Moreover, critics can be passionae in their disparagement of the Agency's drone program of assassinations, labeling it indiscriminate, highly unpopular abroad (even with many people living in the Middle East and Southwest Asia who otherwise feel an affinity toward the United States), and likely to result one day in drone retaliations against the United States.

A recent Agency director, John O. Brennan, expressed dismay on various television shows (for a time he was a CNN consultant) that the CIA had become a quasi-military machine for hunting down and dispatching suspected terrorists rather than focusing on its core mandate of intelligence collection and analysis. Hunting had overshadowed gathering. It was an old refrain. Some thirty years earlier, in the 1970s, Dr. Ray S. Cline, another top Agency analyst suggested that the paramilitary operations in Laos had "diverted [the CIA] from its more basic tasks," as the "covert action pressures on CIA distorted its overall effort"—namely, the collection and assessment of information about world affairs.[3] The Church Committee found that by 1962, spending on paramilitary activities had been chiefly responsible for the fact that the Third Option attracted a larger share of the Agency's overall budget than ever before, a trend that would continue.[4]

Brennan was joined in his disappointment over CIA drone operations by one of the most thoughtful and dedicated congressional overseers for intelligence, SSCI's Angus King. He excoriated the executive branch for being "the prosecutor, the judge, the jury, and the executioner all in one" when it came to drone attacks—a development he saw as "very contrary to the traditions and the laws of this country."[5] Former president Jimmy Carter eloquently underscored the consequences. "Top intelligence and military officials," he wrote, "as well as [human] rights defenders in targeted areas, affirm that the great escalation in drone attacks has turned aggrieved families toward terrorist organizations, aroused civilian populations against us and permitted repressive governments to cite such actions to justify their own despotic behavior."[6]

Further, critics of covert action will never forget the outcome at the Bay of Pigs. Or the moral, legal, constitutional low point in the modern history of US covert action: the misuse of the government's secret powers during the Iran-*contra* affair.

Looking over the Third Option record, an astute journalist and DCI Helms biographer, Thomas Powers writes that these operations have been "callous" and "reckless." They sum up to a "record of crime, blunder, embarrassment and failure."[7] Even Helms, although he was in charge of the Agency during several of its most prominent clandestine interventions abroad, was doubtful of its value. He wrote in a memoir: "We must realize that today's world is far too sophisticated to permit covert action to be wielded about like an all-purpose political chain saw," adding: "At its best, covert action should be used like a well-honed scalpel, infrequently, and with discretion lest the blade lose its edge."[8] One of the leading lights in the Directorate of Plans and the organizer of the Bay of Pigs operation, DDP Richard Bissell concluded that "the long term value [of the Third Option] . . . can be questioned."[9]

Yet DCI Woolsey underscored for a visitor to Langley in 1993 that "there are some cases in which there is nothing else that can be done except covert action." He continued: "You're not going to persuade terrorists not to do something by *démarcheing* them. The same for weapons proliferators. You've got to figure out some way to stop them." Woolsey noted, though, that large-scale PMs were essentially a thing of the past—"*way, way* down from what it would have been four or five years ago."[10] The Obama administration's adoption of a major paramilitary operation in Syria would eventually belie this forecast, though, and underscore the resilience of the Third Option in all shapes and sizes as an attractive policy option for the White House.

As one can see, opinions on the value of covert action vary widely. On balance, this book finds that America's secret approach to foreign policy objectives has been useful in its paramilitary forms as a supplement to overt American warfare, as was the case in Indochina and more recently in the struggles against global terrorism. Further on the plus side (as argued in Chapter 9), the roll-back of the Taliban in Afghanistan immediately after 9/11 was a shining example of how the CIA and the Pentagon can work together to defeat America's foes.

Persuasive, too, are the targeted attacks that have been carried out against prominent terrorist leaders like Bin Laden and al-Baghdadi, although the capture and fair trial of international criminals would be morally superior outcomes. Here is an example of how the latter is possible: The terrorist Mir Aimal Kansi, after making his way to the United States, had killed several CIA officers. Going methodically from car to car and armed with an AK-47, he had gunned them down point-blank at a traffic intersection where, on their way to work in January of 1993, they had stopped at a red light near the entrance to Langley. He escaped to Pakistan, but the United States hunted him down there and brought him back to this country where he was tried and found guilty. The evidence was irrefutable and, moreover, he confessed to the murders. He was put to death in 2002 by lethal injection at the Greensville Correctional Center in Jarratt, Virginia.[11]

Despite the occasional merit of drone assassinations, many observers believe they have been ordered too often and without reliable, consistent coordination with the Pentagon. A strong case can be made for eliminating drone assaults outside of an authorized battlefield; or, for that matter, the use of assassination as an instrument of American foreign policy altogether, short of targeting—with compelling evidence and serious oversight of the operation—murderous leaders of terrorist factions, battlefield combatants, and in self-defense during a time of emergency. (British intelligence is said to have moved away from assassinations as an instrument of foreign policy.)[12] Why invite a retaliation against America's own leaders, who live in an open society and are comparatively easy targets? In addition, assassinations seldom achieve the ostensible goal of bringing peace to a region. Consider the hundreds of assassinations that have taken place between Israelis and Palestinians, tit-for-tat, over the years. Further, America's murder plots have mostly failed in their implementation, as the many CIA attempts against Castro's life attest. So does the persistent bungling of Russian efforts, through its secret "Unit 29155," to eliminate intelligence defectors and others on Moscow's contemporary hit list.[13]

Ongoing Assessments

Part of the challenge in judging the worthiness of any specific covert action lies in weighing the difference between short-term success and long-term disaster. The 1953 coup in Iran arguably had some useful short-term results. Recall DCI Colby's judgment: "The assistance to the Shah . . . was an extremely good move which gave Iran twenty-five years of progress before he was overthrown."[14] Colby has noted in addition that it would be "a mistake to get rid of covert action. Did we overuse it? Probably in some cases. But I think some of the major covert actions were very effective." He referred specifically to "the Laos case, and Western Europe," then added "Afghanistan" [during the Reagan administration]. Colby acknowledged that the Bay of Pigs was a disaster, but he couldn't help wondering: "But what if had worked?"[15] Recall, too, that Helms considered the shah's help in establishing CIA listening posts along the Soviet border a significant service to the United States (Chapter 3).

What does "worked" mean, though? Worked for whom? The 1953 coup in Iran had a mixed outcome. On the positive side for American consumers at least, the shah maintained a cap on the price of Iranian oil exported to the United States. Over the longer haul, though, America's support for the Iranian king exploded in the faces of Washington strategists; and, to this day, the government in Tehran continues to view the United States as an unremitting enemy. The experience of the United States with covert support for the Taliban during the 1980s had long-term negative consequences as well, with the United States fighting its longest war ever against this band of Afghan warriors, beginning in 2001 and finally ending in 2021.

Lacking a crystal ball, efforts to foresee the long-run results of a major covert action is like playing roulette in Vegas. Despite the difficulties ("Mankind does not have the capacity to pierce the fog of the future," Dean Rusk liked to point out),[16] the potential ill effects of the Third Option's unintended consequences should give strategic planners serious pause. The opacity of long-range outcomes ought to lead them to ponder, more deeply than is often the case, what might go wrong over the horizon with a proposed operation. Of course, some policymakers could care less about long-term outcomes; they are just trying to make it through a nasty situation. National security adviser Henry Kissinger, for example, told President Nixon on the topic of withdrawal from the war in Vietnam that what the administration needed was "some formula that holds the thing together a year or two, after which no one will give a damn."[17]

John Deutch, an "outsider" DCI from 1995 to 1997, has said that he believed covert action was "very useful, though we're very bad at it." He continued in an interview: "Historically, it has been used to get rid of governments you didn't like, in the fifties and sixties. Here the record is mixed, and not too pertinent.

However, covert action having to do with proliferation [of unconventional weaponry] and with terrorism is highly useful—to disrupt or preempt these activities. This is terribly important. If you find out that Osama bin Laden has a chemical plant, you may want to go there and destroy it. If you use the U.S. Marine Corps, you've got a military battle on your hands." With his voice trailing off, he added: "But if you do it covertly...."[18] Deutch personally had a rocky relationship with the DO, however, in part because he fired a popular operations officer in Guatemala whom the DCI thought had failed to honor his directive to avoid recruiting locals involved in dubious human rights activities. "You could spend your whole life trying to please the DO—and its retirees," the former director sighed during the interview, slowly shaking his head with unhappy memories.

Yet another DCI outsider, Admiral Stansfield Turner has pointed to the Agency's activities in Afghanistan against the Soviets in the 1980s as "certainly" a useful covert action. Recall from Chapter 1 that he saw value as well in the propaganda programs, noting that "when you get facts into a country where the truth is not a common commodity, you're doing some good."[19]

While some covert actions have been helpful to the United States and its friends overseas, many close observers suggest that skepticism is in order on the question of whether the vast majority have had any significant effect in protecting and advancing this nation's global interests. One talented doubting Thomas is Admiral Dennis Blair, who served as director of National Intelligence (2009–2010) and concluded: "If we'd have none of them [covert actions] we would probably be better off, and certainly no worse off than we are today."[20] One can debate the validity of this sharply negative assessment. This book argues that the Third Option has occasionally registered successes and should be kept at hand. An important caveat accompanies this view, though. With the exception of low-cost truthful propaganda insertions into the media of *non-democratic regimes*, along with low-profile funding for aspiring pro-democracy factions in those countries, the Third Option should be resorted to only in a few specific situations. These include when the United States is faced with an imminent threat; when paramilitary operations might usefully assist the Pentagon in times of authorized US overt warfare; and when the Third Option might thwart terrorist activities aimed at the United States and its allies.

Most important, though, since the world changes and unforeseen events arise, is having a reliable and democratic method for deciding when the Third Option should be used. Here is the *central place that process must claim in any free society*. The glories of a true Republic are representation, debate, and the rule of law. The central theme in this book is that the great gift given to the American people by the nation's founders was a system of governance that requires the involvement of both the legislative and executive branches before the nation commits itself to an important foreign policy initiative. The notion of sole executive authority over foreign policy was roundly rejected by those who drafted the Constitution and, indeed, so has it been to the wisest philosophers down through the march of history. Checks on power, along with policy debate and the rule of law—here are mainstays underpinning the moral goodness in America's use of a covert action, as well as for elevating the chances of a favorable outcome in these endeavors.

Toward this end, a number of considerations should be kept in mind as the nation deliberates over whether to take up a particular Third Option. When one looks at the Ladder of Clandestine Escalation (Chapter 2), what stands out most vividly are the dangers that accompany the high rungs of Threshold Four. These choices involve potential loss of life, man and beast, as well as the widespread alteration or destruction of property, food supplies, and the environment—covert violence. Many if not most Americans might be willing to acknowledge the occasional value of lower rungs on the ladder, but high caution is in order as one ascends. At higher rungs, choices become more contentious; decision makers must be acutely wary and circumspect, understanding that "there are few absolutes in the ethics of covert action," as former DCI Colby once emphasized.[21]

Given the uncertainty always present in international relations, it becomes all the more valuable for these decisions to be made by a group of elected individuals, not just the president or, worse still, unelected bureaucrats in the Operations Directorate. The participation of America's representatives, both in the White House and on Capitol Hill, is vital as well—that is, if the United States hopes to remain one of the world's leading democracies. The most effective Third Options have been those launched with the enthusiastic backing of both Congress and the White House, as with the Agency's intervention in Afghanistan in the 1980s or again in Afghanistan against Al Qaeda and the Taliban in 2001–2002.

Maximizing the Value—and the Virtue—of Covert Action

The wise selection of clandestine operations, along with their skillful implementation and close accountability, are difficult tasks. "Covert action is a dirty mission, hard to manage," an acting DCI Admiral William O. Studeman told the Aspin-Brown Commission in 1995. A commissioner on that panel, former US Senator Wyche Fowler, reached the conclusion that the Third Option was "a dirty-diaper pail."[22] The odds of fielding an effective clandestine intervention abroad can be improved significantly, though, when certain considerations are taken into account by planners and overseers.

Imminent Threat

A debate about the nuances separating one rung from another on the ladder of escalation would become irrelevant if the safety of the United States were in immediate peril, as it was from terrorists on 9/11, or would be in the hypothetical case of a nuclear, biological, or chemical war. *In extremis* the government must resort rapidly to whatever steps will save the country, including any covert actions that might serve as a shield or sword. In most cases, though, time will allow more careful judgment on the wisdom of a proposed Third Option before it is carried out.

Keeping Covert Action at the CIA

The Third Option requires skill and experience, just like anything else if done properly. It should not be handed off for sole management to the NSC staff (the originators in the Reagan administration of the Iran-*contra* scandal); or given over to the Department of Defense, whose job is chiefly to deter and—if necessary—fight overt wars on behalf of the United States. In most instances, the DoD is not well designed for secretive and agile activities. Sometimes, though, the Agency and small teams of Special Forces can combine their skills for specific activities that are advantaged by a "jointness" (in DoD terminology) of civilian and military know-how—what are known by strategists as "hybrid" operations. The Bin Laden take-down in 2011 is a good illustration and, before that, the routing of the Taliban regime in Afghanistan in 2001–2002 as payback for the 9/11 assaults. In recent years, the Department of Defense has shouldered its way into covert action operations. The Intelligence Oversight Committees—SSCI and HPSCI—must be on guard against this tendency toward military encroachment into traditional Agency assignments. Giving the DoD orders for Third Option activities only encourages confusion in the national security arena while undermining expected accountability procedures for covert action set forth in the rigorous Hughes-Ryan procedures (Chapters 7 and 8).[23]

Proportionality

As students of just war theory understand, the severity of a threat should guide a response, whether overt or covert. Terrorists armed with biological weapons will send the US government racing up the Ladder of Clandestine Escalation to curb such an attack with a quick and pinpointed paramilitary intervention by the CIA and Special Forces. If the threat is less potentially catastrophic, as was the Greenpeace protest against French nuclear-weapons testing, the Third Option might be left on the shelf altogether; or, if used, the action would be at a lower rung on the ladder than the one rashly selected by the government of France in 1985 (or, at any rate, its foreign intelligence service). One should climb upward on the ladder only in desperation, as more benign operations fail. Further, in all but the most extraordinary circumstances, the highest rungs on the ladder—involvement in secret wars, assassinations, coups d'état, and other violent operations—should be rejected out of hand, outside of the most dire existential circumstances.

Further, one must be alert to the dangers of a DO tradition of "can-doism"—a high-spiritedness among clandestine officers (as in the military) that they can resolve whatever foreign policy problem the White House might send their way.[24] "No can do" is simply not an acceptable response to most national security operatives. Yet, while guts and determination are admiral traits at times, this attitude can also lead CIA officers to embrace the notion that the ends justify whatever means might be necessary to achieve a goal. As a Canadian historian has put it, a "Donovan tradition" remains alive and well within the CIA—the gung-ho spirit of William Donovan, head of the OSS in the Second World War, who encouraged intelligence officers in that organization "to act unhesitatingly in ambiguous situations," and to "'do something' even if it goes beyond the original mandate."[25]

The Nature of the Target

The notion of directing covert actions against fellow democracies, even an activity as simple as placing truthful propaganda in their news media, represents a significant and unnecessary escalation of this secret approach to foreign policy, although the use of this same form of targeting against authoritarian or totalitarian regimes is morally defensible. True democracies, still a distinct minority of governments around the world, are a global fellowship that should be respected by all of its members and never corroded by any. A reason for violating this principle would have to be compelling. The practice of the Golden Rule is important in American foreign policy and its subset of covert action, just as it is in individual human relations. Would US citizens tolerate, for example, the Germans or the French secretly recruiting intelligence media assets in the United States for the purpose of manipulating American media outlets? Not for a second. As law professor Jack Goldsmith has observed with respect to America's complaints about foreign hacking against its computers, so in the use of covert propaganda: "the key issue is the U.S. government's failure to look in the mirror."[26]

Short-Term, Long-Term Expectations

As underscored throughout this volume, in considering the merits of a covert action wise planners will want to ponder as best they can the question of what unintended consequences might arise over the short and long terms. Did the shah in 1953—already a secluded and unpopular figure in Iran—augur well as a leader for this nation and an ally of the United States? Could the *mujahideen* be trusted with Stinger missiles, and would they—with their 14th-century views—remain a friend of America once the Soviet threat had vanished? And what was their relationship with Al Qaeda? However difficult such questions may be to answer at the time of decision, they warrant much more consideration and "gaming" by experts inside and outside the Intelligence Community than has typically been the case.

Diplomacy Versus War or Covert Action

Solving international disputes through diplomacy—talking instead of fighting or sending in DO assets—has much to recommend it, including lower costs, less potential embarrassment, humaneness, and respect for the Golden Rule at the international level. The First Option—diplomacy—is "Number One" for a reason: it should be the opening step in a nation's efforts to achieve its foreign policy objectives. Yet too often this approach is given short shrift. Compare, for example, the budgets of the Defense Department and the State Department—a spending ratio of about 20:1 in favor of the DoD.

Before a covert action is adopted in any given circumstance, can one honestly say that diplomacy has been given a good chance? Secretary of State Cyrus Vance did not think so when the Carter administration settled on a paramilitary rescue attempt in Iran. He thought he was on the verge of a break-through in achieving release of the US hostages. Whether he was right or wrong, the secretary should have been given more time—a pause that, at any rate, might have allowed better planning for what turned out to be a calamitous covert rescue operation. A conclusion reached by former DCI Gates should always be remembered as the United States confronts vexing challenges in the world arena: "Throwing [covert action] into the breach at the last minute in the absence of any better solution nearly always ensures failure."[27]

The Virtue of Co-Location

Throughout the Intelligence Community, "stovepiping" or "siloing" is an ongoing phenomenon, with each of the nation's spy agencies sheltered unto itself and cooperating only minimally across institutional boundaries—a lack of sharing that was the major criticism of the 9/11 Commission in its examination of why the IC failed to anticipate the Qaeda attack against the United States. When DCI Panetta served at the CIA during the Obama administration, he reached the view that the co-location of analysts and operatives at Agency Headquarters and stations overseas, that is, placing a number of these individuals closer to one another by sharing suites of offices together, was "key to victories in counterterrorism and counterproliferation." He expanded this approach "at home and abroad."[28] Like several other CIA directors before him (Admiral Turner, for example, writes about this headache in his memoirs), Panetta witnessed stovepiping even inside the CIA and vowed to break down the walls between analysts and operatives. These two groups needed to share their thoughts and experiences with one another, for the benefit of more accurate intelligence forecasts as well as more realistic and carefully planned covert actions.

Both DCIs Turner and Webster expressed concern in particular about an uncooperative attitude sometimes exhibited by the Operations Directorate. As Turner put it: "The chief of operations [the DDO] had difficulty getting his act together in order to answer my questions."[29] Judge Webster complained, too, about the poor manner in which information traveled "upstream" from the DO's offices to the DCI (and now the D/CIA) on Langley's Seventh Floor. The Judge said that he could never count on the operations people to give him "all the facts."[30]

Before a covert action of any importance goes forward (including significant modifications of existing operations), the DO should consult regularly with the DA (Directorate of Analysis) to compare notes on their respective understandings of the situation in a target country and what the likely consequences (short and long term) of using the Third Option would be. This is exactly the kind of dialogue that never happened prior to the Bay of Pigs operation, with the end result that the DP operatives never had the benefit of personally witnessing the deep pessimism felt by the DI analysts—several of whom were bona fide experts on Cuba—about the potential problems of an invasion plan. Moreover, lawmakers should regularly quiz "finding" briefers on whether the principle of co-location has been honored in the crafting of a covert action proposal. Having both an analyst and an operative at the SSCI and HPSCI briefings would help lawmakers probe this dimension of effective Third Option planning.

Choosing Assets Well

In determining what assets overseas will be recruited for covert actions, except in extreme circumstances the CIA should hire only local men and women known to have some sense of integrity. Too often in the past, assets have been placed on the Agency's payroll despite their records of abusing human rights in their countries through violent activities, drug trafficking, and terrorism. While it is true that nuns and boy scouts are unlikely recruits to carry out covert actions, neither should this concealed approach to American foreign policy rely on rapists, murders, narcotics peddlers, and other thugs.

Having an Ethical Exit Plan

At the end of the Vietnam War and America's hasty retreat from Indochina in 1975, the CIA left behind multiple files on its local CA and other assets—many of whom, being so identified, were executed by the victorious North Vietnamese and Viet Cong forces as they captured Saigon. Former CIA officer Frank Snepp called public attention to this unfortunate abandonment of files on the Agency's assets left behind, which earned him the fiery wrath of CIA Headquarters and its Publications Review Board for displaying the organization's dirty linen in a widely publicized book.[31]

In an earlier covert action episode that also required a more considered exit strategy, Thomas Powers recalls the plight of local military men who joined with the CIA in its half-hearted and feckless efforts to punish Sukarno for his friendliness toward communists in Indonesia. "One group of officers [the CIA's paramilitary assets] still in the heart of Sumatra, accompanied by a handful of Indonesians facing death if they remained, had to walk out to the coast through several hundred miles of jungle," he writes, "and then put out to sea in rubber boats from which they were later picked up by the U.S. Navy."[32] Not a good way to encourage the recruitment of talented assets in the future. At least, though, these soldiers were picked up. The fate of many foreigners who have risked their lives as Agency assets has been far more tragic, such as Ukrainian émigrés early in the Cold War left to await their execution in Carpathian caves after parachuting into their country with instructions from the CIA to sow havoc against its communist leaders. Or the Khambas in Tibet, the Nationalist Chinese in Burma, members of the Bay of Pigs brigade, the Hmong in Laos, the Kurds in Iraq, and many others. All of these Agency allies were, in the words of conservative critic Ferdinand Mount, "so many causes and peoples briefly taken up by the CIA and then tossed aside like broken toys."[33]

Recall how, when the Agency departed Laos in 1968, the Hmong had to fare for themselves, with tens of thousands fleeing into Thailand and a trickle—for those with the right connections—settled by the Agency in the United States. For the sake of an ethical foreign policy and to gain the trust of potential allies abroad for future covert actions, any Third Option that involves foreigners as assets must have a carefully thought-out and humane strategy of exfiltration and resettlement in case an operation runs awry. Television images coming out of Kabul in August of 2021 suggest that America's planning for that time of exit was far from perfect, too.

Inculcating a Culture of Law and Morality

Intelligence officers can be better trained and encouraged to honor America's laws and constitutional procedures as well as to abide by ethical standards. Much of this book is about the means for achieving those objectives. Few comments have underscored the importance of honor in the world of intelligence more than a statement made by DCI Vice Admiral William F. Raborn Jr. (1965–1967) to the Rockefeller Commission on Intelligence Activities in 1975:

> If some member of the president's staff said, "You do this or you do that," [the intelligence officer's] reply should be to ask him to put it in writing and send it over to me over his signature. Then that gentleman [or gentlewoman] should have guts enough to say when that happens that you can tell the president I will be back over within fifteen or twenty minutes with my letter of resignation, which I will hand him with the word: "Get yourself another boy." And then he will say, "I will further call a press conference and say why I am leaving."

More recently, a former senior intelligence officer suggested to journalist Whipple that the incumbent D/CIA Gina Haspel should have vigorously defended an Agency briefer when President Trump accused the well-regarded officer, publicly and wrongly, of downplaying the dangers presented by the COVID pandemic in early 2020. Haspel had remained silent. This was her posture, too, when Trump went after a CIA whistleblower who alerted HPSCI that the president was attempting to coerce the government of Ukraine for his own political reasons. Trump wanted Kiev officials to besmirch the name of his Democratic political rival, Joe Biden, former vice president in the Obama administration—a misuse of White House powers that triggered impeachment proceedings against Trump. The CIA official interviewed by Whipple thought that Haspel should have told Trump's national security adviser in no uncertain terms that she would resign the next time the president dealt unfairly with an Agency briefer or whistleblower. In Whipple's interviews with Agency personnel, many officers expressed a sense that Haspel, as one put it, had been "seduced by her proximity to presidential power."[34] Others find this characterization unfair, though, pointing out that the whistleblower should have been defended by the DNI, not D/CIA Haspel.

Compared to the US diplomatic corps (especially during the Vietnam War era), resignations in principled protest by CIA officers have been few and far between, even though such departures can provide an important signal to government leaders and citizens alike that the Agency may have taken a serious misstep. A rare illustration at Langley is when analyst John Horton resigned in protest as the national intelligence officer (NIO) for Latin American when DCI William J. Casey insisted on distorting an intelligence estimate regarding Mexico. Casey wanted the intelligence report to make the false claim that Mexico had fallen into political instability because of communist influence—an argument adopted by the DCI because government officials in Mexico City refused to support the Reagan administration's anti-Sandinista policies in Nicaragua.

Honoring Post-1975 Procedures for Covert Action

No covert action should slight the presidential findings process or the congressional reporting requirement laid out initially in the Hughes-Ryan Act and refined by the 1980 and 1991 Intelligence Oversight Acts. Fidelity to the spirit of these laws would insist on specificity in the finding, as well as thorough questioning by lawmakers during the briefing that follows in the secure hearing rooms of SSCI and HPSCI. The fidelity of the assurances from the Agency made during briefings must also be revisited periodically, with reviews by the congressional committees every few months for an ongoing covert action. The purpose would be to provide a check against the intent of a Third Option drifting from A, to B, to C, or even further beyond the boundary promises of the original finding and briefing—the cautionary tale from Clark Clifford discussed earlier in this book.

Examples of a serious probe into findings during briefings to SSCI and HPSCI would include questions from lawmakers such as these:

What has been the previous experience in targeting this regime or group?
What are the precise projected costs of the operation?
Does it have a PM component (which always raises the costs and the risks)?
Does the operation involve a coup attempt or an assassination?
Is the target a high-risk, denied area, such as North Korea, or an elusive terrorist faction?
Did the DO check with the DA on the merits of the proposed covert action (the co-location problem)?
Does the covert action plan have a friendly ally within the target nation who shares America's objectives and can be trusted?

This last requirement is often critical for success, especially in the case of PM ops. A keen observer of intelligence, journalist James Risen, has noted that covert actions work best when they are "pushing on an open door"—that is, in situations where an ally in need of help has interests congruent with those of the United States. This was true, for example, during the early stages of the Cold War when Italy and Greece sought assistance from the United States in resisting communist takeovers; or, at the other end of the Cold War, when the CIA during the Reagan administration backed the popular, pro-democracy Polish labor movement Solidarity.[35]

Colby told the Church Committee in 1975 that "covert action is most successful when you want to help someone who wants the help and doesn't have the means to succeed without it."[36] Kim Roosevelt understood this principle. He believed that his good fortune in Iran in 1953 relied on the fact that the military and the people in that country wanted just what the Eisenhower administration wanted: no more Mossadegh. As Roosevelt told Secretary of State John Foster Dulles, "If [the CIA] is ever going to try something like this again, *we must be absolutely sure that [the] people and army want what we want.* If not, you had better give the job to the Marines!"[37] A good example of how covert actions can function well when conducted alongside a reliable local partner is the CIA-Northern Alliance coalition that, fighting with overt US military forces, quickly defeated the Taliban regime after the 9/11 attacks. An Agency leader in the field during this celebrated paramilitary operation, Gary Berntsen, remembers that the partnership with the Northern Alliance "provided us a native army to work with and an extremely valuable intelligence network to link into."[38]

Continuing the suggested litany of rigorous congressional queries during CA briefings, they would include as well:

> In the case of a joint covert action, what has been the track record in working with the foreign liaison service?

This question is vital. Such operations rachet up the complications and risks, since no two nations have precisely congruent objectives. To what extent is it wise for the CIA to partner with Mossad in counterterrorism operations when the latter is blowing up nuclear scientists on the streets of Tehran?

> Has the Agency thoroughly coordinated the proposed operation with each of the government entities displayed in Figure 8.1, including the State Department on propaganda themes and the CIA's Office of Inspector General?
>
> Important, too, are the DO's answers to Judge Webster's Writs, which need to be examined by both the NSC Subcommittee on Covert Action, and then SSCI and HPSCI.

For example, does the envisioned Third Option violate any US laws? To which one could add: Does the proposed operation honor the concept of balanced government, permitting a meaningful role for Congress in the covert action decision process? This writ highlights the importance of adhering to Hughes-Ryan procedures. Especially: *No more Iran-contras; no more covert actions run by the NSC staff, or others outside the normal decision pathway and the new standards established by the post-1975 rules.*

Further, is the covert action in harmony with with America's overt foreign policy; and, if not, why is that the case? For example, seeking *détente* with another nation while simultaneously carrying out covert action against it is foolish; but it does happen, as in Indonesia during the anti-Sukarno clandestine operations in the 1950s. In addition,

- Is the Third Option consistent with American values, such as fair play and a respect for human rights?
- Would the operation, if exposed, embarrass the American people or, on the contrary, be fully acceptable to them?

The CIA's hiring of the Mafia to bump off Fidel Castro made for an unsavory alliance, to say the least. It gave the mob undue leverage over the US government in return; and worse yet, it deeply bruised the image of the United States around the world.[39]

Good questioning keeps intelligence managers and their officers on their toes. But more is required. Getting the relationship between Congress and the CIA on a proper course in crafting covert actions takes compromise and adjustment both on Capitol Hill and at Langley. Jospeh Wippl, a seasoned former DO officer and Agency station chief in Berlin, has written,

> The CIA must learn to respect Congress, rather than seek to manipulate it. Congress must learn to expect, and accept, risk, embarrassment, and imperfection—all of which are inevitable if the CIA and the other intelligence agencies are to obtain the global intelligence that U.S. leaders require in order to conduct policy. This means that Congress must understand that there simply can be no clean covert action, no trouble-free human intelligence, and no wholly accurate analysis.[40]

The Vicissitudes of America's Third Option

The chairman of the 1975 intelligence investigation committee in the Senate, Frank Church, was a harsh critic of covert action. "I think that covert activities in the past twenty years of the kind that we have engaged in," he said, as the panel's inquiry came to an end, "have done this country much more harm than good." He went on: "Twenty-five years ago, this country had a matchless moral position from which it exercised immense leadership and influence in the world. Anything the United States stood for was automatically endorsed by three-quarters of the governments of the world." In Church's view, the United States had pursued a quarter-century of "methods that were plainly copied from the KGB: coercion, false propaganda, bribery, abduction, attempted assassination, and where are we at the end of that twenty-five years?"[41] His answer: "If we have gained little, what have we lost? Our good name and reputation."[42]

During his Committee's public hearings on the Third Option, Church remarked further that America's clandestine interventions "have been utterly directed toward . . . keeping all kinds of despotisms—corrupt, rotten regimes— in power all over the world. When we have been exposed in having done it, we have been severely damaged, and we have really lost our capacity for moral leadership."[43] Behind the scenes, in conversations with DCI Colby, the senator further railed against America's secret interventions into the Chilean presidential election and subsequent attempts by Salvador Allende to govern. "Traditionally, America has stood for self-determination," Church insisted, adding: "What if a Latin American country interfered in our presidential elections?"

Colby felt strongly, though, that the United States should be able to help fellow democracies resist communist encroachment. The DCI's view led to this further exchange:

CHURCH: "We seem alarmed about freely elected Marxist regimes, but not when right-wing regimes are in power."
COLBY: "Right-wing regimes don't threaten us internationally."[44]

For Church, the harm done to America's reputation around the world by covert actions was a core argument against their continuation. Professor Eliot A. Cohen has noted that "there are no reliable metrics for a nation's reputation."[45] Nonetheless, few could confidently argue that the standing of the United States in the world has gone up with the revelations over the years of the CIA's secret interventions. That standing is complex and related to more than this nation's intelligence activities, of course; but it would be hard to deny that controversial uses of the Third Option have been a factor in its decline.

Church remained convinced that covert action should be resorted to only in extreme situations: to save the United States from great peril or, on some infrequent occasions, to help where America could in the advancement of democracies around the world (as with America's covert aid to allies in Western Europe following the Second World War or as in Portugal, which was in political turmoil at the time of the Senate intelligence investigation in 1975). During his

Committee's probe into the nation's spy powers, he conceded a role for covert action to "avert a nuclear holocaust or save an entire civilization," or to "help democratic political parties" overseas, if such aid "might avert a forcible take-over by a communist minority, heavily subsidized by the Soviets."[46]

Church preferred to have a more discriminating use of covert action. He maintained that almost all of America's foreign policy activities should be assigned to the Department of State, leaving only a few covert actions in the hands of the CIA—strictly paramilitary and sabotage activities. Moreover, he would have reduced the numbers of Third Options under way in 1975 by about 90 percent.[47]

Avoidance of the nuclear war scenario was the only aspect of the Third Option upon which all the expert witnesses during the Chuch Committee hearings on covert action could agree. If the Third Option could prevent Armageddon, then, yes, by all means use it. An effective CIA response in a time of emergency would require, though, an existing, well-training corps of operations officers standing by—a point usually passed over by critics of the Third Option who would just as soon see the Operations Directorate (if not the CIA) disappear.

In their public testimony to the Church Committee, Clark Clifford and Cyrus Vance also recommended reserving the Third Option for adoption only in the rarest of circumstances. "The guiding criterion," advised Clifford, a former secretary of defense and chief author of the National Security Act of 1947, "should be the test as to whether or not a certain covert project *truly affects* our national security." Vance, soon to be Secretary of State in the Carter administration, testified that CAs should be the policy of the United States "only when they are *absolutely essential* to the national security."[48] In fact, though, the adoption of covert action as a policy option has rarely been the last resort, and it is often the first.

The Church Committee witness most negatively disposed toward the Third Option was national security expert and former NSC staffer Morton Halperin. "The possible benefits," he argued, "are far outweighed by the costs to our society of maintaining a capability for covert operations." He found the Third Option "incompatible with our democratic institutions, with congressional and public control over foreign policy decisions, with our constitutional rights, and with the principles and ideals that this Republic stands for in the world."[49] Writing at the time of the Church panel inquiry, the eloquent Harvard Law School professor Roger Fisher sided with Halperin's perspective:

> When we choose our weapons, let's choose ones we are good at using—like the Marshall Plan—not ones that we are bad at—like the Bay of Pigs. To join some adversaries in the grotesque world of poison dart-guns and covert operations is to give up the most powerful weapons we have: idealism, morality, due process

of law, and belief in the freedom of others to disagree, including the right of other countries to disagree with ours.[50]

Forty-three years after the Senate intelligence investigation, scholar Lindsey A. O'Rourke's thoughtful analysis of covert actions led her to this bottom line: "Policymakers should think twice before launching covert regime change. Although, on occasion, these missions have succeeded, more often than not they have backfired on their creators."[51]

~~~

Looking back at Cy Vance's testimony on covert action, his "essential" standard seems overly restrictive and unrealistic today. Sometimes the Third Option has been helpful at lower levels of adoption on the escalation ladder, as with the Agency's assistance to the Christian Democratic Party in Italy during the early stages of the Cold War; or with pro-democracy movements in Portugal, Poland, and elsewhere in later stages. (Colby believed that US clandestine support to anticommunist groups in Europe—East and West—stood with the Laotian intervention as the Agency's most important Third Option successes.)[52] If a carefully orchestrated charge by King George's cavalry can save democracy somewhere, then that possibility should be taken seriously.

Moreover, attempts to provide honest information to captive peoples who are isolated from the rest of the world, by whatever form of an "iron curtain" a dictator may have fabricated, can be a constructive measure. And, of course, overt and covert efforts by Washington officials to assist, legally and ethically, with counterterrorism objectives that protect the United States from another 9/11 attack are imperative. Even carefully calibrated uses of high-rung economic and paramilitary Third Options might be important to initiate in times of emergencies—the Clifford-Vance exceptional circumstances. At these lofty reaches of the escalation ladder, though, care in decision making and accountability must be redoubled by foreign policy planners.

Some forms of covert action are bound to continue, regardless of which political party or president may be in charge of the government in Washington at any given time. Such operations have received a stamp of approval by various administrations, and across party lines, for decades. Most have been small-scale propaganda and political operations, quietly implemented—indeed, these sum to "the vast majority of the hundreds and hundreds of covert action projects carried out by CIA," Dr. Ray S. Cline, a well-regarded CIA insider, reported in 1976.[53] In many cases, these lower-rung operations have helped to advance democratic governments around the world. Realistically, then, one should aim not at eliminating the Third Option altogether but at carefully delineating the bright lines this policy initiative must honor, if covert actions are to remain within legal and moral boundaries.

It bears emphasis: an especially sharp eye is warranted with respect to the extreme variants of the Third Option, whether political (a coup d'état, say), economic (mining foreign harbors to sink commercial ships, as ordered by DCI Casey in Nicaragua), or paramilitary. They have been the main causes of controversy and public damage to the reputation of the CIA and, therefore, of the United States. As an experienced DO operative Robert Baer has written, "Whenever the guns came out, the CIA got itself into trouble.... Better to operate in the shadows and leave the bang-bang to others."[54]

Sanger maintains that the CIA is no longer in the business of manipulating elections or instigating coups; that suitcases stuffed with King George's cavalry have been replaced by suitcases stuffed with an "Internet in a box" to provide foreigners with accurate information.[55] It is true: the United States is now helping democracies and would-be democracies more overtly, through the auspices of the National Endowment for Democracy and other organizations in Washington designed to advance democratic principles around the world in a public manner, and to enhance the opportunity for more people to cast ballots in fair elections. Yet Sanger acknowledges that the United States attempted to oust Hamid Karzai in Afghanistan during the Obama years—and that is not the only example of more traditional covert actions in recent years (Chapter 6).

In general terms, America's clandestine interventions began with a concentration on hindering the progress of communism and aiding US business interests abroad, mainly through the use of propaganda and political action in the 1940s and 1950s. It then moved toward major paramilitary activities in Cuba, Laos, Vietnam, Nicaragua, and Afghanistan in the 1960s and 1980s (after a 1970s lull of introspection about the proper uses of covert action), as well as—steadily— non-proliferation operations to curb the global spread of WMD. Next came an expanding use of the Third Option directed against terrorists in the 1990s. After the 9/11 attacks the next decade, the CIA became increasing reliant on drone attacks in pursuit of its counterterrorism mission. Nevertheless, the Agency's more traditional propaganda, political and economic activities, and even major paramilitary operations do, in fact, continue on—witness the Syrian and Libyan debacles during the Obama years, and the Trump-ordered assassination of Qasem Soleimani. The central question remains: How useful are any of these secret interventions in the future of American foreign policy?

Having sung the praises of some Third Options in previous chapters (and above), the judgment here is that far too many have proven feckless or, more alarming still, harmful to the global standing of the United States—and truly devastating to the target nations. Examining the roster of countries that have suffered from America's clandestine interventions, the German Nobel Laureate for literature Günter Grass appropriately wondered if there was "no country too small or trifling to escape [the Agency's] attention?"[56] Similarly, Senator Church arrived at the conclusion that America's primary CA targets had been "small, weak nations."[57]

Yet, in truth, many of America's covert actions have been focused on well-armed adversaries, too, including the USSR, nations in Eastern Europe, and China (all primary and steady targets for secret propaganda, among other covert actions), as well as established industrialized nations like France and Italy (against internal communist targets during the Cold War). The timelines presented in Figures 3.1 and 5.1 highlight the reality, though, that a large number of small, poor nations have indeed been the victims of Agency operations over the years. As they carried on their struggle for global supremacy, the United States and the Soviet Union moved from the European theater of covert conflict soon after the end of the Second World War to the less confrontational turf of Third World developing countries.

Figure 10.1 provides a profile of the nations examined in Chapters 3 through 6 that were targeted for US covert actions. These nations, selected by the author because of their frequent mention in the public literature, are separated into two groupings: those that were victims of major covert actions (the bold print in Figures 3.1 and 5.1, and the subjects of this book); and those that were the focus of more minor operations (non-bold print). Also examined in Figure 10.1 are the regional settings of covert action targets around the world, again using the list of nations from the timelines presented earlier in Figures 3.1 and 5.1, divided once more into CA targets of major and more minor status.

For these sets of nations in both the "major" and the "minor" categories, the developing world has been in fact the main battle space for the most significant US clandestine interventions reviewed in this book: thirty poor nations, as against seventeen rich ones; and, among the lesser CAs routinely mentioned in the literature, the figures are fifty-four as against twelve, respectively. These targeting results are just as Frank Church and Günter Grass had more intuitively lamented. Yet, as these numbers show, the more developed world has seen its share of covert intrusions as well, especially in the early years of the Cold War when the Soviet empire (the USSR and its Eastern European satellites) was the most frequently targeted region of the world, edged out in more recent decades—although only barely—by Asia. Figure 10.1 is a reminder, too, of how the United States made something of a shift from the well-to-do European nations toward the less risky turf of the world's poor nations as it carried out its clandestine interventions in the post–Hughes-Ryan era: from 59 percent to 73 percent for the "major" category; and 64 percent to 81 percent for the "minor" category.[58]

America's secret machinations may have had some useful returns for a few US corporations and their stockholders, notably in the earlier decades of the

THE MAJOR COVERT ACTION TARGETS**

1947-1974	1975-2020	Overall: 1947-2020

Nation-Targeting Hierarchy

Developing	Developed	Developing	Developed	Developing	Developed
19 nations	13 nations	11 nations	4 nations	30 nations	17 nations

Regional-Targeting Hierarchy

1947-1974	1975-2020	Overall: 1947-2020
USSR/E. Europe (17)	Asia (5)	USSR/E. Europe (21)
Asia (5)	USSR/E. Europe (4)	Asia (10)
Latin America (3)	Middle East (4)	Middle East (7)
Middle East (3)	Latin America (1)	Latin America (4)
W. Europe (3)	Africa (1)	W. Europe (3)
Africa (1)	Western Europe (0)	Africa (2)

THE MINOR COVERT ACTIONS TARGETS**

1947-1974	1975-2020	Overall: 1947-2020

Nation-Targeting Hierarchy

Developing	Developed	Developing	Developed	Developing	Developed
29 nations	10 nations	25 nations	2 nations	54 nations	12 nations

Regional-Targeting Hierarchy

1947-1974	1975-2020	Overall: 1947-2020
Latin America (10)	Africa (11)	Latin America (17)
USSR/E. Europe (10)	Latin America (7)	Africa (15)
Asia (9)	Middle East (4)	Asia (12)
Africa (4)	Asia (3)	USSR/E. Europe (12)
Western Europe (4)	USSR/E. Europe (2)	Middle East (6)
Middle East (2)	Western Europe (0)	Western Europe (4)

Figure 10.1 Covert Action Targeting, by Level of Development and Region, 1947–2020*

*Some nations are counted more than once, if they were targeted more than once at different times over the decades represented here.
**Drawn respectively from Figures 3.1 and 5.1 (in which the major operations explored in this book are in bold); these nations have been, in the author's judgment, the most commonly referred to Third Options in the public record during the modern era.

Cold War. More important, they may have signaled to European and Asian allies the willingness of the United States to stand strong in the worldwide ideological battle between the superpowers. This second proposition, though, was bankrupt as a concept in some parts of the world from the beginning. The forces of nationalism and self-determination were vastly more important than global communism in places like Iran in 1953 and Vietnam in 1964. Did Germany and Japan (for example) ever doubt America's commitment to their defense during the Cold War, given their obvious importance to this nation's own future security and prosperity? It seems unlikely. Did they really care what the US response was to events in (for them) far-away Guatemala City, Santiago, or Managua? Doubtful. It was important for the United States to take a strong stance on the Korean Peninsula in 1950–1953, though, because in the early 1950s global communism carried a high viral load in Asia.

One of the findings that stands out in a review of US clandestine interventions since 1947 is that many of them have left small, poor nations around the world as destitute as ever. The United States would topple one despotic leader or junta only to put in their place another autocrat, this time pro-America. An SOB but our SOB, in the old saying. The people of Iran, Guatemala, South Vietnam, Laos, Cambodia, and down the list, have remained poverty stricken, and their views of the United States no more favorable—and often worse—than before the CIA paid them a visit. Covert action has a place among the instruments of US foreign policy; but it will never be able, magically, to bring about vibrant, democratic societies in places that continue to suffer acutely from the four great demons of global affairs—hunger, poverty, desperation, and chaos—identified long ago by General George C. Marshall when he announced his eponymous plan for European recovery.[59] The venerable wisdom of Lord Salisbury should also always be kept in mind by those in high councils: sometimes it is better to do nothing rather than just doing something.

The Fourth Option

In its conduct of foreign policy, the United States could benefit from closer attention to a Fourth Option: the virtue of leading by example. This means doing the right thing that others, at home and abroad, will respect and admire: acting with a dignity and patience that befits the world's oldest and strongest democracy; staying within the white lines of law and propriety; keeping the high moral ground by pursuing a principled relationship with other nations; helping people overseas, with a more robust program of foreign assistance through the Peace Corps and other programs. An illustration is the US Navy's use of hospital ships to deliver health care abroad. The USNS *Mercy* and USNS *Comfort* visit ports around the globe, especially countries that have suffered from the effects of tsunamis, earthquakes, and hurricanes. The *Comfort*, for instance, has a staff of 900 who tend to 1,000 hospital beds as well as operating rooms, labs, radiology equipment, and dental facilities. Among the countries where the vessel has recently moored are Indonesia, Haiti, and Colombia, bringing help to patients and leaving in their wake new, enduring friendships for the United States. Here is foreign policy at its finest.[60] In this spirit, America's global distribution of COVID-19 vaccines has had the dual attributes of helping to eliminate a deadly global virus while at the same time attracting new friendships for the United States.

"If America has a service to perform in the world—and I believe it has," observed a chairman of the Senate Foreign Relations Committee in the 1960s, J. William Fulbright (D, Arkansas), "it is in large part the service of its own example."[61] Exploding cigars, poison-tipped pens, lethal pills, assassination teams, deadly dart guns, the mining of foreign harbors, the torture, the killing of civilians abroad without clear evidence they are terrorists intent on attacking the United States—these are not the kinds of activities that Americans have traditionally embraced. On the contrary, the United States is the nation that supported the Marshall Plan, that offers assistance to those caught in natural disasters, that champions international human rights. The Fourth Option is the best consort for the First Option, diplomacy, when both are carried out with empathy—and with a hearing aid turned on so that the United States is not just talking to other nations but listening to their hopes and extending a helping hand wherever possible .

Two outstanding American diplomats have echoed Fulbright's sentiments. "When we mine harbors in Nicaragua, we fuzz the difference between ourselves and the Soviet Union," remarked the distinguished diplomat George Ball during the Cold War. "We act out of character, which no great power can do without diminishing itself."[62] More recently, in reaction to President Trump's often erratic and unprincipled conduct of foreign affairs, Roberta Jacobson, a former US ambassador to Mexico with thirty-one years of service at the State Department, rued the abandonment of the moral high ground that America once enjoyed. "The loss of those principles makes us 'like everyone else' in a world where 'everyone does it,'" she writes, adding that this loss "makes us less safe, less prosperous, and less of an example."[63]

In contrast to these views, Trump's remarkably Manichaean D/CIA and later secretary of state, Mike Pompeo, recommended that "the CIA, to be successful, must be aggressive, vicious, unforgiving, relentless."[64]

~ ~ ~

In the inner sanctums of the Oval Office, SCCI, and HPSCI, as well as on Langley's Seventh Floor and in the Roosevelt Room in the White House where NSC meetings take place, which pathway will America's elected officials decide to follow? Will American citizens encourage their elected officials to support a more judicious use of covert action? Or will they walk the blinkered and arrogant

"America First" pathway proposed by Donald Trump and Mike Pompeo? The United States has much work ahead if it wishes to restore its moral leadership in the world, becoming again the beacon of hope and democratic ideals that it once was for freedom-loving people everywhere in the aftermath of the Second World War. Adopting a more discriminating approach to the Third Option is a worthy place to begin.

Acknowledgments

The most important person for me to thank in the preparation of this volume, as with my earlier publications, is Leena Johnson, my wife for the past fifty-two years and my girlfriend for four years before that. Throughout this time, she has been a font of encouragement and guidance as I pursued a career that combined government service along with university research and teaching.

Many colleagues also assisted me along the way in my efforts to understand the subject of covert action—a heavily veiled and controversial instrument of foreign policy hidden deeply within the nation's intelligence bureaucracy. Some of these individuals are present or former officers in the Central Intelligence Agency and must remain anonymous; others are former government officials who took time out of frenetic schedules to discuss the Third Option with me (always avoiding classified information, of course, as does this book), either while still in office or in retirement. They include James J. Angleton, Les Aspin, George Ball, Edward P. Boland, George H. W. Bush, Jimmy Carter, William J. Casey, Frank Church, James R. Clapper, Ray S. Cline, William E. Colby, William J. Daugherty, John M. Deutch, Nicholas Dujmovic, Wyche Fowler, Robert M. Gates, Porter J. Goss, Richard Helms, John Hollister Hedley, Fred Hitz, Karl F. Inderfurth, Frederic F. Manget, Walter F. Mondale, William N. Nolte, Kevin A. O'Brien, Paul R. Pillar, Harry Rositski, James R. Schlesinger, J. Warren Stembridge, William O. Studeman, George Tenet, Michael A. Turner, Stansfield Turner, William H. Webster, and R. James Woolsey. A special thank you to Gregory F. Treverton, former chairman of the National Intelligence Council, who read a first draft of the book and made helpful suggestions—although of course he is in no way responsible for errors that may have occurred in this final version.

Several reports by journalists with an intelligence and foreign policy beat have aided my understanding of America's relations with the rest of the world, as the notes to this book attest. They include Peter Baker, David Brooks, Karen De Young, Thomas L. Friedman, Seymour M. Hersh, David Ignatius, David Martin, Mark Mazzetti, James Risen, David E. Sanger, Charlie Savage, Scott Shane, Tim Weiner, David Wise, and Bob Woodward. Special thanks to Scott for reading an early draft and offering helpful suggestions.

Further, many fine scholars gave of their time and knowledge to assist with this inquiry. In addition to those researchers whom I cite in this book's "Notes" and "Selected Bibliography," I especially want to thank Richard J. Aldrich, Christopher Andrew, James E. Baker, David M. Barrett, James A. Barry, Siegfried

Beer, Richard A. Best Jr., Richard K. Betts, A. Denis Clift, Rory Cormac, Louis Fisher, Peter Gill, Michael Handel, Glenn Hastedt, Michael Herman, Frederick P. Hitz, Arthur S. Hulnick, Peter Jackson, William E. Jackson, Rhodri Jeffreys-Jones, Robert Jervis, James Johnston, David Kahn, Anne Karalekas, Jennifer Kibbe, Wolfgang Krieger, Mark M. Lowenthal, Stephen Marrin, Ernest May, Christopher Moran, William M. Nolte, Joy Patton, Mark Phythian, John Prados, Harry Howe Ransom (a mentor and a pioneer in the field of Intelligence Studies), W. Michael Reisman, Arthur M. Schlesinger, Jr., Paul Schliefsteiner, Frederick A.O. Schwartz Jr., Stan A. Taylor, Patrick F. Walsh, Wesley W. Wark, Michael S. Warner, Stephen R. Weissman, Brad Westerfield (another of the field's pathbreakers), James J. Wirtz (with whom I have had the pleasure for many years of editing a widely adopted anthology of articles on intelligence, published by Oxford University Press), and Amy B. Zegart. Added thanks go to Elizabeth White, the first-rate University of Georgia librarian; and to Australian journalist and researcher Wendy Zuckerman for drawing my attention to some helpful public documents. Last but not least among my research associates, I want to thank my students over the years for their friendship and for what they have taught me; I happily dedicate this volume to them.

Encouragement from family is vital while writing a book. I feel so lucky to have the Swatis—Kristin, Jamil, August, and Loch—cheering me on and I thank them from the bottom of my heart. As well, my appreciation goes to the outstanding administrative team at the University of Georgia, especially President Jere W. Morehead and Dean Matthew R. Auer, and to my first-rate colleagues in the School of Public and International Affairs. I am deeply grateful, moreover, to Niko Pfund, president extraordinaire of Oxford University Press in the United States; to David McBride, the Press's outstanding Social Science editor; the talented and helpful Emily Mackenzie Benitez, project editor, Social Sciences, Holly Mitchell, assistant editor, Social Science; and Jeremy Toynbee, Newgen project manager, for their sure-handed guidance; and to Patterson Lamb for her keen eye in helping with the final manuscript preparation for this, my eighth, book for OUP—one of the finest publishing houses in the world.

Finally, I take my hat off to those men and women at the CIA engaged in the legitimate and useful forms of covert action since 1947, at the direction of the White House and the Congress—and often in dangerous circumstances. The shortcomings associated with the Third Option discussed in these pages should not take away from the fact that the overwhelming majority of public servants at the "the Agency" have served the nation well, across the intelligence spectrum from collection and analysis and counterintelligence to covert action. They have acted morally; they have honored the law; they have kept legislative overseers informed; and they have labored indefatigably on behalf of the American people. They merit our respect and gratitude.

APPENDIX A
Intelligence Leadership in the United States, 1946–2021

Directors, National Intelligence (DNI)

2005–2007	Amb. (ret.) John D. Negroponte
2007–2009	Gen. (ret.) J. M. "Mike" McConnell
2009–2010	Adm. (ret.) Dennis C. Blair
2010–2017	Gen. (ret.) James R. Clapper, Jr.
2017–2019	Dan Coates
2019–2020	Joseph Maguire (Acting)
2020–2021	John Ratcliffe
2021–	Avril D. Haines

Directors, Central Intelligence (DCI), an office terminated in 2004

1946	Adm. Sidney William Souers
1946–1947	Lt. Gen. Hoyt Sanford Vandenberg
1947–1950	Rear Adm. Roscoe H. Hillenkoetter
1950–1953	Gen. Walter Bedell Smith
1953–1961	Allen W. Dulles
1961–1965	John A. McCone
1965–1966	Vice Adm. William F. Raborn, Jr.
1966–1973	Richard Helms
1973	James R. Schlesinger
1973–1976	William E. Colby
1976–1977	George H. W. Bush
1977–1981	Adm. Stansfield Turner
1981–1987	William J. Casey
1987–1991	William H. Webster
1991–1993	Robert M. Gates
1993–1995	R. James Woolsey
1995–1997	John M. Deutch
1997–2004	George J. Tenet
2004	Porter J. Goss

Directors, Central Intelligence Agency (D/CIA)

2005–2006	Porter J. Goss
2006–2009	Gen. Michael Hayden
2009–2011	Leon Panetta
2011–2013	Gen. David Petraeus
2013–2018	John Brennan
2018–2021	Gina Haspel
2021–	William J. Burns

Chair, Senate Select Committee on Intelligence (SSCI)

1976–1977	Daniel K. Inouye, Democrat, Hawaii
1977–1981	Birch Bayh, Democrat, Indiana
1981–1985	Barry Goldwater, Republican, Arizona
1985–1987	David Durenberger, Republican, Minnesota
1987–1993	David L. Boren, Democrat, Oklahoma
1993–1995	Dennis DeConcini, Democrat, Arizona
1995–1997	Arlen Specter, Republican, Pennsylvania
1997–2001	Richard C. Shelby, Republican, Alabama
2001–2003	Bob Graham, Democrat, Florida
2003–2006	Pat Roberts, Republican, Kansas
2007–2008	John D. Rockefeller IV, Democrat, West Virginia
2009–2014	Dianne Feinstein, Democrat, California
2015–2020	Richard M. Burr, Republican, North Carolina
2020–2021	Marco Rubio, Republican, Florida
2021–	Mark Warner, Democrat, Virginia

Chair, House Permanent Select Committee on Intelligence (HPSCI)

1977–1985	Edward P. Boland, Democrat, Massachusetts
1985–1987	Lee H. Hamilton, Democrat, Indiana
1987–1989	Louis Stokes, Democrat, Ohio
1989–1991	Anthony C. Beilenson, Democrat, California
1991–1993	Dave McCurdy, Democrat, Oklahoma
1993–1995	Dan Glickman, Democrat, Kansas
1995–1997	Larry Combest, Republican, Texas
1997–2004	Porter J. Goss, Republican, Florida
2004–2006	Peter Hoekstra, Republican, Michigan
2006–2011	Silvestre Reyes, Democrat, Texas
2011–2014	Mike Rogers, Republican, Michigan
2015–2019	Devin Nunes, Republican, California
2019–	Adam Schiff, Democrat, California

APPENDIX B

The Intelligence Oversight Act of 1980

Title V of the National Security Act of 1947, 50 USC 413

Accountability for Intelligence Activities

Congressional Oversight

Sec.501. (a) To the extent consistent with all applicable authorities and duties, including those conferred by the Constitution upon the executive and legislative branches of the Government, and to the extent consistent with due regard for the protection from unauthorized disclosure of classified information and information relating to intelligence sources and methods, the Director of Central Intelligence and the heads of all departments, agencies, and other entities of the United States involved in intelligence activities shall—
(1) keep the Select Committee on Intelligence of the Senate and the Permanent Select Committee on Intelligence of the House of Representatives (hereinafter in this section referred to as the "intelligence committees") fully and currently informed of all intelligence activities which are the responsibility of, are engaged in by, or are carried out for or on behalf of, any department, agency, or entity of the United States, including any significant anticipated intelligence activity, except that (A) the foregoing provision shall not require approval of the intelligence committees as a condition precedent to the initiation of any such anticipated intelligence activity, and (B) if the President determines it is essential to limit prior notice to meet extraordinary circumstances affecting vital interests of the United States, such notice shall be limited to the chairmen and ranking minority members of the intelligence committees, the Speaker and minority leader of the House of Representatives, and the majority and minority leaders of the Senate;
(2) furnish any information or material concerning intelligence activities which is in the possession, custody, or control of any department, agency, or entity of the United States and which is requested by either of the intelligence committees in order to carry out its authorized responsibilities; and
(3) report in a timely fashion to the intelligence committees any illegal intelligence activity or significant intelligence failure and any corrective action that has been taken or is planned to be taken in connection with such illegal activity or failure.

(b) The President shall fully inform the intelligence committees in a timely fashion of intelligence operations in foreign countries, other than activities intended solely for obtaining necessary intelligence, for which prior notice was not given under subsection (a) and shall provide a statement of the reasons for not giving prior notice.

(c) The President and the intelligence committees shall each establish such procedures as may be necessary to carry out the provisions of subsections (a) and (b).

(d) the House of Representatives and the Senate, in consultation with the Director of Central Intelligence, shall each establish, by rule or resolution of such House, procedures to protect from unauthorized disclosure all classified information and all information relating to intelligence sources and the methods furnished to the intelligence committees or to Members of the Congress under this section. In accordance with such procedures, each of the intelligence committees shall promptly call to the attention of its respective House, or to any appropriate committee or committees of its respective House, any matter relating to intelligence activities requiring the attention of such House or such committee or committees.

(e) Nothing in this Act shall be construed as authority to withhold information from the intelligence committees on the grounds that providing the information to the intelligence committees would constitute the unauthorized disclosure of classified information or information relating to intelligence sources and methods.

Notes

Preface

1. On Franklin, see *Intelligence in the War of Independence*, Central Intelligence Agency, Washington, DC (1975); and on Jefferson: Brian Kilmeade and Don Yaeger, *Thomas Jefferson and the Tripoli Pirates: The Forgotten War That Changed American History* (New York: Random House, 2015); Stephen Knott, *Secret and Sanctioned: Covert Operations and the American Presidency* (New York: Oxford University Press, 1996); and Robert Wallace, "The Barbary Wars," *Smithsonian* 5 (January 1975): 82–91. For the later presidents mentioned here, see Mitchell Rogovin, statement, *Hearings*, Permanent Select Committee on Intelligence, US House of Representatives, 95th Cong., 1st Sess., Part 5 (1976): 1729.
2. Another common nickname for the CIA used by insiders is "the Company."
3. Respectively: *Final Report*, Select Committee to Study Governmental Operations with Respect to Intelligence Activities, US Senate, 94th Cong., 2d Sess. (Washington, DC: US Government Printing Office, 1976): vol I: 9, hereafter cited as the Church Committee; Leon Panetta and Jim Newton, *Worthy Fights: A Memoir of Leadership in War and Peace* (New York: Penguin, 2014): 390); and government officials quoted in Tom Wicker et al., "C.I.A.: Maker of Policy, or Tool?" *New York Times* (April 25, 1966): A1ff.
4. Church Committee, 94th Cong., 2d Sess. and 95th Cong., 1st Sess. (1975–76).
5. Loch K. Johnson, *A Season of Inquiry Revisited: The Church Committee Confronts America's Spy Agencies* (Lawrence: University Press of Kansas, 2015): 56.
6. Quoted by Don Oberdorfer, "Behind the House Vote on 'the Secret War,' a Low-Profile Insider," *Washington Post* (August 6, 1983): A13.
7. Loch K. Johnson, *The Threat on the Horizon: An Inside Account of America's Search for Security After the Cold War* (New York: Oxford University Press, 2011): 288.
8. Miles Copeland, *Beyond Cloak and Dagger: Inside the CIA* (New York: Simon & Schuster,1974): 204–5.
9. Dean Rusk, as told to Richard Rusk and edited by Daniel S. Papp, *As I Saw It* (New York: Norton, 1990): 562. For years, I was a faculty colleague of retired secretary of state Dean Rusk at the University of Georgia, and we met periodically to discuss intelligence, diplomacy, and war-making—a highlight of my enjoyable years in Athens, one of the loveliest towns with one of the best universities in the United States.
10. It would be easy, and entirely wrong, to misconstrue the remarks presented in this book as an attack on the CIA. My experience in government, along with my many interviews with Agency officers since 1975, lead me to believe that this organization's personnel are among the brightest and most dedicated civil servants in Washington.

When I express skepticism about the value of some covert actions (by no means all), I am certainly aware of the bravery, patriotism, and good intentions of those intelligence officers who have sloughed their way through dangerous paramilitary warfare at the Bay of Pigs in Cuba, as well as in Korea, Laos, Vietnam, Afghanistan, and so many other places of interest to the United States around the world; or otherwise placed themselves in harm's way by having to deal at times with unsavory individuals in bad neighborhoods overseas.

More than a hundred CIA officers have given their lives for the United States in paramilitary operations and other intelligence-related duties abroad. One illustration: at Camp Chapman, a remote Agency hideaway near Khost in the Afghan mountain region, several CIA personnel gathered on December 30, 2009, to plan a counterterrorism operation. Key to the meeting was going to be the presence of Dr. Humam Khalil Abu-Mulal al-Balawi, a Jordanian physician with an interest in world affairs and engaged in undercover work for the Agency. The CIA trusted Dr. al-Balawi, who had been reliable in the past, and allowed him into the meeting without the normally rigorous security checks. Once inside, al-Balawi turned out to be a double agent. He detonated a suicide vest he was wearing that killed him and seven Agency officers.

As observed by the protagonist in the great spy tale *Kim*, an intelligence officer "must go alone—alone and at the peril of his head. Then, if he spits, or sits down, or sneezes other than as the people do whom he watches, he may be slain" [Rudyard Kipling, *Kim* (New York: Knopf, 1995, originally published in 1901): 137]. I admire and respect the service of America's intelligence officers; I am only trying in these pages to evaluate the contributions of covert action as an instrument of US foreign policy.

Introduction

1. In general parlance in Washington, DC, "covert action," the "Third Option," the "Quiet Option," "covert operations," "clandestine activities," and "special activities" are used synonymously, although since the end of the Cold War the most widely used expressions are "covert action" and the "Third Option."
2. Commission on the Organization of the Government for the Conduct of Foreign Policy, *Report*, vols. I–VII (June 30, 1975), Washington, DC, quote at vol I: 1.
3. See Fareed Zakaria, *Ten Lessons for a Post-Pandemic World* (New York: Norton, 2020).
4. P. R. Ehrlich et al., "The Long-Term Biological Consequences of Nuclear War," *Science* 222 (December 23, 1983): 145–49.
5. Loch K. Johnson, *American Foreign Policy and the Challenges of World Leadership: Power, Principle, and the Constitution* (New York: Oxford University Press, 2015).
6. Abba Eban, *The New Diplomacy: International Affairs in the Modern Age* (New York: Random House, 1983): 334. On the art of diplomacy, see as well Wolfgang

Ischinger, *World in Danger: German and Europe in an Uncertain Time* (Washington, DC: Brookings Institution Press, 2021).
7. See Michael Beschloss, *Presidents of War* (New York: Crown, 2018); and Charlie Savage, *Power Wars: The Relentless Rise of Presidential Authority and Secrecy* (New York: Little, Brown, 2015).
8. William E. Colby, testimony, Select Committee to Study Governmental Operations with Respect to Intelligence Activities, Rm. S407, Capitol Building (October 23, 1975), Washington, DC (a panel led by Senator Frank Church and hereafter cited as the Church Committee). Colby had appeared before the Murphy Commission two years earlier and offered a warning to its members. Given "the shape of the world," he said, covert action "should not be lightly discarded from our national arsenal" [William E. Colby, testimony, Commission on the Organization of the Government for the Conduct of Foreign Policy, (November 19, 1973), Washington, DC].
9. Ted Shackley, *Spymaster: My Life in the CIA*, with Richard A. Finney (Dulles, VA: Potomac Books, 2005): 38.
10. Richard M. Bissell Jr., with Jonathan E. Lewis and Frances T. Pudlo, *Reflections of a Cold Warrior: From Yalta to the Bay of Pigs* (New Haven, CT: Yale University Press, 1996): 207.
11. James R. Schlesinger, remark to the author, Washington, DC (June 20, 1991).
12. Steve Coll, *Directorate S: The C.I.A. and America's Secret Wars in Afghanistan and Pakistan* (New York: Penguin, 2018): 40. On covert action myths, see Loch K. Johnson, *Spy Watching: Intelligence Accountability in the United States* (New York: Oxford University Press, 2018): 327–49.
13. Gregory F. Treverton, *Reshaping National Intelligence for an Age of Information* (New York: Cambridge University Press, 2001): 174.
14. Henry Kissinger, remark, "Evening News," *NBC Television Network* (January 13, 1978).
15. Author's interview with an operative in the CIA's Operations Directorate, Washington, DC (February 7, 1986). Trying to push history can prompt other nations to push back, leading to conflict. "The most controversial parts of foreign policy—arguably the ones most requiring public debate—are covertly handled by the C.I.A.," observes Professor Daniel Immerwahr of Northwestern University ["The Death of America's Political Imagination," *New York Times* (July 4, 2021): SR4].
16. See, for instance, John Yoo, *Defender in Chief: Donald Trump's Fight for Presidential Power* (New York: St. Martin's Press, 2020).
17. Quoted in David E. Sanger, "Trump Turns Power of State Against Foes, like an Authoritarian," *New York Times* (October 10, 2020): A17.
18. See, for example, Edward S. Corwin, *The President: Office and Powers, 1978–1957*, rev. ed. (New York: New York University Press, 1969); Louis Fisher, *Defending Congress and the Constitution* (Lawrence: University Press of Kansas, 2011); and Richard E. Neustadt, *Presidential Power and the Modern Presidents* (New York: Free Press, 1990). Professor Neustadt underscored the fundamental precept that the Constitution had created a government of "separated institutions *sharing* powers" (29, original emphasis).

19. Justice Louis Brandeis, *Myers v. United States*, 272 US 52, 293 [1926], emphasis added. For essays by some of the nation's founders warning about the dangers of concentrated executive power, see especially *Papers Nos. 4* (written by John Jay), as well as *10* and *51* (both by James Madison) in *The Federalist* (New York: Modern Library, 1937).
20. Pub. L. No. 92-404, 86 Stat. 619 (1972).
21. For a review of this wrestling match between the executive and legislative branches, see Loch K. Johnson, *The Making of International Agreements: Congress Confronts the Executive* (New York: New York University Press, 1984); and Oona A. Hathaway, Curtis A. Bradley, and Jack L. Goldsmith, "The Failed Transparency Regime for Executive Agreements: An Empirical and Normative Analysis," *Harvard Law Review* 134/2 (December 2020): 629-725.
22. Pub. L. No. 88-408, 78 Stat. 384 (1964).
23. Pub. L. No. 87-297, 33, 75 Stat. 631, 634, as amended at 22 U.S.C. 2573 (2012).
24. These statutes were by no means perfect and have sometimes been slighted, or totally ignored, by the executive branch; but most of the time their provisions have been honored and they stand as benchmarks in the struggle over power that the drafters of the Constitution anticipated and encouraged. On the WPR, see John Hart Ely, *War and Responsibility: Constitutional Lessons of Vietnam and Its Aftermath* (Princeton, NJ: Princeton University Press, 1993); and Johnson, *American Foreign Policy*.
25. Robert C. Byrd (D, West Virginia), quoted by Martin Tolchin, "Leadership Role a 'Love-Hate' Affair," *New York Times* (September 21, 1983): B8.
26. Loch K. Johnson, *A Season of Inquiry: The Senate Intelligence Investigation* (Lexington: University Press of Kentucky, 1985).
27. Jill Lepore, *These Truths: A History of the United States* (New York: Norton, 2018): 536.
28. David S. McLellan, *The Cold War in Transition* (New York: Macmillan, 1966): 6. See also John Lewis Gaddis, *The United States and the Origins of the Cold War, 1941–47* (New York: Columbia University Press, 1972).
29. Philip T. Reeker, the Acting Assistant Secretary of State for Europe and Eurasia, warned in 2020 that "by spreading disinformation about coronavirus, Russian malign actors are once again choosing to threaten public safety by distracting from the global health response" [quoted in Edward Wong and Katie Rogers, "Return of Americans Infected on Ship Is Said to Have Infuriated Trump," *New York Times* (February 23, 2020): 9]. See also Ellen Nakashima and Craig Timberg, "Russian Disinformation Operation Relied on Forgeries, Fake Posts on 300 Platforms," *Washington Post* (June 16, 2020): A1.
30. Christopher Andrew, *The Secret World: A History of Intelligence* (New York: Penguin, 2018): 680.
31. Richard Rovere, *Senator Joe McCarthy* (New York: Harcourt, Brace, 1959).
32. Quoted by Robert D. Warth, *Soviet Russia in World Politics* (New York: Twayne, 1963): 320.
33. Harry S. Truman, *Memoirs*, vol. 1 (New York: Doubleday, 1955): 551–52.
34. Merle Miller, *Plain Speaking: An Oral Biography of Harry S. Truman* (New York: Berkley, 1973): 420 note.
35. Andrew, *The Secret World*, 677. The CIA, now age seventy-four, has surpassed the biblical span of threescore and ten.

36. Harry S. Truman, in the *Washington Post* (December 22, 1962), cite by Roger Hilsman, *To Move a Nation* (New York: Dell, 1964): 63; and Harry S. Truman, "Limit CIA Role in Intelligence," *Washington Post* (December 23, 1963): A23, where the former president criticizes the Agency's engagement in "cloak and dagger" operations, as opposed to the original mission he had envisioned of collection and analysis. A researcher came across a similar remark made by Truman earlier in 1963, when he said that the CIA "was not intended as a 'Cloak and Dagger' outfit" [Scott A. Moseman, "Truman and the Formation of the Central Intelligence Agency," *Journal of Intelligence History* 19/2 (June 2020):149–67, quote at 164, based on a Truman memorandum dated December 1, 1963, SRF 24, Truman Library, Missouri].

37. W. Michael Reisman and James E. Baker, *Regulating Covert Action: Practices, Contexts, and Policies of Covert Coercion Abroad in International and American Law* (New Haven, CT: Yale University Press, 1992): 8.

38. *Doolittle Report*, after lead author General James H. Doolittle, Hoover Presidential Commission (1954, originally classified top secret), cited in "Foreign and Military Intelligence," *Final Report*, Church Committee, US Senate (April 26, 1976): 9.

39. See Gaddis, *The United States and the Origins of the Cold War*.

40. B. Hugh Tovar, "Strengths and Weaknesses in Past U.S. Covert Action," in Roy Godson, ed., *Intelligence Requirements for the 1980s: Covert Action* (Washington, DC: National Strategy Information Center, 1981): 194–95.

41. Representative Mendel Rivers (D, South Carolina), quoted by Charles McCarry, "Ol' Man Rivers," *Esquire* (October 1970): 171.

42. Jack London, *The Call of the Wild* (New York: Macmillan, 1903): 76.

43. Anne Karalekas, "A History of the Central Intelligence Agency," in Supplementary Detailed Staff Reports on Foreign and Military Intelligence, Book IV, *Final Report*, Report No. 94-755, Church Committee, US Senate (April 23, 1976): 109.

44. Quoted in the *San Francisco Examiner* (September 16, 1976), as cited by Rhodri Jeffreys-Jones, *The CIA & American Democracy* (New Haven, CT: Yale University Press, 1989): 51.

45. Letter to the author from Harry Howe Ransom, Vanderbilt University (January 30, 2002).

Chapter 1

1. For an additional accounting of covert action practices during the Cold War, see Loch K. Johnson, *America's Secret Power: The CIA in a Democratic Society* (New York: Oxford University Press, 1989): 22–24.

2. Harry Rositzke, *CIA's Secret Operations: Espionage, Counterespionage, and Covert Action* (New York: Reader's Digest Press, 1977): 151. More recently, *Washington Post* journalist Whitlock reports that during the long US war in Afghanistan the CIA recruited "war criminals, drug traffickers, smugglers and ex-communists" to help fight Al Qaeda and the Taliban [Craig Whitlock: *The Afghanistan Papers: A Secret*

History of the War (New York: Simon & Schuster, 2021): 21]. The list of foreign receipients who have benefitted from CIA largess has been long over the years and would include as well governors, parliamentarians, and even religious leaders, really anyone who could help the Agency achieve its Third Option objectives--- mistresses, chauffeurs, and janitors for that matter, if they are in useful places. In 1995, DCI Deutch promulgated a rule---soon known at Langley as the "Deutch rule"---that prohibited DO officers from recruiting for intelligence collection and CA purposes particular heinous individuals in foreign lands, on grounds of their incompatibility with US values. Known murderers and torturers, for instance, could no longer be allowed on the Langely payroll. The DO responded at Agency headquarters with a combination of derisive laughter and anger toward the Director, even though Deutch excluded counterterrorism activities from his prescription. Many of the Directorate's officers viewed him as naïve, as if covert action could be conducted by nuns and boy scouts overseas. Soon after Deutch's departure from the CIA, his "rule" (which some at Langley admired for its ethial stance) was considerably relaxed.

3. Author's interview with retired DCI Stansfield Turner at his residence, McLean, VA (May 1, 1991).
4. See David Shimer, *Rigged: America, Russia, and One Hundred Years of Covert Electoral Interference* (New York: Knopf, 2020).
5. Rory Cormac, "Techniques of Covert Propaganda: The British Approach in the mid-1960s," *Intelligence and National Security* 34/7 (December 2019): 1066. One can't help but wonder if a better "book program" for the United States might have been to spend this money on books and other educational materials for less advantaged families in such locations as Appalachia and America's inner cities, or wherever else poverty haunts this nation's citizenry.
6. See Stuart H. Loory, "The CIA's Use of the Press: 'A Mighty Wurlitzer,'" *Columbia Journalism Review* (September/October 1974): 8–18; and Hugh Wilford, *The Mighty Wurlitzer: How the CIA Played America* (Cambridge, MA: Harvard University Press, 2008).
7. On Laos, see Ted Shackley, *Spymaster: My Life in the CIA* (Dulles, VA: Potomac Books, 2005): 42; and on Poland, Seth G. Jones, *A Covert Action: Reagan, the CIA, and the Cold War Struggle in Poland* (New York: Norton, 2018).
8. Michael A. Turner, "Covert Action: An Appraisal of the Effects of Secret Propaganda," in Loch K. Johnson, ed.,, vol. 3, *Covert Action, Behind the Veils of Secret Foreign Policy* (Westport, CT: Praeger Security International, 2005): 107.
9. Author's interview with Stansfield Turner at his residence, McLean, VA (May 1, 1991). On the Agency's "book program," see Robert M. Gates, *From the Shadows* (New York: Simon & Schuster, 2003): 91, as well as his *Exercise of Power: America Failures, Successes, and a New Path Forward in the Post-Cold War World* (New York: Knopf, 2020): 36–37; and Wilford, *The Mighty Wurlitzer*.
10. Robert L. Grenier, *88 Days to Kandahar: A CIA Diary* (New York: Simon & Schuster, 2015): 75.
11. John Prados, *Presidents' Secret Wars: CIA and Pentagon Covert Operations from World War II to the Persian Gulf* (New York: William Morrow, 1996): 125, 469–70.

Jim Angleton related stories to the author about these attempts to encourage revolution in Hungary [interview, Army-Navy Club, Washington, DC (August 25, 1975)]. The Agency adamantly denies the allegation, though, and the hopes of Hungarian revolutionaries may have been based more on wishful thinking than on a concrete reassurance of help signaled by CIA officers, although certainly the Eisenhower administration spoke often and with great zeal about a "rollback" of the Iron Curtain (more on this case in Chapter 3).

12. See Loch K. Johnson, *Spy Watching: Intelligence Accountability in the United States* (New York: Oxford University Press, 2018).
13. Johnson, *Spy Watching*.
14. On the Agency practice of going after books disliked by its leaders, see David Wise, *The American Police State: The Government Against the People* (New York: Random House, 1976), which discusses the CIA's efforts to stifle the study by Wise and Thomas B. Ross on covert action in Guatemala, entitled *The Invisible Government* (New York: Random House, 1964): 198–203. See as well Morton H. Halperin, "The CIA and Manipulation of the American Press," *First Principles* 3/5 (January 1978): 1–5; David Shamus McCarthy, *Selling the CIA: Public Relations and the Culture of Secrecy* (Lawrence: University Press of Kansas, 2018); Christopher Moran, *Company Confessions: Revealing CIA Secrets* (London: Biteback Publishers, 2015); and John Prados, *The Family Jewels: The CIA, Secrecy, and Presidential Power* (Austin: University of Texas Press, 2013).
15. See Johnson, *Spy Watching*, 201–2.
16. Deepfakes are seemingly authentic videos, audios, or snapshots of an individual doing, or saying, something incriminating that they didn't really do or say. A hypothetical example would be a morphed video speech of Saddam Hussein giving a speech in a Baghdad market square during the 1990s that projected an exaggerated view of his animus toward Shiite Muslims, thereby stirring internal unrest in Iraq, but a tape that was actually manufactured in a CIA lab from an older, real video taken by an Agency asset while Saddam was giving a more benign speech. O'Rourke predicted the emergence of this CIA capability soon [Lindsey A. O'Rourke, *Covert Regime Change: America's Secret Cold War*, Ithaca, NY: Cornell University Press, 2018): 235]; in fact, though, Langley has been using this technique at least since the mid-1990s. On the debut of a Sukarno look-alike as a CIA porno film star meant to discredit the Indonesian leader, see John Ranelagh, *The Agency: The Rise and Decline of the CIA* (New York: Simon & Schuster, 1986): 333.
17. For an example of Agency retribution against a US ambassador viewed by a CIA/COS as too human-rights oriented, see Tim Weiner, *Legacy of Ashes* (New York: Doubleday, 2007): 459.
18. For the Colby quote, see his testimony, "The CIA and the Media," *Hearings*, Subcommittee on Oversight, Permanent Select Committee on Intelligence, US House of Representatives, 95th Cong., 1st and 2d Sess. (December 28, 1978): 88; for the Allende example, Loch K. Johnson, *A Season of Inquiry: The Senate Intelligence Investigation* (Lexington: University Press of Kentucky, 1985): 197; for the Cline remark, "The CIA and the Media," *Hearings*, 90-91; and on CIA-media relations in general, Johnson, *America's Secret Power*, Ch. 9.

19. Peter Brush, a research paper, cited by Stephen Kinzer, *The Brothers: John Foster Dulles, Allen Dulles, and Their Secret World War* (New York: Henry Holt, 2013): 197.
20. James Reston, *Deadline: A Memoir* (New York: Random House, 1991): 209.
21. Rositzke, *CIA's Secret Operations*, 163.
22. Remark to the author by a former British intelligence office, Oxford University, Oxford, England (April 21, 2003). During the Church Committee's hearings on covert action, senior DO officer David Atlee Philips also mentioned this phrase [testimony, "Covert Action," *Hearings*, vol. 7, Church Committee, "Hearings on Covert Action, 1975, US Senate, 94th Cong., 1st. Sess. (December 4–5, 1975)], reprinted in Loch K. Johnson, "From the Intelligence Archives: Witness Testimony from the Church Committee Hearings on Covert Action, 1975," *Intelligence and National Security* 34/6 (October 2019): 899–914, quote at 907. King George III spread funds around Europe in a secret effort to undermine Napoleon [see Andrew Roberts, *Napoleon: A Life* (New York: Viking, 2014): 131]; perhaps that activity is the distant origin of the phrase.
23. Victor Marchetti, "The CIA in Italy: An Interview with Victor Marchetti," in Philip Agee and Louis Wolf, eds., *Dirty Work: The CIA in Western Europe* (Secaucus: Lyle Stuart, 1978): 170
24. Shimer, *Rigged*.
25. Testimony, "Covert Action," *Hearings*, 188.
26. Not every recipient of Agency largess has had to sign a receipt; according to a former CIA officer, Egyptian leader Gamal Abdel Nasser accepted from a DP officer a suitcase crammed with $3 million in the 1950s, no signature required [Miles Copeland, *The Game of Nations: The Amorality of Power Politics* (New York: Simon & Schuster, 1970), as cited by Moran, *Company Confessions*, 226]. The Northern Alliance was more formally known as the United Islamic Front for the Salvation of Afghanistan.
27. "Gesprach mit William E. Colby," *Der Spiegel* 4 (January 23, 1978): 69–115, quote at 75 (author's translation).
28. Conversation with the author, Capitol Building, Washington, DC (July 14, 1975).
29. Remark to journalist Laura Ingraham, Fox News (February 16, 2018).
30. Scott D. Breckinridge Jr., Papers, Ford Public Policy Research Center, University of Kentucky, Lexington, KY, manuscript 063, Box 1, cited in Moran, *Company Confessions*: 170.
31. McGeorge Bundy, Memorandum to the President (January 9, 1964): 1, in *Miscellaneous Records of the Church Committee*, Senate Select Committee on Intelligence, Loch K. Johnson file on "LBJ Library National Security Papers Touching on Assass. And Covert Action in Cuba" (July 21, 1975), declassified on March 8, 2000, Record Number 157-10014-10096, hereafter cited as "LBJ Library Papers." Elsewhere, an Agency operations official underscored for President Johnson's National Security Adviser, Bundy, in a letter that the Agency possessed the "capacity, which is increasing, to sabotage Cuban merchant ships calling at foreign ports" ["Des"—Desmond FitzGerald—to "Mac" (March 6, 1964): 2].
32. For examples of NSC documents with information of this kind: "Cuba, Covert Program," memorandum from Gordon Chase to McGeorge Bundy (no date, but

probably March 1964); and Chase to Bundy (November 12, 1964); LBJ Library Papers. Chase served as the intelligence officer for the National Security Council during the Kennedy and Johnson years.

33. The three major Russian intelligence agencies are the SVR, a civilian organization that replaced the First Directorate of the KGB and is responsible mainly for foreign espionage; the GRU, the chief military intelligence agency; and the FSB, the Federal Security Service, which took over the KGB's internal security duties. Each at one time or another has been assigned to carry out "active measures" at home and abroad, including the assassination of Russian intelligence defectors and those who politically challenge the current Kremlin leadership.

34. For this and some other sly Third Option ideas that journalist David E. Sanger has overheard being discussed by CIA operatives while he was on the intelligence beat, see his *The Perfect Weapon: War, Sabotage and Fear in the Cyber Age* (New York: Crown, 2018): xvi.

35. Central Intelligence Agency, "Cost of Cuban Operations: Fiscal Years 1960–1964" (LBJ Library Papers).

36. Stephen Kinzer, *Poisoner in Chief: Sidney Gottlieb and the CIA Search for Mind Control* (New York: Henry Holt, 2019), quote at 61.

37. Statement (July 15, 1987), quoted by Reisman and Baker, *Regulating Covert Action*, 188, n. 44.

38. Kevin A. O'Brien, "Covert Action: The 'Quiet Option' in International Statecraft," in Johnson, ed., *Strategic Intelligence*, 43. The full quote often attributed to George Orwell is: "People sleep peaceably in their beds at night only because rough men stand ready to do violence on their behalf" [see, among many other uses of this quote, Roger Cohen, "An Obsession the World Doesn't Share," *New York Times* (December 5, 2004): WK6]. A former CIA officer refers to "the paramilitary boys" as being possessed by an "enthusiastic, super-macho style" [Joseph Burkholder Smith, "Nation-Builders, Old Pros, Paramilitary Boys, and Misplaced Persons," *Washington Monthly* (February 1978): 23–30]. Often DO personnel are thought of as men and women of action, while the DA analysts are men and women of words. It is easy, and oversimplified, to stereotype DO officers—or any other CIA personnel. In reality, PM officers come in many forms, from James Bond types to less-imposing individuals who can be just as physically tough, such as DCI Colby; or debonaire CEO types, such as Richard Helms. Nevertheless a large cultural gap does exist between DO operatives and DA analysts. The former are often individuals who were social stars in college, whether athletes, Greek presidents, or club leaders, while the latter focused on making As, planning for advanced academic degrees, and fretting about the environmental fate of the Patagonian toothfish. Many officers in the DO could care less that they have neither met Strunk or White nor read *Moby-Dick*; they prefer a familiarity with krav maga, fast cars on the Autobahn, and fast horses in the Afghan countryside.

39. James R. Clapper with Trey Brown, *Facts and Fears: Hard Truths from a Life in Intelligence* (New York: Viking, 2018): 119. A journalist and author of a recent assessment of the Agency's most recent DCIs comes to a similar conclusion, referring to the Afghan intervention as the "most successful covert operation in modern history"

[Chris Whipple, *The Spy Masters: How the CIA Directors Shape History and the Future* (New York: Scribner, 2020): 13].

40. Weiner, *Legacy of Ashes*, 95.
41. John M. Prini, letter to the editor, *New York Times* (January 2, 2021): A22.
42. Mark Mazzetti and Adam Goldman, "Erik Prince Recruits Ex-Spies to Help Infiltrate Liberal Groups," *New York Times* (March 7, 2020), A1. On Blackwater, see Jeremy Scahill, *Blackwater: The Rise of the World's Most Powerful Mercenary Army* (New York: Nation Books, 2007); and Tim Shorrock, *Spies for Hire: The Secret World of Intelligence Outsourcing* (New York: Simon & Schuster, 2008).
43. *Annual Report*, Permanent Select Committee on Intelligence (HPSCI), U.S. House, 104th Cong., 1st Sess. (1985): 16.
44. Steve Coll, *Directorate S: The C.I.A. and America's Secret Wars in Afghanistan and Pakistan* (New York: Penguin, 2018): 165.
45. Shackley, *Spymaster*, 49.
46. Memorandum from Gordon Chase to McGeorge Bundy (May 14, 1964); LBJ Library Papers.
47. Author's interview with a former DDO, Washington, DC (September 12, 1985).
48. An anonymous officer quoted by Joshua Kurlantzick, *A Great Place to Have a War: America in Laos and the Birth of a Military CIA* (New York: Simon & Schuster, 2016): 201.
49. Gordon Chase, Memorandum for Mr. Bundy, "Special Group Meeting—Cuba" (March 4, 1965): 2; LBJ Library Papers.
50. Author's interview, Washington, DC (June 6, 1983).
51. Quoted by Loch K. Johnson, *The Threat on the Horizon: An Inside Account of America's Search for Security after the Cold War* (New York: Oxford University Press, 2011): 113.
52. CIA Africa Division officer, statement to the CIA Office of the Inspector General (March 14, 1975), declassified and reported in *Alleged Assassination Plots Involving Foreign Leaders: An Interim Report*, Report No. 94-465, Church Committee, "Hearings on Covert Action," US Senate, 94th Cong., 1st Sess. (November 20, 1975): 45–46.
53. In 1977, DCI Stansfield Turner fired other rogue middle-level DO employees after he discovered they had sold explosive devices to unauthorized former Agency operatives; reported by Bob Woodward, "Two Middle-Level CIA Employees Fired by Agency Director Turner," *Washington Post* (April 27, 1977): A1.

Chapter 2

1. Herman Kahn, *On Escalation: Metaphors and Scenarios*. New York: Praeger, 1965): 38.
2. See Loch K. Johnson, "On Drawing a Bright Line for Covert Operations," *American Journal of International Law* 86 (April 1992): 284–309; and Loch K. Johnson, *Secret Agencies: U.S. Intelligence in a Hostile World* (New Haven, CT: Yale University Press, 1996).

3. Quoted by Chris Whipple, *The Spy Masters: How the CIA Directors Shape History and the Future* (New York: Scribner, 2020): 15.
4. Tom Wicker et al., "C.I.A.: Maker of Policy, or Tool?" *New York Times* (April 25, 1966): A1.
5. Robert M. Gates, *From the Shadows* (New York: Simon & Schuster, 1996): 95–96.
6. ABC *Nightly News* (October 29, 2020).
7. Robert M. Gates, *Exercise of Power: America Failures, Successes, and a New Path Forward in the Post–Cold War World.* New York: Knopf, 2020): 37. See, as well, Calder Walton, "Spies, Election Meddling, and Disinformation: Past and Present," *Brown Journal of World Affairs* 26/1 (Fall/Winter 2019): 107–24.
8. Julian E. Barnes, Matthew Rosenberg, and Edward Wong, "China and Russia Sow Disinformation About How U.S. Is Handling the Virus," *New York Times* (March 29, 2020): A12.
9. William J. Broad, "Putin's War on U.S. Science," *New York Times* (April 14, 2020): D1.
10. Michael A. Turner, "Covert Action: An Appraisal of the Effects of Secret Propaganda," in Loch K. Johnson, ed., *Strategic Intelligence*, vol. 3, *Covert Action, Behind the Veils of Secret Foreign Policy* (Westport, CT: Praeger Security International, 2005): 116.
11. Peter Gill and Mark Phythian, *Intelligence in an Insecure World*, 3d ed. (Cambridge, UK: Polity, 2018): 111.
12. Adam Entolus and Evan Osnos, "Last Man Standing," *New Yorker* (February 10, 2020): 40–41. The covert action was called off at the last minute by President George W. Bush, who began to worry that the explosion might accidentally kill pupils in a nearby school for girls. Entolus and Osnos report that CIA Director Gina Haspel encouraged President Donald Trump to strike against Soleimani (49); and they further cite former D/CIA John O. Brennan, an opponent of the assassination, as saying that this decision essentially announced that "anybody would be fair game" (51). If President Trump can order the killing of high-level policy officials overseas, other countries may conclude they have the right to strike down high-level US policy officials, leading to an unraveling of international order. "Trump announced a standard that can be invoked by other countries," constitutional law scholar Louis Fisher emphasized to the author (email, dated July 6, 2020).
13. David E. Sanger, *Confront and Conceal: Obama's Secret Wars and Surprising Use of American Power* (New York: Random House, 2012), as well as his *The Perfect Weapon: War, Sabotage, and Fear in the Cyber Age* (New York: Crown, 2018), the source of the quotes presented here (26). The *Times* has referred to Stuxnet as "the most sophisticated cyberweapon ever deployed" [William J. Broad, John Markoff, and David E. Sanger, "Israel Tests Called Crucial in Iran Nuclear Setback," *New York Times* (January 16, 2011): A1].
14. See James Risen, *State of War: The Secret History of the CIA and the Bush Administration* (New York: Free Press, 2006): 209–12.
15. Email communication to the author from a professional colleague (June 7, 2012), based on his interviews with intelligence officials.
16. Ronen Bergman, "When Israel Hatched a Secret Plan to Assassinate Iranian Scientists," *Politico* (March 6, 2018): 1–7.

17. Gordon Chase, Memorandum for the 303 Committee, "Future of CIA's Cuban Paramilitary Program; Proposed UDT Sabotage Operations" (January 13, 1965): 3, in *Miscellaneous Records of the Church Committee*, Senate Select Committee on Intelligence, Loch K. Johnson file on "LBJ Library National Security Papers Touching on Assass. and Covert Action in Cuba" (July 21, 1975), declassified on March 8, 2000, Record Number 157-10014-10096, cited in this book as "LBJ Library Papers."
18. Miles Copeland, *Beyond Cloak and Dagger: Inside the CIA* (New York: Pinnacle, 1975): 214.
19. Whipple, *The Spy Masters*, 295.
20. Peter Schweizer, *Victory: The Reagan Administration's Secret Strategy That Hastened the Collapse of the Soviet Union* (New York: Atlantic Monthly Press, 1994): 87.
21. Remarks, National Conference of Editorial Writers (1976), quoted in testimony, Gilbert Cranberg, editor, *The Des Moines Register Tribune*, "The CIA and the Media," *Hearings*, Subcommittee on Oversight, Permanent Select Committee on Intelligence, U.S. House of Representatives, 95th Cong., 1st and 2d Sess. (December 28, 1978): 250, emphasis added.
22. Dean Rusk, as told to Richard Rusk and edited by Daniel S. Papp, *As I Saw It* (New York: Norton, 1990): 397.
23. Colleague's remark, University of Georgia, Athens, Georgia (July 4, 2016).
24. Author's interview with former DCI William E. Colby, law office, Washington, DC (January 22, 1991). Many Americans have the same reservations about the holding of foreigners at Guantánamo without trial. Nosenko was finally exonerated and became a "valuable" consultant to the CIA [according to DCI Stansfield Turner, *Notes from the Director*, No. 30 (September 21, 1978): 1, an inside Agency publication].
25. George Black, "The Victims of Agent Orange the U.S. Has Never Acknowledged," *New York Times* (March 16, 2021): A27.
26. Based on Loch K. Johnson, "Inspection of Classified Documents in the LBJ Library Related to Covert Actions Against Chile," Memorandum for Senior Staff, Church Committee (July 21, 1975, declassified on May 11, 1994, by the CIA), reported initially in Loch K. Johnson, *National Security Intelligence: Secret Operations in Defense of the Democracies*, 2d ed. (Cambridge: Polity, 2017): 92–93.
27. Interview conducted with McGeorge Bundy by Loch K. Johnson, University of Georgia (February 11, 1985).
28. In contrast to this choice of foreign targeting, an SSCI member, Bob Graham (D, Florida) has observed that CIA personnel tend to be white, middle-aged men "who stand out like light bulbs" overseas—"male, pale, and Yale," as they were characterized in the 1950s (with an ongoing element of truth today). See Bob Graham with Jeff Nussbaum, *Intelligence Matters* (New York: Random House, 2004): 37–38.
29. See Scott Shane, *Objective Troy: A Terrorist, a President, and the Rise of the Drone* (New York: Crown, 2015).
30. *9/11 Commission Report* (New York: Norton, 2004).
31. See, Michael Scheuer (an Agency veteran and chief of the ALEC Station from 1996 to 1999), *Imperial Hubris: Why the West Is Losing the War on Terror* (New York: Brassey's, 2004). The designation ALEC came from his son's name.

32. Steve Coll, *Ghost Wars: The Secret History of the CIA, Afghanistan, and Bin Laden, from the Soviet Invasion to September 10, 2001* (New York: Penguin, 2004): 530.
33. See Scheuer, *Imperial Hubris*, as well as his *Osama Bin Laden* (New York: Oxford University Press, 2011).
34. An alternative spelling is Qassem Suleimani.
35. Author's interview with retired DCI Turner at his residence, McLean, Virginia (May 1, 1991).
36. W. Michael Reisman and James E. Baker, *Regulating Covert Action: Practices, Contexts, and Policies of Covert Coercion Abroad in International and American Law* (New Haven, CT: Yale University Press, 1992): 70.
37. W. Hays Parks, "Memorandum of Law: Executive Order 12333 and Assassination," *Army Law* (December 1989): 4. The referenced executive order is E.O. No. 12333 [Fed. Reg. 59,941 (December 4, 1981)], original signed by President Gerald R. Ford in February of 1976 as E.O. No. 11905, which states that "no person employed by or acting on behalf of the United States Government shall engage in, or conspire to engage in, assassination." For background on this response from President Ford to the Church Committee investigation, see Loch K. Johnson, *Season of Inquiry: The Senate Intelligence Investigation* (Lexington: University of Kentucky Press, 1985): 195–97.
38. Author's interview with former DCI William E. Colby, Washington, DC (January 22, 1991).
39. Rachael G. Hoffman, "The Age of Assassinations: Monarchy and Nation in Nineteenth-Century Europe," in Jan Rüger and Nicolaus Wachsmann, eds., *Rewriting German History: New Perspectives on Modern Germany* (New York: Palgrave/Macmillan, 2015): 121–41.
40. Neither New Zealand's chief of counterintelligence nor any other representative of its government at the time were ever informed by the French about its deplorable plans in Auckland. The Kiwi CI Chief was furious with French intelligence over this event (conversation with the author, Atlanta, Georgia, May 22, 1992).
41. Copeland, *Beyond Cloak and Dagger*, 203, note. 38;
42. Louis Menand, "Table Talk: How the Cold War Made Georgetown Hot," *New Yorker* (November 10, 2014): 77.

Chapter 3

1. These examples are drawn from the public literature in the "Selected Bibliography" at the end of this book; they are meant to be illustrative rather than definitive. According to former DCI Richard Helms, the Agency conducted "thousands" of covert actions in its early days [cited by Christopher Moran, *Company Confessions: Revealing CIA Secrets* (London: Biteback Publishers, 2015): 241, based on Helms's papers, as well as his comment to colleague William Hood (Georgetown University Special Collections Research Center, Washington, DC)]. The Third Option was aimed at forty-eight countries in 1953 alone, according to Intelligence Studies scholar Harry Howe Ransom

["Strategic Intelligence and Intermestic Politics," in Charles W. Kegley Jr., and Eugene R. Wittkopf, eds., *Perspective on American Foreign Policy: Selected Readings* (New York: St. Martin's, 1983: 303)]; and, reported the Church Committee, the Agency conducted some 900 major covert actions between 1951 and 1975 [Loch K. Johnson, *A Season of Inquiry: The Senate Intelligence Investigation* (Lexington: University Press of Kentucky, 1985)]. Beyond the high-profile cases examined in this and the following chapters stand several other operations in the public domain that are not addressed in these pages. Some of these interventions that are more prominent are included in the timelines of Figures 3.1 and 5.1, in regular (non-bold) print. Although more limited in scope and of less historical moment, these operations were (of course) nonetheless consequential to people living within the targeted nations.

Among other cases not discussed here, but which have been reviewed elsewhere in the scholarly literature are several additional initiatives undertaken during the Eisenhower administration, such as political funding for pro-US Japanese politicians; an assassination plot (failed) against Generalissimo Rafael Trujillo of the Dominican Republic; and destabilization programs against President José Figueres in Costa Rica. The list goes on. The Eisenhower administration was almost as busy trying out the Third Option in different parts of the world as it was in pursuing diplomatic initiatives. The diplomacy was guided by Secretary Foster Dulles, who displayed a proclivity for "pactomania" (critics complained), that is, the fashioning of a dizzying number of pro-American alliances across the latitudes, such as the Southeast Asia Treaty Organization or SEATO. Accompanying Secretary Dulles's energetic uses of the First Option, DCI Allen Dulles was secretly shaping a significant part of America's foreign policy inside the Central Intelligence Agency with the Third Option.

Additional CA illustrations: the Kennedy administration also sought to destabilize the Trujillo government in the Dominican Republic as well as the Nkrumah government in Ghana; the Ibarra and Arosemena regimes in Ecuador; the Jaga regime in British Guiana; and the Frei regime in Chile. The Johnson administration followed on with continuing operations aimed at Chile, plus the launching of a military coup against President Joao Goulart of Brazil and the pursuit of a coup in Greece. For further examples of covert actions not taken up here, see James M. Scott and Jerel A. Rosati, "'Such Other Functions and Duties': Covert Action and American Intelligence Policy," in Loch K. Johnson, ed., *Strategic Intelligence: Covert Action, Behind the Veils of Secret Foreign Policy* (Westport, CT: Praeger Security International, 2007), vol. 3: 83–106).

2. On Truman's initial views on the Agency, see Merle Miller, *Plain Speaking: An Oral Biography of Harry S. Truman* (New York: Berkeley, 1973): 420; on the CIA's own skepticism, see "Review Roundtable: CIA Statement on *Legacy of Ashes* [the Tim Weiner book on the Agency by that title (New York: Penguin, 2008)]," a discussion at the Central Intelligence Agency (August 6, 2007), reprinted in "CIA Statement on *Legacy of Ashes,* 2007," *Intelligence and National Security* 23/6 (December 2008): 887–890.
3. On CIA activities with respect to Greece, for example, see Alonzo L. Hamby, *Man of the People: A Life of Harry S. Truman* (New York: Oxford University Press, 1995): 390.
4. Robert M. Gates, *Exercise of Power: America Failures, Successes, and a New Path Forward in the Post–Cold War World* (New York: Knopf, 2020): 14.

5. See John Lewis Gaddis, *The United States and the Origins of the Cold War, 1941–47* (New York: Columbia University Press, 1972).
6. From a 1957 speech by Mao in Moscow, quoted by Fareed Zakaria, *Ten Lessons for a Post-Pandemic World* (New York: Norton, 2020): 198.
7. See Arthur B. Darling, *The Central Intelligence Agency: An Instrument of Government to 1950* (University Park: Pennsylvania State University Press, 1990). The United States secretly spent an equivalent of about $582 million on these programs, in today's adjusted dollars [David Shimer, *Rigged: America, Russia and One Hundred Years of Electoral Interference* (New York: Knopf, 2020): 40].
8. Rhodri Jeffreys-Jones, *The CIA & American Democracy* (New Haven, CT: Yale University Press, 1989): 51.
9. C. [an anonymous name abbreviation], Leslie, and Peter Sichel, "Book Reviews, Intelligence in Public Media," *Studies in Intelligence* 64/4 (December 2020): 45.
10. Testimony, Church Committee, Select Committee to Study Governmental Operations with Respect to Intelligence Activities, US Senate, 94th Cong., 1st Sess. (October 28, 1975), cited hereafter as the Church Committee.
11. Miles Copeland, *Beyond Cloak and Dagger: Inside the CIA* (New York: Pinnacle, 1975): 208.
12. Anne Karalekas, "A History of Covert Action," in Supplementary Detailed Staff Reports on Foreign and Military Intelligence, Book IV, *Final Report*, Church Committee, Report No. 94–755, US Senate, 94th Cong., 2d Sess. (April 23, 1976): 36.
13. Scott Anderson, *The Quiet Americans: Four CIA Spies at the Dawn of the Cold War—a Tragedy in Three Acts* (New York: Doubleday, 2020): 300.
14. Roger Jeans, *The CIA and Third Force Movements in China During the Early Cold War* (New York: Lexington, 2018): 39.
15. Nicholas Dujmovic, "Review Essay: Covert Action to Promote Democracy in China During the Cold War," *Studies in Intelligence* 64/4 (December 2020): 33.
16. Victor Marchetti and John Marks, *The CIA and the Cult of Intelligence* (New York: Knopf, 1974): 51. See, also, Anderson, *The Quiet Americans*.
17. Nicholas Dujmovic, book review tweet, Center for the Study of Intelligence, CIA (March 29, 2010).
18. Dujmovic, book review tweet.
19. Interview with Victor Marchetti (November 22, 1983), by John Ranelagh, *The Agency: The Rise and Decline of the CIA* (New York: Simon & Schuster, 1986): 219. Marchetti served as the Agency's executive director during the mid-1960s. For the budget data, see David M. Barrett, *The CIA and Congress: The Untold Story from Truman to Kennedy* (Lawrence: University Press of Kansas, 2005): 102.
20. Church Committee, *Final Report* 31. The US overt military budget similarly exploded during these years, tripling from 1949 to 1951 [Jill Lepore, *These Truths: A History of the United States* (New York: Norton 2018): 539].
21. For these statistics, see the book by one of the Agency's top analysts from the 1950s to the 1970s: Ray S. Cline, *Secrets, Spies and Scholars: The Essential CIA* (Washington, DC: Acropolis Books, 1976): 115, 131; as well as Weiner, *Legacy of Ashes*, 53.

22. Gregory F. Treverton, "Covert Action: Forward to the Past?" in Johnson, *Strategic Intelligence*, 3.
23. On the lack of Korean language skills among Agency operatives in Korea in 1952, see Weiner, *Legacy of Ashes*, 57.
24. Declassified secret minutes, staff meeting, Seventh Floor, CIA Headquarters, Langley, VA (October 27, 1952), cited by Ted Gup, *The Book of Honor: Covert Lives and Classified Deaths at the CIA* (New York: Doubleday, 2000): 50.
25. See, respectively, Weiner, *Legacy of Ashes*, 61; and Annie Jacobsen, *Surprise, Kill, Vanish: The Secret History of CIA Paramilitary Armies, Operators, and Assassins* (New York: Little, Brown, 2019): 52–53.
26. Memorandum for the Joint Chiefs of Staff, "Overseas CIA Logistical Support Bases," Office of the Director, Central Intelligence Agency (June 6, 1952), cited in Jacobsen, *Surprise, Kill, Vanish*, 54.
27. Karalekas, "A History of the Central Intelligence Agency," 109, 110.
28. Phyllis Provost McNeil, Aspin-Brown Commission, "The Evolution of the U.S. Intelligence Community—An Historical Perspective," *Preparing for the 21st Century: An Appraisal of U.S. Intelligence, Report of the Commission on the Roles and Capabilities of the United States Intelligence Community* (March 1, 1996), Appendix A: A1-25, reprinted in Loch K. Johnson and James J. Wirtz, *Intelligence: The Secret World of Spies*, 5th ed. (New York: Oxford University Press, 2019): 5–22, quote at 12.
29. Weiner, *Legacy of Ashes*, 84.
30. "The Present Crisis in Iran," paper (undated), *Foreign Relations of the United States, 1950: The Near East, South Asia, and Africa*, vol. 5: 513, 516, US Department of State, cited by Peter Frankopan, *The Silk Roads: A New History of the World* (New York: Knopf, 2016): 394.
31. Roham Alvandi and Mark J. Gasiorowski, "The United States Overthrew Iran's Last Democratic Leader," *Foreign Policy Online* (October 20, 2019): 6.
32. Stephen Dorril, *MI6: Inside the Covert World of Her Majesty's Secret Intelligence Service* (New York: Free Press, 2000): 584.
33. Geoffrey Wawrow, *Quicksand: America's Pursuit of Power in the Middle East* (New York: Penguin, 2010): 139.
34. Stephen Kinzer, *The Brothers: John Foster Dulles, Allen Dulles, and Their Secret World War* (New York: Holt, 2013): 140. One of the CIA planners for the operation believed that "Iran was in real danger of falling behind the Iron Curtain; if that happened it would mean a victory for the Soviets in the Cold War and a major setback for the West in the Middle East" [see Donald N. Wilbur, a 1954 in-house CIA history filed in the National Security Archives at George Washington University, and quoted in Michael Poznansky, "Stasis or Decay? Reconciling Covert War and the Democratic Peace," *International Studies Quarterly* 59 (2015): 815–26, quote at 821].
35. Richard H. Immerman, *John Foster Dulles: Piety, Pragmatism, and Power in U.S. Foreign Policy* (Wilmington, DE: Scholarly Resources, 1999): 65.
36. See Frankopan, *The Silk Roads*, 401.
37. Fredrik Logevall, *JKF: Coming of Age in the American Century, 1917–1956* (New York: Random House, 2020): 467.

38. Milt Bearden and James Risen, *The Main Enemy: The Inside Story of the CIA's Final Showdown with the KGB* (New York: Random House, 2003): 220. The CIA and everyone else failed to predict the demise of the shah and the rise of the mullahs. Agency analysts assumed Iranian socialists would eventually take over (author's interview with former DCI Richard Helms, who also served as US ambassador to Iran from 1973 to 1977, departing two years before the revolution in 1979; Washington, DC, December 12, 1990). Helms observed in the interview cited here that "the Shah was most helpful to us. We had two listening posts in Iran that were very well-situated geographically for picking up emissions from the missile-launching fields in the Soviet Union."
39. Chris Whipple, remark, "The Spymasters," discussion, public forum, Karen J. Greenberg, Director, Center on National Security, Fordham University, New York City (September 29, 2020).
40. Journalist Tim Weiner's interview with John McMahon, in Weiner, *Legacy of Ashes*, 385.
41. Reuel Marc Gerecht [a former CIA operations officer], "Blundering Through History with the C.I.A.," *New York Times* (April 23, 2000): A 24.
42. Wise and Ross, *The Invisible Government*, 121.
43. A judgment reached by the sage Middle East watcher and journalist David Ignatius, *Washington Post* (January 15, 2020): A23.
44. Dwight D. Eisenhower, *The White House Years: A Mandate for Change, 1953–1956* (Garden City, NY: Doubleday, 1963): 422–23.
45. Oral history, Dulles Papers, Seeley G. Mudd Manuscript Library, Princeton University, cited in Kinzer, *The Brothers*, 160. The Soviet Union had no diplomatic ties to Árbenz.
46. See Kinzer, *The Brothers*, 148.
47. Wise and Ross, *Invisible Government*, 179.
48. Quoted in John Lewis Gaddis, *Strategies of Containment: A Critical Appraisal of Postwar American National Security Policy* (New York: Oxford University Press, 1982): 130–31.
49. See John Cooney, *The American Pope: The Life and Times of Francis Cardinal Spellman* (New York: Dell, 1986); and Kinzer, *The Brothers*, 169.
50. On kowtowing to the UFC, see David Atlee Phillips, a former CIA official with responsibilities for Latin America, *The Night Watch* (New York: Atheneum, 1977): 53; and for the murder statistics, William J. Daugherty [another former Agency operative], "Political Action as a Tool of Presidential Statecraft," in Johnson, ed., *Strategic Intelligence*, 127.
51. Anthony Lewis, "Costs of the CIA," *New York Times* (April 25, 1997): A19.
52. Rhodri Jeffreys-Jones, "American Espionage: Lessons from History," *Brown Journal of World Affairs* 26/1 (Fall/Winter 2019): 100.
53. Identity unknown (introduced simply as a "former DO officer"), remarks, Conference on "James Angleton and His Influence on US Counterintelligence," Woodrow Wilson International Center and Georgetown University Center for Security Studies, Washington, DC (March 29, 2013), author's notes.

54. H. Bradford Westerfield, "Introduction," in H. Bradford Westerfield, ed., *Inside CIA's Private World* (New Haven, CT: Yale University Press, 1995): viii.
55. Angleton spoke of this encouragement proudly to the author during an interview on October 24, 1975, Army-Navy Club, Washington, DC (during the Church Committee inquiry); two other operations officers note how the Agency "had encouraged their [the Hungarian] revolt" (C. and Sichel, "Book Reviews," 46).
56. William E. Colby and Peter Forbath, *Honorable Men: My Life in the CIA* (New York: Simon & Schuster, 1978): 134.
57. Ole R. Holsti, "The 'Operational Code' Approach to the Study of Political Leaders: John Foster Dulles' Philosophical and Instrumental Beliefs," *Canadian Journal of Political Science* 3 (1970): 123–155.
58. Tim Weiner, *Legacy of Ashes*, 129–35; Burton Hersh, *The Old Boys: The American Elite and the Origins of the CIA* (New York: Scribner's, 1992): 397–404. The CIA continues to deny that RFE played a role in encouraging the uprising ("CIA Statement on *Legacy of Ashes*," in "Review Roundtable").
59. Hersh, *The Old Boys*, 402.
60. Interviewed by Anderson, *The Quiet Americans*, 467.

Chapter 4

1. See Tom Wicker et al., "C.I.A.: Maker of Policy, or Tool?" *New York Times* (April 25, 1966): A1.
2. Email communication to the author (August 4, 2020).
3. Robert F. Worth, "The M. B. Z. Moment," *New York Times Sunday Magazine* (January 12, 2020): 939.
4. Dulles cable to Léopoldville, dated August 27, 1960, US Government, Select Committee to Study Governmental Operations with Respect to Intelligence Activities (Church Committee), "The CIA Assassination Plot in the Congo, 1960–61," *Alleged Assassination Plots Involving Foreign Leaders: An Interim Report*, Select Committee on Intelligence (hereafter, the Church Committee), US Senate, 94th Cong., 1st Sess. (November 1975): 15.
5. Stephen Kinzer, *Poisoner in Chief: Sidney Gottlieb and the CIA Search for Mind Control* (New York: Henry Holt, 2019): 178. A CIA officer quipped to the Church Committee that he recalled at the time thinking that the hypodermic needle delivered by Gottlieb "wasn't for somebody to get his polio shot up to date" [Loch K. Johnson, *A Season of Inquiry: The Senate Intelligence Investigation* (Lexington: University of Kentucky Press, 1985): 49].
6. Stephen R. Weissman, *American Foreign Policy in the Congo 1960–1964* (Ithaca, NY: Cornell University Press, 1974): 280, and his "An Extraordinary Rendition," *Intelligence and National Security* 25/2 (April 2010): 198–222.
7. Porter Goss, quoted in Eric Ofgang, "School of Spies," *Connecticut Magazine* (October 2020): 56.

8. Martin J. Sherwin, *Gambling with Armageddon: Nuclear Roulette from Hiroshima to the Cuban Missile Crisis* (New York: Knopf, 2020), cited by Elizabeth Kolbert, "This Close," *New Yorker* (October 12, 2020): 71.
9. See Wilbur Crane Eveland, *Ropes of Sand: America's Failure in the Middle East* (New York: Norton, 1980); Matthew Jones, "'The Preferred Plan': The Anglo-American Working Group Report on Covert Action in Syria, 1957," *Intelligence and National Security* 19/3 (2004): 401–15.
10. "Khrushchev Tirade Again Irks Envoys," *New York Times* (November 19, 1956): A1.
11. Email correspondence with the author (May 27, 2020).
12. Quoted in Ofgang, "School of Spies," 59.
13. "CIA Summary of Costs for Cuban Operations, FY 1960–1964" (December 15, 1963), *Miscellaneous Records of the Church Committee*, Senate Select Committee on Intelligence, Loch K. Johnson file on "LBJ Library National Security Papers Touching on Assass. And Covert Action in Cuba" (July 21, 1975), declassified on March 8, 2000, Record Number 157-10014-10096, hereafter cited as "LBJ Library Papers."
14. Peter Wyden, *Bay of Pigs: The Untold Story* (New York: Simon & Schuster, 1979).
15. During the Clinton administration, the CIA under the leadership of DCI John Deutch began an effort known as "co-location," designed to seat at least some analysts and operatives together in the same suite of offices in hopes of engendering an improved synergism between the two important groups that sometimes had differing views on the world [see Loch K. Johnson, *The Threat on the Horizon: An Inside Account of America's Search for Security after the Cold War* (New York: Oxford University Press, 2011)].
16. Rusk comment to the author (October 24, 1982), Athens, Georgia.
17. Anonymous interview, Coral Gables, Florida, conducted by Dexter Filkins, "On the Warpath," *New Yorker* (May 6, 2019): 45.
18. Quoted in Wicker, "C.I.A.: Maker of Policy, or Tool," *New York Times*, (April 25, 1966): A1.
19. Jonathan Schell, *The Unconquerable World: Power, Nonviolence, and the Will of the People* (New York: Henry Holt, 2003): 54.
20. Ted Shackley, with Richard A. Finney, *Spymaster: My Life in the CIA* (Dulles, VA: Potomac Books, 2003): 50; see, also, James H. Johnston, *Murder, Inc.: The CIA Under John F. Kennedy* (Lincoln: University of Nebraska Press, 2019).
21. Richard Helms, with William Hood, *A Look over My Shoulder: A Life in the Central Intelligence Agency* (New York: Random House, 2003): 202–3.
22. For the thirty-two number, see Stansfield Turner, *Burn Before Reading: Presidents, CIA Directors, and Secret Intelligence* (New York: Hyperion, 2005): 98; for five or six, see the interview with DCI Colby (conducted on July 25, 1983) in John Ranelagh, *The Agency: The Rise and Decline of the CIA*, rev. ed. (New York: Simon & Schuster, 1987): 336–37; and the number eight is from the author's interviews with various DO personnel over the years. The National Security Archive has published declassified Agency documents that reveal a CIA plot to kill Fidel Castro's brother as well, Raúl Castro, in the earliest known murder attempt against a Cuban leader during these years. The plan was to have a chartered Cubana Airlines airplane, in which

Raúl was a passenger, have an "accidental" crash. The CIA rescinded the scheme at the last moment, but word never reached the pilot (who had been promised $10,000 for his deed). The pilot's resolved failed at the crucial moment in the flight, though. Perhaps he had come to realize that a crash—a "water ditch"—might kill him as well. The plane safely continued on to its Prague destination. See Peter Kornbluh, ed., "CIA Assassination Plot Targeted Cuba's Raul Castro," *Briefing Book No. 756*, National Security Archives (April 16, 2021).

23. Evan Thomas, "The Real Cover-Up," *Newsweek* (November 21, 1993): 24; see, Johnston, Murder, Inc. For antecedents of the fountain pen approach to assassination developed by scientists in the intelligence services of Germany and Japan during the Second World War, see Stephen Kinzer, *Poisoner in Chief: Sidney Gottlieb and the CIA Search for Mind Control* (New York: Henry Holt, 2019): 26, 31. As Kinzer also notes, the Agency's Second World War precursor, the OSS, had experimented with the development of "truth serums" and poison dart guns (77).

24. Church Committee, "The CIA Assassination Plot in the Congo, 1960–61," *Alleged Assassination Plots*, 108 ff.

25. Testimony, Richard Helms, former CIA Director, "Foreign and Military Intelligence," *Final Report*, Church Committee (June 13, 1975), Washington, DC: US Government Printing Office; and Church Committee, *Alleged Assassination Plots*, 149.

26. Tim Weiner, *Legacy of Ashes: The History of the CIA* (New York: Doubleday, 2007): 187; and for Helms on the retaliation danger of assassinations, see David Frost's interview with him, *Studies in Intelligence* (September 1993).

27. Church Committee, *Alleged Assassination Plots*, 149.

28. Press conference, Capitol Hill (June 6, 1975), Washington, DC (author's notes).

29. Adam Zamoyski, *Napoleon: A Life* (New York: Basic Books, 2018): 356–57.

30. Church Committee, *Alleged Assassination Plots*, 263. Chairman Church told the media, though, that it "strains credulity" to think that Presidents Eisenhower, Kennedy, and Johnson had been unaware of the assassination plots against Castro [*Baltimore Sun* (October 6, 1975), quoted in LeRoy Ashby and Rod Gramer, *Fighting the Odds: The Life of Senator Frank Church* (Pullman: Washington State University Press, 1994): 476].

31. LBJ Library Papers, memo from NSC staffer Gordon Chase (probably for National Security adviser McGeorge Bundy), dated December 2, 1963. Ironically, by 1968 the Johnson administration was actually warning the Cuban regime (through the Department of State) of assassination plots against Castro under way at the hands of Cuban exiles beyond the Agency's control. As National Security Adviser Walt Rostow wrote to the president on June 20, 1968, "CIA, Defense, and State agreed that, should an assassination or an assassination attempt take place, the U.S. skirts should be clean" (memo, LBJ Library Papers).

32. LBJ Library Papers, memo, Bundy to Lyndon B. Johnson (December 12, 1963). In the next month, Bundy would forward a memo to the president in opposition to further CIA "sabotage attacks [against Cuba] on the ground that they are illegal, ineffective, and damaging to our broader policy" (memo to the president dated January 9, 1964, LBJ Library Papers).

33. Gordon Chase NSC memo-for-the-record, entitled "U.S. Policy Towards Cuba" and dated December 2, 1963 (LBJ Library Papers). National Security Adviser Bundy reminded the president in a memo on December 12, 1963, to tell the media that the White House would "take every available means to stop and turn back the spread of Communism in this hemisphere." On the December 1963 sabotage attacks: CIA, Review of Current Program of Covert Action Against Cuba, Annex I (January 25, 1964); LBJ Library Papers.
34. McGeorge Bundy ("McG. B."), Memorandum to the president (June 26, 1965); LBJ Library Papers.
35. A. J. Langgurth, *Our Vietnam: The War, 1954–1975* (New York: Simon & Schuster, 2000): 33. Max Hastings writes that Ho had traveled to the United States in his youth and found it "fascinating" [*Vietnam: An Epic Tragedy, 1945–1975* (New York: HarperCollins, 2018): 6]; and Stanley Karnow cites a speech Ho gave in Hanoi in which, although he hated the French, he told the crowd in 1945 that the United States should be regarded as a "good friend" because "it is a democracy without territorial ambitions" [*Vietnam: A History* (New York: Viking 1983): 147].
36. News conference (April 7, 1954), *Public Papers of the President,* Dwight D. Eisenhower, Office of the Federal Register, National Archives, 1960): 382–83.
37. Joseph Burkholder Smith, "Nation-Builders, Old Pros, Paramilitary Boys, and Misplaced Persons," *Washington Monthly* (February 1978): 23–30, quote at 25.
38. Website posting, National Security Archive, Washington, DC (November 1, 2020).
39. William E. Colby and Peter Forbath, *Honorable Men: My Life in the CIA* (New York: Simon & Schuster, 1978): 272; and interview with Colby, "Gesprach mit William E. Colby," *Der Speigel* 4 (January 23, 1978): 69–115 (author's translation), quote at 106.
40. Richard Helms, with William Hood, *A Look over My Shoulder*, 255. The number of fighters in a North Vietnamese combat division is difficult to pinpoint precisely. Sometimes these divisions were 10,000 strong; sometimes 7,000; and sometimes less, given how malaria and other jungle diseases eroded the North Vietnamese troop strength, which drew chiefly upon recruits from the north who had little or no experience in jungle living, with all of its unaccustomed parasites that attacked their bodies. A rough calculus, though, would suggest that a division would amount to some 8,500 soldiers or, for three divisions, a total of about 25,500 war fighters—an appreciable figure diverted into Laos from the South Vietnam killing fields. The author expresses his appreciation to Michael Leonard, a defense analyst, West Point alum, and decorated two-tour intelligence officer during the Vietnam War, for his insights into this battlefield math.
41. See Joshua Kurlantzick, *A Great Place to Have a War: America in Laos and the Birth of a Military CIA* (New York: Simon & Schuster, 2016).
42. Wicker, "C.I.A.: Maker of Policy."
43. Kurlantzick, *A Great Place to Have a War*, 177, citing a study by Karen J. Coates and Jerry Redfern, "Eternal Harvest: The Legacy of American Bombs in Laos," *Occasional Paper 49*, Japan Policy Research Institute, Oakland, California (June 2014): 1–4.
44. Helms, *A Look over My Shoulder*, 261-62.

45. Author's interview with Helms, Washington, DC (December 12, 1990). In this conversation, the former DCI expressed strong reservations about any covert action that was large in scope, considering these doomed to fail. "It's chiefly a question of size," he said, adding that "if the thing gets above a certain size, it's unmanageable and isn't covert anymore." Yet his favorite operation in Laos was hardly small-scale.

46. The quote is from Douglas Blaufarb, the Agency's COS in Laos during the middle of this episode; see John Prados, *Safe for Democracy: The Secret Wars of the CIA* (Chicago: Ivan R. Dee, 2006): 361. Lionel Rosenblatt, president emeritus of Refugees International, recalls that the Hmong had been put "into this meat grinder, mostly to save US soldiers from fighting and dying [in Vietnam]," quoted in Douglas Martin, "Gen. Yang Pao, Laotian Who Aided U.S. Dies at 81," *New York Times* (January 8, 2001): A17. On the Kurds, see Chris Whipple, *The Spy Masters: How the CIA Directors Shape History and the Future* (New York: Scribner, 2020). America's overt military forces have been guilty of leaving local allies in the lurch, too, as when America departed from Vietnam in 1975 and Afghanistan in 2021.

47. Based on a Kurlantzick interview with a witness to this comment: Joseph Lazarsky, Alexandria, Virginia (February 2006), in Kurlantzick, *A Great Place to Have a War*, 19. At least, though, some individually heroic CIA operatives helped about 25,000 Hmong flee to safety in Thailand [see Brian Phelan, "Thailand: Plight of the Meo," *Far Eastern Economic Review* (August 29, 1975): 20–22].

48. On the Chile case, see Gregory F. Treverton, *Covert Action: The Limits of Intervention in the Postwar World* (New York: Basic Books, 1987); as well as Church Committee, *Alleged Assassination Plots*; "Covert Action in Chile," *Hearings*, Church Committee, US Senate, 94th Cong., 1st Sess. (December 4 and 5, 1975).

49. Treverton, *Covert Action*, 100. For a CIA perspective on the covert actions against Allende, see David Atlee Phillips, *The Night Watch* (New York: Atheneum, 1977).

50. Officers at the CIA are not wild about the idea of dedicating their careers in intelligence, sometimes in dangerous locations, for the sake of advancing Corporate America; they see as far more noble a devotion to protecting the people of the United States in an uncertain world. As a highly regarded DCI has put it, "You know, I'm prepared to give my life for my country, but not for a company" [Robert M. Gates, speech, Economic Club of Detroit (April 13, 1992): 9]. The most famous early American intelligence officer, Nathan Hale (a statue of whom stands in front of the CIA's Headquarters Building at Langley), did not say on the eve of his execution by the British in 1776: "I regret that I have but one life to give for the Union Wharf Company."

51. In the 1970s, Senator Frank Church probed into US-Chilean relations first as chair of the Subcommittee on Multinational Corporations (part of the Foreign Relations Committee, on which the senator was a senior member and later chair), and then as chair of the better-known Senate Select Committee on Intelligence investigative panel; see Ashby and Gramer, *op.cit.*: 491.

52. Interviewed by Whipple, *op.cit.*: 44.

53. On July 23, 1971: Weiner, *Legacy of Ashes, op.cit.*: 315, quoting from *The Haldeman Diaries: Inside the Nixon White House*, CD Rom (New York: Sony, 1944).

54. Interviewed by journalist Bob Simon, "60 Minutes," CBS Television (September 9, 2001).
55. This quote, from June 27, 1970, has been widely reported; see, for instance, Seymour M. Hersh, "The Price of Power," *Atlantic Monthly* (December 1982): 24.
56. As related to the author by Senator Frank Church on July 2, 1975, Washington, D.C.
57. Congressional testimony quoted by his leading biographer John Lewis Gaddis, *George F. Kennan, An American Life* (New York: Penguin, 2011): 592.
58. A Kilpatrick column published in 1976 and cited by Ashby and Gramer, *Fighting the Odds*, 489.
59. According to the author's interview with a senior DO officer (February 14, 1977), Washington, DC.
60. Thomas Meaney, "The Wages of Realism," *The New Yorker* (May 18, 2020): 63.
61. See Church Committee, *Alleged Assassination Plots*; and Jonathan Haslam, *The Nixon Administration and the Death of Allende's Chile* (London: Verso, 2005): 194.
62. Treverton, *Covert Action*, 142-43.
63. Church Committee, *Alleged Assassination Plots*, 227.
64. Cable reprinted in Church Committee, *Alleged Assassination Plots*, 231.
65. Haslam, *The Nixon Administration*, 221.
66. National Security Archive, George Washington University, Washington, DC (October 22, 2020).
67. Gregory F. Treverton, "Covert Action: Forward to the Past," in Loch K. Johnson, ed., *Strategic Intelligence: Covert Action, Behind the Veils of Secret Foreign Policy*, vol. 3 (Westport, CT: Praeger Security International, 2007): 5. Treverton was one of the lead investigators during the Church Committee's inquiry into the Agency's Chilean covert actions.
68. For the first quote: author's interview (October 10, 1980), Washington, DC; and, for the second, Frederick L. Wettering, "Covert Action: The Disappearing 'C,'" *International Journal of Intelligence and Counterintelligence* 16 (Winter 2003–2004): 561–72, quote at 563.
69. Letter to the author from former president George H. W. Bush (January 23, 1994).

Chapter 5

1. John Tunney (D, CA) and Dick Clark (D, Iowa) were both US senators, Tunney a one-termer and the son of the former heavyweight boxing champ Gene Tunney, and Clark another fearless, one-termer critical of American foreign policy, in the manner of the other half of the Iowa delegation in the Senate, Harold Hughes—a co-sponsor of the Hughes-Ryan Act (featured in Chapter 7). The Tunney-Clark law passed on January 27, 1976 (*Congressional Record*: 1057); for an account, see Thomas M. Franck and Edward Weisband, *Foreign Policy by Congress* (New York: Oxford University Press, 1979): 51–55.

2. Angola was the location of an imaginative, if fatuous, effort by the Directorate of Operations to recruit a senior KGB officer stationed there, by way of a "compromise" covert action (*kompromat*, in Soviet spytalk). One of the DO's more adventurous officers opened a brothel in Angola's capital city, one fully equipped with hidden cameras. The plan was to take interesting photographs of KGB operatives, then threaten to send the images to their family and friends unless they cooperated with the CIA. Alas, though, the first Soviet intelligence officer in this experiment was so proud of his physical prowess that the only response he offered was to ask if he could buy some of the pictures. He could have cared less who saw them, for in his view they only added to his macho status [see John Stockwell, the CA organizer in this case, who relates this "honeytrap" episode in his book entitled *In Search of Enemies: A CIA Story* (New York: Norton, 1978)]. This was not the only experiment in which the Intelligence Community tried using a House of the Rising Son as a method for attempted clandestine manipulation [see, for example, another account in Stephen Kinzer, *Poisoner in Chief: Sidney Gottlieb and the CIA Search for Mind Control* (New York: Henry Holt, 2019: 144–45)].
3. Jeff Gerth, "Military's Information War Is Vast and Often Secretive," *New York Times* (December 11, 2005): A1.
4. See Karl F. Inderfurth and Loch K. Johnson, *Fateful Decisions: Inside the National Security Council* (New York: Oxford University Press, 2004).
5. Zbigniew Brzezinski, *Power and Principle: Memoirs of a National Security Advisor, 1977–1981* (New York: Farrar, Straus & Giroux, 1985); Carl Bernstein and Marco Politi, *His Holiness, John Paul II and the Hidden History of Our Time* (New York: Doubleday, 1996); and Robert M. Gates, *From the Shadows* (New York: Simon & Schuster, 1996).
6. Author's conversation with DCI Turner, McLean, Virginia (April 1, 1985).
7. Quoted by Ray Takeyh, "The Other Carter Doctrine," *Foreign Affairs* (February 26, 2021): 6, based on recently declassified government documents.
8. Ronald Reagan, "A Time for Choosing," speech (October 27, 1964); and remarks, National Association of Evangelicals, Annual Convention, Orlando, FL (March 8, 1983).
9. Ronald Reagan, *An American Life: The Autobiography* (New York: Simon & Schuster, 1990): 216.
10. For these recollections, see Chris Whipple, *The Spy Masters: How the CIA Directors Shape History and the Future* (New York: Scribner, 2020): 111.
11. William J. Casey, "The Hidden Struggle for Europe," *Draft Manuscript* (1976): 11, William J. Casey Papers, Box 26, Folder 9, Hoover Institution Archives, Stanford University, Stanford, CA, as quoted by Seth G. Jones, *A Covert Action: Reagan, the CIA, and the Cold War Struggle in Poland* (New York: Norton, 2018): 56.
12. Senate Select Committee on Secret Military Assistance to Iran and the Nicaraguan Opposition and House Select Committee to Investigate Covert Arms Transactions with Iran, *Joint Hearings, McFarland Testimony*, vol. 100–7, Part II, July 14, 1987): 224 (Washington, DC: US Government Printing Office, 1988), cited hereafter as the Inouye-Hamilton Committee.

13. President Reagan, remarks to Jewish Leaders during a White House briefing on "United States Assistance for the Nicaraguan Democratic Resistance" (March 5, 1986).
14. For the last and most restrictive, making it clear that the United States was prohibited from overthrowing the incumbent government of Nicaragua, see Department of Defense Appropriations Act, 1985, Pub. L. No. 98-473, 066, 98 Stat. 1935 (1984).
15. Author's interview with DCI Judge William H. Webster, CIA Headquarters, Langley, VA (May 2, 1991).
16. Rather than turning their heads, it would have been laudable for those at Langley who opposed the illegal Iran-*contra* activities to have tried stopping them early in the proceedings, by—if necessary—talking directly with the president and other NSC principals about their concerns, or with the Intelligence Oversight Board on the President's Foreign Intelligence Advisory Board (IOB/PFIAB) and the congressional oversight committees. Whistleblowing can be career-jeopardizing, however, and it is far easier to assume the posture of the ostrich, with one's head in the ground. When asked why he went along with the profoundly unethical FBI COINTELPRO operations in the 1960s, a right-hand man to the Bureau director J. Edgar Hoover explained to the Church Committee investigators that he had no choice but to go along. He had a house mortgage to pay and two kids in college; he couldn't afford to lose his job [William C. Sullivan, testimony to two Church Committee senior staffers (the author and a colleague), Boston, Massachusetts (June 10, 1975)].
17. Inouye-Hamilton Committee, *Joint Hearings, Lt. Col. North Testimony*, vol. 100–7, Part I (July 8, 1987): 317–18. North, who was a Casey disciple, testified that he had originally heard this phrase from the DCI.
18. Laurence H. Tribe, "Reagan Ignites a Constitutional Crisis," *New York Times* (May 20, 1987): A31.
19. Bill Moyers, *The Secret Government: The Constitution in Crisis*, PBS Documentary (1987).
20. William G. Miller, staff director of the Church Committee and the first SSCI staff director, interviewed by Gregory F. Treverton, *Covert Action: The Limits of Intervention in the Postwar World* (New York: Basic Books, 1987): 252.
21. Inouye-Hamilton Committee, *Joint Hearings, Adm. John M. Poindexter Testimony*, vol. 6: (July 21, 1987): 159.
22. Inouye-Hamilton Committee, *Joint Hearings, Fawn Hall Testimony*, vol. 100–7 (June 9, 1987): 552.
23. Inouye-Hamilton Committee, *Joint Hearings, Lt. Col. North Testimony*, vol. 100–7, Part I (July 9, 1987): 245.
24. Press conference remark, Washington, DC (May 7, 1987), quoted in William S. Cohen and George J. Mitchell, *Men of Zeal: A Candid Inside Story of the Iran-Contra Hearings* (New York: Viking, 1988): 76. In addition, see the exhaustive study on the Iran-*contra* affair by Malcolm Byrne, *Iran-Contra: Reagan's Scandal and the Unchecked Abuse of Presidential Power* (Lawrence: University Press of Kansas, 2014).
25. Byrne, *Iran-Contra*, 78, citing recollections from the administration's secretary of state George Shultz, who cleverly steered clear of personal involvement in the

affair—although at least in outline the secretary clearly knew what was going on [see US Office of the Independent Counsel, *Final Report*, vol. 1 (Washington, DC: US Government Printing Office, 1988): 338].

26. Cohen and Mitchell, *Men of Zeal*, 87.
27. Robert Parry and Peter Kornbluh, "Iran-Contra's Untold Story," *Foreign Policy* 72 (Fall 1988): 3–29.
28. Inouye-Hamilton Joint Committee, *Joint Hearings, Elliott Abrams Testimony*, vol. 100–5, Exhibit EA-28.
29. Cohen and Mitchell, *Men of Zeal*, 115. Abrams testified further that he "could have been more forthcoming, but I frankly was not going to be the first person to step up and do that. . . . So long as others who knew the details [of the affair], as much as I, who knew more than I, were keeping their silence on this, I was going to keep my silence" (Inouye-Hamilton Committee, *Joint Hearings*, 122).
30. Elliott Abrams, *Undue Process: A Story of How Political Differences Are Turned into Crimes* (New York: Free Press, 1993): 171. In the Trump administration, Abrams served as the US special representative for Venezuela as that country was in the throes of domestic unrest. The language he chooses here reminds one of the dangerous philosophy---"attitude" would be a less lofty characterization---that seemed to animate the January 6, 2021, insurgents in Washington.
31. Inouye-Hamilton Committee, *Joint Hearings*, 126.
32. Inouye-Hamilton Committee, *Joint Hearings*, 280.
33. Author's interview with retired DCI Stansfield Turner at his residence, McLean, VA (May 1, 1991).
34. George Crile, *Charlie Wilson's War* (New York: Grove, 2003): 339.
35. See Milt Bearden and James Risen, *The Main Enemy: The Inside Story of the CIA's Final Showdown with the KGB* (New York: Random House, 2003); Steve Coll, *Ghost Wars: The Secret History of the CIA, Afghanistan, and Bin Laden, from the Soviet Invasion to September 10, 2011* (New York: Penguin, 2004); and Crile, *Charlie Wilson's War*.
36. Bearden and Risen, *The Main Enemy*, 214.
37. The 70 percent figure is from Crile, *Charlie Wilson's War*, 437, as well as the 28,000 figure: 511; Bearden and Risen put the casualty figure at 15,000, based on what the Soviets have reported: 358.
38. Coll reports on an added expense of this covert action: the United States provided $3.2 billion in military weaponry and equipment, including advanced F-16 fighter aircraft, to Pakistan in exchange for its support of the *mujahideen* in Afghanistan (*Ghost Wars*, 62).
39. For these tonnage figures, see Bearden and Risen, *The Main Ememy*, 218–19, 312.
40. Crile, *Charlie Wilson's War*, 4. As noted in Chapter 1, other knowledgeable observers have seconded this appraisal, including former DNI James R. Clapper.
41. Author's interview, Athens, GA (October 6, 1987).
42. Cited by Christopher Moran, *Company Confessions: Revealing CIA Secrets* (London: Biteback, 2015): 241, drawing on Helms's papers [comment from Helms to William Hood (March 16, 1998), Georgetown University Special Collections Research Center, Washington, D.C.].

43. James M. Scott and Jerel A. Rosati, "'Such Other Functions and Duties': Covert Action and American Intelligence Policy," in Loch K. Johnson, ed., *Strategic Intelligence: Covert Action, Behind the Veils of Secret Foreign Policy* (Westport CT: Praeger Security International, 2007, vol. 3): 83–106; and Jones, *A Covert Action*, 302. See also David F. Rudgers, *Creating the Secret State: The Origins of the Central Intelligence Agency, 1943–1947* (Lawrence: University Press of Kansas, 2000); and William J. Daugherty, *Executive Secrets: Covert Action and the President* (Lexington: University Press of Kentucky, 2004). Daugherty, an experienced DO hand and one of the hostages captured by militants in Iran during the Carter administration, refers to this operation as "the most successful political action program ever" ("Political Action as a Tool of Statecraft," Johnson, ed., *Strategic Intelligence*, 128).
44. Michael A. Turner, "Covert Action: An Appraisal of the Effects of Secret Propaganda," in Johnson, *Strategic Intelligence*, 114.
45. Jones, *A Covert Action*, 309.
46. Letter to the author from former president George H. W. Bush (dated January 23, 1994). This same budget estimate emerged in the author's interview with DCI R. James Woolsey, CIA Headquarters Building, Langley, Virginia (September 29, 1993).
47. Charles G. Cogan, "Partners in Time: The CIA and Afghanistan," *World Policy Journal* 10 (Summer 1993): 73–82, quote at 80.
48. Author's interview, Washington, DC (March 21, 1995).
49. See Loch K. Johnson, *Threat on the Horizon: An Inside Account of America's Search for Security After the Cold War* (New York: Oxford University Press, 2011).
50. Johnson, *Threat on the Horizon*, 259.
51. Author's interview with DCI R. James Woolsey, CIA Headquarters, Langley, VA (September 29, 1993).
52. John Deutch, speech, National Press Club, Washington, DC (September 12, 1995), author's notes.
53. Deutch, speech (September 12, 1995).. See Whipple, *The Spymasters*, 167; and Johnson, *Threat on the Horizon*, 284.
54. For an authoritative account, see Wesley K. Clark, "How We Succeeded in Kosovo," *Brown Journal of World Affairs* 26/1 (Fall/Winter 2019): 165–78. At the time, Clark was the Supreme Allied Commander Europe and leader of the NATO response to Serbia's shocking paramilitary operations.
55. Clark, "How We Succeeded in Kosovo," 169.

Chapter 6

1. Loch K. Johnson, *The Threat on the Horizon: An Inside Acount of America's Search for Security After the Cold War* (New York: Oxford University Press, 2011).
2. George Tenet, with Bill Harlow, *At the Center of the Storm: My Years at the CIA* (New York: HarperCollins, 2007): 225.
3. Steve Coll, *Directorate S: The C.I.A. and America's Secret Wars in Afghanistan and Pakistan* (New York: Penguin, 2018): 81.

4. See Gary Schroen, *First In, An Insider's Account of How the CIA Spearheaded the War on Terror in Afghanistan* (New York: Ballantine Books, 2005).
5. Coll, *Directorate S*, 664. This is a rather different scene from the one of the Taliban taking over in Kabul as the US military exited Aghanistan in August of 2021.
6. Gregory F. Treverton, "Covert Action: Forward to the Past?" In Loch K. Johnson, ed., *Strategic Intelligence: Covert Action, Behind the Veils of Secret Foreign Policy*, vol. 3 (Westport, CT: Praeger Security International, 2007): 1–22, quote at 16.
7. Scott Shane, Mark Mazzetti, and Robert F. Worth, "Secret Assault on Terrorism Widens on Two Continents," *New York Times* (August 15, 2010): A1.
8. The quote is from an email comment to the author in October 2020 from a retired DO officer who wishes to remain anonymous; for the tenfold estimate, see Micah Zenko, "Obama's Embrace of Drone Strikes Will Be a Lasting Legacy," *New York Times* (January 16, 2016): A23.
9. Mark Mazzetti, Adam Goldman, and Michael S. Schmidt, "Behind the Sudden Death of a $1 Billion Secret C.I.A. War in Syria," *New York Times* (August 2, 2017): A1. On this case, see also Armin Krishnan, "Controlling Partners and Proxies in Pro-Insurgency Paramilitary Operations: The Case of Syria," *Intelligence and National Security* 34/4 (June 2019): 544–60.
10. BBC, cited by Krishnan, "Controlling Partners and Proxies."
11. Michael D. Shear, Helene Cooper, and Eric Smidt, "U.S. Ends Efforts to Train Rebels in Syria," *New York Times* (October 10, 2015): A1.
12. Armin Krishnan, "Controlling Partners and Proxies," 554.
13. Mark Mazzetti and Ali Younes, "C.I.A. Arms for Syrian Rebels Supplied Black Market, Officials Say," *New York Times* (June 26, 2016): A1.
14. See Mark Mazzetti and Ali Younes, "Thefts Redirect Arms from C.I.A.," *New York Times* (June 27, 2016): A1. In the wake of a failed covert action, the argument seems to arise with regularity that the operation would have succeeded if (for instance) only President John F. Kennedy had provided air support to destroy the Cuban Air Force during the Bay of Pigs invasion; or, concerning the use of the Third Option in Syria during the Obama administration, if only more money had been spent on the build-up of the rebel paramilitary army [see, respectively, the interview responses of die-hards in Dexter Filkins, "On the Warpath," *New Yorker* (May 6, 2019): 45; and Mazzetti, Goldman, and Schmidt, "Behind the Sudden Death"].
15. See the account in Louis Fisher, *President Obama: Constitutional Aspirations and Executive Actions* (Lawrence: University Press of Kansas, 2018).
16. Stephen R. Weissman, "Covert Action, Congressional Inaction," *Foreign Affairs* (December 2, 2020): 2.
17. Mark Bowden, *Black Hawk Down: A Story of Modern Warfare* (New York: Penguin, 1999).
18. Schroen, *First In, An Insider's Account*, 38.
19. See Leon Panetta and Jim Newton on these deliberations, *Worthy Fights: A Memoir of Leadership in War and Peace* (New York: Penguin, 2014): 299; and for the quote: Whipple, *The Spymasters*, 255. Ambiguities persist over the degree to which the DoD should be assigned what are essentially paramilitary activities [Loch K. Johnson,

Spy Watching: Intelligence Accountability in the United States (New York: Oxford University Press, 2018: 328); and Jennifer D. Kibbe, "Covert Action and the Pentagon," in Loch K. Johnson, ed., *Strategic Intelligence: Covert Action, Behind the Veils of Secret Foreign Policy* (Westport, CT: Praeger Security International, 2007, vol. 3: 131–44)]. For some basic definitional distinctions, see Michael E. DeVine, *Covert Action and Clandestine Activities of the Intelligence Community: Selected Definitions*, Brief R4517, Congressional Research Service (June 14, 2019).

20. For more on US military Special Forces creeping into the covert action domain, a touchy subject between Langley and the Pentagon, see Jennifer D. Kibbe, "Covert Action, Pentagon Style," in Loch K. Johnson, ed., *The Oxford Handbook of National Security Intelligence* (New York: Oxford University Press, 2010: 569–86). For an example of the Federal Bureau of Investigation (FBI) edging into this turf as well, in Latin America, see Darren E. Tromblay, *The FBI Abroad: Bridging the Gap Between Domestic and Foreign Intelligence* (Boulder, CO: Lynne Rienner, 2020): 218–19.
21. See Scott Shane, *Objective Troy* (New York: Tim Duggan Books, 2015): 71.
22. Eric Schmitt, "U.S. Commandos Use Secretive Missiles to Kill Qaeda Leaders in Syria," *New York Times* (September 24, 2020): A1.
23. On these developments, see Nicholas Schmidle, "Getting bin Laden," *New Yorker* (August 8, 2011); Charles Savage and Eric Schmitt, "Biden Secretly Limits Counterterrrorism Drone Strikes Away from War Zones," *New York Times* (March 3, 2021); and Eric Schmitt and Christoph Koetti, "Remote C.I.A. Base in the Sahara Steadily Grows," *New York Times* (March 8, 2021). See also Ellen Nakashima and Missy Ryan, "Biden Orders Temporary Limits on Drone Strikes Outside of War Zones," *Washington Post* (March 4, 2021).
24. James Risen, *State of War: The Secret History of the CIA and the Bush Administration* (New York: Simon & Schuster, 2006): 221. In 2020, Risen has observed that this drift toward a military use of the CIA has come at the expense of global collection and analysis, leaving the United States insufficiently informed about events and conditions in China and many other places (telephone conversation with the author, May 4, 2020).
25. See Mark Mazzetti, "C.I.A. to Focus More on Spying: A Difficult Shift," *New York Times* (May 24, 2013): A1
26. See John O. Brennan, *Undaunted: My Fight Against America's Enemies, at Home and Abroad* (New York: Celaden Books, 2021); and Mazzetti, "C.I.A. to Focus More on Spying."
27. Quoted by Tim Weiner, *Legacy of Ashes: The History of the CIA* (New York: Doubleday, 2007): 238.
28. Charlie Savage, "Spy Chief," *New York Times Book Review* (November 1, 2020): 13.
29. See Coll, *Directorate S*, 338.
30. See Shane, *Objective Troy*.
31. Mark Mazzetti, *The Way of the Knife: The CIA, a Secret Army, and a War at the Ends of the Earth* (New York: Penguin, 2013): 311.
32. David Ignatius, "How Kash Patel Rose from Obscure Hill Staffer to Key Operative in Trump's Battle with the Intelligence Community," *Washington Post* (April 16, 2021).

33. See John L. Helgerson, *CIA Briefings of Presidential Candidates, 1952–1992: Getting to Know the President*, Center for the Study of Intelligence (Washington, DC: Central Intelligence Agency, no date but probably 1994).
34. While serving as assistant to Les Aspin when he chaired the Aspin-Brown Commission on Intelligence in 1995–96, the commissioners asked the author to prepare a study for the panel on the value of several year's worth of recent *PDB*s, when compared to leading public media sources. Sometimes the media were superior, as (for example) on current party politics in Germany; most of the time, though, the *PDB* added value to the public reporting, thanks to the Intelligence Community's worldwide network of intelligence sources (whether human or machine, such as a surveillance satellite). This study remains classified, but its non-classified broad outlines are presented in Johnson, *Threat on the Horizon*.
35. Quoted by Serge Schmemann, "His Incompetent Statesmanship," *New York Times* (October 18, 2020): SR7; and Eliza Collins, "Trump: I Consult Myself on Foreign Policy," *Politico* (March 16, 2016).
36. "Jake Sullivan to the Rescue," *The Economist* (December 5, 2020): 35.
37. Richard Helms, interviewed by Loch K. Johnson, "Spymaster Richard Helms," *Intelligence and National Security* 18 (Autumn 2003): 24–44.
38. On the overall increase in drone attacks during the Trump administration, accompanied by a relaxation in accountability rules for target selection, see Kelsey D. Atherton, a defense technology journalist, in "Trump Inherited the Drone War but Ditched Accountability," *Foreign Policy* (March 22, 2020). See, as well, Julian E. Barnes and Eric Schmitt, "Pentagon Weighs Sharp Drawback in Support for C.I.A.," *New York Times* (December 11, 2020): A25.
39. On the Biden administration reappraisal of CIA drone attacks, see Charlie Savage and Eric Schmitt, "Biden Secretly Limits Counterterrorism Drone Strikes Away from War Zones," *New York Times* (March 3, 2021): A12.
40. Connie Bruck, "The Guantánamo Failure," *New Yorker* (August 1, 2016): 34.
41. John O. Brennan, former D/DIA, remarks, Panel on "Iran, Iraq, and Beyond," Center on National Security, Fordham University, New York City (January 30, 2020).
42. W. Michael Reisman, remarks, "Covert Action," panel presentation, International Studies Association, Annual Meeting, Washington, DC (March 29, 1994).
43. Karen J. Greenberg, "Killing Qassim Suleimani Was Illegal. And Predictable," *New York Times* (January 6, 2020): A 24.
44. Adam Entous and Evan Osno, "Last Man Standing," *New Yorker* (February 10, 2020): 40.
45. Edward Wong, "Seek an End to the 'Forever War,'" *New York Times* (February 3, 2020): A14.
46. See James R. Clapper, with Trey Brown, *Facts and Fears: Hard Truths from a Life in Intelligence* (New York: Viking, 2018).
47. James R. Clapper, remark, Jackson Institute for Global Affairs Discussion Forum, Yale University (held on the Internet, October 20, 2020).
48. Paul R. Kolbe, "With Hacking, the United States Needs to Stop Playing the Victim," *New York Times* (December 23, 2020): A15.
49. Kolbe, "With Hacking, the United States Needs to Stop Playing the Victim."

Chapter 7

1. James E. Baker, "From Cold War to Long War: Covert Action in a Legal Context," in Loch K. Johnson, ed., *Strategic Intelligence: Covert Action, Behind the Veils of Secret Foreign Policy* (Westport, CT: Praeger Security International, 2007): 159. See also Loch K. Johnson, "A Centralized Intelligence System: Truman's Dream Deferred," *American Journal of Intelligence* 23 (Autumn/Winter 2005): 6–16; Merle Miller, *Plain Speaking: An Oral Biography of Harry S. Truman* (New York: Berkeley, 1973); David F. Rudgers, *Creating the Secret State: The Origins of the Central Intelligence Agency, 1943–1947* (Lawrence: University Press of Kansas, 2000); Douglas T. Stuart, *Creating the National Security State: A History of the Law that Transformed America* (Princeton, NJ: Princeton University Press, 2008); Michael Warner, "Central Intelligence: Origin and Evolution," in Michael Warner, ed., *Central Intelligence: Origins and Evolution* (Washington, DC: Center for the Study of Intelligence, Central Intelligence Agency, 2001); and Amy B. Zegart, *Flawed by Design: The Evolution of the CIA, JCSA, and NSC* (Stanford, CA: Stanford University Press, 1999). For an insider suggestion that covert actions were already under way before enactment of the National Security Act in 1947, see Nicholas Dujmovic, "Review Essay: Covert Action to Promote Democracy in China During the Cold War," *Studies in Intelligence* 64/4 (December 2020): 34.
2. Quoted by Victor Marchetti and John D. Marks, *The CIA and the Cult of Intelligence* (New York: Knopf, 1974): 70.
3. Quoted in John Hedley, "The Intelligence Community: Is It Broken? How to Fix It," *Studies in Intelligence* 39 (1996): 17.
4. See Michael Allen, *Blinking Red: Crisis and Compromise in American Intelligence After /11* (Washington, DC: Potomac Books, 2015).
5. Stansfield Turner, *Burn before Reading: Presidents, CIA Directors, and Secret Intelligence* (New York: Hyperion, 2005): 254, 262.
6. Interview with Houston (June 29, 1990) by journalist Ronald Kessler, *Inside the CIA: Revealing the Secrets of the World's Most Powerful Spy Agency* (New York: Simon & Schuster, 1992): 238; and Sarah-Jane Corke, *U.S. Covert Operations and Cold War Strategy: Truman, Secret Warfare, and the CIA, 1945–53* (London: Routledge, 2008): 181, note 12. See, also, Bianca Adair, "The Quiet Warrior: Rear Admiral Sidney Souers and the Emergence of CIA's Covert Action Authority," *Studies in Intelligence* 65/2 (June 2021): 1-18.
7. Anne Karalekas, "A History of Covert Action," in Supplementary Detailed Staff Reports on Foreign and Military Intelligence, Book IV, *Final Report*, Select Committee to Study Governmental Operations with Respect to Intelligence Activities (hereafter, the Church Committee), Report No. 94-755, US Senate, 94th Cong., 2d Sess. (April 23, 1974): 105.
8. Ray S. Cline, *Secrets, Spies and Scholars: The Essential CIA* (Washington, DC: Acropolis Book 1976): 97; see also *Final Report*, Book I, Church Committee, US Senate, 94th Cong., 2d Sess. (December 4, 1975): 105.
9. Department of State (US), "Note on U.S. Covert Actions," *Foreign Relations of the United States, 1977–1980*, vol. XIX (South Asia), Washington, DC (2019): 35.

10. Pub.L. 110, 50 U.S.C. 401. The concept of "sources and methods" is both important and worrisome: important because the CIA deals every day with sensitive materials (such as top-secret documents and electronic devices) and must also shelter the names of its foreign agents for their own safety, so the concern for sources and methods is legitimate. Yet the gauzy phrase has also been used by the Agency to stiffarm lawmakers and their staffs who are attempting to understand and monitor the nation's intelligence activities. Too often, CIA personnel tell their supervisors on Capitol Hill, and even in the White House: "No, we can't discuss that program with you, because the sources and methods are too delicate and perishable to review outside of small groups at Langley or in Agency stations overseas---even with congressional overseers." Thus, "sources and methods" can be a slippery means for evading accountability.
11. Bruce D. Berkowitz and Allan E. Goodman, *Best Truth: Intelligence in the Information Age* (New Haven, CT: Yale University Press, 2000): 125.
12. Author's interview with retired DCI Stansfield Turner at his residence, McLean, VA (May 1, 1991).
13. "The CIA Assassination Plot in the Congo, 1960–61," *Alleged Assassination Plots Involving Foreign Leaders: An Interim Report* (Church Committee), US Senate, 94th Cong., 2d Sess. (November 1975): 10.
14. Karalekas, "A History of Covert Action," 26.
15. On the NSC, see John Gans, *White House Warriors: How the National Security Council Transformed the American Way of War* (New York: Liveright, 2019); and Karl F. Inderfurth and Loch K. Johnson, eds., *Fateful Decisions: Inside the National Security Council* (New York: Oxford University Press, 2004).
16. F. Clifton Berry Jr., *Inside the CIA: The Architecture, Art & Atmosphere of America's Premier Intelligence Agency* (Montgomery, AL: Community Communications, 1997): 21.
17. Quoted by Stewart Alsop, *The Center: People and Power in Political Washington* (New York: Harper & Row, 1968): 250.
18. On Kennan, see John Lewis Gaddis, *George F. Kennan: An American Life* (New York: Penguin, 2011).
19. Frederick P. Hitz, "The Importance and Future of Espionage," in Loch K. Johnson, ed., *Strategic Intelligence: The Intelligence Cycle*, vol. 2 (Westport, CT: Praeger, 2007): 75–93, quote at 77.
20. Karalekas, "A History of Covert Action," 32.
21. Two other important executive orders dealing with intelligence are E.O. 12036 (signed by President Carter and in support of strong congressional oversight of intelligence), and E.O. 12333 (signed by President Reagan, which tilted toward greater discretionary powers for the CIA)—although both are secondary in effect to the formal legal language embedded in the 1980 Intelligence Oversight Act. The Reagan E.O. was known in Washington, for short, as "twelve-triple-three." See *Public Papers of the Presidents of the United States* (Washington, DC: US Government Printing Office, 1979 and 1981, respectively).

22. Phillip J. Cooper, "Executive Orders," in Leonard W. Levy and Louis Fisher, eds., *Encyclopedia of the American Presidency*, vol. 2 (New York: Simon & Schuster, 1994): 584.
23. Loch K. Johnson, *The Threat on the Horizon: An Inside Account of America's Search for Security after the Cold War* (New York: Oxford University Press, 2011): 340.
24. Karalekas, "A History of Covert Action," 92, original emphasis.
25. Cited by Greg Miller, "As the U.S. Spied on the World, the CIA and the NSA bickered," *Washington Post* (March 6, 2020): A1. Historian Richard H. Immerman found that "Wisner was accountable to virtually no one" [*The Hidden Hand: A Brief History of the CIA* (Chichester, UK: Wiley, 2014): 28].
26. Peter Grose, *A Gentleman Spy: The Life of Allen Dulles* (New York: Houghton Mifflin, 1994); Leonard Mosley, *Dulles: A Biography of Eleanor, Allen, and John Foster Dulles and Their Family Network* (New York: Dial, 1978).
27. Karalekas, "A History of Covert Action," 41.
28. Richard Helms with William Hood, *A Look over My Shoulder: A Life in the Central Intelligence Agency* (New York: Random House, 2003): 185.
29. Johnson, *Threat on the Horizon*, 180–81.
30. Church Committee, *Hearings: Covert Action*, vol. 7: 8; Church Committee, *Final Report*, Book I: 145; and Karalekas, "A History of Covert Action," 45.
31. Church Committee, *Final Report*, Book I: 47. See this source, also, for the Committee's finding that the DP's personnel roster rapidly expanded by a count of 1,000 new officers in the early days of the Kennedy administration: 112.
32. DCI Helms once told a group of journalists: "The nation must, to a degree, take it on faith that we . . . are honorable men devoted to her service" [Washington, DC (April 14, 1971), cited by Harry Howe Ransom, "Congress, Legitimacy and the Intelligence Community," paper, Western Political Science Association, Annual Convention, San Francisco, CA (April 4, 1976)]. The title of Colby's memoir is *Honorable Men*.
33. "Note on U.S. Covert Actions," *Foreign Relations of the United States, 1977–1980*, vol. 14, South Asia (US Department of State (2019): 35–45.
34. John Prados and Arturo Jimenez-Bacardi, eds., "The High Command of the Secret War: Exhibits from the CIA, 1961–1974," in *New Collection of Declassified Documents Illuminates the Role of Presidents and Top Advisers in Guiding and Sanctioning CIA Activities from Cuba to Africa, 1961–1974*, National Security Archives Briefing Book #667, Washington, DC (March 4, 2019): 9. The sources in this chapter from the Kennedy and Ford Libraries (below) are also from this collection of declassified documents.
35. Marchetti and Marks noted that during the 1960s, the Agency used "about two thirds of its funds and its manpower for covert operations and their support" [Victor Marchetti and John Marks, *The CIA and the Cult of Intelligence* (New York: Knopf, 1974): 94]. On Helms's lack of enthusiasm for the Third Option, see Thomas Powers, *The Man Who Kept the Secrets: Richard Helms and the CIA* (New York: Knopf, 1979): 28, 101.
36. During the Iran-*contra* intelligence scandal, National Security Adviser John M. Poindexter provided in his testimony to the congressional investigative committee

a vivid illustration. "I made a very deliberate decision not to ask the president," he testified, "so that I could insulate him from the decision and provide some future deniability for the President if it ever leaked out" ["The Iran-Contra Affair," *Hearings*, Select Committee on Secret Military Assistance to Iran and the Nicaraguan Opposition (the Inouye-Hamilton Joint Committee), 100th Cong., 1st Sess. (July 15, 1978), Washington, DC: 17]. Senator Dan Inouye was a Democrat from Hawaii and SSCI's first chairman; Lee Hamilton, a Democrat from Indiana and HPSCI's second chairman (after Eddie Boland).

37. Prados and Jimenez-Bacardi, eds., "The High Command of the Secret War," 5.
38. "CIA Reorganization," memorandum from Arthur M. Schlesinger Jr. to President John F. Kennedy (June 30, 1961), Kennedy Presidential Library, *John F. Kennedy Papers*, National Security File, Departments and Agencies, Box 271, Folder, "CIA 5/1961–8/1961."
39. Department of State, U. Alexis Johnson, Memorandum for 40 Committee, "Request for Funds for President to Pass to President Bokassa of the Central African Republic in Forgery Case" (July 10, 1972), Gerald R. Ford Presidential Library, *Gerald R. Ford Papers*, Presidential Handwriting File, Box 31, Folder, "Intelligence (8)."
40. Henry Steele Commager, "Intelligence: The Constitution Betrayed," *New York Review of Books* (September 30, 1976): 32.
41. Karalekas, "A History of Covert Action," 93.
42. Colby's remarks to the Church Committee (October 31, 1975), in Loch K. Johnson, *A Season of Inquiry: The Senate Intelligence Investigation* (Lexington: University Press of Kentucky, 1985): 108.
43. James Abourezk, a Democrat, represented South Dakota in the US House at the time, then went on to serve in the US Senate. For the lopsided voting against the Abourezk Amendment, see the *Congressional Record* (October 2, 1974): 33482.
44. An amendment to the Foreign Assistance Act of 1974, Pub. L. No. 93-559, 32, 88 Stat. 1795, 1804 (1974).
45. Senator Hughes, a former truck driver built with the heft of an NFL linebacker, was in his first term as a senator. He had been a reform-minded governor of Iowa and came to Washington as part of the "Watergate Class." He served only a single term, frustrated by the Senate's notorious resistance to change. Leo Ryan, a foreign policy specialist, was appalled by the Allende coup revelations in the *Times* and led the effort to bring greater accountability to covert actions. In 1978, he would be gunned down by private security guards at a compound in Guyana, South America, run by the US religious leader Jim Jones. Representative Ryan had traveled to Guyana at the request of constituents to check on the safety of their children, who had run away from home to join the cult at "Jonestown." The youngsters and other cult members were killed by poison-laced Kool-Aid that Jones forced them to drink just before Ryan arrived. In the wake of this mayhem, Jones took his own life.
46. Karalekas, "A History of Covert Action," 89.
47. 50 U.S.C. 403.
48. Author's interview with DCI R. James Woolsey, CIA Headquarters, Langley, VA (September 29, 1993).

NOTES TO PAGES 183–192   319

49. Ray S. Cline, *The CIA Under Reagan, Bush and Casey* (Washington, DC: Acropolis Books, 1981): 293.
50. John Ranelagh, *The Agency: The Rise and Decline of the CIA* (New York: Simon & Schuster, 1986): 616.
51. An additional intelligence law related to the Third Option that followed in the footsteps of the 1980 oversight law was the Intelligence Identities Protection Act of 1982 [Pub. L. 97-200, 50 U.S.C. 421 (2012)]. Under this statute, anyone who reveals the identity of a DO or any other intelligence officer is subject to criminal legal proceedings. A disgruntled Agency officer by the name of Philip Agee had published a book that listed many of his colleagues by name, an "outing" that destroyed their careers and put them in danger from any CIA-hater or terrorist organization. Thus far, two people have been convicted under the statute. For more detail on all of these intelligence laws, see Stephen Dycus, Arthur L. Berney, William C. Banks, Peter Raven-Hansen, and Stephen I. Vladeck, *National Security Law*, 6th ed. (New York: Wolters Kluwer, 2016); and Loch K. Johnson, *Spy Watching: Intelligence Accountability in the United States* (New York: Oxford University Press, 2018).
52. See John Oseth, *Regulating U.S. Intelligence Operations: A Study in the Definition of National Interest* (Lexington: University Press of Kentucky, 1985): 122–41.
53. *Congressional Record* (February 9, 1978): 3110–41.
54. A GOP staffer on the Hill once offered a description of an Agency congressional liaison officer he had met. The CIA man had behaved as if "Washington was a foreign country and he was the station chief in hostile terrain, mounting operations against the Congress" [interviewed by Gregory F. Treverton, in his *Covert Action: The Limits of Intervention in the Postwar World* (New York: Basic Books, 1987): 260].
55. Title V of the National Security Act of 1947 (50 U.S.C. 413), Accountability for Intelligence Activities: The Intelligence Oversight Act of 1980), Pub. L. No. 96-450, 94 Stat. 1975 (1981).
56. Treverton, *Covert Action*, 250.
57. "The Iran-Contra Affair," *Hearings* (the Inouye-Hamilton Joint Committee); Tower Commission, *Report of the President's Special Review Board* (Washington, DC: US Government Printing Office, February 26, 1987).
58. 50 U.S.C. 3517: Inspector General for Agency Act.
59. Pub. L. 102-88, 601–603, 105 Stat. 429, 441–445 (1991), as amended (50 U.S.C. 3091–3094. This statute amended the National Security Act of 1947, repealed the Hughes-Ryan Amendment of 1974, and codified into law Executive Order 12333.
60. For the full text of this letter, see H.R. Rep. No. 166, U.S. House, 102d. Cong., 1st Sess. (1991): 27.
61. Pub. L. 109-148, 1005(e), 119 Stat. 2680, 2739–2740.
62. Clark Clifford, testimony, *Hearings*, vol. 7, Church Committee, US Senate, 94th Cong., 2d Sess. (December 4, 1975): 51–52. Even inside the Agency, DCI Stansfield Turner claimed that he never knew what the DO was up to most of the time [*Secrecy and Democracy: The CIA in Transition* (Boston: Houghton Mifflin, 1985)].
63. Quoted in the *Washington Star* (November 12, 1975), as cited by Treverton, *Covert Action*, 252.

64. Arthur L. Liman, with Peter Israel, *Lawyer: A Life of Counsel and Controversy* (New York: Public Affairs, 1998): 318–20.
65. Edward S. Corwin, *The President: Office and Powers, 1987–1957* (New York: New York University Press, 1957): 201.

Chapter 8

1. James R. Clapper, remark, Jackson Institute for Global Affairs Discussion Forum, Yale University (a virtual meeting held on October 20, 2020).
2. Robert M. Gates, "The CIA and American Foreign Policy," *Foreign Affairs* 66/2 (1987–88): 215–30.
3. Interview conducted with Dulles by political scientist Harry Howe Ransom, "Congress, Legitimacy and the Intelligence Community," research paper presentation, Western Political Science Association, Annual Convention, San Francisco, California (April 4, 1976): 7.
4. Richard B. Russell Library, Oral History No. 86, taped by Hughes Cates (February 22, 1977), University of Georgia, Athens, GA.
5. William E. Colby, quoted by Bob Wiedrich, "Can Congress Keep A Secret?" *Chicago Tribune* (February 3, 1976): A16.
6. Senator Frank Church, quoted by Tom Braden, "What's Wrong with the CIA?" *Saturday Review* 2 (April 5, 1975): 14.
7. Former DNI James R. Clapper, email remarks to the author (July 3, 2020).
8. Former DNI James R. Clapper, email remarks to the author (July 3, 2020).
9. Author's interview with a DDO, Washington, DC (November 16, 1980). A COS stationed in Mexico, say, might come up the idea based on extensive experience in the country that so-and-so working for such-and-such newspaper might be a good media asset for the Agency and could plant a certain theme into her columns. Here are the beginnings of a suggestion for a covert propaganda operation, stemming from the ground truth realities and knowledge that a chief of station copes with every day. On occasion, the Agency has apparently gone a step further in the field. According to a CIA operations officer: "We made the [covert] action programs up ourselves after we had collected enough intelligence to make them appear required by the circumstances" [Joseph Burkholder Smith, "Nation-Builders, Old Pros, Paramilitary Boys, and Misplaced Persons," *Washington Monthly* (February 1978): 28].
10. Author's interview with senior DO officer, Washington, DC (January 24, 1976).
11. Letter from FitzGerald to Bundy (March 6, 1964): 1, in *Miscellaneous Records of the Church Committee*, Senate Select Committee on Intelligence, Loch K. Johnson file on "LBJ Library National Security Papers Touching on Assass. and Covert Action in Cuba" (July 21, 1975), declassified on March 8, 2000, Record Number 157-10014-10096, cited in this book as "LBJ Library Papers."
12. Miles Copeland, *The Game Player: Confessions of CIA's Original Political Operator* (London: Aurum Press, 1989): 125, original emphasis.

13. Scott Anderson, *The Quiet Americans: Four CIA Spies at the Dawn of the Cold War—a Tragedy in Three Acts* (New York: Doubleday, 2020): 458.
14. See Loch K. Johnson, *Bombs, Bugs, Drugs, and Thugs: Intelligence and America's Quest for Security* (New York: New York University Press, 2000); also Henry A. Crumpton, *The Art of Intelligence: Lessons from a Life in the CIA's Clandestine Service* (New York: Penguin, 2009).
15. Quoted by Ronald Kessler, *The CIA at War: Inside the Secret Campaign Against Terror* (New York: St. Martin's, 2004): 100.
16. See the testimony of an incumbent DDO, *Hearings*, Aspin-Brown Commission on Intelligence (April 6, 1995, Washington, DC), summarized in Loch K. Johnson, *The Threat on the Horizon: An Inside Account of America's Search for Security after the Cold War* (New York: Oxford University Press, 2011): 112–13.
17. On Charlie Wilson, see Chapter 5; on Gingrich, see Richard A. Clarke, *Against All Enemies: Inside America's War on Terror* (New York: Free Press, 2004): 103, reinforced by the present author's interview with a senior DCI aide, Washington, DC (November 20, 1996); and on Carter, the author's interview with a senior Carter administration official, Washington, DC (February 22, 1979).
18. Chris Whipple, *The Spy Masters: How the CIA Directors Shape History and the Future* (New York: Scribner, 2020): 73.
19. Robert M. Gates, *From the Shadows* (New York: Simon & Schuster, 1996): 379.
20. Interview quote from David Shimer, "When the CIA Interferes in Foreign Elections," *Foreign Affairs This Week*, www.foreignaffairs.com (June 21, 2020): 12.
21. Author's interview, Washington, DC (June 11, 1984). More recently, a retired head of the Agency's Office of Legal Counsel with twenty-four years of service at the CIA has noted in reference to covert action and the new rules for intelligence accountability: "You always had the two camps [inside the CIA]: those who felt that their hands were too tied, and those who felt the restrictions were wise and appropriate" [Robert Eatinger, quoted by Zach Dorfman, Kim Zetter, Jenna McLaughlin, and Sean D. Naylor, "Secret Trump Order Gives CIA More Powers to Launch Cyberattacks," *News.Yahoo* (July 15, 2020)]. In a recent tell-all account of his short stint as national security adviser in the Trump administration, John Bolton calls for a "scraping" of the Obama-era approach to cyber covert actions with their fidelity to the post-Church Committee approval and oversight procedures, replacing them with "a more agile, expeditious decision-making structure" [John Bolton, *The Room Where It Happened: A White House Memoir* (New York: Simon & Schuster, 2020): 176].
22. David E. Sanger, *The Perfect Weapon: War, Sabotage, and Fear in the Cyber Age* (New York: Crown, 2018): 222–23.
23. Crumpton, *The Art of Intelligence*, 206.
24. Email communication to the author (August 30, 2020). Another senior official said that most of the nation's covert actions during the Obama years never required a separate finding; they were operations that already fell under carry-over findings from the Bush II administration [email communication to the author (October 24, 2020)]. This is a related, and equally troubling, phenomenon; covert actions need to be fine-tuned and tailored to confront immediate global conditions—by senior decision

makers, not only operatives in the field—rather than just sliding forward from one administration to another.
25. Memorandum from Arthur M. Schlesinger Jr. to President John F. Kennedy (September 5, 1962), Kennedy Presidential Library, Boston, MA.
26. Interviewed by Anderson, *The Quiet Americans*: 388.
27. Stansfield Turner, *Secrecy and Democracy: The CIA in Transition* (Boston: Houghton Mifflin, 1985): 169.
28. Inouye-Hamilton Joint Committee, "Witness Testimony: Iran-Contra Affair," *Report*, S. Rept. No. 100-216 and H. Rept. No. 100-433, Select Committee on Secret Military Assistance to Iran and the Nicaraguan Opposition, 100 Cong., 1st Sess., US House and Senate (November 1987): 379.
29. See Mark M. Lowenthal, *Intelligence: From Secrets to Policy*, 4th ed. (Washington, DC: CQ Press, 2009): 944–95. Torricelli went on to win a Senate seat from New Jersey, but evidence regarding his misuse of campaign funds spoiled plans for a second term.
30. Gregory F. Treverton, "Covert Action: Forward to the Past?" in Loch K. Johnson, ed., *Strategic Intelligence: Covert Action, Behind the Veils of Secret Foreign Policy*, vol. 3 (Westport, CT: Praeger Security International, 2007):19.
31. For a comparison of all the DCIs with respect to their willingness to adopt constitutional safeguards against the abuse of secret power, see Loch K. Johnson, *Spy Watching: Intelligence Accountability in the United States* (New York: Oxford University Press, 2018).
32. Greg Miller and Ellen Nakashima, "President's Intelligence Briefing Book Repeatedly Cited Virus Threat," *Washington Post* (April 27, 2020): A1.
33. See Loch K. Johnson, "The National Security State Gone Awry: Returning to First Principles," in Karen J. Greenberg, ed., *Reimagining the National Security State: Liberalism on the Brink* (New York: Cambridge University Press, 2020): 37–70; and Loch K. Johnson, "The Spy Power, Technological Innovations, and the Human Dimensions of Intelligence: Recent Presidential Abuse of America's Secret Agencies," *Journal of Intelligence, Conflict, and Warfare* 4/1 (2021).
34. Senator John McCain, remarks, "Meet the Press," *NBC Television* (November 21, 2004).
35. Kean Commission (led by former Governor Thomas H. Kean, R, New Jersey), *The 9/11 Commission: Final Report of the National Commission on Terrorist Attacks upon the United States* (New York: Norton, 2004): 420.
36. *Congressional Record* (December 9, 2014).
37. Author's interviews with SSCI and HPSCI staffers, Washington, DC (April 22, 1984 and July 25, 1986, respectively).
38. The letter was dated April 9, 1984, and published in the *Washington Post* on April 11, 1984: A17.
39. Johnson, *Spy Watching*, 307-7.
40. For a more detailed examination, see Johnson, *Spy Watching*.
41. Kathleen Clark, "'A New Era of Openness?' Disclosing Intelligence to Congress Under Obama," *Constitutional Commentary* 26 (2010): 14.

42. Quoted by Tom Braden, "What's Wrong with the CIA?" *Saturday Review* (April 5, 1975): 14.
43. Quoted by Associated Press (October 7, 1986), as cited in Malcolm Byrne, *Iran-Contra: Reagan's Scandal and the Unchecked Abuse of Presidential Power* (Lawrence: University Press of Kansas, 2014): 254.
44. David E. Sanger, "Congress-N.S.A. Tussle over Ukraine Records Breaks into the Open," *New York Times* (January 20, 2020). Similarly, Acting DNI Richard Grenell reportedly declined to appear before HPSCI in March of 2020, "citing apprehension about his preparedness to address sensitive subjects that tend to upset the president" [Seung Min Kim and Ellen Nakashima, "Trump's Acting Intelligence Chief Declines to Meet with Congress for Election Threats Briefing," *Washington Post* (March 10, 2020): A1]. Under rules of confidentiality, a high-level US intelligence officer told the author of this book that the Defense Department did not want the media to know about the early intelligence warning-reports on COVID-19 "since it would blow away Trump's 'blind-sided' narrative" [that is, the president's claim that he had never been briefed by the Intelligence Community about the virus threat]; email correspondence (March 14, 2020).
45. A charter HPSCI member, Norman Mineta (D, California) once lamented: "We are like mushrooms. They [CIA officers] keep us in the dark and feed us a lot of manure" [quoted in *Newsweek* (October 10, 1983): 38].
46. William S. Cohen and George J. Mitchell, *Men of Zeal: A Candid Inside Story of the Iran-Contra Hearings* (New York: Viking, 1988): 251. For a similar experience on a joint congressional panel investigating the 9/11 intelligence failures, see Senator Bob Graham with Jeff Nussbaum, *Intelligence Matters: The CIA, the FBI, the Saudis, and the Failure of America's War on Terrorism* (New York: Random House, 2004).
47. Peter Baker et al., "7 Days in January: Secret Orders a Deadly Strike and a World on Edge," *New York Times* (January 12, 2020): SR11.
48. Karen DeYoung, "Senior Administration Officials Struggle to Explain Intelligence Behind Killing of Soleimani," *Washington Post* (January 12, 2020): A1.
49. Inouye-Hamilton Committees, *Hearings*, vol. 100–102 (May 11 and 12, 1987): 16–17, 86.
50. For other examples of Helms being less than candid with members of Congress engaged in their accountability duties, see "The Two Oaths of Richard Helms," *Case C14-83-525*, Kennedy School of Government, Harvard University (1983); and Johnson, *Spy Watching*.
51. Author's interview with Representative Hamilton, Athens, GA (April 9, 2008).
52. Inouye-Hamilton Joint Committee, *Hearings*, Select Committee on Secret Military Assistance to Iran and the Nicaraguan Opposition, 100 Cong., 1st Sess., US House and Senate (November 1987): 142.
53. An Internet discussion forum, sponsored by the Biden Presidential Campaign Organization (August 30, 2020).
54. Email communication to the author (May 28, 2010).
55. James Risen, *State of War: The Secret History of the CIA and the Bush Administration* (New York: Free Press, 2006): 57.

56. See the *Congressional Quarterly Almanac*, vol. XLVII, 102d Cong., 1st Sess.: 482.
57. Mike Soraghan, "Reyes Backs Pelosi on Intel Briefings," *The Hill* (May 1, 2009): 1.
58. Mark M. Lowenthal, *Intelligence: From Secrets to Policy*, 6th ed. (Washington, DC: CQ Press, 2015): 234.
59. Whipple, *The Spy Masters*, 233.
60. For a study of the quality of questioning by members of the congressional Intelligence Committees, see Loch K. Johnson, "Playing Ball with the CIA: Congress Supervises Strategic Intelligence," in Paul E. Peterson, ed., *The President, the Congress, and the Making of American Foreign Policy* (Norman: University of Oklahoma Press, 1994): 49–73.
61. For a more detailed account of this dramatic turning point in the history of accountability for covert actions, see Johnson, *Spy* Watching, 133–36.
62. Cohen and Mitchell, *Men of Zeal*, 287.
63. Elizabeth Williamson and Julian E. Barnes, "With Intelligence Nominee, Trump Ensures an Ally Will Have the Post," *New York Times* (March 20, 2020): A1. On the distinctions among cheerleaders, ostriches, and other species of intelligence overseer on Capital Hill, see Johnson, *Spy Watching*.
64. David Ignatius, "Trump's Choking Hazard: Cutting Off Intelligence to Congress," *Washington Post* (August 31, 2020).
65. Inouye-Hamilton Committee, *Testimony of Caspar W. Weinberger*: 208–9.
66. Quoted by David Ignatius, "The U.S. Needs to Know What Went Wrong," *Washington Post* (March 31, 2020): A21.
67. Jane Mayer, "Enabler-in-Chief," *New Yorker* (April 20, 2020): 66.

Chapter 9

1. *Principled Spying: The Ethics of Secret Intelligence* (Washington, DC: Georgetown University Press, 2018): 198.
2. B. Hugh Tovar, "Covert Action," in Roy Godson, ed., *Intelligence Requirements for the 1990s: Collection, Analysis, Counterintelligence, and Covert Action* (Lexington, MA: Heath, 1989): 224.
3. Loch K. Johnson, *The Threat on the Horizon: An Inside Account of America's Search for Security after the Cold War* (New York: Oxford University Press, 2011): 280.
4. "A Looming Metamorphosis for the Intelligence Community," research paper, Georgetown Law School Conference on Intelligence (November 7, 2019), Washington, DC.
5. Steve Coll, *Directorate S: The C.I.A. and America's Secret Wars in Afghanistan and Pakistan* (New York: Penguin, 2018): 356.
6. Harry Rositzke, *CIA's Secret Operations: Espionage, Counterespionage and Covert Action* (New York: Reader's Digest Press, 1977): 206. Writing in a memoir, long-serving DP officer Michael Burke took a position in agreement with Rositzke: "Given the black-and-white definition of the Cold War, there is no shillyshallying about

morality. Who is not with me is against me" [*Outrageous Good Fortune* (Boston: Little, Brown, 1984): 143].

7. "Paper No. 51," *The Federalist* (New York: Modern Library, 1937): 335–41.
8. Attorney General Barr provides an illustration of this approach to governance. "Bill's view on the separation of powers was not overlapping authority keeping all branches in check [the Madisonian model], but keeping the other branches neutralized, leaving a robust executive power to rule," observes law professor Douglas Kmiec, who proceeded Barr as head of the Office of Legal Counsel in the Department of Justice [quoted by Emily Bazelon, "Who Is Bill Barr?" *New York Times* (October 27, 2019): 4]. Elsewhere Barr has said that "the Constitution itself places *no limit* on the president's authority to act on matters which concern him or his own conduct" [Mattathias Schwartz, "The Advocate," *New York Times Sunday Magazine* (June 7, 2020): 42, emphasis added].
9. Quoted in Mark Mazzetti, "Expanded Power, Vested in a Mercurial President," *New York Times* (January 5, 2020): A1.
10. Robert L. Grenier, *88 Days to Kandahar: A CIA Diary* (New York: Simon & Schuster, 2015): 392.
11. See Loch K. Johnson, *Spy Watching, Intelligence Accountability in the United States* (New York: Oxford University Press, 2018), and *A Season of Inquiry Revisited: The Church Committee Confronts America's Spy Agencies* (Lawrence: University Press of Kansas, 2015).
12. Loch K. Johnson, *Season of Inquiry: The Senate Intelligence Investigation* (Lexington: University Press of Kentucky, 1985): 50; and the author's interview with McGeorge Bundy, National Security Adviser to President John F. Kennedy, Athens, Georgia (October 6, 1987).
13. *Alleged Assassination Plots Involving Foreign Leaders, An Interim Report*, Select Committee to Study Governmental Operations with Respect to Intelligence Activities [the Church Committee], US Senate, 94th Cong., 1st Sess. (Washington, DC, November 1975).
14. Quoted in Stephen Kinzer, *The Brothers: John Foster Dulles, Allen Dulles, and Their Secret World War* (New York: Times Books, 2013): 196.
15. London: Chatto and Windus, 1954 (originally published in 1933).
16. For the first account, see Tom Wicker et al., "C.I.A. Operations: A Plot Scuttled," *New York Times* (April 25, 1966): A1; the second cites the deputy secstate at the time, Ulysses Alexis "Alex" Johnson, in John Prados and Arturo Jimenez-Bacardi, eds., *New Collection of Declassified Documents Illuminates the Role of Presidents and Top Advisers in Guiding and Sanctioning CIA Activities from Cuba to Africa, 1961–1974*, National Security Archives Briefing Book #667, Washington, DC (March 4, 2019). This venture is mentioned as well in Victor Marchetti and John Marks, *The CIA and the Cult of Intelligence* (New York: Knopf, 1974): 72, with the implication that the ship did leave Havana harbor on its mission.
17. David M. Barrett, Villanova University, emails to the author (August 11, 2020 and October 20, 2020). Professor Barrett, the author of *Congress and the CIA: The Untold Story from Truman to Kennedy* (Lawrence: University Press of Kansas, 2005), is a

master at searching through dusty governmental archives to find evidence about past US intelligence activities. He is presently at work on another book on relations between Langley and Capitol Hill during the Kennedy years. The author is grateful to him for sharing his insights into this sugar story, and the "rice paddy" incident that follows.
18. Barrett emails to the author (August 11, 2020, and October 20, 2020).
19. James Risen, *State of War: The Secret History of the CIA and the Bush Administration* (New York: Free Press, 2006): 81–82.
20. Joint Chiefs of Staff, Memorandum for the Secretary of Defense, "Cuban Actions" JCS 2304/244-1 (undated, but following a March 21, 1964, request from the Johnson White House for "new ideas related to Cuba," and before the end of October in 1964 when the DoD delivered its response to the White House; see Note 21): 1–4, in *Miscellaneous Records of the Church Committee*, Senate Select Committee on Intelligence, Loch K. Johnson file on "LBJ Library National Security Papers Touching on Assass. and Covert Action in Cuba" (July 21, 1975), declassified on March 8, 2000, Record Number 157-10014-10096, cited earlier in this book as "LBJ Library Papers."
21. Memo, R. C. Bowman to Bundy, "Square Dance" (November 12, 1964), with JSC attachment date October 30, 1964); LBJ Library Papers.
22. Based on Loch K. Johnson, "Inspection of Classified Documents in the LBJ Library Related to Covert Actions Against Chile," Top Secret Memorandum for Senior Staff, Church Committee (July 21, 1975, declassified on May 11, 1994 by the CIA), LBJ Library Papers, reported initially in Loch K. Johnson, *National Security Intelligence: Secret Operations in Defense of the Democracies*, 2d ed. (Cambridge: Polity, 2017): 92–93.
23. Gordon Chase, Memorandum for Mr. Bundy, "Special Group Meeting—Cuba" (March 4, 1965): 1; LBJ Library Papers.
24. Chase, Memorandum for Mr. Bundy.
25. John McCone, DCI, "Memorandum on Cuban Policy (April 25, 1963), John F. Kennedy Presidential Library, *John F. Kennedy Papers*, National Security File, Country File, Box 51, Folder, "Cuba: Subjects-Intelligence Material" (4/1963).
26. Roger Hilsman, *To Move a Nation* (New York: Dell, 1964): 314–15; and the author's conversations with Professor Rusk at the University of Georgia in June of 1982.
27. Robert Wallace and H. Keith Melton, with Henry Robert Schlesinger, *Spycraft: The Secret History of the CIA's Spy Techs, from Communism to Al-Qaeda* (New York: Plume/Penguin, 2009).
28. Johnson, *Season of Inquiry: The Senate Intelligence Investigation*, 73.
29. Webster had served as a judge in Missouri before becoming FBI director and then CIA director; and Deutch was a professor of chemistry and provost at MIT before, and after, serving in the DoD and as DCI.
30. Stansfield Turner, *Secrecy and Democracy: The CIA in Transition* (Boston: Houghton Mifflin, 1985): 178.
31. Journalist David E. Sanger notes a variation of this standard: "The simple test applied to covert actions at the CIA: if this operation was splashed across the front pages of the *Times* and the *Post*, would someone have to resign in disgrace?" [*The Perfect Weapon: War, Sabotage, and Fear in the Cyber Age* (New York: Crown, 2018): 76].

32. Remarks, Aspin-Brown Commission staff interviews, Washington, DC (1996), quoted in Johnson, *Threat on the Horizon*, 281. For other useful guidelines, such as a sensitivity to the Just War principle of proportionality, see Omand and Phythians, *Principled Spying*, and Jan Goldman, ed., *Ethics of Spying* (Lanham, MD: Scarecrow Press, 2006).
33. Vice President Al Gore observed at an NSC meeting: "That's a no-brainer. Of course it's a violation of international law, that's why it's a covert action" [quoted by a White House counterterrorism guru who served in several administrations, Richard A. Clarke, *Against All Enemies: Inside America's War on Terror* (New York: Free Press, 2004): 144].
34. Author's interview with DCI Judge William H. Webster, CIA Headquarters, Langley, VA (May 2, 1991).
35. Les Aspin, speech, "Foreign Intelligence Legal and Democratic Controls," American Enterprise Institute, Washington, DC (December 12, 1979): 2.
36. See Chris Whipple, *The Spy Masters: How the CIA Directors Shape History and the Future* (New York: Scribner, 2020): 169–70. In a standard internal memo on calculating the odds of CA success, an NSC document from the Johnson administration opined that the "chances of total success [in blowing up a major Cuban power plant, with the target destroyed and no one caught] are less than 50–50 while the chances of partial success (target destroyed, people caught) are only somewhat better than 50–50." The White House decided to drop the proposal, "primarily because of its high probability of failure and because of the Soviet dimension"—that is, some signs that the USSR was apparently about to cut back on aid to Cuba, a direction the administration did not want to reverse by inflaming Cuban pleas to Moscow for help in thwarting US operations against the island. [Gordon Chase, Memorandum for the Record, "Meeting with the President" (December 19, 1963): 3; LBJ Library Papers].
37. Robert M. Gates, *Duty: Memoirs of a Secretary at War* (New York: Knopf, 2014): 219. See also James R. Clapper with Trey Brown, *Facts and Fears: Hard Truths from a Life in Intelligence* (New York: Viking, 2018): 451. According to several sources, the prophecies of probable success expressed to the president by members of his national security team ranged from 40 to 95 percent.
38. The Agency's interventions in Iran in 1953 and Guatemala in 1954, often well regarded, are not addressed in the rankings that follow, on grounds that these two countries were less pressing as targets for covert action than the ones that are presented. This is true as well for Angola and Indonesia. Several other examples of the Third Option discussed in Chapters 3 through 6 are not addressed either in the "Best" or "Worst" tabulations, because they were relatively secondary events in the grand scheme of America's foreign policy initiatives. It should be remembered, as well, that the CIA has engaged in hundreds of other covert actions, but they fall outside the scope of this book because of their lower historical importance and for reasons of limited space in this book. And, of course, there are additional examples of the Third Option that can only be scrutinized by outside eyes sometime in the future, because they remain either unknown at all to the public or perhaps known but still officially

classified. Experience suggests, however, that the most significant ones have made their way into the public record.

39. Oliver L. North, with William Novak, *Under Fire: An American Story* (New York: HarperCollins, 1991): 272. A more recent example of the Agency's elimination of evidence that might implicate its officers in criminal activity is when DDO Jose A. Rodriquez Jr. destroyed the videotapes of torture activities carried out by the Operations Directorate in the wake of the 9/11 attacks [see his "Don't We Want to Stop Terrorism?" *Washington Post* (December 12, 2014): B1].

40. See James H. Johnston, *Murder, Inc.: The CIA Under John F. Kennedy* (Lincoln: University of Nebraska Press/Potomac Books, 2019): 48. The attorney general especially feared all-out war with the Soviet Union if Castro were assassinated during the crisis.

41. Russia's President Putin has maintained, when outed on his interference in the 2016 US presidential elections, that America engages in the same activity around the world. If the United States can manipulate elections (including against the Russians, he argued), then why should Americans be surprised when they are given some of their own medicine? This argument of moral equivalence between US and Russian covert action is deeply flawed. In most cases, the Agency promotes the advancement of democracy around the world while Moscow has been out to destroy the free and open societies. (Obvious, and regrettable, US exceptions to this rule have included actions against the democratic regimes of Guatemala, Nicaragua, and Chile, among a few others.) However false this notion of moral equivalence is, the argument provides fodder for the Russian propaganda mills.

The Russians were correct in one sense: the White House spread at least as much disinformation about the United States as did Moscow in 2020, especially President Trump's dismissal of his defeat in that year's presidential election as a product of fraudulent voting by Democrats, along with his subsequent campaign to trash—without an iota of evidence—the legitimacy of the entire election. Trump proved he could do more to erode the foundations of democracy in the United States with his Twitter account and his incitement of followers to use violence against the Congress than could the mighty Russian SVR and GRU combined. Presidential scholar Michael Beschloss has referred to the January 6, 2021, Trump-inspired attacks against Capitol Hill as a "near death" experience for America's democracy (remark, MSNBC, January 24, 2021). For those six hours of mayhem, the world's oldest democracy seemed more like a tinhorn dictatorship that had ordered out its brownshirts to destroy free government in the cause of false patriotism.

42. Armin Krishnan, "Controlling Partners and Proxies in Pro-Insurgency Paramilitary Operations: The Case of Syria," *Intelligence and National Security* 34/4 (June 2019): 544–60, quote at 554.

43. Karen De Young, "Senior Administration Officials Struggle to Explain Intelligence Behind Killing of Soleimani," *Washington Post* (January 12, 2020): A1.

44. Author's interview with retired DCI Turner at his residence, McLean, Virginia (May 1, 1991).

Chapter 10

1. Author's interviews, which have included many Seventh Floor officials at Langley. Among them: ten DCIs from Richard Helms forward, who collectively led the Agency from 1966 through 2004, plus DNI James R. Clapper Jr. (2010-17). Most of the interviews that inform this book, though, were conducted with active or former DP and DO personnel, Agency attorneys, and congressional liaison personnel, along with scores of lawmakers on SSCI and HPSCI as well as staff on those committees. These sessions have numbered more than 600. For published examples of some of the formal sessions with DCIs, and with DNI Clapper, see the author's essays in the journal *Intelligence and National Security*, "A Conversation with James R. Clapper Jr., The Director of National Intelligence in the United States," 30 (February 2015): 1–25; "A Remembrance: Admiral Stansfield Turner, Naval Officer as DCI," 53 (June 2018): 587–97; "William E. Colby: Spymaster During the 'Year of the Intelligence Wars,'" 22 (April 2007): 250–69; "Spymaster Richard Helms," 18 (Autumn 2003): 638–63; as well as Loch K. Johnson, *Spy Watching: Intelligence Accountability in the United States* (New York: Oxford University Press, 2018), Ch. 11.
2. Haass's op-ed reflects the testimony he provided to the Aspin-Brown Commission on the topics of intelligence gathering and covert action, along the lines of an op-ed piece of his at the time: Richard N. Haass, "Don't Hobble Intelligence Gathering," *Washington Post* (February 15, 1996): A27. On his appearance before the Commission, see Loch K. Johnson, *Threat on the Horizon: An Inside Account of America's Search for Security After the Cold War* (New York: Oxford University Press, 2011).
3. Ray S. Cline, *Secrets, Spies and Scholars: The Essential CIA* (Washington, DC: Acropolis Books, 1976): 215.
4. Select Committee to Study Governmental Operations with Respect to Intelligence Activities Intelligence (Church Committee), *Final Report*, vol. IV, US Senate, 94th Cong., 2d Sess., Sen. Rept. No. 94-755 (Washington, DC: US Government Printing Office, 1976): 67.
5. Quoted by Karen J. Greenberg, "Rethinking How We Try Terrorists," *American Scholar* (Summer 2016): 15.
6. Jimmy Carter, "A Cruel and Unusual Record," *New York Times* (June 25, 2012): A17.
7. Thomas Powers, *The Man Who Kept the Secrets: Richard Helms and the CIA* (New York: Knopf, 1979): xi.
8. Richard Helms, with William Hood, *A Look over My Shoulder: My Life in the Central Intelligence Agency* (New York: Random House, 2003): 184.
9. Richard Bissell, *Reflections of a Cold Warrior: From Yalta to the Bay of Pigs* (New Haven, CT: Yale University Press, 1996): 220. As the chief architect of the Bay of Pigs operations, he would have had good reason to doubt even the short-term effects as well.
10. R. James Woolsey, interview with the author, CIA Headquarters, Langley, VA (September 29, 1993), original emphasis. A *démarche* is a petition or protest presented through diplomatic channels.

11. Loch K. Johnson, *National Security Intelligence: Secret Operations in Defense of the Democracies*, 2d ed. (Cambridge, UK: Polity, 2017): 122.
12. Rory Cormac, *Disrupt and Deny: Spies, Special Forces, and the Secret Pursuit of British Foreign Policy* (Oxford: Oxford University Press, 2018); and David Omand and Mark Phythian, *Principled Spying: The Ethics of Secret Intelligence* (Washington, DC: Georgetown University Press, 2018): 181.
13. See, respectively, Stansfield Turner, *Burn Before Reading: Presidents, CIA Directors, and Secret Intelligence* (New York: Hyperion, 2005): 98; and, on Russia, Michael Schwirtz, "Secret Spy Unit in Russia Aims to Jolt Europe," *New York Times* (October 9, 2019): A1.
14. Remarks, *Larry King Live*, CNN Television (February 2, 1987).
15. Author's interview with former DCI William E. Colby, law office, Washington, DC (January 22, 1991)
16. Remark to the author (July 4, 1984), Athens, Georgia.
17. Recorded Oval Office conversation (August 3, 1972), quoted by Steve Coll, *Directorate S: The C.I.A. and America's Secret Wars in Afghanistan and Pakistan* (New York: Penguin, 2018): 486. John Rizzo, the Agency's senior attorney during the controversial post-9/11 period when the CIA adopted waterboarding and other shameful techniques against suspect terrorists, once observed that with respect to these methods: "I don't think the long-term effects were ever explored [at Langley] in any real depth" [Sam Roberts, "John Rizzo, 73, Lawyer for C.I.A. Who Backed Waterboarding, Dies," *New York Times* (August 13, 2021, B11]. This, despite the fact that the Directorate for Analysis has more thinkers and intellectuals---"analysts"---by far than any other federal government agency.
18. Author's interview with retired DCI John Deutsch, MIT campus, Boston, MA (October 29, 1998).
19. Author's interview with retired DCI Stansfield Turner at his residence, McLean, VA (May 1, 1991).
20. Quoted by Mark Mazzetti, *The Way of the Knife: The CIA, A Secret Army, and a War at the Ends of the Earth* (New York: Penguin, 2013): 81, based on his interview with Admiral Blair.
21. William E. Colby, "Public Policy, Secret Action," *Ethics and International Affairs* 3 (1989): 69.
22. Johnson, *The Threat on the Horizon*, 200 and 281, respectively.
23. See Jennifer D. Kibbe, "Covert Action, Pentagon Style," in Loch K. Johnson, ed., *The Oxford Handbook of National Security Intelligence* (New York: Oxford University Press, 2010): 569–86; Jennifer D. Kibbe, "The Rise of the Shadow Warriors," *Foreign Affairs* 83 (2004): 102–15; and Johnson, *Spy Watching*, 327–28.
24. On this DO attitude, see William R. Johnson, "Clandestinity and Current Intelligence," *Studies in Intelligence* 20/3 (Fall 1976): 15–69, reprinted in H. Bradford Westerfield, ed., *Inside CIA's Private World* (New Haven, CT: Yale University Press, 1995), quote at 57.
25. Sarah-Jane Corke, *U.S. Covert Operations and Cold War Strategy: Truman Secret Warfare, and the CIA, 1945–53* (London: Routledge, 2008): 12–13.

26. From an interview with Jack Goldsmith by David E. Sanger, *The Perfect Weapon: War, Sabotage, and Fear in the Cyber Age* (New York: Crown, 2018): xxiii.
27. Robert M. Gates, *Exercise of Power: American Failures, Successes, and a New Path Forward in the Post–Cold War World* (New York: Knopf, 2020): 42.
28. Quoted in Greg Miller, "CIA to Station More Analysts Overseas as Part of Its Strategy," *Washington Post* (April 30, 2010): A1. On the challenges of bridging the DO and DI (and now DA) cultures, see Charles G. Cogan, "The In-Culture of the DO," *Intelligence and National Security* 8 (January 1993): 78–86.
29. Author's interview with Admiral Stansfield Turner, McLean, VA (May 1, 1985).
30. Johnson, *Threat on the Horizon*, 154.
31. Frank Snepp, *Decent Interval* (New York: Random House, 1979), see especially the "Postscript," 573–80; and for the story of the Agency's vendetta against the Snepp, see his, *Irreparable Harm: A Firsthand Account of How One Agent Took on the CIA in an Epic Battle over Free Speech* (New York; Random House, 1999).
32. Powers, *The Man Who Kept the Secrets*, 114.
33. Ferdinand Mount, "Spook's Disease," *National Review* 32 (March 7, 1980): 300. On the treatment of the Kurds, see the Pike Committee, *Report*, US House of Representatives, 94th Cong., 1st Sess. (1975), never released by Congress but leaked in full to the *Village Voice* (February 6, 1976). In a rebuttal, a senior DO officer once told this book's author: "These people wanted to fight and would have anyway—we only helped them do what they wanted to do" [author's interview, Washington, DC (June 6, 1983)].
34. Chris Whipple, *The Spy Masters: How the CIA Directors Shape History and the Future* (New York: Scribner, 2020): 326–27.
35. James Risen, telephone conversation with the author (May 4, 2020); the examples are the author's.
36. Cited in Loch K. Johnson, *A Season of Inquiry: The Senate Intelligence Investigation* (Lexington: University Press of Kentucky, 1985): 103, based on "Covert Action," *Hearings*, Select Committee on Intelligence (Church Committee), US Senate, vol. 7, 94th Cong., 1st Sess. (December 4, 1975): 144–203. These hearings are reprinted in Loch K. Johnson, "Witness Testimony from the Church Committee Hearings on Covert Action, 1975," *Intelligence and National Security* 34/6 (October 2019): 899–913.
37. Kermit Roosevelt, *Countercoup: The Struggle for Control of Iran* (New York: McGraw-Hill 1979): 210, emphasis added.
38. Gary Berntsen and Ralph Pezzullo, *Jawbreaker: The Attack on Bin Laden and Al-Qaeda* (New York: Crown, 2005): 313.
39. Frank Church, "Covert Action: Swampland of American Foreign Policy," *Bulletin of the Atomic Scientists* (February 1976): 7–11. For a discussion of the advantages of establishing an oversight algorithm for covert action accountability, see Johnson, *Spy Watching*, 461.
40. Joseph Wipple, "The History of the Central Intelligence Agency and Congress," *Intelligence and National Security* 26/1 (February 2011): 119.
41. Senator Frank Church, *Testimony*, Committee on Government Operations, US Senate, 94th Cong., 1st Sess. (January 21, 1976): 11. In mid-February of 1976, he would

tell an audience in Chicago that America's efforts to murder foreign officials in small countries with "Latin leaders [and] black leaders" was "shameful" [Loch K. Johnson, *A Season of Inquiry: The Senate Intelligence Investigation* (Lexington: University Press of Kentucky, 1985): 193].

42. Church, "Covert Action: Swampland," quote at 11; reprinted in Loch K. Johnson and James J. Wirtz, eds., *Intelligence: The Secret World of Spies*, 5th ed. (New York: Oxford University Press, 2019), quote at 236.
43. Church, "Covert Action: Swampland," *Hearings*.
44. This conversation took place in Senate Church's office, Russell Building, US Senate (July 14, 1975), author's notes.
45. Eliot A. Cohen, "Military Delusions," *New York Times Book Review* (January 5, 2020): 9.
46. Church, "Covert Action: Swampland," 239. During his Committee's hearings on covert action, Church said with respect to encouraging democracy in Portugal that, if exposed, the United States could say: "Yes, were there and we are proud of it, because what we tried to do clearly conformed with our traditional values as a nation. We stand for that." (Johnson, *Season of Inquiry*: 148).
47. These comments by Senator Church are based on Johnson, *A Season of Inquiry*: 114, plus additional conservations between the senator and the author during 1975.
48. Clifford and Vance, testimony, "Covert Action," *Hearings*, 53 and 54, respectively (emphasis added in both cases).
49. Morton Halperin, "Covert Action," *Hearings*, 60.
50. Roger Fisher, "The Fatal Flaw in Our Spy System," *Boston Globe* (February 1, 1976): A19.
51. Lindsey A. O'Rourke, *Covert Regime Change: America's Secret Cold War* (Ithaca, NY: Cornell University Press, 2018): 238.
52. Remarks, Pacem in Terris IV Convocation, Washington, DC (December 4, 1975), author's notes.
53. Cline, *Secrets, Spies and Scholars*, 130.
54. Robert Baer, *See No Evil: The True Story of a Ground Soldier in the CIA's War on Terrorism* (New York: Three Rivers Press, 2002): 33.
55. Sanger, *The Perfect Weapon*, 177.
56. Günter Grass, "Solidarity with the Sandinistas," *The Nation* 236 (March 12, 1983): 301.
57. Church, "Covert Action: Swampland," 8.
58. It should be reemphasized that these categories are based on the volume of scholarly and anecdotal literature on the most well-known major and minor CAs, not a complete universe of every Agency covert action since 1947 by any means. This full history remains locked up in CIA vaults. The major category, recall, consists of nations that are largely agreed on by scholars as the most significant CAs over the years. The minor category, those few smaller nations that steadily appear in the public research on covert action, is a less reliable set, because there have been thousands of these operations and targetings over the decades; this listing of fifty-four "minor" targets is only a subset of what is widely reported as a much larger universe of US covert actions around the world since 1947 (although the major ones are examined in this book).

However incomplete, this profile does provide a sense of the the CIA's national targets and their regional locations. Further left out of Figure 10.1 is the targeting of non-state terrorists and foreign cyberattackers, the origins of which are still being sorted out by counterintelligence specialists, with most evidence pointing so far to the handiwork of Russia's SVR, which hacked the United States routinely from 2016 to 2020.

59. From an address at Harvard University, quoted by Anthony Lewis, "When We Could Believe," *New York Times* (June 12, 1987): A31.
60. See Karen J. Greenberg, "American Ships Are Sending the Wrong Message Overseas," *TomDispatch.com* (December 20, 2018). Professor Greenberg of Fordham University chastises the United States for converting other Navy ships into floating prisons for the apprehension of suspected drug smugglers, who often languish aboard without legal counsel and in the most inhospitable conditions—including brutal treatment. Another side of American foreign policy.
61. Remarks, *Congressional Record* (May 17, 1966): 10808.
62. Remarks, "Should the CIA Fight Secret Wars?," a roundtable discussion, *Harper's* (September 1984): 37–44.
63. Roberta Jacobson, "What Trump and Corruption Cost Us," *New York Times* (October 14, 2019): A27.
64. Presidential candidate Trump, Republican Presidential Debate, Manchester, New Hampshire (February 6, 2016); and D/CIA Mike Pompeo, speech (2017), cited in Luke Mogelson, "The Afghan Way of Death," *New Yorker* (October 28, 2019): 43.

Abbreviations and Codenames

It is annoying to read a book that has too many abbreviations, acronyms, and codenames—akin to reading a dense Department of Defense manual. It is equally aggravating, though, to read a longer phrase over and over in a book, such as the "Central Intelligence Agency" instead of simply "CIA." This book has tried to keep the shorthand terms that flood Washington's national security establishment to a minimum here, but sometimes they are useful for purposes of parsimony. Further, they reflect daily practice in Washington, DC, giving the reader a sense of the documents and diction that fuel discourse in the nation's national security circles. Here is a list of the ones used:

Abbreviations

ABC	Anybody But Communists (an American foreign policy slogan in the modern era)
AG	Attorney General
Agency, the	Central Intelligence Agency (insider name for)
ARVN	Army of the Republic of Vietnam (U.S. ally in South Vietnam)
BBC	British Broadcasting Corporation
BND	Bundesnachtrichtendienst (German foreign intelligence service)
CA	covert action (the Third Option)
CA/CT	the use of covert action for counterterrorism
CAS	Covert Action Staff (DO/CIA)
CAT	Civil Air Transport (a CIA proprietary)
CIA	Central Intelligence Agency
CIG	Central Intelligence Group
CIS	Counterintelligence Staff (DO/CIA)
CPSU	Communist Party of the Soviet Union
Company, the	Central Intelligence Agency (insider name for)
CBJC	Congressional Budget Justification Book (with classified Annex)
C/JCS	Chair, Joint Chiefs of Staff (Pentagon)
COS	chief of station, the top CIA official in a foreign country

COVID-19	Coronavirus, spread globally from origins in China, beginning in 2019
CPSU	Communist Party of the Soviet Union
CRF	Contingency Reserve Fund
CT	Counterterrorism
CTC	Counterterrorism Center (CIA)
CT/CA	counterterrorism/covert action operation
DA	Directorate of Administration (now Directorate of Support)
DA	Directorate of Analysis (previously Directorate of Intelligence)
DC	District of Columbia
DCI	Director of Central Intelligence (the title of the nation's spy chief until the end of 2004)
D/CIA	Director of the Central Intelligence Agency (established in 2004 to replace the DCI designation)
DDCI	Deputy Director, Central Intelligence (CIA)
DDO	Deputy Director for Operations (CIA)
DDP	Deputy Director for Plans (CIA)
DGSE	Direction Générale de la Sécurité Extérieure (French foreign intelligence service)
DI	Directorate of Intelligence
DNI	Director of National Intelligence
DO	Directorate of Operations (CIA)
DoD	Department of Defense
DoJ	Department of Justice
DoS	Department of State
DP	Directorate of Plans (CIA), precursor of the DO
DMZ	demilitarized zone (Korea)
DS	Directorate of Support
DTA	Detainee Treatment Act (2005), prohibiting torture by U.S. government agencies
EDC	European Defense Community
E.O. (or e.o.)	executive order
ERP	European Recovery Program (Marshall Plan)
FBI	Federal Bureau of Investigation
FDR	Franklin Delano Roosevelt (America's 32d President)
First Option	diplomacy (the Treaty Power)
FISA	Foreign Intelligence Surveillance Act (1978)
FISC	Foreign Intelligence Surveillance Court
5412 Committee	CA/NSC panel (also known as the Special Group or SP)

ABBREVIATIONS AND CODENAMES 337

FNLA	National Front for the Liberation of Angola
40 Committee	CA/NSC panel during the Nixon and Ford Administrations, formerly the 303 Committee
Fourth Option	the policy option of setting a good example—legally, morally—in world Affairs
FSA	Free Syrian Army
FSB	Federal Security Service of the Russian Federation, KGB successor for internal security
GCHQ	Government Communications Headquarters, the British signals intelligence agency
GID	General Intelligence Directorate (Jordanian Intelligence service, also Known as the Mukhabarat)
GOP	Grand Old Party (the Republican Party in the United States)
GRU	Soviet, and now Russian, military intelligence service
HAWK	a U.S. surface-to-air missile
HPSCI	House Permanent Select Committee on Intelligence
humint	human intelligence (espionage assets)
IC	Intelligence Community
ICBMs	intercontinental ballistic missiles
ICD	Intelligence Community Directive
ICTY	International Criminal Tribunal for former Yugoslavia
IOB/PFIAB	Intelligence Oversight Board on the President Foreign Intelligence Advisory Board
INS	*Intelligence and National Security* (journal)
INR	Intelligence and Research Bureau (Department of State)
IRPTA	Intelligence Reform and Terrorism Prevention Act (2004)
ISI	Directorate for Inter-Services Intelligence (Pakistani intelligence service)
ISIS	Islamic State in Iraq and Syria (also known as ISIL, the Islamic State in Iraq and the Levant; and, in Arabic, *Dawlat*, or, insultingly, *Daesh*)
JCS	Joint Chiefs of Staff (DoD)
JSOC	Joint Special Operations Command (DoD)
KGB	Committee for State Security (Soviet foreign intelligence service during the Cold War, replaced by the SVR)
Langley	CIA Headquarters compound near McLean in northern Virginia
MI6	British foreign intelligence service (also known as Strategic Intelligence Service, or SIS
MIT	Massachusetts Institute of Technology (Boston)
MON	Memorandum of Notification (regarding covert action alterations)

MONGOOSE	a 1960's program to overthrow the Fidel Castro regime in Cuba (CIA)
MPSA	Popular Movement for the Liberation of Angola
NAFTA	North American Free Trade Agreement
NATO	North Atlantic Treaty Organization
NBCs	nuclear, biological, and chemical weaponry
NCPC	National Counterproliferation Center (ODNI)
NCTC	National Counterterrorism Center (White House and ODNI)
NED	National Endowment for Democracy, a bipartisan NGO in the United States openly supporting democracy movements around the world
NGA	National Geospatial-Intelligence Agency
NGO	Non-Governmental Organization
NIO	national intelligence officer
NIP	National Intelligence Program (U.S. Intelligence Community)
NKVD	Stalin's secret police
NPC	Nonproliferation Center (CIA)
NSA	National Security Agency (also, National Student Association)
NSAM	National Security Action Memorandum
NSC	National Security Council
NSC4/A	NSC/CA Directive (1947)
NSC10/2	NSC/CA Directive (1948)
NSC68	NSC/CA Directive (1950)
NSC 10/5	NSC/CA Directive (1951)
NSC 5412/1	NSC/CA Directive (1955)
NSC 5421/2	NSC/CA Directive (1955)
NSCID	National Security Council Intelligence Directive
NSDM	National Security Decision Memorandum
NSPG	National Security Planning Group (Reagan administration covert action panel)
NSSM	National Security Study Memorandum
NVN	North Vietnam
OAS	Organization of American States
OBL	Osama bin Laden
ODNI	Office of the Director of National Intelligence
OED	Oxford English Dictionary
OEOB	Old Executive Office Building (also known today as the Eisenhower Building)
O/JCS	Office of the Joint Chiefs of Staff (U.S. Department of Defense)
OMB	Office of Management and Budget (part of the U.S. presidency)
OPC	Office of Policy Coordination/CIA

OSO	Office of Special Operations/CIA
OSS	Office of Strategic Services (WWII)
PDB	*President's Daily Brief*
PDC	Christian Democratic Party (Chile)
PDD	Presidential Decision Directive
PFIAB	President's Foreign Intelligence Advisory Board
PIAB	President's Intelligence Advisory Board
PPG	Presidential Policy Guidance
PRB	Publication Review Board (CIA)
PM ops	paramilitary operations
PSB	Psychological Strategy Board (CIA)
PSP	Cuban Communist Party
RDI	rendition, detention, and interrogation of suspected terrorists (CIA)
RFE	Radio Free Europe (CIA clandestine radio station)
RL	Radio Liberty (CIA clandestine radio station)
RNC	Republican National Committee
SA	special activities (covert action)
SAD	Special Activities Division (part of the CIA Operations Directorate)
SALT	Strategic Arms Limitation Talks (between the United States and the Soviet Union)
SAVAC	Iranian secret police under the Shah
SCC	Special Coordinating Committee (Carter Administration CA panel)
SEALS	Sea, Air, and Land teams (U.S. Navy)
SEATO	Southeast Asia Treaty Organization
SecDef	Secretary of Defense
Second Option	overt military intervention (the War Power)
SecState	Secretary of State
SG	Special Group (National Security Council)
SIS	Secret Intelligence Service or MI6 (British foreign intelligence agency)
SOE	Special Operations Executive (U.K.)
SOF	Special Operations Forces (DoD)
SOG	Special Operations Group (PM/CAS/CIA)
SOP	Standard Operating Procedure
SPG	Special Procedures Group/CIA
SSCI	Senate Select Committee on Intelligence
Stasi	East German intelligence service (Cold War)
Stinger	US portable, shoulder-held, surface-to-air missile

Stuxnet	a virus injected into Iranian computers by the CIA and Mossad
SVR	Foreign Intelligence Service of the Russian Federation (replacing the First Directorate of the KGB, responsible for foreign espionage)
Third Option	covert action (CIA)
TOW	Tube-launched, optically tracked, wire-guided US anti-tank missile
303 Committee	CA/NSC panel (also known as the Special Group following the 5214 Committee in 1964)
UAE	United Arab Emirates
UAV	unmanned aerial vehicle (drone)
UDT	Underwater Demolition Team
UFC	United Fruit Company (US)
UK	United Kingdom
UN	United Nations
Unit 29155	Assassination group, contemporary Russian intelligence service
UNITA	National Union for the Total Independence of Angola
USD	United States dollars
USMCA	United States-Mexico-Canada Agreement
USNS	United States naval ship
VC	Viet Cong (South Vietnamese Communists)
WI-ROGUE	codename for a specific, and reckless, CIA operative in the 1960s
WMD	weapons of mass destruction
WPR	War Powers Resolution

Codenames for selected covert actions explored in this book

Name	Administration	Target Nation	Years
Valuable/BG Fiend	Truman/Eisenhower	Albania	1950–53
TPAjax	Eisenhower	Iran	1953
PB/Success	Eisenhower	Guatemala	1954
Omega	Eisenhower	Egypt	1955
Archipelago	Eisenhower	Indonesia	1957
Zapata	Eisenhower/JFK	Cuba	1961
Mongoose	JFK/LBJ	Cuba	1961–64
ZR/Rifle	JFK	Cuba	1961–63

Name	Administration	Target Nation	Years
Momentum	JFK/LBJ/Nixon	Laos	1962–68
Phoenix	LBJ/Nixon	Vietnam	1967–71
Eagle Claw	Carter	Iran	1979
Cyclone	Carter/Reagan	Afghanistan	1979–89
Staunch/Toys	Reagan	Iran/Nicaragua (*contras*)	1983–86
QR/Helpful	Carter/Reagan/Bush I	Poland	1979–90
Merlin	Clinton	Iran	2000
Enduring Freedom	Bush II	West Afghanistan	2001–03
Anaconda	Bush II	East Afghanistan	2001–03
Olympic Games	Bush II/Obama	Iran	2005–10
Geronimo (Neptune Spear)	Obama	Pakistan	2011
Timber Sycamore	Obama	Syria	2013

Selected Bibliography

An Overview of Covert Action

Adler, Emanuel. "Executive Command and Control in Foreign Affairs: The CIA's Covert Activities." *Orbis* 23 (Fall 1979): 671–95.

Aldrich, Richard J. *The Clandestine Cold War in Asia, 1945–65: Western Intelligence, Propaganda and Special Operations*. London: Frank Cass, 2000.

Aldrich, Richard J. *The Hidden Hand: Britain, America and Cold War Secret Intelligence, 1945–1964*. London: John Murray, 2001.

Andrew, Christopher, and Oleg Gordievsky. *KGB: The Inside Story*. London: Hodder & Stoughton, 1990.

Andrew, Christopher, and Vasili Mitrokhin. *The World Was Going Our Way: The KGB and the Battle for the Third World*. New York: Basic Books, 2005.

Barry, James A. "Covert Action Can Be Just." *Orbis* 37 (Summer 1993): 375–90.

Berkowitz, Bruce D., and Allan E. Goodman. *Best Truth: Intelligence in the Information Age*. New Haven, CT: Yale University Press, 2000.

Blackstock, Paul W. *The Strategy of Subversion*. Chicago: Quadrangle Books, 1964.

Brennan, John O. *Undaunted: My Fight Against America's Enemies, at Home and Abroad*. New York: Celaden Books, 2021.

Burke, Michael. *Outrageous Good Fortune*. Boston: Little, Brown, 1984.

Carson, Austin. *Secret Wars: Covert Conflict in International Politics*. Princeton, NJ: Princeton University Press, 2018.

Church, Frank. "Covert Action: Swampland of American Foreign Policy." *Bulletin of the Atomic Scientists* 32 (February 1976): 7–11.

Clapper, James R., with Trey Brown. *Facts and Fears: Hard Truths from a Life in Intelligence*. New York: Viking, 2018.

Cline, Ray S. *Secrets, Spies and Scholars: The Essential CIA*. Washington, DC: Acropolis Books, 1976.

Colby, William E. "The CIA's Covert Action." *Center Magazine* (March–April 1975): 71–80.

Copeland, Miles. *The Game of Nations*. New York: Simon & Schuster, 1969.

Copeland, Miles. *Beyond Cloak and Dagger: Inside the CIA*. New York: Simon & Schuster, 1974.

Copeland, Miles. *The Game Player: Confessions of CIA's Original Political Operator*. London: Aurum Press, 1989.

Corn, David. *Blond Ghost: Ted Shackley and the CIA's Crusades*. New York: Simon & Schuster, 1994.

Corson, William R. *The Armies of Ignorance*. New York: Dial Press, 1977.

Currey, Cecil B. *Edward Lansdale: The Unquiet American*. Boston: Houghton Mifflin, 1988.

Damrosch, Lori Fisler. "Covert Operations." *American Journal of International Law* 84 (October 1989): 795–805.

Daugherty, William J. "The Role of Covert Action." In Loch K. Johnson, ed., *Handbook of Intelligence Studies*. New York: Routledge, 2007.

Downes, Alexander B., and Mary Lauren Lilley. "Overt Peace, Covert War? Covert Intervention and the Democratic Peace." *Security Studies* 19/2 (2010): 222–306.

Dulles, Allen W. *The Craft of Intelligence*. New York: Harper & Row, 1963.

Emerson, Steven. *Secret Warriors: Inside the Covert Military Operations of the Reagan Era*. New York: Putnam, 1988.

Forsythe, David P. "Democracy, War, and Covert Action." *Journal of Peace Research* 29/4 (2009): 385–95.

Fulbright, J. William, with Seth P. Tillman. *The Price of Empire*. New York: Pantheon, 1989.

Fuller, Christopher J. *See It/Shoot It: The Secret History of the CIA's Lethal Drone Program*. New Haven, CT: Yale University Press, 2017.

Gates, Robert M. *Exercise of Power: America Failures, Successes, and a New Path Forward in the Post–Cold War World*. New York: Knopf, 2020.

Gill, Peter, and Mark Phythian. *Intelligence in an Insecure World*, 3d ed. Cambridge, UK: Polity, 2018.

Goodman, Allan E., and Bruce D. Berkowitz. *The Need to Know: The Report of the Twentieth Century Fund Task Force on Covert Action and American Democracy*. New York: Twentieth Century Fund Press, 1992.

Gustafson, Kristian. "'Direct Political Repercussions': Clausewitzian Philosophy and Covert Action," paper, Panel on "Covert Action in Today's Globalizing World." International Studies Association Annual Meeting, Toronto, Canada (March 27, 2019).

Hancock, Larry. *Creating Chaos: Covert Political Warfare from Truman to Putin*. London: OR Books, 2018.

Helms, Richard, with William Hood. *A Look over My Shoulder*. New York: Random House, 2003.

Inderfurth, Karl F., and Loch K. Johnson, eds. *Fateful Decisions: Inside the National Security Council*. New York: Oxford University Press, 2004.

Jacobsen, Annie. *Surprise, Kill, Vanish: The Secret History of CIA Paramilitary Armies, Operators, and Assassins*. New York: Little, Brown, 2019.

Jervis, Robert. "Intelligence and Foreign Policy." *International Security* 11 (Winter 1986–87): 141–61.

Johnson, Chalmers. *The Sorrows of Empire*. New York: Metropolitan Books, 2004.

Johnson, Loch K. *A Season of Inquiry: The Senate Intelligence Investigation*. Lexington: University Press of Kentucky, 1985. [Reprinted as A Season of Inquiry Revisited: The Church Committee confronts America's Spy Agencies (Lawrence, University Press of Kansas), 2015].

Johnson, Loch K. "Verdeckte Aktionen und die CIA: Amerikas geheime Aussenpolitik." In Wolfgang Krieger, ed., *Geheimdienste in der Weltgeschichte*, 260–74. München: Verlag C.H. Beck, 2003.

Krishnan, Armin. *Why Paramilitary Operations Fail*. Basingstoke: Palgrave, 2018.

Krishnan, Armin. *Covert Operations and Gray Zone Conflict: The Threat to U.S.* New York: Rowman & Littlefield, 2021.

Kolko, Gabriel. *Confronting the Developing World: United States Foreign Policy, 1945–1980*. New York: Pantheon, 1988.

Lobel, Jules. "Covert Operations." In Leonard W. Levy and Louis Fisher, eds., *Encyclopedia of the American Presidency*, vol. 1, 318–21. New York: Simon & Schuster, 1994.

Lowenthal, Mark M. *Intelligence: From Secrets to Policy*, 8th ed. Thousand Oaks, CA: Sage and CQ Presses, 2020.

McGarvey, Patrick J. *The CIA: The Myth and the Madness*. New York: Saturday Review, 1972.
Martin, David C., and John Walcott. *Best Laid Plans: The Inside Story of America's War on Terror*. New York: Touchstone, 1989.
Mayer, Jane. "The Predator War: What Are the Risks of the C.I.A.'s Covert Drone Program?" *New Yorker* (October 19, 2009).
Menand, Louis. "Table Talk: How the Cold War Made Georgetown Hot." *New Yorker* (November 10, 2014): 77.
Newsom, David D. "When Covert Action Is Successful." *Christian Science Monitor* (April 28, 1983): 23.
Panetta, Leon, and Jim Newton. *Worthy Fights: A Memoir of Leadership in War and Peace*. New York: Penguin, 2014.
Patton, Joy. *Predicting Indigenous Leader Survival in Regimes Targeted by CIA Covert Action*. PhD dissertation, University of Southern Mississippi, 2019.
Phillips, David Atlee. "The CIA, Covert and Overt, Always Survives Its Critics." *Los Angeles Times* (October 18, 1987) Pt. 5: 3.
Pillar, Paul. *Terrorism and U.S. Foreign Policy*. Washington, DC: Brookings Institution Press, 2001.
Pincus, Walter. "CIA Turns to Boutique Operations: Covert Action Against Terrorism, Drugs, Arms." *Washington Post* (September 14, 1997): A6.
Powers, Thomas. *Intelligence Wars: American Secrets History from Hitler to Al-Qaeda*. New York: New York Review of Books, 2002.
Prados, John. "The Future of Covert Action." In Loch K. Johnson, ed., *Handbook of Intelligence Studies*, 289–300. New York: Routledge, 2007.
Prados, John. *The Family Jewels: The CIA, Secrecy, and Presidential Power*. Austin: University of Texas Press, 2013.
Prados, John. *The Ghosts of Langley: Into the CIA's Heart of Darkness*. New York: Free Press, 2017.
Prouty, L. Fletcher. *The Secret Team: The CIA and Its Allies in Control of the United States and the World*. Englewood Cliffs, NJ: Prentice-Hall, 1973.
Ransom, Harry Howe. *The Intelligence Establishment*. Cambridge, MA: Harvard University Press, 1970.
Ransom, Harry Howe. "Strategic Intelligence and Intermestic Politics." In Charles W. Kegley Jr. and Eugene R. Wittkopf, eds., *Perspectives on American Foreign Policy: Selected Readings*. New York: St. Martin's Press, 1983.
Ranelagh, John. *The Agency: The Rise and Decline of the CIA*, rev. ed. New York: Simon & Schuster, 1987.
Rositzke, Harry. "America's Secret Operations: A Perspective." *Foreign Affairs* 53/2 (January 1975): 341–44.
Scott, Len V. "Secret Intelligence, Covert Action and Clandestine Diplomacy." In Len V. Scott and Peter Jackson, eds., *Understanding Intelligence in the Twenty-First Century: Journeys in Shadows*. London: Routledge, 2004.
Shackley, Theodore. *The Third Option: An American View of Counterinsurgency*. Pleasantville, NY: Reader's Digest, 1981.
Shultz, Richard H. Jr. "Covert Action." In Roy Godson, ed., *Intelligence Requirements for the 1990s: Collection, Analysis, Counterintelligence, and Covert Action*, 166–200. Lexington, MA: Heath, 1989.
Smith, Joseph Burkholder. *Portrait of a Cold Warrior*. New York: Ballantine, 1976.

Stout, Mark. "Covert Action in the Age of Social Media." *Georgetown Journal of International Affairs* 18/2 (2017): 94–103.
Tenet, George, with Bill Harlow. *At the Center of the Storm: My Years in the CIA*. New York: HarperCollins, 2007.
Tovar, B. Hugh. "Strengths and Weaknesses in Past U.S. Covert Action." In Roy Godson, ed., *Intelligence Requirements for the 1980s: Covert Action*, rev. ed., 71–81. Washington, DC: National Strategy Information Center, 1983.
Tovar, B. Hugh. "Covert Action." In Roy Godson, ed., *Intelligence Requirements for the 1990s: Collection, Analysis, Counterintelligence, and Covert Action*. 200–24. Lexington, MA: Heath, 1989.
Treverton, Gregory F. "Covert Action: From 'Covert' to Overt." *Daedalus* 116 (Spring 1987): 57–64.
Warner, Michael. *The CIA Under Harry Truman*. Washington, DC: CIA, 1994.
Warner, Michael, ed. *Central Intelligence Agency: Origins and Evolution*. Washington, DC: CIA, 2001.
Warner, Michael. *The Rise and Fall of Intelligence: An International Security History*. Washington, DC: Georgetown University Press, 2014.
Whipple, Chris. *The Spymasters: How the CIA Directors Shape History and the Future*. New York: Simon & Schuster, 2020.
Winks, Robin W. *Cloak & Gown: Scholars in the Secret War, 1939–1961*. New York: William Morrow, 1987.
Wirtz, James J. "Life in the 'Gray Zone': Observations for Contemporary Strategists." *Defense & Security Analysis* 33/2 (2017): 106–14.
Woods, Randall B. *Shadow Warrior: William Egan Colby and the CIA*. New York: Basic Books, 2013.
Zegart, Amy. "The Value of Cheap Fights: Drones and the Future of Coercion." *Journal of Strategic Studies* 43/1 (February 2018): 6–46.

History

Adair, Bianca. "The Quiet Warrior: Rear Admiral Sidney Souers and the Emergence of CIA's Covert Authority." *Studies in Intelligence* 65/2 (June 2021): 1–18.
Agee, Philip. *Inside the Company: CIA Diary*. New York: Penguin, 1975.
Anderson, Elizabeth E. "The Security Dilemma and Covert Action: The Truman Years." *International Journal of Intelligence and Counterintelligence* 11/4 (1998): 403–27.
Anderson, Scott. *The Quiet Americans: Four CIA Spies at the Dawn of the Cold War—A Tragedy in Three Acts*. New York: Doubleday, 2020.
Andrew, Christopher. *For the President's Eyes Only*. New York: HarperCollins, 1995.
Andrew, Christopher. *The Secret World: A History of Intelligence*. New York: Penguin, 2018.
Bailey, Norman. *The Strategic Plan that Won the Cold War: National Security Decision Directive 75*, 2d ed. McLean, VA: Potomac Foundation, 1998.
Barnes, Trevor. "The Secret Cold War: The CIA and American Foreign Policy in Europe, 1946–1956, Parts I and II." *Historical Journal* 24 (June 1981): 399–415; and 25 (September 1982): 649–70.
Barnes, Trevor. "Democratic Deception: American Covert Operations in Post-War Europe." In David A. Charters and Maurice A. J. Tugwell, eds., *Deception Operations: Studies in the East-West Context*, 297–305. London: Brassey's, 1990.

Bissell, Richard. "Reflections on the Bay of Pigs: Operation ZAPATA." *Strategic Review* 8 (Fall 1984): 66–70.
C. (an anonymous abbreviation), Leslie, and Peter Sichel. "Book Reviews, Intelligence in Public Media." *Studies in Intelligence* 64/4 (December 2020): 45–51.
Clarridge, Duane R. *A Spy for All Seasons: My Life in the CIA*. New York: Scribner's, 1997.
Cline, Ray S. *The CIA Under Reagan, Bush and Casey*. Washington, DC: Acropolis, 1981.
Codevilla, Angelo. "The CIA: What Have Three Decades Wrought." *Strategic Review* (Winter 1980): 68–71.
Cogan, Charles G. "The In-Culture of the DO." *Intelligence and National Security* 8 (January 1993): 78–86.
Cogan, Charles G. "Hunters Not Gathers: Intelligence in the Twenty-First Century." *Intelligence and National Security* 19/2 (2004): 304–21.
Colby, William E. *Lost Victory: A Firsthand Account of America's Sixteen-Year Involvement in Vietnam*. Chicago: Contemporary Books, 1989.
Colby, William E. "Skis and Daggers." *Studies in Intelligence* (Winter 1999–2000): 53–60.
Corke, Sarah-Jane. *US Covert Operations and Cold War Strategy: Truman, Secret Warfare and the CIA, 1947–53*. London: Routledge, 2008.
Corke, Sarah-Jane. "The Eisenhower Administration and Psychological Warfare." *Intelligence and National Security* 24/2 (April 2009): 156–74.
Cormac, Rory. "Techniques of Covert Propaganda: The British Approach in the Mid-1960s." *Intelligence and National Security* 34/7 (December 2019): 1064–69.
Curry, Cecil B. *Edward Lansdale: The Unquiet American*. Boston: Houghton Mifflin, 1988.
Darling, Arthur B. *The Central Intelligence Agency: An Instrument of Government, to 1950*. University Park: Pennsylvania State University Press, 1990.
Downes, Alexander B., and Mary Lauren Lilley. "Overt Peace, Covert War? Covert Intervention and the Democratic Peace." *Security Studies* 19/2 (2010): 266–306.
Dravis, Michael W. "Storming Fortress Albania: American Covert Operations in Microcosm, 1949–54." *Intelligence and National Security* 7/4 (October 1992): 99–123.
Dujmovic, Nicholas. Book review tweet. Center for the Study of Intelligence, CIA (March 29, 2010).
Dujmovic, Nicholas. "Drastic Actions Short of War: The Origins and Application of CIA's Covert Paramilitary Function in the Early Cold War." *Journal of Military History* 76/3 (July 2012): 21–36.
Dujmovic, Nicholas. "Review Essay: Covert Action to Promote Democracy in China During the Cold War." *Studies in Intelligence* 64/4 (December 2020): 31–35.
Eizenstat, Stuart E. *President Carter: The White House Years*. New York: St. Martin's Press, 2018.
Evan, Thomas. *The Very Best Men: The Daring Early Years of the CIA*. New York: Simon & Schuster, 1995.
Eveland, Wilbur Crane. *Ropes of Sand: America's Failure in the Middle East*. New York: Norton, 1980.
Frost, David. "Interview with Richard Helms." *Studies in Intelligence* (September 1993).
Gaddis, John Lewis. *The United States and the Origins of the Cold War, 1941–47*. New York: Columbia University Press, 1972.
Gates, Robert M. *From the Shadows*. New York: Simon & Schuster, 1996.
Gerber, Theodore P., and Jane Zavisca. "Does Russian Propaganda Work?" *Washington Quarterly* 39/2 (2016): 79–98.

SELECTED BIBLIOGRAPHY

Gerecht, Reuel Marc. "Blundering Through History with the C.I.A." *New York Times* (April 23, 2000): A 24.

Glennon, Michael J. *National Security and Double Government*. New York: Oxford University Press, 2015.

Grose, Peter. *Gentleman Spy*. Boston: Houghton Mifflin, 1994.

Grose, Peter. *Operation Rollback: America's Secret War Behind the Iron Curtain*. Boston: Houghton Mifflin, 2000.

Grow, Michael. *U.S. Presidents and Latin American Interventions: Pursuing Regime Change in the Cold War*. Lawrence: University Press of Kansas, 2008.

Gup, Ted. *The Book of Honor: The Secret Lives and Deaths of CIA Operatives*. New York: Doubleday, 2000.

Hamilton, John Maxwell. *Manipulating the Masses: Woodrow Wilson and the Birth of American Propaganda*. Baton Rouge: Louisiana State University Press, 2020.

Hazard, Elizabeth. *Cold War Crucible*. Boulder, CO: East European Monographs, 1996.

Hersh, Burton. *The Old Boys: The American Elite and the Origins of the CIA*. New York: Scribner's, 1992.

Hixson, Walter L. *Parting the Curtain: Propaganda, Culture and the Cold War, 1945–1964*. London: St. Martin's Press, 1997.

Holm, Richard L. "Recollections of a Case Officer in Laos, 1962–1964." *Studies in Intelligence* 47/1 (2003): 1–17.

Immerman, Richard H. *The Hidden Hand: A Brief History of the CIA*. Chichester, UK: Wiley, 2014.

Jeans, Roger. *The CIA and Third Force Movements in China During the Early Cold War*. New York: Lexington, 2018.

Jeffreys-Jones, Rhodri. *The CIA and American Democracy*, 3d. ed. New Haven, CT: Yale University Press, 2003.

Jeffreys-Jones, Rhodri. "American Espionage: Lessons from History." *Brown Journal of World Affairs* 26/1 (Fall/Winter 2019): 93–106.

Johnson, Loch K. *America's Secret Power: The CIA in a Democratic Society*. New York: Oxford University Press, 1986.

Karalekas, Anne. "A History of Covert Action." In Supplementary Detailed Staff Reports on Foreign and Military Intelligence, Book IV, *Final Report*. Select Committee to Study Governmental Operations with Respect to Intelligence Activities (Church Committee), Report No. 94-755, US Senate, 94th Cong., 2d Sess. (April 23, 1976): 25–93.

Kessler, Ronald. *Inside the CIA: Revealing the Secrets of the World's Most Powerful Spy Agency*. New York: Simon & Schuster, 1992.

Kibbe, Jennifer D. "Covert Action and the Pentagon." In Loch K. Johnson, ed., *Strategic Intelligence: Covert Action, Behind the Veils of Secret Foreign Policy*, vol. 3: 131–44. Westport, CT: Praeger Security International, 2007.

Kilmeade, Brian, and Don Yaeger. *Thomas Jefferson and the Tripoli Pirates: The Forgotten War That Changed American History*. New York: Random House, 2015.

Kinzer, Stephen. *Overthrow: America's Century of Regime Change from Hawaii to Iraq*. New York: Times Books, 2006.

Kinzer, Stephen. *The Brothers: John Foster Dulles, Allen Dulles, and Their Secret World War*. New York: Holt, 2013.

Knott, Stephen F. *Secret and Sanctioned: Covert Operations and the American Presidency*. New York: Oxford University Press, 1996.

Leary, William M. "CIA Air Operations in Laos, 1955–1974." *Studies in Intelligence* 43/3 (Winter 1999–2000): 16–24.

Leary, William M. *Perilous Missions: Civil Air Transport and CIA Covert Operations in Asia.* Tuscaloosa: University of Alabama Press, 1984.

Leary, William M., ed. *The Central Intelligence Agency: History and Documents.* Tuscaloosa: University of Alabama Press, 1984.

Leary, William M., and William Stueck. "The Chennault Plan to Save China: U.S. Containment in Asia and the Origin of the CIA's Aerial Empire, 1949–1950." *Diplomatic History* 8 (Fall 1984): 149–64.

Loory, Stuart H. "The CIA's Use of the Press: 'A Mighty Wurlitzer.'" *Columbia Journalism Review* (September/October 1974): 8–18.

Marchetti, Victor, and John D. Marks. *The CIA and the Cult of Intelligence.* New York: Knopf, 1974.

Marchetti, Victor. "Propaganda and Disinformation: How the CIA Manufactures History." *Journal of Historical Review* 9 (Fall 1989): 305–320.

McGehee, Ralph W. *Deadly Deceits: My 25 Years in the CIA.* New York: Sheridan Square, 1983.

McNeil, Phyllis Provost. In the Aspin-Brown Commission. "The Evolution of the U.S. Intelligence Community—An Historical Perspective." *Preparing for the 21st Century: An Appraisal of U.S. Intelligence, Report of the Commission on the Roles and Capabilities of the United States Intelligence Community* (March 1, 1996), Appendix A: A1–!25. Reprinted in Loch K. Johnson and James J. Wirtz, eds.. *Intelligence: The Secret World of Spies,* 5th ed. New York: Oxford University Press, 2019: 5–22.

Moran, Christopher. *Company Confessions: Revealing CIA Secrets.* London: Biteback, 2015.

Morley, Jefferson. *Our Man in Mexico: Winston Scott and the Hidden History of the CIA.* Lawrence: University Press of Kansas, 2008.

Moseman, Scott A. "Truman and the Formation of the Central Intelligence Agency." *Journal of Intelligence History* 19/2 (June 2020): 149–66.

Nashel, Jonathan. *Edward Lansdale's Cold War.* Amherst: University of Massachusetts Press, 2005.

National Security Archives. George Washington University, Washington, D.C.

O'Brien, Kevin A. "Interfering with Civil Society: CIA and KGB Covert Political Action During the Cold War." *International Journal of Intelligence and Counterintelligence* 8 (Winter 1995): 431–56.

O'Brien, Kevin A. "Covert Action: The 'Quiet Option' in International Statecraft." In Loch K. Johnson, ed., *Strategic Intelligence: Covert Action, Behind the Veils of Secret Foreign Policy.* vol. 3: 23–60. Westport, CT: Praeger Security International, 2007.

O'Toole, G. J. A. *Honorable Treachery: A History of US Intelligence, Espionage, and Covert Action from the American Revolution to the CIA.* New York: Atlantic Monthly Press, 1991.

Peake, Hayden B. "Harry S. Truman on CIA Covert Operations." *Studies in Intelligence* 25/1 (Spring 1980): 31–41.

Peterzell, Jay. *Reagan's Secret Wars.* Washington, DC: Center for National Security Studies, 1984.

Pike Committee. "The CIA Report the President Doesn't Want You to Read: The Pike Papers." *Village Voice* (February 16 and 23, 1975).

Powers, Thomas. *The Man Who Kept the Secrets: Richard Helms and the CIA.* New York: Knopf, 1979.

Prados, John. *President's Secret Wars: CIA and Pentagon Covert Operations Since World War II*. New York: William Morrow, 1986.

Prados, John. *Safe for Democracy: The Secret Wars of the CIA*. Chicago: Ivan R. Dee, 2006.

Prados, John. *The Family Jewels: The CIA, Secrecy, and Presidential Power*. Austin: University of Texas Press, 2013.

Prados, John, and Arturo Jimenez-Bacardi, eds. *New Collection of Declassified Documents Illuminates the Role of Presidents and Top Advisers in Guiding and Sanctioning CIA Activities from Cuba to Africa, 1961–1974*. National Security Archives Briefing Book #667. Washington, DC (March 4, 2019).

Rositzke, Harry. *The CIA's Secret Operations: Espionage, Counterespionage, and Covert Action*. Pleasantville, NY: Reader's Digest Press, 1977.

Rudgers, David F. "The Origins of Covert Action." *Journal of Contemporary History* 35/2 (April 2000).

Rudgers, David F. *Creating the Secret State: The Origins of the Central Intelligence Agency, 1943–1947*. Lawrence: University Press of Kansas, 2000.

Schlesinger, Arthur M. Jr. *The Imperial Presidency*. New York: Popular Library, 1974.

Schweizer, Peter. *The Reagan Administration's Secret Strategy That Hastened the Collapse of the Soviet Union*. New York: Atlantic Monthly Press, 1994.

Scott, James M., and Jerel A. Rosati. "'Such Other Functions and Duties': Covert Action and American Intelligence Policy." In Loch K. Johnson, ed., *Strategic Intelligence: Covert Action, Behind the Veils of Secret Foreign Policy*, vol. 3: 83–106. Westport CT: Praeger Security International, 2007.

Scott-Smith, Giles. *The Politics of Apolitical Culture: The Congress for Cultural Freedom, the CIA and Postwar American Hegemony*. London: Routledge, 2002.

Shackley, Ted, with Richard A. Finney. *Spymaster: My Life in the CIA*. Lincoln: University Press of Nebraska/Potomac, 2005.

Smith, Richard Harris. *OSS: The Secret History of America's First Central Intelligence Agency*. Guilford, CT: Lyons, 2005.

Stern, Gary. "Covert Action and the Bush Administration." *First Principles* 15/1 (February 1990): 4–5.

Stockton, Bayard. *Flawed Patriot: The Rise and Fall of CIA Legend Bill Harvey*. Washington, DC: Potomac Books, 2006.

Saunders, Frances Stonor. *Who Paid the Piper? The CIA and the Cultural Cold War*. London: Granta, 1999.

Stuart, D. T. *Creating the National Security State: A History of the Law that Transformed America*. Princeton, NJ: Princeton University Press, 2008.

Talbot, David. *The Devil's Chessboard: Allen Dulles, the CIA, and the Risk of America's Secret Government*. New York: Harper, 2015.

Tonsetic, Robert L. *Special Operations in the American Revolution*. New York: Casemate, 2013.

Troy, Thomas F. *Donovan and the CIA: A History of the Establishment of the Central Intelligence Agency*. Frederick, MD: University Publications of America, 1981.

Truman, Harry S. *Memoirs*, vol. 2: *Years of Trial and Hope: 1946–1952*. Garden City, NY: Doubleday, 1956.

Truman, Harry S. "Limit CIA Role to Intelligence." *Washington Post* (December 22, 1963): A11.

Turner, Stansfield. *Secrecy and Democracy: The CIA in Transition*. Boston: Houghton Mifflin, 1985.

Turner, Stansfield. *Burn Before Reading: Presidents, CIA Directors, and Secret Intelligence*. New York: Hyperion, 2005.

US Government, Select Committee to Study Governmental Operations with Respect to Intelligence Activities (Church Committee). "The CIA Assassination Plot in the Congo, 1960–61." *Alleged Assassination Plots Involving Foreign Leaders: An Interim Report*, US Senate, 94th Cong., 2d Sess. (November, 1975).

US Government. "Covert Action in Chile." *Hearings*, Select Committee to Study Governmental Operations with Respect to Intelligence Activities (Church Committee), US Senate, 94th Cong., 1st Sess. (December 4 and 5, 1975).

US Government, Select Committee to Study Governmental Operations with Respect to Intelligence Activities (Church Committee). *Final Report*. US Senate, 95th Cong., 1st Sess. (1976).

Wallace, Robert. "The Barbary Wars." *Smithsonian* 5 (January 1975): 82–91.

Walters, Vernon A. *Silent Missions*. New York: Doubleday, 1978.

Weiner, Tim. *Legacy of Ashes: The History of the CIA*. New York: Doubleday, 2007.

Whitlock, Craig. *The Afghanistan Papers: A Secret History of the War*. New York, Simon & Schuster, 2021.

Wilford, Hugh. *The Mighty Wurlitzer: How the CIA Played America*. Cambridge, MA: Harvard University Press, 2008.

Wilford, Hugh. *America's Great Game: The CIA's Secret Arabists and the Shaping of the Modern Middle East*. New York: Basic Books, 2013.

Willmetts, Simon. "Quiet Americans: The CIA in Early Cold War Culture." *Journal of American Studies* 47/1 (2013): 127–47.

Winters, Francis X. *The Year of the Hare: America in Vietnam, January 25, 1963–February 15, 1964*. Athens: University of Georgia Press, 1997.

Wittner, Lawrence S. *American Intervention in Greece, 1943–1949: A Study in Counterrevolution*. New York: Columbia University Press, 1986.

Yoon, Mi Yung. "Explaining U.S. Intervention in Third World Internal Wars, 1945–1989." *Journal of Conflict Resolution* 41/4 (1997): 580–602.

Zegart, Amy. *Flawed by Design: The Evolution of the CIA, JCS, and NSC*. Stanford, CA: Hoover Institution Press, 2001.

Case Studies

Abrahamian, Ervand. *The Coup: 1953, the CIA, and the Roots of Modern U.S.-Iranian Relations*. New York: New Press, 2012.

Ahern, Thomas L. Jr. *The Way We Do Things: Black Entry Operations into North Vietnam, 1961–64*. Center for the Study of Intelligence. Washington, DC: Central Intelligence Agency, 2005.

Ahern, Thomas L. Jr. *Undercover Armies: CIA and Surrogate Warfare in Laos*. Washington, DC: Center for the Study of Intelligence (CIA), 2006.

Ahern, Thomas L. Jr. *Declassified: CIA and Counterinsurgency in Vietnam*. Lexington: University Press of Kentucky, 2009.

Alvandi, Roham, and Mark J. Gasiorowski. "The United States Overthrew Iran's Last Democratic Leader." *Foreign Policy Online* (October 20, 2019).

Ambrose, Stephen E., with Richard H. Immerman. *Ike's Spies: Eisenhower and the Intelligence Establishment*. New York: Anchor Books, 1981.

Baer, Robert. *See No Evil*. New York: Crown, 2002.

Barrett, David M. "Congress, the CIA, and Guatemala." *Studies in Intelligence* 45/10 (Winter– Spring 2002): 23–30.

Bayandor, Darioush. *Iran and the CIA: The Fall of Mosaddeq Revisited*. New York: Palgrave Macmillan, 2010.

Bearden, Milt. "Lessons from Afghanistan." *New York Times* (March 2, 1998): A17.

Bearden, Milt, and James Risen. *The Main Enemy: The Inside Story of the CIA's Final Showdown with the KGB*. New York: Random House, 2003.

Békés, Csaba. "The 1956 Hungarian Revolution and World Politics." *Cold War International History Project, Working Paper No. 16*. Washington, DC: Woodrow Wilson International Center for Scholars, 1956.

Bergen, Peter L. *Manhunt: The Ten-Year Search for Bin Laden from 9/11 to Abbottabad*. New York: Crown, 2012.

Bernstein, Carl, and Marco Politi. *His Holiness, John Paul II and the Hidden History of Our Time*. New York: Doubleday, 1996.

Berntsen, Gary, and Ralph Pezzullo. *Jawbreaker: The Attack on Bin Laden and Al-Qaeda: A Personal Account by the CIA's Key Field Commander*. New York: Crown, 2005.

Bittman, Ladislav. *The Deception Game*. Syracuse, NY: Syracuse University Press, 1972.

Blight, James G., and Peter Kornbluh, eds. *Politics of Illusion: The Bay of Pigs Invasion Reexamined*. Boulder, CO: Lynne Rienner, 1998.

Bohning, Don. *The Castro Obsession: U.S. Covert Operations Against Cuba, 1959–1965*. New York: Oxford University Press, 2005.

Boot, Max. *The Road Not Taken: Edward Lansdale and the American Tragedy in Vietnam*. New York: Norton/Liveright, 2018.

Bowden, Mark. *Guests of the Ayatollah: The First Battle in America's War with Militant Islam*. New York: Atlantic Monthly Press, 2006.

Brands, Hal. "Making the Conspiracy Theorist a Prophet: Covert Action and the Contours of United States-Iraq Relations." *International History Review* 33/3 (2011): 381–408.

Carbonell, Néstor T. *Why Cuba Matters: New Threats in America's Backyard*. New York: Archway/Simon & Schuster, 2020.

Callather, Nick. *Secret History: The CIA's Classified Account of Its Operations in Guatemala, 1952–1954*. Palo Alto, CA: Stanford University Press, 1999.

Carson, Austin. "Facing Off and Saving Face: Covert Intervention and Escalation Management in the Korean War." *International Organization* 70 (Winter 2016): 103–31.

Chapman, Peter. *Bananas: How the United Fruit Company Shaped the World*. New York: Grove Atlantic, 2008.

Charters, David A. "Breaking Cover: The Bay of Pigs Intervention." In David A. Charters and Maurice A.J. Tugwell, eds., *Deception Operations: Studies in the East–West Context*, 353–55. London: Brassey's, 1990.

Chesney, Robert. "Who May Be Killed? Anwar Al-Awlaki as a Case Study in the International Legal Regulation of Lethal Force." *Yearbook of International Humanitarian Law* 13 (August 2010): 6–8.

Church Committee. *Alleged Assassination Plots Involving Foreign Leaders*. S. Rept. 94-465. Washington, DC: US Government Printing Office, November 20, 1975.

Church Committee. "Covert Action in Chile: 1963–1973." *Staff Reports*. Washington, DC: US Government Printing Office, December 1975.

Cockburn, Leslie. *Out of Control: The Story of the Reagan Administration's Secret War in Nicaragua, the Illegal Arms Pipeline, and the Contra Drug Connection.* New York: Atlantic Monthly Press, 1987.

Cogan, Charles G. "Partners in Time: The CIA and Afghanistan." *World Policy Journal* 10 (Summer 1993): 73–82.

Cohen, Eliot A. "'Only Have the Battle': American Intelligence and the Chinese Intervention in Korea, 1950." *Intelligence and National Security* 5/1 (January 1990): 243–56.

Colby, Jacob. *The Business of Empire: United Fruit, Race, and U.S. Expansion in Central America.* Ithaca, NY: Cornell University Press, 2001.

Colby, William E., and Peter Forbath. *Honorable Men: My Life in the CIA.* New York: Simon & Schuster, 1978.

Coll, Steve. *Ghost Wars: The Secret History of the CIA, Afghanistan, and Bin Laden, from the Soviet Invasion to September 10, 2011.* New York: Penguin, 2004.

Coll, Steve. *Directorate S: The C.I.A. and America's Secret Wars in Afghanistan and Pakistan.* New York: Penguin, 2018.

Conboy, Kenneth. *The Cambodian Wars: Clashing Armies and CIA Covert Operations.* Lawrence: University Press of Kansas, 2013.

Conboy, Kenneth, and James Morrison. *The CIA's Secret War in Tibet.* Lawrence: University Press of Kansas, 2011.

Conboy, Kenneth, and James Morrison. *Feet to the Fire: CIA Covert Operations in Indonesia, 1957–1958.* Annapolis: Naval Institute Press, 1999.

Cormac, Rory. "Disruption and Deniable Interventionism: Explaining the Appeal of Covert Action and Special Forces in Contemporary British Policy." *International Relations* 31/2 (2017): 169–91.

Cormac, Rory. *Disrupt and Deny: Spies, Special Forces, and the Secret Pursuit of British Foreign Policy.* Oxford, England: Oxford University Press, 2018.

Cormac, Rory, and Oliver Daddow. "Covert Action Failure and Fiasco Construction: William Hague's 2011 Libyan Venture." *Journal of European Public Policy* 25/5 (2018): 690–707.

Cottam, Richard W. *Iran and the United States: A Cold War Case Study.* Pittsburgh: University of Pittsburgh Press, 1988.

Crile, George. *Charlie Wilson's War.* New York: Grove, 2003.

Crumpton, Henry A. *The Art of Intelligence.* New York: Penguin, 2012.

Cullather, Nick. *Secret History: The CIA's Classified Account of Its Operations in Guatemala, 1952–1954.* Stanford, CA: Stanford University Press, 1999.

Deeks, Ashley. "Arming Syrian Rebels: Lethal Assistance and International Law." *Lawfare* (May 1, 2013).

Devlin, Larry. *Chief of Station: Fighting the Cold War in a Hot Zone.* New York: Public Affairs, 2007.

Draper, Theodore. *A Very Thin Line: The Iran-Contra Affairs.* New York: Hill and Wang, 1991.

Duffy, Gloria, "Crisis Mangling and the Cuban Brigade." *International Security* 8 (Summer 1983): 67–87.

Faddis, Charles S. *The CIA War in Kurdistan: The Untold Story of the Northern Front in the Iraq War.* Havertown, PA: Casemate, 2020.

Fischer, Benjamin B. "Solidarity, the CIA, and Western Technology." *International Journal of Intelligence and Counterintelligence* 25/3 (2012): 427–69.

Fraser, Andrew. "Architecture of a Broken Dream: The CIA and Guatemala, 1952–54," *Intelligence and National Security* 20/3 (September 2005): 234–51.
Gasiorowski, Mark J., and Malcolm Byrne, eds. *Mohammad Mossadeq and the 1953 Coup in Iran*. Syracuse, NY: Syracuse University Press, 2003.
Gasiorowski, Mark J. "The 1953 Coup D'Etat in Iran." *International Journal of Middle East Studies* 19/3 (August 1987): 261–86.
Gadney, Reg. *Cry Hungary! Uprising 1956*. New York: Atheneum, 1986.
Gleijeses, Piero. "Ships in the Night: The CIA, the White House and the Bay of Pigs." *Journal of Latin American Studies* 27/1 (1995): 1–42.
Gleijeses, Piero. *Shattered Hope: The Guatemalan Revolution and the United States, 1944–1954*. New York: Cambridge University Press, 1999.
Gleijeses, Piero. "The CIA's Paramilitary Operations During the Cold War: An Assessment." *Cold War History* 16/3 (2016): 291–306.
Goode, James A. *The United States and Iran: In the Shadow of Musaddiq*. New York: Palgrave Macmillan, 1997.
Gorst, Anthony, and W. Scott Lucas. "The Other Collusion: Operation Straggle and Anglo-American Intervention in Syria, 1955–1956." *Intelligence and National Security* 4 (Summer 1989): 576–95.
Granville, Johanna C. *The First Domino: International Decision Making During the Hungarian Crisis of 1956*. College Station: Texas A&M University Press, 2004.
Granville, Johanna C. "Caught with Jam on Our Fingers: Radio Free Europe and the Hungarian Revolution in 1956." *Diplomatic History* 29/5 (2005): 234–56.
Grenier, Robert L. *88 Days to Kandahar: A CIA Diary*. New York: Simon & Schuster, 2008.
Grile, George. *Charlie Wilson's War*. New York: Grove, 2003.
Gustafson, Kristian C. "CIA Machinations in Chile in 1970: Reexamining the Record." 47 *Studies in Intelligence* 3 (2003): 35–50.
Gustafson, Kristian C. *Hostile Intent: U.S. Covert Operations in Chile, 1964–1974*. Washington, DC: Potomac Books, 2007.
Gustafson, Kristian C., and Christopher Andrew. "The Other Hidden Hand: Soviet and Cuban Intelligence in Allende's Chile." *Intelligence and National Security* 33/3 (2018): 407–21.
Hamilton-Merritt, Jane. *Tragic Mountain: The Hmong, the Americans, and the Secret Wars for Laos, 1942–1992*. Bloomington: Indiana University Press, 1999.
Handy, Jim. *Revolution in the Countryside: Rural Conflict and Agrarian Reform in Guatemala, 1944–1954*. Chapel Hill: University of North Carolina Press, 1994.
Higgins, Trumbull. *The Perfect Failure: Kennedy, Eisenhower, and the CIA at the Bay of Pigs*. New York: Norton, 1987.
Haslam, Jonathan. *The Nixon Administration and the Death of Allende's Chile: A Case of Assisted Suicide*. London: Verso, 2005.
Immerman, Richard H. *The CIA in Guatemala: The Foreign Policy of Intervention*. Austin: University of Texas Press, 1982.
Inouye-Hamilton Joint Committee. "Witness Testimony: Iran-Contra Affair." *Hearings*. 100 Cong., 1st Sess., U.S. House and Senate (July/August 1987).
Inouye-Hamilton Joint Committee. *Report*, S. Rept. No. 100-216 and H. Rept. No. 100-433. Select Committee on Secret Military Assistance to Iran and the Nicaraguan Opposition, 100 Cong., 1st Sess., US House and Senate (November 1987).
Jackson, Wayne G. *Allen Welsh Dulles as Director of Central Intelligence: Covert Activities*, vol. III (declassified on April 26, 1994).

Johnson, A. Ross. *Radio Free Europe and Radio Liberty: The CIA Years and Beyond.* Stanford, CA: Stanford University Press, 2010.

Johnston, James H. *Murder, Inc.: The CIA Under John F. Kennedy.* Lincoln: University of Nebraska Press, 2019.

Jones, Clive. "'Where the State Feared to Tread': Britain, Britons, Covert Action and the Yemen Civil War, 1962–64." *Intelligence and National Security* 21/5 (2006): 717–37.

Jones, Clive. *Britain and the Yemen Civil War, 1962–1965: Ministers, Mercenaries and Mandarins: Foreign Policy and the Limits of Covert Action.* Brighton, UK: Sussex Academic Press, 2010.

Jones, Howard. *The Bay of Pigs.* New York: Oxford University Press, 2010.

Jones, Matthew. "'The Preferred Plan': The Anglo-American Working Group Report on Covert Action in Syria, 1957." *Intelligence and National Security* 19/3 (2004): 401–15.

Jones, Seth G. *A Covert Action: Reagan, the CIA, and the Cold War Struggle in Poland.* New York: Norton, 2018.

Kahana, Ephraim. "Covert Action: The Israeli Experience," in Loch K. Johnson, ed., *Strategic Intelligence: Covert Action, Behind the Veils of Secret Foreign Policy,* vol. 3: 61-82. Westport, CT: Praeger Security International, 2007.

Kaufman, Michael T. *Mad Dreams, Saving Graces: Poland, A Nation in Conspiracy.* New York: Random House, 1989.

Kim, Jaechun, and David Hundt. "Popular Consent and Foreign Policy Choices: War Against the Philippines and Covert Action in Chile." *Australian Journal of International Affairs* 66/1 (2012): 52–69.

Koh, Harold Hongju. "Why the President (Almost) Always Wins in Foreign Affairs: Lessons of the Iran-Contra Affair." *Yale Law Journal* 97 (June 1988): 1255–342.

Kornbluh, Peter, ed. *Bay of Pigs Declassified: The Secret CIA Report on the Invasion of Cuba.* New York: New Press, 1998.

Krishnan, Armin. "Controlling Partners and Proxies in Pro-Insurgency Paramilitary Operations: The Case of Syria." *Intelligence and National Security* 34/4 (June 2019): 544–60.

Kurlantzick, Joshua. *A Great Place to Have a War: America in Laos and the Birth of a Military CIA.* New York: Simon & Schuster, 2016.

Lemarchand, Rene. "The CIA in Africa." *Journal of Modern African Studies* (September 1976): 401–26.

Lindsey, Jon R. "Stuxnet and the Limits of Cyber Warfare." *Security Studies* 22/3 (2013): 363–404.

Little, Douglas. "Cold War and Covert Action: Syria 1945–58." *Middle Eastern Journal* (Winter 1990): 69–75.

Lockhart, James. *Chile, the CIA and the Cold War: A Transatlantic Perspective.* Edinburgh: Edinburgh University Press, 2019.

Lucas, Scott, and Alistair More. "The Hidden Alliance: The CIA and MI-6 Before and After Suez." *Intelligence and National Security* 15 (Summer 2000): 95–120.

Lundberg, Kirsten. "Politics of a Covert Action: The U.S., the Mujahideen, and the Stinger Missile." *Intelligence Studies Case No. 1566.0.* Kennedy School of Government, Harvard University (November 9, 1999).

McGehee, Ralph W. "The C.I.A. and the White Paper on El Salvador." *Nation* (April 11, 1981): 423–25.

McGehee, Ralph W. *Deadly Deceits: My 25 Years in the CIA.* New York: Sheridan Square, 1983.

Maddrell, Paul. "Corruption, Oligarchy and the Covert Action of the Putin Crime Family." Paper, Panel on "Covert Action in Today's Globalizing World." International Studies Association, Annual Meeting, Toronto, Canada (March 27, 2019).

Marchio, James D. "Resistance Potential and Rollback: US Intelligence and the Eisenhower Administration's Policies Toward Eastern Europe, 1953–56." *Intelligence and National Security* 10/2 (April 1995): 145–64.

Mawby, Spencer, "The Clandestine Defence of Empire: British Special Operations in Yemen, 1951–64." *Intelligence and National Security* 17/3 (2002): 105–30.

Mazzetti, Mark. *The Way of the Knife: The CIA, a Secret Army, and a War at the Ends of the Earth*. New York: Penguin, 2013.

McCurdo, Torey L. "The Economics of Overthrow: The United States, Britain and the Hidden Justification of Operations TPAJAX." *Studies in Intelligence* 56/2 (2012): 12–18.

Miller, James E. "Taking Off the Gloves: The United States and the Italian Elections of 1948." *Diplomatic History* 7/1 (Winter 1983).

Ofgang, Eric. "School of Spies." *Connecticut Magazine* (October 2020): 51–63.

Omang, Joanne. "A Historical Background to the CIA's Nicaragua Manual." In *The CIA's Nicaragua Manual: Psychological Operations in Guerrilla Warfare*. New York: Vintage, 1985.

Osgood, Kenneth. *Total Cold War: Eisenhower's Secret Propaganda Battle at Home and Abroad*. Lawrence: University Press of Kansas, 2006.

Parker, James E. *Code-Name Mule: The CIA's Secret War in Laos*. Annapolis, MD: United States Naval Institute Press, 1992.

Persico, Joseph E. *Casey: From the OSS to the CIA*. New York: Viking, 1990.

Pisani, Sallie. *The CIA and the Marshall Plan*. Lawrence: University Press of Kansas, 1991.

Prados, John. *William Colby and the CIA: The Secret Wars of a Controversial Spymaster*. Lawrence: University Press of Kansas, 2007.

Qureshi, Lubna K. *Nixon, Kissinger, and Allende: U.S. Involvement in the 1973 Coup in Chile*. Lanham, MD: Lexington Books, 2009.

Rabe, Stephen G. *US Intervention in British Guiana: A Cold War Story*. Chapel Hill: University of North Carolina Press, 2005.

Rahnema, Ali. *Behind the 1953 Coup in Iran: Thugs, Turncoats, Soldiers, and Spooks*. London: Cambridge University Press, 2014.

Rasenberger, Jim. *The Brilliant Disaster: JFK, Castro, and America's Doomed Invasion of Cuba's Bay of Pigs*. New York: Scribner's, 2011.

Reisch, Alfred A. *Hot Books in the Cold War: The CIA-Funded Secret Western Book Distribution Program Behind the Iron Curtain*. Budapest: Central European University Press, 2013.

Risen, James. *State of War: The Secret History of the CIA and the Bush Administration*. New York: Simon & Schuster, 2006.

Robarge, David. "CIA's Covert Operations in the Congo: 1960–1968: Insights from Newly Declassified Documents." *Studies in Intelligence* 58 (September 2014): 1–9.

Roosevelt, Kermit. *Countercoup: The Struggle for the Control of Iran*. New York: McGraw-Hill, 1979.

Sanger, David E. *Confront and Conceal: Obama's Secret Wars and Surprising Use of American Power*. New York: Broadway Paperbacks (Random House), 2012.

Schlesinger, Stephen, and Stephen Kinzer. *Bitter Fruit: The Story of the American Coup in Guatemala*. Cambridge, MA: Harvard University Press, 2005.

Schroen, Gary C. *First In: How the CIA Spearheaded the War on Terror in Afghanistan.* New York: Random House, 2005.
Shane, Scott. *Objective Troy.* New York: Tim Duggan Books, 2015.
Shimer, David. "When the CIA Interferes in Foreign Elections." *Foreign Affairs This Week,* 1–16. www.foreignaffairs.com (June 21, 2020):
Shultz, Richard H., and Roy Godson. *Dezinformatsia: Active Measures in Soviet Strategy.* New York: Pergamon-Brassey, 1984.
Sigmund, Paul E. *The Overthrow of Allende and the Politics of Chile, 1964–1976.* Pittsburgh: University of Pittsburgh Press, 1977.
Smith, Joseph Burkholder. *Portrait of a Cold Warrior.* New York: Putnam, 1976.
Smith, Joseph Burkholder. "The CIA in Vietnam: Nation-Builders, Old Pros, Paramilitary Boys, and Misplaced Persons." *Washington Monthly* (February 1978): 23–30.
Snepp, Frank. *Decent Interval.* New York: Random House, 1977.
Takeyh, Ray. "The Other Carter Doctrine." *Foreign Affairs* (February 26, 2021).
Thomas, Ronald C. Jr. "Influences on Decision-making at the Bay of Pigs." *International Journal of Intelligence and Counterintelligence* 3 (Winter 1989): 537–48.
Triay, Victor. *Bay of Pigs: An Oral History of Brigade 2506.* Gainesville: University of Florida Press, 2001.
Tower Commission. *Report of the President's Special Review Board* [on the Iran-*contra* Affair]. Washington, DC: US Government, February 26, 1987.
Vandenbroucke, Lucien S. "Anatomy of a Failure: The Decision to Land at the Bay of Pigs." *Political Science Quarterly* 99/3 (1984): 471–91.
Walters, Vernon A. "The Uses of Political and Propaganda Covet Action in the 1980s." In Roy Godson, ed., *Intelligence Requirements for the 1980s: Covert Action.* Washington, DC: National Strategy Information Center, 1981.
Warner, Michael. *Hearts and Minds: Three Case Studies of the CIA's Covert Support of American Anti-Communist Groups in the Cold War, 1949–1967.* Langley, VA: Central Intelligence Agency, 1999.
Warner, Roger. *Backfire: The CIA's Secret War in Laos and Its Link to the War in Vietnam.* New York: Simon & Schuster, 1995. Updated as *Shooting at the Moon: The Story of America's Clandestine War in Laos.* Lebanon, NH: Steerforth Press, 1998.
Waters, Robert, and Gordon Daniels. "The World's Longest General Strike: The AFL-CIO, the CIA, and British Guiana." *Diplomatic History* 29/2 (April 2005): 279–307.
Waters, Ronald W. "The Clark Amendment: An Analysis of U.S. Policy Choices in Angola." *The Black Scholar: Journal of Black Studies and Research* 12 (July/August 1981): 2–11.
Weiner, Tim. "Covert Action in Iraq: Call in the CIA and Cross Your Fingers." *New York Times* (September 15, 1996), Sec. 4: 3.
Weissman, Stephen R. "CIA Covert Action in Zaire and Angola: Patterns and Consequences." *Political Science Quarterly* 94 (Summer 1979): 263–86.
Weissman, Stephen R. "An Extraordinary Rendition." *Intelligence and National Security* 25/2 (April 2010): 198–222.
Wilbur, Donald N. *CIA Clandestine Service History: Overthrow of Premier Mosaddeq of Iran, November 1952–August 1953.* Washington, DC: Central Intelligence Agency, March 1954 (declassified in 2000).
Wilford, Hugh. "'Essentially a Work of Fiction': Kermit 'Kim' Roosevelt, Imperial Romance, and the Iran Coup of 1953." *Diplomatic History* 40/5 (November 2016): 922–47.

Wise, David, and Thomas Ross. *The Invisible Government*. New York: Random House, 1964.
Woolsey, R. James. "Iraqi Dissidents Railroaded—by U.S." *Wall Street Journal* (June 10, 1998): A24.
Wyden, Peter. *Bay of Pigs: The Untold Story*. New York: Simon & Schuster, 1979.
Yoon, Mi Yung. "Explaining U.S. Intervention in Third World Internal Wars, 1945–1989." *Journal of Conflict Resolution* 41/4 (1997): 580–602.
Zilinskas, Raymond A. "Cuban Allegations of Biological Warfare by the United States: Assessing the Evidence." *Critical Reviews in Microbiology* 25/3 (1999): 173–227.

Policy and Legal Implications

Aspin, Les. "Covert Action: Questions to Answer." *First Principles* 6 (May 1981): 9–11.
Aspin-Brown Commission. *Preparing for the 21st Century: An Appraisal of U.S. Intelligence*. Commission on the Roles and Capabilities of the United States Intelligence Community. Washington, DC: US Government Printing Office, March 1, 1996.
Baker, James E. "From Cold War to Long War to Gray War: Covert Action and Drone Warfare in US Legal Context." In Loch K. Johnson, ed., *Essentials of Strategic Intelligence*. Santa Barbara, CA: ABC-Clio/Praeger, 2015.
Baker, James E. "Covert Action: United States Law in Substance, Process, and Practice." In Loch K. Johnson, ed., *The Oxford Handbook of National Security Intelligence*, 587–607. New York: Oxford University Press, 2010.
Baker, James E. "From Cold War to Long War: Covert Action in U.S. Legal Context." In Loch K. Johnson, ed., *Strategic Intelligence: Covert Action, Behind the Veils of Secret Foreign Policy*, 157–76. Westport, CT: Praeger Security International, 2007.
Barry, James A. "Managing Covert Political Action: Guideposts from Just War Theory." In Jan Goldman, ed., *Ethics of Spying*, 248–65. Lanham, MD: Scarecrow Press, 2006.
Bauer, Bob, and Jack Goldsmith. *After Trump: Reconstructing the Presidency*. Washington, DC: Lawfare Press, 2020.
Berkowitz, Bruce D., and Allan E. Goodman. "The Logic of Covert Action." *National Interest* 51 (Spring 1998): 38–46.
Berkowitz, Bruce D. "Is Assassination an Option?" *Hoover Digest* (2000): 1–5.
Best, Richard, and Andrew Feikert. *Special Operations Forces (SOF) and CIA Paramilitary Operations: Issues for Congress*. Washington, DC: Congressional Research Service Reports for Congress, 2006.
Boland, Edward P. "Covert Actions and the Congress." Letter to the Editor. *New York Times* (June 8, 1978): A26.
Brzezinski, Zbigniew. *Power and Principle: Memoirs of the National Security Advisor, 1977–1981*. New York: Farrar, Straus and Giroux, 1983.
Byman, Daniel, and Ian A. Merritt. "The New American Way of War: Special Operations Forces in the War of Terrorism." *Washington Quarterly* 41 (2018): 79–93.
Callanan, James. *Covert Action in the Cold War: US Policy, Intelligence, and CIA Operations*. New York: I. B. Tauris, 2010.
Charters, David A. "The Role of Intelligence Services in the Direction of Covert Paramilitary Operations." In Alfred C. Maurer et al., eds., *Intelligence: Policy and Process*. London: Westview, 1985.

Charters, David A., and Maurice A. J. Tugwell, eds. *Deception Operations: Studies in the East- West Context*. London: Brassey's, 1990.
Chomeau, John B. "Covert Action's Proper Role in U.S. Policy." *International Journal of Intelligence and Counterintelligence* 2 (Fall 1988): 407–13.
Clarke, Richard A. *Against All Enemies*. New York: Free Press, 2004.
Cline, Ray S. "Covert Action Is Needed for United States Security." In Don Mansfield and Gary J. Buckley, eds., *Conflict in American Foreign Policy*, 72–77. Englewood Cliffs, NJ: Prentice-Hall, 1985.
Cline, Ray S. "Covert Action as a Presidential Prerogative." *Harvard Journal for Law and Public Policy* 12/2 (Spring 1989): 357–70.
Cohen, William S., and George J. Mitchell. *Men of Zeal*. New York: Penguin, 1988.
Cooper, Chester L. "The CIA and Decisionmaking." *Foreign Affairs* 50 (January 1972): 223–36.
Cormac, Rory, and Richard J. Aldrich. "Grey Is the New Black: Covert Action and Implausible Deniability." *International Affairs* 94 (2018): 477–94.
Damrosch, Lori Fisler. "Politics Across Borders: Nonintervention and Nonforcible Influence over Domestic Affairs." *American Journal of International Law* 83 (January 1989): 6–13.
Daugherty, William J. "Covert Action: Strengths and Weaknesses." In Loch K. Johnson, ed., *The Oxford Handbook of National Security* Intelligence, 608–28. New York: Oxford University Press, 2010.
Daugherty, William J. "The Role of Covert Action." In Loch K. Johnson, ed., *Handbook of Intelligence Studies*, 279–88. New York: Routledge, 2007.
Daugherty, William J. "Political Action as a Tool of Presidential Statecraft." In Loch K. Johnson, ed., *Strategic Intelligence: Covert Action, Behind the Veils of Secret Foreign Policy*, vol. 3, 119–30. Westport, CT: Praeger Security International, 2007.
Daugherty, William J. "Approval and Review of Covert Action Programs Since Reagan." *International Journal of Intelligence and Counterintelligence* 17 (Spring 2004): 62–80.
Daugherty, William J. *Executive Secrets: Covert Action and the Presidency*. Lexington: University Press of Kentucky, 2004.
Downes, Alexander B., and Lindsey A. O'Rourke. "You Can't Always Get What You Want: Why Foreign-Imposed Regime Change Seldom Improves State Relations." *International Security* 41/2 (2016): 43–89.
Dycus, Stephen, and Arthur L. Berney, William C. Banks, and Peter Raven-Hansen. *National Security Law*, 3d ed. New York: Aspen, 2002.
Dycus, Stephen, and Arthur L. Berney, William C. Banks, Peter Raven-Hansen, and Stephen I. Vladeck. *National Security Law*, 6th ed. New York: Wolters Kluwer, 2016.
Eyth, Marcus. "The CIA and Covert Operations: To Disclose or Not to Disclose—That Is the Question." *Brigham Young University Journal of Public Law* 17/1 (2002): 45–72.
Fuller, Christopher J. *See It, Shoot It: The Secret History of the CIA's Lethal Drone Program*. New Haven, CT: Yale University Press, 2017.
Gates, Robert M. "The CIA and American Foreign Policy." *Foreign Affairs* 66 (Winter 1987/88): 215–30.
Gelb, Leslie H., "Should We Play Dirty Tricks in the World?" *New York Times Magazine* (December 21, 1975): 10ff.
Godson, Roy, ed. *Intelligence Requirements for the 1980s*. Washington, DC: National Strategy Information Center, 1979.

Godson, Roy, Richard Kerr, and Ernest May. *Intelligence Requirements for the 1990s*. Working Group on Intelligence Reform. Washington, DC, 1992.

Godson, Roy, Ernest R. May, and Gary Schmitt. *U.S. Intelligence at the Crossroads: Agendas for Reform*. Washington DC: Brassey's, 1995.

Goldsmith, Jack L. "The Remarkably Open Syrian Covert Action." *Lawfare* (July 23, 2013).

Goldsmith, Jack L. "Questions About CIA v. DOD Drone Strikes." *Lawfare* (May 13, 2014).

Goodman, Allan. "Does Covert Action Have a Future?" *Parameters* 18/2 (1988): 74–80.

Gross, Richard C. "Different Worlds: Unacknowledged Special Operations and Covert Action." *Strategy Research Project*, US Army War College (2009).

Haass, Richard N. "Don't Hobble Intelligence Gathering." *Washington Post* (February 15, 1996): A27.

Halperin, Morton H. "Decision-Making for Covert Operations." *Society* (March-April 1975): 45–51.

Halperin, Morton H. "The CIA and Manipulation of the American Press." *First Principles* 3/5 (January 1978): 1–5.

Halperin, Morton H. "Covert Operations: The Real Issue." *First Principles* 5/7 (May 1980): 1–5.

Halperin, Morton H. "Prohibiting Covert Operations." *First Principles* 12/2 (April 1987): 1ff.

James, Patrick, and Glenn E. Mitchell. "Targets of Covert Pressure: The Hidden Victims of the Democratic Peace." *International Interactions* 21/1 (1995): 85–107.

Janis, Irving. *Groupthink*, 2d ed. Boston: Houghton Mifflin, 1982.

Johnson, Loch K. "The CIA and the Media." *Intelligence and National Security* 1 (May 1986): 143–69.

Johnson, Loch K. "Smart Intelligence." *Foreign Policy* 89 (Winter 1992–93): 67–75.

Johnson, Loch K. *Secret Agencies: U.S. Intelligence in a Hostile World*. New Haven, CT: Yale University Press, 1996.

Johnson, Loch K. "Intelligence Analysis and Planning for Paramilitary Operations." *Journal of National Security Law & Policy* 5 (2012): 481–506.

Johnson, Loch K., and James J. Wirtz, eds. *Intelligence: The Secret World of Spies*, 5th ed. New York: Oxford University Press, 2018.

Joseph, Michael F., and Michael Poznansky. "Media Technology, Covert Action, and the Politics of Exposure." *Journal of Peace Research* 55/3 (2018): 320–35.

Kessler, Ronald. *The CIA at War: Inside the Secret Campaign Against Terror*. New York: St. Martin's Press, 2004.

Kibbe, Jennifer D. "Covert Action, Pentagon Style." In Loch K. Johnson, ed., *The Oxford Handbook of National Security Intelligence*, 569–86. New York: Oxford University Press, 2010.

Kibbe, Jennifer D. "Covert Action and the Pentagon." In Loch K. Johnson, ed., *Strategic Intelligence: Covert Action, Behind the Veils of Secret Foreign Policy*, vol. 3, 107–18. Westport, CT: Praeger Security International, 2007,

Kornbluh, Peter, ed. *Bay of Pigs Declassified: The Secret CIA Report on the Invasion of Cuba*. New York: New Press, 1988.

Kornbluh, Peter. "The Iran-Contra Scandal: A Postmortem." *World Policy Journal* (Winter 1987–88): 41–47.

Kreps, Sarah E. *Drones: What Everyone Needs to Know*. New York: Oxford University Press, 2016.

Lefever, Ernest W. "Don't Reject Covert Action." *USA Today* (September 18, 1991): A10.

Lian, Yi-Zheng. "China Has a Vast Influence Machine, and You Don't Even Know It." *New York Times* (May 21, 2018): A25.

Lindsay, Jon R. "Stuxnet and the Limits of Cyber Warfare." *Security Studies* 22/3 (2013): 365–404.

Luttwak, Edward N. "How to Administer Covert Operations." *New York Times* (November 17, 1986): A21.

Mayer, Jane. "Outsourcing Torture." *The New Yorker* (February 6, 2005).

McMurdo, Torey. "The Economics of Overthrow: The United States, Britain, and the Hidden Justification of Operation TPAJAX." *Studies in Intelligence* 56/2 (2012): 15–26.

Moses, Hans. *The Clandestine Service of the Central Intelligence Agency*. 1. Intelligence Profession Series. McLean, VA: Association of Former Intelligence Officers, 1983.

Murphy Commission. *Report to the President: The Organization of the Government for the Conduct of Foreign Policy*. Washington, DC: Government Printing Office, June 1975.

O'Rourke, Lindsey A. *Covert Regime Change: America's Secret Cold War*. Ithaca, NY: Cornell University Press, 2018.

Parks, W. Hays. "Memorandum of Law: Executive Order 12333 and Assassination." *Army Law* (December 1989): 1–12.

Perina, Alexandra H. "Black Holes and Open Secrets: The Impact of Covert Action on International Law." *Columbia Journal of Transnational Law* 53/3 (2015): 507–83.

Peterzell, Jay. "Legal and Constitutional Authority for Covert Operations." *First Principles*, 1–5. Washington, DC: Center for National Security Studies, 1985.

Poznansky, Michael. "Feigning Compliance: Covert Action and International Law." *International Studies Quarterly* (2019): 1–13.

Poznansky, Michael. *In the Shadow of International Law: Covert Action in the Postwar World*. New York: Oxford University Press, 2020.

Prados, John. "The Future of Covert Action." In Loch K. Johnson, ed., *Handbook of Intelligence Studies*, 289–300. New York: Routledge, 2007.

Ransom, Harry Howe. "The Uses and Abuses of Secret Power." *Worldview* 18 (May 1975): 11–15.

Rizzo, John. *Company Man: Thirty Years of Controversy and Crisis in the CIA*. New York: Simon & Schuster, 2014.

Rhode, David. *In Deep: The FBI, the CIA, and the Truth About America's "Deep State."* New York: Norton, 2020.

Robinson, Linda. "The Future of Special Operations: Beyond Kill and Capture." *Foreign Affairs* 91 (2012): 110–12.

Rogovin, Mitchell [CIA Counsel]. *Hearings*. Statement, Permanent Select Committee on Intelligence, US House of Representatives, 94th Cong., 1st Sess. Part 5 (1976), 1729, 1732–33.

Sanger, David E. *The Perfect Weapon: War, Sabotage, and Fear in the Cyber Age*. New York: Crown, 2018.

Scheuer, Michael. *Imperial Hubris: Why the West Is Losing the War on Terror*. New York: Brassey's, 2004.

Scheuer, Michael. *Osama Bin Laden*. New York: Oxford University Press, 2011.

Schwarz, Elke. "Pursuing Peace: The Strategic Limits of Drone Warfare." *Intelligence and National Security* 32/4 (June 2017): 422–25.

Shimer, David. *Rigged: America, Russia, and One Hundred Years of Covert Electoral Interference*. New York: Knopf, 2020.

Shultz, Richard H. Jr. *Transforming US Intelligence for Irregular War: Task Force 714 in Iraq*. Washington, DC: Georgetown University Press, 2020.

Spaniel, William, and Michael Poznansky. "Credible Commitment in Covert Affairs." *American Journal of Political Science* 62/3 (2018): 668–81.

Smith, Gregory L. "Secret but Constrained: The Impact of Elite Opposition on Covert Operations." *International Organization* 73/3 (2019): 685–707.

Smith, Joseph Burkholder. "Nation-Builders, Old Pros, Paramilitary Boys, and Misplaced Persons." *Washington Monthly* (February 1978): 23–30.

Stempel, John D. "Covert Action and Diplomacy." In Loch K. Johnson, ed., *Strategic Intelligence: Covert Action, Behind the Veils of Secret Foreign Policy*, vol. 3:145–56. Westport, CT: Praeger Security International, 2007.

Stern, Gary M. "Covert Paramilitary Operations." *First Principles* 13 (February/March 1988): 1, 10–14.

Stiefler, Todd. "CIA's Leadership and Major Covert Operations: Rogue Elephants or Risk-Averse Bureaucrats?" *Intelligence and National Security* 19 (Winter 2004): 632–54.

Stockwell, John. *In Search of Enemies: A CIA Story*. London: Andre Deutsch, 1978.

Treverton, Gregory F. *Covert Action: The Limits of Intervention in the Postwar World*, 148–78. New York: Basic Books, 1987.

Treverton, Gregory F. *Reshaping National Intelligence for an Age of Information*. New York: Cambridge University Press, 2001.

Turner, Michael A. "Covert Action: An Appraisal of the Effects of Secret Propaganda." In Loch K. Johnson, ed., *Strategic Intelligence: Covert Action, Behind the Veils of Secret Foreign Policy*, vol. 3, 107–18. Westport, CT: Praeger Security International, 2007.

Turner, Robert F. "Coercive Covert Action and the Law." *Yale Journal of International Law* 20/2 (Summer 1995): 427–49.

Turner, Stansfield. "From an ex-CIA Chief: Stop the 'Covert' Operation in Nicaragua." *Washington Post* (April 21, 1983): C1.

Turner, Stansfield. "CIA Covert Action at What Price?" *Christian Science Monitor* (May 31, 1984): 14.

Tuttle, Andrew C. "Secrecy, Covert Action, and Counterespionage: Intelligence Challenges for the 1990s." *Harvard Journal for Law and Public Policy* 12/2 (Spring 1989): 523–40.

Üngör, Ugur Ümit. *Paramilitarism: Mass Violence in the Shadow of the State*. New York: Oxford University Press, 2020.

US House of Representatives. "The CIA and the Media." Hearings. Subcommittee on Oversight, Permanent Select Committee on Intelligence, 1979.

Walsh, Lawrence E. *Firewall: The Iran-Contra Conspiracy and Cover-Up*. New York: Norton, 1997.

Walton, Calder. "Spies, Election Meddling, and Disinformation: Past and Present." *Brown Journal of World Affairs* 26/1 (Fall/Winter 2019): 107–24.

Warner, Michael. "A Matter of Trust: Covert Action Reconsidered." *Studies in Intelligence* 63/4 (December 2019): 33–41.

Weissman, Mikael, Niklas Nilsson, Björn Palmertz, and Pere Thunholm, eds. *Hybrid Warfare: Security and Asymmetric Conflict in International Relations*. New York: I. B. Tauris, 2021.

Wettering, Frederick L. "[C]overt Action: The Disappearing "C."" *International Journal of Intelligence and Counterintelligence* 16 (Winter 2003–2004): 561–72.

Wicker, Tom. " 'Covert' Means Fiasco." *New York Times* (October 10, 1989): A29.

Willard-Foster, Melissa. *Topping Foreign Governments: The Logic of Regime Change*. Philadelphia: University of Pennsylvania Press, 2019.
Wise, David. "CIA Should Forget Covert Actions." *Cleveland Plain Dealer* (September 16, 1996): 9B.
Woods, Chris. *Sudden Justice: America's Secret Drone Wars*. New York: Oxford University Press, 2015.
Woodward, Bob. *Veil: The CIA Secret Wars, 1981–87*. New York: Simon & Schuster, 1987.
Yoo, John. *Defender in Chief: Donald Trump's Fight for Presidential Power*. New York: St. Martin's Press, 2020.

Ethical Considerations

Ball, George, and Ray S. Cline. "Should the CIA Fight Secret Wars?" *Harper's* (September 1984): 27–44.
Barnds, William J. "Intelligence and Foreign Policy: Dilemmas of a Democracy." *Foreign Affairs* 47 (January 1969): 281–95.
Barnes, Jamal. "Black Sites, 'Extraordinary Renditions' and the Legitimacy of the Torture Taboo." *International Politics* 53/2 (2016): 198–219.
Beitz, Charles R. "Covert Intervention as a Moral Problem." *Ethics and International Affairs* 3/94 (1989): 45–60.
Bloomfield, Lincoln P. Jr. "Legitimacy of Covert Action: Sorting Out the Moral Responsibilities." In Jan Goldman, ed., *Ethics of Spying*, 193–205. Lanham, MD: Scarecrow Press, 2006.
Church, Frank. "Do We Still Plot Murders? Who Will Believe We Don't?" *Los Angeles Times*, (June 14, 1983): Pt. 2, 5.
Colby, William E. "Public Policy, Secret Action." *Ethics and International Affairs* 3 (1989): 69.
Falk, Richard A. "CIA Covert Acton and International Law." *Society* 12 (March/April 1975): 39–44.
Fisher, Roger. "The Fatal Flaw in Our Spy System." *Boston Globe* (February 1, 1976): A21.
Fulbright, J. William. "We Must Not Fight Fire with Fire." In Young Hum Kim, ed., *The Central Intelligence Agency: Problems of Secrecy in a Democracy*, 24–36. Lexington, MA: Heath, 1968.
Godfrey, E. Drexel Jr. "Ethics and Intelligence." *Foreign Affairs* 56 (April 1978): 624–42.
Godson, Roy. *Dirty Tricks or Trump Cards: U.S. Covert Action and Counterintelligence*. New Brunswick, NJ: Transaction, 2000.
Goldman, Jan, ed. *Ethics of Spying*. Lanham, MD: Scarecrow Press, 2006.
Goulden, Joseph C., with Alexander W. Raffio. *The Death Merchant: The Rise and Fall of Edwin P. Wilson*. New York: Simon & Schuster, 1984.
Johnson, Loch K. "On Drawing a Bright Line for Covert Operations." *American Journal of International Law* 86 (April 1992): 284–309.
Lefever, Ernest W. "Can Covert Action Be Just?" *Policy Review* 12 (Spring 1980): 115–22.
Lewis, Anthony. "Costs of the CIA." *New York Times*, April 25, 1997: A19.
Mount, Ferdinand. "Spook's Disease." *National Review* 32 (March 7, 1980): 300.
Moyers, Bill. *The Secret Government: The Constitution in Crisis*. WNET and WETA Public Television (1987).

Omand, David, and Mark Phythian. *Principled Spying: The Ethics of Secret Intelligence*. Washington, DC: Georgetown University Press, 2018.
Psychological Operations in Guerrilla Warfare [written by an anonymous CIA officer]. New York: Random House, 1985.
Poznansky, Michael. "Stasis or Decay? Reconciling Covert War and the Democratic Peace." *International Studies Quarterly* (2015): 815–26.
Ransom, Harry Howe. "Don't Make the C.I.A. a K.G. B." *New York Times* (December 24, 1981): A23.
Rodriguez, Jose A. Jr., with Bill Harlow. *Hard Measures: How Aggressive CIA Action After 9/11 Saved American Lives*. New York: Threshold Editions, 2012.
Treverton, Gregory F. "Covert Action and Open Society." *Foreign Affairs* 65 (Summer 1987): 995–1014.
Treverton, Gregory F. "Imposing a Standard: Covert Action and American Democracy." *Ethics and International Affairs* 3/1 (March 1989): 27–43.
Turner, Stansfield, and George Thibault. "Intelligence: The Right Rules." *Foreign Policy* 48 (Fall 1982): 122–38.
Valentine, Douglas. *The Phoenix Program*. New York: William Morrow, 1990.
Wicker, Tom, John W. Finney, Max Frankel, and E. W. Kenworthy. "C.I.A.: Maker of Policy, or Tool?" *New York Times* (April 25, 1966): A1.
Wrage, Stephen D. "A Moral Framework for Covert Action." *Fletcher Forum* 4 (Summer 1980): 10–15.
Zenko, Micah, and Sarah Kreps. *Limiting Armed Drone Proliferation*. New York: Council on Foreign Relations Press, 2014.

Controlling Covert Action

Aspin, Les. "Covert Acts Need Even More Oversight." *Washington Post* (February 24, 1980): B7.
Baker, James E. "Covert Action: United States Law in Substance, Process, and Practice." In Loch K. Johnson, ed., *The Oxford Handbook of National Security* Intelligence, 587–607. New York: Oxford University Press, 2010.
Baker, James E., and W. Michael Reisman. *Regulating Covert Action: Practices, Contexts and Policies of Covert Coercion Abroad in International and American Law*. New Haven, CT: Yale University Press, 1992.
Barrett, David M. *Congress and the CIA: The Untold Story from Truman to Kennedy*. Lawrence: University Press of Kansas, 2005.
Block, Lawrence, and David B. Rivkin Jr. "The Battle to Control the Conduct of Foreign Intelligence and Covert Operations: The Ultra-Whig Counterrevolution Revisited." *Harvard Journal of Law & Public Policy* 12 (1989): 303–42.
Born, Hans, Loch K. Johnson, and Ian Leigh, eds. *Who's Watching the Spies? Establishing Intelligence Service Accountability*. Washington, DC: Potomac Books, 2005.
Byrne, Malcolm. *Iran-Contra: Reagan's Scandal and the Unchecked Abuse of Presidential Power*. Lawrence: University Press of Kansas, 2014.
Carlucci, Frank C. "Legislative Control of Covert Action." *Testimony*. Select Committee on Intelligence, US Senate, 1988.

Cinquegrana, Americo R. "Dancing in the Dark: Accepting the Invitation to Struggle in the Context of 'Covert Action': The Iran-Contra Affair and the Intelligence Oversight Process." *Houston Journal of International Law* 177 (1988): 177–87.

Cogan, Charles G. "Covert Action and Congressional Oversight: A Deontology." *Studies in Conflict and Terrorism* 16/2 (April 1993): 87–97.

Clark, Kathleen. "'A New Era of Openness?' Disclosing Intelligence to Congress Under Obama." *Constitutional Commentary* 26 (2010): 14.

Cohen, William S. "Congressional Oversight of Covert Actions: The Public's Stake in the Forty-Eight Hour Rule." 12 *Harvard Journal of Law and Public Policy* (1989): 285.

Connor, William E. "Reforming Oversight of Covert Actions After the Iran-Contra Affair: A Legislative History of the Intelligence Authorization Act for FY 1991." 32 *Virginia Journal of International Law* (1992): 871–912.

Cummings, Alfred. *Sensitive Covert Action Notifications: Oversight Options for Congress.* Congressional Research Service (CRS), 7-5700 (July 7, 2009).

Fisher, Louis. *The Constitution and 9/11: Recurring Threats to America's Freedoms.* Lawrence: University of Kansas Press, 2008.

Fowler, Senator Wyche Jr. "Congress and the Control of Covert Operations: Legislative Controls." *First Principles* 9 (March/April 1984): 1, 4–7.

Franck, Thomas M., and Edward Weisband. *Foreign Policy by Congress* (New York: Oxford University Press, 1979): 51–55.

Gates, Robert M. Remarks. "Legislative Oversight of Intelligence Activities: The U.S. Experience." S. *Report 103-88,* Select Committee on Intelligence, US Senate, 103d Cong, 2d Sess. (October 1994): Appendix 10.

Glennon, Michael J. "The Boland Amendment and the Power of the Purse." *Christian Science Monitor* (June 15, 1987): A14.

Hamilton, Alexander, John Jay, and James Madison. *The Federalist.* New York: Modern Library, 1937.

Hastedt, Glenn. "The Constitutional Control of Intelligence." *Intelligence and National Security* 1 (May 1986): 255–71.

Hersh, Seymour M. "Congress Is Accused of Laxity on C.I.A.'s Covert Activity." *New York Times* (June 1, 1978): A1.

Highsmith, Newell L. "Policing Executive Adventurism: Congressional Oversight of Military and Paramilitary Operations." *Harvard Journal of Legislation* 19 (1982): 327–54.

Johnson, Loch K. "The CIA: Controlling the Quiet Option." *Foreign Policy* 39 (Summer 1980): 143–53.

Johnson, Loch K. "The U.S. Congress and the CIA: Monitoring the Dark Side of Government." *Legislative Studies Quarterly* 5 (November 1980): 477–99.

Johnson, Loch K. "Paramilitary Operations." *First Principles* 9/4 (March/April 1984): 1–4.

Johnson, Loch K. "The Contemporary Presidency: Presidents, Lawmakers, and Spies: Intelligence Accountability in the United States." *Presidential Studies Quarterly* 34 (December 2004): 828–37.

Johnson, Loch K. "Accountability and America's Secret Foreign Policy: Keeping a Legislative Eye on the Central Intelligence Agency." *Foreign Policy Analysis* 1 (March 2005): 99–120.

Johnson, Loch K. *Spy Watching: Intelligence Accountability in the United States.* New York: Oxford University Press, 2018.

Kibbe, Jennifer D. "The Rise of the Shadow Warriors." *Foreign Affairs* 83 (2004): 102–15.

Leahy, Patrick J. "CIA, Covert Action, and Congressional Oversight." *Christian Science Monitor* (March 31, 1988): 13.

Lilla, Mark, and Mark Moore. "The Two Oaths of Richard Helms." *Intelligence Studies Case No. 525.0*. Kennedy School of Government, Harvard University, Cambridge, MA (January 1, 1983).

Marwick, Christine M. "New Charters for Intelligence: S.2525." *First Principles* 3/7 (March 1978): 1–8.

O'Connell, Anne Joseph. "Intelligence Oversight." In Matthew J. Morgan, ed., *The Impact of 9/11 and the New Legal Landscape*, 158–73. New York: Palgrave Macmillan, 2009.

Oseth, John. *Regulating U.S. Intelligence Operations: A Study in the Definition of National Interest*. Lexington: University Press of Kentucky, 1985.

Phillips, David Atlee. *The Night Watch: 25 Years of Peculiar Service*. New York: Atheneum, 1977.

Schlesinger, Arthur M. Jr. "Reform of the CIA?" *Wall Street Journal* (February 25, 1976): A10.

Schwarz, F.A.O. Jr. *Democracy in the Dark: The Seduction of Government Secrecy*. New York: Free Press, 2015.

Schwarz, F.A.O. Jr., and A. Z. Huq. *Unchecked and Unbalanced: Presidential Power in a Time of Terror*. New York: New Press, 2007.

Snider, L. Britt. *The Agency and the Hill: CIA's Relationship; with Congress, 1946–2004*. Washington, DC: Center for the Study of Intelligence (CIA), 2008.

Steele, Douglas. "Covert Action and the War Powers Resolution: Preserving the Constitutional Balance." *Syracuse Law Review* 39 (1988): 1139.

Tower Commission. *President's Special Review Board*. New York: Bantam & Times Books, 1987.

Treverton, Gregory F. "Covert Action and Open Society." *Foreign Affairs* 65 (Summer 1987): 995–1014.

Treverton, Gregory F. "Controlling Covert Action." In Glenn P. Hastedt, ed., *Controlling Intelligence*, 113–33. London: Cass, 1991.

Treverton, Gregory F. "Covert Action: Forward to the Past?" In Loch K. Johnson, ed., *Strategic Intelligence: Covert Action, Behind the Veils of Secret Foreign Policy*, vol. 3: 1–22. Westport, CT: Praeger Security International, 2007.

Turner, Stansfield. "Covert Common Sense: Don't Throw the CIA Out with the Ayatollah." *Washington Post* (November 23, 1986): A24.

US Government. "The Iran-Contra Affair." *Hearings*. Select Committee on Secret Military Assistance to Iran and the Nicaraguan Opposition, the Inouye-Hamilton Joint Committee, 100th Cong., 1st Sess. (July/August 1987).

US Government. *Report of the President's Special Review Board* (Tower Commission). Washington, DC (February 26, 1987).

Van Puyvelde, Damien. *Outsourcing US Intelligence: Contractors and Government Accountability*. Edinburgh: Edinburgh University Press, 2019.

Walden, Jerrold R. "The CIA: A Study in the Arrogation of Administrative Powers." *George Washington Law Review* 39 (October 1970): 98.

Weissman, Stephen R. "Covert Action, Congressional Inaction." *Foreign Affairs* (December 2, 2020).

About the Author

Loch K. Johnson has written several books and articles on America's intelligence agencies. Most recently, the books include *National Security Intelligence: Secret Operations in Defense of the Democracies*, 2d ed. (Polity, 2017, and *Spy Watching: Intelligence Accountability in the United States* (Oxford, 2018). In Congress, he served as special assistant to the chairman of the Senate Select Committee on Intelligence (the Church Committee); as a staff aide on the Senate Foreign Relations Committee; as the first staff director of the Subcommittee on Intelligence Oversight, House Permanent Select Committee on Intelligence; as a senior staff member on the Subcommittee on Trade and International Economic Policy, House Committee on Foreign Affairs; and as special assistant to Chairman Les Aspin of the Aspin-Brown Presidential Commission on the Roles and Missions of Intelligence.

Born in Auckland, New Zealand, Professor Johnson received his PhD in political science from the University of California, Riverside. In post-doctoral activities, he was awarded an American Political Science Association (APSA) Congressional Fellowship. Professor Johnson has won the "Certificate of Distinction" from the National Intelligence Study Center in Washington, DC; the "Studies in Intelligence" Award from the Center for the Study of Intelligence in Washington, DC; the "Best Article Award" from the Century Foundation's Understanding Government Project; and the V.O. Key "Best Book" Prize from the Southern Political Science Association, co-authored with Charles S. Bullock III. He has served as secretary of the APSA and as the inaugural chair of its Intelligence Studies Organized Group. He was, also, president of the International Studies Association (ISA), South.

Professor Johnson was the senior editor of the international journal *Intelligence and National Security* for seventeen years, and was a member of the editorial advisory board for other journals, including *Foreign Policy Analysis* and the *Journal of Intelligence History*. He has been a Phi Beta Kappa Visiting Scholar and a member of the Phi Beta Kappa National Board for the Visiting Scholar Program. As well, he taught at Yale University and at Oxford University, as a Distinguished Visiting Scholar. In 2014, he was presented with the "Distinguished Scholar" Award bestowed by the Intelligence Studies Section of the ISA, and in 2015 the Lifetime Achievement Award from the International Association for Intelligence Education in Washington, DC.

ABOUT THE AUTHOR

At the University of Georgia, Loch Johnson was Regents Research Professor of Public and International Affairs, as well as Distinguished Meigs Teaching Professor. From 1997–2001, he led the founding of the university's School of Public and International Affairs; and in 2012, the consortium of fourteen universities in the Southeast Conference (SEC) selected him as its inaugural Professor of the Year. He was also awarded the Faculty Service Award at the University of Georgia and delivered the Graduate Commencement Address at the university in 2019. He is now retired from the university and lives with his wife in Salisbury, Connecticut, gateway to the scenic Northwest Hills of that state.

Index

For the benefit of digital users, indexed terms that span two pages (e.g., 52–53) may, on occasion, appear on only one of those pages.

Abourezk Amendment, 182
Abourezk, James (D, South Dakota), 318n.42
Abrams, Elliott, 130, 214, 310n.28
accountability, 5–6, 7–8, 37–38, 98, 107, 129, 132, 150–51, 153–54, 177, 181, 182, 203, 212, 268
    CIA view toward, 177, 201, 214–15
    congressional, 107, 181, 183, 186, 210, 251, 268
    difficulties of, 214–15, 248–49
    game-playing, 207, 210, 213, 214–15
    ingredients for success, 218
    post-Hughes-Ryan failures, 243–44, 245, 246, 249–51
    post-Hughes-Ryan successes, 237, 239, 242
    presidential, 183
    prodded by *New York Times* reporting, 318n.44
    specificity, importance of, 155, 186, 191, 212, 214, 265
    staff role in Congress, 215
Acheson, Dean, 12
active measures (Soviet Union and Russia), 11, 36, 44, 268–69, 293n.33
    assassinations, 292–93n.32
    assassination of Prime Minister Indira Gandhi, 44–45
    attacks against US hospital computers, 44–45
    bioweapons, 44–45
    COVID-19 (coronavirus), 44–45
    Ebola and flu outbreaks, 44–45
    Kompromat ("compromise" operation), 308n.2
    propaganda: AIDs in Africa, 44–45
    US bioengineering, manipulation of global radio waves, and spread of hazardous chemicals, 44–45
Acton, Lord, 225
Adams, John, 182
Aderholt, Gen. Heinie, 102
advising and training foreign assets, 48

Afghanistan, 1–2, 120–21, 124, 145, 152, 161, 162, 202, 236–39, 252–53
    Reagan administration paramilitary activities in, 131–35, 237–39, 257–58
    Bush II administration paramilitary activities against, 144–45, 200–1, 228, 236–37
Africa, 11–12, 38–39, 55–56, 92, 93, 117–19, 163, 252
Agee, Philip, 319n.51
"Agency, the" (CIA nickname), xi
Agent Orange, 56
agitprop, 44–45
Agriculture, Department of, 189
Al Hurra TV, 26–27
Al Shiraa (Beirut), 127
Al Qaeda, 4, 38, 57–58, 134, 141–42, 143–44, 146, 236, 252–53
al-Awlaki, Anwar, 153
al-Baghdadi, Abu Bakr (ISIS), 253, 254, 256
al-Balawi, Dr. Humam Khalil Abu-Mulal, 287n.10
al-Nahyan, Mohammed bin Zayed, 93–94
Albania, 72–73
Alec Station (CIA), 58–60
Alfhem (Swedish freighter), 84
all-source fusion, 13
Allen, Charlie, 40
Allende, Salvador, 26, 51–52, 102–4, 110, 117, 119, 178, 180, 318n.44
Alliance for Progress, 16
Alexander II, Tsar (Russia), 61–62
Alexander III, Tsar (Russia), 61–62
ambassadors, US, 50, 198
"America First" (Trump administration), 276
American foreign policy, instruments of, 2–3
American Revolution, 100
Amin, Hafizullah, 131
Anaconda, 108, 144–45
analysis, intelligence, 12–13, 29, 74, 88, 173, 175, 176, 199, 264
    lack of outreach in the US, 81
    surpassed by PM activities, 101

Anderson, Scott, 197–98
Andrew, Christopher, 11, 287n.10
Angleton, James J., 28, 198, 290–91n.11
Angola, 32, 124, 308n.2, 327n.37
    Marxist revolutionaries, 144
    US oil interests, 144
Anglo-Iranian Oil Company, 77
Antarctica, 109
ante facto reporting to Congress (prior notice of a proposed operation), 187–89, 215
anti-communism, 11–12, 19, 32, 71, 78–79, 83, 91, 112, 123–24, 239, 241, 272
    Angola, 120
    Chile, 109
    Cuba, 94, 96, 103
    Congo, 94
    fearmongering, for political advantage, 11–12
    global, 104, 239, 266–67
    Mexico, 264–65
    Nicaragua, 264–65
Antoine duc d'Eghien, Prince Louis, 102
Arabian Sea, 55–56
Arab Spring, 143, 146
Árbenz Guzmán, Jacobo, 83–88, 93, 97
"Archipelago," Operation (Indonesia), 89
Arellano, Archbishop Mariano Rossell y, 88
Aristotle, 204
Armas (Castillo-Armas), Colonel Carlos, 86, 87
Arms Export Control Act of 1976, 125, 126–27
arms merchants, 36
Army, US, 57–58
Asia, 11–12, 75
Aspin, Les (D, Wisconsin), xv, 211, 216–17, 233–34, 236
Aspin-Brown Commission, xiv, 38–39, 140, 223, 253
Assad, Bashar, 146–47, 248
Assassination Manual (Nicaragua), 37–38, 127
assassination plots ("executive action"; "neutralizing"), 34–35, 39, 49–50, 52–59, 61–62, 76, 89, 91–92, 93, 105, 148–49, 226–27, 241, 251, 253, 256, 297n.35
    Allende, 104
    assets for, 94
    authority for, 97–98, 101–2, 304n.30
    banned by executive order, 126–27
    Bin Laden, Osama, 148–51
    Blackleaf 40, 100
    botulinum, 100
    British rejection of, 256
    Castro, 100
    Chile, 104
    CIA as killing machine, 100, 106, 153

    cobra venom, 100
    curare, 100
    dart-gun, 100–232, 270–71, 276, 304n.23
    Diem, Ngo Dinh, 72, 104–5
    drones, use of, 148. *See also* drones
    DS&T, 96
    "execution squad," 38–39
    executive order on, 148
    exploding cigar, 100
    fountain pen approach, 100, 303–4n.22
    fungi toxins, 100
    Mafia, 100
    Manual, 37, 127
    methods, 100
    Murder, Inc., 100
    "Phoenix," Operation, 105
    poisons, 94, 100, 232
    Polish security forces, 136
    Potassium cyanide, 100
    saxitoxin, 100
    shellfish toxins, 100, 232
    Somalian warlords and, 148
    Soviet, 131
    strychnine, 100
    "targeted killings," 154, 158
    threat to world order, 160–61, 245–46
    warrant procedure (proposed), 154
    "ZR/RIFLE," Operation, 100
assets (CIA), 21–22, 38–39, 168, 172, 197, 263–65
agents provocateurs, 28
atomic spies, 12
attorney general, 204
attorney general guidelines, 172
Auckland, New Zealand, 64

Baer, Robert, 266, 272
Baker, James A., 129
Baker, James E., 14, 43, 167
balancing, defensive, 52
Balkans, 140
Ball, George, 276
Baltic nations, 15
Barbary Pirates (North Africa), xi
Barr, Attorney General William "Bill," 225, 325n.8
Barrett, David M., 325–26n.17
Batista y Zaldivar, Fulgencio, 95–96, 245
Bay of Pigs, 94–38, 100, 178–79, 203, 226–27, 252, 255, 264, 270–71, 309n.14
Bayh, Birch (D, Indiana), 209
BBC, 137
Bearden, Milt, 310n.35

Beckett, Thomas, 101
Belgium, 95, 246
Berkowitz, Bruce D., 168
Berntsen, Gary, 267
Beschloss, Michael, 328n.41
"BG/FIEND," Operation, 72
Biden, Hunter, 265–66
Biden administration, 153, 157
Biden, President Joe, 154, 156–57, 265
Bin Laden, Osama (OBL), 58–59, 141–42, 144–45, 149, 236, 253 , –54, 256, 260
assassination plots against, 149–51, 236–37
Bissell, Richard, 97–98, 255
Black, Cofer, 149–50
Black Hawk Down (book and film), 149
"black sites," 36–37, 55, 291n.14
Blackleaf, 40, 100
Blackwater (Xe Services, Academi), 36–37
Blair, Adm. Dennis, 258
blow back (replay), 29–30, 53
Bokassa, Jean-Bedel, 179–80
Boland Amendments, 126–27, 186, 192, 208, 217–18, 242
Boland, Edward P. "Eddie," xiv, 126, 210, 217, 218, 317n.35
Bolton, John, 321n.21
Bombay *Free Press Journal*, 44–45
Bond, James, 176
Boren, David L., 209
Bosnia, 140
Bowman, R.C., 231
Bradbury, Roger, 223
Brandeis, Louis, 8, 225
Brazil, 297–98n.1
Breckinridge, Scott D., Jr., 32
Brennan, John O., 51, 153, 158, 254–55, 295n.12
British Broadcasting Company, 23–24
British foreign intelligence service, MI6 (Secret Intelligence Service, SIS), 31, 48–49, 72, 73, 80, 82
British Guiana, 297–98n.1
Bross, John, 31
Bruni, Sultan of, 126–27
Brzezinski, Zbigniew ("Zbig"), 43, 121
Buchanan, James, 249
Buckley, William, 52, 124–25, 243
budget, intelligence, 19, 121, 124, 131, 138–39, 145, 146, 174–75, 176, 179–80, 183–84, 317n.34
annual national intelligence (US), 23, 157, 195
early expenditures, 75, 76
Peace Dividend, 139

private funding, 86, 126–27
unvouchered funds, 168
Bundesnachrichtendienst (BND, German foreign intelligence agency), 74
Bundy, McGeorge "Mac," 57, 103, 134–35, 191–92, 197, 231, 304n.32, 305n.33
Bunga (parasite), 56–57, 231
Bureau of Intelligence and Research (State Department), 199
Bureau of Investigative Journalism, 153
Burke, Michael, 324–25n.6
Burma (now Myanmar), 103–4, 106, 264
Bush, Barbara, 141
Bush II administration, 143–44, 152, 226
Bush, President George H. W. (Bush I, R, Texas), 61, 128, 131, 138, 207, 295n.12, 311n.44
assassination plot against, 141
DCI, 112, 131, 180
letter to Congress, 183, 190–91, 215
pocket-veto, 190
Bush, President George W. (Bush II, R, Texas), 49, 158, 160, 188, 215–16, 295n.12
response to, 9/11, 143–48
business interests, U.S, role in guiding covert action, 78–79, 83–84, 85–86, 96, 97, 107–9, 112, 132–2, 271, 272, 273
Byrd, Robert C. (West Virginia), 288n.25

"C," Leslie, and Peter Sichel, 302n.55
Cabot, John Moors, 84
Call of the Wild, 15
Cambodia, 103–4, 275
Canada, 95–96, 122, 245, 260
cannibalism, 51
capitalism, 12, 124
Carter administration, 27, 43, 120, 134, 186, 200, 202, 215, 237, 242, 249–51, 262, 266
Carter, President Jimmy (D, Georgia), 122, 217, 316n.20
drone critic, 255
US embassy crisis in Iran, 52, 120–23
case officer (CIA), 21–22
Case-Zablocki Act, 9–10
Casey, William J., 123–24, 130, 132, 175, 204, 206, 207, 209–10, 218, 234, 237–38, 265–66, 272
Castillo-Armas, Colonel Carlo, 85–86
Castro, Fidel, 26, 50, 95–103, 180, 228
assassination of John F. Kennedy, 100
radicalization of, 94
Catholic Church, 26
Center for Counterterrorism (CTC/CIA), 198
Center for Nonproliferation (CNP/CIA), 198

Center for the Study of Intelligence (CIA), 174
Central African Republic, 179–80
Central America, 83–84, 85–86, 123–24, 125, 132, 134, 210
Central Intelligence Agency (CIA, "the Agency"), xi, 226–27
  advisers, 46, 48
  call for more aggressive behavior, 268
  Covert Action Staff (CAS), 291n.14
  "C.I.A. Did It, The" 58f
  Comptroller, 177, 199
  Counterintelligence Staff (CIS), 198, 291n.14
  domestic spy scandal (Operation "CHAOS"), 10
  early attitudes toward, 69, 167–68
  establishment of, 9, 13, 16
  extreme circumstances, 269–70
  few protest resignations, 265–66
  foreign liaison, 267
  General Counsel, 199
  infrastructure ("plumbing"), 21–22
  initial lack of enthusiasm for covert action, 69
  Inspector General (IG/CIA), 177, 267
  Inspector General Act (CIA), 184–90,
  Legal Counsel, 199
  legislative liaison staff, 186, 319n.52
  Miami Station, 229
  need for agility, 202, 203
  officers from Ivy League, 71
  paramilitary specialty, 145
  propaganda specialist seconded to the NSC, 129
  "publish or perish" syndrome, 197–98
  reporting to Congress, 181, 194
  quarters, early (CIA), 169–70
  self-preservation as *raison d'état*, 223, 226, 247–48
  station, chief of (COS), 21–22, 179, 194–95, 197, 207–8, 232, 265, 268, 320n.9
  stations (CIA), 197, 207–8
  stockpiled armaments, 35
  training facility ("The Farm," "Camp Swampy"), 37
  weaponry, 85, 89
  whistle-blower, 265
  White House relations, 95, 124
  wide discretionary authority, 194
  witting circle, 183, 227
Central Intelligence Agency Act (1949), 168
Central Intelligence Agency, Director of (D/CIA), 167
Central Intelligence, Director of (DCI), 167
Chad, 35–36, 124, 152, 270

"CHAOS," Operation, 179–80, 226–27
character and reputation, 51, 75, 87, 233, 244, 268–69, 272
Charles McC. Mathias Jr. (R, Maryland), 97–98
Chase, Gordon, 38
Che Guevara, 94
cheerleaders, 208–9, 218–19
checks-and-balances, 7–8, 10, 192, 194, 205, 224–25, 257–58
Cheney, Dick (R, Wyoming), 130, 225, 226
Chile, xiv–xv, 6–8, 31, 110, 179–80, 183
  Allende regime, 26, 29, 51–52, 246, 265–66, 269
  Christian Democratic Party (PDC), 107–8
  covert action against, 107–12
  democracy, 243, 328n.40
  Frei regime, 297–98n.1
  lack of US vital interests in, 110
  military, 103–4
  Pinochet regime, 112
  truckers strike, 111
China, Communist, 2, 3, 15, 69–71, 106, 133, 162, 252–53, 309n.23
  Army, 101, 133
  COVID-19, 45
  cyberwarfare, 161
  nuclear weaponry of, 1
  propaganda against, 27, 29
  Tibet, 89–90
Christ, Jesus, 228
Church Committee, xiv, 25–26, 32, 38–39, 98–99, 104, 111–12, 120, 138, 150, 172, 178, 179–80, 182, 192, 227, 234, 245–46, 249–51, 254–55, 268–69, 297–98n.1
  "Intelligence Wars," 180, 181, 207–8
  "time of troubles," 180
Church, Frank (D, Idaho), xv, 102, 109, 120, 194–95, 240, 265–66, 272–73, 304n.30
Churchill, Winston S., 5, 8, 77
CIA Inspector General Act (1987), 190
Clandestine Service, 174–75
Clapper, James R., 158, 161, 162, 191, 194, 197, 329n.1
Clark, Dick (D, Iowa), 307n.1
Clark, Gen. Wesley, 140
Clarke, Richard A., 327n.33
Clifford, Clark, 13–14, 191–92, 270
Cline, Ray S., 29, 266, 271–72
Clinton administration, 32, 49, 59–60, 102, 138–39, 141, 143–44, 149
Clinton, President Bill (D, Arkansas), 28, 56, 139
Cogan, Charles, 138

Cohen, Eliot A., 269
Cohen, Roger, 293n.37
Cohen, William S. (R, Maine), 131, 218
COINTELPRO, 226–27
Colby, William E., 5, 29, 32, 55, 61, 91, 104, 105, 119–20, 175, 180–81, 192, 194–95, 257, 259, 267, 269, 271, 290n.8, 317n.31
Cold War, 11, 14, 110–11, 252, 253, 273
  détente, 138
  end of, 138
  turned hot, 95
Cold War II, 124, 238
Cole (USNS), 58–59, 141–42, 143
Coll, Steve, 6, 37, 59, 144, 223, 310n.32
collection and analysis, of intelligence, 14–69, 87–88, 122, 289n.37
co-location, of DI and DO officers, 177, 262–63, 266, 303n.15
Columbia, 275–76
Combest, Larry (R, Texas), 210–11
Comfort, USNS, 275–76
communism, 12, 124
  global threat, 15, 79–80, 168, 169
  overstated as threat, 267
"Company, the" (CIA nickname), 285n.2
Congo, Democratic Republic of, 20–21, 38–39, 93–95, 245–30
  CIA chief of station, 94
Congress (legislative branch), 8, 102, 131, 151, 172, 244. *See also* lawmakers
  accountability, 172, 203, 208–9, 212, 233, 248–49
  Appropriations Committees, 132, 181, 184, 187, 195–97, 212
  attitudes toward CIA, 208–9, 265, 268
  cheerleading, 216–17
  CIA attitudes toward, 174, 212
  colloquy, 188
  dance of legislation, 187
  debate, 184
  hearings, 213, 215–16, 263
  intelligence reporting to, 153, 181, 183–84
  pork-barrel activities, 211
  power of the purse, 183, 189, 207, 210, 215–16
  questioning during findings briefings, 208, 251, 266
  role-playing by lawmakers, 208–9, 216
  secrecy and, 203
  slow rolling, 217–18
  staff, role of, 215
  subpoena powers, 183
  Trump administration contempt for, 213–14, 216–17
Congressional Budget Justification Book (CBJC), 195–97
Connolly, Gerald (D, Virginia), 213–14
Constitution (US), 7, 10, 62–63, 64, 126–27, 180, 181, 183, 188–89, 191–93, 204, 205, 217, 218, 219, 236, 248–49.
  See also law
  "Article CIA," 245, 246
  Article I, 7–8, 126, 127, 216, 224, 227, 235, 242–44
  Article II, 7–8, 126, 187, 206, 209–10, 224–26, 246, 325n.8
  attacks against, 60, 128, 205, 242–43
  "Constitutional Intelligence in America" ("C.I.A."), 192, 206, 251
  ethical component related to intelligence, 192, 224–27, 234–35
  Founding Convention, 7–8, 225, 244
  process and procedures, importance of, 234–35, 258–59, 265, 268
  powers delineated, 7–8, 10, 150–51, 183
  representative government as a virtue, 227
containment doctrine, 15–16, 172–73, 238, 240
Contingency Reserve Release Fund, 175–76, 200, 218
Cooper, Philip J., 172
Coors, Joseph, 127
Copeland, Miles, 285n.8, 292n.26
Corsica, 30–31
Cormac, Rory, 24–25, 296n.21
Corwin, Edward S., 180, 193
Costa Rica, 297–98n.1
Council on Foreign Relations, 253
counterinsurgency, 179
counterintelligence, 13, 46, 53–54, 157, 182, 241, 291n.14, 297n.38
Counterintelligence Staff (CIS/CIA), 198
counterproliferation, 262
counterterrorism, 46, 58–59, 262, 271, 272, 291n.14
Counterterrorism Center (CTC/CIA), 59, 149–50
covert action, 1, 5, 158, 286n.1,
  agricultural operations, 56–57
  approval procedures, 174, 178, 179, 181
  beginnings, in modern era, 15–16, 168
  best successes, 236–42, 258, 266
  budgets, 74, 94, 101, 136
  call for a more discriminating use of, 2, 268, 276–77

covert action (*cont.*)
　"compromise" operation
　　("honeytrap"), 308n.2
　coups, 59–60
　criminalizing of, 239, 243
　decision pathways, 195, 196*f*, 197–99
　definition of, 1, 29, 190
　devolution of authority, 179
　difficulties of studying, 5
　dirty mission, 259
　environmental operations, 56
　ethics of, 3, 40, 93, 225–26, 233, 250*f*
　economic operations, 33, 111
　electronic operations, 161
　evolution (and fluctuations), 69, 70*f*, 112–13, 118*f*, 119–20, 138, 159*f*, 268–69, 272
　extreme forms of, 63, 266, 272
　first major failure (Indonesia), 90
　forms of, 19, 75
　freedom of the press violations overseas, 47–48
　"gaming," 262
　Golden Ages, 80, 124, 142, 145, 153, 163
　good intentions of, 211, 248, 266, 287n.10, 306n.49, 317n.31
　history and, 5, 96
　hubris, 96
　hunting, 150
　international "noise levels," 103
　joint operations with allies, 48–49, 72, 95, 267
　"knavish tricks," 6
　Ladder of Clandestine Escalation, 40, 63
　local partners, value of, 51, 266–67
　luck, 151. *See also* odds of success.
　lull in practice of, 104
　management of assets, 38–39
　methods ("tradecraft"), 16, 229, 231–32, 246, 265, 272
　militarization of, 152
　mining foreign harbors, 7
　mobsters and, 30, 51
　mostly small-scale propaganda and political operations, 271–72
　My Lai level of immorality, 60
　non-lethal operations, 119, 136
　objectives of, 3, 4, 5, 6, 12, 269–70
　odds of success, 27–28, 38, 56, 85–86, 131, 199, 200–1, 234, 236, 245, 251, 257, 258–59, 327n.36
　"overt-covert" action, 36, 145, 146
　paramilitary operations, 34, 55, 59
　"pocket of privilege," 176
　poisoning of rice paddies in South Vietnam, 54–55
　political operations, 51
　porno movies, use of, 89
　post-Hughes-Ryan, 117
　practiced by other nations, 5, 14, 15, 24, 49, 256, 288n.29
　presidential attraction to, 14
　privatization of, 36, 126–27
　process and procedure, importance of, 201–2, 206, 258–59
　pursued incautiously, 261
　rarely appropriate, 266
　rationale for, 6–7, 87–88
　Red Zones, 227–32
　rogue elephant behavior, xiv, 5–6, 36–39, 60, 126, 127, 130, 174, 186, 201, 202, 204, 211, 213, 243–44
　sabotage, 33, 56, 99–100, 103, 292n.31, 304n.32
　security support in Third World nations, 35
　short-term versus long-term results, 99, 134, 257
　small, weak nations as victims, 272–75. *See also* targeting
　Smell Test, 228
　spending on, 48, 51–52
　supervision of, 5–6
　support of right-wing dictators, 247, 269
　synonyms for, 5–6, 286n.1, 287n.10
　targeting, 19, 71, 244, 249–51, 250*f*, 267, 272–73, 274*f*, 275
　Third Option, 1
　Title 50, US Military Code, 149–50
　tradecraft, xii, 23, 29, 100, 202, 291n.14
　unintended consequences, 81, 95, 134–35, 257, 262
　use of Eastern European émigrés, 71–72, 172–73
　weaponry, 35, 50, 51–52
　worst failures, 242–49
Covert Action Staff (CAS), 34–35, 197–99
COVID-19 (coronavirus), 2, 44, 207, 268, 288n.29, 323n.44
"cowboy," 36–37. *See also* assets
Croatia, 140
Cruise missiles, 58–59, 60
Crumpton, Henry A., 321n.23
Cuba, covert operations against. 50, 56–57, 95–103, 110, 244–45, 252. *See also* Bay of Pigs
　Angola, support for, 117–19
　Brigade 2506, 95, 263
　Communist Party (PSP), 94

Cuban Air Force, 312n.14
Cuban Communist Party (PSP), 96
  exiles, 38
  missile crisis, 99, 110, 244, 245
  Ortodoxo Party, 94
  "Zapata," Operation (Bay of Pigs), 94–96
cultures, intelligence (US), 94
cut-outs, 6–7, 44
cyberattacks (cyberterrorism, cyberwarfare), 2, 49, 55–56, 62, 161–62, 245
cyberdefense, 161
cyber-peace treaty, 162
cyberterrorism, 161–62
"Cyclone," Operation, 237
Czechoslovakia, 15, 84, 92, 135

Daugherty, William J., 310n.41
DCI Covert Action Checklist, 234–35
DeConcini, Dennis, 209
democracy, 8, 240, 257–58, 266
demons of global affairs: hunger, poverty, desperation, chaos, 275
deep state, 157
deepfakes, 29, 291n.16
Defense, Department of (DoD or Pentagon), 13, 23, 33, 54–55, 101, 152, 168, 231–32, 323n.44
  budget, 261
  CIA as an auxiliary unit of, 152, 170–72, 174
  CIA budget, 175–76
  covert actions, 230, 231
  Jawbreaker teams, 144
  joint ("hybrid" or "jointness") operations with CIA, 145, 150, 152, 256, 257, 259, 260
  Joint Special Operations Command (JSOC), 150
  Navy SEALS, 151
  opposes creation of strong Intelligence Director, 167–68
  Special Forces, 122, 144, 149, 150, 231
  Secretary of, 152
  Title 10, US Military Code, 149–50, 151
Defense Intelligence Agency (DIA), 23, 157
democratic values and principles, 134–35, 183, 192, 194–95, 201–2, 204–6, 217, 223–24, 239, 241, 244, 249, 258–59, 268–69, 271–72, 276–77
despots and right-wing regimes, 265–66
Detainee Treatment Act (DTA) of 2005, 191
Deutch, John, 28, 140, 141, 172, 233, 234, 236, 251, 257–58, 303n.15
developing nations (Third World), 97, 163, 267, 273

DeVos, Betsy, 36
dezinformatsia, 44–45
Diem, Ngo Dinh, 72, 104–5
Dien Bien Phu, battle of, 104–5
diplomacy, 5, 245, 251, 262, 268
  disputes over, 9
  executive agreements, 9
  international agreements, 9
  statutory agreements, 9
Direction Générale de la Sécurité Extérieure (DGSE), 63
directives, intelligence, 191. *See also*, executive orders and directives
Director, Central Intelligence (DCI), 5, 13, 20–21, 20f, 29–30, 175, 191, 197
Director, Central Intelligence Agency (D/CIA), 51, 152, 195–97
Director, National Intelligence (DNI), 22, 35–36, 152, 195–97, 216–17, 265
  working in tandem with D/CIA, 197
Directorate of Administration (DA), 184
Directorate of Analysis (DA), 184, 199, 263
Directorate of Intelligence (DI), 74, 98, 175, 199, 245
Directorate of Operations (DO/CIA), 20–21, 21f, 51, 123, 140, 153, 179–81, 198–99, 226, 253, 257–58, 259, 263, 270, 327–28n.38
  "can-doism," 261
  budgets, 74
  independence, 262
  infrastructure ("plumbing"), 21–22
  Near East Division, 134
  need for well-trained and ready corps of operatives, 266
Directorate of Plans (DP), CIA, 20–21, 27, 87–88, 90, 98, 104, 132, 174–77, 180, 238, 253
  building an infrastructure, 170–71
  "knuckle-draggers," 88
  "pocket of privilege," 176
Directorate of Science and Technology (DS&T), 94
Directorate of Support (DS), 175
directorates (CIA), 20–21, 20f
  cultural chasm among, 98
Dirksen, Everett (R, Illinois), 249
"dirty tricks," xiv, 121
"disposal problem," 37–38
Dominican Republic, 297–98n.1
domino theory, 78–79, 86–87, 110, 123, 300n.33, 305n.33
Donovan tradition, 261
Donovan, William (OSS), 261

drones (Unmanned Aerial Vehicles, UAV) attacks, 57–58, 60, 101, 140, 145, 245, 256
    accidental civilian deaths, 153
    accountability, 154, 159–60,
    Afghanistan, 152
    controversies, 154–55, 251, 254
    counterterrorism and, 152–55
    country targets, 152, 163
    efforts to reduce civilian casualties and property damage, 152
    frequency, 149, 152, 158
    "goodbye list," 153–54
    Hellfire missiles, 152
    introduction of, 152
    King of Covert Action, 148–49
    lack of CIA and DoD coordination, 154
    lethality, 152
    "Ninja" (R9X), 152
    Pakistan, 152
    Predator, 152
    presidential authority, 154
    Reaper, 152, 160
    reform proposals, 154–55
    signature strikes, 149
    "targeted killings" (or "hits"), 155
    targeting procedures, 153–55
drug trafficking, 198
Dulles, Allen, DCI, 76–77, 85–86, 94, 95, 101, 104–5, 155, 169–70, 174–76
    favors covert action, 176
    secrecy and, 194, 213
    Warren Commission member, 100
Dulles brothers, 78–79, 84–85, 88, 100–1, 104
Dulles, John Foster, 76–77, 79–80, 90, 93, 96, 175, 267, 297–98n.1
Dujmovic, Nicholas, 315n.1
Durenberger, David (R, Minnesota), 213

"Eagle Claw," Operation, 122
Eastern Europe, 11, 15, 24, 43, 71–72, 73, 89–90, 135, 137, 162, 171, 252–53
Eatinger, Robert, 321n.21
economic covert action, 33, 111, 229–32
economics, global, 4, 104
Ecuador, 297–98n.1
Egypt, 55, 73–74, 88, 94, 133, 143
Eisenhower administration, 14, 15, 16, 72–73, 102, 138–39, 245–46, 297–98n.1
    anti-communism of, 101
    Asia, 93
    assassination plots, 102
    Congo, 102, 245
    Cuba, 94
    Egypt, 88, 96
    Guatemala, 83
    Hungary, 89–90, 91
    Indonesia, 88, 96
    Iran, 78
    Laos, 93
Eisenhower, President Dwight David (R, Kansas), 15, 76–77, 83, 93, 94, 207
    global economic resources, comments on (rubber, tin, tungsten), 104
El Mercurio, 26
El Salvador, 31
electronic covert action, 59–60, 159–60
electronic espionage, US, 80
"Elimination by Illumination," Operation, 228
Emmanuel II, Victor; Emmanuel III, Victor; and Umberto I, Kings (Italy), 61–62
empathy, international, 276
"Enduring Freedom," Operation, 144–45
Enterprise, The, 126–27, 160, 186, 192, 207–8, 210, 242–43
Entolus, Adam, 295n.12
environmental operations, 4, 54, 293n.37
    Agent Orange (and other chemicals), 54
    sabotage, 54
ethical evaluations of key covert actions, xiii, 275–76
    Afghanistan (1979–1919), 235–36
    Afghanistan (2001–2011) and Bin Laden, 234–35
    ambiguities, 40
    Chile (1962-1973), 242–43
    Congo (1960-1961), 241–42
    Cuba (1960-1964), 240–41
    intelligence ethics as an oxymoron, 223
    Iran and Nicaragua (1984-1987), 239–40
    Italy and Containment (1947-1950), 237–38
    Laos (1962-1968), 236–37
    Poland and Solidarity (1978-1991), 238–39
    Syria (2013-2017), 243–44
    war situations, 61
ethics, 36–37, 40, 45–46, 49–50, 56–59, 60, 76, 98, 101, 102, 103–4, 120–21, 123–24, 203, 243, 258–59, 266, 324–25n.6
    contrasts with Russia and the Soviet Union, 328n.40
    embarrassment and, 233, 234
    football analogy, 207, 227, 229
    Fourth Option, 268
    Golden Rule, 261, 262, 269
    Just War theory, 260–61
    lost US advantages, 265–66
    moral leadership, 269, 275–77

moral profile, 249, 250f
oxymoron, 223
process, 227, 233
proportionality, 260–61
Red Zones, 203
seeking the high ground, 268
survival of democracy, 224–25
Ethiopia, 124
ethnic cleansing, 140
Europe, 45, 61–62, 69–71, 252, 253, 267, 269–70
European Defense Community (EDC), 74
ex post facto reporting (notice *after* an operation), 188–89, 215
executive international agreements, 9
executive orders (e.o.s) and directives on intelligence, 169, 172, 184, 297n.35
  Directive NSC 10/2 (1948), 171
  Directive NSC 68 (1950), 171
  Directive NSC 10/5 (1951), 171
  Directive NSC 5412/1 (1955), 177
  Directive NSC 5421/2 (1955), 177
  E.O. 11905 (Ford), 126–27, 149, 172, 297n.35
  E.O. 12036 (Carter), 316n.20
  E.O. 12333 (Reagan), 297n.35, 316n.20
  key documents, nomenclature, 172
  list of key NSC intelligence documents, 172
  National Security Decision Directive (NSDD)-75, 172
  secret codicils, 172
exfiltration (exit of assets) and resettlement, 122, 264–65
extraordinary rendition (abduction or "snatch" operations), detention, and interrogation, 34–35, 52–53, 54–55, 60

Far East, 20, 174
Farouk, King, 73–74
Federal Bureau of Investigation (FBI), 153, 157, 309n.20
Federalist Paper No. 51, 224
Feinstein, Dianne (D, California), 208–9
Figueres, President José, 297–98n.1
finding, 122, 181, 182, 184, 185f, 200, 203–4, 251, 265
  briefing to Congress, 184, 263
  carry-over, 321–22n.24
  examples of findings, 185f
  generic ("Worldwide" or overly broad), 202–4, 216–17
First Option, 5, 97, 261, 262, 268
First Persian Gulf War, 28, 141
Fisher, Louis, 295n.12
Fisher, Roger, 270–71

FitzGerald, Desmond, 197, 292n.30
5412 Committee (NSC), 177–78
FNLA, National Front of the Liberation of Angola, 32, 117–19
Fleming, Ian, 176
Florida, 96
Flynn, Gen. Michael, 157
Ford, President Gerald R. (R, Michigan), 15–16, 31, 119, 126–27, 181, 297n.35
Ford administration, 31, 43, 119, 126–27, 136, 148, 181, 217–18
  executive order on assassinations, 172–73, 253
Foreign Intelligence Surveillance Act (FISA), 154
Foreign Intelligence Surveillance Court (FISC), 154
40 Committee, 154–55, 178–79, 191–92
foreign policy, American instruments of, 4
"forever wars," 1–2
Fourth Option (leading by example), 275–77
"Foxtrot" team (Afghanistan), 31–32
Fowler, Wyche (D, Georgia), 211, 223, 259
France, 9, 15, 31, 64, 252
Franklin, Benjamin, xi
Free Syrian Army, 146
Friedrich III, Kaiser (Germany), 61–62
"frugal option," covert action as, 5–6
FSB (Russian domestic intelligence service), 292–93n.32
Fulbright, J. William (D, Arkansas), 276

game-playing, 210
Gang of Eight, 188, 190, 201, 212–13, 234, 237
Gang of Four, 212–13
Gang of None, 213
Gang of One, 213
Gang of Two, 212–13
Gates, Robert M., 43, 44–45, 69, 124, 175, 194, 198, 199, 207, 209, 215, 262, 306n.49
George, Claire, 130
Gerber, Burton, 108–9
Germany, 15, 24, 31, 53–54, 73, 102–3, 252, 303–4n.22, 310n.32
"Geronimo," Operation, 150
Gestapo (Nazi Germany), 63
Ghana, 297–98n.1
Gill, Peter, 48–49
Gingrich, Newt (R, Georgia), 198
global interdependence, 4
Goldsmith, Jack, 225–26, 261
Goldwater, Barry (R, Arizona), 209–10, 218
Goodman, Allen E., 168

GOP, 96
Gorbachev, President Mikhail, 138
Gore, Vice President Al, 327n.33
Goss, Porter (R, Florida), 94, 175, 210–11
Gottlieb, Dr. Sidney, 94
Goulart, President Joao (Brazil), 297–98n.1
Government Communications Headquarters (GCHQ/UK), 49
governmental powers, distrust of, 6
Graham, Bob (D, Florida), 209, 296n.28
Grant, President Ulysses S., xi
Grass, Günter, 272–73
Greece, 15, 72, 252, 297–98n.1
Green Party (Germany), 24
Greenberg, Karen J., 160
Greenpeace, 63–64, 260–61
Gregg, Donald, 126–27
Grenada, 162
Grenell, Richard, 323n.44
Grenier, Robert L., 27
GRU (Russian military intelligence), 71–72, 123–24, 292–93n.32, 328n.40
Guantánamo, 55
Guatemala, 37, 83–88, 94, 95, 110, 205–6, 247, 252, 253–54, 275, 327n.37
    CIA chief of station, 84
    land reform, 84
    mired in poverty, 88
Guatemalan Army of Liberation, 86
Guevara, Che, 95–96
Gulag Archipelago, 25
Gulf of Abadan, 78
Gulf of Aden, 130
Gulf of Tonkin Resolution, 9
Guyana, 31, 318n.44
Guzmán, Jacobo Árbenz, 83–86

Haass, Richard N., 253
hacking, 160, 260
Haines, Avril, 195–97
Haiti, 275–76
Hale, Nathan, 306n.49
Hall, Fawn, 128
Halperin, Morton, 270
Hamilton, Lee H. (D, Indiana), 34–35, 129, 167, 208, 210–11, 214, 317n.35
Harriman, Averell, 230
Harris, Kamala (D, California), 209
Hart, Philip (D, Michigan), 249
Harvey, William, 245
Haspel, Gina, 158, 265
Hastings, Max, 305n.35

hearing aid, importance of for US foreign policy 268
Helms, Richard, 56, 99–100, 101–2, 105–7, 109, 111, 119–20, 134–35, 140, 153, 175, 178–79, 180, 234, 293n.37, 297–98n.1, 317n.31, 329n.1
    amnesia and, 214
    Dance of the Seven Veils, 214
Henderson, Ambassador Loy, 79
Henry II, King, 101, 102
Hersh, Burton, 91–92
Hillenkoetter, Rear Adm. Roscoe H., 168
history, 6–7, 81, 96, 123
Hitler, 4, 64–65, 124, 157
Hitz, Fred, CIA Inspector General, 171–72
Hmong (Meo) tribesman (Laos), 106–7, 147, 240, 254, 264, 306n.46
Ho Chi Minh, 29–30, 104–104, 305n.35
Ho Chi Minh Trail, 105–6
Hoekstra, Peter (R, Michigan), 210–11, 215–16
Honduras, 243–44
Hoover Commission, 14
Hoover, J. Edgar, 309n.15
Horn of Africa, 148
Horton, John, 265–66
hostage situations, 54–55
House Appropriations Subcommittee on Defense, 131–32
House Permanent Select Committee on Intelligence (HPSCI), vi, 4, 37–38, 111–12, 125, 127, 132, 148, 150, 153, 182, 183, 186, 192, 205–6, 210, 226, 227, 259, 265, 323n.44
Houston, Lawrence R., 168
Huddleston, Walter "Dee" (D, Kentucky), 184–86
Hughes, Harold (D, Iowa), 182, 307n.1, 318n.44
    Hughes-Ryan Act, 102–3, 117, 125, 126–27, 133, 136, 150–51, 181–84, 201, 202, 213, 216, 233, 242, 266
    importance of, 181, 182, 183, 184, 186, 195, 198–99, 204, 213–14, 235–36
    language of, 182
    limits of, 245
    pre-Hughes-Ryan era, 235–36
    reporting to Congress, 212–18
"Huk" (Hukbalahap), Philippines, 72
human rights, 4, 60, 120–22, 186, 198–99, 255, 268
human trafficking, 197–98
humint, 141, 171–72
Hungary, 15, 27–28, 44, 90–92, 135, 290n.10, 302n.56

"hunting" versus "gathering," 254–55
Hurras al-Din, 152

Ibarra and Arosemena regimes (Ecuador), 297–98n.1
Immerman, Richard H., 79–80, 317n.25
Immerwahr, Daniel, 287n.15
Impeachment proceedings, possible (against President Reagan), 128–29
imperial presidency, 9, 128
India, 77
Indochina, 107
Indonesia, 89–90, 96, 264, 268, 275–76
Inouye, Daniel K. (D, Hawaii), 208, 209, 317n.35
Inouye-Hamilton Committee, 184, 202, 213, 217, 219
Insurgency (domestic), of 2021, 2
intelligence, US
    all-source fusion, 13
    annual budget, 23
    collection and analysis, 10, 12–13, 149, 150–51, 152, 154, 173, 174, 176, 183, 254–55, 309n.23
    "entity," 189, 216,
    failure, 262
    flat, networked, 200–1
    liaison, 148
    political football, 207
    pork-barrel politics, 211
    privatization of, 36
    reform, 120, 192
    sharing of, 262
    "stovepipes" ("silos"), 9, 13, 262–63
    survival machine, 223
    threat assessment, 2
Intelligence Charter of 1978, proposed, 184–86
Intelligence Community (IC), 3, 22, 22f, 143–44, 149, 152, 167
    budget for, 23
    "tribal federation," 167
intelligence exceptionalism, 194, 235, 239
Intelligence Identities Protection Act of 1982, 319n.49
Intelligence Oversight Act of 1980 (Accountability for Intelligence Activities Act), 126, 150–51, 190–91, 192, 212, 215, 216, 233, 242, 266
Intelligence Oversight Act of 1991 (Intelligence Authorization Act of 1991), 186, 190–91, 192, 212–13
Intelligence Oversight Board, 309n.15

Intelligence Reform and Terrorism Prevention Act (IRTPA, 2004), 167, 191, 195
intermediate-range nuclear force (INF), 24
international agreements, 9
International Telephone and Telegraph (ITT), 108, 109
internationalists, 102
internet, 152, 272
Iran, 2–3, 15, 60, 76–83, 95, 123, 147, 198, 257, 267, 273–75
    assassination of Major General Qasem Soleimani, 57, 60, 159–61, 295n.12
    coup against (1953), 76–83, 252, 253–54, 257, 327n.37
    fundamentalist theocrats of, 80–81
    Iranian Communist Party (Tudeh), 78
    Islamic Revolutionary Guard Corps Quds Force, 158, 159–60
    nuclear weapons program, 49–50
    strategic importance of, 77, 300n.33
    US embassy hostage crisis, 52, 120–23, 245, 249–51, 261
Iran-*contra* scandal, 52, 123–31, 140, 163, 184, 192, 204, 226–27, 237–38, 242–44, 245, 249–51, 255, 309n.15
    blow to Constitution, 192
    blow to Third Option, 135
    criminalizing policy, 243
    Russia and, 146
Iraq, 57, 94, 152, 162
    Army, importance of, 82
    First Persian Gulf War, 28, 57–58, 141
    Second Persian Gulf War, 1–2, 144, 149
    Soleimani assassination, 159–61
    Voice of Free Iraq, 28
    WMDs, 152
ISI (Pakistani intelligence service), 133
ISIS, 4. *See* Islamic State in Iraq and Syria
Islamic Revolutionary Guard, 161
Islamic State in Iraq and Syria (ISIS), also known as Islamic State of Iraq and the Levant, as well as the Islamic State (or *Dalat* in Arabic), 2–3, 4, 57–58, 146–47, 253
isolationism, 12
Israel, 49, 125, 130
    assassinations, 256
    intelligence, 28
Italy, 11, 15, 71, 73, 240–41, 252, 271
    Christian Democratic Party, 23, 31, 71, 266, 271
    Communist Party, 23, 31, 71, 240

Jacobson, Roberta, 276
Jaga regime (British Guiana), 297–98n.1
January 6, 2021 (1/6), 2, 62–63, 82, 265–66, 328n.40
Japan, 4, 31, 102–3, 253, 297–98n.1, 303–4n.22
Jaruzelski, Gen. Wojciech, 135–36, 137–38
Jefferson, President Thomas, xi
Jeffreys-Jones, Rhodri, 71, 87
jihadists, 40, 45–46, 132, 143–44, 146–47, 148–49
Jimenez-Bacardi, Arturo, 178, 179, 187
Johnson administration (Lyndon B.), 30, 33, 103, 179, 182, 297–98n.1, 327n.35
  Chile, 102
  Cuba, 100, 304n.31
  Vietnam, 102, 181
Johnson, Andrew, 249
Johnson, Lyndon B. (D, Texas), 9, 100, 103, 179
Johnston, James H., 328n.39
Joint Chiefs of Staff (DoD), 56–57, 173, 178, 231
jointness, 13, 260
Jones, Jim, 318n.44
Jones, Seth G., 135, 138
Jordan, 148
  General Intelligence Directorate, GID (or "Mukhabarat"), Jordanian intelligence service, 148
Joseph, Emperor Franz (Austria), 61–62
journalists, US, 172–73
Just War, principle of proportionality, 260–61, 327n.32
Justice, Department of, 152, 153–54, 226, 325n.8

Kahn, Herman, 40
Kalaris, George, 291n.14
Kansi, Mir Aimal, 256
Karalekas, Anne, 15–16, 169, 182
Karnow, Stanley, 305n.35
Karzai, Hamid, 272
Katyn Massacre (Poland), 63
Kennan, George F., 71, 109, 171, 174
Kennedy administration, 16, 30–31, 38, 56–57, 94, 102, 178, 211, 228, 229, 245–46, 297–98n.1
  anti-communist philosophy, 102
  assassination plots, 99
  Chile, 102
Kennedy, President John F (D, Massachusetts)., 37–38, 94, 95, 97–99, 100, 178, 179, 229–30, 312n.14
Kennedy, Robert F. "Bobby," 100, 245, 328n.39
Kenya, 141–42

KGB (Soviet foreign intelligence, Cold War), 11, 31, 44–45, 56–57, 71–72, 123–24, 186, 245, 268–69, 292–93n.32, 308n.2
  catchment basins, 71–72
  moles, 73, 74
Khambas (Tibet), 264
Khomeini, Ayatollah Ruhollah, 80–81, 122
Khost (Afghanistan), 59–60, 285–86n.10
Khrushchev, Soviet President Nikita, 95
  secret speech (1956), 28, 198
  Cuba, 99
Kilpatrick, James, 109–10
Kim, 287n.10
Kim Il Sung, 76
King, Angus (I, Maine), 211, 255
King George's cavalry, 31, 47, 76–77, 82, 89, 91, 136, 144, 148, 271, 272
Kinzer, Stephen, 34, 94, 300n.33, 303–4n.22, 308n.2
Kipling, Rudyard, 287n.10
Kissinger, Henry, 6–7, 53, 109–11, 117–19, 217–18, 225, 243, 247, 257
Kmiec, Douglas, 325n.8
Kolbe, Paul R., 162
Korea, 162
  North Korea, 2–3, 4, 157, 173, 265
  South Korea, 173, 253
Korean War, 8, 15, 74–76, 79, 103–4, 162–63, 173, 252
Kosovo, 140
Krishman, Armin, 147, 248
kulaks, 11
Kultura, 27
Kurds, 102, 147, 264
Kurlantzick, Jushua, 107
Kuwait, 141

Ladd, Alan, 79–80
Ladder of Clandestine Escalation, 42f, 229, 232–33, 235, 236, 244, 249, 251, 259, 271. *See also* covert action
Langley, VA (CIA Headquarters), 104, 157, 169–70, 200–1
Lansdale, Lt. Col. Edward G., 72
Laos, 56, 93, 102, 103–4, 105–7, 147, 162–63, 239–40, 252, 254, 264, 271, 275
Latin America, 11–12, 61, 98, 247, 252
law, 150–51, 167, 174, 179–81, 202, 258–59, 265, 270, 275–76, 304n.32
  American, 127, 224, 267
  Attorney General, 202
  authorized battlefields, 154
  destruction of, 60, 62–63, 191–92

due process, 270–71
God's, 128
guide for covert actions, 234–35
habeas corpus, 55
intellectual property, 161
intelligence, 117, 125–26, 129–30, 150, 152, 153–54, 162, 224
  National Security Act foundations, 167–68
  international, 45–46, 57–58, 98, 154, 179, 254, 327n.33
  Law of the Seas, 51–52
  military, US, 149–50
  Nurnberg defense, 226
  US, as nation of, 181
lawmakers (members of Congress), 6, 181
Lebanon, 48–49, 90, 124, 127
Lee, Mike (R, Utah), 213–14
Leonard, Michael, 305n.40
Lewis, Anthony, 87
liberation theology, 91, 173
Libya, 145, 147
Liman, Arthur L., 192
Lincoln, Abraham, 64, 157, 249
London, Jack, 15
Long, Huey (D, Louisiana), 249
Louis, Prince Antoine duc d'Enghien, 98
Lowenthal, Mark M., 215–16
luck (chance), role of in covert action, 82, 122, 151
Lumumba, President Patrice (Congo), 38–39, 93–95, 102, 245

MacArthur, Gen. Douglas, 69–71, 173
Macedonia, 140
Machiavelli, 51
Mackenzie, Compton, 228
Madison, James, 194–95, 224, 225, 325n.8
Mafia, 30–31, 94, 268
Maghreb, 2
Magsaysay, Ramon, 72
Mali, 152
Manhattan Project, 12
Mao Zadong, 69–72
Marchetti, Victor, 317n.34, 325n.16
Marks, John, 317n.34, 325n.16
Marshall, George C., 275
Marshall Plan, 30–31, 69–71, 241, 253, 270–71, 276
Masood, Ahman Shah, 144
mass rape, 140
Mathias, Charles "Mac" (R, Maryland), 101
Mazzoli, Roman (D, Kentucky), 211, 217

McCain, John (R, Arizona), 208–9, 291n.14
McCarthy, Senator Joseph (R, Wisconsin), 11–12, 15, 249
McCarthyism, 8, 15, 79
McCone, John A., 102, 109, 178–79, 231–32
McConnell, Mitch (R, Kentucky), 219
McCurdy, Dave (D, Oklahoma), 210–11
McFarlane, Robert C. "Bud," 129–30, 208, 214
McGhee, George, 79
McLellan, David S., 11
McMahon, John, 81
McNamara, Robert S., 55, 103, 230
Meaney, Thomas, 110–11
media assets, 20–21
Memoranda of Notification (MON), 203
Menard, Louis, 65
Mercy, USNS, 275–76
"Merlin," Operation, 49
Mexico, 265–66, 268
micromanagement, 177, 183
Middle East, 26–27
  drone strikes, 162
  Iranian coup (1953), 77
  oil, 71
Milosevic, President Slobodan, 140–41
"MINARET," Operation, 226–27
mind-control, 34–35
Mitchell, George J. (D, Maine), 130, 218
Mobutu, Joseph, 94–95
Monat, Der, 27
Mondale, Walter F. "Fritz" (D, Minnesota), 120, 121
"Mongoose," Operation, 72, 97, 99–100, 102, 178, 229–30, 241
"Momentum," Operation, 105–6, 107
Monroe, Marilyn, 90
Montesquieu, 225
Moscow Youth Festival, 30
Mossad, 48–50, 216, 267
Mossadegh, Mohammed, 77–83, 265
Mount, Ferdinand, 264
Moyers, Bill, 127
Mozambique, 119
MPLA Party (Angola), 32–33, 69
Mueller, Robert S. III, 44
Mughniyah, Imad ("Maurice"), 48–49, 216
mujahideen (Afghanistan), 35–36, 53–54, 120–21, 133, 134, 135, 144, 237–38, 252–53, 254, 260–61, 262, 310n.36
mules (Chinese), 133
mullahs (Iran), 80–81, 123
Mukhabarat (Jordan), 148
Murphy Commission on Foreign Policy, 1–2, 5

My Lai, 36–37, 63
Myanmar, 106

Napoleon, 102
Nasser, Gamal Abdel, 73–74, 88, 93–94, 104, 292n.26
National Counterproliferation Center (NCPC), 198
National Endowment for Democracy (NED), 143, 199, 271
National Geospatial-intelligence Agency (NGA), 23
National Intelligence, Director of (DNI), 167–68
National Intelligence Estimates (NIEs), 176
National Intelligence Officer (NIO), 263
National Intelligence Program (NIP), 195
National Intelligence Reorganization and Reform Act of 1978 ("Grand Intelligence Charter"), 184–86
National Reconnaisance Office (NRO), 23
National Security Act of 1947, 13, 14, 69, 75, 167, 169, 266
  "other functions and duties" clause, 13–14, 167–68, 235
National Security Adviser, 178
National Security Agency (NSA), 23, 49, 149, 215, 226–27, 236
National Security Archive, 105, 111–12
National Security Council, 8, 55–56, 78, 95–96, 171, 179, 197, 227, *See also* executive orders and directives,
  covert action working group, 200
  Deputies Committee, 153, 200
  intelligence panels, 179–80, 200
  Principals Committee, 153, 200
  Special Group (Augmented), 95–96
  staff, 123–24, 125, 129, 130–31, 132, 184, 208, 216
  Subcommittee on Covert Action, 200, 202, 266
  top officials, 175
National Security Planning Group, 200
National Student Association, 30
nationalism, 94, 100–1, 273–75
natural disasters, 268
Nazis, 5, 11, 157, 170–71
Near East, 162
"Neptune Spear," Operation, 102, 149–51, 234
new media, 47–48
New York Times, 29, 42, 44–45, 106, 117, 145, 153, 179–80, 181, 183, 203, 233, 234, 236, 318n.44, 326n.31

"*New York Times* test" (covert action causing public embarrassment), 233, 234, 268
New Yorker drawing, 58f
Newsweek, 25, 27
New Zealand, 230, 297n.40
Nicaragua, xiv, 4, 36, 37, 51–52, 86, 123, 125–27, 145, 161–62, 209–10, 243, 247, 265–66, 272, 276
  CIA assassination *Manual*, 126–27
  contras, 126–27
  mining harbors in, 207, 268
  Sandinistas, 125
Nicholas II, Tsar (Russia), 61–62
Niger, 152
9/11 (September 11, 2001), 134, 143, 163, 172, 186, 238, 252
9/11 Commission, 253
Nisour Square (Baghdad), 36–37
Nixon administration, 26, 107–8, 110–11, 112, 178, 179–80, 247–48
Nixon, President Richard M. (R, California), 89–90, 95–96, 107–8, 109, 225, 243
Nkrumah government (Ghana), 297–98n.1
NKVD (Stalin regime intelligence agency), 63
non-interventionist norms, 179
nonproliferation, 257–58, 266–67
Nonproliferation Center (NPC), 198
Noriega, Manuel, 61
North American Free Trade Agreement (NAFTA), 139
North Atlantic Treaty Organization, 71, 102–3, 129–30, 138, 140–41, 240, 248
North, Lt. Col. Oliver L., 126–27, 208, 212, 243–44
Northern Alliance (Afghanistan), 31–32, 51, 144, 148, 236, 267
Nosavan, Gen. Phoumi, 93
Nosenko, Yuriy, 55
nuclear, biological, chemical (NBC) and radiological weapons, 3, 63
nuclear weapons, 12
nuclear winter, 3
Nunes, Devin (R, California), 36–37, 211
Nürnberg defense, 228
Nusra Front (al-Nusra; or, more recently, Hayat Tahrir al-Sham and Hurras al-Din), an Al Qaeda affiliate, 146–47, 151

Obama administration, 145, 146–47, 148, 149–50, 152, 157, 255–56, 266, 321n.21
Obama, President Barack (D, Illinois), 143–44, 145, 159–60, 234
  as the Covert Action President, 145

Office of the Director of National Intelligence (ODNI), 264
Office of Inspector General (IG/CIA), 21f, 265
Office of Policy Coordination (OPC), 171, 173–75
Office of Special Operations (OSO), 171–72, 174–75
Office of Strategic Services (OSS), 20, 119–20, 124, 169, 176
oil, US and British interests in Iranian, 77, 80
Old Executive Office Building (OEOB), 178
"Olympic Games," Operation, 49
Omand, David, 223, 327n.32
"Omega," Operation (Egypt), 88
Organization of American States (OAS), 231
Ortega, Daniel, 125
Ortodoxo Party (Cuba), 96
O'Rourke, Lindsey A., 271
Orwell, George, 35, 293n.37
Osnos, Evan, 160, 295n.12
Oswald, Lee Harvey, 100
overt-covert action, 36

Pahlevi, Mohammed Reza, 80
Pakistan, 133, 149, 152, 156, 236, 237, 310n.36
  accidental drone deaths of civilians, 153
  "West Point" equivalent (in Abbottabad), 149, 151
Palestinians, use of assassination, 256
Panama, 61
pandemics, 2, 4
Panetta, Leon E. (R, California), xiv, 150–51, 199, 214, 262–63
paramilitary operations, CIA, 34–39, 95, 105–6, 145, 254–55, 263, 266
  first major, long-lasting one, 101
  first significant one, 86
  in times of imminent threat, 257
  "knuckle-draggers," 88
  "paramilitary boys," 293n.37
  suicide missions, 76, 173
  supervision of, 38
  value of in overt warfare, 233
Parks, W. Hays, 61
participant observation, 5
Pathet Lao (Laos), 106, 107, 254
patriotic terrorism, 287n.10
Pawley, William, 86
"PB/Success," Operation, 85
Peace Corps, 97
Pearl Harbor, 2, 5
Pelosi, Nancy (D, California), 213–14
Pepsi Cola, 108

Perez, Professor Louis A., 97
"perspectives" (propaganda), 20, 199
Persian Gulf, 230
Pezzullo, Ralph, 267
Philby, Kim, 73
Philippines, 15, 72
Philips, David Atlee, 292n.21
"Phoenix," Operation, 105
Phythian, Mark, 48–49, 223, 327n.32
Pike Committee, 112, 181
Pike, Otis (D, New York), 112
Pinochet, Gen. Augusto, 112, 247
Plato, 204
plausible denial, doctrine of, 53, 128–29, 130, 133, 149, 179, 181, 182, 183, 184, 190, 198–99, 231, 232, 317n.35
Poindexter, Admiral John M., 52, 127–28, 208, 225, 317n.35
Point Four Program, 241, 253
Poland, 15, 25, 27, 30, 52, 63, 71, 121, 124, 241–42
  covert action in, 121, 135–39, 252–53, 271
  Soviet invasion of, potential, 135
  workers and trade unions, 137–38
policymaking and process, 195, 203–4, 233, 257–58
Policy Planning Staff (State Department), 171
political covert action, 30, 137, 171
  bribery, as, 31–32, 74
  methods, 25–26, 32–33, 180
  money as the mother's milk of covert action, 135–36
Polk, President James K., xi
Pompeo, Mike (R, Kansas), 156, 157, 276–77
Pope, Alexander Lawrence, 89–90
Pope John Paul II, 121, 124
Pope Pius XI, 26
Popieluszko, Father Jerzy, 136–37
Portugal, 269–70, 271
Powers, Thomas, 255, 263
Prados, John, 178, 179
President's Daily Brief (PDB), 155, 176, 207, 310n.32
President's Foreign Intelligence Advisory Board or PFIAB (now called the President's Intelligence Advisory Board or PIAB), 309n.15
presidency, US
  authority for covert action, 56
  imperial, 9, 126, 172–73, 209–10, 288n.19
Presidential Policy Guidance (PPG), 153
Prince, Erik, 36–37

propaganda, secret ("perception
    enhancement"), 19, 43–44, 121–22, 252–
    53, 258, 260, 271–72
  black (false, disinformation), 23–24, 43–44,
    46, 53, 100
  blow back (replay), 29–30, 51
  book program, 25, 121–22, 252–53
  British approach to, 24–25
  criticism of, 27, 47–48
  early days at CIA, 14, 25–26, 170
  gray, 23–24
  Guatemala, uses in, 86
  inside the US, 28–29
  Iran, US uses in, 82
  letter-writing campaigns (Italy), 23
  Madison Avenue influence, 171
  methods, 20–21, 23–24, 29, 82, 89, 136–37
  "Mighty Wurlitzer," 25–26, 111
  night letters, 27
  "perspectives" (themes), 14, 20, 199
  rumor campaigns, 82
  Soviet, 14
  white, 23–24
  Xerox equipment, 137
proportionality, 260–61
PSP (Cuban Communist Party), 96
Psychological Strategy Board (PSB), 174
public diplomacy, 207–8
Publications Review Board (PRB), 264
Puerto Rico, 229–30
Putin, Vladimir V., 11, 33, 45, 159–60, 328n.40

Qaddafi, Muammar, 148
Qatar, 146
"QR/HELPFUL," Operation, 135
"quiet option," covert action as, 5–6

Raborn, Vice Adm. William F., Jr., 178–79, 265
radio broadcasts (CIA), 170–71
Radio Free Europe, 26–28, 44, 90, 137, 302n.56
Radio Liberty, 26–27, 137
Radio Marti, 99–100
Radio Sawa, 26–27
Radio Solidarity, 137
radiological weapons, 63
Rainbow Warrior, 63, 230
Ramparts, 30
Ranelagh, John, 182
Ransom, Harry Howe, 297–98n.1
Ratcliffe, John (R, Texas), 218–19
"ratlines," 25
Reagan administration, 37–38, 121, 124, 132,
    134, 162–63, 182, 186, 199, 216

Reagan, President Ronald (R, California), 123,
    128–29, 162, 237, 243, 316n.20
realpolitik, 102
Reeker, Philip T., 288n.29
Reisman, W. Michael, 14, 61, 160
  rendition, detention, and interrogation (RDT,
    or "snatch" operations), 34–35, 54–55, 60
Republican National Committee (RNC), 90
Republican Party, 79
resistance groups, CIA in Eastern Europe, 173
  émigré volunteers, 173
  stay-behind program, 173
Reston, James, 29–30
Rhodesia, 119
Risen, James, 93, 152, 266–67, 310n.35
Rivers, Mendel (D, S. Carolina), 289n.40
Robinson, Keith (R, Virginia), 211
Rockefeller (Vice President Nelson)
  Commission on Intelligence Activities
    (1975), 265
Rockefeller, John D., IV (D, West Virginia), 209
Rodriquez, Jose A. Jr., 327–28n.38
rollback (of Iron Curtain), 73, 90, 91, 173,
    290n.10
Romania, 15
Roosevelt, President Franklin D. (D, New York),
    81–82, 249
Roosevelt, Kermit "Kim," 81–82, 267
Roosevelt, President Teddy (R, New York), and
    big stick diplomacy 51
Rosati, Jerel A., 135
Rosenblatt, Lionel, 306n.45
Rositzke, Harry, 30, 223, 324–25n.6
Ross, Thomas, 83
Rostow, Walt, 304n.31
Rositzke, Harry, 223
Royal Lao Government, 105–6
Rudman, Warren B. (R, New Hampshire), 128
Rusk, Dean, xiv, 8, 10, 54, 98, 100–1, 103, 194,
    232, 257
Russia, 2–3, 59, 71–72, 162, 248, 252–53
  intelligence services, contemporary,
    293n.33
  intelligence tampering with US elections, 44,
    156, 157, 161, 201, 219
  military, 36, 146
  nuclear weaponry of, 3
  possible responses to cyberattacks
    by, 160–61
  propaganda, 11, 328n.40
  Syria, 147, 248
  underground, 252–53
Ryan, Leo (D, New York), 182, 318n.44

Saddam Hussein, 28, 61, 141, 149, 230
Sahara, 125
samizdat, 121–22
Sandinista Party (Nicaragua), 125
Sanger, David E., 49, 272, 287n.17
satellites, 23
Saudi Arabia, 3, 127, 146–47, 207, 209
SAVAK, 83
Savary, René, 102
Schelling, Thomas, 99
Schiff, Adam (D, California), 210–11, 213, 219
Schlesinger, Arthur M. Jr., 128, 179, 203
Schlesinger, James R., 6, 179–80
Schneider, General René, 111–12, 246
Schwartz, Mattathias, 325n.8
Scott, James M., 135
Second Option, 5
Second Persian Gulf War, 148
self-determination, 269, 273–75
Senate Foreign Relations Committee (SFRC), 109–10, 268
Senate Select Committee on Intelligence (SSCI), 29, 127, 132, 148, 150, 153, 181, 183, 186, 192, 203, 210, 226, 227, 259, 265
separation of powers doctrine, 224–25
Serbia, 139
Serbia-Montenegro, 140
Shackley, Ted, 37
shah, Iranian, 80, 253–54, 257, 262
 criticism of, 81, 83, 87
 positive contributions made to Iran, 81
shaming, 161
"SHAMROCK," Operation, 226–27
Shane, 79–80
sheep-dip, 34–35
shellfish toxin, 100
Sherman, Gen. William Tecumseh, 33
Shiites and Sunnis, 124, 145
Shultz, George, 309n.24
Sichel, Peter, 203
Slovenia, 140
Smith, Joseph Burkholder, 320n.9
Smith, Gen. Walter Bedell ("Beetle"), 75–76, 174–75
snake-eater, 35
"snatch" teams, 34
Snepp, Frank, 264
social media, 27
socialism, perceived dangers of, 102
SolarWinds, 2–3
Soleimani, Major General Qasem, 60, 159–61, 225–26, 249–51, 295n.12
 alternatives to assassination, 161

 assassination rejected by President Bush II, 158
 assassination rejected by President Obama, 158
 congressional hearings on, 213–14
 intelligence officials reject Trump hypothesis on immediacy of Soleimani threat, 158
Solidarity Movement (Poland), 27, 52, 121, 135–38, 199, 241–42, 266–67
Solzhenitsyn, Aleksandr, 25
Somalia, 2, 149, 152
sources and methods, 9, 168, 213–14
Southeast Asia Treaty Organization (SEATO), 297–98n.1
South-West Africa, 119
Southwest Asia, 131
Soviet (Red) 40th Army, 131, 132, 133
Soviet Union (USSR), 5, 6, 11, 12–13, 14, 15, 43, 109, 121, 162, 200, 245, 269–70, 276
 Air Force, 94
 Angola and, 117–19
 Aswan Dam (Egypt), 88
 collapse of, 137
 dissidents, 25
 ICBMs, 94
 invasion of Hungary, 91
 missile-testing, US spying on, 80
 nuclear weapons of, 9
 possible expansion in Middle East, 77
 proposed submarine base in Cuba, 102
 Western Hemisphere, interest in, 102
Space Force Agency, 22
Span, Johnny Michael "Mike," 144
special activities, 5–6, 124, 252
Special Activities (SA) Division, 34–35, 148–49
Special Coordinating Committee, 200
Special Forces, 34–35
Special Group (SG) on Counterinsurgency, 178, 197
Special Group (Augmented), 99–100, 178
Special Operations Executive (UK), 124
Special Operations Group (SOG or "Ground Branch"), 34–35, 106, 144, 150, 198–99
Special Procedures Group (SPG, or Special Projects Group), 170–71
Spector, Arlen (R, Pennsylvania), 209
Spellman, Francis Cardinal, 86
Spy Power, 4, 5, 10, 16
"Square Dance," Operation, 56–57, 231
Stalin, Joseph, 11, 12, 15, 28, 60, 78–79, 170–71
Stasi (East Germany), 44–45

State, Department of, 88, 125, 143, 168, 178, 231–32, 270, 304n.31
   budget, 261
   CIA as auxiliary unit of, 170–71, 174
   CIA cooperation with, 199
   embassies under terrorist attacks, 141
   Policy Planning Staff, 171
   propaganda coordination with CIA, 267
   public diplomacy, 205
   tensions with CIA, 171, 179–80
   Secretary of, 152
   Voice of America, 137
statutory international agreements, 9
"Staunch," Operation, 125
stay-behind guerrilla forces and resistance groups (Eastern Europe), 35, 73, 172–73
Stinger missiles, 35–36, 53–54, 119, 133, 237, 262
Stockwell, John, 308n.2
Studeman, Admiral William O., 6–7, 259
Stuxnet, 49
Sudan, 142
Sukarno, President, 89–90, 264
Sullivan and Cromwell (law firm), 78–79, 85, 174–75
Sullivan, William C., 309n.15
Sultan of Brunei, 127
Sung, Kim II, 76
Supreme Court, 8, 9–10
Sûreté de l'État (Belgian intelligence service), 95
SVR (post-Cold War Russian foreign intelligence service), 292–93n.32, 328n.40, 332n.54
Swalwell, Eric (D, California), 211
Syria, 3, 5, 71, 73–74, 88, 96, 145, 245, 251, 253
   drone targeting, 151–52
   major covert action against, 146–48, 248–51

Taliban (Afghanistan), 131, 134–35, 144, 236, 237–38, 252–53, 256, 257
Tanzania, 141–42
Tarnak Farms (Afghanistan), 55–56
Taylor, Adm. Rufus, 167
Tea Party, 156
"techies," 141
techint, 141
Technical Services Division (CIA),
Tenet, George J., 56, 144, 209
terrorism, 4, 260, 266–67
   Age of Terrorism, 141–42, 143
   aerial terrorism, 143–44
   counterterrorism, 144, 145, 257–58
   domestic, 4

   international, 2, 48–49, 138, 139, 224–25, 257, 259
Thailand, 55, 103–4, 291n.14
Third Force, 71–72
Third Option, 1
threat assessment, 2
303 Committee (NSC), 178
   Special Group (Augmented), for Operation "Mongoose," 178
   Special Group on Counterinsurgency, 178
Tibet, 90, 264
"Timber Sycamore," Operation, 146–48
   high desertion rates, 146–47
Time, 25, 27, 84
Tito, 244
Torricelli, Robert G. (D, New Jersey), 205–6, 322n.29
torture ("interrogation in depth"), 29, 37–38, 54–55, 60, 172, 182, 186, 191, 210–11, 226, 229, 291n.14, 327–28n.38
   intelligence method, 291n.14,
   SSCI on, 291n.14
Tovar, B. Hugh, 223
Tower Commission, 184
"Toys," Operation, 125
"TPAjax," Operation, 80
Treaty Power, 4–5, 16, 75
Treverton, Gregory F., 75, 111, 112, 145, 187, 206, 307n.67, 319n.54
Tribe, Laurence H., 127
Trujillo, Rafael, 297–98n.1
Truman administration, 11, 16, 79, 168, 173
Truman Doctrine, 69–71, 241, 253
Truman, Harry S. (D, Missouri), 8, 12, 14, 173, 289n.36
   creation of CIA, 12–13, 167
   criticism of, 69, 79
   lack of enthusiasm for covert action, 14, 69, 288n.29
Trump administration, 4, 11, 16, 72, 155, 264–65
Trump, President Donald J. (R, New York and Florida), 2, 5, 7, 22, 36–37, 44, 60, 95, 98–99, 155, 207, 213–14, 225, 249, 264, 265, 276–77, 295n.12
   claims to be his own intelligence director, 156, 216
   contempt for Congress, 213–14, 219
   encouragement of US domestic insurgency (2021), 82
   erratic foreign policy, 276–77
   eschews daily intelligence reporting, 155–56, 323n.46

impeachment of, 264–65
orders assassination of Maj. Gen. Qasem
    Soleimani, 60, 159–60
prides his intelligence instincts, 156
President Putin, and, 158
relations with CIA, 155–58
threat to democracy, 249, 265, 328n.40
waterboarding, 158
truth serums, 303–4n.22
Tunney, Gene, 307n.1
Tunney, John (D, California), 307n.1
Tunney-Clark Amendment (1975), 119, 307n.1
Turkey, 146–48, 248, 252
Turner, Michael, 47–48
Turner, Adm. Stansfield, 27, 55, 61, 123, 131,
    167–68, 172–73, 203, 204, 210, 217–18,
    233, 236, 251, 258, 263, 316n.12, 319n.57
Tyler, President John, xi

Ukraine, 30–31, 35, 71, 264–65
Underwater Demolition Teams, 33, 50
unintended consequences, of covert action, 134,
    257, 262
Union Wharf Company, 306n.49
Unit 8200 (Israeli intelligence), 49
Unit 29155 (Russian intelligence), 256
UNITA (National Union for the Total
    Independence of Angola), 117–19
United Arab Emirates (UAE), 59–60, 93–94
United Fruit Company (La Frutera), 83–84, 86,
    87, 253–54
United Nations, 87, 95, 231
    International Criminal Tribunal on
        Yugoslavia, 141
United States,
    Air Force, 72, 85, 106–7, 144
    Army, 232
    global reputation of, 42, 51, 87, 265, 268–69
    Marine Corps, 267
    military, 272
    Military Code (Title 10 and Title 50),
        149, 154–55
    Navy, 264, 275–76
    presidential elections, 2016, 2020, 44
    terrorist attacks against, 55–56
    world leader, 12
USA Today/Ipsos poll on Soleimani
    assassination, 160–61

"Valuable," Operation, 72
Vance, Cyrus, 262, 270, 271
Viet Cong (VC), 105, 230
Vietnam, 100–1, 104–62, 267

Vietnam, North, 101, 305n.42
Vietnam, South, 72, 104, 105, 162–63, 230,
    239, 275
Vietnam War, 1–2, 9, 44–45, 50, 51–52, 56, 75,
    102, 104–5, 107, 162–63, 179–80, 181, 230,
    254, 256, 257, 264, 273–75
Virgin Mary, 228
Voice of America, 137
Voice of Liberation (*La Voz de la Liberación*),
    Guatemala, 86–87

Walêsa, Lech, 134
    wins Nobel Prize for Peace, 136–37
    becomes President of Poland, 138
War Power, 4, 5, 7, 9, 16
War Powers Resolution (WPR), 9–10
Warner, Mark (D, Virginia), 209
Warren Commission, 100
Warsaw Pact, 92
Washington, President George, xi, 225, 249
Washington Post, 29, 210, 326n.31
waterboarding, 158, 291n.14
Watergate scandal, 102, 107–8, 180, 181,
    318n.44
weaponry, conventional,
    CIA Stinger missiles and other weaponry,
        132–33, 147
    French-make anti-armor Milan missiles,
        133, 134
    Saudi tank-destroying missiles, 146
    Soviet Army MI-24D attack
        helicopters, 132–33
    SPG-9s 73 recoilless rifles, 132–33
weapons of mass destruction (WMD), 3, 140,
    143, 182, 224–25, 259, 266–67
    bacteriological, 44–45
    nerve gas, 146
    proliferators, 138–39, 140, 144, 198, 255–56
Webster, Judge William H., 126, 233–35,
    236, 263
"Webster's Writs," 233–5, 236, 251, 263, 267
Weiner, Tim, 76, 101
Weinberger, Casper, 219
Weissman, Stephen R., 148
Western democracies, 11–12
Western Hemisphere, 110
Whipple, Chris, 265, 293n.38, 321n.18
whistleblowing, 265
Wilbur, Donald N., 300n.33
Wilhelm I, Kaiser (Germany), 61–62
Wilson, Charlie (D, Texas), 132, 198, 237–38
Wippl, Joseph, 268
WI/ROGUE, 38–39, 197

Wise, David, 83
Wisner, Frank G. "Wis," 32, 85, 91–92, 139, 174, 317n.24
witting circle, 187–88
Woolsey, R. James, 32, 139, 140, 141, 183, 255–56, 311n.44
World War, First, 12
World War, Second, 1–2, 11, 12, 13–14, 53–54, 60, 69–71, 101, 124, 240
"wrecking," 11
Wyden, Ron (D, Oregon), 211

Yale University, 50, 160
Year of the Intelligence Wars, 210
Yemen, 58–59, 141–42, 143, 152, 153
Yugoslavia, 244

Zablocki, Clement J. (D, Wisconsin), 9
Zahar Kili encampment (Afghanistan), 56–57
"Zapata," Operation (Bay of Pigs), 97–98
zero-sum view of world politics, 91, 100–1, 102, 104, 109, 124, 276
"ZR/RIFLE," Operation, 100